1 MONTH OF
FREE
READING

at
www.ForgottenBooks.com

---◇---

By purchasing this book you are eligible for one month membership to ForgottenBooks.com, giving you unlimited access to our entire collection of over 1,000,000 titles via our web site and mobile apps.

To claim your free month visit:
www.forgottenbooks.com/free976604

ISBN 978-0-260-85180-2
PIBN 10976604

DEPARTMENT OF AGRICULTURE

NOTICE OF PROPOSED AMENDMENTS

1) Heading of Part: Animal Diagnostic Laboratory Act

2) Code Citation: 8 Ill. Adm. Code 110

3) Section Numbers: Proposed Action: Section Numbers: Proposed Action

110.50	Amended	110.110	Amended
110.80	Amended	110.120	Amended
110.90	Amended		

4) Statutory Authority: AN ACT authorizing the Department of Agriculture to establish animal disease laboratories" (Ill. Rev. Stat. 1987, ch. 8, par. 105.11).

5) A Complete Description of the Subjects and Issues Involved:

Increases in some laboratory fees are proposed. Many of these fees have not been increased since they became effective July 1, 1984. The budget for operating the laboratories is only partially related to the work load experienced by the laboratories. A major portion of the work load comes from practicing veterinarians and is dependent upon their decision and that of the animal owner. This increased work load without any increase in budget has resulted in a budget problem that may prevent conducting of the requested tests and examinations presented to the laboratories. Without any other method of controlling accessions, fees are being increased in an effort to somewhat discourage the submission of samples. Also, many of the increases will reflect fee charges that are more compatible to those of surrounding states and private industry.

Additional language has been added to clarify what areas the necropsy tests cover. Where only a necropsy is requested without any tests, the fee will remain at $15.

Serologic tests on paired, acute and convalescent specimens are considered one accession and are presently billed as such. The added language clarifies that policy.

New laboratory services which the Department can now conduct and the fees which will be charged for such services are being added. The new services include the Wisconsin mastitis test, the FeLV-FeLT test, Porcine fetal fluid IgG test, Feline lentivirus test, herbicide screen, Cyclopiazonic acid test, drug screen, sulfa residue, water quality screen, and cremation.

Our laboratory personnel advise us that the Microtiter test is a more accurate name for the Leptospirosis test, and six serotypes are run under that test.

We are removing the language that permitted the rabies test to be conducted without charge when there was human exposure. The Department does not charge

DEPARTMENT OF AGRICULTURE

NOTICE OF PROPOSED AMENDMENTS

for State mandated tests; however, rabies is not a State mandated regulatory test. Often we do not receive information to indicate human exposure until billing time when we are told that they should not have been billed. A fee on all rabies tests will simplify the situation. Section 110.50(d) already requires doubling of the fee for out-of-state animals so the "rabies out-of-state testing..$10" is unnecessary language and is being removed.

The test for Feline Leukemia is also conducted at the Galesburg laboratory. This oversight is being corrected.

Toxoplasmosis can be conducted on species other than canine and feline so we are removing the words "canine and feline".

In testing for metals, a test for mercury, molybdenum and cadmium will be offered as a separate test. The screen for 26 metals using inductively coupled plasma emission spectrometry is no longer available through the Department's laboratories. Originally, this test was made available in accordance with a cooperative arrangement with a university laboratory.

Clarifying language is proposed for the individual mycotoxin test.

The aflatoxin by minicolumn test has been replaced by a more sensitive thin-layer chromatography test.

6) Will this proposed rule replace an emergency rule currently in effect? No

7) Does this rulemaking contain an automatic repeal date? No

8) Does this proposed amendment contain incorporations by reference? No

9) Are there any other amendments pending on this Part? No

10) Statement of Statewide Policy Objectives: This rulemaking does not impose any additional mandatory requirements on units of local government in such a way that would necessitate additional expenditures from local revenues.

11) Time, Place and Manner in which interested persons may comment on this proposed rulemaking:

A public hearing on the proposed amendments will be held on January 10, 1989, at 10:00 a.m., Department of Agriculture, State Fairgrounds, Springfield, Illinois. Persons unable to attend the hearing may present their comments on the proposed rulemaking in writing to the Director, Department of Agriculture, State Fairgrounds, Springfield, Illinois 62794-9281. Mailed comments must be postmarked no later than January 5, so they will be available for consideration at the public hearing. All comments received will be fully considered by the agency and the Advisory Board of Livestock Commissioners.

DEPARTMENT OF AGRICULTURE

NOTICE OF PROPOSED AMENDMENTS

The public hearing on the proposed rulemaking will run concurrent with a public meeting of the Advisory Board of Livestock Commissioners.

This proposed rulemaking may have an impact on small businesses. In accordance with Sections 3.01 and 4.03 of the Illinois Administrative Procedure Act, small businesses may present their comments to the Director as outlined above.

12) Initial Regulatory Flexibility Analysis:
   A) Date rule was submitted to the Business Assistance Office of the Department of Commerce and Community Affairs: Nov. 4, 1988
   B) Types of small businesses effected: Veterinarians or other persons who request animal diagnostic laboratory services of the Department of Agriculture.
   C) Reporting, bookkeeping or other procedures required for compliance: The amendments establish the services and the charges for such services that are performed at the Department's animals diagnostic laboratories. The person requesting the services must pay the fees as set forth in the rules.
   D) Types of professional skills necessary for compliance: Basic management.

The full text of the Proposed Amendments begins on the next page:

DEPARTMENT OF AGRICULTURE

NOTICE OF PROPOSED AMENDMENTS

TITLE 8: AGRICULTURE AND ANIMALS
CHAPTER I: DEPARTMENT OF AGRICULTURE
SUBCHAPTER b: ANIMALS AND ANIMAL PRODUCTS
(EXCEPT MEAT AND POULTRY INSPECTION ACT REGULATIONS)

PART 110
ANIMAL DIAGNOSTIC LABORATORY ACT

Section
110.10   Definitions
110.20   Submitting Specimens
110.30   Payment For Laboratory Services
110.40   Tests Not Covered By Fee Schedule
110.50   Minimum Fees
110.60   Euthanasia Fees
110.70   Clinical Pathology Fees
110.80   Histopathology Fees
110.90   Microbiology Fees
110.100   Parasitology Fees
110.110   Toxicology Fees
110.120   Miscellaneous Fees
110.130   Meats Chemistry Fees

AUTHORITY: Implementing and authorized by "AN ACT authorizing the Department of Agriculture to establish animal disease laboratories" (Ill. Rev. Stat. 1987 1985, ch. 8., par. 105.11).

SOURCE: Adopted and codified at 8 Ill. Reg. 9047, effective July 1, 1984; amended at 9 Ill. Reg. 4471, effective March 22, 1985; amended at 9 Ill. Reg. 19638, effective January 1, 1986; amended at 10 Ill. 9733, effective May 21, 1986; amended at 11 Ill. Reg. 10163, effective May 15, 1987; amended at 12 Ill. Reg. 3379, effective January 25, 1988; amended at 13 Ill. Reg. _____, effective _____.

Section 110.50 Minimum Fees

   a) A minimum accession fee of $5 per accession shall be charged on all accessions originating from Illinois animals, with the exception of samples for trichinosis testing for which the minimum accession fee is $1. If such fees for the individual tests exceed the minimum fee, no minimum fee shall be charged. Persons submitting specimens for which there are no charges for the laboratory procedure shall be exempt from the minimum fee.

DEPARTMENT OF AGRICULTURE

NOTICE OF PROPOSED AMENDMENTS

b) The necropsy fee is $35 ~~15~~ per accession for all species and~~,~~ cadavers ~~or multiple tissues~~ submitted where more than one test is needed. If multiple tissue specimens are submitted where more than one test is needed, the fee is $30 per accession. In cases where only a necropsy is performed without any tests, the fee is $15. The necropsy fee will include a test ~~tests~~ in pathology, microbiology, parasitology and toxicology as indicated by the necropsy. The necropsy fee does not include electron microscopy examination, toxicologic screens, water and feed analysis, serology or herd surveys.

c) Electron microscopy and toxicologic tests (other than a screen for metals and pesticides) shall be performed only after consultation with and with approval from the person who requested the laboratory services at the fees set forth in this Part.

d) All fees, including the minimum accession and necropsy fee, shall be doubled on all out-of-state animals, unless a specific charge is noted.

e) Serologic tests on paired, acute and convalescent specimens will be billed as one accession at the fee set forth in this Part.

(Source: Amended at 13 Ill. Reg. _____, effective _____)

Section 110.80 Histopathology Fees

a) The following are the fees for histopathology:

1) Biopsy......................... 12.50 C, G
2) Multiple Tissues............... 25.00 ~~15.00~~ C, G

b) In the event some specialty testing situation is requested by the person requesting the laboratory services, other fixatives are available. Please consult the respective diagnostic laboratory for the specific fee.

(Source: Amended at 13 Ill. Reg. _____, effective _____)

Section 110.90 Microbiology Fees

The following are the fees for microbiology:

DEPARTMENT OF AGRICULTURE

NOTICE OF PROPOSED AMENDMENTS

a) Bacteriology, Mycoplasma and Fungi

1) Aerobic or anaerobic culture without
   sensitivity testing.................10.00 ~~6.00~~ C, G
2) Aerobic culture with sensitivity
   testing............................15.00 ~~10.00~~ C, G
3) Anaerobic culture (includes sensitivity
   test)............................. 15.00 C, G
4) Milk samples for mastitis evaluation
   1-4 specimens.....................15.00 ~~10.00~~ C, G
   (additional specimens, each at)....2.00 ~~1.50~~ C, G
   Wisconsin mastitis test
   1-10 specimens, each.............. 2.00 C
   (additional specimens, each at)... 1.00 C
5) Leptospirosis - 6% serotypes Microtiter test
   ~~Microscopic agglutination~~ - per specimen 2.00 C, G
6) Canine brucellosis - per specimen.... 5.00 C,G,S
7) Fluorescent Antibody Test (FA).....10.00 ~~5.00~~ C, G
8) Escherichia coli serotyping........... 3.00 G
9) Campylobacter (culture)............... 4.00 C, G
10) Salmonella Serotyping................ 1.00 C, G
    Salmonella isolation using enrichment
    media............................. 6.00 C, G
11) Hemophilus (culture)................. 3.00 C, G
12) Nasal Swabs--Bordetella.............. 2.00 C, G
13) Listeria (culture).................. 4.00 C, G
14) Haemophilus equigenitalis (CEM)...... 4.00 C, G
15) Spirochetes (swine dysentery--Treponema
    sp.)............................. 3.00 C, G
16) Johne's Bacillus (first specimen)..... 5.00 C, G
    (each additional specimen)........... 1.00 C, G
17) Prepare and Supply Transport Media (per
    tube)............................. 1.00 C, G
18) Return culture for bacterin production
    per organism...................... 2.00 C, G
19) Mycology Testing.................... 6.00 C, G
20) Microscopic examination............. 3.00 C
21) Mycoplasma Testing.................. 6.00 C, G
22) Somatic Cell Count
    (1-10 specimens, each)............. 2.00 C
    (Each additional specimen)......... 1.00 C
23) E. Coli or Metritis (1-4 specimens)..... 10.00 C, G
    (each additional specimen)......... 1.30 C, G

b) Virology

DEPARTMENT OF AGRICULTURE

NOTICE OF PROPOSED AMENDMENTS

1) Electron Microscopy - fecal.............. 10.00 C
2) Pseudorabies Serology (positive or
   negative)............................ no charge C, G
   Pseudorabies Serology Out-of-State....... 3.00 C, G
   Pseudorabies Serology (positive or
   negative) and end titer.................. 3.00 C, G
   Additional serology test to determine
   pseudorabies vaccine usage (1-10
   specimens, each)......................... 1.00 C, G
   (Each additional specimen)............... .50 C, G
   Pseudorabies Serology (request for screen
   at dilution of 1:2)...................... 3.00 C, G
3) Fluorescent Antibody Test
   (each disease).....................10.00 5.00 C, G
4) Rabies other-than-human-exposure......... 5.00 C, G
   Rabies-out-of-state-specimen............10.00 C, G
5) Virus Isolation in Cell Culture.......... 15.00 C, G
6) Viral Serology (each disease)
   (1-5 specimens, each).................... 3.00 C, G
   (Each additional specimen)............... 1.00 C, G
7) Feline Leukemia........................... 10.00 C, G
8) Feline Infectious Peritonitis (F.I.P.)... 5.00 C
9) Canine parvo-virus (ELISA) fecal......... 5.00 C, G
10) Canine parvo-virus serum................. 5.00 C
11) Canine distemper on serum................ 5.00 C
12) Rota-virus on fecal..................... 10.00 C
13) Semen testing (export)................... 10.00 C
14) Swine enterovirus (8 serotypes)......... 12.00 C
15) FeLV-FeLV................................ 15.00 C
16) Porcine fetal fluid IgG.................. 3.00 C
17) Feline lentivirus (FeLV)................ 10.00 C

c) Chlamydia Isolation in Cell Culture.......... 15.00 C, G

d) Miscellaneous serology

1) Toxoplasmosis (canine-and-feline)........ 5.00 C
2) Vibrio Agglutination Test (Campylobacter) 2.00 S
3) EIA-AGID................................. 5.00 S
4) Mare Immunological Pregnancy Test (35-60
   days post-service)....................... 15.00 C
5) Aleutian Disease-Mink
   (immunoelectrophoresis).................. .20 S
6) Out-of-State brucellosis serology........ .50 C,G,S
7) Brucellosis testing other than bovine,
   porcine and canine....................... .50 C,G,S

DEPARTMENT OF AGRICULTURE

NOTICE OF PROPOSED AMENDMENTS

8) Bluetongue (1-5 specimens, each)....... 3.00 C, S
   (Each additional specimen)............. 2.00 C, S
9) Bovine leukosis (1-5 specimens, each)... 3.00 C, S
   (Each additional specimen)............. 1.00 C, S
10) Vesicular stomatitis................... 3.00 C
11) Complement Fixation Serology
   (1-5 specimens, each).................. 3.00 C
   (Each additional specimen)............. 1.00 C
   Note: The Complement Fixation Serology
   tests include testing for anaplasmosis,
   and chlamydia.

(Source: Amended   at 13 Ill. Reg. _____, effective
_____)

Section 110.110 Toxicology Fees

a) A maximum charge of $100 50 shall be assessed Illinois
   residents. There is no maximum charge for
   out-of-state residents.

b) Toxicology Work-up:

   Maximum $50 25 per animal or $100 50 per herd (Illinois
   animals)

c) Metals

1) Arsenic or Selenium
   1-3 specimens, each................20.00 10.50 C
   each additional specimen...........10.00 4.00 C
2) Lead, Mercury Copper, Cadmium, Zinc,
   Thallium, Calcium, Sodium, Magnesium,
   Potassium, Iron, Chromium, Cobalt,
   Nickel, or Manganese or Molybdenum
   1-3 specimens, each.................... 5.00 C
   each additional specimen.............. 3.00 C
3) Cadmium, Molybdenum and Mercury
   1-3 specimens, each................10.00 C
   (each additional specimen)............. 6.00 C
3) A-screen-for-25-metals-(elements)
   is-available-using-inductively-coupled
   plasma-emission-spectrometry.
   Serum-or-plasma-specimen............25.00 C
   Specimens-requiring-digestion.......40.00 C

d) Insecticide Screen

DEPARTMENT OF AGRICULTURE

NOTICE OF PROPOSED AMENDMENTS

1) Organochlorines, organophosphates.40.00 ~~20.00~~ C
2) Carbamates...............................30.00 ~~15.00~~ C
3) Individual insecticide................... 10.00 C

e) Herbicides

1) Phenoxy compounds....................40.00 ~~20.00~~ C
2) <u>Individual analysis of any</u>
   <u>herbicide from screen................. 20.00 C</u>
   ~~Others (as individuals).............10.00 C~~
3) <u>Herbicide screen (heterocyclic</u>
   <u>nitrogen derivatives, dintroanailines,</u>
   <u>urea, carbamate and anilide</u>
   <u>compounds)............................. 50.00 C</u>
4) <u>Imidazole compounds.................... 50.00 C</u>

f) Rodenticides

1) Anticoagulant screen.................... 25.00 C
2) Zinc Phosphide.......................... 10.00 C
3) Strychnine and other alkaloids......... 10.00 C
4) Yellow Phosphorus....................... 5.00 C
5) Individual anticoagulant............... 10.00 C
6) Fluoracetate (1080).................... 20.00 C

g) Mycotoxins

1) Screen (aflatoxins, T-2, DAS, Vomitoxin,
   Zearalenone).......................50.00 ~~25.00~~ C
2) Milk or urine aflatoxin.............20.00 ~~10.00~~ C
3) Ochratoxin..........................30.00 ~~20.00~~ C
4) Citrinin............................30.00 ~~20.00~~ C
5) <u>Individual analysis</u> ~~quantitation~~ <u>of any</u>
   <u>mycotoxin from screen</u>.............20.00 ~~10.00~~ C
6) ~~Aflatoxin by Minicolumn.............10.00 C~~
   <u>Cyclopiazonic acid (CPA)................. 30.00 C</u>
7) <u>Blacklight for Aspergillus flavus</u>....... 2.00 C
8) Endophyte testing
   Staining................................. 12.50 C
   Grow-out................................. 15.00 C

h) Miscellaneous Analysis

DEPARTMENT OF AGRICULTURE

NOTICE OF PROPOSED AMENDMENTS

1) Feed microscopy......................... 10.00 C
2) Nitrate:
   Ground Materials (first specimen)..... 8.00 C
   (each additional specimen)... 4.00 C
   Forages (first specimen).............. 12.00 C
   (each additional specimen).... 5.00 C
   On Vitreous humor..................... 9.00 C
3) Cyanide................................. 10.00 C
   Cyanide (screen-picric acid).......... 5.00 C
4) Ammonia (Urea Toxicosis)
   first specimen........................ 10.00 C
   (each additional specimen).......... 5.00 C
5) Carboxyhemoglobin, Methemoglobin,
   Sulfahemoglobin
   (first specimen)...................... 15.00 C
   (each additional specimen).......... 5.00 C
6) Sulfate................................. 5.00 C
7) Creosote, Petroleum Products.......... 15.00 C
8) pH...................................... 1.00 C
9) Urea................................... 10.00 C
10) Total chlorides, feeds or water....... 5.00 C
11) Monensin or other ionophone (each)25.00 ~~10.00~~ C
12) Water chlorine......................... 5.00 C
13) Water nitrate, nitrite (each)......... 5.00 C
14) Water hydrogen sulfide................. 5.00 C
15) Water hardness......................... 5.00 C
16) Pentachorophenol (PCP or Penta)....... 15.00 C
17) Bone--Percent Ash, Ca, Po4........... 12.00 C
18) Ca, Po4 (in feed)..................... 10.00 C
19) Ergot alkaloids....................... 15.00 C
20) Antibiotics in feed (each)........... 15.00 C
21) Vitamin Analysis (each).............. 10.00 C
22) Feed Quality Analysis.............30.00 ~~15.00~~ C
23) Protein and moisture analysis........ 7.50 C
24) Gas chromatographic/mass
    spectrophotometric analysis (each
    sample)..............................50.00 ~~25.00~~ C
25) Cholinesterase:
    Blood (first specimen)................ 7.50 C
    (Each additional specimen)...... 4.00 C
    Brain (first specimen)................ 12.50 C
    (Each additional specimen)...... 8.00 C
26) Drug screen............................. 25.00 C
27) <u>Sulfa residue (each sulfa drug)....... 5.00 C</u>
28) <u>Water quality screen (CH, OP,</u>
    <u>Carbamates, Herbicides, Lead).........100.00 C</u>

DEPARTMENT OF AGRICULTURE

NOTICE OF PROPOSED AMENDMENTS

(Source: Amended at 13 Ill. Reg. _____, effective
_____)

Section 110.120 Miscellaneous Fees

a) Swine health checks at slaughter facilities:
    Reproductive and serology for sows
    (1-5 head)................................. 25.00
    each additional animal..................... 4.00
    Market swine health check
    (12 head maximum)......................50.00 40.00
    (Contact the Galesburg laboratory for information)

b) Water potability test (Coliform and Enterococcus--
    Millipore Method and Nitrates)............. 8.00 C

c) Return of shipping container...............
    ....current postal rate C,G,S

d) Field trip by Department laboratory
    personnel to take specimens................ 50.00 C, G

e) Cremation................................... 50.00 G

(Source: Amended at 13 Ill. Reg. _____, effective
_____)

DEPARTMENT OF AGRICULTURE

NOTICE OF PROPOSED AMENDMENTS

1) **Heading of Part:** Animal Welfare Act

2) **Code Citation:** 8 Ill. Adm. Code 25

3) **Section Numbers:**   **Proposed Action:**

    25.20   Amended
    25.30   Amended
    25.50   Amended
    25.130   Amended

4) **Statutory Authority:** Animal Welfare Act (Ill. Rev. Stat. 1987, ch. 8,
pars. 302.1, 318, and 319).

5) **A Complete Description of the Subjects and Issues Involved:**

We are updating references to the Code of Federal Rules by citing the latest
edition which is the 1988 edition. This change will eliminate the need to
keep old CFR's on file in the agency and carried by our inspection personnel.
Also, it is easier for the public to locate the rule in a library when the
current version is cited. These amendments will not impose any additional
requirements.

We are updating reference to the Journal of the American Veterinary Medical
Association for the convenience of the public in locating the document. It is
easier to locate a more recent issue in a library. The proposed adoption of
the 1986 journal does not change the current requirement that only equipment
approved by the American Veterinary Medical Association be used for euthanasis
therefore, this change will not impose any additional requirements. The
address of the American Veterinary Medical Association has been added to
comply with requirements of the Illinois Administrative Procedure Act.

6) **Will this proposed rule replace an emergency rule currently in effect?** No

7) **Does this rulemaking contain an automatic repeal date?** No .

8) **Does this proposed amendment contain incorporations by reference?** None
that require approval in accordance with Section 6.02(b) of the Illinois
Administrative Procedure Act.

9) **. Are there any other amendments pending on this Part?** No

10) **Statement of Statewide Policy Objectives:** This rulemaking does not impose
any additional mandatory requirements on units of local government in such a
way that would necessitate additional expenditures from local revenues. The
current rules require that only equipment that has been approved by the American
Veterinary Medical Association be used for euthanasis. The adoption of a
later version of the Journal of the American Veterinary Medical Association

which identifies such equipment does not create any additional requirements on units of local government. Updating references to the 1988 Code of Federal Rules will not impose additional requirements on units of local government.

11) Time, Place and Manner in which interested persons may comment on this proposed rulemaking:

A public hearing on the proposed amendments will be held on January 10, 1989, at 10:00 a.m., Department of Agriculture, State Fairgrounds, Springfield, Illinois. Persons unable to attend the hearing may present their comments on the proposed rulemaking in writing to the Director, Department of Agriculture, State Fairgrounds, Springfield, Illinois 62794-9281. Mailed comments must be postmarked no later than January 5, so they will be available for consideration at the public hearing. All comments received will be fully considered by the agency and the Advisory Board of Livestock Commissioners.

The public hearing on the proposed rulemaking will run concurrent with a public meeting of the Advisory Board of Livestock Commissioners.

This proposed rulemaking may have an impact on small businesses. In accordance with Sections 3.01 and 4.03 of the Illinois Administrative Procedure Act, small businesses may present their comments to the Director as outlined above.

12) Initial Regulatory Flexibility Analysis:
   A) Date rule was submitted to the Business Assistance Office of the Department of Commerce and Community Affairs: Nov. 4, 1988
   B) Types of small businesses affected: Pet shop operators, dog dealers, kennel operators, cattery operator, pounds, and animal shelters.
   C) Reporting, bookkeeping or other procedures required for compliance: Insure proper ventilation, provide nutrition, and provide humane care and treatment of all animals as set forth in the rules.
   D) Types of professional skills necessary for compliance: Basic management.

The full text of the Proposed Amendments begins on the next page:

TITLE 8: AGRICULTURE AND ANIMALS
CHAPTER I: DEPARTMENT OF AGRICULTURE
SUBCHAPTER b: ANIMALS AND ANIMAL PRODUCTS (EXCEPT MEAT AND POULTRY INSPECTION ACT REGULATIONS)

PART 25
ANIMAL WELFARE ACT

Section
25.10   Definitions
25.15   Incorporations By Reference
25.20   Buildings and Premises
25.30   General Care of Animals
25.40   Dogs Brought into Illinois
25.50   Shipment of Mammals and Birds
25.60   Health of Animals at Time of Release
25.70   Department May Restrict The Sale of Animals
25.80   Quarantine
25.90   Records
25.100   Consent Statement and Inspection
25.110   Animals Prohibited from Sale
25.120   Boarding and Training
25.130   Pounds and Animal Shelters

AUTHORITY: Implementing and authorized by the Animal Welfare Act (Ill. Rev. Stat. 1987, ch. 8, par. 301 et seq.) and the Illinois Diseased Animals Act (Ill. Rev. Stat. 1987, ch. 8, par. 168 et seq.).

SOURCE: Regulations Relating to the Animal Welfare Act, filed May 17, 1974, effective May 27, 1974; filed October 6, 1976, effective October 16, 1976; codified at 5 Ill. Reg. 10438; amended at 7 Ill. Reg. 1724, effective January 28, 1983; amended at 12 Ill. Reg. 8265, effective May 2, 1988.

Section 25.20 Buildings and Premises

   a) All buildings and premises shall be maintained in a sanitary condition and the licensee shall:

       1) Have equipment available for proper storage or disposal of waste material to control vermin and insects.

       2) Dispose of dead animals in compliance with "AN ACT in relation to the disposal of dead animals" (Ill. Rev. Stat. 1987, ch. 8, par. 149 et seq.) and rules enacted pursuant to that Law (8 Ill. Adm. Code 85).

Compliance with this State Law shall not exempt licensee from compliance with local ordinances.

3) Take effective control measures to prevent infestation of animals and premises with external parasites and vermin.

4) Provide water from a source having sufficient pressure to properly sanitize and clean kennels, runs, equipment, and utensils.

5) Provide hand washing facilities.

b) All buildings shall be constructed so as to provide adequate shelter for the comfort of the animals and shall provide adequate facilities for separation of diseased animals to avoid exposure to healthy and salable animals.

c) Floors of buildings housing or displaying animals shall be of permanent construction to enable thorough cleaning and sanitizing. Dirt and unfinished wood floors are unacceptable. Cleaning shall be performed daily, or more often if necessary, to prevent any accumulation of debris, dirt or waste.

d) Cages shall be constructed of a material that is impervious to urine and water and able to withstand damage from gnawing and chewing.

1) The cages must be cleaned and sanitized at least once daily, or more often if necessary.

2) All empty cages shall be kept clean at all times.

3) Cages shall be of sufficient size to allow the animal to comfortably stand, sit, or lie, and offer freedom of movement.

4) An ambient temperature as defined in the rules for the Federal Animal Welfare Act (9 CFR 3.2; 1988 1987) shall be maintained for warmblooded animals. In the case of coldblooded animals, the temperature that is compatible to the well-being of the species shall be maintained.

e) Runs shall be constructed of material of sufficient strength and design to confine the animal(s).

1) They shall be kept in good repair and condition.

2) For new construction or remodeling, the licensee shall provide runs surfaced with concrete or other impervious material.

3) Surface of the run shall be designed to permit the surface to be cleaned and kept free from excessive accumulation of animal waste.

4) Provisions must be made for adequate drainage.

f) Cages or aquariums for housing of small animals, birds, or fish shall provide space not less than 2 1/2 times the body volume of living creatures contained therein.

g) If animals are group-housed, they shall be maintained in compatible groups without overcrowding. No female dog or cat in estrus shall be placed in a pen with male animals, except for breeding purposes.

(Source: Amended at 13 Ill. Reg. _____, effective _____)

Section 25.30 General Care of Animals

a) All persons or establishments licensed under this Act shall comply with all sections of the Humane Care for Animals Act (Ill. Rev. Stat. 1987, ch. 8, par. 701 et seq.).

b) Sufficient clean water and fresh food shall be offered to each animal daily as prescribed in the rules for the Federal Animal Welfare Act (9 CFR 3.5-3.7; 1988 1987). In the case of young animals, they shall be fed more than once daily. Reptiles, fish or amphibians shall be fed and cared for in accordance with the eating pattern and environmental conditions compatible with each individual species.

c) The licensee or his representative shall be present for general care and maintenance of the animals at least once daily.

d) Aquariums containing fish shall be kept in a clean healthful condition. Live algae shall not be considered an unhealthful condition. Any dead fish shall be removed from aquariums daily.

DEPARTMENT OF AGRICULTURE

NOTICE OF PROPOSED AMENDMENTS

e) Adult cats shall be provided with litter pans at all times. The pans shall be cleaned and sanitized at least once daily or more often if necessary.

(Source: Amended   at   13   Ill.   Reg.   _____ ,   effective
_____)

Section 25.50 Shipment of Mammals and Birds

a) Animals shall be transported in crates constructed of a smooth, durable material which is easily cleaned and shall:

1) Have a solid floor which may have a false bottom above it.

2) Be so constructed as prescribed in the rules for the Federal Animal Welfare Act (9 CFR 3.11 - 3.17; 1988 1987) as to provide maximum safety for the particular animal or animals being transported.

3) Have openings on 2 sides and the top to assure adequate ventilation.

b) In all cases, the crates shall be large enough to provide space for the animals to lie down in an extended position and to allow ease of movement when standing or turning around as prescribed in the rules for the Federal Animal Welfare Act (9 CFR 3.11 - 3.17; 1988 1987). When the temperature is over 85° F., increased space shall be provided within reason.

c) The crates shall be cleaned before use for each trip.

d) Food and water containers shall be cleaned and sanitized before each trip.

e) If bedding is used it shall be clean, dry, and relatively dust-free.

f) Animals in transit for 4 or more hours shall be offered food 2 hours before loading and fresh water about 30 minutes before loading.

g) The person or persons responsible for the welfare of the animal or animals while in transit shall:

DEPARTMENT OF AGRICULTURE

NOTICE OF PROPOSED AMENDMENTS

1) Offer the animals food at least once each 24 hours, except that newly weaned young shall be offered suitable food at 4-hour intervals.

2) Offer all animals water at 12-hour intervals at least, except that water shall be offered at 4-hour intervals when the temperature reaches 90° F.

3) Clean the crate or crates at least every 24 hours and, if bedding is used, shall provide clean bedding.

4) Inspect each animal at 4-hour intervals, or oftener.

h) No female obviously near parturition shall be transported.

i) Trucks transporting animals shall provide protection from the sun in hot weather, and protection from cold weather. Adequate ventilation shall be provided in hot weather, and the trucks shall be draft-free in cold weather. Provisions shall be made for warming an area carrying weaned young if the temperature falls below 50° F., and for unweaned young if the temperature falls below 65° F.

(Source: Amended   at   13   Ill.   Reg.   _____ ,   effective
_____)

Section 25.130 Pounds and Animal Shelters

Persons licensed to operate Pounds and Animal Shelters shall comply with the following rules in addition to the other rules already prescribed.

a) Licensee shall make a record of each animal received, including the date it was received, the source, and the eventual disposition.

b) Approved equipment as described in the Journal of the American Veterinary Medical Association, 930 North Meacham Road, Schaumburg, Illinois 60196 (February 1, 1986) July 1, 1978, shall be used for euthanasia.

c) Licensee shall accept any animal for which the person wishing to dispose of the animal is willing to sign an affidavit of ownership giving his name, address, telephone number, reasons for wishing to dispose of the ani-

DEPARTMENT OF AGRICULTURE

NOTICE OF PROPOSED AMENDMENTS

mal, and description of the animal, including distinguishing marks and pertinent medical information, if any.

d) Any animal presented to a pound or shelter in an injured, diseased, or ill condition shall be examined by and, if feasible, treated by a licensed veterinarian. If the veterinarian deems that, for humane reasons, the animal should be euthanized, his recommendations for euthanasia shall be followed.

e) Licensee operating a pound for a municipality or other political subdivision shall, in a conspicuous place at the establishment, post the hours the facility will be open with an attendant on duty to release estrayed pets back to their owner. Any expense incurred during the period of impoundment shall be paid by the owner prior to release of the impounded animal.

(Source: Amended at 13 Ill. Reg. _____, effective _____)

DEPARTMENT OF AGRICULTURE

NOTICE OF PROPOSED AMENDMENTS

1) Heading of Part: Bovine Brucellosis

2) Code Citation: 8 Ill. Adm. Code 75

3) Section Numbers: Proposed Action:

   75.5   Amended
   75.190   Amended

4) Statutory Authority: Illinois Bovine Brucellosis Eradication Act (Ill. Rev. Stat. 1987, ch. 8, pars. 139, 140, 142, and 143).

5) A Complete Description of the Subjects and Issues Involved:

We are updating a reference to the Illinois Revised Statutes by citing the latest edition which is the 1987 edition. This change will eliminate the need to keep old Illinois Revised Statutes on file in the agency. Also, it is easier for the public to locate the rule in a library when the current version is cited. This amendment will not impose any additional requirements.

Calves under 2 months of age entering Illinois from states (Class C) that still have high incidents of bovine brucellosis are entering Illinois marketing channels once they become older. These animals pose a potential risk to Illinois herds. The amendment is intended to keep these animals from moving once they are in the State and to reduce the potential exposure of Illinois cattle to Brucellosis. An entry permit is required on all shipments of calves from Class C states that are under two months of age and are not accompanied by their dams. Such calves will be quarantined until shipped to slaughter or neutered. Calves that are neutered will not be able to enter the breeding channels once they become older. The quarantine will keep them from moving once they are in the State and reduce the chance of them entering feeding channels. The quarantine will be released once the animals are slaughtered or neutered. The calves must be accompanied by a Certificate of Veterinary Inspection and identified with an official eartag. The eartag numbers will be recorded on the Certificate. At present, there is only one Brucellosis Class C state.

6) Will this proposed rule replace an emergency rule currently in effect? No

7) Does this rulemaking contain an automatic repeal date? No

8) Does this proposed amendment contain incorporations by reference? No

9) Are there any other amendments pending on this Part? No

10) Statement of Statewide Policy Objectives: This rulemaking does not impose any additional mandatory requirements on units of local government in such a way that would necessitate additional expenditures from local revenues.

DEPARTMENT OF AGRICULTURE

NOTICE OF PROPOSED AMENDMENTS

11) Time, Place and Manner in which interested persons may comment on this
proposed rulemaking:

A public hearing on the proposed amendments will be held on January 10, 1989,
at 10:00 a.m., Department of Agriculture, State Fairgrounds, Springfield,
Illinois. Persons unable to attend the hearing may present their comments
on the proposed rulemaking in writing to the Director, Department of
Agriculture, State Fairgrounds, Springfield, Illinois 62794-9281. Mailed
comments must be postmarked no later than January 5, so they will be
available for consideration at the public hearing. All comments received
will be fully considered by the agency and the Advisory Board of Livestock
Commissioners.

The public hearing on the proposed rulemaking will run concurrent with a
public meeting of the Advisory Board of Livestock Commissioners.

This proposed rulemaking may have an impact on small businesses. In accordance with Sections 3.01 and 4.03 of the Illinois Administrative Procedure Act,
small businesses may present their comments to the Director as outlined above.

12) Initial Regulatory Flexibility Analysis:
   A) Date rule was submitted to the Business Assistance Office of the
      Department of Commerce and Community Affairs: Nov. 4, 1988
   B) Types of small businesses affected: Owners of calves from Bovine
      Brucellosis Class C states; veterinarians.
   C) Reporting, bookkeeping or other procedures required for compliance:
      An entry permit must be obtained on shipments of calves under 2 months
      of age entering Illinois from Brucellosis Class C states. All such
      calves will be quarantined until shipped to slaughter or neutered.
      All calves must be accompanied by the Certificate of Veterinary
      Inspection and shall be individually identified by official eartags.
      The eartag numbers must be recorded on the Certificate of Veterinary
      Inspection.
   D) Types of professional skills necessary for compliance:
      Basic management, recordkeeping.

The full text of the Proposed Amendments begins on the next page!

DEPARTMENT OF AGRICULTURE

NOTICE OF PROPOSED AMENDMENTS

TITLE 8:   AGRICULTURE AND ANIMALS
CHAPTER I: DEPARTMENT OF AGRICULTURE
SUBCHAPTER b: ANIMALS AND ANIMAL PRODUCTS
(EXCEPT MEAT AND POULTRY INSPECTION ACT REGULATIONS)

PART 75
BOVINE BRUCELLOSIS

AUTHORITY: Implementing and authorized by the Illinois Bovine
Brucellosis Eradication Act (Ill. Rev. Stat. 1987 1985, ch. 8,

DEPARTMENT OF AGRICULTURE

NOTICE OF PROPOSED AMENDMENTS

par. 134 et seq.y as amended by P.A. 85-0333, effective January 1, 1988).

SOURCE: Regulations Relating to Bovine Brucellosis, filed January 17, 1972, effective January 27, 1972; amended, filed May 3, 1972, effective May 13, 1972; filed Dec. 6, 1972, effective Dec. 16, 1972; filed June 20, 1973, effective June 20, 1973; filed Dec. 14, 1973, effective Dec. 24, 1973; filed Aug. 19, 1975, effective Aug. 29, 1975; filed Mar. 12, 1976, effective March 22, 1976; filed June 21, 1976, effective July 1, 1976; filed Dec. 29, 1976, effective Jan. 8, 1977; amended at 2 Ill. Reg. 24, p. 55, effective June 15, 1978; amended at 3 Ill. Reg. 34, p. 96, effective Aug. 24, 1979; amended at 5 Ill. Reg. 720, effective January 2, 1981; codified at 5 Ill. Reg. 10453; amended at 7 Ill. Reg. 1737, effective January 28, 1983; amended at 7 Ill. Reg. 1733, effective February 2, 1983; amended at 8 Ill. Reg. 5891, effective April 23, 1984; amended at 9 Ill. Reg. 4483, effective March 22, 1985; amended at 9 Ill. Reg. 19647, effective January 1, 1986; amended at 10 Ill. Reg. 9741, effective May 21, 1986; amended at 11 Ill. Reg. 10169, effective May 15, 1987; amended at 12 Ill. Reg. 3386, effective January 22, 1988; amended at 13 Ill. Reg. _____, effective _____.

NOTE: CAPITALIZATION DENOTES STATUTORY LANGUAGE.

Section 75.5 Definitions

The definitions for this Part shall be as stated in 8 Ill. Adm. Code 20.1. The following definition shall also apply:

"Act" means the Illinois Bovine Brucellosis Eradication Act (Ill. Rev. Stat. 1987 1985, ch. 8, par. 134 et seq.y as amended by P.A. 85-0333, effective January 1, 1988).

"Registered animal" means an animal for which individual records of ancestry are recorded and maintained by a breed association whose purpose is the improvement of the bovine species, and for which individual registration certificates are issued and recorded by such breed association. The breed associations recognized by the Division are those recognized by the United States Department of Agriculture (9 CFR 51.1, 1988 1987).

(Source: Amended at 13 Ill. Reg. _____, effective _____)

Section 75.190 Additional Requirements on Cattle from States Designated as Class B and Class C States

DEPARTMENT OF AGRICULTURE

NOTICE OF PROPOSED AMENDMENTS

a) In addition to other entry requirements, a prior permit must be obtained for dairy, feeding or breeding cattle, except those consigned direct to slaughter or calves under 6 months of age except as further provided for in this Section, entering Illinois from states designated by the U.S. Department of Agriculture as Class B and Class C under provisions of the Brucellosis Eradication Uniform Methods and Rules as recommended and approved by the United States Animal Health Association (P.O. Box 28176, Suite 205, 6924 Lakeside Avenue, Richmond, Virginia 23228-0176) and by the U.S. Department of Agriculture (July 1, 1986). Such prior permits shall be obtained by contacting the Division of Animal Industries, Illinois Department of Agriculture, State Fairgrounds, P.O. Box 19281, Springfield, Illinois 62794-9281, telephone 217/782-4944. Information regarding the origin, destination and description of the cattle along with the number of animals in the shipment is necessary for obtaining a permit.

b) Breeding cattle 12 months of age or over from such states shall be placed under quarantine and in isolation until retested and negative to an official test for brucellosis conducted not less than 45 days nor more than 120 days after entering Illinois.

c) All female cattle born after July 1, 1985, if more than 4 months of age, except spayed heifers (female cattle may be spayed after entry into Illinois with prior approval from the Division which will be given upon receipt of the name of the veterinarian who will be performing the operation) or those consigned directly to slaughter, entering Illinois from Class B or Class C states must be official calfhood vaccinates and vaccination status shall be recorded on the official interstate health certificate. In lieu of calfhood vaccination, cattle from Class B states entering Illinois for feeding purposes only may be identified with a hot iron brand on either or both jaws or either hip using the letter F of not less than three inches in height.

d) Female cattle, except those consigned directly to slaughter, entering Illinois from Class C states shall, in addition to present entry requirements now on file, either originate from a certified brucellosis-free herd or be spayed and be officially identified by a hot iron brand on either or both jaws or on either hip using an open spade design (e.g., as used in playing cards) of

DEPARTMENT OF AGRICULTURE

NOTICE OF PROPOSED AMENDMENTS

not less than three inches in height. Certification of spaying by an accredited veterinarian is to be shown on the official interstate health certificate. Female cattle may be spayed after entry into Illinois with prior approval from the Division which will be given upon receipt of the name of the veterinarian who will be performing the operation.

e) Calves under two months of age not accompanied by their dams may be imported from Class C states if they meet the following requirements:

1) An entry permit shall be obtained on all shipments. All such calves shall be quarantined until shipped to slaughter or neutered (spayed or castrated).

2) All calves shall be accompanied by the Certificate of Veterinary Inspection and shall be individually identified by official eartags. The eartag numbers shall be recorded on the Certificate.

(Source: Amended at 13 Ill. Reg. _____, effective _____)

DEPARTMENT OF AGRICULTURE

NOTICE OF PROPOSED AMENDMENTS

1) Heading of Part: Definitions

2) Code Citation: 8 Ill. Adm. Code 20

3) Section Number: Proposed Action:

20.1   Amendment

4) Statutory Authority: Illinois Swine Disease Control and Eradication Act (Ill. Rev. Stat. 1987, ch. 8, par. 515); Illinois Feeder Swine Dealer Licensing Act (Ill. Rev. Stat. 1987, ch. 111, par. 215); Illinois Livestock Dealer Licensing Act (Ill. Rev. Stat. 1987, ch. 111, par. 415); Illinois Bovine Tuberculosis Eradication Act (Ill. Rev. Stat. 1987, ch. 8, par. 104); Illinois Bovine Brucellosis Eradication Act (Ill. Rev. Stat. 1987, ch. 8, par. 143); Illinois Swine Brucellosis Eradication Act (Ill. Rev. Stat. 1987, ch. 8, par. 14R1); Illinois Dead Animal Disposal Act (Ill. Rev. Stat. 1987, ch. 8, par. 160); Illinois Diseased Animals Act (Ill. Rev. Stat. 1987, ch. 8, par. 169); Livestock Auction Market Law (Ill. Rev. Stat. 1987, ch. 121 1/2, pars. 215a and 218); "AN ACT in relation to hatcheries, poultry flocks and the produce thereof" (Ill. Rev. Stat. 1987, ch. 8, par. 132.3); and Illinois Pseudorabies Control Act (Ill. Rev. Stat. 1987, ch. 8, par. 805).

5) A Complete Description of the Subjects and Issues Involved:

Reference to the Chicago-Joliet Marketing Center is being deleted as this public stockyards has ceased operations. This deletion will not create any impact on the regulated public.

We are updating references to the Code of Federal Rules by citing the latest edition which is the 1988 edition. This change will eliminate the need to keep old CFR's on file in the agency and carried by our inspection personnel. Also, it is easier for the public to locate the rule in a library when the current version is cited. These amendments will not impose any additional requirements.

6) Will this proposed rule replace an emergency rule currently in effect? No

7) Does this rulemaking contain an automatic repeal date? No

8) Does this proposed amendment contain incorporations by reference? No

9) Are there any other amendments pending on this Part? No

10) Statement of Statewide Policy Objectives: Rulemaking does not affect units of local governments.

DEPARTMENT OF AGRICULTURE

NOTICE OF PROPOSED AMENDMENTS

11) Time, Place and Manner in which interested persons may comment on this
proposed rulemaking:

A public hearing on the proposed amendments will be held on January 10, 1989,
at 10:00 a.m., Department of Agriculture, State Fairgrounds, Springfield,
Illinois. Persons unable to attend the hearing may present their comments
on the proposed rulemaking in writing to the Director, Department of
Agriculture, State Fairgrounds, Springfield, Illinois 62794-9281. Mailed
comments must be postmarked no later than January 5, so they will be
available for consideration at the public hearing. All comments received
will be fully considered by the agency and the Advisory Board of Livestock
Commissioners.

The public hearing on the proposed rulemaking will run concurrent with a
public meeting of the Advisory Board of Livestock Commissioners.

This proposed rulemaking may have an impact on small businesses. In accordance with Sections 3.01 and 4.03 of the Illinois Administrative Procedure Act,
small businesses may present their comments to the Director as outlined above.

12) Initial Regulatory Flexibility Analysis:
   A) Date rule was submitted to the Business Assistance Office of the
      Department of Commerce and Community Affairs: November 4, 1988
   B) Types of small businesses affected: Public stockyards, marketing centers,
      owners of cattle.
   C) Reporting, bookkeeping or other procedures required for compliance:
      None. These are definitions.
   D) Types of professional skills necessary for compliance:
      None.

The full text of the Proposed Amendments begins on the next page!

DEPARTMENT OF AGRICULTURE

NOTICE OF PROPOSED AMENDMENTS

TITLE 8: AGRICULTURE AND ANIMALS
CHAPTER I: DEPARTMENT OF AGRICULTURE
SUBCHAPTER b: ANIMALS AND ANIMAL PRODUCTS
(EXCEPT MEAT AND POULTRY INSPECTION ACT REGULATIONS)

PART 20
DEFINITIONS

Section
20.1   Definitions

AUTHORITY: Implementing and authorized by Section 15 of the Illinois Swine Disease Control and Eradication Act (Ill. Rev. Stat.
1987, ch. 8, par. 515); implementing and authorized by Section 15
of the Illinois Feeder Swine Dealer Licensing Act (Ill. Rev.
Stat. 1987, ch. 111, par. 215); implementing and authorized by
Section 15 of the Illinois Livestock Dealer Licensing Act (Ill.
Rev. Stat. 1987, ch. 111, par. 415); implementing and authorized
by Section 18 of the Illinois Bovine Tuberculosis Eradication Act
(Ill. Rev. Stat. 1987, ch. 8, par. 104); implementing and
authorized by Section 10 of the Illinois Bovine Brucellosis Eradication Act (Ill. Rev. Stat. 1987, ch. 8, par. 143); implement-
ing and authorized by Section 7 of the Illinois Swine Brucellosis
Eradication Act (Ill. Rev. Stat. 1987, ch. 8, par. 1481); implementing and authorized by Section 12 of the Illinois Dead Animal
Disposal Act (Ill. Rev. Stat. 1987, ch. 8, par. 160); implementing and authorized by Section 2 of the Illinois Diseased Animals
Act (Ill. Rev. Stat. 1987, ch. 8, par. 169); implementing and
authorized by Sections 8a and 11 of the Livestock Auction Market
Law (Ill. Rev. Stat. 1987, ch. 121 1/2, pars. 215a and 218);
implementing and authorized by Section 2.3 of "AN ACT in relation
to hatcheries, poultry flocks and the produce thereof" (Ill. Rev.
Stat. 1987, ch. 8, par. 132.3); implementing and authorized by
Section 5 of the Illinois Pseudorabies Control Act (Ill. Rev.
Stat. 1987, ch. 8, par. 805).

SOURCE: Regulations Relating to the Division of Meat, Poultry and
Livestock Inspection, Definitions, filed January 27, 1966, effective January 27, 1966; amended May 3, 1972, effective May 14,
1972; codified at 5 Ill. Reg. 10437; amended at 8 Ill. Reg. 5915,
effective April 23, 1984; amended at 9 Ill. Reg. 18404, effective
November 19, 1985; amended at 10 Ill. Reg. 9747, effective May
21, 1986; amended at 12 Ill. Reg. 8275, effective May 2, 1988;
amended at 13 Ill. Reg. _____, effective _____.

Section 20.1 Definitions

a) The term "Department" or "Department of Agriculture", unless otherwise indicated, means the Department of Agriculture of the State of Illinois.

h) The term "Division" or "Division of Animal Industries" means the Division of Animal Industries of the Illinois Department of Agriculture.

c) The term "Animal and Plant Health Inspection Service" means the Animal and Plant Health Inspection Service of the United States Department of Agriculture.

d) The term "brucellosis" means the disease wherein an animal is infected with Brucella micro-organisms irrespective of the occurrence or absence of clinical signs.

e) The term "official test" means any test for the detection of a reportable disease in Illinois as defined in 8 Ill. Adm. Code 85.10 approved by the Department and the Animal and Plant Health Inspection Service which is based on a standard test which is approved by the American Association of Veterinary Laboratory Diagnosticians and the United States Department of Agriculture and conducted in an approved laboratory.

f) The term "suspicious animal" or "suspect" means an animal which has given a positive reaction to an official test and whose test results are less than that which would result in a classification of reactor.

g) The term "infected animal", "positive animal" or "reactor" means an animal which has given a positive reaction to any official test or in which evidence of the disease has been found in the body or in the body discharges.

h) The term "approved laboratory" means one of the animal disease laboratories operated by the Division, the State-Federal Serology Laboratory, the Laboratories of Veterinary Diagnostic Medicine at the College of Veterinary Medicine, University of Illinois, or a laboratory approved by the Animal Health Official of the exporting state to conduct official tests.

i) The term "ring test" or "BRT" -- brucellosis ring test, means the diagnostic test of milk or cream to detect the presence of brucellosis in the herd in which such milk or cream sample was produced.

j) "Infectious disease" means the reaction resulting from the introduction into the body of a specific disease-producing organism or its toxic product.

k) "Contagious disease" means a specific infectious disease which is readily transmitted from host to host by direct contact or by means of intermediate hosts.

l) The term "infestation" or "infested with" means the invasion of the body by animal parasites.

m) The term "quarantine" means a condition in which one or more animals shall be kept separate and apart from and not allowed to come in contact in any way with other animals.

n) The term "restriction" or "restricted" means a condition in which one or more animals shall be kept on certain designated premises and shall not be allowed to come in contact in any way with animals from other premises.

o) A "Certified Brucellosis-Free Herd" is one in which at least two annual negative official tests for brucellosis have been conducted on all animals in the herd 6 months of age or over and for which a certificate has been issued by the Animal Health Official of the state of origin and the Animal and Plant Health Inspection Service.

p) A "Tuberculosis-free Accredited Herd" is one for which a certificate of accreditation has been issued by the Animal Health Official of the state of origin and the Animal and Plant Health Inspection Service.

q) The term "accredited veterinarian" means a veterinarian who is licensed by the state in which he practices, is approved by the animal health authority of that state, and is accredited by the United States Department of Agriculture.

r) A "recognized slaughtering establishment" is an establishment where slaughtering is conducted under Federal or State inspection.

s) The term "public stockyards" means a stockyards where trading in livestock is conducted, where yarding, feeding, and watering facilities are provided by the stockyard, transportation, or similar company, and where

State and/or Federal inspection is maintained for the inspection of livestock for communicable disease, such as ~~Chicago-Joliet Marketing Center, they located at Joliet,~~ National Stockyards located at East St. Louis~~,~~ and Peoria Union Stockyards located at Peoria.

t) A "Marketing Center" is a licensed livestock auction market which has been designated as a "Specifically Approved Stockyard" by the Department and the United States Department of Agriculture (9 CFR 78.44 (1988 ~~1987~~)). Incorporation by reference does not include any later amendments or editions beyond the date specified. Marketing Centers shall enter into a Memorandum of Understanding with the United States Department of Agriculture and the Department and comply with the standards set forth in that Memorandum.

u) A "consignment" means a document issued by the owner or shipper of livestock, designating the name of the owner and/or shipper; place of origin; stockyards, packing plant, or marketing center of destination; date of shipment; and number and description of livestock, certified to by the owner or shipper, kept in possession of the carrier and delivered to a stockyard, packing plant, or marketing center of destination upon acceptance. This consignment shall be held by the stockyards, packing plant, or marketing center for a period of not less than six months for inspection by the legally authorized officials of the United States Department of Agriculture and the Department and other officials having police powers.

v) The term "health certificate" or "certificate of health" or "interstate health certificate" or "certificate of veterinary inspection" means a legible record, made on an official form of the state of origin, or the Animal and Plant Health Inspection Service, and issued by an accredited veterinarian of the state of origin, a veterinarian in the employ of the Animal and Plant Health Inspection Service, or a veterinarian in the employ of the United States Armed Services, which shows that the animals or birds listed thereon meet the health requirements of the state of destination. The health certificate shall contain the name and address of the consignor, the name and address of the consignee, and an accurate description or identification of the animals or birds involved, and shall also indicate the health status of the animals or birds, including the dates and

results of required tests and dates of vaccination, if any. The two copies of the health certificate that are labeled "Division Copy" shall be submitted to the Division within 30 days of issuance.

w) An "approved health certificate" is one that has been so endorsed by the Animal Health Official of the state of origin.

x) The term "State Inspector" means an Animal Health Inspector employed by the Division of Animal Industries of the Illinois Department of Agriculture.

y) The term "Federal Inspector" means an Animal Health Technician employed by the Animal and Plant Health Inspection Service of the United States Department of Agriculture.

z) The term "feeder female cattle" means female bovines 6-18 months of age which have not been tested for brucellosis prior to sale.

aa) The term "Director" means the Director of the Illinois Department of Agriculture.

bb) The term "feeder swine" or "feeding swine" means swine under 6 months of age, weighing less than slaughter weight and not requiring testing as breeding swine or swine consigned directly to slaughter.

cc) The term "Market Cattle Identification Program" means the brucellosis testing program of market cattle that is part of the National Brucellosis Eradication Program (9 CFR 78 (1988 ~~1987~~)). Incorporation by reference does not include any later amendments or editions beyond the date specified. In accordance with the authority stated in the Illinois Bovine Brucellosis Eradication Act (Ill. Rev. Stat. 1987, ch. 8, par. 135), the Department has entered into a cooperative agreement with the United States Department of Agriculture to identify brucellosis infected herds.

dd) The term "negative exposed cattle" means a test negative animal in an infected herd.

(Source: Amended at 13 Ill. Reg. _____, effective _____)

ILLINOIS REGISTER

DEPARTMENT OF AGRICULTURE

NOTICE OF PROPOSED AMENDMENTS

1) Heading of Part: Diseased Animals

2) Code Citation: 8 Ill. Adm. Code 85

3) Section Numbers: Proposed Action:

85.5	Amendment
85.10	Amendment
85.15	Amendment
85.50	Amendment
85.75	Amendment

4) Statutory Authority: Illinois Diseased Animals Act (Ill. Rev. Stat. 1987, ch. 8, pars. 169, 179, 180, and 189)

5) A Complete Description of the Subjects and Issues Involved:

We are updating references to the Code of Federal Rules by citing the latest edition which is the 1988 edition. This change will eliminate the need to keep old CFR's on file in the agency and carried by our inspection personnel. Also, it is easier for the public to locate the rule in a library when the current version is cited. These amendments will not impose any additional requirements.

On August 16, 1988, the Secretary of the U.S. Department of Agriculture declared salmonella enteritidis a hazardous disease to the poultry industry. Salmonella enteritidis has occurred with increasing frequency in the northeastern United States during the past several years. A recent discovery indicated that salmonella enteritidis can be spread from an infected hen through an intact egg. Salmonella enteritidis has been identified at a hatchery in Illinois. The amendment will require any veterinarian, producers of table eggs, or other person who has knowledge of the disease to report the disease to the Department immediately after discovery. Through reporting, the Department will gain valuable information on the extent of the infection and how fast it is spreading.

We are updating reference to the Bovine Tuberculosis Eradication Uniform Methods and Rules, which has been republished as of March 31, 1988. This amendment will not impose any additional compliance requirements on goats.

6) Will this proposed rule replace an emergency rule currently in effect? No

7) Does this rulemaking contain an automatic repeal date? No

8) Does this proposed amendment contain incorporations by reference? No

9) Are there any other amendments pending on this Part? No

DEPARTMENT OF AGRICULTURE

NOTICE OF PROPOSED AMENDMENTS

10) Statement of Statewide Policy Objectives: Rulemaking does not affect units of local governments.

11) Time, Place and Manner in which interested persons may comment on this proposed rulemaking:

A public hearing on the proposed amendments will be held on January 10, 1989, at 10:00 a.m.,, Department of Agriculture, State Fairgrounds, Springfield, Illinois. Persons unable to attend the hearing may present their comments on the proposed rulemaking in writing to the Director, Department of Agriculture, State Fairgrounds, Springfield, Illinois 62794-9281. Mailed comments must be postmarked no later than January 5, so they will be available for consideration at the public hearing. All comments received will be fully considered by the agency and the Advisory Board of Livestock Commissioners.

The public hearing on the proposed rulemaking will run concurrent with a public meeting of the Advisory Board of Livestock Commissioners.

This proposed rulemaking may have an impact on small businesses. In accordance with Sections 3.01 and 4.03 of the Illinois Administrative Procedure Act, small businesses may present their comments to the Director as outlined above.

12) Initial Regulatory Flexibility Analysis:
   A) Date rule was submitted to the Business Assistance Office of the Department of Commerce and Community Affairs: November 4, 1988
   B) Types of small businesses affected: Owners of cattle; veterinarians; producers of table eggs; persons transporting diseased livestock; owners of goats.
   C) Reporting, bookkeeping or other procedures required for compliance: The amendments adopt the latest printed versions of the Bovine Tuberculosis Eradication Uniform Methods and Rules and the Code of Federal Rules, which will not impose any additional compliance requirements.

   Any veterinarian, producers of table eggs, or other person having knowledge of salmonella enteritidis must report the disease to the Department immediately after discovery.

   D) Types of professional skills necessary for compliance: Basic management, reporting and recordkeeping.

The full text of the Proposed Amendments begins on the next page:

DEPARTMENT OF AGRICULTURE

NOTICE OF PROPOSED AMENDMENTS

TITLE 8: AGRICULTURE AND ANIMALS
CHAPTER I: DEPARTMENT OF AGRICULTURE
SUBCHAPTER b: ANIMALS AND ANIMAL PRODUCTS
(EXCEPT MEAT AND POULTRY INSPECTION ACT REGULATIONS)

PART 85
DISEASED ANIMALS

Section
85.5   Definitions
85.7   Incorporation by Reference
85.10   Reportable Diseases
85.15   Truck Cleaning and Disinfection
85.20   Disposal of Sick, Diseased, or Crippled Animals at
        Stockyards
85.25   Sale of Livestock Quarantined Because of Disease
85.30   Identification Ear Tags for Livestock
85.35   Identification Tags Not to be Removed
85.40   Livestock for Immediate Slaughter Not to be
        Diverted En Route
85.45   Anthrax
85.50   Goats
85.55   Scrapie in Sheep
85.60   Bluetongue
85.65   Sheep Foot Rot (Repealed)
85.70   Cattle Scabies
85.75   Cattle Scabies -- Additional Requirements on Cattle
        from Certain Designated Areas
85.80   Sheep
85.85   Diseased Animals
85.90   Copy of Health Certificate Shall be Furnished
85.95   Requests for Permits
85.100 Consignments to Stockyards, Recognized Slaughtering
        Centers, or Marketing Centers
85.103 Obligation of Transportation Company and Truck Operators
85.110 Additional Requirements on Cattle From Designated States

AUTHORITY: Implementing and authorized by the Illinois Diseased
Animals Act (Ill. Rev. Stat. 1987, ch. 8, par. 168 et seq.) and
Section 6 of the Illinois Bovine Brucellosis Eradication Act
(Ill. Rev. Stat. 1987, ch. 8, par. 139).

SOURCE: Regulations Relating to Diseased Animals, filed January
17, 1972, effective January 27, 1972; filed August 19, 1975,
effective August 29, 1975; filed December 29, 1976, effective
January 8, 1977; amended at 2 Ill. Reg. 24, p. 12, effective June
15, 1978; amended at 3 Ill. Reg. 33, p. 337, effective August 17,
1979; amended at 5 Ill. Reg. 724, effective January 2, 1981; cod-

DEPARTMENT OF AGRICULTURE

NOTICE OF PROPOSED AMENDMENTS

ified at 5 Ill. Reg. 10456; amended at 7 Ill. Reg. 1746, effective January 28, 1983; amended at 8 Ill. Reg. 5925, effective
April 23, 1984; amended at 9 Ill. Reg. 4469, effective March 22,
1985; amended at 9 Ill. Reg. 18411, effective November 19, 1985;
amended at 10 Ill. Reg. 20464, effective January 1, 1987; amended
at 12 Ill. Reg. 8283, effective May 2, 1988; amended at 13 Ill.
Reg. _____, effective _____.

Section 85.5 Definitions

For the purpose of these rules, the following definitions shall
apply:

"Accredited veterinarian" means a veterinarian who is
licensed by the state in which he practices, is approved
by the animal health authority of that state, and is
accredited by the United States Department of Agriculture (9 CFR 160, 161 and 162; 1988 1987).

"Division" means the Division of Animal Industries of
the Illinois Department of Agriculture, State Fairgrounds, P.O. Box 19281, Springfield, Illinois
62794-9781.

"Recognized slaughtering center" means an establishment
where slaughtering is conducted under Federal or State
inspection.

(Source: Amended at 13 Ill. Reg. _____, effective
_____)

Section 85.10 Reportable Diseases

a) Suspected cases of the following diseases shall be
   reported immediately to the Department:

   anthrax
   avian influenza
   bluetongue
   brucellosis -- bovine, swine, equine and caprine
   contagious equine metritis
   equine viral encephalitides
   fowl typhoid
   hog cholera
   Mycoplasma gallisepticum -- turkeys
   Mycoplasma synoviae -- turkeys
   Newcastle disease

paratuberculosis -- (Johne's disease)
piroplasmosis
pseudorabies -- (Aujeszky's disease)
psittacosis -- (ornithosis)
pullorum disease
rabies
salmonella enteritidis
salmonella typhimurium -- poultry
scabies -- cattle and sheep
scrapie
tuberculosis# -- bovine
vesicular conditions of any type
any contagious or infectious disease presently
considered as "exotic", i.e., not known to exist
in the United States

b) Any herd owner, flock owner, veterinarian or other person having knowledge of the disease, failing to report a
suspect case of any of the above diseases immediately
after discovery, or who is responsible for the spread of
the disease, shall be subject to penalty as provided by
law.

c) Reports of any of the above diseases shall be made to
the Division, telephone 217/782-4944.

(Source: Amended   at   13   Ill.   Reg. _____, effective
_____)

Section 85.15 Truck Cleaning and Disinfection

Any truck or other conveyance in which diseased livestock is
transported shall be cleaned and disinfected immediately after
the diseased livestock is unloaded as prescribed in the Code of
Federal Regulations (9 CFR 71.7, 71.10-71.12; 1988 1983).

(Source: Amended   at   13   Ill.   Reg. _____, effective
_____)

Section 85.50 Goats

a) Part A -- Brucellosis in Goats

1) When a serologic test for brucellosis in goats discloses one or more reactors, the entire herd shall
be placed under quarantine and the reactor(s) immediately isolated from the remainder of the herd,
reactor tagged and branded, and slaughtered. After

removal of the reactor(s), the entire herd shall be
retested at time intervals and the number of times
as requested by the Division. The length of the
quarantine period shall be determined by the Division.

2) All brucellosis agglutination blood tests of goats
shall be made at an approved laboratory.

h) Part B -- Requirements for Establishing and Maintaining
Certified Brucellosis-Free Herds of Goats

1) General Requirements

A) Certified brucellosis-free herd certificates,
which shall be valid for one year, unless
revoked in accordance with the procedures as
adopted by the United States Animal Health Association (P.O. Box 28176, Suite 205, 6924 Lakeside Avenue, Richmond, Virginia 23228-0176) and
as outlined for cattle certificate revocation in
the Brucellosis Eradication Uniform Methods and
Rules, effective July 1, 1986, published by the
United States Department of Agriculture, Animal
and Plant Health Inspection Service, shall be
issued by the Division.

B) Certificates shall be extended for a period of
one year upon evidence of a negative herd retest
and compliance with all requirements for maintenance of a certified brucellosis-free herd.

C) A "herd" shall be considered as including all
animals 6 months of age and over and shall consist of at least 5 animals.

D) All animals in the herd shall be identified by
registration number, individual tattoo, or ear
tag.

E) All official blood tests of goats shall be conducted at an approved laboratory.

2) To Qualify for Certification

A) Herds shall be certified upon completion of 2
consecutive negative complete herd tests not
less than 10 nor more than 14 months apart.

B) Animals classified as suspects, in herds that
are otherwise negative, must be retested at 30-
day intervals until their status has been determined. If the suspects are sold or otherwise
disposed of before their status has been determined, the entire herd must be retested to
achieve a negative herd status. If the suspects
are classified as reactors upon retest, the herd
is considered to be infected. Diseased goats
may only be consigned directly to a slaughtering
facility and must be accompanied by a "Permit
for Movement, VS Form 1-27".

C) If on the initial herd test, or as a result of
any retests of animals in the herd, one or more
reactors are disclosed, the entire herd shall be
placed under quarantine and the reactor(s) immediately isolated from the remainder of the herd,
reactor tagged and branded, and slaughtered.
After removal of the reactor(s), the entire herd
shall be retested at time intervals and the number of times as requested by the Division. The
length of the quarantine period shall be determined by the Division.

3) To Qualify for Recertification

A) A negative herd test conducted within 60 days
prior to the anniversary date is required for
continuous certification. Upon receipt of a
negative herd test, the Division shall extend
certification for 12 months from the anniversary
date.

B) If the annual test for recertification is conducted within 60 days following the anniversary
date and all the animals are negative, certification will be restored and the certification
period will be 12 months from the anniversary
date.

C) If the annual test for recertification is not
conducted within 60 days following the anniversary date, certification is cancelled and
recertification requirements are then the same
as for initial certification.

D) If suspects or reactors are disclosed on a
recertification test, their disposition and herd
retest requirements shall be the same as specified in 8 Ill. Adm. Code 85.50(b)(2)(B) and (C).

E) All official blood tests of goats shall be conducted at an approved laboratory.

4) Additions to Certified Brucellosis-Free Herds

A) Animals originating from other certified herds
may be added without tests.

B) Animals originating from herds not certified may
be added; provided, they are negative to an
official brucellosis test within 60 days prior
to addition, are held in isolation from other
members of the certified herd for a minimum
period of 30 days and are retested and negative
at the end of this isolation period.

C) Purchased additions shall not receive new herd
status for sale or exhibition purposes until
they have been members of the herd for at least
30 days and are included in a complete herd
retest.

c) Part C -- Requirements for Establishing and Maintaining
Accredited Tuberculosis-Free Herds of Goats

1) General Requirements

A) Accredited tuberculosis-free herd certificates,
which shall be valid for one year, unless
revoked in accordance with the procedures outlined in the Bovine Tuberculosis Eradication
Uniform Methods and Rules, effective March 31,
1988 January 4, 1983, with amendments through
February 20, 1987, Part III B, Accredited Herd
Plan for Dairy Goats, shall be issued by the
Division (9 CFR 77.1 (1988 1987)).

B) Certificates may be extended for a period of one
year upon evidence of a negative herd retest and
compliance with all requirements for maintenance
of an accredited tuberculosis-free herd.

C) A "herd" shall be considered as including all animals 12 months of age and over and shall consist of at least 5 animals.

D) All animals in the herd shall be identified by registration number, individual tattoo, or ear tag.

E) All official tuberculin tests shall be conducted by an accredited veterinarian or a veterinarian in the employ of the Illinois Department of Agriculture or the United States Department of Agriculture.

2) To Qualify for Accreditation

A) Herds shall be accredited upon completion of 2 consecutive negative complete herd tests not less than 10 nor more than 14 months apart.

B) If a reaction to the tuberculin test is disclosed, the veterinarian reading the test shall, within 24 hours, notify the Division by collect telephone call and make arrangements for a veterinarian trained in conducting the comparative-cervical test to retest the animal within 10 days of the original injection. If the animal is identified as a reactor as a result of the comparative-cervical test, personnel from either the Illinois Department of Agriculture or the United States Department of Agriculture will issue a quarantine, supervise disposition of animals, and conduct additional tests on members of the herd.

3) To Qualify for Reaccreditation

A) A negative herd test conducted within 60 days prior to the anniversary date is required for continuous accreditation. Upon receipt of a negative herd test, the Division shall extend accreditation for 12 months from the anniversary date.

B) If the annual test for reaccreditation is conducted within 60 days following the anniversary date, certification will be restored and the

accreditation period will be 12 months from the anniversary date.

C) If the annual test for reaccreditation is not conducted within 60 days following the anniversary date, accreditation is cancelled and reaccreditation requirements are then the same as for initial accreditation.

D) If a reaction to the tuberculin test is disclosed at the time of the reaccreditation test, the procedure outlined in 8 III. Adm. Code 85.50(b)(2)(B) shall be followed.

4) Additions to Accredited Tuberculosis-Free Herds

A) Animals originating from other accredited herds may be added without tests.

B) Animals originating from herds not accredited may be added; provided, they are negative to an official test for tuberculosis within 60 days prior to addition and are retested and negative to an official tuberculin test not sooner than 60 days from the date the previous test was conducted.

C) Purchased additions shall not receive new herd status for sale or exhibition purposes until they have been members of the herd for at least 60 days and are included in a complete herd retest.

d) Part D - Other Contagious Diseases. All goats, including dairy goats, will not be allowed to be exhibited in Illinois and must be removed immediately from the exhibition area if showing signs of any of the following conditions:

1) Lesions of contagious ecthyma (sore mouth).

2) Active lesions of ringworm with resulting loss of hair.

3) Caseous lymphadenitis as evidenced by draining abscesses.

DEPARTMENT OF AGRICULTURE

NOTICE OF PROPOSED AMENDMENTS

(Source: Amended at 13 Ill. Reg. _____, effective
_____)

Section 85.75 Cattle Scabies -- Additional Requirements on Cattle from Certain Designated Areas

a) A prior permit must be obtained from the Division before
    cattle, except those consigned direct to slaughter, may
    enter Illinois from certain designated areas determined
    to have high incidence of cattle scabies. The Director
    of the Department shall have authority to specify the
    designated areas from which movement of cattle into
    Illinois will be restricted.

b) Cattle from such areas, except those consigned to a
    recognized exhibition and moved from Illinois following
    exhibition (county and State fairs, other State-support-
    ed exhibitions, and breed registry exhibitions); dairy
    cattle; or those consigned direct to slaughter, shall be
    dipped for cattle scabies within 10 days prior to entry
    or treated in accordance with the procedures as set
    forth in 9 CFR 73.12 (1988 1987)).

c) Each such animal shall be treated with a solution of
    approved acaricide and water or other method of treat-
    ment approved by the United States Department of Agri-
    culture (9 CFR 73.10 and 73.12; 1988 1987)).

(Source: Amended at 13 Ill. Reg. _____, effective
_____)

DEPARTMENT OF AGRICULTURE

NOTICE OF PROPOSED AMENDMENTS

1) Heading of Part: Illinois Bovine Tuberculosis Eradication Act

2) Code Citation: 8 Ill. Adm. Code 80

3) Section Numbers: Proposed Action:

80.10   Amendment
80.20   Amendment
80.110   Amendment

4) Statutory Authority: Illinois Bovine Tuberculosis Eradication Act (Ill.
Rev. Stat. 1987, ch. 8, par. 87.5, 92, 93, 94, 95, 98.6, and 104)

5) A Complete Description of the Subjects and Issues Involved:

We are updating references to the Bovine Tuberculosis Eradication Uniform
Methods and Rules, which has been republished as of March 31, 1988. These
amendments will not impose any additional compliance requirements on cattle.

We are updating a reference to the Illinois Revised Statutes by citing the
latest edition which is the 1987 edition. It is easier for the public to
locate the Act in a library when the current version is cited. This amendment
will not impose any additional requirements on the regulated public.

6) Will this proposed rule replace an emergency rule currently in effect? No

7) Does this rulemaking contain an automatic repeal date? No

8) Does this proposed amendment contain incorporations by reference? No

9) Are there any other amendments pending on this Part? No

10) Statement of Statewide Policy Objectives: Rulemaking does not affect
units of local governments.

11) Time, Place and Manner in which interested persons may comment on this
proposed rulemaking:

A public hearing on the proposed amendments will be held on January 10, 1989,
at 10:00 a.m., Department of Agriculture, State Fairgrounds, Springfield,
Illinois. Persons unable to attend the hearing may present their comments
on the proposed rulemaking in writing to the Director, Department of
Agriculture, State Fairgrounds, Springfield, Illinois 62794-9281. Mailed
comments must be postmarked no later than January 5, so they will be
available for consideration at the public hearing. All comments received
will be fully considered by the agency and the Advisory Board of Livestock
Commissioners.

DEPARTMENT OF AGRICULTURE

NOTICE OF PROPOSED AMENDMENTS

The public hearing on the proposed rulemaking will run concurrent with a public meeting of the Advisory Board of Livestock Commissioners.

This proposed rulemaking may have an impact on small businesses. In accordance with Sections 3.01 and 4.03 of the Illinois Administrative Procedure Act, small businesses may present their comments to the Director as outlined above.

12) Initial Regulatory Flexibility Analysis:
   A) Date rule was submitted to the Business Assistance Office of the Department of Commerce and Community Affairs: November 4, 1988
   B) Types of small businesses affected: Owners of cattle; veterinarians.
   C) Reporting, bookkeeping or other procedures required for compliance: None. The amendments adopt the latest printed versions of the Bovine Tuberculosis Eradication Uniform Methods and Rules and the Illinois Revised Statutes, which will not impose any additional compliance requirements.
   D) Types of professional skills necessary for compliance: Basic management and recordkeeping.

The full text of the Proposed Amendments begins on the next page!

DEPARTMENT OF AGRICULTURE

NOTICE OF PROPOSED AMENDMENTS

TITLE 8: AGRICULTURE AND ANIMALS
CHAPTER I: DEPARTMENT OF AGRICULTURE
SUBCHAPTER b: ANIMALS AND ANIMAL PRODUCTS (EXCEPT MEAT AND POULTRY INSPECTION ACT REGULATIONS)

PART 80
ILLINOIS BOVINE TUBERCULOSIS ERADICATION ACT

Section
80.10   Requirements for Illinois Tuberculosis-Free Accredited Herd
80.20   When Indemnity Will Be Paid on Tests
80.30   Herds Quarantined Because of Suspected Tuberculosis Infection
80.40   Identification Tags Not To Be Removed
80.50   Infected Herd Depopulation (Repealed)
80.60   Cattle for Immediate Slaughter (Repealed)
80.70   Feeding or Grazing Cattle (Repealed)
80.80   Female Cattle--Beef Breeds--18 Months and Over (Repealed)
80.90   Sale of Quarantined Feeding or Grazing Cattle (Repealed)
80.100   Release of Feeding or Grazing Cattle from Quarantine (Repealed)
80.110   Dairy or Beef Cattle or Steers
80.120   Tuberculin Tests

AUTHORITY: Implementing and authorized by the Illinois Bovine Tuberculosis Eradication Act (Ill. Rev. Stat. 1987, ch. 8, par. 87 et seq.).

SOURCE: Regulations Relating to Bovine Tuberculosis, filed January 17, 1972, effective January 27, 1972; filed June 21, 1976, effective July 1, 1976; filed December 29, 1976, effective January 8, 1977; amended at 2 Ill. Reg. 24, p. 1, effective June 15, 1978; codified at 5 Ill. Reg. 10455; amended at 7 Ill. Reg. 1742, effective January 28, 1983; amended at 8 Ill. Reg. 17809, effective October 1, 1984; amended at 9 Ill. Reg. 4503, effective March 22, 1985; amended at 9 Ill. Reg. 18432, effective November 19, 1985; emergency amendment at 11 Ill. Reg. 5326, effective March 13, 1987, for a maximum of 150 days; amended at 11 Ill. Reg. 10183, effective May 15, 1987; amended at 12 Ill. Reg. 8295, effective May 2, 1988; amended at 13 Ill. Reg. _____, effective _____.

Section 80.10   Requirements for Illinois Tuberculosis-Free Accredited Herd

A cattle herd qualifies as a tuberculosis-free accredited herd when it meets the requirements of the Bovine Tuberculosis Eradi-

DEPARTMENT OF AGRICULTURE

NOTICE OF PROPOSED AMENDMENTS

cation Uniform Methods and Rules (March 31, 1988 ~~January 4, 1982, with amendments through February 20, 1982~~) for such herds as approved by the United States Animal Health Association (P.O. Box 26176, Suite 205, 6924 Lakeside Avenue, Richmond, Virginia 23228-0176) and the United States Department of Agriculture, Animal and Plant Health Inspection Service, for the establishment and maintenance of a tuberculosis-free accredited herd of cattle. This incorporation by reference does not include any future amendments or editions beyond the date specified.

(Source: Amended at 13 Ill. Reg. _____, effective _____)

Section 80.20 When Indemnity Will Be Paid on Tests

Indemnity will be paid to owners of dairy and breeding cattle which react to the tuberculin test administered by accredited veterinarians and are destroyed provided:

a) The entire herd is tuberculin tested. Tuberculosis reactors found when there is not a complete herd test are not eligible for indemnity.

b) Feeder cattle and steers are not eligible for indemnity except when an entire herd is depopulated due to tuberculosis infection.

c) The appraisal is made by a regularly employed State or Federal veterinarian and subject to the requirements of Sections 6, 7, and 8 of the Illinois Bovine Tuberculosis Eradication Act (Ill. Rev. Stat. 1987 ~~1983~~, ch. 8, para. 92, 93, and 94). The appraisal value of the animal shall be based upon the breeding value of such animal at the moment of appraisal, taking into consideration the age, breed, health status, weight and market value at slaughter.

(Source: Amended at 13 Ill. Reg. _____, effective _____)

Section 80.110 Dairy or Beef Cattle or Steers

All dairy or beef cattle or steers being exhibited in the State of Illinois from Accredited Tuberculosis Free States as defined under the Bovine Tuberculosis Eradication Uniform Methods and Rules (March 31, 1988 ~~January 4, 1982, with amendments through February 20, 1982~~) as approved by the United States Animal Health Association (P.O. Box 28176, Suite 205, 6924 Lakeside Avenue,

---

DEPARTMENT OF AGRICULTURE

NOTICE OF PROPOSED AMENDMENTS

Richmond, Virginia 23228-0176) and the United States Department of Agriculture shall be accompanied by an official certificate of health issued by an accredited veterinarian. This incorporation by reference does not include any future amendments or editions beyond the date specified. No tuberculin test is required for cattle originating from Accredited Tuberculosis Free States. Cattle being exhibited in Illinois from a state that is not Tuberculosis Accredited Free shall be accompanied by an an official certificate of health issued by an accredited veterinarian showing:

a) Cattle originated from an accredited tuberculosis-free herd. Accredited herd number and date of last test shall be recorded on the certificate and the cattle shall be identified by ear tag number, tattoo number or registration name and number, OR

b) Cattle originating out-of-state were negative to a tuberculin test conducted within 60 days prior to exhibition, OR

c) If Illinois is not an Accredited Tuberculosis Free State, cattle originating in Illinois were negative to a tuberculin test conducted within 90 days prior to exhibition.

(Source: Amended at 13 Ill. Reg. _____, effective _____)

DEPARTMENT OF AGRICULTURE

NOTICE OF PROPOSED AMENDMENTS

1) Heading of Part: Illinois Dead Animals Disposal Act

2) Code Citation: 8 Ill. Adm. Code 90

3) Section Numbers: Proposed Action:

   90.10   Amended
   90.110   Amended

4) Statutory Authority: Illinois Dead Animal Disposal Act (Ill. Rev. Stat. 1987, ch. 8, pars. 158, 160, and 165).

5) A Complete Description of the Subjects and Issues Involved:

We are updating references to the Illinois Revised Statutes by citing the latest edition which is the 1987 edition. This change will eliminate the need to keep old Illinois Revised Statutes on file in the agency. Also, it is easier for the public to locate the rule in a library when the current version is cited. These amendments will not impose any additional requirements.

We are adding a statement that disposal by burial must be in compliance with the Illinois Environmental Protection Act to eliminate possible confusion by the public that compliance with Agriculture's rules does not mean that they do not have to comply with EPA requirements. This clarification was requested by the Illinois Environmental Protection Agency. The disposal by burning requirements already make reference to the Environment Protection Act, and this amendment will make the language in the two subsections consistent. The amendment does not add any additional requirements because the public must comply with the Illinois Environmental Protection Act requirements anyway.

6) Will this proposed rule replace an emergency rule currently in effect? No

7) Does this rulemaking contain an automatic repeal date? No

8) Does this proposed amendment contain incorporations by reference? None that require approval in accordance with Section 6.02(b) of the Illinois Administrative Procedure Act.

9) Are there any other amendments pending on this Part? No

10) Statement of Statewide Policy Objectives: This rulemaking does not impose any additional mandatory requirements on units of local government in such a way that would necessitate additional expenditures from local revenues.

11) Time, Place and Manner in which interested persons may comment on this proposed rulemaking:

DEPARTMENT OF AGRICULTURE

NOTICE OF PROPOSED AMENDMENTS

A public hearing on the proposed amendments will be held on January 10, 1989, at 10:00 a.m., Department of Agriculture, State Fairgrounds, Springfield, Illinois. Persons unable to attend the hearing may present their comments on the proposed rulemaking in writing to the Director, Department of Agriculture, State Fairgrounds, Springfield, Illinois 62794-9281. Mailed comments must be postmarked no later than January 5, so they will be available for consideration at the public hearing. All comments received will be fully considered by the agency and the Advisory Board of Livestock Commissioners.

The public hearing on the proposed rulemaking will run concurrent with a public meeting of the Advisory Board of Livestock Commissioners.

This proposed rulemaking may have an impact on small businesses. In accordance with Sections 3.01 and 4.03 of the Illinois Administrative Procedure Act, small businesses may present their comments to the Director as outlined above.

12) Initial Regulatory Flexibility Analysis:
  A) Date rule was submitted to the Business Assistance Office of the Department of Commerce and Community Affairs: Nov. 4, 1988
  B) Types of small businesses affected: Renderers, blenders, collection centers, and persons disposing of animals, poultry, fish, or parts of bodies thereof on their farms.
  C) Reporting, bookkeeping or other procedures required for compliance: Disposal by burial must be in compliance with the Illinois Environmental Protection Act.
  D) Types of professional skills necessary for compliance: Basic management.

The full text of the Proposed Amendments begins on the next page:

DEPARTMENT OF AGRICULTURE

NOTICE OF PROPOSED AMENDMENTS

TITLE 8: AGRICULTURE AND ANIMALS
CHAPTER I: DEPARTMENT OF AGRICULTURE
SUBCHAPTER b: ANIMALS AND ANIMAL PRODUCTS (EXCEPT MEAT
AND POULTRY INSPECTION ACT REGULATIONS)

PART 90
ILLINOIS DEAD ANIMAL DISPOSAL ACT

Section
90.10   Plant Facilities
90.20   Plant Premises
90.30   Annual Truck Permits (Repealed)
90.40   Truck Operator's Records (Repealed)
90.50   Odors and Insects Shall Be Controlled
90.60   Salmonella Control For Renderers and Blenders
90.70   Inspection of Premise (Repealed)
90.80   Identification of Receptacles
90.90   Records (Repealed)
90.100   Transportation and Transactions (Repealed)
90.110   On-The-Farm Disposal
90.120   Collection Center
90.130   Disposal By Collection Center of Unusable Materials

AUTHORITY: Implementing and authorized by the Illinois Dead Animal Disposal Act (Ill. Rev. Stat. 1987 1983, ch. 8, par. 149.1 et
seq.).

SOURCE: Regulations Relating to the Disposal of Dead Animals,
filed January 17, 1972, effective January 27, 1972; filed December 6, 1972, effective December 16, 1972; codified at 5 Ill. Reg.
10458; amended at 7 Ill. Reg. 852, effective January 10, 1983;
amended at 8 Ill. Reg. 5937, effective April 23, 1984; amended at
13 Ill. Reg. _____, effective _____.

Section 90.10 Plant Facilities

If, upon first inspection, the facility of the renderer, blender
or collection center fails to meet the requirements set forth in
Section 10 of the Illinois Dead Animal Disposal Act (Ill. Rev.
Stat. 1987 1983, ch. 8, par. 158) and the rules of this Part, the
applicant shall be granted sixty (60) days in which to correct
the deficiencies specified. At the end of the period for cor-
recting the deficiencies, another inspection shall be made. If
upon inspection the deficiencies have been corrected, a license
shall be issued.

(Source: Amended at 13 Ill. Reg. _____, effective
_____)

DEPARTMENT OF AGRICULTURE

NOTICE OF PROPOSED AMENDMENTS

Section 90.110 On-The-Farm Disposal

Persons disposing of animals, poultry, fish, or parts of bodies
thereof, other than to a licensed renderer, shall comply with the
following:

a) Disposal by Burning

    1) No open burning will be permitted.

    2) Any disposal by burning must be performed with an
        incinerator that is in compliance with the Illinois
        Environmental Protection Act (Ill. Rev. Stat. 1987
        1983, ch. 111 1/2, par. 1001 et seq.).

b) Disposal by Burying

    1) Location shall be in an area where runoff will not
        contaminate water supplies.

    2) Depth shall be sufficient to allow at least a six-
        inch compacted soil cover over the uppermost part of
        the carcass.

    3) The abdominal cavity of large carcasses shall be
        punctured to allow escape of putrefactive gasses.

    4) Lime or other chemical agent shall not be used to
        prevent decomposition.

    5) Precautions shall be taken at the site of burial
        necessary to prevent any disturbance by animal or
        mechanical means.

    6) If a disposal pit is employed for daily or routine
        deposits, there shall be a minimum six-inch com-
        pacted soil cover after each deposition.

    7) Any disposal by burial shall also be in compliance
        with the Illinois Environmental Protection Act.

(Source: Amended at 13 Ill. Reg. _____, effective
_____)

DEPARTMENT OF AGRICULTURE

NOTICE OF PROPOSED AMENDMENTS

1) Heading of Part: Livestock Dealer Licensing

2) Code Citation: 68 Ill. Adm. Code 610

3) Section Numbers: Proposed Action:

   610.10   Amended
   610.20   Amended
   610.30   Amended
   610.40   Amended
   610.60   Amended

4) Statutory Authority: Illinois Livestock Dealer Licensing Act (Ill. Rev. Stat. 1987, ch. III, pars. 415, and 420.1).

5) A Complete Description of the Subjects and Issues Involved:

We are updating references to the Illinois Revised Statutes by citing the latest edition which is the 1987 edition. This change will eliminate the need to keep old Illinois Revised Statutes on file in the agency. Also, it is easier for the public to locate the rule in a library when the current version is cited. These amendments will not impose any additional requirements.

The original intent of permitting livestock dealers to purchase untested breeding cattle was to provide relief for small cattle owners who may not have the facilities for testing cattle prior to sale. All livestock dealers should have facilities to test their cattle, and if the cattle are originating from a farm owned and/or operated by the livestock dealer, the cattle should be brucellosis tested. This change in the regulation will still provide relief for the small cattle owners, but require livestock dealers to test their cattle.

6) Will this proposed rule replace an emergency rule currently in effect? No

7) Does this rulemaking contain an automatic repeal date? No

8) Does this proposed amendment contain incorporations by reference? No

9) Are there any other amendments pending on this Part? No

10) Statement of Statewide Policy Objectives: This rulemaking does not impose any additional mandatory requirements on units of local government in such a way that would necessitate additional expenditures from local revenues.

11) Time, Place and Manner in which interested persons may comment on this proposed rulemaking:

DEPARTMENT OF AGRICULTURE

NOTICE OF PROPOSED AMENDMENTS

A public hearing on the proposed amendments will be held on January 10, 1989, at 10:00 a.m., Department of Agriculture, State Fairgrounds, Springfield, Illinois. Persons unable to attend the hearing may present their comments on the proposed rulemaking in writing to the Director, Department of Agriculture, State Fairgrounds, Springfield, Illinois 62794-9281. Mailed comments must be postmarked no later than January 5, so they will be available for consideration at the public hearing. All comments received will be fully considered by the agency and the Advisory Board of Livestock Commissioners.

The public hearing on the proposed rulemaking will run concurrent with a public meeting of the Advisory Board of Livestock Commissioners.

This proposed rulemaking may have an impact on small businesses. In accordance with Sections 3.01 and 4.03 of the Illinois Administrative Procedure Act, small businesses may present their comments to the Director as outlined above.

12) Initial Regulatory Flexibility Analysis:
  A) Date rule was submitted to the Business Assistance Office of the Department of Commerce and Community Affairs: Nov. 4, 1988
  B) Types of small businesses affected: Livestock dealers
  C) Reporting, bookkeeping or other procedures required for compliance: A livestock dealer must test breeding cattle originating directly from a farm owned and/or operated by the dealer.
  D) Types of professional skills necessary for compliance: Basic management.

The full text of the Proposed Amendments begins on the next page:

DEPARTMENT OF AGRICULTURE

NOTICE OF PROPOSED AMENDMENTS

TITLE 68: PROFESSIONS AND OCCUPATIONS
CHAPTER II: DEPARTMENT OF AGRICULTURE

PART 610
LIVESTOCK DEALER LICENSING

AUTHORITY: Implementing and authorized by the Illinois Livestock Dealer Licensing Act (Ill. Rev. Stat. 1987 1983, ch. 111, par. 401 et seq.).

SOURCE: Rules and Regulations Relating to the Livestock Dealer Licensing Act, filed January 17, 1972, effective January 27, 1972; amended May 3, 1972, effective May 13, 1972; June 20, 1973, effective July 1, 1973; April 5, 1976, effective April 15, 1976; 2 Ill. Reg. No. 34, page 166, effective August 24, 1978; codified at 5 Ill. Reg. 10573; amended at 8 Ill. Reg. 5973, effective April 23, 1984; amended at 13 Ill. Reg. _____, effective

Section 610.10   Entry Requirements

All livestock imported into the State shall meet Illinois entry requirements as may be set forth in those Acts listed in Section 19.1 of the Illinois Livestock Dealer Licensing Act (Ill. Rev. Stat. 1987 1983, ch. 111, par. 420.1). Livestock dealers shall submit to the Division, on Division Form M-106, weekly reports of all out-of-state livestock.

DEPARTMENT OF AGRICULTURE

NOTICE OF PROPOSED AMENDMENTS

(Source: Amended at 13 Ill. Reg. _____, effective _____)

Section 610.20   Breeding Cattle Health Requirements

a) All Illinois breeding cattle, six months of age and over, purchased by a licensed livestock dealer shall comply with one of the following:

  1) Be negative to a brucellosis test within 60 days prior to purchase; test valid for one change of ownership or premises, except that such cattle may change ownership or premises one or more times in the 14-day period immediately following the date of the negative test, or

  2) Be officially calfhood vaccinated and under 24 months of age, or

  3) Be consigned direct from farm of origin to a livestock auction market and shall meet the requirements of the Livestock Auction Market Law (Ill. Rev. Stat. 1987 1983, ch. 121 1/2, par. 208 et seq.) and rules pursuant thereto (8 Ill. Adm. Code 40.100 and 40.110), or

  4) Be untested but subject to brucellosis test within 48 hours after purchase and prior to commingling with other cattle if originating directly from a farm owned and/or operated other than by a licensee.

b) All breeding cattle sold by the livestock dealer, except direct to slaughter, shall be accompanied by a negative brucellosis blood test as provided in the Illinois Bovine Brucellosis Eradication Act (Ill. Rev. Stat. 1987 1983, ch. 8, par. 134 et seq.), or shall be official calfhood vaccinates under 24 months of age.

c) Any cattle which, upon being tested for brucellosis for the livestock dealer, are classified as reactors or suspects shall automatically come under jurisdiction of the Illinois Bovine Brucellosis Eradication Act and rules (8 Ill. Adm. Code 75.70(b)).

(Source: Amended at 13 Ill. Reg. _____, effective _____)

Section 610.30   Swine Health Requirements

DEPARTMENT OF AGRICULTURE

NOTICE OF PROPOSED AMENDMENTS

a) All Illinois breeding swine 4 months of age and over purchased by a licensed livestock dealer shall comply with the Illinois Swine Brucellosis Eradication Act (Ill. Rev. Stat. 1987 ~~1983~~, ch. 8, par. 148f et seq.).

h) All breeding swine sold or purchased by a licensed livestock dealer through a livestock auction market shall comply with the requirements of the Livestock Auction Market Law and rules (8 Ill. Adm. Code 40.170(e)).

(Source: Amended at 13 Ill. Reg. _____, effective _____)

Section 610.40 Prevention of Spread of Livestock Diseases

All other species of breeding livestock, to wit: cattle and sheep, shall comply with the laws and rules as listed in Section 19.1 of the Illinois Livestock Dealer Licensing Act (Ill. Rev. Stat. 1987 ~~1983~~, ch. 111, par. 402) relating to such livestock.

(Source: Amended at 13 Ill. Rev. _____, effective _____)

Section 610.60 Slaughter Animals

Livestock dealers purchasing animals for slaughter purposes only shall:

a) Keep slaughter animals isolated from all breeding animals.

h) Be sold within 10 days of purchase direct to a public stockyard or recognized slaughter establishment under State or Federal supervision.   Slaughter cattle from farm of origin may be consigned direct to a recognized slaughter establishment, or public stockyard, or licensed livestock auction market under State or Federal supervision (except the type of cattle mentioned in 8 Ill. Adm. Code 610.60(c)).

c) Maintain records on each head of livestock purchased in accordance with Section 17 of the Illinois Livestock Dealer Licensing Act (Ill. Rev. Stat. 1987 ~~1983~~, ch. 111, par. 417).   Livestock purchased at less than prevailing market price, such as, "downer" cows, cows with epithelioma (cancer eye), crippled animals, and animals whose general physical appearance would indicate they are not healthy or are suffering from malnutrition shall

be consigned directly to a recognized slaughtering establishment under State or Federal supervision.

(Source: Amended at 13 Ill. Reg. _____, effective _____)

DEPARTMENT OF AGRICULTURE

NOTICE OF PROPOSED AMENDMENTS

1) Heading of Part: Meat and Poultry Inspection Act

2) Code Citation: 8 Ill. Adm. Code 125

3) Section Numbers: Proposed Action:

    125.60   Amended
    125.80   Amended

4) Statutory Authority: The Meat and Poultry Inspection Act (Ill. Rev. Stat. 1987, ch. 56 1/2, pars. 311 and 316)

5) A Complete Description of the Subjects and Issues Involved:

The rules are being amended to reference the latest printed edition of the Illinois Revised Statutes, which is the 1987 edition. This change is for the purpose of keeping references up to date.

The Director renamed the Division of Meat, Poultry and Livestock Inspection. The new name is the Division of Animal Industries. Further, the post office assigned a different zip code to the Department of Agriculture. The rules are amended to reflect these changes.

We are increasing the overtime charges by $2.40 an hour and holiday charges by $1.40 an hour. The proposed rate for overtime inspection is $15 per hour and $10 per hour for inspection performed on holidays. The U.S. Department of Agriculture has increased their overtime and holiday charges to $24.68 per hour, which means the Illinois Department of Agriculture is still performing the same service at much less cost to the licensee. The present charges have been in effect since January, 1985. Since the licensee must request that the Department provide overtime and/or holiday meat and poultry inspection, any expense for overtime or holidays is at the option of the establishment.

If the establishment fails to pay the overtime charges within 30 days, a penalty will be assessed. If the overtime charge is less than $50, a $25 penalty is assessed for every 30 days overdue, and if the overtime charge is $50 or more, a $50 penalty is assessed for every 30 days overdue. The establishment of the overdue penalty is to encourage payment on time.

6) Will this proposed rule replace an emergency rule currently in effect? No

7) Does this rulemaking contain an automatic repeal date? No

8) Does this proposed amendment contain incorporations by reference? No

9) Are there any other amendments pending on this Part? No

DEPARTMENT OF AGRICULTURE

NOTICE OF PROPOSED AMENDMENTS

10) Statement of Statewide Policy Objectives: Rule does not affect units of local governments.

11) Time, Place and Manner in which interested persons may comment on this proposed rulemaking:

A public hearing on the proposed amendments will be held January 10, 1989, at 10:00 a.m., Department of Agriculture, State Fairgrounds, Springfield, Illinois. Persons unable to attend the hearing may present their comments on the proposed rulemaking in writing to the Director, Department of Agriculture, State Fairgrounds, Springfield, Illinois 62794-9281. Mailed comments must be postmarked no later than January 5, so they will be available for consideration at the public hearing. All comments received will be fully considered by the agency.

The public hearing on the proposed rulemaking will follow the public meeting of the Advisory Board of Livestock Commissioners.

This proposed rulemaking may have an impact on small businesses. In accordance with Sections 3.01 and 4.03 of the Illinois Administrative Procedure Act, small businesses may present their comments to the Director as outlined above.

12) Initial Regulatory Flexibility Analysis:
    A) Date rule was submitted to the Business Assistance Office of the Department of Commerce and Community Affairs: Nov. 4, 1988
    B) Types of small businesses affected: Processors and/or slaughterers of meat and/or poultry.
    C) Reporting, bookkeeping or other procedures required for compliance: Payment of the charges incurred for overtime and holiday inspection services performed by Department employees within 30 days and payment of any penalty incurred for late payments.
    D) Types of professional skills necessary for compliance: Basic management.

The full text of the Proposed Amendments begins on the next page:

DEPARTMENT OF AGRICULTURE

NOTICE OF PROPOSED AMENDMENTS

TITLE 8: AGRICULTURE AND ANIMALS
CHAPTER I: DEPARTMENT OF AGRICULTURE
SUBCHAPTER c: MEAT AND POULTRY INSPECTION ACT

PART 125
MEAT AND POULTRY INSPECTION ACT

SUBPART A: GENERAL PROVISIONS FOR BOTH MEAT AND/OR
POULTRY INSPECTION

DEPARTMENT OF AGRICULTURE

NOTICE OF PROPOSED AMENDMENTS

AUTHORITY: Implementing and authorized by The Meat and Poultry Inspection Act (Ill. Rev. Stat. 1987 ~~1985~~, ch. 56 1/2, par. 301 et seq., ~~as amended by PrAr 85-245, effective September 9, 1987~~) and The Civil Administrative Code of Illinois (Ill. Rev. Stat. 1987 ~~1985~~, ch. 127, par. 16).

SOURCE: Adopted at 9 Ill. Reg. 1782, effective January 24, 1985; peremptory amendment at 9 Ill. Reg. 2337, effective January 28, 1985; peremptory amendment at 9 Ill. Reg. 2980, effective February 20, 1985; peremptory amendment at 9 Ill. Reg. 4856, effective April 1, 1985; peremptory amendment at 9 Ill. Reg. 9240, effective June 5, 1985; peremptory amendment at 9 Ill. Reg. 10102, effective June 13, 1985; peremptory amendment at 9 Ill. Reg. 11673, effective July 17, 1985; peremptory amendment at 9 Ill. Reg. 13748, effective August 23, 1985; peremptory amendment at 9 Ill. Reg. 15575, effective October 2, 1985; peremptory amendment at 9 Ill. Reg. 19759, effective December 5, 1985; peremptory amendment at 10 Ill. Reg. 447, effective December 23, 1985; peremptory amendment at 10 Ill. Reg. 1307, effective January 7, 1986; peremptory amendment at 10 Ill. Reg. 3318, effective January 24, 1986; peremptory amendment at 10 Ill. Reg. 3880, effective February 7, 1986; peremptory amendment at 10 Ill. Reg. 11478, effective June 25, 1986; peremptory amendment at 10 Ill.

DEPARTMENT OF AGRICULTURE

NOTICE OF PROPOSED AMENDMENTS

Reg. 14858, effective August 22 1986; peremptory amendment at 10
Ill. Reg. 15305, effective September 10, 1986; peremptory amendment at 10 Ill. Reg. 16743, effective September 19, 1986; peremptory amendment at 10 Ill. Reg. 18203, effective October 15,
1986; peremptory amendment at 10 Ill. Reg. 19818, effective
November 12, 1986; peremptory amendment at 11 Ill. Reg. 1696,
effective January 5, 1987; peremptory amendment at 11 Ill. Reg.
2930, effective January 23, 1987; peremptory amendment at 11 Ill.
Reg. 9645, effective April 29, 1987; peremptory amendment at 11
Ill. Reg. 10321, effective May 15, 1987; peremptory amendment at
11 Ill. Reg. 11184, effective June 5, 1987; peremptory amendment
at 11 Ill. Reg. 14830, effective August 25, 1987; peremptory
amendment at 11-Ill. Reg. 18799, effective November 3, 1987; peremptory amendment' at 11 Ill. Reg. 19805, effective November 19,
1987; peremptory amendment at 12 Ill. Reg. 2154, effective January 6, 1988; amended at 12 Ill. Reg. 3417, effective January 22,
1988; peremptory amendment at 12 Ill. Reg. 4879, effective February 25, 1988; peremptory amendment at 12 Ill. Reg. 6313, effective March 21, 1988; peremptory amendment at 12 Ill. Reg. 6819,
effective March 29, 1988; peremptory amendment at 12 Ill. Reg.
13621, effective August 8, 1988; peremptory amendment at 12 Ill.
Reg. _19116_ , effective _November 1, 1988_ ; amended at 13 Ill.
Reg. _____, effective _____.

SUBPART A: GENERAL PROVISIONS FOR BOTH MEAT AND/OR
            POULTRY INSPECTION

Section 125.60 Administrative Hearings; Appeals

a) All decisions and actions of the Department are subject
    to the Illinois Administrative Procedure Act (Ill. Rev.
    Stat. _1987_ 1983, ch. 127, par. 1001 et seq.) and the
    Department's Administrative Rules (8 Ill. Adm. Code 1)
    which pertain to administrative hearings, petitions,
    contested cases, declaratory rulings and availability of
    Department files for public access. Administrative
    hearings are governed by the Illinois Administrative
    Procedure Act, Subpart B of the Department's Administra-
    tive Rules, and Section 19(F) of The Meat and Poultry
    Inspection Act.

b) Any appeal from a decision of an inspector shall be made
    either orally or in writing to the regional supervisor.
    Any appeal from a decision of a regional supervisor
    shall be made either orally or in writing to the Bureau
    Chief, Bureau of Meat and Poultry Inspection, Division
    of _Animal Industries_ Meat, Poultry and Livestock
    Inspection, Department of Agriculture, Springfield,

DEPARTMENT OF AGRICULTURE

NOTICE OF PROPOSED AMENDMENTS

Illinois _62794-9281_ 62706 (217/782-_6684_ 4944). The
regional supervisor or the Bureau Chief shall respond to
an appeal within 72 hours from the time the appeal is
received or the appellant may proceed to the next higher
level of appeal. Any appeal from a decision of the
Bureau Chief shall be made in writing to the Superintendent, Division of _Animal Industries_ Meat, Poultry and
Livestock Inspection and an administrative hearing shall
be held.

(Source: Amended at 13 Ill. Reg. _____, effective
_____)

Section 125.80 Schedule of Operations; Overtime; Penalties

a) The Department incorporates by reference 9 CFR 307.4(a),
    307.4(d), and 381.37(a) and (d) (1984). References to 9
    CFR 307.6(b) and 381.39(b) in the incorporated 'language
    shall be interpreted to mean as set forth in this Sec-
    tion.

b) The basic workweek and workday shall be those days and
    hours as on file and approved by the Department of Cen-
    tral Management Services in accordance with the Person-
    nel Code (Ill. Rev. Stat. _1987_ 1983, ch. 127, par.
    63b101 et seq.) and the rules for that Act (80 Ill. Adm.
    Code 303.300). The work schedule of the official estab-
    lishment and any requests for changes in the work sched-
    ule shall be submitted in writing by the licensee to the
    regional supervisor. However, minor deviations (one
    hour or less) from the daily operating schedule shall be
    approved by the inspector if the request is received on
    the day before the change is to occur and the change is
    only for that particular day.

c) Overtime charges for inspection services rendered shall
    be as follows:

    1) For inspection on a Saturday, Sunday or on a workday
        at times other than the hours as set forth in the
        approved work schedule, the rate shall be _$15.00_
        $13.60 per hour or any fraction of an hour.

    2) For inspection on holidays, the rate shall be _$10.00_
        $8.40 per hour or any fraction of an hour.

DEPARTMENT OF AGRICULTURE

NOTICE OF PROPOSED AMENDMENTS

3)   If the establishment fails to pay the overtime
      charges within 30 days from the date of billing, the
      following penalty shall be incurred:

      A)   If the overtime charge is less than $50.00, a
            $25.00 penalty shall be assessed for every 30
            days overdue.

      B)   If the overtime charge is $50.00 or more, a
            $50.00 penalty shall be assessed for every 30
            days overdue.

      C)   If the account is more than 60 days overdue, a
            formal hearing shall be held in accordance with
            Section 125.60, and the licensee will be asked
            to show cause why the establishment's license
            should not be suspended.

d)   The overtime charge shall be for the actual time the
      inspector is performing the inspection service. Travel
      expenses and the minimum overtime that will be billed is
      as follows:

      1)   When an inspector has departed the official estab-
            lishment after the completion of his/her regular
            workday and is recalled to perform inspection ser-
            vice, the minimum overtime that will be charged
            shall be two hours.

      2)   For inspection service rendered on Saturday, Sunday
            or on a holiday, the minimum overtime that will be
            charged is two hours.

      3)   When an inspector is required to return to the
            establishment after the completion of his/her regu-
            lar work day or on a Saturday, Sunday or holiday,
            the official establishment will be billed for mile-
            age charged by the inspector in accordance with
            Travel Regulations (80 Ill. Adm. Code 2800) In addi-
            tion to the overtime charged.

(Source: Amended at 13 Ill. Reg. _____, effective
_____)

DEPARTMENT OF AGRICULTURE

NOTICE OF PROPOSED AMENDMENTS

1)   Heading of Part: Illinois Pseudorabies Control Act

2)   Code Citation: 8 Ill. Adm. Code 115

3)   Section Numbers: Proposed Action:

     115.10   Amended
     115.20   Amended

4)   Statutory Authority: Illinois Pseudorabies Control Act (Ill. Rev. Stat,
1987, ch. 8, pars. 805 and 809).

5)   A Complete Description of the Subjects and Issues Involved:

We are updating references to the Code of Federal Rules and to the Illinois
Revised Statutes by citing the latest edition. This change will eliminate
the need to keep old CFR's on file in the agency and carried by our inspection
personnel. Also, it is easier for the public to locate the Act and rules in
a library when the current versions are cited. These amendments will not
impose any additional requirements.

We are adding another method which a swine producer may use to obtain release
of a pseudorabies quarantine. Pseudorabies quarantines will be released when
a negative test has been made on the complete breeding herd at least 45 days
after the last known exposed swine have left the premises. With the addition
of this test, there will be three methods available from which to choose for
releasing quarantine.

6)   Will this proposed rule replace an emergency rule currently in effect? No

7)   Does this rulemaking contain an automatic repeal date? No

8)   Does this proposed amendment contain incorporations by reference? None
that require approval in accordance with Section 6.02(b) of the Illinois
Administrative Procedure Act.

9)   Are there any other amendments pending on this Part? No

10) Statement of Statewide Policy Objectives: This rulemaking does not affect
units of local government.

11) Time, Place and Manner in which interested persons may comment on this
proposed rulemaking:

A public hearing on the proposed amendments will be held on January 10, 1989,
at 10:00 a.m., Department of Agriculture, State Fairgrounds, Springfield,
Illinois. Persons unable to attend the hearing may present their comments
on the proposed rulemaking in writing to the Director, Department of

DEPARTMENT OF AGRICULTURE

NOTICE OF PROPOSED AMENDMENTS

Agriculture, State Fairgrounds, Springfield, Illinois 62794-9281. Mailed comments must be postmarked no later than January 5, so they will be available for consideration at the public hearing. All comments received will be fully considered by the agency and the Advisory Board of Livestock Commissioners.

The public hearing on the proposed rulemaking will run concurrent with a public meeting of the Advisory Board of Livestock Commissioners.

This proposed rulemaking may have an impact on small businesses. In accordance with Sections 3.01 and 4.03 of the Illinois Administrative Procedure Act, small businesses may present their comments to the Director as outlined above.

12) Initial Regulatory Flexibility Analysis:
    A) Date rule was submitted to the Business Assistance Office of the
       Department of Commerce and Community Affairs: Nov. 4, 1988
    B) Types of small businesses affected: Swine producers.
    C) Reporting, bookkeeping or other procedures required for compliance:
       For release of quarantine, a negative test of the complete breeding
       herd must be made at least 45 days after the last known exposed swine
       have left the premises. This test has been added as an alternative
       method for releasing the quarantine.
    D) Types of professional skills necessary for compliance:
       Basic management.

The full text of the Proposed Amendments begins on the next page:

DEPARTMENT OF AGRICULTURE

NOTICE OF PROPOSED AMENDMENTS

TITLE 8:   AGRICULTURE AND ANIMALS
CHAPTER I: DEPARTMENT OF AGRICULTURE
SUBCHAPTER b: ANIMALS AND ANIMAL PRODUCTS
(EXCEPT MEAT AND POULTRY INSPECTION ACT REGULATIONS)

PART 115
ILLINOIS PSEUDORABIES CONTROL ACT

Section
115.10   Definitions
115.15   Incorporation by Reference
115.20   Pseudorabies Quarantines
115.30   General Requirements for Qualified Pseudorabies
          Negative, Controlled Vaccinated and Feeder Swine
          Pseudorabies Monitored Herds
115.40   Requirements for Establishing and Maintaining
          Qualified Pseudorabies Negative Herds
115.50   Requirements for Establishing and Maintaining
          Pseudorabies Controlled Vaccinated Swine Herds
115.60   Requirements for Establishing and Maintaining
          Feeder Swine Pseudorabies Monitored Herds
115.70   Pseudorabies Test Requirements for Intrastate Movement
115.80   Pseudorabies Testing of Feeder Swine
115.90   Feeder Swine
115.100   Breeding Animals Consigned to Slaughter

AUTHORITY: Implementing and authorized by the Illinois Pseudorabies Control Act (Ill. Rev. Stat. 1987, 1985, ch. 8, par. 801 et seq. ᵧ as amended by P.A. 85-0165, effective January 1, 1988 and P.A. 85-0171, effective January 1, 1988).

SOURCE: Adopted at 12 Ill. Reg. 3394, effective January 22, 1988; amended at 13 Ill. Reg. _____, effective _____.

Section 115.10   Definitions

The definitions for this Part shall be as set forth in the general definitions Section (8 Ill. Adm. Code 20.1). Also, the following definitions shall apply to this Part:

"Act" means the Illinois Pseudorabies Control Act (Ill. Rev. Stat. 1987 1985, ch. 8, par. 801 et seq. ᵧ as amended by P.A. 85-0165, effective January 1, 1988 and P.A. 85-0171, effective January 1, 1988).

"Official test" or "test" means any serologic test for the detection of pseudorabies (serum neutralization (SN), for example) as approved by the United States

Department of Agriculture (9 CFR 85.1, 1988 1987) and conducted in an approved laboratory.

(Source: Amended · at 13 Ill. Reg. _____, effective _____)

Section 115.20 Pseudorabies Quarantines

a) When pseudorabies has been diagnosed in a swine herd, such herd shall be placed under quarantine when:

1) It has been determined that there have been multiple swine deaths on the premises that are attributable to pseudorabies AND that swine are actually ill of a disease clinically diagnosed as pseudorabies; OR

2) Pseudorabies (Aujeszky's disease) has been confirmed by diagnosis by an approved laboratory; OR

3) One or more swine are positive to an official test for pseudorabies. Positive swine may be retested once. The results of the retest will be considered final.

b) Quarantined animals shall not be sold, loaned or traded except for slaughter. Such swine may be shipped to any market, except those which release swine for breeding or feeding purposes. Examples of markets which shall not receive such swine for slaughter are livestock auction markets, other markets licensed as feeder swine dealers, or order buyers and other slaughter buyers releasing swine for breeding or feeding purposes.

c) Pseudorabies quarantines shall be released when:

1) All swine on the premises have been shipped to slaughter, the premises have been cleaned and disinfected, and the premises have remained vacant for at least 30 days; OR

2) Two negative official pseudorabies tests at least 30 days apart have been obtained on a representative sample of the breeding swine in the herd 6 months of age and over not less than 45 days after the last positive animal has been shipped to slaughter. In herds of 35 animals or less, a representative sample is all or 10 animals, whichever is less. In herds of 36 to 299 animals, a representative sample is 30%

or 30 animals, whichever is less. In herds of 300 animals or more, a representative sample is a minimum of 10%. ; OR

3) A negative test has been made on the complete breeding herd at least 45 days after the last known exposed swine have left the premises.

4) 3) The Department shall require additional herd tests prior to release of quarantine when epidemiologic evidence, such as, the presence of pseudorabies on neighboring farms or indications of reintroduction of infection into the herd is apparent.

(Source: Amended at 13 Ill. Reg. _____, effective _____)

DEPARTMENT OF CENTRAL MANAGEMENT SERVICES

NOTICE OF PROPOSED AMENDMENT

1) The Heading of the Part: Day Care

2) The Code Citation: 89 Ill. Adm. Code 1300

3) Section Number: Proposed Action:

   1300.340   Amend

4) Statutory Authority: Implementing the State Agency Employees Child Care
   Services Act (Ill. Rev. Stat. 1987, ch. 127, pars. 3001 et seq.) and
   authorized by Sections 67.06 and 67.24 of the Civil Administrative Code of
   Illinois (Ill. Rev. Stat. 1987, ch. 127, pars. 63b13.6 and 63b13.24).

5) A Complete Description of the Subjects and Issues Involved: Public Act
   85-1337 mandated the amendment. The change makes the recommendation of
   vendor by the DCMS committee binding on the using agency.

6) Will this proposed amendment replace an emergency rule currently in
   effect? No.

7) Does this rulemaking contain an automatic repeal date? No.

8) Does this proposed amendment contain incorporation by reference? No.

9) Are there any proposed amendments pending to this Part? No.

10) Statement of Statewide Policy Objectives: Rulemaking does not affect
    units of local government.

11) Time, Place, and Manner in which interested persons may comment on this
    proposed rulemaking: Interested persons may submit written comments
    within 45 days of the date of publication to:

              John Brazaitis
              Department of Central Management Services
              720 Stratton Building
              Springfield, Illinois 62706
              217-782-9669

12) Initial Regulatory Flexibility Analysis: Does not affect small business.

The full text of the Proposed Amendment begins on the next page:

DEPARTMENT OF CENTRAL MANAGEMENT SERVICES

NOTICE OF PROPOSED AMENDMENT

TITLE 89: SOCIAL SERVICES
CHAPTER XI: DEPARTMENT OF CENTRAL MANAGEMENT SERVICES

PART 1300
DAY CARE

SUBPART A: GENERAL

Section
1300.110   Summary
1300.120   Definitions
1300.130   Application

SUBPART B: DETERMINATION OF NEED

Section
1300.200   Request for Child Care Services
1300.210   Determination of Need
1300.220   Recommendation to Director
1300.230   Director's Determination
1300.240   Assistance of the Department

SUBPART C: REQUEST FOR PROPOSAL AND AWARD

Section
1300.300   Request for Proposal
1300.310   Minimal Requirement for Request for Proposal
1300.320   Evaluation of Proposal
1300.330   Evaluation by Committee
1300.340   Selection by Director

AUTHORITY: Implementing the State Agency Employees Child Care Services Act
(Ill. Rev. Stat. 1987, ch. 127, pars. 3001 et seq.) and authorized by Sections
67.06 and 67.24 of the Civil Administrative Code of Illinois (Ill. Rev. Stat.
1987, ch. 127, pars. 63b13.6 and 63b13.24).

SOURCE: Emergency Rules adopted at 10 Ill. Reg. 7926, effective May 7, 1986
for a maximum of 150 days; adopted at 11 Ill. Reg. 8930, effective April 23,
1987; amended at ____ Ill. Reg. _____, effective _____.

Section 1300.340 Selection by Director

After considering the recommendations of the Committee the Director of the
State Agency shall select a the vendor recommended by the Committee to
provide Child Care Services. Such-selection-shall-be-based-on-the-criteria-
contained-in-Section-1300.320-and-shall-give-due-weight-to-the-
recommendation-of-the-Committee.

(Source: Amended at _____ Ill. Reg. _____, effective _____)

DEPARTMENT OF CENTRAL MANAGEMENT SERVICES

NOTICE OF PROPOSED AMENDMENTS

1) The Heading of the Part: Standard Procurement

2) The Code Citation: 44 Ill. Adm. Code 1

3) Section Number: Proposed Action:

   1.2215   Amend

4) Statutory Authority: Ill. Rev. Stat. 1987 ch. 127, par. 132-601 et seq.

5) A Complete Description of the Subjects and Issues Involved: This proposed rulemaking makes the following changes:

   1.2215(b)   State universities are now subject to the Act. Later sections recognize that universities may comply differently than other agencies.

   1.2215(c)   Only those contracts funded in whole or in part by appropriated funds will be considered subject to the Act.

   1.2215(e)   Added language that any agency may request an exemption and identifying information that must be included in the request.

   1.2215(h)(5) Reminds agencies that advance and progress payments can be used on set-aside contracts (construction contracts may, however, not use advance payments).

   1.2215(h)(8) Universities may have different rules regarding use of sheltered markets.

   1.2215(j)(3) Now use self-certified in place of temporarily certified. Self-certified has become more widely used. The meaning has not, however, changed. Later uses of the term temporarily certified have been changed.

   1.2215(j)(5)(B) Added new internal reference.

   1.2215(j)(8) The Minority and Female Business Enterprise Council will accept vendor certifications performed by other entities such as the Department of Transportation and Chicago Regional Purchasing Council provided that entities standards meet those set forth in these rules. The Council will annually review those agencies' requirements to determine whether they continue to meet Council requirements.

DEPARTMENT OF CENTRAL MANAGEMENT SERVICES

NOTICE OF PROPOSED AMENDMENTS

   1.2215(j)(11) A new eligibility test has been added. Companies with annual sales of $14 million or more are excluded unless they can show that receiving a particular contract would have a definite positive impact on minority or female employment. Later sections have been renumbered to reflect this additional test.

   1.2215(j)(16). States that vendors are certified as minority or female owned for a period of one year and refers readers to another section regarding recertification.

   1.2215(j)(17) If the bidder is not certified, its name will be removed from the list of certified bidders.

   1.2215(j)(17) These sections are being deleted in favor of new section
   1.2215(j)(18) (j)(18). The new section gives a more detailed statement
   old numbers   of the process that vendors may utilize to challenge a decision that the bidder does not qualify as minority or female owned. The initial decision of the Secretary can be challenged by asking the Secretary to reconsider. The Secretary must render a decision within 6 months or else the certification will be considered denied. Thereafter, the decision can be reviewed by a committee made up of Council members. Finally, the entire Council may consider the matter. A new subsection "S" has been added to require that notice be sent to the Council by certified mail or if hand delivered, noted in the mail log.

   1.2215(j)(19) The current language on decertification of a vendor is being replaced with new language. The review procedures of the new subsection (18) would be available to the bidder.

   1.2215(j)(20) Firms that send in recertification material in a timely manner will remain certified until the Secretary has a chance to review the material.

   1.2215(m)(4)   Indicates that universities may establish their own rules regarding penalties that may be assessed against vendors who are not qualified for the programs.

   1.2215(o)   This is rewritten to show that universities do not have to submit an annual plan for proposed compliance with the Act but they must submit quarterly progress reports. Defines what information the universities must provide.

6) Will this proposed amendment replace an emergency rule currently in effect? No.

DEPARTMENT OF CENTRAL MANAGEMENT SERVICES

NOTICE OF PROPOSED AMENDMENTS

7) Does this rulemaking contain an automatic repeal date? No.

8) Does this proposed amendment contain incorporation by reference? No.

9) Are there any proposed amendments pending to this Part? No.

10) Statement of Statewide Policy Objectives: Rulemaking does not affect units of local government.

11) Time, Place, and Manner in which interested persons may comment on this proposed rulemaking:

    Ben Bagby
    Department of Central Management Services
    720 Stratton Building
    Springfield, Illinois 62706
    217-782-9669

    Small businesses are especially encouraged to ask questions and submit comments for review.

12) Initial Regulatory Flexibility Analysis:

    A). Date rule was submitted to the Business Assistance Office of the Department of Commerce and Community Affairs: November 1, 1988

    B) Types of small businesses affected: Any small business which is owned and controlled by minority or female individuals and which desire to participate in the Minority and Female-owned Business Program.

    D) Reporting, bookkeeping or other procedures required for compliance: Must complete forms provided by the State and provide copies of supporting material.

    D) Types of professional skills necessary for compliance: None.

The full text of the Proposed Amendment begins on the next page:

DEPARTMENT OF CENTRAL MANAGEMENT SERVICES

NOTICE OF PROPOSED AMENDMENTS

TITLE 44: GOVERNMENT CONTRACTS, PROCUREMENTS AND PROPERTY MANAGEMENT
SUBTITLE A: PROCUREMENT AND CONTRACT PROVISIONS
CHAPTER I: DEPARTMENT OF CENTRAL MANAGEMENT SERVICES

PART 1
STANDARD PROCUREMENT

SUBPART A: GENERAL

Section
1.100   Authority
1.110   Policy
1.120   Applicability
1.130   Definitions

SUBPART B: APPROVAL OF PROCUREMENT RULES

Section
1.200   Approval Required
1.210   When Approved
1.220   Filing of Rules
1.230   Standard Form of Rules
1.240   Non-Standard Form of Rules
1.250   Length of Approval

SUBPART C: PROCUREMENT RESPONSIBILITY

Section
1.300   General
1.310   Department of Central Management Services
1.320   Department of Transportation
1.330   Capital Development Board
1.340   Procuring Agency Responsibility
1.350   Delegation of Procurement Authority

SUBPART D: SOURCES OF SUPPLY

Section
1.400   Open Source of Supply
1.410   Special Sources
1.420   Directed Source

SUBPART E: METHODS OF PROCUREMENT

Section
1.500   General
1.510   Competition Encouraged
1.520   Source Selection

DEPARTMENT OF CENTRAL MANAGEMENT SERVICES

NOTICE OF PROPOSED AMENDMENTS

DEPARTMENT OF CENTRAL MANAGEMENT SERVICES

NOTICE OF PROPOSED AMENDMENTS

DEPARTMENT OF CENTRAL MANAGEMENT SERVICES

NOTICE OF PROPOSED AMENDMENTS

DEPARTMENT OF CENTRAL MANAGEMENT SERVICES

NOTICE OF PROPOSED AMENDMENTS

AUTHORITY: The Illinois Purchasing Act (Ill. Rev. Stat. 1987, ch. 127, par. 132.1 et seq.); Illinois Small Business Purchasing Act (Ill. Rev. Stat. 1987, ch. 127, par. 132.21, et seq.); AN ACT in relation to State purchases of printing paper, stationery and envelopes (Ill. Rev. Stat. 1987, ch. 127, par. 132.101, et seq.); State Printing Contracts Act (Ill. Rev. Stat. 1987, ch. 127, par. 132.201, et seq.); the Minority and Female Business Enterprise Act (Ill. Rev. Stat. 1987, ch. 127, par. 132.601 et seq.).

DEPARTMENT OF CENTRAL MANAGEMENT SERVICES

NOTICE OF PROPOSED AMENDMENTS

SOURCE: Adopted at 7 Ill. Reg. 100, effective December 17, 1982, amended at 7 Ill. Reg. 13481, effective October 4, 1983; amended at 7 Ill. Reg. 13844, effective October 12, 1983; codified at 8 Ill. Reg. 14941; Sections 1.2210, 1.2220, 1.2230, 1.224C recodified to Section 1.2210 at 9 Ill. Reg. 6118; amended at 10 Ill. Reg. 923, effective January 2, 1906; amended at 10 Ill. Reg. 18707, effective October 22, 1986; amended at 11 Ill. Reg. 7225, effective April 6, 1987; amended at 11 Ill. Reg. 7595, effective April 14, 1987; amended at 12 Ill. Reg. _____, effective_____.

Section 1.2215 Minority and Female-Owned Business

a) Introduction

   The Minority and Female Business Enterprise Act (Ill. Rev. Stat. 1987, ch. 127, par. 132.601 et seq.) (Act) authorizes the establishment of sheltered markets for minority and female-owned business, sets a minimum 10% expenditure goal for State contracts, and creates the Minority and Female Business Enterprise Council (Council) to oversee the Minority and Female Business Enterprise Act.

b) Goal

   The Governor, all departments, officers, boards, commissions, institutions and bodies politic and corporate of the State excepting, including the governing boards of the various State colleges and universities (from this point forward referred to as state agency or agency unless specifically exempted) and excepting other constitutional officers, shall establish a goal that at least 10% of the dollar value of State contracts be awarded to minority and female-owned businesses. Contracts representing 50% of the dollar value associated with the established goal shall be awarded to minority-owned businesses and the other 50% awarded to female-owned businesses.

c) Contracts and Expenditures Subject to Act

   1) Agencies subject to the goal established above shall include under this program all contracts they might establish, whether bid or not, and all funds available for expenditure, including, but not limited to, those derived from state, federal, local, grant and other sources, funded in whole or in part with funds appropriated by the General Assembly, unless exempted elsewhere in this Part. Funds shall be excluded from the Minority and Female Business Enterprise Act program if receipt of those funds would be jeopardized by including them in the program.

   2) The following are not considered to be contracts or resulting expenditures subject to the Act:

DEPARTMENT OF CENTRAL MANAGEMENT SERVICES

NOTICE OF PROPOSED AMENDMENTS

   A) employee wages, salary and other payroll related costs

   B) contracts between State agencies not including payments to private vendors

   C) contracts with other governmental entities

   D) refunds of money

   E) payments of money to individuals or groups in the nature of reimbursement, settlement, entitlement, or assistance

   F) where the contract is subject to federal reimbursement

d) Council Review of Contract Categories

   The Council shall, pursuant to Section 7(2) of the Minority and Female Business Enterprise Act, review each appropriation object as found in "AN ACT in relation to State finance" (Ill. Rev. Stat. 1987, ch. 127, par. 145f) and detail objects found in the Comptroller's Uniform Statewide Accounting System Manual. If after investigation it is determined that one or more minority or female-owned firms are currently capable of providing goods or services in particular categories, those categories shall remain as subject to the goal. If, however, investigation shows no minority or female-owned firms are currently engaged in providing the particular good or service in question then the Council shall consider removing the category and associated expenditures from the goal for the current fiscal year. Such removal shall occur only if the Council also finds that there is no reasonable expectation that minority or female-owned firms will enter the field during that fiscal year. Any action to remove a category from the goal under this Section shall be by written resolution passed by the Council. Pursuant to Section 7(2) of the Minority and Female Business Enterprise Act the Council has determined that the following detail objects are exempt from the goal.

   Assistance Payments to Individuals
   Association Dues
   Awards and Grants to Students
   Awards, Benefits and Treatment Expenses - Injured Employees
   Burial Expense Awards
   Community Services for DMHDD and Chemically Dependent
   Court of Claims Awards
   Debt Retirement
   Electricity
   Employee Tuition Fees
   Fire Protection Services
   Gas (Natural Gas)
   Grants for Educational Purposes - School Districts

DEPARTMENT OF CENTRAL MANAGEMENT SERVICES

NOTICE OF PROPOSED AMENDMENTS

Grants for Educational Purposes - Higher Education
Grants to Local Governments (other)
Grants to Non-Profit Organizations
Grants to Other State Agencies
Grants to or on behalf of Veterans and their Dependents
Industrial Commission Awards or Settlement Awards for Injured
   Employees
Interviewee Expenses
Land (Relocation Costs)
Land Relocation Costs (Highways)
Land, Relocation Costs (Waterways)
Land, Right of Way and Easements
Land, Rights of Way and Easements (Highway)
Land, Rights of Way and Easements (Waterways)
Legislative Staff Services
Loans
Lottery Prizes
Operating Taxes, Licenses and Fees
Payments into Pension Funds
Payments to Local Governments for Employees
Pensions, Annuities and Benefits
Postage and Postal Charges
Purchase of Investments
Refunds
Registration Fees and Conference Expenses
Reimbursement for Living Expenses for State Wards Outside State
   Institutions
Reimbursements to Governmental Units
Retirement
Revenue Stamps
Shared Revenue Payments
Shared Waterway Agreements
Social Security
Taxes and Transfers
Tort Claims
Tuition, Training Supplies and Equipment for Aided Persons
Unemployment Compensation Payments
University Central Data Processing Services
University Central Supply Services
University Central Telecommunication Services

DEPARTMENT OF CENTRAL MANAGEMENT SERVICES

NOTICE OF PROPOSED AMENDMENTS

from the goal. Justification of the exemption request must include
documentation of outreach efforts to identify and use MBE's and
FBE's, the anticipated expenditures in each area where an exemption
is requested and the total agency appropriation. Upon written
request by any State agency the Council shall exempt specific
contracts from the goal if the agency can show that a diligent effort
failed to locate one or more minority or female-owned businesses that
could perform the contract at a reasonable price. A diligent effort
requires solicitation of appropriate vendors from the master vendor
list maintained by the Council, checking with the Council for updates
to the list, and advertising in the official State Newspaper and
locally if in the judgment of the procuring agency if it is more
likely to reach minority and female-owned business. In addition,
when the decision to procure is first made the procuring agency shall
provide as much information about the procurement as is then
available to the Secretary and shall provide a copy of the Invitation
for Bid, Request for Proposal or other solicitation information when
in final form. Whether price quoted is reasonable will be determined
by the Council based upon current market prices, historical prices,
prices received by other agencies for similar goods or services, the
policy of the Minority and Female Business Enterprise Act to promote
minority and female-owned business and other such relevant factors.
Any action regarding a request for specific exemption shall be by
resolution passed by the Council.

f)   Goal Measurement

   1)   The goal shall be measured on a full fiscal year basis. The
        goal shall be measured against the total amount of covered
        expenditures. Expenditures not covered are those mentioned in
        subsection (c)(2), (d) and (e) above.

   2)   Certain procuring agencies such as the Department of Central
        Management Services and the Capital Development Board are
        responsible for establishing contracts for other (user)
        agencies. Those procuring agencies shall be responsible for
        meeting the goal for such contracts even though the user agency
        may have the appropriation to fund the contract. To properly
        account for the goal in these situations the following
        procedures shall be followed:

DEPARTMENT OF CENTRAL MANAGEMENT SERVICES

NOTICE OF PROPOSED AMENDMENTS

B) Those amounts reported by user agencies to Department of Central Management Services shall be assigned by the Secretary to the appropriate procuring agency. Such amounts will be included in the amount upon which the procuring agency goal is based. This procedure does not result in money actually being transferred from the user agency to the procuring agency. Rather, the transfer is for compliance plan accounting purposes only.

C) If a procuring agency delegates procurement authority to a user agency, the procuring agency's goal base shall be reduced in amount of the delegation and the user agency's goal base shall be increased in like amount.

D) If the user agency transfers money from a line subject to procuring agency authority, the procuring agency's goal base shall be reduced by that amount and the user agency's goal base in the major or minor object code receiving the transfer shall be increased.

g) Minority and Female Status

1) Minority or female-owned business refers to for-profit enterprises regardless of form of organization (sole proprietorship, partnership or corporation).

2) A female-owned business shall be counted or included for sheltered market and goal purposes as a female-owned business regardless of the ethnicity of the female owner or owners.

3) For a business to qualify as minority-owned, only those minorities who are male shall be counted or included for sheltered market and goal purposes except that a firm which is owned 50% by minority males and 50% by minority females shall be considered a minority-owned business for purposes of the Act.

h) Sheltered Market

1) Procuring agencies are authorized to limit prospective vendors to minority and-or female-owned businesses or to require that vendors utilize minority and female-owned subcontractors for certain categories of contracts or for specific contracts. When a sheltered market set-aside is made the advertisement and-or bid document, if applicable, shall clearly state the contract is available for only minority and-or female-owned business. Sheltered market set-asides may be effective for such period of time and for such number of contracts as the Procuring Agency determines is necessary to reach the goal.

DEPARTMENT OF CENTRAL MANAGEMENT SERVICES

NOTICE OF PROPOSED AMENDMENTS

2) Sheltered market set-asides shall be used by procuring agencies as the primary means of meeting the contracting goal when the quarterly progress reports indicate the goal established in the agency's compliance report is not or will not be met and the goal is not modified by mutual agreement between the agency and the Department.

3) Each procuring agency shall notify the Secretary in writing ten days prior to establishment of a set-aside.

4) If the procuring agency determines that acceptance of the set-aside bid will result in payment of an unreasonable price, the procuring agency shall reject the bids. The agency shall then either rebid under the set-aside or withdraw the set-aside designation for the particular procurement. Before a set-aside may be withdrawn, the procuring agency shall submit to the Secretary a written statement detailing why the price given is unreasonable. The Secretary shall respond within three working days approving the withdrawal of the sheltered market if, based upon current market prices, historical prices, prices received by other agencies for similar goods or services, the policy of this Act to promote minority and female-owned business and other such relevant factors, the price appears to be unreasonable. If the Secretary determines the price is reasonable the request to withdraw will be denied. If no answer is received the set-aside may be withdrawn. When a set-aside is withdrawn, the procuring agency shall notify each minority or female-owned firm that bid explaining why the set-aside was withdrawn. The procuring agency shall provide a copy of the notice to the Secretary.

5) Procuring agencies shall consider reducing or eliminating bond requirements when allowed by law and when the reduced bond amount would adequately protect the State's interests.

6) Procuring-agencies-shall-consider-use-of-progress-or-advance payments.--Advance-payments-would-have-to-comply-with-Section 9.05-of-"AN-ACT-in-relation-to-State-Finance"-(Ill.-Rev.-Stat. 1985,-ch.-127,-par.-145f). Any contract awarded to a minority or female-owned business pursuant to this Section may contain a provision allowing advance or progress payments or both. A construction contract may not contain an advance payment provision. The advance or progress payment provision may be added to a contract at any time by agreement of the parties. Procuring agencies shall consider initiating use of such provisions and shall consider requests from minority and female-owned businesses to include such provisions in State contracts. Section 9.05 of "AN ACT in relation to State Finance" (Ill. Rev. Stat. 1987, ch. 127, par. 145f) may be applicable to contracts with such provisions.

DEPARTMENT OF CENTRAL MANAGEMENT SERVICES

NOTICE OF PROPOSED AMENDMENTS

7) Only certified minority and female-owned businesses may participate in sheltered markets.

8) The governing boards of State colleges and universities are not required to comply with this subsection (h) and may establish their own rules governing topics described in this subsection (h).

1) Subcontracting

1) Agency goals may be satisfied in part by counting expenditures made by State vendors to certified minority and female-owned businesses as subcontractors.

2) Agencies may require that vendors agree to contract with minority or female-owned business as subcontractors so that up to 10% of the project costs are paid to the minority or female-owned subcontractor.

3) Agencies shall not require that a vendor enter into subcontracts with minority and female-owned business when subcontracting is not necessary for the vendor to perform.

4) When minority or female-owned subcontractors are required, the vendor may be required to designate them by name and anticipated expenditure as a part of the bid. Alternatively the bid may merely require that the vendor hire the necessary subcontracting to meet the subcontractor expenditure requirement.

5) If no vendor can locate minority or female-owned subcontractors willing to subcontract or if a designated minority or female-owned subcontractor is later unable or unwilling to perform, the vendor shall be excused from having to comply with the requirement provided a good faith effort was made to locate or replace the needed minority or female-owned subcontractor.

6) Good Faith Effort

A) A good faith effort shall, at a minimum, consist of the following:

i) contacting the Minority and Female Business Enterprise Division of the Department of Central Management Services (Division) at least 15 days prior to need and requesting referrals from the certified vendor list and from any other list maintained by the Division.

ii) advertising in the Official State Newspaper or a local newspaper as time permits.

DEPARTMENT OF CENTRAL MANAGEMENT SERVICES

NOTICE OF PROPOSED AMENDMENTS

iii) contacting appropriate organizations such as unions, contractor associations, and minority or female oriented organizations.

B) Any vendor claiming good faith relief must fully document, in writing, the steps taken to obtain minority and female-owned subcontractors. The procuring agency may require additional information if the submittal does not meet the criteria stated above.

7) If a good faith exception is given, the procuring agency shall notify the Secretary of the Minority and Female Business Enterprise Council of the exception and shall include all pertinent information.

8) A vendor who obtains a contract requiring hiring of minority and female-owned subcontractors and who fails to do so and who does not qualify for a good faith exception is subject to having the contract cancelled and shall be liable for any damages the State may suffer because of the cancellation and need to find a substitute contractor.

j) Minority and Female-Owned Business Certification

1) Each minority and female-owned business, whether in a direct or subcontract relationship with the State, must be certified in accordance with the provisions of this Part established by the Council before the business is eligible to bid for or accept a contract or subcontract under the set-aside authorized by subsection (h). The primary purpose of the certification process is to determine if ownership is by minorities or females and to determine if minorities or females have operational control of the firm.

2) No agency may count expenditures with a non-certified vendor toward meeting the goal.

3) Vendors shall be temporarily self-certified upon submission of the Bidder's Application Form issued by the Department of Central Management Services and approved by the Council provided the information on the form is complete and accurate and indicates on its face that it is a minority or female-owned business as defined by the Act. This temporary self-certification is valid until revoked for failure to provide additional information necessary to complete the Bidder's Application Form or for failure to comply with program eligibility requirements of the Minority and Female Business Enterprise Act or of this Part.

4) The full certification procedure is more detailed and requires

that the Secretary (Manager of the Minority and Female Business Enterprise Division of the Department of Central Management Services) make determinations. The Secretary shall present, annually, a plan for subjecting temporarily self-certified firms to the full certification procedure. Such plan shall give first priority to those temporarily self-certified firms who have been or are about to be awarded a contract under the program. After that, priority will be determined by the date of the bidder's application form. In addition, the Secretary will in the event of an internal or third party challenge to the status of any temporarily self-certified firm conduct a full certification. The full certification procedure is outlined below.

5) Application

A) The firm seeking certification must obtain a MBE-FBE application package which includes:

   i) A letter of transmittal summarizing the program.

   ii) Form IL-401-1318 Application for MBE-FBE Certification.

   iii) Form IL-401-1319 Application for MBE-FBE Joint Venture Certification Application.

B) Form IL-401-1318 or IL-401-1319 must be completed, and all required attachments to meet the tests under subsections (j)(11), (j)(12), (j)(13) and (j)(14) and (j)(15), or a written explanation of their absence, must be submitted before a determination of eligibility can be made. A sufficient explanation for the absence of required attachments is that they do not exist or do not apply to the applicant. An application package may be obtained from the Minority and Female Business Enterprise Division of the Department of Central Management Services (Division). The completed form must be returned to the Division.

6) File Preparation

A) The Division staff will establish a file for each application received and the following information will be recorded into an alphabetized log, entitled "MBE-FBE Application Received":

   i) date of application
   ii) date received
   iii) name of firm
   iv) name of principal (usually the President)

   v) address
   vi) telephone number
   vii) type of certification sought (MBE or FBE)
   viii) nature of the firm's business (products or services provided)

B) The same information will be recorded in the applicant's file on a form entitled "Receipt of Application Report".

7) The Initial File Review for Accuracy and Completeness

The file will be reviewed to ensure the following:

A) All portions of the application form have been completed (including required attachments), marked not applicable (N-A.) or a satisfactory explanation for lack of completeness has been provided.

B) The application form is signed by the owner or manager and notarized. The notary cannot be an owner or a shareholder.

C) Missing documents or explanation of their absence will be noted, and the applicant will be requested to comply with an information request. If the applicant has indicated the firm has certified status through another organization, but no letter of certification has been included, the letter shall be requested at this time.

D) Beginning at this point, notes on all phone calls and other contacts with the applicant will be recorded on the MBE-FBE interview form.

8) Second File Review Other MBE-FBE Certifications

~~The Division staff will determine if the applicant has been previously certified by another agency, and if the requirements of the agency equal or exceed those standards set forth by this procedure. Upon verification of the previous certification, the Division staff may recommend automatic approval to the Secretary and the Secretary may so certify.~~ The Division staff shall ensure that the other entities' certification requirements continue to equal or exceed the standards set forth in this Part and can therefore be accepted by the Council. The Division will accomplish this by annually reviewing the other entities' requirements and verifying they equal or exceed standards of this Part. If the other entities requirements no longer equal or exceed the requirements of this Part and they refuse to make needed adjustments, the Division will no longer accept that entities' certifications. The

DEPARTMENT OF CENTRAL MANAGEMENT SERVICES

NOTICE OF PROPOSED AMENDMENTS

Division will review each such certifications, beginning with
the most recent, and act to revoke certifications of those
vendors who do not meet the requirements of this Part.
Certifications previously issued by that other entity will be
honored until revoked by the Secretary.

9)   Additional Data Collections

If the applicant has not been previously certified as a MBE-FBE,
the Division staff will conduct a personal interview with the
applicant which may include a telephone interview and-or an
announced on-site visit. During the on-site visit, the Division
staff will use Form IL-401-1318 or Form IL-401-1319, whichever
is appropriate and the site visit checklist to collect
information to verify the application. The on-site visit will
be completed upon review and approval of the completed
application. The on-site visit may be triggered at any point
during the certification process to verify compliance or at any
point prior to the time of recertification.

10) Determination of Eligibility

Upon completion of a thorough examination of all information
gathered from all sources (the application form, site visit,
prior history, and other source data), the Division staff will
begin the process to determine eligibility. The goal should be
to complete the entire certification process within 60 days of
completion of the initial review under subsection (j)(7)
including determination of eligibility, submission of
recommendation to the Secretary and completion of the
certification decision. Each element in the determination
process is based upon the requirements of the Act and the
eligibility standards determined by the Minority and Female
Business Enterprise Council, and therefore must be satisfied
before an applicant can be certified. Each standard must be
answered completely before another one is considered. If a firm
fails to meet one of the eligibility standards, no further
consideration shall be given to the application and the
certification shall be denied or a certified firm shall be
decertified, and notified of the appeal process.

11) First Test

A business which has annual gross sales for its most recent
fiscal year of less than $14 million is eligible for the
program. A business with gross sales of $14 million or more in
its most recent fiscal year is eligible to participate in the
program if the business can show that if it were to receive a

DEPARTMENT OF CENTRAL MANAGEMENT SERVICES

NOTICE OF PROPOSED AMENDMENTS

particular contract or subcontract there would be a significant
impact on employment of minority or female individuals or in the
use of minority or female owned subcontractors or suppliers.
For the impact to be significant in terms of employment, the
business would have to hire new employees with a full time
equivalence to 50% of their work force and at least 51% of those
new hires must be minority or female individuals. For the
impact to be significant in terms of use of subcontractors or
suppliers, the business must direct 75% of the value of the
contract to minority or female owned subcontractors or
suppliers. If the business makes contractual commitments
regarding hiring or use of subcontractors or suppliers and
agrees to appropriate enforcement mechanisms, such as bonding or
damage provisions, the Council will approve award of a contract
to such business.

12) Second Test

The first second test the applicant must meet is whether the
firm is owned and controlled by a person who is a citizen or
lawful permanent resident of the United States. Proof of
citizenship or permanent residency must be confirmed by a birth
certificate, naturalization papers, permanent resident status
documents, passports or other documents.

1213) Second Third Test

A)   The second third test is whether the applicant firm is
     owned or controlled by a person who is a minority or female.

B)   Documentation such as birth certificates, passports,
     naturalization papers, Indian rolls, is required, if
     available, as proof that the owners are in one of the
     eligible groups (see Section 2 of the Act):

     i)   Black - a person having origins in any of the black
          racial groups in Africa

     ii) Hispanic - a person of Spanish or Portuguese culture
          with origins in Mexico, South or Central American or
          the Caribbean (regardless of race)

     iii) American Indian or Alaskan Native - a person having
          origins in any of the original people of North
          American.

     iv) Asian American - a person having origins in any of the
          original peoples of the Far East, Southeast Asia, the
          Indian Subcontinent or the Pacific Islands.

DEPARTMENT OF CENTRAL MANAGEMENT SERVICES

NOTICE OF PROPOSED AMENDMENTS

v) Female - a person who is a citizen or lawful, permanent resident of the United States, and who is of the female gender.

C) If a person does not have documentary evidence or if it is not sufficient, the Secretary will consider, amongst other evidence submitted, whether the person is identified with or commonly recognized as belonging to an eligible group, has held himself out to be a member of one of the groups, has acted like a member of the community of one of the groups, and would be identified by a person at large as one of the groups.

1214) Third Fourth Test

The third fourth test which must be met by an applicant is that the firm must be at least fifty-one percent (51%) owned by one or more minority or by one or more females or in the case of a corporation, at least fifty-one percent (51%) of the stock must be owned by one or more minority persons or one or more females. The ownership shall be real, substantial and continuing. To determine interest in the firm, as the standards indicate, the committee must look beyond the ownership stated as a matter of form. Real is defined as a bona fide investment in the firm done at arms length and in good faith. Substantial is defined as the investment necessary to initiate a business in light of the type of work to be done, the organization of the concern, and the potential resources of the financial relationship with other businesses. The application should be carefully reviewed to determine:

A) If the minority or female ownership is 51% or more

B) If the minority or female owners obtain ownership by gift or inheritance or make substantial contribution in terms of expertise, money, etc. The contribution is analyzed in such a way as to disclose whether the investment in the firm reflects the asserted ownership interest. The Secretary will consider the following, amongst others, as indicators of insufficient contribution:

i) minimal cash outlay or personal investment

ii) a promise or agreement to contribute capital

iii) a note payable to the firm or other owners who are not minority or female.

iv) contributions for services rather than capital, except where services are unique, specialized or of a value commensurate with the ownership value of such services.

v) no recourse loans where the borrower assumes no liability for repayment upon default

vi) no recourse stock purchases wherein the purchaser assumes no liability upon default of payment other than transaction of shares.

C) Indicators of insufficient stock transactions include, but are not limited to, the following:

i) minimal cash outlay or personal investment

ii) a promise or agreement to buy stock

iii) stock issued, but not purchased.

iv) stock certificates purchased but not in the possession of the minority or female owner

v) stock held in trust or as a guardian for a minor

D) The minority or female owner must, except in the case of gift or inheritance, provide evidence of payment, monetary or in kind or experience for their share of the ownership. Examples of evidence include but are not limited to cancelled checks, bookkeeping entries, signed agreements. The following items will also be reviewed:

i) stock certificates,
ii) stock transfer ledgers,
iii) proof of stock purchases (if any),
iv) stockholder agreements (if any),
v) partnership agreements (if any),
vi) profit sharing agreements (if any),
vii) buy-out-rights agreements, and
viii) other related documents.

E) It will be determined if the minority or female owner paid the investment with a loan from a non-minority or male former employer or stockholder. Lack of proof of payment monetary or in kind will result in denial of certification or decertification.

1415) The Fourth Fifth Test

DEPARTMENT OF CENTRAL MANAGEMENT SERVICES

NOTICE OF PROPOSED AMENDMENTS

The ~~fourth~~ fifth test the applicant must meet is that the minority or female person be in direct control of the day to day operations of the firm, as well as have the power to make major decisions on management, policy, fiscal, and operational matters. To make the determination the following items will be reviewed for evidence of non-minority or male control:

A) Articles of incorporation will be reviewed to determine whether the minority or female owner was involved at the time of incorporation and in what way. If the minority or female owner was not involved at the time of incorporation, the time when he or she became involved in the firm and the ~~manner~~ in which it was done will be determined.

B) Corporate By-Laws will be reviewed to determine:

     i)   the duties of the directors and officers who occupy these positions,

     ii) the voting rights of the shareholders, and

     iii) any restrictive language which may ~~effect~~ affect the minority or female stockholder's voting rights.

C) Stock options-shareholders agreements which if exercised, will dilute or eliminate minority or female control.

D) Does the minority or female make decisions independently?

E) Review of resumes should determine whether the minorities or females have sufficient background including education and training for responsibilities assigned. However, no minimum educational or training requirements are imposed.

F) The following will be determined:

     i)   the minority or female owner continues to work for a non-minority firm. If so, what is the relationship of the firm to the applicant firm?

     ii) Who in the firm negotiates contracts loans, prepares estimates and makes other management and supervisory decisions?

~~15~~16) Notification of Approval

When the Secretary has determined that all conditions of this Part have been met, the Secretary will notify the applicant by letter that such approval is made. ~~and~~ This approval is for

DEPARTMENT OF CENTRAL MANAGEMENT SERVICES

NOTICE OF PROPOSED AMENDMENTS

a period of one year from the date of the letter and may be renewed in accordance with subsection (j)(20).~~, and further, that s~~Such approval may be rescinded at any time within the year if it is determined that the applicant no longer satisfies the eligibility standards for a MBE-FBE. At this time the applicant is entered into the state's MBE-FBE Directory and the Division file as a certified MBE-FBE.

~~16~~17) Notification of Denial

When the Secretary determines that the applicant firm does not meet the requirements of this Part and the Act, the Secretary shall send a letter by certified mail to the applicant setting forth the rationale for the determination, inviting the applicant to provide additional information in the areas of concern and advising the applicant of the appeal review process. The Secretary shall remove the applicant from the list of certified vendors.

~~17) Notification of Appeal~~

~~A) Upon receipt by an applicant firm of a certified letter advising of a potential denial or decertification and requesting additional information, applicant firm may submit a letter of appeal with reasons why the denial or decertification is invalid. This letter of approval must be received by certified mail in the Secretary's office within 45 days from the date of the notice from the Secretary. Failure of the applicant to respond within 45 days of receipt of the certified letter will cause automatic denial of certification or immediate administrative decertification.~~

~~B) If the applicant appeals on or prior to the deadline, the Secretary will review the appeal.~~

~~C) If the Secretary can now approve the firm, the notification of approval letter will be sent to the applicant, and the applicant firm will be entered into the MBE-FBE Directory as a certified MBE-FBE.~~

~~D) If the Secretary is still unable to certify the applicant firm as a MBE-FBE, the Secretary shall send a letter so advising the applicant and additionally, advising that the appeal, together with the file, has been submitted to the Council. The Council will notify the applicant by certified mail of a date to participate in a hearing before the Council for a final determination. Within a reasonable time, (no longer than 45 days) the Council will set the date, time, and place for a hearing and~~

DEPARTMENT OF CENTRAL MANAGEMENT SERVICES

NOTICE OF PROPOSED AMENDMENTS

have-the-Secretary-notify-all-parties-and-witnesses-of-the
hearing-schedule-by-certified-mail.

18)-Hearing

The-format-for-an-appeal-hearing-before-the-Council-shall-be
informal,-the-rules-of-evidence-will-not-apply.--The-hearing
shall:

A)   be-conducted-by-the-chairperson-who-shall-convene-the
     meeting-and-state-the-name-case-number-and-the-date-on
     which-the-hearing-is-conducted-and-that-the-hearing-is
     informal-and-the-rules-of-evidence-do-not-apply.--The
     Secretary-or-representative-staff-shall-be-present.--The
     chairperson-of-the-council-shall-explain-to-the-applicant
     who-the-Council-is-and-its-responsibility-for-hearing-the
     applicant.

B)   allow-the-petitioner-a-full-opportunity-to-properly
     identify-himself-and-his-company,-to-present-the-case
     completely-and-to-ask-questions-regarding-the-nature-of
     the-certification-denial.

C)   allow-the-Council-to-hear-the-applicant,-ask-and-obtain-
     answers-to-relevant-questions.--No-decision-shall-be-made
     immediately-but-the-applicant-will-be-advised-that-the
     Council-will-make-a-final-determination-and-notify-the
     applicant-immediately-after-such-determination-is-made.
     The-Council-may-approve-the-firm-and-have-the-firm-so
     notified-and-listed-in-the-Directory-of-Certified
     MBEs-FBEs.--Decertified-firms-will-be-removed-from-the
     Directory-of-Certified-MBEs-FBEs.--The-decisions-of-the
     Council-are-final,-and-the-firm's-representative-will-be
     so-notified.--The-firm-may-reapply-twelve-months-from-the
     date-of-the-final-determination.--The-representative-of
     the-aggrieved-firm-may-pursue-the-matter-through-the
     court-system.

19) Review and Reconsideration

     A)   The Secretary shall inform the applicant of the decision
          within six months of receipt of the request for
          reconsideration. If the decision is not favorable to the
          applicant, the Secretary shall inform the applicant of
          additional reviews that are available. If the Secretary
          fails to inform the applicant within the six month period
          the reconsideration request will be considered denied and
          the applicant may ask for review by the Council's
          Certification Committee.

DEPARTMENT OF CENTRAL MANAGEMENT SERVICES

NOTICE OF PROPOSED AMENDMENTS

B)   The applicant may request that the Council's Certification
     Committee, made up of at least five parties appointed by
     the Council's chair, review the reconsideration decision of
     the Secretary. This request must be submitted to the
     Secretary in writing and must be actually received by the
     Secretary no later than 45 days after applicant received
     the Secretary's decision. The request must state why
     applicant believes the Secretary's decision is wrong, must
     address all points raised in the Secretary's decision and
     must include any supporting documentation.

C)   Upon receipt of the request for review, the Secretary shall
     contact the Council's Certification Committee, inform them
     of the request, and establish a date and time to meet and
     review relevant information. The Secretary will attempt to
     schedule the meeting between 15 and 30 days after receipt
     of the request for review . The meeting shall be held in
     Springfield or Chicago unless the Committee agrees to meet
     at some other location. The applicant will be informed of
     the meeting schedule by letter mailed at least 10 days
     prior to the meeting date.

D)   Prior to the meeting the Secretary shall provide each
     Committee member with a copy of the request for review and
     of the Secretary's file on the matter. In addition, the
     Secretary shall prepare and submit to the Committee a draft
     response to the points raised in the request for review.
     Each Committee member shall review the files prior to the
     meeting. Any Committee member may ask questions of the
     Secretary and the Secretary shall ensure that the questions
     and answers are provided to each Committee member.

E)   The meeting shall not be open to the public. Only the
     applicant, the applicant's representative, the Secretary,
     the Secretary's necessary assistants, the Committee members
     and necessary witnesses may be present. Although the
     applicant may have an attorney or other representative
     assist at the meeting, applicant must be present if any
     representative is present and applicant must respond to
     questions of the Committee. The meeting shall be conducted
     in an informal manner within these procedures and all
     information obtained shall be considered.

F)   The Committee Chair shall call the meeting to order, shall
     announce the matter at issue and explain how the meeting
     will be conducted. Each party in attendance shall be
     identified. The Chair shall briefly restate the reasons
     given for the Secretary's decision and open the floor to
     the applicant.

DEPARTMENT OF CENTRAL MANAGEMENT SERVICES

NOTICE OF PROPOSED AMENDMENTS

G) The applicant may make an opening statement but must respond to each of the reasons given in the Secretary's decision. The applicant may call and question any witnesses. The Committee may ask questions of the applicant, the Secretary or any other person present. The Secretary may comment at any time and when applicant is finished the Secretary may call any witnesses. Both applicant and Secretary may make closing statements.

H) After listening to the applicant and the Secretary, the Committee shall dismiss all persons present. The Committee shall meet in private to discuss the matter and shall make a decision from information obtained from the meeting. The decision will be based upon majority vote of the Committee.

I) If the decision is favorable to the applicant, the Committee shall inform the Secretary. The Secretary will place the applicant on the list of certified vendors. The Secretary shall notify the applicant, the Committee and the Council of this action.

J) If the decision is adverse to the applicant, the Committee shall inform the Secretary. The Secretary shall notify the applicant and the Council of this action. The applicant shall also be informed of the Committee's reasons and told of the next review procedure. Notice to the applicant shall be by certified mail.

K) The applicant may ask that the full Council review an adverse decision of the Certification Committee. The request must be submitted to the Secretary in writing and must actually be received by the Secretary no later than 15 days after applicant received the Committee's decision. This request must state why applicant believes the Committee's decision is wrong, must address all points raised in the Committee's decision and must include any supporting documentation.

L) The Secretary shall provide each Council member with a copy of the second request and a copy of the Secretary's file on the matter for review. In addition, the Secretary shall prepare and submit to the Council a draft response to the points raised in the second request for review. The Secretary shall consult with the Committee prior to submitting the draft.

M) The Council shall consider the second request at the next regularly scheduled Council meeting provided that the second request was received by the Secretary at least 21

DEPARTMENT OF CENTRAL MANAGEMENT SERVICES

NOTICE OF PROPOSED AMENDMENTS

days prior to the Council meeting. If received after that time the matter will be considered at the next following Council meeting. The applicant will be told of the location, date and time of the meeting.

N) The Council shall consider only the written information provided or produced by the applicant, the Certification Committee and the Secretary. The Council may, on its own request that the applicant address the Council or respond to specific questions. Although applicant may have an attorney or other representative assist at the meeting, the applicant must be available to respond to Council questions. The Council will allow the applicant to address the Council if such request is made as part of the second request.

O) After reviewing all information obtained, the Council shall vote to uphold the Committee's decision, overturn the Committee's decision or have the matter sent back to the Committee for reconsideration with instructions from the Council.

P) If the decision is favorable to the applicant, the Council shall inform the Secretary. The Secretary shall place the applicant on the list of certified vendors. The Secretary shall inform the applicant.

Q) If the decision is adverse to the applicant, the Council shall inform the Secretary. The Secretary shall notify the applicant.

R) If the decision is to send the matter back to the Committee, the process shall continue from that point until resolved at the Committee or Council level.

S) For purposes of this level of subsection, all notices shall be evidenced by certified mail receipt and-or an entry in the certification log maintained by the Minority and Female Business Enterprise Division.

19) Decertification

A) An approval shall be rescinded and a firm decertified if the firm no longer qualifies as a minority or female-owned business under the Act or this Part.

B) Upon receipt of information which questions the validity of a MBE-FBE's certification, the Division shall conduct an investigation as provided for within this procedure, on-site visit, telephone interview, staff interviews.

DEPARTMENT OF CENTRAL MANAGEMENT SERVICES

NOTICE OF PROPOSED AMENDMENTS

examination-of-the-records-eter-to-determine-if-there-is
a-valid-reason-to-begin-the-decertification-process.
Prior-to-decertification-the-MBE-FBE-will-be-notified-by
and-advised-of-the-appeal-process-and-additional
information-will-be-requested.--After-receipt-of-such-a
letter,-the-appeal-process-is-open-to-the-firm-and-the
firm-may-follow-that-process-through-to-a-final
determination-by-the-Council.---Decertification-may-also
occur-as-a-result-of-a-challenge-from-a-third-party.---If
such-a-challenge-occurs-the-procedures-outlined-in-the
following-section-should-be-followed.

19) Decertification

A) A firm that is certified (either self or full) may have
   that status challenged by the State or some third-party.

B) Upon receipt of information which questions the validity of
   a M-FBE certification, the Secretary shall conduct an
   investigation which may include on-site or telephone
   Interviews, review of existing records submitted pursuant
   to subsection (j)(5)(B) or collection and examination of
   new records to supplement, explain or clarify records
   previously submitted.

C) If the investigation results in a finding that the firm is
   not or no longer eligible for M-FBE status, the Secretary
   shall notify the firm that it is decertified. The review
   and reconsideration procedures found in subsection (j)(18)
   are available to the firm that is given a decertification
   letter. After decertification the applicant may not apply
   for readmission to the program until one year has passed
   since the date of decertification. A certification of the
   applicant by another entity shall not be accepted during
   the one year period following decertification.

20) Challenge-Procedure

A) The-purpose-of-the-challenge-procedure-is-to-determine
   whether-a-business-enterprise-presumed-to-be-a-minority
   or-female-owned-business-enterprise-is-in-fact-a
   legitimate-MBE-FBE-as-defined-in-Sec.-(1)-of-the-Act.
   The-procedure-provides-that-any-third-party-may-challenge
   the-status-of-any-minority-or-female-owned-business
   enterprise-seeking-or-enjoying-certification-under-the
   State-of-Illinois-MBE-FBE-certification-program.

B) The-challenge-must-be-in-writing,-allege-that-the
   challenged-firm-does-not-meet-the-eligibility
   requirements-of-the-Act-or-this-Part-and-be-submitted-to
   the-Secretary.

C) If-the-Secretary-determines-there-is-no-reason-to-believe
   the-challenge-is-valid,-as-determined-by-subsection
   (j)(20)(B),-the-proceedings-will-be-terminated-and-the
   challenger-notified-in-writing.

D) If-the-Secretary-determines-there-is-validity-to-the
   challenge-under-subsection-(j)(20)(B),-the-Secretary-will
   notify-the-challenged-party-in-writing-that-his-her
   status-as-a-MBE-FBE-has-been-challenged.---The-notice-will
   identify-the-challenging-party-and-summarize-the-grounds
   for-the-challenge.---The-notice-will-also-request-the
   MBE-FBE-to-provide-information-responding-to-the
   challenge.

E) The-Secretary-will-evaluate-the-evidence-and-make-a
   proposed-determination-as-to-whether-specific-eligibility
   requirements-of-the-Act-or-this-Part-which-have-been
   challenged-is-met-or-not.---This-decision-will-be
   submitted-along-with-complete-file-to-the-Council.
   Within-45-days,-the-Council,-will-issue-a-proposed
   determination-to-the-challenger-and-the-MBE-FBE.

F) Within-a-reasonable-time-the-Council-will-provide-an
   opportunity-to-both-parties-for-an-informal-hearing-to
   respond-to-the-proposed-determination.

G) Following-the-hearing-the-Council-will-inform-the-parties
   in-writing-and-state-its-reasons-for-the-decision-to
   certify-or-not-certify-based-on-the-eligibility
   requirements-of-this-Act-or-this-Part-which-has-been
   challenged.

H) The-denial-is-final-and-may-be-appealed-through-the-courts
   by-the-aggrieved-party.--The-MBE-FBE-and-or-joint-venture
   may-correct-the-deficiencies-in-the-firm-and-apply-for
   certification-twelve-months-after-the-date-of-the-denial
   of-certification.

21) Recertification Process

A) Forty-five days prior to expiration of a certification the
   Division staff will identify the firm and mail certified
   with return receipt an application for Certification as a

Minority Business Enterprise-Female Business Enterprise. A cover letter will advise the firm to complete and return the application prior to the 15th day before the expiration of the current certification. Firms that fail to meet this deadline will be decertified.

B) If the applicant submits the material in a timely manner, the original certification shall remain in effect until the Secretary completes the recertification process.

BC) Upon receipt of the recertification application the Division staff will review it for changes which affect eligibility under the Act or this Part.

CD) If no such changes have occurred, the Secretary will grant recertification. If changes in the business give rise to questions regarding eligibility, the Secretary will notify the firm requesting clarification and/or additional information.

DE) When all questions of eligibility have been clarified, the Secretary will issue a new certification good for a period of one year.

EF) If the Secretary determines that the firm is not eligible, a denial letter will be sent and the firm is eligible to initiate the appeal process.

k) Minority and Female-Owned Business List

1) The Council shall maintain a list of businesses that have been certified as minority or female-owned businesses. This list shall be made available to all procuring agencies.

2) Any lists of minority or female-owned business maintained by procuring agencies shall be forwarded to the Council.

l) Change of Status

1) Any contract awarded under a set-aside may not be assigned to another vendor without permission of the Secretary.

2) Should a vendor who received a contract under the set-aside cease to qualify as minority or female-owned during contract performance because of subsequent business transfer, reorganization or other similar actions, the procuring agency may cancel the contract immediately without penalty to the State.

3) Any change of the minority and female business status of a certified minority and female business shall be reported to the Council by both the vendor and the procuring agency.

m) Penalty to Vendor

The following penalties may be assessed in accordance with the Minority and Female Business Enterprise Act.

1) Refusal to supply proof or additional proof of status when claiming minority or female status shall result in suspension from participation in sheltered market programs for a period not to exceed one year.

2) Refusal to supply additional proof of status pursuant to subsections (j)(4) and (j)(6) above after receiving a contract under a set-aside shall result in suspension from receiving any additional State contracts for a period of one year and if in the State's interest, cancellation of existing set-aside contracts without penalty to the State. In determining whether to cancel an existing set-aside contract, the State shall consider the cost of utilizing another vendor, availability of another vendor, delivery time and other such factors.

3) Accepting a contract under any sheltered market procurement when the vendor does not qualify as a minority or female-owned business pursuant to subsections (i)(4)and (i)(6) above shall result in suspension from all State bidding and contracting for a period of one year. If it is in the State's interest the contract may be cancelled immediately without penalty to the state. In determining whether it is in the State's interest to cancel an existing set-aside contract, the State shall consider the cost of utilizing another vendor, the availability of another vendor, delivery time and other such factors. In addition, if the vendor knowingly misrepresented its status the amount of profit applicable to amounts paid to the vendor shall be withheld from any amounts owed to the vendor. If the amount owed the vendor is insufficient to off-set profits the vendor shall be liable to pay back to the State any balance thereof. The profit rate shall be deemed 20% unless a lesser or greater amount can be conclusively proved.

4) Governing boards of State colleges and universities may establish rules governing penalties.

n) If the Secretary finds a business in violation of the Minority and Female Business Enterprise Act or of this Part, the Secretary shall report such violation to the Illinois Attorney General. Any such violation found by any State agency or any person should be reported to the Secretary as soon as practicable after the finding.

DEPARTMENT OF CENTRAL MANAGEMENT SERVICES

NOTICE OF PROPOSED AMENDMENTS

a)   Agency Compliance

    1)   Each agency, other than the governing boards of State colleges
      and universities, shall submit a compliance plan annually. The
      Council shall establish the format and timetable for submission
      of the plan. The Council shall approve the plan if it meets the
      requirements of this Part and the Minority and Female Business
      Enterprise Act.

    2)   Each agency shall submit quarterly reports that outlines its
      progress under the program. The governing boards of State
      colleges and universities shall submit an annual report
      identifying by university and by campus their total
      appropriation, expenditures by major object code, expenditures
      with minority and female owned businesses broken down by major
      object code, expenditures with minority and female owned
      businesses broken down by ethnicity, and the names and addresses
      of minority and female business receiving contracts or
      subcontracts. The annual report shall also identify any
      significant accomplishments relating to the program.

    3)   The Council on its own motion or upon request of a procuring
      agency shall recommend ways in which the procuring agency may
      reach its goal. Upon finding by the Council that a procuring
      agency's compliance plan, as presently adopted or implemented,
      is insufficient to reach the agency goal, the Council shall
      recommend ways in which the agency can reach its goal. Such
      recommendations shall include but not be limited to the
      following (See Act, Section 2):

        A)   *assurances of stronger and better focused solicitation
          efforts to obtain more minority and female owned businesses
          as potential sources of supply;*

        B)   *division of job or project requirements, when economically
          feasible, into tasks or quantities to permit participation
          of minority and female owned businesses;*

        C)   *elimination of extended experience or capitalization
          requirements, when programmatically feasible, to permit
          participation of minority and female owned businesses;*

        D)   *identification of specific proposed contracts as
          particularly attractive or appropriate for participation by
          minority and female owned business, such identification to
          result from and be coupled with efforts to subparagraphs
          (i) through (iii);*

        E)   *implementation of those regulations established for the use
          of the sheltered market process.*

DEPARTMENT OF CENTRAL MANAGEMENT SERVICES

NOTICE OF PROPOSED AMENDMENTS

    4)   If the compliance plans or quarterly reports indicate the agency
      goal will not be reached, the Council will request the agency
      head to appear before the Council and explain the agency's
      non-compliance. If the Council determines the agency is not
      making a serious effort to reach the goal, the Council will then
      prepare a report for submission to the Governor with
      recommendations for remedial action.

(Source: Amended at 12 Ill. Reg. _____, effective_____)

ILLINOIS REGISTER

OFFICE OF THE COMPTROLLER

NOTICE OF PROPOSED AMENDMENTS

1) Heading of the Part: Public Radio and Television Station Grants.

2) Code Citation: 74 Ill. Adm. Code 280.

3) Section numbers: Proposed action:

        280.10   Amendment
        280.30   Amendment
        Appendix A   New Section
        Appendix B   New Section

4) Statutory authority: Ill. Rev. Stat. 1987, ch. 127, pars. 1551, 1552.

5) A complete description of the subjects and issues involved: These
    amendments allow for participation in the Community Service Grants
    Program by public radio and television stations whose fiscal year time
    periods differ from that of the State of Illinois.

6) Will these proposed amendments replace any emergency rules currently
    in effect? No.

7) Does this rulemaking contain an automatic repeal date? No.

8) Do these proposed amendments contain incorporations by reference? No.

9) Are there any proposed amendments pending on this Part? No.

10) Statement of Statewide Policy Objectives: Not applicable.

11) Time, place and manner in which interested persons may comment on
    these proposed amendments: Interested persons or organizations may
    submit written comments or requests to comment within 45 days of
    publication of this notice to:

                Kirby VanZandt
                Office of the Comptroller
                201 State House
                Springfield, Illinois 62706

12) Initial regulatory flexibility analysis: These amendments do not
    affect small businesses.

The full text of the proposed amendments is as follows:

OFFICE OF THE COMPTROLLER

NOTICE OF PROPOSED AMENDMENTS

TITLE 74: PUBLIC FINANCE
CHAPTER II: COMPTROLLER

PART 280
PUBLIC RADIO AND TELEVISION STATION GRANTS

Section	
280.5	Foreword
280.10	Definitions
280.15	Operating Grants
280.20	Applications Content
280.25	Grant Limitations
280.30	Application Times
Appendix A	Corporation for Public Broadcasting Qualification Criteria for Radio Community Service Grants
Appendix B	Corporation for Public Broadcasting Qualification Criteria for Television Community Service Grants

AUTHORITY: Implementing and authorized by "AN ACT to provide for State grants
to certain public radio and television stations in the State of Illinois and
for related purposes" (Ill. Rev. Stat. 1987, ch. 127, par. 1551 et
seq.){Public Act-84-1040, effective November-16, 1985}.

SOURCE: Adopted at 4 Ill. Reg. 37, p. 597, effective August 29, 1980;
codified at 5 Ill. Reg. 10598; amended at 10 Ill. Reg. 10115, effective May
28, 1986; amended at ___ Ill. Reg._____, effective_____.

Section 280.10 Definitions

"Act" means "AN ACT to provide for State grants to certain public
radio and television stations in the State of Illinois and for related
purposes" (Ill. Rev. Stat. 1987, ch. 127, par. 1551 et seq.){Public
Act-84-1040, effective-November-26, 1985}.

"Actual Operating Cost" means the total sum expended for the operations and maintenance of an Illinois public radio or television
station during the station's fiscal year ending prior to October 1July
1 of the fiscal year for which funds are appropriated for grants under
this Act, and includes programming and production costs, all administrative costs, all public information costs, all fund raising costs,
all broadcasting costs and all in-kind expenses relating to the above.
However, the term "actual operating costs" does not include the costs
of acquiring fixed assets, depreciation on fixed assets, production
costs underwritten by public broadcasting entities, costs attributable
to instructional activities of the educational institution, whether on
closed circuit or not, costs of operating a commercial (profit-making)
business enterprise, including a for-profit subsidiary, or an individual, and all in-kind expenses related to the above.

OFFICE OF THE COMPTROLLER

NOTICE OF PROPOSED AMENDMENTS

"Comptroller" means the Comptroller of the State of Illinois or his designated representative for receiving grant applications pursuant to the Act.

"Eligible station" means a public radio or television station in full-time operation which meets the minimum grant criteria of the Corporation for Public Broadcasting (see Appendices A and B of this Part) before applying for a grant under the Act is receiving grants from the Corporation for Public Broadcasting.

"Illinois Public Radio Station" or "Radio Station" means a non-commercial public radio broadcasting station licensed as such by the Federal Communications Commission to and operating from a community within this State which is eligible to receive grants under the Act.

"Illinois Public Television Station" or "Television Station" means a non-commercial public television broadcasting station licensed as such by the Federal Communications Commission to and operating from a community within this State which is eligible to receive grants under the Act.

"Public Broadcasting Entities" means the Corporation for Public Broadcasting, any licensee or permitee of a television or radio broadcasting station which is eligible to be licensed by the Federal Communications Commission as a non-commercial educational radio or television broadcasting station, or any non-profit institution engaged primarily in the production, acquisition, distribution, or dissemination of educational and cultural television or radio programs.

"Station" means any eligible radio or television station.

(Source: Amended at_____III. Reg._____, effective_____.)

Section 280.30   Application Times

Unless a written request for an extension of time beyond February 1October 1 to a specified date is approved by the Comptroller for good cause shown, an application for grant shall be made on or before February 1October 1 of each year that appropriations have been made available to the Comptroller for distribution pursuant to the Act. This provision shall not apply to fiscal year 1986; the deadline date for fiscal year 1986 shall be June 15, 1986.

(Source: Amended at_____Ill. Reg._____, effective_____.)

Appendix A   Corporation for Public Broadcasting ("CPB") Qualification Criteria for Radio Community Service Grants

OFFICE OF THE COMPTROLLER

NOTICE OF PROPOSED AMENDMENTS

a) Licensing and Power: The station must be designated by the Federal Communications Commission as a noncommercial, educational radio station. The station must have transmitter power sufficient to provide primary signal coverage in the community of license.

b) Management and Staff: The following conditions must be satisfied:

    1) A minimum of five full-time professional radio station staff must be employed on an annual (12 month) basis. At least three full-time staff members should be employed in managerial and/or programming positions. Minimum staff cannot be paid with Community Service Grant funds.

    2) Full-time, professional, radio station staff includes permanent personnel with demonstrated skill and expertise in the management, programming, production, promotion, development, or engineering areas of radio station operation, paid no less than the minimum federal hourly wage plus regular health benefits, whose terms of employment require the exercise of full-time duties in one or more of these areas. The term "full-time" will be understood to be the number of hours that constitute the normal acceptable work week at each institution or station.

    3) Custodial and clerical staff, students whose student status is a condition of employment, interns and trainees, do not meet the definition of this criterion, nor do personnel teaching or holding academic duties in excess of the equivalent of one three-hour credit course per quarter or semester.

    4) Persons employed on a non-permanent basis, such as on a public service employment training grant, cannot be considered full-time professional radio station staff to meet this criterion.

c) Facilities: A station must have sufficient, professionally equipped on-air and production facilities to allow for broadcast of programming of high technical quality including the capability for simultaneous local production and origination. In addition, sufficient office space must be provided.

d) Broadcast Operations: The station's minimum operational schedule must be 18 consecutive hours per day, 365 days per year. However, AM stations which are restricted by the terms of their licenses to less than the minimum broadcast schedule required by the CPB policy will be eligible for assistance if all other criteria are met.

OFFICE OF THE COMPTROLLER

NOTICE OF PROPOSED AMENDMENTS

e) Programming: The following conditions must be satisfied:

    1) The station's daily broadcast schedule must be devoted
        primarily to general audience programming of good quality
        which serves demonstrated community needs of an educa-
        tional, informational, and cultural nature, within its
        primary signal area.

    2) A program schedule designed to further the principles of
        religious philosophies does not meet the definition of this
        criterion.

    3) A program schedule designed primarily for in-school or
        professional in-service audiences does not meet the
        definition of this criterion.

    4) Stations licensed to political organizations do not meet
        the definition of this criterion.

    5) Radio applicants in areas already served by a CPB-qualified
        radio station must propose a substantially different
        program service from the existing CPB-qualified station(s)
        in the area and clearly identify the varying needs and
        interests of the audience to be served. For the purposes
        of this criterion, counter-scheduling programs already
        available from a CPB-qualified station in the market does
        not, by itself, constitute a substantially different
        service.

    6) The station must originate a significant, locally produced
        program service designed to serve its community of li-
        cense.

f) Non-Federal Income: Each grantee must have a minimum
    non-federal annual income of $150,000.

(Source: Added at _____Ill. Reg._____, effective_____.)

Appendix B   Corporation for Public Broadcasting ("CPB") Qualification
              Criteria for Television Community Service Grants

    a) Management: Each grantee must have a staff headed by a manager
        or other chief executive officer who:

        1) has the responsibility and authority to determine when and
            what material shall be broadcast over the station; and

        2) has the responsibility and authority to administer dis-
            bursements under a budget authorized by the governing
            board of the licensee.

OFFICE OF THE COMPTROLLER

NOTICE OF PROPOSED AMENDMENTS

b) Staff: The following conditions must be satisfied:

    1) Each grantee must have no less than ten staff, which
        includes five full-time staff with regular health benefits,
        one of which is the manager or chief executive officer, and
        the equivalent of five additional full-time personnel, paid
        no less than the minimum federal hourly wage. The term
        "full-time" will be understood to be the number of hours
        that constitute the normal acceptable work week at each
        institution or station. Likewise, each "equivalent
        full-time" position will mean equal to the number of hours
        for a normal work week at each stations.

    2) Minimum staff cannot be paid with Community Service Grant
        funds.

    3) Persons employed on a non-permanent basis, such as on a
        public service employment training program grant or a CPB
        training grant, cannot be considered full-time professional
        television station staff to meet this criteria.

    4) Personnel used to meet the five full-time staff requirement
        may not teach or hold academic duties in excess of the
        equivalent of one three credit hour course per quarter or
        semester.

c) Joint or Dual Licensee: When more than one grantee is operated
    by one licensee, each such grantee in addition to the above,
    must be headed by a manager or other chief executive officer who
    reports directly to the governing board of the licensee; or in
    the case of university licensees, each general manager should
    report on an equal basis to the next level of governing superi-
    ors.

d) Non-Federal Income: Each grantee must have a minimum non-federal
    annual income of $300,000.

e) Studio/Production Facilities: Each grantee must have studio and
    production facilities and regularly produce and broadcast
    locally originated programming.

f) Broadcast Operations: Each grantee must:

    1) during the first full year of on-air operation commencing
        immediately following issuance of Program Test Authority,
        broadcast on a minimum schedule of six days per week,
        fifty-two weeks per year, for a total of at least 2,500
        hours or 48 hours a week and

OFFICE OF THE COMPTROLLER

NOTICE OF PROPOSED AMENDMENTS

2) for all stations during the second such full year of operation and in all succeeding years, broadcast on a schedule of seven days per week, fifty-two weeks per year, for a total of at least 3,000 hours or 57 hours a week.

g) Programming: The following conditions must be satisfied:

1) The station's daily broadcast schedule must be devoted primarily to programming of good quality which serves demonstrated community needs of an educational, informational and cultural nature, within its primary signal area.

2) A program schedule designed to further the principles of religious philosophies does not meet the definition of this criterion.

3) Stations licensed to political organizations do not meet the definition of this criterion.

4) CPB will provide Community Service Grant assistance to all eligible television stations that meet current criteria regardless of overlapping broadcast signals. However, a grantee seeking qualification in a market where a CPB-qualified television station already exists must demonstrate the intention to provide a substantially different program service or a new service to a substantial number of unserved homes. For the purpose of this criterion, counter-scheduling programs already available from a CPB-qualified station in the market does not, by itself, constitute a substantially different service.

(Source: Added at_____Ill. Reg._____, effective_____.)

STATE BOARD OF EDUCATION

NOTICE OF PROPOSED AMENDMENTS

1) Heading of the Part: Pupil Transportation Reimbursement

2) Code Citation: 23 Ill. Adm. Code 120

3) Section Numbers:

Section Numbers:	Proposed Action:
120.10	Amendment
120.60	Amendment
120.110	Amendment
120.130	New Section
120.200	Amendment
120.210	Amendment
120.235	New Section

4) Statutory Authority: Ill. Rev. Stat. 1987, ch. 122, pars. 29-5, 29-5.2, 29-17

5) A Complete Description of the Subjects and Issues Involved: These proposed amendments implement provisions of two laws passed in 1987, P.A. 85-271 and P.A. 85-871. The former requires the chief administrative officer of each school to notify custodians of qualifying students that reimbursement under the Parental Transportation Grant program is available. The latter, P.A. 85-871, makes changes in that program, including stipulating that qualifying pupils must be Illinois residents and specifying the application deadline for reimbursement (June 30). The rules also establish procedures for reimbursement for the installation of 28-inch seat backs as required by law and clarify the reimbursement available for underground storage tanks.

6) Will this proposed rule replace an emergency rule currently in effect? No

7) Does this rulemaking contain an automatic repeal date? ___ Yes   X No

8) Does this proposed amendment contain incorporations by reference? No

9) Are there any other proposed amendments pending on this Part? No

10) Statement of Statewide Policy Objectives: Adoption of these amendments will not create or enlarge a state mandate.

STATE BOARD OF EDUCATION

NOTICE OF PROPOSED AMENDMENTS

1) <u>Time, Place, and Manner in which interested persons may comment on this proposed rulemaking</u>: Written comments may be submitted within 45 days of the publication of this notice to:

   Marcia Salisbury
   Illinois State Board of Education
   100 North First Street
   Springfield, Illinois 62777
   (217) 782-5256

12) <u>Initial Regulatory Flexibility Analysis</u>: These amendments will not affect small businesses.

The full text of the Proposed Rule(s) begins on the next page:

STATE BOARD OF EDUCATION

NOTICE OF PROPOSED AMENDMENTS

TITLE 23: EDUCATION AND CULTURAL RESOURCES
SUBTITLE A: EDUCATION
CHAPTER I: STATE BOARD OF EDUCATION
SUBCHAPTER c: FINANCE

PART 120
PUPIL TRANSPORTATION REIMBURSEMENT

SUBPART A: SCHOOL REIMBURSEMENT

SUBPART B: CUSTODIAN REIMBURSEMENT FOR PUPIL TRANSPORTATION

AUTHORITY: Implementing and authorized by Article 29 of The School Code (Ill. Rev. Stat. 1987, ch. 122, par. 29-1 et seq.).

SOURCE: Adopted at 10 Ill. Reg. 19438, effective October 31, 1986; amended at 10 Ill. Reg. 21675, effective December 11, 1986; amended at 12 Ill. Reg. 4147, effective February 5, 1988; amended at ___ Ill. Reg. _____, effective _____.

NOTE: Capitalization indicates statutory language.

SUBPART A: SCHOOL REIMBURSEMENT

Section 120.10   Definitions

"Buildings" - A district leased, leased/purchased or owned structure
or portion of a structure that houses pupil transportation vehicles
and/or equipment used for servicing the district's pupil
transportation vehicles, such as a school bus storage building or
pupil transportation maintenance garage.

"Chief mechanic" - The person who directly supervises the school
district's mechanics and maintenance personnel for pupil
transportation vehicles and who also performs the duties of school
bus mechanic when necessary.

"Contract" - A written agreement between two parties, for a specific
period of time and amount for compensation, that is enforceable by
law.

"Contractual pupil transportation service" - Pupil transportation
services provided for a set fee under a contract with an independent
carrier.

"District owned and operated pupil transportation service" - Pupil
transportation service provided by a school district that owns and
operates the approved safety inspected vehicle(s), exercises
managerial control over facilities and personnel used in the pupil
transportation service, and also employs and supervises the school
bus driver(s).

"Equipment" - Items, other than vehicles, costing $500 or more and
having a useful life of more than one year.

"Independent Carrier" - An individual, partnership, corporation,
firm, organization, association or other legal entity not subject to
control by a school district, which enters into a contract with a
school district to provide pupil transportation services. An entity
does not qualify as an independent carrier if its contract with the
district requires that it do one or more of the following:

  employ existing school district drivers, mechanics, and
  administrative and clerical personnel;

  pay salaries as stipulated by the school district;

  employ or discharge employees solely at the discretion of the
  school district;

employ specific types and numbers of administrative personnel.

"Lease" - A written contract between two parties whereby the lessee
agrees to pay the lessor a specified sum of money for the use of the
lessor's transportation equipment, building and/or vehicles for a
specific period of time with no option to purchase.

"Lease/purchase agreement" - A written contract between two parties
whereby the lessee agrees to pay the lessor a specified sum of money
for the use of the lessor's transportation equipment, building
and/or vehicles for a specific period of time, and the contract
contains a clause permitting the lessee the option to purchase the
equipment and/or vehicles at a specified price within a specified
period of time.

"Materials, parts, and supplies" - Items costing less than $500 or
having a useful life of one year or less.

"Principal cost or capital cost" -

  For purchased vehicles, equipment and/or buildings/property the
  principal cost is the cash cost (list price less any discount,
  revenue from sale of district-owned item, and/or trade-in
  allowance) plus the prior year's undepreciated balance of the
  traded district-owned vehicle, equipment or building/property
  excluding all financing charges whether explicit or implicit.

  For leased or leased/purchased vehicles, equipment and/or
  buildings/property the principal cost is the fair market value
  of the vehicle, equipment and/or building/property at the time
  of acquisition.

"Prorated cost" - A cost incurred for multiple functions. In
accounting for such cost, the total cost shall be prorated on a
verifiable basis among the appropriate account function codes.

"Pupil transportation vehicles" - School buses and other vehicles
used for transporting pupils.

"School bus driver" - A person who possesses a valid school bus
driver's permit, and drives a pupil transportation vehicle to
transport pupils.

"School bus maintenance personnel" - Individuals whose duties are to
maintain the district owned or operated pupil transportation
vehicles.

STATE BOARD OF EDUCATION

NOTICE OF PROPOSED AMENDMENTS

"School day" - THAT PERIOD OF TIME WHICH THE PUPIL IS REQUIRED TO BE IN ATTENDANCE AT SCHOOL FOR INSTRUCTIONAL PURPOSES.

"Site improvement" - Any addition or improvement to a site leased, leased/purchased, or owned that is directly related to the district pupil transportation services, including but not limited to, underground fuel storage tanks.

"Transportation Fund" - An accounting entity as described in Section 17-8 of The School Code (Ill. Rev. Stat. 1985 1987, ch. 122, par. 17-8), to account for revenue and expenditures related to pupil transportation services.

"Transportation related building and building maintenance costs" - The portion of depreciation of buildings, and site improvements and costs of operation and maintenance of buildings and site improvements directly related to a school district's pupil transportation program. These costs are chargeable to and paid from the Educational Fund or Operations, Building and Maintenance Fund as prescribed in Section 17-7 of The School Code (Ill. Rev. Stat. 1985 1987, ch. 122, par. 17-7).

"Transportation supervisory salary costs" - That portion of the salary and related employee benefits of school district employee(s) who are documented as supervising a school district's pupil transportation programs (Regular, Vocational, Special Education and Nonreimbursable). For districts that do not employ a full or part-time transportation supervisor, a superintendent's/director of special education's salary and related employee benefits shall be prorated as detailed in Section 120.80(b)(3) of this Part. These salary and related employee benefit costs shall be paid from the Transportation Fund.

"Useful life" - The period of time during which the item is expected to be suitable for pupil transportation service.

(Source: Amended at ___ Ill. Reg. ____, effective _____)

Section 120.60 Reimbursable Annual Depreciation Allowances

a) Annual depreciation allowances shall be based on the principal cost of pupil transportation vehicles or equipment for items costing $800 or more and with a useful life in excess of one year.

1) When a vehicle and/or equipment costing $500 or more is purchased, leased for 30 days or more, or leased/purchased any time during the fiscal year, a full year's depreciation is claimable for that year.

STATE BOARD OF EDUCATION

NOTICE OF PROPOSED AMENDMENTS

2) When a vehicle and/or equipment is sold, destroyed, or traded-in any time during the fiscal year, no depreciation may be claimed for that year.

3) Vehicles and/or equipment leased for 30 days or more, leased/purchased or purchased, and sold or destroyed within the same fiscal year must use a prorated principal cost based on the following formula:

(Principal costs divided by 12 months) X number of months in possession of the district = prorated principal cost.

b) Pupil transportation vehicles that are purchased, leased/purchased, or leased for 30 days or more by the district shall be subject to a 20 percent annual depreciation allowance based on the principal cost.

c) Pupil transportation equipment not installed in the vehicle that is purchased or leased/purchased or leased for more than 30 days by the district shall be subject to a ten percent annual depreciation allowance based on the principal cost.

d) The depreciation of buildings/property that are purchased, leased/purchased, or leased for more than 30 days, is based on an annual depreciation rate of 2% of the principal cost.

e) The depreciation of storage tanks or fueling stations that are purchased, leased/purchased, and/or leased for more than 30 days is based on an annual depreciation rate of 5% of the principal cost.

e) f) Repairs or modifications to pupil transportation vehicles costing $500 or more and extending the useful life of the vehicle by more than one year must be capitalized and shall be subject to a 33 1/3 percent annual depreciation allowance.

f) g) Depreciation of site improvement(s) costing $500 or more and having a useful life of more than one year, made to the building(s) or property used for pupil transportation purposes, is subject to a five percent annual depreciation allowance based on the principal cost, including installation fees.

(Source: Amended at ___ Ill. Reg. ____, effective _____)

Section 120.110 Reporting Requirements

According to the date set forth in Section 29-5 of The School Code, districts shall annually report, on the State Board of Education form entitled "Annual Claim for Pupil Transportation Reimbursement," the information described in subsections (a) through (b) (a) of this Section.

STATE BOARD OF EDUCATION

NOTICE OF PROPOSED AMENDMENTS

a) For regular pupil transportation services, the school districts
    shall annually, pursuant to Section 29-5 of The School Code, report
    the following items:

    1) Total number of enrolled pupil days in the regular pupil
        transportation service, to be compiled on the State Board of
        Education form, "Resident Pupils Transported Work Sheet" for
        each of the following:

        A) Pupils residing one and one-half miles or more from their
            assigned attendance center;

        B) Pupils residing less than one and one-half miles from
            their assigned attendance center;

        C) Pupils residing less than one and one-half miles from
            their assigned attendance center with vehicular hazard
            approval; and

        D) Pupils transported at times other than at the beginning or
            end of the school day.

    2) Total number of days pupils were transported during the regular
        school term.

    3) Total number of pupils, to be compiled on the "Resident Pupils
        Transported Work Sheet" in the following categories:

        A) Public school pupils transported during the regular school
            term;

        B) Nonpublic school pupils transported during the regular
            school term; and

        C) Public and nonpublic school pupils transported during the
            summer school term.

    4) Total number of vehicle miles traveled to and from school
        during the regular school term.

    5) Expenditures and deductions as set forth in Sections 120.50
        through 120.80.

b) For vocational pupil transportation services, the school districts
    shall annually report the following items:

    1) Total number of pupils transported during the regular school
        term;

STATE BOARD OF EDUCATION

NOTICE OF PROPOSED AMENDMENTS

    2) Total number of vehicular miles traveled during the regular
        school term; and

    3) Expenditures and deductions as set forth in Sections 120.50
        through 120.80.

c) For special education pupil transportation services, the school
    districts shall annually report the following information:

    1) Total number of special education pupils transported during the
        regular school term;

    2) Total number of special education pupils transported during the
        summer school term;

    3) Total number of vehicular miles traveled during the regular and
        summer school term; and the

    4) Expenditures and deductions as set forth in Sections 120.50
        through 120.80.

d) For nonreimbursable pupil transportation services, the school
    districts shall annually report the:

    1) Total number of vehicle miles traveled during the regular
        school term; and

    2) Expenditures as set forth in Sections 120.50 through 120.80 of
        this Part.

e) The following forms shall be submitted annually to the State Board
    of Education.

    1) "Annual Claim for Pupil Transportation Reimbursement"

    2) "Pupil Transportation Depreciation Schedule," which records the
        district's calculation of the annual depreciation allowance
        pursuant to Section 120.60 of this Part.

f) The following forms shall be retained by the school district for
    audit purposes:

    1) "Resident Pupils Transported Work Sheet"

    2) "Pupil Transportation Indirect Cost Work Sheet," which records
        the information developed pursuant to Section 120.80 of this
        Part.

(Source: Amended at ___ Ill. Reg. ____, effective _____)

STATE BOARD OF EDUCATION

NOTICE OF PROPOSED AMENDMENTS

Section 120.130 Seat Back Reimbursement

a) A school district's additional cost resulting from the installation
of 28-inch seat backs by the original bus manufacturer is eligible
for reimbursement in accordance with Section 29-17 of The School
Code (Ill. Rev. Stat, 1987, ch. 122, par. 29-17).

b) For 28-inch seat back installation reimbursement, the school
district shall annually report:

1) The number of school buses purchased or leased by, or operated
under a contract for, the school district in which 28-inch seat
backs were installed during the school year; and

2) The district's additional cost for each school bus resulting
from the installation of 28-inch seat backs.

c) To document its claim, the district shall retain itemized or other
equivalent billing information from the original bus manufacturer
verifying the cost of installation and the amount of the district's
claim.

(Source: Added at ___ Ill. Reg. ____, effective _____)

SUBPART B: CUSTODIAN REIMBURSEMENT FOR PUPIL TRANSPORTATION

Section 120.200 Definitions

"Affidavit" means a written and notarized statement signed by the
custodian in which it is stated that to the best knowledge and
belief of the custodian the pupil transportation expenses claimed
for the school year indicated are accurate.

"Contemporaneous Records" means documentary evidence of expenditures
or mileage accumulated for pupil transportation such as cancelled
checks, receipts from public or private carriers or calculations
based on odometer readings.

"CUSTODIAN" MEANS, WITH RESPECT TO A QUALIFYING PUPIL, AN ILLINOIS
RESIDENT WHO IS THE PARENT, OR PARENTS, OR LEGAL GUARDIAN OF SUCH
QUALIFYING PUPIL.

"ONE AND ONE-HALF MILES DISTANCE" MEANS THE DISTANCE FROM THE EXIT
OF THE PROPERTY WHERE THE PUPIL RESIDES TO THE POINT WHERE PUPILS
ARE NORMALLY UNLOADED AT THE SCHOOL ATTENDED; SUCH DISTANCE SHALL BE
MEASURED BY DETERMINING THE SHORTEST DISTANCE ON NORMALLY TRAVELED
ROADS OR STREETS (Ill. Rev. Stat. 1986 1987, ch. 122, par. 29-3).

STATE BOARD OF EDUCATION

NOTICE OF PROPOSED AMENDMENTS

"QUALIFYING PUPIL" MEANS AN INDIVIDUAL WHO:

IS A RESIDENT OF THE STATE OF ILLINOIS; AND

IS UNDER THE AGE OF 21 AT THE CLOSE OF THE SCHOOL YEAR FOR
WHICH REIMBURSEMENT IS SOUGHT; AND

DURING THE SCHOOL YEAR FOR WHICH REIMBURSEMENT IS SOUGHT WAS A
FULL-TIME PUPIL ENROLLED IN A KINDERGARTEN THROUGH 12TH GRADE
EDUCATIONAL PROGRAM; AND

DID NOT LIVE WITHIN 1 1/2 MILES FROM THE SCHOOL IN WHICH THE
PUPIL WAS ENROLLED OR HAVE ACCESS TO TRANSPORTATION PROVIDED
ENTIRELY AT PUBLIC EXPENSE TO AND FROM THAT SCHOOL AND A POINT
WITHIN 1 1/2 MILES OF THE PUPIL'S RESIDENCE, MEASURED IN A
MANNER CONSISTENT WITH SECTION 29-3 of The School Code; OR

DID LIVE WITHIN 1 1/2 MILES FROM THE SCHOOL IN WHICH THE PUPIL
WAS ENROLLED AS MEASURED IN A MANNER CONSISTENT WITH SECTION
29-3 OF THE SCHOOL CODE, DID NOT HAVE ACCESS TO TRANSPORTATION
PROVIDED ENTIRELY AT PUBLIC EXPENSE TO AND FROM THAT SCHOOL,
AND CONDITIONS WERE SUCH THAT WALKING WOULD HAVE CONSTITUTED A
SERIOUS SAFETY HAZARD TO THE SAFETY OF THE PUPIL DUE TO VEHICULAR
TRAFFIC.

"QUALIFIED TRANSPORTATION EXPENSES" MEANS COSTS REASONABLY INCURRED
BY THE CUSTODIAN TO TRANSPORT, FOR THE PURPOSES OF ATTENDING
REGULARLY SCHEDULED DAY-TIME CLASSES, A QUALIFYING PUPIL BETWEEN
SUCH QUALIFYING PUPIL'S RESIDENCE AND THE SCHOOL AT WHICH SUCH
QUALIFYING PUPIL IS ENROLLED AND SHALL INCLUDE AUTOMOBILE EXPENSES
AT THE STANDARD MILEAGE RATE ALLOWED BY THE UNITED STATES INTERNAL
REVENUE SERVICE AS REIMBURSEMENT FOR BUSINESS TRANSPORTATION
EXPENSE, AS WELL AS PAYMENTS TO MASS TRANSIT CARRIERS, PRIVATE
CARRIERS, AND CONTRACTUAL FEES FOR TRANSPORTATION.

"SCHOOL" MEANS A PUBLIC OR NONPUBLIC ELEMENTARY OR SECONDARY SCHOOL
IN ILLINOIS, ATTENDANCE AT WHICH SATISFIES THE REQUIREMENTS OF
SECTION 26-1 of The School Code (Ill. Rev. Stat. 1986 1987, ch. 122,
par. 26-1).

"Serious Safety Hazard" — THE DETERMINATION OF WHAT CONSTITUTES A
SERIOUS SAFETY HAZARD SHALL IN EACH CASE BE MADE BY THE ILLINOIS
DEPARTMENT OF TRANSPORTATION IN ACCORDANCE WITH GUIDELINES WHICH
THAT DEPARTMENT SHALL PROMULGATE in 92 Ill. Adm. Code 557
(Transportation).

(Source: Amended at ___ Ill. Reg. ____, effective _____)

STATE BOARD OF EDUCATION

NOTICE OF PROPOSED AMENDMENTS

Section 120.210 Custodians Eligible for Reimbursement

a) This Subpart establishes the procedures for reimbursing custodians for qualified transportation expenses as provided in Section 29-5.2 of The School Code (Ill. Rev. Stat. ~~1985~~ 1987, ch. 122, par. 29-5.2).

b) The custodian must complete a claim form, provided by the State Board of Education, no later than June 30 of each year ~~within 21 calendar days after the close of the regular school year~~. The claim form will be available at each school attendance center for which the State Board of Education has a mailing address on file.

   1) In cases where a qualifying pupil resides within 1 1/2 miles of the pupil's school but for whom walking constitutes a serious hazard to the safety of the pupil due to vehicular traffic, the custodian must first request a determination of a serious safety hazard from the Illinois Department of Transportation, except that any custodian who previously received a determination that a serious safety hazard exists need not resubmit such a request for 4 years.

   2) The custodian's request for a determination of a serious safety hazard must be completed on a form provided by the Superintendent of the Educational Service Region for the county in which the custodian resides and must be returned to that Educational Service Region Superintendent by February 1 of the school year for which reimbursement will be sought.

c) The custodian shall certify on the claim form provided by the State Board of Education that:

   1) the custodian is the parent or legal guardian of the pupil(s) for whom expenses are being claimed;

   2) during the school year for which reimbursement is being claimed, the pupil(s) attended regularly scheduled day-time classes as full-time student(s) in a kindergarten through grade 12 program at the public or nonpublic school;

   3) the pupil(s) resided 1 1/2 miles or more from the school attended and did not have access to transportation to and from school provided entirely at public expense; or these pupils lived within 1 1/2 miles from the school attended, the Illinois Department of Transportation has determined, within the last 4 years, that walking would constitute a serious hazard to the safety of the pupils due to vehicular traffic, the hazardous conditions remain unchanged, and the pupils did not have access to transportation to and from school provided entirely at public expense;

STATE BOARD OF EDUCATION

NOTICE OF PROPOSED AMENDMENTS

   4) the custodian paid the amount claimed to transport the pupil(s) to and from school during the school year for which the claim is being submitted; and

   5) that if requested within three years after the close of the school year for which reimbursement is claimed, the custodian will provide the State Superintendent of Education with either contemporaneous records verifying the amount claimed or an affidavit verifying the amount claimed and notification of a serious safety hazard issued by the Illinois Department of Transportation when the pupil(s) claimed lived within 1 1/2 miles of the school attended.

(Source: Amended at __ Ill. Reg. ___, effective _____)

Section 120.235 Responsibilities of Public and Nonpublic Chief Administrative Officers

THE CHIEF ADMINISTRATIVE OFFICER OF EACH SCHOOL SHALL NOTIFY CUSTODIANS OF QUALIFYING STUDENTS THAT REIMBURSEMENT IS AVAILABLE. NOTIFICATION SHALL OCCUR BY THE FIRST MONDAY IN NOVEMBER OF THE SCHOOL YEAR FOR WHICH REIMBURSEMENT IS AVAILABLE (Ill. Rev. Stat. 1987, ch. 122, par. 29-5.2(h)).

(Source: Added at ___ Ill. Reg. ___, effective _____)

1) Heading of the Part: Sex Equity

2) Code Citation: 23 Ill. Adm. Code 200

3) Section Numbers: Proposed Action:
   200.10   Amendment
   200.30   Amendment
   200.40   Amendment
   200.80   Amendment
   200.100   Amendment

4) Statutory Authority: Ill. Rev. Stat. 1987, ch. 122, pars. 27-1, 34-18(11)

5) A Complete Description of the Subjects and Issues Involved: Section
   200.30 (Applicability) has been revised to delete the exception of a
   district serving a city having a population exceeding 500,000
   inhabitants. (The applicability of the State Board's rules was extended
   to cover the Chicago school system by P.A. 85-410, which took effect on
   January 1, 1988.) The change in Section 200.40(e) is also made in order
   to reflect the rules' broadened applicability.

   Standards for athletic interest surveys have been added to Section
   200.80 pursuant to discussions with the Joint Committee on
   Administrative Rules. They address the administration and content of
   the survey which districts are required to conduct at least every four
   years.

   Other technical changes have been made in several sections to update
   statutory citations as applicable.

6) Will this proposed rule replace an emergency rule currently in effect?
   No

7) Does this rulemaking contain an automatic repeal date? Yes X No

8) Does this proposed amendment contain incorporations by reference? No

9) Are there any other proposed amendments pending on this Part? No

10) Statement of Statewide Policy Objectives: These rules will not create
    or enlarge a State mandate.

STATE BOARD OF EDUCATION

NOTICE OF PROPOSED AMENDMENTS

11) Time, Place, and Manner in which interested persons may comment on this
    proposed rulemaking: Written comments may be submitted within 45 days
    of the publication of this notice to:

        Patricia Poole
        Illinois State Board of Education
        Suite 14-300
        100 West Randolph Street
        Chicago, Illinois 60601
        (312) 917-3226

12) Initial Regulatory Flexibility Analysis: These amendments will not
    affect small businesses.

The full text of the Proposed Rule(s) begins on the next page:

STATE BOARD OF EDUCATION

NOTICE OF PROPOSED AMENDMENTS

TITLE 23: EDUCATION AND CULTURAL RESOURCES
SUBTITLE A: EDUCATION
CHAPTER I: STATE BOARD OF EDUCATION
SUBCHAPTER e: INSTRUCTION

PART 200
SEX EQUITY

Section
200.10   Definitions
200.20   State Policy
200.30   Applicability
200.40   Administration
200.50   Treatment of Students
200.60   Educational Programs and Activities
200.70   Counseling Services
200.80   Extracurricular Programs and Activities
200.90   Compliance and Enforcement
200.100   Effects of Other Requirements

AUTHORITY: Implementing Title IX of the Education Amendments of 1972 (20 U.S.C. 1681 et seq.), Article I, Section 18 of the Illinois Constitution, and Sections 10-22.5, 27-1, and 34-18(1) of The School Code (Ill. Rev. Stat. 1987, ch. 122, pars. 10-22.5, 27-1, and 34-18(1)), and authorized by Sections 2-3.6, 27-1, and 34-18(1) of The School Code (Ill. Rev. Stat. 1987, ch. 122, pars. 2-3.6, 27-1, and 34-18(1)).

SOURCE: Adopted at 10 Ill. Reg. 18014, effective October 3, 1986; amended at ____ Ill. Reg. _____, effective _____.)

Section 200.10 Definitions

"Comparable" means similar in quality and quantity, taking into consideration all relevant facts and circumstances.

"Contact Sports" means those sports whose purpose or major activity involves bodily contact: e.g., basketball, boxing, football, ice hockey, rugby, and wrestling.

"Counseling" means all guidance activities, personal counseling, guidance-related evaluation and testing, provision of vocational and career information and advice, scheduling assistance, and any other guidance services provided to students by any person acting under the authorization of an educational system.

"Course" means any district-sponsored class regardless of the location of class meetings, nature of instruction, or type or age of student.

STATE BOARD OF EDUCATION

NOTICE OF PROPOSED AMENDMENTS

"Discrimination" means the violation of individuals' state or federal equal rights guarantees (U.S. Constitution, Amendment 14; 20 U.S.C. 1681 et seq.; Illinois Constitution, Article I, Sections 2, 18; Ill. Rev. Stat. 1986 1987, ch. 122, pars. 10-22.5, 27-1, and 34-18(1), whether intended or unintended.

"Disparate Interest Levels" means that, according to the results of a school's written student athletics interest survey (conducted pursuant to the requirements set forth in Section 200.80(b)(1)), the total number of students of one sex who wish to participate in all athletics exceeds by more than 50% the total number of students of the other sex who wish to participate in all athletics. Disparate interest levels do not in and of themselves evidence discrimination.

"Disproportionate Enrollment" means that students of one sex constitute at least 75% of a school's participants in a given program, course, or activity. Disproportionate enrollment does not in and of itself evidence discrimination.

"Educational System" means any local public education agency in its entirety, including elementary, secondary and unit districts, area vocational education centers, and special education cooperatives.

"Equal Access" means availability of opportunity without discrimination on the basis of sex, going beyond simple admission to a course or activity to include full and unrestricted participation in educational and experiential processes.

"Prime Time" means that time period which is most desirable locally for a given activity.

"Program" means a series of courses or set of activities leading toward identified educational or experiential student outcomes.

"School" means any attendance center within an educational system.

"Sex Bias" means the attribution of behaviors, abilities, interests, values and/or roles to a person or group of persons on the basis of their sex.

"Sexual Harassment" means unwelcome sexual advances, requests for sexual favors, and other verbal or physical conduct of a sexual nature.

"Sexual Intimidation" means any behavior, verbal or nonverbal, which has the effect of subjecting members of either sex to humiliation, embarrassment or discomfort because of their gender.

STATE BOARD OF EDUCATION

NOTICE OF PROPOSED AMENDMENTS

"Significant Assistance" means the payment of dues, fees, or other remuneration in return for the provision of services or benefits, or any other collaboration that significantly facilitates the functioning of any agency, organization, or person outside an educational system.

(Source: Amended at _____ Ill. Reg. _____, effective _____)

Section 200.30 Applicability

These rules are applicable to all public school districts, ~~except those in a city having a population exceeding 500,000 inhabitants.--A school district organized under the provisions of Article 34 of The School Code shall comply with the provisions of Section 34-18(1) concerning the promulgation of guidelines for equal access to programs supported from school district funds (Ill. Rev. Stat. 1985, ch. 122, par. 34-18(1)).~~ Nothing contained herein shall be construed as relieving ~~such~~ a school district of its duty to comply with Title IX of the Education Amendments of 1972 (20 U.S.C. 1681 et seq.) or its implementing regulations (34 CFR 106).

(Source: Amended at _____ Ill. Reg. _____, effective _____)

Section 200.40 Administration

a) All policies and practices of educational systems shall comply with Title IX of the Education Amendments of 1972 (20 U.S.C. 1681 et seq.), Article I, Section 18 of the Illinois Constitution, and Sections 10-22.5, ~~and~~ 27-1, and 34-18(1) of The School Code (Ill. Rev. Stat. ~~1985~~ 1987, ch. 122, pars. 10-22.5, ~~and~~ 27-1, and 34-18(1)).

b) Each educational system shall have a written policy on sex equity stating that it does not discriminate on the basis of sex in the provision of programs, activities, services, or benefits and that it guarantees both sexes equal access to educational and extracurricular programs and activities.

c) Each system shall have a written grievance procedure available for use by any individual(s) wishing to present a complaint alleging that the system has discriminated against a student or students on the basis of their sex.

    1) Such procedure shall specify the steps to be taken in initiating and processing a grievance, shall identify all parties to be involved at each step of the procedure, shall include specific timelines for completion of each step and rendering of a written decision, and shall provide for final appeal of grievance decisions made at the system level to the system's governing board.

STATE BOARD OF EDUCATION

NOTICE OF PROPOSED AMENDMENTS

    2) Such procedure shall inform complainants of their right to further appeal the decision of the system's governing board to the Superintendent of the appropriate Educational Service Region pursuant to Section 3-10 of The School Code and, thereafter, to the State Superintendent of Education pursuant to Section 2-3.8 of The School Code, as provided in subsection (b) of Section 200.90.

d) Each system shall take reasonable measures to assure that employees, students and parents are informed of the system's sex equity policy and grievance procedure, e.g., through the use of policy manuals and student handbooks.

e) Each educational system shall, within one year of ~~the effective date of~~ becoming subject to this Part and at least every four years thereafter, evaluate its policies and practices in terms of the requirements of this Part to identify sex discrimination and shall develop a written sex equity plan to modify any policy or practice that does not meet the requirements of this Part and to take remedial steps to eliminate the effects of any discrimination resulting from such policy or practice.

    1) The sex equity evaluation shall include an examination of course enrollment data to identify any instances of disproportionate enrollment on the basis of sex and, where discrimination may have contributed to such disproportionality, the sex equity plan shall seek to redress any such disproportionality identified.

    2) Inservice training implementing the sex equity plan shall be provided by the system to school district administrators and to certificated and noncertificated personnel as needed.

f) Except as provided in subsection (a)(4) of Section 200.80, an educational system may not on the basis of sex designate or otherwise limit the use of any facility or portion thereof, related services, equipment or supplies. This subsection shall not apply to shower and toilet facilities, locker rooms, and dressing areas. All such accommodations and all related support and maintenance services shall be comparable for both sexes.

g) Except as provided in subsection (a)(4) of Section 200.80, an educational system may not provide significant assistance to or enter into any agreement with any organization, group, business or individual that discriminates against students on the basis of sex.

STATE BOARD OF EDUCATION

NOTICE OF PROPOSED AMENDMENTS

h)   An educational system shall not institute organizational changes or
     employment practices which would result in discrimination against
     students of either sex.

i)   A system shall maintain records documenting compliance with this
     Part, e.g., reports of sex equity evaluations and plans, remediation
     efforts and inservice activities, data collection and analyses,
     grievances and their disposition; such records shall be made
     available to State Board enforcement authorities upon request.

(Source: Amended at _____ Ill. Reg. _____, effective _____)

Section 200.80 Extracurricular Programs and Activities

a)   General Practices

     1)   Except as provided in subsection (b)(1)(A) of this Section,
          students of both sexes shall have equal access to all
          extracurricular programs and activities, including clubs,
          committees, service or honor organizations, intramural sports
          programs, interscholastic athletics and other after-school
          activities which are offered by a system.

     2)   Except as provided in subsection (b)(1)(A) of this Section,
          extracurricular programs and activities offered by a system
          shall not use titles which imply that membership or
          participation is restricted on the basis of sex.

     3)   A system shall not provide significant assistance to any
          association or conference whose purpose is to organize or
          regulate interscholastic competition if that association or
          conference discriminates on the basis of sex in the provision
          of benefits or services to students.

     4)   Schools may cooperate with single sex youth organizations that
          are tax exempt and whose membership has traditionally been
          limited to members of one sex and principally to persons who
          are under 19 years of age, provided that comparable activities
          shall be available for both sexes.

b)   Selected Activity Areas

     1)   Athletics (Interscholastic and Intramural)

          A)   Both sexes shall be accorded equal opportunities to
               participate in athletics programs.

STATE BOARD OF EDUCATION

NOTICE OF PROPOSED AMENDMENTS

          i)   Single-sex teams are permitted for contact sports or
                when selection for team membership is based upon
                competitive skill, provided the interests and
                abilities of both sexes are accommodated.

          ii)   In a noncontact sport, when a team is provided only
                for members of one sex, members of the excluded sex
                must be allowed to compete for a place on the team
                if their overall athletic opportunities have been
                limited in comparison with those of the other sex.

          iii) Where a coeducational team in a given sport does not
                accommodate the interests and abilities of members
                of both sexes, separate teams shall be afforded by
                sex. For example, if the level of interest
                determined pursuant to subsection (b)(1)(B)
                indicates that 30 students of one sex and 30
                students of the other sex want to participate in a
                particular sport, but only one student of the first
                sex is able to qualify to compete while 20 students
                of the other sex do so, a coeducational team does
                not accommodate the interests and abilities of both
                sexes.

     B)   Within one year of the effective date of becoming subject
          to this Part and at least once every four years
          thereafter, a system shall assess student athletics
          interest by administering a written survey to all
          students. Such surveys shall be conducted in accordance
          with the following specifications:

          i)   The survey shall be designed to measure the
                athletics interest of students as participants
                rather than as spectators;

          ii)   Students of both sexes shall be surveyed;

          iii) The same survey forms listing the same sports
                options shall be used by students of both sexes;

          iv)   On the survey form, sports shall not be designated
                by gender (e.g., list "basketball" not "boys'
                basketball" or "girls' basketball");

          v)   Survey forms shall at least include the sports
                currently available in the system, and shall include
                provision for students to indicate interest in
                sports other than those listed by the system on the
                survey forms; and

STATE BOARD OF EDUCATION

NOTICE OF PROPOSED AMENDMENTS

vi) Students surveyed shall include at least those currently enrolled in the system.

C) Survey results shall be used in planning for the future as well as in assessing current program comparability. If survey data indicate that the overall levels of student interest in the range of alternatives being provided are disparate between the sexes and such disparity may be the result of discrimination, the system shall initiate efforts to reduce such disparity.

D) C) Based upon the results of the interest survey, existing offerings and other pertinent factors (e.g., budget, facilities, available competition, etc.), a system shall provide comparable continuity in sports opportunities for students of both sexes (i.e., students have the opportunity to acquire skills at successive levels, over time, within a given sport).

E) D) The nature and extent of the athletics programs offered by a system shall accommodate the interests and abilities of both sexes to a comparable degree. Factors to be considered in assessing program comparability include but are not necessarily limited to the following:

    i) Selection of sports offered,

    ii) Levels of competition within sports,

    iii) Length of sports seasons,

    iv) Scheduling of athletics opportunities throughout the calendar year,

    v) Scheduling of practices and games during prime time,

    vi) Use of facilities for practice and competition,

    vii) Ratio of coach(es) to athletes,

    viii) Quality of coaching and officiating (e.g., credentials, experience and compensation),

    ix) Assignment and compensation of coaches and officials,

    x) Supplies and equipment,

STATE BOARD OF EDUCATION

NOTICE OF PROPOSED AMENDMENTS

    xi) Allowances for travel and per diem,

    xii) Medical and training services,

    xiii) Publicity for teams and individual participants,

    xiv) Overall distribution of athletic budget funds.

2) Music

A) Choruses segregated by sex shall not be allowed; however, choral groups based upon vocal range and quality are allowable.

B) Instrumental music skill acquisition and performance shall be based upon students' individual interests and abilities, regardless of their sex.

3) Speech and Drama

A) Competitive speaking events shall be open to both sexes.

B) Materials limited to a single sex (e.g., a monologue specific to one sex) may be used as long as comparable opportunities are provided for both sexes.

4) Miscellaneous

A) Activities such as cheerleading, pompom squads, color guards, school safety patrol, teacher/office aides, and library assistants shall be open to students of both sexes.

    i) Participation criteria, selection procedures, or uniform restrictions which would discriminate on the basis of sex shall not be applied.

    ii) Criteria for the utilization of such groups shall not discriminate on the basis of sex.

B) A king or queen of an activity may be selected; however, comparable opportunities for students of both sexes shall be provided.

C) If a system sponsors mother-son, father-daughter, mother-daughter, or father-son activities, comparable activities shall be available for both sexes, and the special needs of children from single-parent families shall be accommodated.

(Source: Amended at _____ Ill. Reg. _____, effective _____)

E BOARD OF EDUCATION

OF PROPOSED AMENDMENTS

er Requirements

his Part is not obviated or alleviated by any
b, organization, athletic league or other
he eligibility or participation of any
ex in any program or activity operated by any

1. Reg. _____, effective _____)

POLLUTION CONTROL BOARD

NOTICE OF PROPOSED AMENDMENTS

1) The Heading of the Part: Air Quality Standards

2) Code Citation: 35 Ill. Adm. Code 243

3)
Section Number:	Proposed Action:
243.108	Amend
243.120	Add

4) Statutory Authority: Illinois Environmental Protection Act
(Ill. Rev. Stat. 1987, ch. 111½, pars. 1010 and 1027).

5) A Complete Description of the Subjects and Issues
Involved: Sections 108 and 109 of the Clean Air Act
authorize the United States Environmental Protection Agency
("USEPA") to review and revise the health and welfare
criteria upon which the national primary and secondary
ambient air quality standards ("NAAQS") are based. On July
1, 1987, USEPA promulgated revisions to the NAAQS for
particulate matter (52 Fed. Reg. 24634). The use of the
"total suspended particulate matter" ("TSP") indicator for
particulate matter was replaced by an indicator that
includes only those particles with an aerodynamic diameter
less than or equal to 10 micrometers ("PM_{10}"). A primary
24-hour PM_{10} standard of 150 micrograms per cubic meter
(ug/M^3) with no more than one exceedance per year was
adopted, as was an annual PM_{10} standard of 50 ug/m^3,
expected annual arithmetic mean. Secondary standards
identical to the primary standards in all respects were
also adopted. The Illinois Environmental Protection Agency
has, therefore, proposed that these PM_{10} standards be
adopted as Illinois standards, suitable for utilization in
the Illinois State Implementation Plan ("SIP"). These
amendments are to be read in conjunction with the
amendments to Part 211.

6) Will this proposed rule replace an emergency rule currently
in effect? No.

7) Does this rulemaking contain an automatic repeal
date? _____ Yes __X__ No
If "yes," please specify the date: _____

8) Does this proposed amendment contain incorporations by
reference? Yes.

POLLUTION CONTROL BOARD

NOTICE OF PROPOSED AMENDMENTS

9) Are there any other amendments pending on this Part? No.
    Section Numbers: Proposed Action: Ill. Reg. Citation:

10) Statement of Statewide Policy Objective:

    (1)   This rulemaking proposes an ambient air quality
            standard for PM_{10}. It does not, in and of itself,
            require any action of a unit of local government,
            school district, or community college district.
            Therefore, it does not create or expand a state
            mandate.

    (2)   Further, this proposal is in response to a federal
            rulemaking adopted by the United States
            Environmental Protection Agency. Therefore, there
            is some question as to whether it is "state-
            initiated" so as to fall within the definition of
            "state mandate" set forth at Ill. Rev. Stat. 1987,
            ch. 85, par. 2203. Comment is requested on this
            issue.

11) Time, Place and Manner in which interested persons may
    comment on this proposed rulemaking:

    Send written comments concerning R88-28 within 45 days of
    publication in the Illinois Register to the Clerk of the
    Pollution Control Board, 100 West Randolph Street, Suite
    11-500, Chicago, Illinois 60601.

12) Initial Regulatory Flexibility Analysis:

    A) Date rule submitted to Business Assistance Office of
        the Department of Commerce and Community Affairs::
        November 3, 1988.

    B) Types of small businesses affected: Any small
        business that emits particles with an aerodynamic
        diameter less than or equal to 10 micrometers.

    C) Reporting, bookkeeping or other procedures required
        for compliance: None.

    D) Types of professional skills necessary for
        compliance: Those measurement and computational
        skills necessary to accomplish the measurement methods
        described in 40 CFR 50, Appendices J and K, 1987.

POLLUTION CONTROL BOARD

NOTICE OF PROPOSED AMENDMENTS

The full text of the proposed rule(s) begins on the next page:

POLLUTION CONTROL BOARD

NOTICE OF PROPOSED AMENDMENTS

TITLE 35: ENVIRONMENTAL PROTECTION
SUBTITLE B: AIR POLLUTION
CHAPTER I: POLLUTION CONTROL BOARD
SUBCHAPTER 1: AIR QUALITY STANDARDS AND EPISODES

PART 243
AIR QUALITY STANDARDS

SUBPART A: GENERAL PROVISIONS

AUTHORITY: Implementing Section 10 and authorized by Section 27 of the Environmental Protection Act (Ill. Rev. Stat. 1987, ch. 111 1/2, pars. 1010 and 1027).

SOURCE: Adopted as Chapter 2: Air Pollution, Part III: Air Quality Standards, in R71-23, 4 PCB 191, filed and effective April 14, 1972; amended in R80-11, 46 PCB 125, at 6 Ill. Reg. 5804, effective April 22, 1982; amended in R82-12, at 7 Ill. Reg. 9906, effective August 18, 1983; codified at 7 Ill. Reg. 13579; amended in R88-28 at ___ Ill. Reg. _____, Effective _____.

POLLUTION CONTROL BOARD

NOTICE OF PROPOSED AMENDMENTS

SUBPART A: GENERAL PROVISIONS

Section 243.108   Incorporations by Reference

The following materials are incorporated by reference:

a)   High volume sampler method, 40 CFR 50, Appendix B (1982), 36 Fed. Reg. 22,388, November 25, 1971.

b)   Pararosaniline method, 40 CFR 50, Appendix A (1982).

c)   Non-dispersive infrared spectrometry technique, 40 CFR 50, Appendix C (1982), 36 Fed. Reg. 22,391, November 25, 1971.

d)   Colorimetric method, 36 Fed. Reg. 22,396, November 25, 1971.

e)   Ozone-ethylene reaction method, 40 CFR 50, Appendix D (1982), 36 Fed. Reg. 22392, November 25, 1971.

f)   Lead, 40 CFR 50, Appendix G (1982), 43 Fed. Reg. 46,258, October 5, 1978, as amended at 44 Fed. Reg. 37,915, June 29, 1979; 46 Fed. Reg. 44,163, September 3, 1981.

g)   40 CFR 50, Appendix J, 1987

h)   40 CFR 50, Appendix K, 1987

(Board note: The incorporations by reference listed above contain no later amendments or editions.)

(SOURCE: Amended at ___ Ill. Reg. _____ effective _____)

SUBPART B: STANDARDS AND MEASUREMENT METHODS

Section 243.120 PM_{10}

a)   Standards. The ambient air quality standards for PM_{10} are:

1)   An annual arithmetic mean concentration of 50 micrograms per cubic meter; and

2)   A maximum 24-hour concentration of 150 micrograms per cubic meter, not to be exceeded more than once per year.

POLLUTION CONTROL BOARD

NOTICE OF PROPOSED AMENDMENTS

b)   Measurement Method. For determining conformance with the PM_{10} air quality standards, PM_{10} shall be measured by the method described in 40 CFR 50, Appendix J, (incorporated by reference in Section 243.108). The computations necessary for analyzing particulate matter data to determine attainment of the PM_{10} standards are described in 40 CFR 50, Appendix K (incorporated by reference in Section 243.108).

(SOURCE: Added at ____ Ill. Reg. effective _____)

POLLUTION CONTROL BOARD

NOTICE OF PROPOSED AMENDMENTS

1)   The Heading of the Part: Definitions and General Provisions

2)   Code Citation: 35 Ill. Adm. Code 211

3)
Section Number:	Proposed Action:
211.101	Amend
211.122	Amend

4)   Statutory Authority: Illinois Environmental Protection Act (Ill. Rev. Stat. 1987, ch. 111½, pars. 1010 and 1027).

5)   A Complete Description of the Subjects and Issues Involved: Sections 108 and 109 of the Clean Air Act authorize the United States Environmental Protection Agency ("USEPA") to review and revise the health and welfare criteria upon which the national primary and secondary ambient air quality standards ("NAAQS") are based. On July 1, 1987, USEPA promulgated revisions to the NAAQS for particulate matter (52 Fed. Reg. 24634). The use of the "total suspended particulate matter" ("TSP") indicator for particulate matter was replaced by an indicator that includes only those particles with an aerodynamic diameter less than or equal to 10 micrometers ("PM_{10}"). A primary 24-hour PM_{10} standard of 150 micrograms per cubic meter (ug/m^3) with no more than one exceedance per year was adopted, as was an annual PM_{10} standard of 50 ug/m^3, expected annual arithmetic mean. Secondary standards identical to the primary standards in all respects were also adopted. The Illinois Environmental Protection Agency has, therefore, proposed that these PM_{10} standards be adopted as Illinois standards, suitable for utilization in the Illinois State Implementation Plan ("SIP"). These amendments are to be read in conjunction with the amendments to Part 243.

6)   Will this proposed rule replace an emergency rule currently in effect? No.

7)   Does this rulemaking contain an automatic repeal date?   Yes ____ X ____ No
   If "yes," please specify the date: _____

8)   Does this proposed amendment contain incorporations by reference? Yes.

POLLUTION CONTROL BOARD

NOTICE OF PROPOSED AMENDMENTS

9)   Are there any other amendments pending on this Part? Yes.

      Section Numbers: Proposed Action: Ill. Reg. Citation:
      211.122   Amend   12 Ill. Reg. 15294

10)   Statement of Statewide Policy Objective:

      (1)   This rulemaking proposes an ambient air quality
             standard for PM_{10}. It does not, in and of itself,
             require any action of a unit of local government,
             school district, or community college district.
             Therefore, it does not create or expand a state
             mandate.

      (2)   Further, this proposal is in response to a federal
             rulemaking adopted by the United States
             Environmental Protection Agency. Therefore, there
             is some question as to whether it is "state-
             initiated" so as to fall within the definition of
             "state mandate" set forth at Ill. Rev. Stat. 1987,
             ch. 85, par. 2203. Comment is requested on this
             issue.

11)   Time, Place and Manner in which interested persons may
      comment on this proposed rulemaking:

      Send written comments concerning R88-28 within 45 days of
      publication in the Illinois Register to the Clerk of the
      Pollution Control Board, 100 West Randolph Street, Suite
      11-500, Chicago, Illinois 60601.

12)   Initial Regulatory Flexibility Analysis:

      A)   Date rule submitted to Business Assistance Office of
            the Department of Commerce and Community Affairs::
            November 3, 1988.

      B)   Types of small businesses affected: · Any small
            business that emits particles with an aerodynamic
            diameter less than or equal to 10 micrometers.

      C)   Reporting, bookkeeping or other procedures required
            for compliance: None.

      D)   Types of professional skills necessary for
            compliance: Those measurement and computational

POLLUTION CONTROL BOARD

NOTICE OF PROPOSED AMENDMENTS

      skills necessary to accomplish the measurement methods
      described in 40 CFR 50, Appendices J and K, 1987.

The full text of the proposed rule(s) begins on the next page:

POLLUTION CONTROL BOARD

NOTICE OF PROPOSED AMENDMENTS

TITLE 35: ENVIRONMENTAL PROTECTION
SUBTITLE B: AIR POLLUTION
CHAPTER I: POLLUTION CONTROL BOARD
SUBCHAPTER c: EMISSION STANDARDS AND LIMITATIONS
FOR STATIONARY SOURCES

PART 211
DEFINITIONS AND GENERAL PROVISIONS

SUBPART A: GENERAL PROVISIONS

Section
211.101   Incorporations by Reference
211.102   Abbreviations and Units

SUBPART B: DEFINITIONS

Section
211.121   Other Definitions
211.122   Definitions

Appendix A   Rule into Section Table
Appendix B   Section into Rule Table

AUTHORITY: Implementing Sections 9 and 10 and authorized by
Section 27 of the Environmental Protection Act (Ill. Rev. Stat.
1987, ch. 111½, pars. 1009, 1010 and 1027).

SOURCE: Adopted as Chapter 2: Air Pollution, Rule 201:
Definitions, R71-23, 4 PCB 191, filed and effective April 14,
1972; amended in R74-2 and R75-5, 32 PCB 295, at 3 Ill. Reg. 5,
p. 777, effective February 3, 1979; amended in R78-3 and 4, 35
PCB 75 and 243, at 3 Ill. Reg. 30, p. 124, effective July 28,
1979; amended in R80-5, at 7 Ill. Reg. 1244, effective January
21, 1983; codified at 7 Ill. Reg. 13590; amended in R82-1 (Docket
A) at 10 Ill. Reg. 12624, effective July 7, 1986; amended in R85-
21(A) at 11 Ill. Reg. 11747, effective June 29, 1987; amended in
R86-34 at 11 Ill. Reg. 12267, effective July 10, 1987; amended in
R86-39 at 11 Ill. Reg. 20804, effective December 14, 1987;
amended in R82-14 and R86-37 at 12 Ill. Reg. 787, effective
December 24, 1987; amended in R86-18 at 12 Ill. Reg. 7284,
effective April 8, 1988; amended in R86-10 at 12 Ill. Reg. 7621,
effective April 11, 1988; amended in R88-28 at ___ Ill.
Reg. _____, effective _____.

SUBPART A: GENERAL PROVISIONS

Section 211.101   Incorporations by Reference

POLLUTION CONTROL BOARD

NOTICE OF PROPOSED AMENDMENTS

The following materials are incorporated by reference:

a)   "Evaporation Loss from Floating Roof Tanks," American
     Petroleum Institute Bulletin 2517, 1962

b)   Ringelmann Chart, Information Circular 833 (Revision of
     1C7718), Bureau of Mines, U.S. Department of Interior,
     May 1, 1967

c)   Standard Industrial Classification Manual,
     Superintendent of Documents, Washington, D.C. 20402,
     1972

d)   American Society for Testing and Materials, 1916 Race
     Street, Philadelphia, PA 19103

     A.S.T.M.D-86
     A.S.T.M.D-240-64
     A.S.T.M.D-323
     A.S.T.M. D-369-69(1971)
     A.S.T.M.D-396-69
     A.S.T.M.D-900-55
     A.S.T.M.D-975-68
     A.S.T.M.D-1826-64
     A.S.T.M.D-2015-66
     A.S.T.M.D-2880-71

e)   40 CFR 51.100, 1987

(Board note: The incorporations by reference listed above
contain no later amendments or editions.)

(SOURCE: Amended at ___ Ill. Reg.
effective _____)

SUBPART B: DEFINITIONS

Section 211.122   Definitions

     "Accumulator": The reservoir of a condensing unit
     receiving the condensate from a surface condenser.

     "Acid Gases": For the purposes of the Environmental
     Protection Act (the Act) (Ill. Rev. Stat. 1985, ch. 111
     ½ par. 1009.4), hydrogen chloride, hydrogen fluoride
     and hydrogen bromide, which exist as gases, liquid mist,
     or any combination thereof.

POLLUTION CONTROL BOARD

NOTICE OF PROPOSED AMENDMENTS

"Actual Heat Input": The quantity of heat produced by the combustion of fuel using the gross heating value of the fuel.

"Aeration": The practice of forcing air through bulk stored grain to maintain the condition of the grain.

"Afterburner": A device in which materials in gaseous effluents are combusted.

"Air Dried Coating": Coatings that dry by the use of air or forced air at temperatures up to 363.15 K (194 F).

"Annual Grain Through-Put": Unless otherwise shown by the owner or operator, annual grain through-put for grain-handling operations, which have been in operation for three consecutive years prior to June 30, 1975, shall be determined by adding grain receipts and shipments for the three previous fiscal years and dividing the total by 6. The annual grain through-put for grain-handling operations in operation for less than three consecutive years prior to June 30, 1975, shall be determined by a reasonable three-year estimate; the owner or operator shall document the reasonableness of his three-year estimate.

"Architectural Coating": Any coating used for residential or commercial buildings or their appurtenances, or for industrial buildings which is site applied.

"Asphalt": The dark-brown to black cementitious material (solid, semisolid or liquid in consistency) of which the main constituents are bitumens which occur natrually or as a residue of petroleum refining.

"Asphalt Prime Coat": A low-viscosity liquid asphalt applied to an absorbent surface as the first of more than one asphalt coat.

"Automobile": Any first division motor vehicle as that term is defined in the Illinois Vehicle Code (Ill. Rev. Stat. 1985, ch. 95½, pars 1-100 et seq.).

POLLUTION CONTROL BOARD

NOTICE OF PROPOSED AMENDMENTS

"Automobile or Light-Duty Truck Manufacturing Plant": A facility where parts are manufactured or finished for eventual inclusion into a finished automobile or light-duty truck ready for sale to vehicle dealers, but not including customizers, body shops and other repainters.

"Batch Loading": The process of loading a number of individual parts at the same time for degreasing.

"Bead-Dipping": The dipping of an assembled tire bead into a solvent-based cement.

"British Thermal Unit": The quantity of heat required to raise one pound of water from 60 F to 61 F (abbreviated btu).

"Bulk Gasoline Plant": Any gasoline storage and distribution facility that receives gasoline from bulk gasoline terminals by delivery vessels and distributes gasoline to gasoline dispensing facilities.

"Bulk Gasoline Terminal": Any gasoline storage and distribution facility that receives gasoline by pipeline, ship or barge, and distributes gasoline to bulk gasoline plants or gasoline dispensing facilities.

"Can Coating": The application of a coating material to a single walled container that is manufactured from metal sheets thinner than 29 gauge (0.0141 in).

"Certified Investigation" A report signed by Illinois Environmental Protection Agency (Agency) personnel certifying whether a grain-handling operation (or portion thereof) or grain-drying operation is causing or tending to cause air pollution. Such report must describe the signatory's investigation, including a summary of those facts on which he relies to certify whether the grain-handling or grain-drying operation is causing or threatening or allowing the discharge or emission of any contaminant into the environment so as to cause or tend to cause air pollution in Illinois, either alone or in combination with contaminants from other sources, or so as to violate regulations or standards adopted by the Pollution Control Board (Board) under the Environmental Protection Act (Act). The certified investigation shall be open to a reasonable public inspection and may be copied upon payment of the actual cost of reproducing the original

POLLUTION CONTROL BOARD

NOTICE OF PROPOSED AMENDMENTS

"Choke Loading": That method of transferring grain from
the grain-handling operation to any vehicle for shipment
or delivery which precludes a free fall velocity of
grain from a discharge spout into the receiving
container.

"Cleaning and Separating Operation": That operation
where foreign and undesired substances are removed from
the grain.

"Clear Coating": Coatings that lack color and opacity
or are transparent using the undercoat as a reflectant
base or undertone color.

"Coal Refuse": Waste products of coal mining, cleaning
and coal preparation operations containing coal, matrix
material, clay and other organic and inorganic material.

"Coating Applicator": Equipment used to apply a surface
coating.

"Coating Line": An operation where a surface coating is
applied to a material and subsequently the coating is
dried and/or cured.

"Coating Plant": Any building, structure or
installation that contains a coating line and which is
located on one or more contiguous or adjacent properties
and which is owned or operated by the same person (or by
persons under common control).

"Coil Coating": The application of a coating material
to any flat metal sheet or strip that comes in rolls or
coils.

"Cold Cleaning": The process of cleaning and removing
soils from surfaces by spraying, brushing, flushing or
immersion while maintaining the organic solvent below
its boiling point. Wipe cleaning is not included in
this definition.

"Complete Combustion": A process in which all carbon
contained in a fuel or gas stream is converted to carbon
dioxide.

POLLUTION CONTROL BOARD

NOTICE OF PROPOSED AMENDMENTS

"Component": Any piece of equipment which has the
potential to leak volatile organic material including,
but not limited to, pump seals, compressor seals, seal
oil degassing vents, pipeline valves, pressure relief
devices, process drains and open ended pipes. This
definition excludes valves which are not externally
regulated, flanges, and equipment in heavy liquid
service. For purposes of Subpart Q (35 Ill. Adm. Code
215), this definition also excludes bleed ports of gear
pumps in polymer service.

"Concentrated Nitric Acid Manufacturing Process": Any
acid producing facility manufacturing nitric acid with a
concentration equal to or greater than 70 percent by
weight.

"Condensate": Hydrocarbon liquid separated from its
associated gasses which condenses due to changes in the
temperature or pressure and remains liquid at standard
conditions.

"Conveyorized Degreasing": The continuous process of
cleaning and removing soils from surfaces utilizing
either cold or vaporized solvents.

"Crude Oil": A naturally occurring mixture which
consists of hydrocarbons and sulfur, nitrogen or oxygen
derivatives of hydrocarbons and which is a liquid at
standard conditions.

"Crude Oil Gathering": The transportation of crude oil
or condensate after custody transfer between a
production facility and a reception point.

"Custody Transfer": The transfer of produced petroleum
and/or condensate after processing and/or treating in
the producing operations, from storage tanks or
automatic transfer facilities to pipelines or any other
forms of transportation.

"Cutback Asphalt": Any asphalt which has been liquified
by blending with petroleum solvents other than residual
fuel oil and has not been emulsified with water.

"Degreaser": Any equipment or system used in solvent
cleaning.

POLLUTION CONTROL BOARD

NOTICE OF PROPOSED AMENDMENTS

"Delivery Vessel": Any tank truck or trailer equipped with a storage tank that is used for the transport of gasoline to a stationary storage tank at a gasoline dispensing facility, bulk gasoline plant or bulk gasoline terminal.

"Distillate Fuel Oil": Fuel oils of grade No. 1 or 2 as specified in detailed requirements for fuel oil A.S.T.M. D-369-69 (1971).

"Dry Cleaning Facility": A facility engaged in the cleaning of fabrics using an essentially nonaqueous solvent by means of one or more solvent washes, extraction of excess solvent by spinning and drying by tumbling in an airstream. The facility includes, but is not limited to, washers, dryers, filter and purification systems, waste disposal systems, holding tanks, pumps and attendant piping and valves.

"Dump-Pit Area": Any area where grain is received at a grain-handling or grain-drying operation.

"Effective Grate Area": That area of a dump-pit grate through which air passes, or would pass, when aspirated.

"Effluent Water Separator": Any tank, box, sump or other apparatus in which any organic material floating on or entrained or contained in water entering such tank, box, sump or other apparatus is physically separated and removed from such water prior to outfall, drainage or recovery of such water.

"Emission Rate": Total quantity of any air contaminant discharge into the atmosphere in any one-hour period.

"End Sealing Compound Coat": A compound applied to can ends which functions as a gasket when the end is assembled on the can.

"Excess Air": Air supplied in addition to the theoretical quantity necessary for complete combustion of all fuel and/or combustible waste material.

"Excessive Release": A discharge of more than 295g (0.65 pounds) of mercaptans and/or hydrogen sulfide into the atmosphere in any five minute period.

POLLUTION CONTROL BOARD

NOTICE OF PROPOSED AMENDMENTS

"Existing Grain-Drying Operation": Any grain-drying operation the construction or modification of which was commenced prior to June 30, 1975.

"Existing Grain-Handling Operation": Any grain-handling operation the construction or modification of which was commenced prior to June 30, 1975.

"Exterior Base Coat": An initial coating applied to the exterior of a can after the can body has been formed.

"Exterior End Coat": A coating applied by rollers or spraying to the exterior end of a can.

"External Floating Roof": A storage vessel cover in an open top tank consisting of a double deck or pontoon single deck which is supported by the petroleum liquid being contained and is equipped with a closure seal between the deck edge and tank wall.

"Extreme Performance Coating": Coatings designed for exposure to any of the following: the ambient weather conditions, temperatures above 368.15 K (203 F), detergents, abrasive and scouring agents, solvents, corrosive atmospheres, or other similar extreme environmental conditions.

"Fabric Coating": The coating of a textile substrate.

"Final Repair Coat": The repainting of any coating which is damaged during vehicle assembly.

"Firebox": The chamber or compartment of a boiler or furnace in which materials are burned, but not the combustion chamber or afterburner of an incinerator.

"Flexographic Printing": The application of words, designs and pictures to a substrate by means of a roll printing technique in which the pattern to be applied is raised above the printing roll and the image carrier is made of elastomeric materials.

"Floating Roof": A roof on a stationary tank, reservoir or other container which moves vertically upon change in volume of the stored material.

POLLUTION CONTROL BOARD

NOTICE OF PROPOSED AMENDMENTS

"Freeboard Height": For open top vapor degreasers, the distance from the top of the vapor zone to the top of the degreaser tank. For cold cleaning degreasers, the distance from the solvent to the top of the degreaser tank.

"Fuel Combustion Emission Source": Any furnace, boiler or similar equipment used for the primary purpose of producing heat or power by indirect heat transfer.

"Fuel Gas System": A system for collection of refinery fuel gas including, but not limited to, piping for collecting tail gas from various process units, mixing drums and controls and distribution piping.

"Fugitive Particulate Matter": Any particulate matter emitted into the atmosphere other than through a stack, provided that nothing in this definition or in 35 Ill. Adm. Code 212, Subpart K shall exempt any source from compliance with other provisions of 35 Ill. Adm. Code 212 otherwise applicable merely because of the absence of a stack.

"Gas Service": Means that the component contains process fluid that is in the gaseous state at operating conditions.

"Gasoline": Any petroleum distillate having a Reid vapor pressure of 4 pounds or greater.

"Gasoline Dispensing Facility": Any site where gasoline is transferred from a stationary storage tank to a motor vehicle gasoline tank used to provide fuel to the engine of that motor vehicle.

"Grain": The whole kernel or seed of corn, wheat, oats, soybeans and any other cereal or oil seed plant; and the normal fines, dust and foreign matter which results from harvesting, handling or conditioning. The grain shall be unaltered by grinding or processing.

"Grain-Drying Operation": Any operation, excluding aeration, by which moisture is removed from grain and which typically uses forced ventilation with the addition of heat.

POLLUTION CONTROL BOARD

NOTICE OF PROPOSED AMENDMENTS

"Grain-Handling and Conditioning Operation": A grain storage facility and its associate grain transfer, cleaning, drying, grinding and mixing operations.

"Grain-Handling Operation": Any operation where one or more of the following grain-related processes (other than grain-drying operation, portable grain-handling equipment, one-turn storage space, and excluding flour mills and feed mills) are performed: receiving, shipping, transferring, storing, mixing or treating of grain or other processes pursuant to normal grain operations.

"Green Tire Spraying": The spraying of green tires, both inside and outside, with release compounds which help remove air from the tire during molding and prevent the tire from sticking to the mold after curing.

"Green Tires": Assembled tires before molding and curing have occurred.

"Gross Heating Value": Amount of heat produced when a unit quantity of fuel is burned to carbon dioxide and water vapor, and the water vapor condensed as descibed in A.S.T.M. D-2015-66, D-900-55, D-1826-64 and D-240-64.

"Heavy Liquid": Liquid with a true vapor pressure of less than 0.3 kPa (0.04 psi) at 294.3 K (70 F) or 0.1 Reid Vapor Pressure as determined by A.S.T.M. method D-323; or which when distilled requires a temperature of 300 F or greater to recover 10% of the liquid as determined by A.S.T.M. method D-86.

"Heavy Metals": For the purposes of Section 9.4 of the Act, elemental, ionic, or combined forms of arsenic, cadmium, mercury, chromium, nickel and lead.

"Heavy, Off-Highway Vehicle Products": For the purposes of Section 215.204(k), heavy off-highway vehicle products shall include: heavy construction, mining, farming or material handling equipment; heavy industrial engines; diesel-electric locomotives and associated power generation equipment; and the components of such equipment or engines.

"Hot Well": The reservoir of a condensing unit receiving the condensate from a barometric condenser.

POLLUTION CONTROL BOARD

NOTICE OF PROPOSED AMENDMENTS

"Housekeeping Practices": Those activities specifically
defined in the list of housekeeping practices developed
by the Joint EPA - Industry Task Force and included
herein under 35 Ill. Adm. Code 212.461.

"Incinerator": Combustion apparatus in which refuse is
burned.

"Indirect Heat Transfer": Transfer of heat in such a
way that the source of heat does not come into direct
contact with process materials.

"In-Process Tank": A container used for mixing,
blending, heating, reacting, holding, crystallizing,
evaporating, or cleaning operations in the manufacture
of pharmaceuticals.

"Interior Body Spray Coat": A coating applied by spray
to the interior of a can after the can body has been
formed.

"Internal Transferring Area": Areas and associated
equipment used for conveying grain among the various
grain operations.

"Large Appliance Coating": The application of a coating
material to the component metal parts (including but not
limited to doors, cases, lids, panels and interior
support parts) of residential and commercial washers,
dryers, ranges, refrigerators, freezers, water heaters,
dishwashers, trash compactors, air conditioners and
other similar products.

"Light-Duty Truck": Any second division motor vehicle,
as that term is defined in the Illinois Vehicle Code,
(Ill. Rev. Stat. 1985, ch. 95½ pars. 1-100 et seq.)
weighing less than 3854 kilograms (8500 pounds) gross.

"Liquid-Mounted Seal": A primary seal mounted in
continuous contact with the liquid between the tank wall
and the floating roof edge around the circumference of
the roof.

"Liquid Service": Means that the equipment or component
contains process fluid that is in a liquid state at
operating conditions.

POLLUTION CONTROL BOARD

NOTICE OF PROPOSED AMENDMENTS

"Load-Out Area": Any area where grain is transferred
from the grain-handling operation to any vehicle for
shipment or delivery.

"Low Solvent Coating": A coating which contains less
organic solvent than the conventional coatings used by
the industry. Low solvent coatings include water-borne,
higher solids, electro-deposition and powder coatings.

"Magnet Wire Coating": The application of a coating of
electrically insulating varnish or enamel to conducting
wire to be used in electrical machinery.

"Major Dump Pit": Any dump pit with an annual grain
through-put of more than 300,000 bushels, or which
receives more than 40% of the annual grain through-put
of the grain-handling operation.

"Major Metropolitan Area (MMA)": Any county or group of
counties which is defined by the following Table:

MAJOR METROPOLITAN AREAS IN ILLINOIS (MMA's)

MMA	COUNTIES INCLUDED IN MMA
Champaign-Urbana	Champaign
Chicago	Cook, Lake, Will, DuPage, McHenry, Kane, Grundy, Kendall, Kankakee
Decatur	Macon
Peoria	Peoria, Tazewell
Rockford	Winnebago
Rock Island -- Moline	Rock Island
Springfield	Sangamon
St. Louis (Illinois)	St. Clair, Madison
Bloomington -- Normal	McLean

"Major Population Area (MPA)": Areas of major
population concentration in Illinois, as described
below:

The area within the counties of Cook; Lake; DuPage;
Will; the townships of Burton, Richmond, McHenry,
Greenwood, Nunda, Door, Algonquin, Grafton and the
municipality of Woodstock, plus a zone extending
two miles beyond the boundary of said municipality

POLLUTION CONTROL BOARD

NOTICE OF PROPOSED AMENDMENTS

located in McHenry County; the townships of Dundee,
Rutland, Elgin, Plato, St. Charles, Campton,
Geneva, Blackberry, Batavia, Sugar Creek and Aurora
located in Kane County; and the municipalities of
Kankakee, Bradley and Bourbonnais, plus a zone
extending two miles beyond the boundaries of' said
municipalities in Kankakee County.

The area within the municipalities of Rockford and
Loves Park, plus a zone extending two miles beyond
the boundaries of said municipalities.

The area within the municipalities of Rock Island,
Moline, East Moline, Carbon Cliff, Milan, Oak
Grove, Silvis, Hampton, Greenwood and Coal Valley,
plus a zone extending two miles beyond the
boundaries of said municipalities.

The area within the municipalities of Galesburg and
East Galesburg, plus a zone extending two miles
beyond the boundaries of said municipalities.

The area within the municipalities of Bartonville,
Peoria and Peoria Heights, plus a zone extending
two miles beyond the boundaries of said
municipalities.

The area within the municipalities of Pekin, North
Pekin, Marquette Heights, Creve Coeur and East
Peoria, plus a zone extending two miles beyond the
boundaries of said municipalities.

The area within the municipalities of Bloomington
and Normal, plus a zone extending two miles beyond
the boundaries of said municipalities.

The area within the municipalities of Champaign,
Urbana and Savoy, plus a zone extending two miles
beyond the boundaries of said municipalities.

The area within the municipalities of Decatur, Mt.
Zion, Harristown and Forsyth, plus a zone extending
two miles beyond the boundaries of said
municipalities.

The area within the municipalities of Springfield,
Leland Grove, Jerome, Southern View, Grandview,

POLLUTION CONTROL BOARD

NOTICE OF PROPOSED AMENDMENTS

Sherman and Chatham, plus a zone extending two
miles beyond the boundaries of said municipalities.

The area within the townships of Godfrey, Foster,
Wood River, Fort Russell, Chouteau, Edwardsville,
Venice, Nameoki, Alton, Granite City and
Collinsville located in Madison County; and the
townships of Stites, Canteen, Centreville,
Caseyville, St. Clair, Sugar Loaf and Stookey
located in St. Clair County.

"Manufacturing Process": A process emission source or
series of process emission sources used to convert raw
materials, feed stocks, subassemblies or other
components into a product, either for sale or for use as
a component in a subsequent manufacturing process.

"Metal Furniture Coating": The application of a coating
material to any furniture piece made of metal or any
metal part which is or will be assembled with other
metal, wood, fabric, plastic or glass parts to form a
furniture piece including, but not limited to, tables,
chairs, wastebaskets, beds, desks, lockers, benches,
shelving, file cabinets, lamps and room dividers. This
definition shall not apply to any coating line coating
metal parts or products that is identified under the
Standard Industrial Classification Code for Major Groups
33, 34, 35, 36, 37, 38, 39, 40 or 41).

"Miscellaneous Fabricated Product Manufacturing
Process":

A manufacturing process involving one or more of
the following applications, including any drying
and curing of formulations, and capable of emitting
volatile organic material:

Adhesives to fabricate or assemble non-
furniture components or products

Asphalt solutions to paper or fiberboard

Asphalt to paper or felt

Coatings or dye to leather

Coatings to plastic

POLLUTION CONTROL BOARD

NOTICE OF PROPOSED AMENDMENTS

Coatings to rubber or glass

Curing of furniture adhesives in an oven which would emit in excess of 10 tons of volatile organic material per year if no air pollution control equipment were used

Disinfectant material to manufactured items

Plastic foam scrap or "fluff" from the manufacture of foam containers and packaging material to form resin pellets

Resin solutions to fiber substances

Rubber solutions to molds

Viscose solutions for food casings

The storage and handling of formulations associated with the process described above.

The use and handling of organic liquids and other substances for clean-up operations associated with the process described above.

"Miscellaneous Formulation Manufacturing Process":

A manufacturing process which compounds one or more of the following and is capable of emitting volatile organic material:

Adhesives

Asphalt solutions

Caulks, sealants or waterproofing agents

Coatings, other than paint and ink

Concrete curing compounds

Dyes

Friction materials and compounds

POLLUTION CONTROL BOARD

NOTICE OF PROPOSED AMENDMENTS

Resin solutions

Rubber solutions

Viscose solutions

The storage and handling of formulations associated with the process described above.

The use and handling of organic liquids and other substances for clean-up operations associated with the process described above.

"Miscellaneous Metal Parts and Products": For the purpose of 35 Ill. Adm. Code 215.204, miscellaneous metal parts and products shall include farm machinery, garden machinery, small appliances, commercial machinery, industrial machinery, fabricated metal products and any other industrial category which coats metal parts or products under the Standard Industrial Classification Code for Major Groups 33, 34, 35, 36, 37, 38 or 39 with the exception of the following: coating lines subject to 35 Ill. Adm. Code 215.204(a)-(i) and (k), automobile or light-duty truck refinishing, the exterior of marine vessels and the customized top coating of automobiles and trucks if production is less than thirty-five vehicles per day.

"Miscellaneous Organic Chemical Manufacturing Process":

A manufacturing process which produces by chemical reaction, one or more of the following organic compounds or mixtures of organic compounds and which is capable of emitting volatile organic materials:

Chemicals listed in 35 Ill. Adm. Code 215. Appendix D.

Chlorinated and sulfonated compounds

Cosmetic, detergent, soap or surfactant intermediaries or specialties and products

Disinfectants

Food additives

POLLUTION CONTROL BOARD

NOTICE OF PROPOSED AMENDMENTS

Oil and petroleum product additives

Plasticizers

Resins or polymers

Rubber additives

Sweeteners

Varnishes

The storage and handling of formulations associated with the process described above.

The use and handling of organic liquids and other substances for clean-up operations associated with the process described above.

"Mixing Operation": The operation of combining two or more ingredients, of which at least one is a grain.

"New Grain-Drying Operation": Any grain-drying operation the construction or modification of which is commenced on or after June 30, 1975.

"New Grain-Handling Operation": Any grain-handling operation the construction of modification of which is commenced on or after June 30, 1975.

"One Hundred Percent Acid": Acid with a specific gravity of 1.8205 at 30 C in the case of sulfuric acid and 1.4952 at 30 C in the case of nitric acid.

"One-Turn Storage Space": That space used to store grain with a total annual through-put not in excess of the total bushel storage of that space.

"Opacity": A condition which renders material partially or wholly impervious to transmittance of light and causes obstruction of an observer's view. For the purposes of these regulations, the following equivalence between opacity and Ringelmann shall be employed:

Opacity Percent	Ringelmann
10	0.5

POLLUTION CONTROL BOARD

NOTICE OF PROPOSED AMENDMENTS

20	1.
30	1.5
40	2.
60	3.
80	4.
100	5.

"Open Top Vapor Degreasing": The batch process of cleaning and removing soils from surfaces by condensing hot solvent vapor on the colder metal parts.

"Operator of Gasoline Dispensing Facility": Any person who is the lessee of or operates, controls or supervises a gasoline dispensing facility.

"Organic Material": Any chemical compound of carbon including diluents and thinners which are liquids at standard conditions and which are used as dissolvers, viscosity reducers or cleaning agents, but excluding methane, carbon monoxide, carbon dioxide, carbonic acid, metallic carbonic acid, metallic carbide, metallic carbonates and ammonium carbonate.

"Organic Materials": For the purposes of Section 9.4 of the Act, any chemical compound of carbon including diluents and thinners which are liquids at standard conditions and which are used as dissolvers, viscosity reducers, or cleaning agents, and polychlorinated dibenzo-p-dioxins, polychlorinated dibenzofurans and polynuclear aromatic hydrocarbons shall be considered to be organic materials. Methane, carbon monoxide, carbon dioxide, carbonic acid, metallic carbonic acid, metallic carbide, metallic carbonates and ammonium carbonate shall not be considered to be organic materials for the purposes of Ill. Rev. Stat. 1985, ch. 111 ½ par. 1009.4.

"Organic Vapor": Gaseous phase of an organic material or a mixture of organic materials present in the atmosphere.

"Overvarnish": A coating applied directly over ink or printing.

"Owner of Gasoline Dispensing Facility": Any person who has legal or equitable title to a stationary storage tank at a gasoline dispensing facility.

POLLUTION CONTROL BOARD

NOTICE OF PROPOSED AMENDMENTS

"Packaging Rotogravure Printing": Rotogravure printing
upon paper, paper board, metal foil, plastic film and
other substrates, which are, in subsequent operations,
formed into packaging products or labels for articles to
be sold.

"Paint Manufacturing Plant": a plant that mixes,
blends, or compounds enamels, lacquers, sealers,
shellacs, stains, varnishes or pigmented surface
coatings.

"Paper Coating": The application of a coating material
to paper or pressure sensitive tapes, regardless of
substrate, including web coating on plastic fibers and
decorative coatings on metal foil.

"Particulate Matter": Any solid or liquid material,
other than water, which exists in finely divided form.

"Petroleum Liquid": Crude oil, condensate or any
finished or intermediate product manufactured at a
petroleum refinery, but not including Number 2 through
Number 6 fuel oils as specified in A.S.T.M. D-396-69,
gas turbine fuel oils Numbers 2-GT through 4-GT as
specified in A.S.T.M. D-2880-71 or diesel fuel oils
Numbers 2-D and 4-D, as specified in A.S.T.M. D-975-68.

"Petroleum Refinery": Any facility engaged in producing
gasoline, kerosene, distillate fuel oils, residual fuel
oils, lubricants, or other products through
distillation, cracking, extraction or reforming of
unfinished petroleum derivatives.

"Pharmaceutical": Any compound or mixture, other than
food, used in the prevention, diagnosis, alleviation,
treatment or cure of disease in man and animal.

"Photochemically Reactive Material": Any organic
material with an aggregate of more than 20 percent of
its total volume composed of the chemical compounds
classified below or the composition of which exceeds any
of the following individual percentage composition
limitations. Whenever any photochemically reactive
material or any constituent of any organic material may
be classified from its chemical structure into more than
one of the above groups of organic materials it shall be

POLLUTION CONTROL BOARD

NOTICE OF PROPOSED AMENDMENTS

considered as a member of the most reactive group, that
is, the group having the least allowable percent of the
total organic materials.

A combination of hydrocarbons, alcohols, aldehydes,
esters, ethers or ketones having an olefinic or cyclo-
olefinic types of unsaturation: 5 percent. This
definition does not apply to perchloroethylene or
trichloroethylene.

A combination of aromatic compounds with eight or more
carbon atoms to the molecule except ethyl-benzene: 8
percent.

A combination of ethylbenzene, ketones having branched
hydrocarbon structures or toluene: 20 percent.

PM_{10}": particulate matter with an aerodynamic diameter
equal to or less than 10 micrometers as defined in 40
CFR 51.100 (incorporated by reference in Section
211.101). Ambient air concentrations for PM_{10} are
usually expressed in micrograms per cubic meter (ug/m^3).

"Pneumatic Rubber Tire Manufacture": The production of
pneumatic rubber tires with a bead diameter up to but
not including 20.0 inches and cross section dimension up
to 12.8 inches, but not including specialty tires for
antique or other vehicles when produced on equipment
separate from normal production lines for passenger or
truck type tires.

"Polybasic Organic Acid Partial Oxidation Manufacturing
Process": Any process involving partial oxidation of
hydrocarbons with air to manufacture polybasic acids or
their anhydrides, such as maleic anhydride, phthalic
anhydride, terephthalic acid, isophthalic acid,
trimelletic anhydride.

"Portable Grain-Handling Equipment": Any equipment
(excluding portable grain dryers) that is designed and
maintained to be movable primarily for use in a non-
continuous operation for loading and unloading one-turn
storage space, and is not physically connected to the
grain elevator, provided that the manufacturer's rated
capacity of the equipment does not exceed 10,000 bushels
per hour.

"Portland Cement Process": Any facility manufacturing portland cement by either the wet or dry process.

"Power Driven Fastener Coating": The coating of nail, staple, brad and finish nail fasteners where such fasteners are fabricated from wire or rod of 0.0254 inch diameter or greater, where such fasteners are bonded into coils or strips, such coils and strips containing a number of such fasteners, which coils and strips are manufactured for use in power tools, and which fasteners must conform with formal standards for specific uses established by various federal and national organizations including Federal Specification FF-N-105b of the General Services Administration dated August 23, 1977 (does not include any later amendments or editions; U.S. Army Armament Research and Development Command, Attn: DRDAR-TST, Rock Island, IL 61201), Bulletin UM-25d of the U.S. Department of Housing and Urban Development - Federal Housing Administration dated September 5, 1973 (does not include any later amendments or editions; Department of HUD, 547 W. Jackson Blvd., Room 1005, Chicago, IL 60606), and the Model Building Code of the Council of American Building Officials, and similar standards. For the purposes of this definition, the terms "brad" and "finish nail" refer to single leg fasteners fabricated in the same manner as staples. The application of coatings to staple, brad, and finish nail fasteners may be associated with the incremental forming of such fasteners in a cyclic or repetitious manner (incremental fabrication) or with the forming of strips of such fasteners as a unit from a band of wires (unit fabrication).

"PPM (Vol) - (Parts per Million) (Volume)": A volume/volume ratio which expresses the volumetric concentration of gaseous air contaminant in a million unit volumes of gas.

"Pressure Tank": A tank in which fluids are stored at a pressure greater than atmospheric pressure.

"Prime Coat": The first film of coating material applied in a multiple coat operation.

"Prime Surfacer Coat": A film of coating material that touches up areas on the surface not adequately covered by the prime coat before application of the top coat.

"Process": Any stationary emission source other than a fuel combustion emission source or an incinerator.

"Process Weight Rate": The actual weight or engineering approximation thereof of all materials except liquid and gaseous fuels and combustion air, introduced into any process per hour. For a cyclical or batch operation, the process weight rate shall be determined by dividing such actual weight or engineering approximation thereof by the number of hours of operation excluding any time during which the equipment is idle. For continuous processes, the process weight rate shall be determined by dividing such actual weight or engineering approximation thereof by the number of hours in one complete operation, excluding any time during which the equipment is idle.

"Production Equipment Exhaust System": A system for collecting and directing into the atmosphere emissions of volatile organic material from reactors, centrifuges and other process emission sources.

"Publication Rotogravure Printing": Rotogravure printing upon paper which is subsequently formed into books, magazines, catalogues, brochures, directories, newspaper supplements or other types of non-packaging printed materials.

"Reactor": A vat, vessel or other device in which chemical reactions take place.

"Reasonably Available Control Technology (RACT)": the lowest emission limitation that an emission source is capable of meeting by the application of control technology that is reasonably available considering technological and economic feasibility.

"Refinery Fuel Gas": Any gas which is generated by a petroleum refinery process unit and which is combusted at the refinery, including any gaseous mixture of natural gas and fuel gas.

"Refinery Unit, Process Unit or Unit": A set of components which are a part of a basic process operation such as distillation, hydrotreating, cracking or reforming of hydrocarbons.

"Residual Fuel Oil": Fuel oils of grade No. 4, 5 and 6 as specified in detailed requirements for fuel oils A.S.T.M. D-396-69 (1971).

"Restricted Area": The area within the boundaries of any "municipality" as defined in the Illinois Municipal Code, plus a zone extending one mile beyond the boundaries of any such municipality having a population of 1000 or more according to the latest federal census.

"Ringelmann Chart": The chart published and described in the Bureau of Mines, U.S. Department of Interior, Information Circular 8333 (Revision of IC7718) May 1, 1967, or any adaptation thereof which has been approved by the Agency.

"Roadway": Any street, highway, road, alley, sidewalk, parking lot, airport, rail bed or terminal, bikeway, pedestrian mall or other structure used for transportation purposes.

"Roll Printing": The application of words, designs and pictures to a substrate usually by means of a series of hard rubber or metal rolls each with only partial coverage.

"Rotogravure Printing": The application of words, designs and pictures to a substrate by means of a roll printing technique in which the pattern to be applied is recessed relative to the non-image area.

"Safety Relief Valve": A valve which is normally closed and which is designed to open in order to relieve excessive pressures within a vessel or pipe.

"Sandblasting": The use of a mixture of sand and air at high pressures for cleaning and/or polishing any type of surface.

"Set of Safety Relief Valves": One or more safety relief valves designed to open in order to relieve excessive pressures in the same vessel or pipe.

"Sheet Basecoat": A coating applied to metal when the metal is in sheet form to serve as either the exterior or interior of a can for either two-piece or three-piece cans.

"Shotblasting": The use of a mixture of any metallic or non-metallic substance and air at high pressures for cleaning and/or polishing any type of surface.

"Side-Seam Spray Coat": A coating applied to the seam of a three-piece can.

"Smoke": Small gas-borne particles resulting from incomplete combustion, consisting predominately but not exclusively of carbon, ash and other combustible material, that form a visible plume in the air.

"Smokeless Flare": A combustion unit and the stack to which it is affixed in which organic material achieves combustion by burning in the atmosphere such that the smoke or other particulate matter emitted to the atmosphere from such combustion does not have an appearance density or shade darker that No. 1 of the Ringelmann Chart.

"Solvent Cleaning": The process of cleaning soils from surfaces by cold cleaning, open top vapor degreasing or conveyorized degreasing.

"Specialty High Gloss Catalyzed Coating": commercial contract finishing of material prepared for printers and lithographers where the finishing process uses a solvent-borne coating, formulated with a catalyst, in a quantity of no more than 12,000 gallons/year as supplied, where the coating machines are sheet fed and the coated sheets are brought to a minimum surface temperature of 190 F., and where the coated sheets are to achieve the minimum specular reflectance index of 65 measured at a 60 degree angle with a gloss meter.

"Splash Loading": A method of loading a tank, railroad tank car, tank truck or trailer by use of other than a submerged loading pipe.

"Stack": A flue or conduit, free-standing or with exhaust port above the roof of the building on which it is mounted, by which air contaminants are emitted into the atmosphere.

"Standard Conditions": A temperature of 70 F and a pressure of 14.7 pounds per square inch absolute (psia).

POLLUTION CONTROL BOARD

NOTICE OF PROPOSED AMENDMENTS

"Standard Cubic Foot (scf)": The volume of one cubic foot of gas at standard conditions.

"Startup": The setting in operation of an emission source for any purpose.

"Stationary Emission Source": An emission source which is not self-propelled.

"Stationary Storage Tank": Any container of liquid or gas which is designed and constructed to remain at one site.

"Submerged Loading Pipe": Any loading pipe the discharge opening of which is entirely submerged when the liquid level is 6 inches above the bottom of the tank. When applied to a tank which is loaded from the side, any loading pipe the discharge of which is entirely submerged when the liquid level is 18 inches or two times the loading pipe diameter, whichever is greater, above the bottom of the tank. The definition shall also apply to any loading pipe which is continuously submerged during loading operations.

"Sulfuric Acid Mist": Sulfuric acid mist as measured according to the method specified in 35 Ill. Adm. Code 214.101(b).

"Surface Condenser": A device which removes a substance from a gas stream by reducing the temperature of the stream, without direct contact between the coolant and the stream.

"Top Coat": A film of coating material applied in a multiple coat operation other than the prime coat, final repair coat or prime surfacer coat.

"Transfer Efficiency": The weight or volume of coating adhering to the material being coated divided by the weight or volume of coating delivered to the coating applicator and multiplied by 100 to equal a percentage.

"Tread End Cementing": The application of a solvent-based cement to the tire tread ends.

POLLUTION CONTROL BOARD

NOTICE OF PROPOSED AMENDMENTS

"True Vapor Pressure": The equilibrium partial pressure exerted by a petroleum liquid as determined in accordance with methods described in American Petroleum Institute Bulletin 2517, "Evaporation Loss From Floating Roof Tanks" (1962).

"Turnaround": The procedure of shutting down an operating refinery unit, emptying gaseous and liquid contents to do inspection, maintenance and repair work, and putting the unit back into production.

"Undertread Cementing": The application of a solvent-based cement to the underside of a tire tread.

"Unregulated Safety Relief Valve": A safety relief valve which cannot be actuated by a means other than high pressure in the pipe or vessel which it protects.

"Vacuum Producing System": Any reciprocating, rotary or centrifugal blower or compressor, or any jet ejector or device that creates suction from a pressure below atmospheric and discharges against a greater pressure.

"Valves Not Externally Regulated": Valves that have no external controls, such as in-line check valves.

"Vapor Balance System": Any combination of pipes or hoses which creates a closed system between the vapor spaces of an unloading tank and a receiving tank such that vapors displaced from the receiving tank are transferred to the tank being unloaded.

"Vapor Collection System": all piping, seals, hoses, connections, pressure-vacuum vents, and other possible sources between the gasoline delivery vessel and the vapor processing unit and/or the storage tanks and vapor holder.

"Vapor Control System": Any system that prevents release to the atmosphere of organic material in the vapors displaced from a tank during the transfer of gasoline.

"Vapor-Mounted Primary Seal": A primary seal mounted with an air space bounded by the bottom of the primary seal, the tank wall, the liquid surface and the floating roof.

POLLUTION CONTROL BOARD

NOTICE OF PROPOSED AMENDMENTS

"Vinyl Coating": The application of a topcoat or printing to vinyl coated fabric or vinyl sheets.

"Volatile Organic Liquid": any liquid which contains volatile organic material.

"Volatile Organic Material":

any organic material which participates in atmospheric photochemical reactions unless specifically exempted from this definition. Volatile organic material emissions shall be measured by the reference methods specified under 40 CFR 60, Appendix A (1986) (no future amendments or editions are included), or, if no reference method is applicable, may be determined by mass balance calculations.

For purposes of this definition, the following are not volatile organic materials:

Chlorodifluoromethane
Chloropentafluoroethane
Dichlorodifluoromethane
Dichlorotetrafluoroethane
Ethane
Methane
Methylene chloride
1,1,1, Trichloroethane
Trichlorofluoromethane
Trichlorotrifluoroethane
Trifluoromethane

"Volatile Petroleum Liquid": Any petroleum liquid with a true vapor pressure that is greater than 1.5 psia (78 millimeters of mercury) at standard conditions.

"Wastewater (Oil/Water) Separator": Any device or piece of equipment which utilizes the difference in density between oil and water to remove oil and associated chemicals of water, or any device, such as a flocculation tank or a clarifier, which removes petroleum derived compounds from waste water.

"Weak Nitric Acid Manufacturing Process" Any acid producing facility manufacturing nitric acid with a concentration of less than 70 percent by weight.

POLLUTION CONTROL BOARD

NOTICE OF PROPOSED AMENDMENTS

"Woodworking": The shaping, sawing, grinding, smoothing, polishing and making into products of any form or shape of wood.

(SOURCE: Amended at ___ Ill. Reg. effective _____)

DEPARTMENT OF PUBLIC HEALTH

NOTICE OF PROPOSED AMENDMENTS

1) Heading of the Part:

Clinical Laboratories and Blood Banks

2) Code Citation:

77 Ill. Adm. Code 450

3) Section Numbers: Proposed Action:

450.440   New Section
450.450   New Section
450.1300   New Section
450.1310   New Section
450.1320   New Section
450.1330   New Section

4) Statutory Authority:

Illinois Clinical Laboratory Act
Ill. Rev. Stat. 1987, ch. 111 1/2, par. 621-101 et seq., as amended by
Public Act 85-1251, effective August 30, 1988.

5) A Complete Description of the Subjects and Issues Involved:

This rulemaking specifies what laboratory tests are considered health
screening tests, what entities can perform health screening activities,
and how health screening activities are to be conducted.

The Department has solicited and received numerous recommendations
concerning what laboratory tests should be listed as health screening
tests. After a review of all recommendations and the recent legislation,
the Department has decided upon the following approach.

In response to HB 3911 and HB 3303, the Department proposes to adopt only
two specific exclusive lists of tests: (1) a list of tests for health
screening, which is included in this rulemaking and (2) a list of tests
for the registration class which the Department anticipates proposing in
February of 1989 under HB 3303. All remaining tests would be either
"simple" or "complex" under the provisions of HB 3303. The lists of tests
would be as follows:

A "HEALTH SCREENING" test "MEANS THE PERFORMANCE OF ANY OF THE DEPARTMENT
LISTED TESTS FOR THE PURPOSE OF ASSESSING A PHASE OF THE GENERAL STATE OF
HEALTH OF HUMAN SUBJECTS" in the context of an off-site health screening
event such as a health fair. Tests designed as health screening tests may
be conducted at the principal location of the laboratory without the
protocol required by these rules.

A. Health Screening Test list pursuant HB 3911 - Public Act 85-1251,
effective August 30, 1988.

DEPARTMENT OF PUBLIC HEALTH

NOTICE OF PROPOSED AMENDMENTS

5) A Complete Description of the Subjects and Issues Involved: (continued)

1. Blood total cholesterol testing by finger stick method, and
2. Blood glucose testing by finger stick method.

B. DRAFT registration class tests pursuant to HB 3303 - Public Act
85-1025, effective June 30, 1988.

1. Any tests performed by a Physician, Dentist or Podiatrist;
2. Hematocrit;
3. Hemoglobin;
4. Blood lead level testing;
5. Chemical Urinalysis testing;
6. Sickle cell anemia testing;
7. Sperm count testing;
8. Pin worm testing;
9. Blood cholesterol testing;
10. Blood glucose testing;
11. Occult blood testing;
12. Urine pregnancy testing (semi-quantitative chorionic
    gonadotropin), and
13. Triglycerides.

Under the existing clinical laboratory rules (77 Ill. Adm. Code
450.30(b)(7)) and until new rules pursuant to HB 3303 are adopted circa
July 1, 1989, local health department laboratories are exempt from
licensure in the following situation:

PUBLIC HEALTH LABORATORIES WHICH MEET THE PROVISIONS OF SECTION 1-103(e)
OF THE ILLINOIS CLINICAL LABORATORY ACT AND WHICH RESTRICT THEIR CLINICAL
LABORATORY TESTING TO THE FOLLOWING: SMEARS AND CULTURES FOR NEISSERIA
GONORRHEAE, WET MOUNTS FOR YEAST OR TRICHOMONAS, SYPHILIS SEROLOGY,
SEMI/QUANTITATIVE CHORIONIC GONADOTROPIN, GLUCOSE, URINALYSIS (LIMITED TO
DIP-STICK AND MICROSCOPIC FOR RED AND WHITE CELLS), HEMATOCRIT,
HEMOGLOBIN, AND RBC SICKLE CELL SCREENING.

Pursuant to HB 3911 and emergency rules to be adopted circa October 28,
1988, local health departments will also be able to conduct health
screenings without a license or permit if done on a not for profit or free
of charge basis. The health screening tests can be in addition to those
tests presently permissible without a license.

Both the present rules and the health screening rules will be combined and
explained further in future amendments pursuant to HB 3303 which will be
drafted later this year.

6) Will this Rulemaking Replace an Emergency Rule Currently in Effect?

Yes _X_   No ___

7) Does this Rulemaking Contain an Automatic Repeal Date? Yes ___ No _X_

DEPARTMENT OF PUBLIC HEALTH

NOTICE OF PROPOSED AMENDMENTS

If "yes," please specify the date: _____

8) **Does this Rulemaking Contain Any Incorporations By Reference?**

Yes ___ No _X_

If "yes," please specify type: 6.02(a)___ or 6.02(b)___

9) **Are there any other Proposed Amendments Pending on this Part?**

Yes ___ No _X_.

If Yes:

Section Numbers   Proposed Action   Ill. Reg. Citation

10) **Statement of Statewide Policy Objectives:**

This rulemaking neither expands or contracts a state mandate.

11) **Time, Place, and Manner in which Interested Persons May Comment on this Rulemaking:**

Interested persons may present their comments concerning these rules by writing to Mr. Robert John Kane, Division of Governmental Affairs, Illinois Department of Public Health, 525 West Jefferson, Second Floor Springfield, Illinois 62761 within 45 days after this issue of the Illinois Register.

These rules may have an impact on small businesses. In accordance with Sections 3.01 and 4.03 of the Illinois Administrative Procedure Act, any small business may present their comments in writing to Robert John Kane at the above address.

Any small business (as defined in Section 3.10 of the Illinois Administrative Procedure Act) commenting on these rules shall indicate their status as such, in writing, in their comments.

NOTICE OF PUBLIC HEARING ON EMERGENCY AMENDMENTS AND PROPOSED AMENDMENTS

The Department will conduct public hearings on these EMERGENCY RULES and the identical PROPOSED AMENDMENTS at the following times and places:

Date, Time and Location of Public Hearings:

1:00 PM
December 8, 1988
Illinois Department of Public Health

DEPARTMENT OF PUBLIC HEALTH

NOTICE OF PROPOSED AMENDMENTS

First Floor Training Room
525 West Jefferson
Springfield, Illinois 62761

10:00 AM
December 9, 1988
Ninth Floor, Room 40
State of Illinois Center
100 West Randolph Street
Chicago, Illinois 60601

Other Pertinent Information:

The hearings will be for the sole purpose of gathering public comment. Persons interested in presenting testimony at this hearing are advised that the Department will adhere to the following procedures in the conduct of the hearing:

1. Each person presenting oral testimony shall provide to the hearing officer a written (preferably typed) copy of such testimony at the time the oral testimony is presented. No oral testimony shall be accepted without such written copy of the testimony being provided.

2. Each person presenting oral testimony will be limited to fifteen (15) minutes for the presentation of such testimony.

3. No person will be recognized to speak for a second time until all persons wishing to testify have done so. All testimony shall conclude at the specific times except that an individual in the midst of presenting testimony shall be allowed to complete his/her testimony.

4. In order to provide for a balanced presentation of views and to facilitate the orderly conduct of the hearing, the Hearing Officer may impose such other rules of procedure, including the order of call of witnesses, as he/she deems necessary.

12) **Initial Regulatory Flexibility Analysis:**

A) **Date Rulemaking was Submitted to the Business Assistance Office of the Department of Commerce and Community Affairs:**

October 27, 1988

B) **Type of Small Businesses Affected:**

Local health departments, clinical laboratories and other entities which conduct health screening.

C) **Reporting, Bookkeeping or Other Procedures Required for Compliance:**

Submission of a testing protocol, personnel information and health screening event reporting.

DEPARTMENT OF PUBLIC HEALTH

NOTICE OF PROPOSED AMENDMENTS

D) Types of Professional Skills Necessary for Compliance:

    Physician and laboratory technician skills.

The Proposed Amendments are identical to the Notice of the Emergency
Amendments which appear on page 19518 of this issue of the Illinois Register.

DEPARTMENT OF PUBLIC HEALTH

NOTICE OF PROPOSED RULES

1) Heading of the Part:

    Private Sewage Mound Code

2) Code Citation: 77 Ill. Adm. Code 906

3) Section Numbers: Proposed Action:

    906.10   New Section
    906.20   New Section
    906.25   New Section
    906.30   New Section
    906.40   New Section
    906.50   New Section
    906.60   New Section
    906.70   New Section
    APPENDIX A   New Section
    906.ILLUSTRATION A   New Section
    906.ILLUSTRATION B   New Section
    906.ILLUSTRATION C   New Section
    906.ILLUSTRATION D   New Section
    906.ILLUSTRATION E   New Section
    906.ILLUSTRATION F   New Section
    906.ILLUSTRATION G   New Section
    906.ILLUSTRATION H   New Section
    906.ILLUSTRATION I   New Section
    906.EXHIBIT A   New Section
    906.EXHIBIT B   New Section
    906.EXHIBIT C   New Section
    906.EXHIBIT D   New Section
    906.EXHIBIT E   New Section
    906.EXHIBIT F   New Section
    906.EXHIBIT G   New Section
    906.EXHIBIT H   New Section
    906.EXHIBIT I   New Section

4) Statutory Authority:

    Ill. Rev. Stat. 1987, ch. 111 1/2, par. 116.301 et seq.

5) A Complete Description of the Subjects and Issues Involved:

    These new rules establish criteria for the design and construction of a
    new type of sewage disposal system which can be used when other types of
    private sewage disposal systems are inappropriate.

6) Will this Rulemaking Replace an Emergency Rule Currently in Effect?

    Yes ___   No _X_

7) Does this Rulemaking Contain an Automatic Repeal Date? Yes ___ No _X_

   If "yes," please specify the date: _____

8) Does this Rulemaking Contain Any Incorporations By Reference?

   Yes _X_ No ___

   If "yes," please specify type: 6.02(a)___ or 6.02(b)___

9) Are there any other Proposed Amendments Pending on this Part?

   Yes ___ No _X_

   If Yes:

Section Numbers	Proposed Action	Ill. Reg. Citation

10) Statement of Statewide Policy Objectives:

   Please specify: To establish rules which reflect new technology for
   the proper disposal of domestic sewage.

11) Time, Place, and Manner in which Interested Persons May Comment on
   this Rulemaking:

   Interested persons may present their comments concerning these rules
   by writing to Mr. Robert John Kane, Division of Governmental Affairs,
   Illinois Department of Public Health, 525 West Jefferson, Second Floor
   Springfield, Illinois 62761 within 45 days after this issue of the
   Illinois Register.

   These rules may have an impact on small businesses. In accordance
   with Sections 3.01 and 4.03 of the Illinois Administrative
   Procedure Act, any small business may present their comments in
   writing to Robert John Kane at the above address.

   Any small business (as defined in Section 3.10 of the Illinois
   Administrative Procedure Act) commenting on these rules shall indicate
   their status as such, in writing, in their comments.

12) Initial Regulatory Flexibility Analysis:

   A) Date Rulemaking was Submitted to the Business Assistance Office of
      the Department of Commerce and Community Affairs:

   B) Type of Small Businesses Affected:

      Licensed private sewage disposal contractors.

   C) Reporting, Bookkeeping or Other Procedures Required for Compliance:

      None

   D) Types of Professional Skills Necessary for Compliance:

      Private sewage disposal contractor's license.

The full text of the Proposed Rules begins on the next page:

DEPARTMENT OF PUBLIC HEALTH

NOTICE OF PROPOSED RULES

TITLE 77: PUBLIC HEALTH
CHAPTER I: DEPARTMENT OF PUBLIC HEALTH
SUBCHAPTER r: WATER AND SEWAGE

PART 906
PRIVATE SEWAGE MOUND CODE

DEPARTMENT OF PUBLIC HEALTH

NOTICE OF PROPOSED RULES

906.EXHIBIT I   Friction Loss in Schedule 40 Plastic Pipe

AUTHORITY: Implementing and authorized by the Private Sewage Disposal Licensing Act (Ill. Rev. Stat. 1987, ch. 111 1/2, pars. 116.301 et seq.)

SOURCE: Adopted at 13 Ill. Reg. _____, effective _____.

Section 960.10 Applicability

a)   The rules of this Part are promulgated by the Illinois Department of Public Health in order to establish requirements for the design and construction of mounds in Illinois which are to be used as private sewage disposal systems. All such mounds must be constructed in accordance with the requirements of this Part.

b)   Plan approval must be obtained from the Department or local authority prior to beginning any construction of a mound system in accordance with Section 905.190 of the Private Sewage Disposal Code (77 Illinois Administrative Code, Part 905). All individuals who construct such systems must be licensed as a Private Sewage Disposal System Installation Contractor.

Section 906.20 Definitions

"Absorption Area" means the area of coarse aggregate in the absorption bed or trenches in a mound.

"Basal Area" means the area of natural soil under a mound which is effective in absorbing effluent.

"Dosing" means the application of sewage under pressure to a sewage disposal system at constant intervals or in constant amounts per application.

"Mound" means a soil absorption sewage treatment system that is elevated above the natural ground surface in a suitable fill material.

"Permeable Soil" means soil which has a percolation rate between 18 and 180 minutes. (See Appendix A, Illustration G of the Private Sewage Disposal Code for meaning of percolation rate and percolation test procedure.)

"Shallow Permeable Soil" means pervious soil over crevriced or porous bed rock, 5 1/2 feet or less in thickness.

"Slowly Permeable Soil" means soil having a percolation rate of between 180 and 360 minutes.

Section 906.25   Incorporated Materials

a) The following federal and state regulations, standards, and statutes are incorporated or referenced in various sections of this part.

   1) American Society for Testing and Materials (ASTM) required standards for approved plastic pipe and published by:

      American Society for Testing and Materials
      1916 Race Street
      Philadelphia, PA 19103

b) All incorporations by reference of federal regulations and the standards of nationally recognized organizations refer to the regulations and standards on the date specified and do not include any additions or deletions subsequent to the date specified.

c) All citations to federal regulations in this Part concern the specified regulation in the 1986 Code of Federal Regulations, unless another date is specified.

d) All materials incorporated by reference are available for inspection and copying at the Department's Central Office, Division of Environmental Health, 525 West Jefferson, Springfield, Illinois 62761.

Section 906.30   Soil and Site Requirements

In order to be suitable for mound construction, the site shall meet the following requirements and those listed in Appendix A, Exhibit A.

a) Percolation Rates. Percolation rates shall be used to determine the suitability of the site for accepting effluent. Percolation tests shall be performed according to the procedure outlined in Appendix A, Illustration G of the Private Sewage Disposal Code (77 Ill. Adm. Code, 905). Excepting that, percolation tests shall be performed at a depth of 20-24 in. from the natural surface. However, in cases where a more slowly permeable soil horizon is above this depth the percolation tests shall be conducted in the more slowly permeable soil horizon. Those results shall be used in the design of the mound. For shallow permeable soils over pervious bedrock, the percolation test shall be run at a depth of 12-18 in. below the natural surface. For permeable soils with high water tables, the percolation test shall be run at a depth of 20-24 in. below the natural surface.

b) Depth to Pervious Rock or Seasonal High Water Table. There shall be a minimum of 24 in. of unsaturated natural soil between the soil

surface and pervious bedrock or the seasonal high water table, including a perched water table, at the proposed mound site. High water tables can be determined by direct observation or by soil mottling. Occurrence of grey and red soil mottling patterns can be used to indicate periodic saturation with water.

c) Rocky Soils. If the soil contains 50% rock fragments or more by volume in the upper 24 in. of soil, the mound basal area shall be 25% larger than that normally required.

d) Slopes. The mound shall be placed upslope and not at the base of the slope of the existing ground. On a site where there is a complex slope, (two directions), the mound shall be situated such that the liquid is not concentrated in one area downslope. Upslope runoff shall be diverted around the mound. For the more permeable soils where the percolation rate is 18-179 min., slopes shall not exceed 12%. For tighter soils where the percolation rate is 180-360 min., slopes shall not exceed 6%.

e) Flood Plains. Construction of mound systems shall not be allowed in flood plains, drainage ways or depressions.

f) Sites with Trees and Large Boulders. Sites with large trees, numerous smaller trees or large boulders are unsuitable for the mound system. If no other site is available, the trees shall be cut off at ground level, leaving the stumps. An increase in mound basal area shall be required where stumps are involved, so that sufficient soil is available to accept the effluent. The increase in mound area shall equal the surface area of the stumps on the mound site.

g) Site Preparation

   1) Vegetation shall be cut and removed from the site prior to construction. The site must then be plowed with a mold board plow 7-8 in. deep with the plowing done perpendicular to the slope. Plowing shall not be done with the furrow running up and down the slope. Chisel plowing may be used in place of mold board. Roto tilling is prohibited. However, roto tilling may be used to incorporate the vegetative cover in unstructured soil such as sand.

   2) Site preparation shall not take place when the soil is too wet. The soil shall be considered too wet when a soil sample taken at a depth of 7-8 in. beneath the surface can be rolled between the palms of the hands into a continuous ribbon of soil. If the soil crumbles, site preparation can then proceed.

   3) Once the site is plowed, all construction machinery and other vehicles shall be kept off the mound site. The fill material

shall be deposited on the site with a backhoe or pushed on from the side, using a track type tractor, keeping 6 in. of fill beneath the tracks. At no time shall ruts be made in the plowed area. The fill shall be placed immediately after site preparation to avoid the possibility of precipitation falling on the plowed area.

4) All work shall be performed from the ends and upslope side, especially on fine textured soils.

Section 906.40 Fill Material

a) Below Absorption Area

1) A mound system shall be provided with a fill material beneath the absorption area (trenches or bed). One of the following fill materials shall be used.

A) FA-1
B) FA-2
C) FA-3
D) FA-8
E) FA-9

2) These materials are classified and graded in accordance with Illinois Department of Transportation, Division of Highways specifications for fine aggregate. These materials shall meet the gradation specifications as shown for these five fine aggregates in Appendix A, Exhibit B.

b) Above the Absorption Area. The cap (area above the bed or trenches) shall consist of a fine textured soil to allow plant growth. Sands are not allowed since they drain rapidly and allow more infiltration of precipitation into the absorption area. Top soil shall be placed to a depth of 6 in. over the entire mound to promote good vegetation cover. The cap soil shall be seeded and fertilized.

Section 906.50 Mound Design

a) A mound system shall include a septic tank for pre-treatment of sewage. The septic tank and piping between the septic tank and the pumping chamber shall conform to the applicable rules in the Private Sewage Disposal Code (77 Ill. Adm. Code, 905).

b) The design of the mound shall be based upon the expected daily waste-water volume using the data contained in Appendix A, Illustration A, of the Private Sewage Disposal Code, (77 Ill. Adm. Code, 905.) and the soil percolation rate. Mounds shall be sized

such that they can accept the daily waste water flow without surface seepage, and the basal area, which is the natural soil area beneath the mound, shall be sufficiently large to conduct the effluent into the underlying top soil. The system shall also be designed to avoid encroachment of the water table into the mound.

c) Where a mound is intended to serve more than a 4 bedroom residence, the system shall be designed in accordance with the procedure outlined in Section 906.60.

d) Design of the Absorption Area

1) Sizing the absorption area. The size of the absorption area is dependent upon the daily waste water flow. The design infiltration capacity of the fill material shall be 1.2 gal/ft²/day.

2)

A) System configuration. The absorption area within the mound shall be constructed as trenches or beds. An illustration of construction using trenches and bed are shown in Appendix A, Illustration A through D. The location of the water table and soil permeability will dictate whether a trench or bed shall be used. In slowly permeable soils, two or three narrow parallel trenches shall be used instead of a bed. Trench widths shall be between 24 and 48 inches. For permeable soils a narrow rectangular bed may be used. Bed widths shall not be greater than 10 ft.

B) On sloping sites, the trenches and beds shall be situated perpendicular to the slope in order to prevent the concentration of effluent into a small area as it moves laterally down slope. Sufficient basal area shall be provided so all the effluent infiltrates into the natural soil before it reaches the toe of the mound. With a trench system, the trench spacing shall be such that the effluent from an upslope trench shall be absorbed by the natural soil before reaching the area under the next trench downslope.

C) The bottom of the absorption area within the bed and trenches shall be level and at the same elevation.

e) Mound Dimensions

1) Mound height. The mound height shall consist of the fill depth (D & E), the trench or bed depth (F), and the cap and top soil

depth (G & H) as shown in Appendix A, Illustration A through D for trench and bed construction respectively. A minimum of 1 foot of fill is required under the bed or trenches. For sites where the soil depth is less than 3 feet over creviced bedrock, the fill depth (D) shall be a minimum of 2 feet.

2) Bed or trench depth (F). The depth of the bed or trenches shall be at least 10 inches. A minimum of 6 in. of aggregate shall be placed beneath the distribution pipe. Clean, 1/2-2 inch stone shall be used. The use of soft limestone is prohibited.

3) Cap and top soil (H & G). The depth of soil over the aggregate at the apex (H) shall be a minimum of 1.5 ft. For a 3 parallel trench system, the depth shall be a minimum of 2 ft. At the outer edge of the gravel the cap and top soil shall be at least 1 ft. deep. The cap shall be topsoil or finer textured subsoil. A minimum of 6 inches of topsoil shall be placed over the entire mound. The top soil shall be seeded with grass seed to control erosion.

4) Side and end slopes. Side and end slopes shall be no steeper than one foot vertical rise in 3 feet horizontal.

f)   Basal Area

1) The basal area is the natural soil-fill interface of the mound. The basal area required shall be dependent upon the soil and site conditions. For level sites, the total basal area beneath the mound can be used. For sloping sites the only basal area which may be considered for design is the area beneath and downslope of the bed or trenches (see Appendix A, Exhibit C). The percolation rate of the natural soil shall determine the mound area required. For the percolation rates shown the following design loading rates shall be used:

A)   60 min - 1.2 gal/ft²/day
B)   180 min -   .74 gal/ft²/day
C)   360 min -   .24 gal/ft²/day

2) If sufficient basal area is not available for the given design and site conditions, additional fill shall be used to make the mound wider for a level site or the fill used to extend the downslope width on a sloping site until sufficient area is available.

Section 906.60   Distribution System (for sewage flows of less than 800 gallons per day)

a)   Piping System. The piping distribution system for the mound shall consist of a manifold pipe and small diameter laterals with perforations. The perforations shall be drilled at 30"-36" intervals along the invert of the lateral. Perforations shall be installed perpendicular to the pipe axis. Perforation diameters shall be between 3/16" and 1/4". If the distance between the end of the lateral and the nearest perforation is greater than 1/2 the perforation spacing used, another hole shall be installed in or near the end cap of the lateral. A typical distribution system for a mound is shown in Appendix A, Illustration E. For a trench system, one lateral shall be required per trench; for a bed system, up to 3 laterals may be used. Laterals shall extend to within 6 inches of the end of the bed or trench. Lateral spacing shall be a maximum of 3 ft. for beds in small mounds only (1-4 bedroom sized system). Pipe diameter will depend upon the length of bed or trenches. The allowable lateral lengths for various size diameter pipes and various hole spacings are given in Appendix A, Exhibit D. The system shall be designed and placed so that the laterals and manifold drain after every dosing. If the mound is downslope of the pumping chamber, the manifold shall be on top of the laterals so the manifold drains, or cross-to-cross construction used. For systems which are to treat a flow of more than 800 gallons per day, the manifold and lateral network must be designed in accordance with Section 906.70. All piping shall be Schedule 40 Polyvinyl Chloride (ASTM Standard D1785/76) or Schedule 40 Acrylonitrile/Butadiene/Styrene (ASTM Standard D1527/77).

b)   Pumping System. The components of the pumping system shall consist of the pumping chamber, pump, pump controls and alarm system as shown in Appendix A, Illustration F. The dosing volume shall be ten times the total lateral pipe void volume or one-fourth the estimated daily sewage flow, whichever is greater. Appendix A, Exhibit F lists the void volumes for various sizes of pipe. The daily volume of sewage shall be determined using Appendix A, Illustration A of the Private Sewage Disposal Code (77 Ill. Adm. Code 905.)

1)   Pumping Chamber Requirements.

A)   Pumping Chamber. Appendix A, Illustration F gives a cross-section of a typical pumping chamber. The volume shall be sufficient to provide the desired dosing volume, space for controls, space for setting the pump on a pedestal, and extra volume for a malfunction and flow-back after pump shuts off. Appendix A, Exhibit G establishes pumping chamber sizes for the various sized systems. Larger tanks may be used, but they may limit the flexibility of adjusting the desired dosing quantity. Sufficient volume must be available to provide for the dose volume, pump pedestal and controls.

B) The pumping chamber shall be waterproof. Waterproofing shall consist of sealing all joints and coating the outside of the tanks. The pumping chamber shall be filled with water after being installed and back filled to prevent the pumping chambers from floating out of position due to hydrostatic pressures, unless the tank is installed in dry soil. A riser pipe shall extend at least 6 in. above the ground surface. All electrical controls shall be mounted outside the tank. The pump disconnect shall be accessible for easy pump removal in the event of pump failure.

2) Pump Selection. The pump shall be a submersible pump designed for corrosive liquids and shall be capable of maintaining at least 2 feet of head at the distal ends of the laterals. The pump switch shall be controlled by a float in the pumping chamber, set so that the required dosing volume is discharged during each pumping cycle. A check valve between the pump and the piping network manifold shall not be allowed.

3) Pump and Alarm Control. The control system for the pumping chamber shall consist of a control for operating the pump and an alarm system to detect when the system is malfunctioning. Pump controls shall be selected which give flexibility in adjusting the on-off depth. Example of acceptable controls are shown in Appendix A, Illustration F. Pump controls shall be adjusted to pump the required dose of sewage plus the volume of sewage which flows back to the pumping chamber after shut-off.

4) Electrical and Alarm System. The alarm system shall consist of an audible and visual alarm in the home or facility building. This system shall be on a circuit separate from the pump. The electrical controls shall be placed outside the pumping chamber.

5) Siphons. Siphons can be designed where sufficient elevation exists between the mound and the siphon chamber. However, the siphon shall be designed to deliver the same flow rate at the same head at the distribution system as a pump system. The distribution system consisting of manifold and laterals shall be designed so that it will drain after each siphon. This shall be accomplished by placing the manifold above the laterals.

Section 906.70   Distribution System (for sewage flows in excess of 800 gallons per day)

a) Design criteria for laterals.

1) The variation in discharge rates from the perforations in any lateral shall not exceed ten percent.

2) The variation in discharge rates between the perforations of any two laterals shall not exceed 15%.

3) The pressure at the distal ends of the lateral shall be at least 2.5 feet of water.

b) Perforations. The perforation requirements of this Section shall be used in place of those of Section 906.40.

1) The perforations shall be spaced uniformly along the laterals and at an interval not to exceed 10 feet.

2) Perforations shall be installed perpendicular to the centerline of the lateral and along the lateral invert.

3) Perforation diameter shall be between 1/4 and 5/8 inches.

4) To facilitate the draining of laterals between dosing cycles, a perforation shall be installed at the distal end of each lateral near the crown of the pipe.

c) Network Configuration

1) The laterals shall be installed in seepage beds. The lateral spacing shall equal the perforation spacing. The perforations of adjacent laterals in the bed shall be staggered.

2) Mounds employing multiple beds may be used. Also, multiple mounds may be employed. If bed elevations are not all equal, then this fact must be considered in the design of the pipe network in order to provide uniform dosing of effluent.

3) Manifold-to-lateral connections shall be made using tee-to-tee construction, with the manifold below the laterals (see Appendix A, Illustration G). If the design is such that the manifold does not drain between dosing cycles, then insulation or some other means shall be provided to prevent freezing. In addition, provisions shall be made for manual draining of the manifold.

4) Two separate distribution networks may be employed, with each network receiving alternate doses of effluent through the use of alternating pumps, valves, or siphons.

5) Siphons or siphon breaks shall be used in networks where the low water level in the pumping chamber is above the lateral inverts.

DEPARTMENT OF PUBLIC HEALTH

NOTICE OF PROPOSED RULES

d) Pumping Chamber

1) Dosing volume. Dosing volume shall be determined by dividing the average daily sewage flow by the dosing frequency for the particular soil type, as is shown in Appendix A, Illustration H. Dosing Volume shall be at least five times the pipe volume of the network. The dosing volume is the amount of liquid pumped or siphoned during each cycle minus the amount which drains back from the system after each dose.

2) Reserve capacity. If a single pump is used, a reserve capacity equal to one day's average sewage flow shall be provided. A reserve capacity is not required if multiple pumps or siphons are used.

3) A high water alarm switch shall be installed 2-3 inches above the pump or siphon activation level. The switch shall be on a circuit separate from the pump controls.

4) The pump or pumps shall be of a submersible type, designed for corrosive liquids. The control switches shall be corrosion resistant. All electrical contacts and relays shall be mounted outside the chamber. Provisions shall be made to prevent gases in the chamber from following the electrical conduits into the control box.

DEPARTMENT OF PUBLIC HEALTH

NOTICE OF PROPOSED RULES

Section 906.ILLUSTRATION A   Plan View of a Mound Utilizing Two Trenches as the Absorption Area

ILLINOIS REGISTER

DEPARTMENT OF PUBLIC HEALTH

NOTICE OF PROPOSED RULES

Section 906.ILLUSTRATION B   Cross-Section of a Mound Using Trenches for the
                             Absorption Area

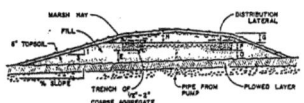

DEPARTMENT OF PUBLIC HEALTH

NOTICE OF PROPOSED RULES

Section 906.ILLUSTRATION C   Plan View of a Mound Utilizing a Bed as the
                             Absorption Area

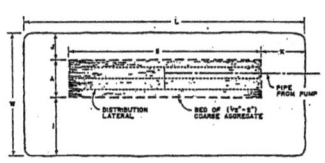

Section 906.ILLUSTRATION D   Cross-Section of a Mound Using a Bed for the
                             Absorption Area

Section 906.ILLUSTRATION E   Mound Distribution System

END MANIFOLD DISTRIBUTION NETWORK

ILLINOIS REGISTER

DEPARTMENT OF PUBLIC HEALTH

NOTICE OF PROPOSED RULES

Section 906.ILLUSTRATION E   Mound Distribution System (continued)

CENTRAL MANIFOLD DISTRIBUTION NETWORK

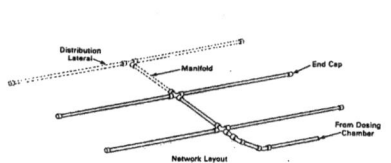

DEPARTMENT OF PUBLIC HEALTH

NOTICE OF PROPOSED RULES

Section 906.ILLUSTRATION F   Typical Pumping Chamber

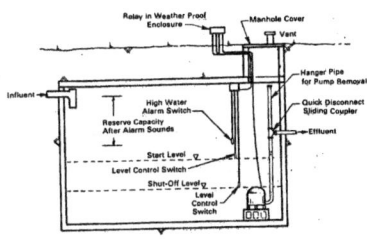

DEPARTMENT OF PUBLIC HEALTH

NOTICE OF PROPOSED RULES

Section 906.ILLUSTRATION G   Tee-To-Tee Lateral/Manifold

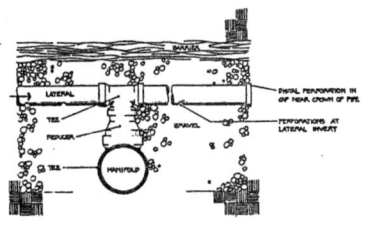

DEPARTMENT OF PUBLIC HEALTH

NOTICE OF PROPOSED RULES

Section 906.ILLUSTRATION H   Dosing Frequencies for Various Soil

Soil Texture	Dosing Frequency
Sand	4 doses/day
Sandy loam	1 dose/day
Loam	Frequency not critical*
Silt loam; silty clay loam	1 dose/day*
Clay	Frequency not critical*

*Long-term resting provided by alternating fields may be desirable.

DEPARTMENT OF PUBLIC HEALTH

NOTICE OF PROPOSED RULES

Section 906.ILLUSTRATION I   Maximum Manifold Length (ft) for Various Manifold Diameters Given the Lateral Discharge Rate and Lateral Spacing

Lateral Discharge Rate		Manifold Diameter - 1 1/4"					Manifold Diameter - 1 1/2"					Manifold Diameter - 2"				
End Manifold	Central Manifold	Lateral Spacing (ft)					Lateral Spacing (ft)					Lateral Spacing (ft)				
		2	4	6	8	10	2	4	6	8	10	2	4	6	8	10
10	5	4	8	6	11	10	10	5	6	8	10	12	16	24	24	30
20	10	4	4	6			4	4	6	8	10	4	8	12	16	20
30	15	2					2	4	6			6	8	6	8	10
40	20											4	4	6	8	10
50	25											2	4	6	8	
60	30											2	4			
70	35											2	4			
80	40											2				
90	45											2				
100	50											2				

Lateral Discharge Rate		Manifold Diameter - 3"					Manifold Diameter - 4"					Manifold Diameter - 6"				
End Manifold	Central Manifold	Lateral Spacing (ft)					Lateral Spacing (ft)					Lateral Spacing (ft)				
		2	4	6	8	10	2	4	6	8	10	2	4	6	8	10
10	5	24	40	48	56	70	42	64	84	96	110	84	136	174	206	240
20	10	16	24	30	32	40	26	40	54	64	70	54	84	108	128	150
30	15	12	16	24	24	30	20	28	36	48	50	42	64	84	96	110
40	20	10	12	18	16	20	16	24	30	32	40	34	52	66	80	90
50	25	8	12	12	16	20	14	20	24	32	40	30	44	60	72	80
60	30	6	8	12	16	20	12	16	24	24	30	26	40	48	64	70
70	35	6	8	12	8	10	10	16	18	24	30	24	36	48	56	60
80	40	6	8	6	8	10	10	12	18	16	20	22	32	42	48	60
90	45	4	8	6	8	10	8	12	16	16	20	20	28	42	48	50
100	50	4	4	6	8	10	8	12	12	16	20	18	28	36	40	50
110	55	4	4	6	8	10	8	12	12	16	20	16	24	36	40	40
120	60	4	4	8	8	10	6	8	12	16	10	16	24	30	32	40
130	65	4	4	6	8	10	6	8	12	16	10	14	24	30	32	40
140	70	2	4	6	8		6	8	12	8	10	14	20	24	32	40
150	75	2	4	6			6	8	12	8	10	14	20	24	32	30
160	80	2	4	6			6	8	6	8	10	12	20	24	32	30
170	85	2	4	6			4	8	6	8	10	12	20	24	28	30
180	90	2	4				4	8	6	8	10	12	16	24	24	30
190	95	2	4				4	8	6	8	10	10	16	18	24	30
200	100	2	4				4	4	6	8	10	10	16	18	24	30

DEPARTMENT OF PUBLIC HEALTH

NOTICE OF PROPOSED RULES

Section 906.EXHIBIT A   Soil and Site Factors that Restrict Mound Systems

Restricting Factors:

	Soil Group		
	Slowly Permeable Soils	Permeable Soils With Pervious Bedrock	Permeable Soils With High Water Tables
Percolation rate*	180-360 min.	18-180 min.	18-180 min.
Depth to pervious rock	24 in.	24 in.	24 in.
Depth to high water tables	24 in.	24 in.	24 in.
Minimum depth to impermeable soil layer or rock strata	60 in.	60 in.	60 in.
Depth to 50% by volume rock fragments	24 in.	24 in.	24 in.
Slope	6%	12%b	12%b

*   Percolation test depth at 24 in., 12 in., and 24 in., for slowly permeable, shallow soils and high water table soils, respectively, unless there is a more restrictive horizon above. If perched water is at 24 in., test depth should be held to 16 in.

b   For percolation rate of 18-90 minutes max. slope is 12% and for 18-360 minutes, max. slope is 6%.

DEPARTMENT OF PUBLIC HEALTH

NOTICE OF PROPOSED RULES

Section 906.EXHIBIT B   Fine Aggregate Gradations

Sieve Size

Percent Passing

Grad. No.	3/8	No. 4	No. 8	No. 10	No. 16	No. 40	No. 50	No. 80	No. 100	No. 200
FA 1	100	97±3			65±20		16±13		5±5	
FA 2	100	97±3			65±20		20±10		5±5	
FA 3	100	97±3		80±15		50±20		25±15		3±3
FA 4	100				5±5					
FA 5	100	92±8							20±20	15±15
FA 6		92±8							20±20	5±5
FA 7		100		97±3		75±15		35±10		3±3
FA 8			100			60±20			3±3	2±2
FA 9			100				20±15		5±5	
FA10				100		90±10		60±30		7±7

DEPARTMENT OF PUBLIC HEALTH

NOTICE OF PROPOSED RULES

Section 906.EXHIBIT C   Downslope and Upslope Width Corrections for Mounds on Sloping Sites

Slope %	Downslope (I) Correction Factor	Upslope (J) Correction Factor
0	1.00	1.00
2	1.06	.94
4	1.14	.89
6	1.22	.86
8	1.32	.80
10	1.44	.77
12	1.57	.73

ILLINOIS REGISTER

DEPARTMENT OF PUBLIC HEALTH

NOTICE OF PROPOSED RULES

Section 906.EXHIBIT D Allowable Lateral Lengths (Feet) for Three Pipe Diameters, Three Perforation Sizs, and Two Perforations Spacings (Use Design Method in Section 906.60 if system is to treat flow from more than 4 bedrooms)

Perforation Spacing (in)	Perforation Diameter (in)	Pipe Diameter		
		(1 in)	(1-1/4 in)	(1-1/2 in)
30	3/16	34	52	70
	7/32	30	45	57
	1/4	25	38	50
36	3/16	36	60	75
	7/32	33	51	63
	1/4	27	42	54

DEPARTMENT OF PUBLIC HEALTH

NOTICE OF PROPOSED RULES

Section 906.EXHIBIT E   Dosing Quantity for Various Sized Homes

Home Size No. Bedrooms	Gallons Day	Dosing Quantity* Gal/Dose
1	200	50
2	400	100
3	600	150
4	800	200

*   Each system must be checked to determine if this quantity is at least 10 times the lateral void volume.

DEPARTMENT OF PUBLIC HEALTH

NOTICE OF PROPOSED RULES

DEPARTMENT OF PUBLIC HEALTH

NOTICE OF PROPOSED RULES

Section 906.EXHIBIT F   Void Volume for Various Diameter Pipes

Section 906.EXHIBIT G   Pumping Chamber Sizes for Various Sized Homes

Diameter inch	Volume gal/ft/length
1	.041
1 1/4	.064
1 1/2	.092
2	.164
3	.368
4	.655
6	1.470

Home Size No. Bedrooms	Minimum Pumping Chamber Size Gallons
1	250-500
2	250-500
3	500-750
4	500-750

ILLINOIS REGISTER

DEPARTMENT OF PUBLIC HEALTH

NOTICE OF PROPOSED RULES

Section 906.EXHIBIT H   Perforation Discharge Rates in Gallons per Minute Versus Perforation Diameter and In-Line Pressure

In-Line Pressure (ft)	Perforation Diameter (in)						
	1/4	5/16	3/8	7/16	1/2	9/16	5/8
1.0	0.74	1.15	1.66	2.26	2.95	3.73	4.60
1.5	0.90	1.41	2.03	2.76	3.61	4.57	5.64
2.0	1.17	1.82	2.62	3.57	4.66	5.90	7.28
3.0	1.28	1.99	2.87	3.91	5.10	6.46	7.97
3.5	1.38	2.15	3.10	4.22	5.51	6.98	8.61
4.0	1.47	2.30	3.31	4.51	5.89	7.46	9.21
4.5	1.56	2.44	3.52	4.79	6.25	7.91	9.77
5.0	1.65	2.57	3.71	5.04	6.59	8.34	10.29

DEPARTMENT OF PUBLIC HEALTH

NOTICE OF PROPOSED RULES

Section 906.EXHIBIT I   Friction Loss in Schedule 40 Plastic Pipe

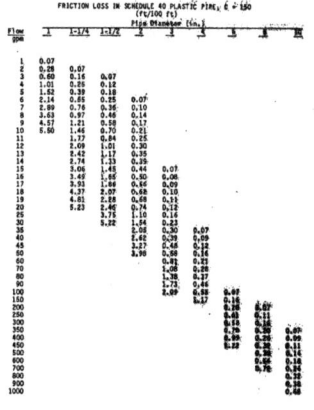

DEPARTMENT OF TRANSPORTATION

NOTICE OF PROPOSED AMENDMENTS

1) Heading of Part: Disadvantaged, Minority and Woman-Owned
Businesses

2) Code Citation: 92 Ill. Adm. Code   10

3) Section Numbers: Proposed Action:

        10.30   Amendment
        10.40   Amendment
        10.50   Amendment
        10.60   Amendment
        10.70   Amendment
        10.80   Amendment

4) Statutory Authority: Ill. Rev. Stat. 1987, ch. 121, pars.
3-101, 3-103, and 4-201.1; and Ill.
Rev.Stat. 1987, ch. 127, par. 132.5

5) A complete description of the subjects and issues involved:

By this rulemaking, the Department proposes to increase the
length of time a firm must remain out of the DBE program
before reapplying for certification eligibility. The
Department has determined that the original ninety day time
limit, imposed by the Department to provide firms with an
opportunity to correct deficiencies not in compliance with
the eligibility standards, is insufficient time for the
firm to make significant changes which would render the
firm eligible for certification. Upon adoption of this
rule, firms which are denied recertification or decertified
will have one hundred-eighty calendar days in which to
reapply and correct deficiencies detailed in the Notice of
Denial.

There may be a negative economic effect on firms regulated
by the rule, however, the approximate economic impact is
unknown. During the 180-day period of ineligibility
(currently 90 days), a firm may still participate as a
subcontractor on IDOT projects, but any services performed
cannot be applied toward attainment of the DBE contract
goal. The amount of work a firm might lose as a result of
not having DBE certification is impossible to determine due
to the variables that exist in the industry.

6) Will this proposed rulemaking replace an emergency rule
currently in effect? No

DEPARTMENT OF TRANSPORTATION

NOTICE OF PROPOSED AMENDMENTS

7) Does this rulemaking contain an automatic repeal date? No

8) Does this proposed amendment contain incorporations by
reference? These conform to Section 6.02(a) of the
Illinois Administrative Procedure Act.

9) Are there any other amendments pending on this Part? No

10) Statement of Statewide Policy Objectives: This rule does
not affect units of local government.

11) Time, Place, and Manner in which interested persons may
comment on this proposed rulemaking:

Any interested party may submit written comments or
arguments concerning this proposed rule. Written
submissions shall be filed with:

        Mr. S. Rowan Woolfolk, Bureau Chief
        Bureau of Small Business Enterprises
        Department of Transportation
        Office of Finance and Administration
        2300 South Dirksen Parkway, Rm. 338
        Springfield, Illinois 62764
        (217) 785-5947

Comments received within thirty days of the date of
publication of this Illinois Register will be considered.
Comments received after that time will be considered, time
permitting.

12) Initial Regulatory Flexibility Analysis:

A) Date rule was submitted to D.C.C.A.: November 3, 1988

B) Types of small businesses affected: This amendment
will affect those firms which provide any of the
construction, engineering or material supplier
services listed in the categories in the Certification
Application form. This amendment will affect a
fraction of firms currently certified with the
Department. Of the 450 certified firms, it is
impossible to determine the number of companies which
will be denied recertification or which will be
decertified and will, therefore, be unable to be
counted for goal credit under this program.

C) Reporting, bookkeeping or other procedures required
   for compliance: Reporting requirements for the DBE/WBE
   business owner remain the same. DBE/WBE applicants
   and participants must annually submit a recertification application to IDOT for program eligibility, in
   accordance with the federal regulation 49 CFR 23.53.

D) Types of professional skills necessary for compliance:
   No new professional skills are necessary for
   compliance.

The full text of the Proposed Amendments begin on the next page:

DEPARTMENT OF TRANSPORTATION

NOTICE OF PROPOSED AMENDMENTS

TITLE 92: TRANSPORTATION
CHAPTER I: DEPARTMENT OF TRANSPORTATION
SUBCHAPTER a: GENERAL

PART 10
DISADVANTAGED, MINORITY AND WOMAN-OWNED BUSINESSES

Section
10.10   Purpose
10.20   Incorporation By Reference of Federal Regulations
10.30   Definitions
10.40   Eligibility Standards
10.50   Certification
10.60   Recertification
10.70   Decertification
10.80   Challenge

AUTHORITY: Implementing and authorized by Section 5 of the Illinois
Purchasing Act (Ill. Rev. Stat. 1987, ch. 127, par. 132.5) and by Sections
3-101, 3-103, and 4-201.1 of the Illinois Highway Code (Ill. Rev. Stat.
1987, ch. 121, pars. 3-101, 3-103 and 4-201.1).

SOURCE: Adopted at 11 Ill. Reg. 13645, effective August 3, 1987; amended
at __ Ill. Reg. _____, effective _____.

Section 10.30 Definitions

As used in this Part:

"Applicant" means a concern that submits an application for
certification or recertification as a DBE, MBE or WBE.

"Bureau" means the Bureau of Small Business Enterprises of the
Illinois Department of Transportation.

"Bureau Chief" means the Department's Bureau Chief of the Bureau of
Small Business Enterprises or his designee.

"Certification Analyst" means an employee of the Illinois
Department of Transportation whose duties include an in-depth
examination of certification applications for disadvantaged,
minority and woman-owned businesses.

"Certification Manager" means the Manager of the Certification
Section of the Bureau of Small Business Enterprises of the Illinois
Department of Transportation or his designee.

"Certification Review Committee" means the Illinois Department of

DEPARTMENT OF TRANSPORTATION

NOTICE OF PROPOSED AMENDMENTS

Transportation's Committee on Disadvantaged, Minority, and Woman-Owned Business Certification. The Bureau Chief, ex officio, is clerk of the Certification Review Committee. Other members include: the Director of the Office of Finance and Administration or designee, the Director of Highways or designee, the Director of the Office of Planning and Programming or designee, the Director of the Division of Aeronautics or designee, the District Engineer or designee and the Manager, Certification Section, Bureau of Small Business Enterprises.

"Concern" means any business entity organized for profit and includes an individual sole proprietor, partnership without limited partners, corporation or professional association.

"Contract" shall have the meaning defined in 49 CFR 23.5 which is incorporated by reference at Section 10.20.

"Contractor" shall have the meaning defined in 49 CFR 23.5 which is incorporated by reference at Section 10.20.

"Department" means the Illinois Department of Transportation.

"Disadvantaged business" or "DBE" shall have the meaning defined in 49 CFR 23.62 which is incorporated by reference at Section 10.20.

~~"Field examination" means the observation of the applicant in its normal surroundings by such means as visual observation, the posing of verbal questions, and an ascertainment of the general pattern of operations of the concern.~~

"Joint venture" shall have the meaning defined in 49 CFR 23.5 and 49 CFR 25, Schedule B which are incorporated by reference at Section 10.20.

"Management Committee" means the Bureau Chief, the Certification Manager, the Manager of the Policy and Support Services Section and the Manager of the Labor-EEO & DBE-WBE Contract Compliance Section of the Bureau of Small Business Enterprises of the Illinois Department of Transportation.

"Minority" shall have the meaning defined in 49 CFR 23.5 which is incorporated by reference at Section 10.20.

"Minority business enterprise" or "MBE" shall have the meaning defined in 49 CFR 23.5 which is incorporated by reference at Section 10.20.

DEPARTMENT OF TRANSPORTATION

NOTICE OF PROPOSED AMENDMENTS

"On-site visit" means the observation of the applicant in its normal surroundings by such means as visual observation, the posing of verbal questions, and an ascertainment of the general pattern of operations of the concern.

"Program" means a Disadvantaged, Minority and Woman-Owned Business Enterprise Program adopted pursuant to 49 CFR 23.41 which is incorporated by reference at Section 10.20.

"Secretary" means the Secretary of the Illinois Department of Transportation or his designee.

"Small business concern" shall have the meaning defined in 49 CFR 23.62 which is incorporated by reference at Section 10.20.

"Socially and economically disadvantaged individuals" shall have the meaning defined in 49 CFR 23.62 and 49 CFR 23, Subpart D, Appendix C which are incorporated by reference at Section 10.20.

"USDOT departmental element" shall have the meaning defined as "departmental element" in 49 CFR 23.5 which is incorporated by reference at Section 10.20.

"Woman-owned business" or "WBE" means a small business concern which is at least 51 per centum owned by one or more women or, in the case of a publicly owned business, at least 51 per centum of the stock of which is owned by one or more women, and whose management and daily business operations are controlled by one or more of the women owners.

(Source: Amended at ___ Ill. Reg. _____, effective _____)

Section 10.40 Eligibility Standards

a) Only concerns and joint ventures certified by the Department as disadvantaged, minority or woman-owned are eligible to be counted toward the applicable disadvantaged, minority or woman-owned business goals established in contracts let by the Department. To ensure that this Part benefits only qualified applicants, the eligibility standards shall be used by the Department to determine whether an applicant is owned and controlled by one or more minorities in the case of an MBE, women in the case of a WBE, or socially and economically disadvantaged individuals in the case of a DBE. The determination of eligibility for certification or recertification shall be governed by the eligibility standards. An applicant for certification or recertification shall prove that it satisfies the eligibility standards. For example, an individual applying for certification is required to submit documentation verifying ethnicity, including but not limited to, a birth certificate, tribal certificate, Bureau of Indian Affairs card, and Armed Services Discharge Papers. An applicant for certification in accordance with either Section 10.50(h)(1), 10.60(k)(1) or 10.70(f)(1), in addition to proving that it satisfies all eligibility standards, shall prove that it has corrected all deficiencies listed in the Notice of Denial or Decertification. These standards of eligibility must be met before an applicant can be certified. If a firm fails to meet one of the eligibility standards, no further consideration need be given to the application, and the certification shall be denied.

1) An applicant shall be certified or recertified as a DBE, in accordance with the procedures set forth in Sections 10.50 and 10.60, if the applicant meets the definition of a DBE as determined by the eligibility standards.

2) An applicant shall be certified or recertified as an MBE, in accordance with the procedures set forth in Sections 10.50 and 10.60, if the applicant meets the definition of an MBE as determined by the eligibility standards.

3) An applicant shall be certified or recertified as a WBE, in accordance with the procedures set forth in Section 10.50 and 10.60, if the applicant meets the definition of a WBE as determined by the eligibility standards.

b) The Department adopts by reference the An applicant shall meet all eligibility standards set forth in 49 CFR 23.53(a)(1) through (a)(6) inclusive and 49 CFR 23.53(c) and (d) which are incorporated by reference at Section 10.20.

c) An applicant whose principal place of business is located in a state other than Illinois shall be certified by that state in accordance with its program prior to certification by the Department.

d) An applicant shall possess all necessary, valid licenses, operating authority or certification of authority to do business in this state prior to certification by the Department.

e) In accordance with the standards set forth in 49 CFR 23.53(a)(2), the Department shall give consideration to the following circumstances in determining eligibility in this Part:

1) Applicants which are newly formed or whose ownership or control has changed within two years prior to the application for certification shall be examined to determine if the firm meets the criteria for an independent business and that the ownership is not merely pro forma.

2) A previous or continuing employer-employee relationship between or among present owners of an applicant shall be examined to ensure that the eligible owner has the management responsibility, control and capability provided for in the eligibility standards.

3) Any relationship between an applicant and a business, concern, firm or individual which is not eligible for certification shall be examined to determine if the relationship conflicts with the ownership and control requirements of the eligibility standards. Such relationships include but are not limited to the following:

A) shared employees;

B) shared or leased equipment;

C) shared or leased office space;

D) shared or leased storage space or equipment storage yards;

E) financial investment, loans or assistance;

F) interlocking management; and

G) management or technical services.

4) Applicants which are not operational shall not be eligible for certification pursuant to this Part. In order to be considered operational, a concern shall be established in business and shall demonstrate the actual performance, control, management and supervision of work in the categories of work for which certification is sought or the ability and the expertise to perform, control, manage and supervise the work in the categories of work for which certification is sought.

(Source: Amended at ___ Ill. Reg. _____, effective _____)

Section 10.50 Certification

DEPARTMENT OF TRANSPORTATION

NOTICE OF PROPOSED AMENDMENTS

a) Any applicant which desires certification as a DBE, MBE or WBE under this Part shall file with the Certification Section of the Bureau of Small Business Enterprises a Certification Application in a form approved by the appropriate USDOT departmental element, together with all supporting information, including but not limited to, assumed name certificates, partnership agreements, corporate bylaws and signed loan agreements, which are required by the Certification Application and 49 CFR 23, Schedule A, incorporated by reference herein. Applicants which desire certification as a joint venture under this Part shall file with the Certification Section of the bBureau, in addition to the Certification Application, the Joint Venture Certification Application in a form approved by the appropriate USDOT departmental element, together with all supporting information, including but not limited to, capital contribution schedules, profit/loss allocation between the ventures, work resumes and separate individual capital accounts, which are required by the Joint Venture Certification Application and 49 CFR 23, Schedule B, incorporated by reference herein. The applications may be obtained from the Bureau. All portions of the appropriate applications shall be completed, and all required attachments must be submitted before a determination of eligibility will be made.

b) The Certification Section shall date and time-stamp the application when received and assign it to a Certification Analyst for examination and review. The Certification Analyst will ensure that all portions of the application have been completed or marked not applicable and that all required attachments have been submitted. The applicant will be requested to supply missing information or attachments.

c) When the Certification Analyst verifies that the application is complete, a desk an audit will be conducted on the eligibility of the applicant.

    1) The applicant may be requested to supply additional information or documentation to verify the contents of the application or to aid in the eligibility determination. Examples of such information and documentation include but are not limited to the following:

        A) evidence of equity contribution, such as personal bank account statement, loan documents and/or copy of equity contribution check,

        B) evidence of required license/authority to transact

DEPARTMENT OF TRANSPORTATION

NOTICE OF PROPOSED AMENDMENTS

        business in the State of Illinois,

        C) bank signature card,

        D) bank resolution,

        E) income tax records, and

        F) evidence of stock transfer(s).

    2) The applicant shall supply additional information or documentation which is requested by the Certification Analyst in order to make an eligibility determination. An applicant which does not supply such additional information or documentation shall not be certified.

d) The Certification Analyst shall arrange for a field-examination of the applicant when questions remain unanswered after the certification desk audit and cannot be resolved by written correspondence or telephone contact an on-site visit to the offices of the applicant and to any job sites on which the applicant is working at the time of the audit. The Certification Analyst shall further arrange for the personal interview of the principal owners of the applicant.

e) Upon completion of the desk audit and any field examination, the Certification Analyst shall draft an audit determination. The audit determination shall set forth the findings and conclusions of the desk audit and any field examination and shall make a recommendation either to certify or not certify the applicant. The Certification Analyst shall be governed by the standards for eligibility set forth in Section 10.40 of this Part.

f) The Management Committee shall render a decision regarding certification of the applicant based upon the audit determination and the record assembled by the Certification Analyst, but the Management Committee shall not be required to follow the Certification Analyst's recommendation. Applicants shall not be certified unless the Management Committee finds that the audit determination and record establish that the applicant meets the eligibility standards set forth in Section 10.40 of this Part. Applicants shall not be denied certification unless the Management Committee finds that the applicant has not met its burden of establishing compliance with the eligibility standards. An audit determination upon which a finding cannot be made shall be returned to the Certification Section with a statement of deficiencies.

DEPARTMENT OF TRANSPORTATION

NOTICE OF PROPOSED AMENDMENTS

g) A letter of approval and certificate shall be mailed by the
    Certification Manager to applicants granted certification. The
    Certificate of DBE/MBE/WBE Certification is effective for a
    period of one year from the date of the approval letter. Joint
    venture certification is effective for specific contracts only.
    Certificates shall remain the property of the Department.

h) A Notice of Denial, which contains a statement of the reasons why
    the applicant has not been certified and the provision(s) of the
    eligibility standards which support the denial, shall be mailed
    by the Certification Manager to applicants denied certification.
    Service shall be by certified mail, return receipt requested.
    Except as provided in 49 CFR 23.55, the denial of certification
    shall be final for all contracts being let at the time of the
    denial. Applicants denied certification may:

    1) Correct deficiencies listed in the Notice of Denial and
        reapply for certification after the passage of ~~ninety~~ one
        hundred-eighty calendar days from receipt of the Notice of
        Denial by filing a Certification Application; or

    2) File an appeal in writing, signed and dated, with the
        United States Department of Transportation within one
        hundred-eighty calendar days from the date of the
        Department's Notice of Denial.

i) The Bureau shall maintain a DBE/MBE/WBE Directory of certified
    concerns. A joint venture certified for a particular contract
    will not be listed in the Directory.

j) ~~At any time there is a change in the ownership or control of a
    certified DBE, MBE or WBE, the certification lapses and the
    concern shall be deleted from the DBE/MBE/WBE Directory. A
    certified DBE, MBE or WBE which has changed its ownership or
    control shall notify the Certification Section of the Bureau
    without delay and shall surrender its Certificate. The concern
    which has surrendered its Certificate may file a new Certifica-
    tion Application.~~ Once certified, a concern is eligible to be
    counted toward the applicable disadvantaged, minority or woman-
    owned business goals established in contracts let or administered
    by the Department. Certification does not guarantee any contract
    or subcontract. As a condition of certification, a concern will
    be required to assure on all contracts or subcontracts, for which
    the concern will be counted toward a goal, that it will perform a
    commercially useful function in the work of the contract. The
    concern is considered to perform a commercially useful function
    when it is responsible for a distinct element of the work of

DEPARTMENT OF TRANSPORTATION

NOTICE OF PROPOSED AMENDMENTS

    a contract and carrying out its responsibilities by actually
    performing, managing and supervising the work involved. Failure
    to perform a commercially useful function is a violation of the
    eligibility standards.

k) At any time there is a change in the ownership or control of a
    certified DBE, MBE or WBE, the concern shall be deleted from the
    DBE/MBE/WBE Directory. A certified DBE, MBE or WBE which has
    changed its ownership or control shall notify the Certification
    Section of the Bureau without delay and shall surrender its
    Certificate. The concern which has surrendered its Certificate may file a
    new Certification Application.

(Source: Amended at __ Ill. Reg. _____, effective _____)

Section 10.60 Recertification

a) Once certified, any concern for which there has been no change in
    ownership or control and which desires to remain certified as a
    DBE, MBE or WBE under this Part shall annually file with the
    Certification Section of the Bureau a Recertification Application
    in a form approved by the appropriate USDOT departmental element,
    together with all supporting information required by the applica-
    tion and 49 CFR 23, Schedule A, incorporated by reference herein.
    The application may be obtained from the Bureau. All portions of
    the application shall be completed, and all required attachments,
    including but not limited to, current financial statements, copies
    of current shareholder meeting minutes and work resumes must be
    submitted before a determination of eligibility for recertifica-
    tion can be made. Joint ventures shall not be recertified.

b) The certification of a concern which does not file a Recertifi-
    cation Application prior to the expiration of its period of certi-
    fication will lapse and the concern will be deleted from the
    DBE/MBE/WBE Directory. The Department shall allow a five business
    day period of grace after the expiration during which time a
    Recertification Application will be accepted. The certifica-
    tion of a DBE, MBE or WBE that has timely filed a Recertifica-
    tion Application shall continue pending the consideration of the
    renewal.

c) The Certification Section shall date and time-stamp the applica-
    tion when received and assign it to a Certification Analyst for
    examination and review. The Certification Analyst will ensure
    that all portions of the application have been completed or marked
    not applicable and that all required attachments have been submit-

ted. The applicant will be requested to supply missing information or attachments.

d) When the Certification Analyst verifies that the Recertification
Application is complete, ~a~ ~desk~ an audit will be conducted on the
eligibility of the applicant.

1) The applicant may be requested to supply additional information or documentation (see Section 10.50(c)(1)) to verify
the contents of the application or to aid in the eligibility
determination.

2) The applicant shall supply additional information or documentation which is requested by the Certification Analyst
in order to make an eligibility determination. An applicant
which does not supply such additional information or documentation shall not be recertified.

e) The Certification Analyst shall arrange for ~a~ ~field~ ~examination~
~of~ an on-site visit to the applicant when questions remain
unanswered after the ~recertification~ ~desk~ audit and cannot be
resolved by written correspondence or telephone contact.

f) Upon completion of the ~desk~ audit ~and~ ~any~ ~field~ ~examination,~ the
Certification Analyst shall draft an audit determination. The
audit determination shall set forth the findings and conclusions
of the ~desk~ audit ~and~ ~any~ ~field~ ~examination~ and shall make a
recommendation either to recertify or not recertify the applicant.
The Certification Analyst shall be governed by the standards for
eligibility set forth in Section 10.40 of this Part.

g) The Management Committee shall render a decision regarding
recertification of the applicant based upon the audit determination and the record assembled by the Certification Analyst, but
the Management Committee shall not be required to follow the
Certification Analyst's recommendation. Applicants shall not be
recertified unless the Management Committee finds that the audit
determination and record establish that the applicant meets the
eligibility standards of Section 10.40 or that no changes have
occurred since the applicant's last certification or recertification. Applicants shall not be denied recertification unless the
Management Committee finds that the applicant has not met its
burden of establishing compliance with the eligibility standards.
An audit determination upon which a finding cannot be made shall
be returned to the Certification Section with a statement of
deficiencies.

h) A letter of approval and certificate shall be mailed by the
Certification Manager to applicants granted recertification.
DBE/MBE/WBE recertification is effective one year from the date
of the approval letter. Certificates shall remain the property
of the Department.

i) A Notice of Denial, which contains a statement of the reasons why
the applicant has not been recertified and the provision(s) of
the eligibility standards which support the denial, shall be
mailed by the Certification Manager to applicants denied recertification. Service shall be by certified mail, return receipt
requested. The denial of recertification shall be final for all
contracts being let at the time of the denial unless the applicant
files a Request for Review by the Certification Review Committee.

j) An applicant denied recertification may file a written Request
for Review by the Certification Review Committee within twenty
business days of receipt of the Notice of Denial. The Request
for Review shall be filed with the Bureau Chief. If the applicant
does not file a Request for Review within twenty business days of
receipt of the Notice of Denial, then the applicant shall be
deemed to have waived its opportunity to file a Request for
Review. The filing of the Request shall stay the effect of the
Notice of Denial pending determination of the review.

1) The Request for Review shall detail the assailed findings,
indicate the error(s) made in the application of the eligibility standards and shall be confined to factual and legal
issues essential to the ultimate and just determination of
the review. The Request shall not exceed ten pages in
length, excluding a separate preface and summary of the
argument which shall not exceed one page. A reply to the
Request shall be filed by the Certification Manager within
ten business days of receipt of the Request and shall be
restricted to the same requirements as to length and format.

2) The decision of the Certification Review Committee shall be
made on the record of the application including all submissions, the audit determination and the Notice of Denial.
No new or additional documentation or information shall be
considered by the Certification Review Committee without a
showing by the party presenting such documentation or
information that it was not available or, through due
diligence, could not have been made available. When there
is insufficient information to render a decision and/or
clarify information submitted in the Request for Review,
the Certification Review Committee, upon fifteen calendar

days notice to the applicant and the Certification Manager, may schedule a meeting at a time and date convenient to all parties, at which time both parties may make oral presentations addressing the issues in the Request for Review.

3)   If the Certification Review Committee does not agree with the audit recommendation to deny recertification and believes the eligibility standards contained in 49 CFR 23 have been met, the recommendation for denial of recertification will be reversed. The file shall be returned to the Certification Manager with directions to recertify the applicant in accordance with Section 10.60(h).

4)   If the Certification Review Committee affirms the denial of recertification, then the decision of the Certification Review Committee affirming the Notice of Denial shall be mailed to the applicant within ten business days. Service shall be by certified mail, return receipt requested.

k)   Except as provided in 49 CFR 23.55, the denial of recertification shall be final for all contracts being let at the time of the denial. Applicants denied recertification may do either one of the following:

1)   Correct deficiencies listed in the Notice of Denial and reapply for certification after the passage of ninety one hundred-eighty calendar days from the date of the Certification Review Committee decision by filing a Certification Application; or

2)   File an appeal in writing, signed and dated, with the United States Department of Transportation within one hundred-eighty calendar days from the date of the Certification Review Committee decision.

1)   At any time there is a change in the ownership or control of a certified DBE, MBE or WBE, the certification lapses and the applicant shall be deleted from the DBE/MBE/WBE Directory. A certified DBE, MBE or WBE which has changed its ownership or control shall notify the Certification Section of the Bureau without delay and shall surrender its Certificate. The concern which has surrendered its certificate may file a new Certification Application.

(Source: Amended at ___ Ill. Reg. _____, effective _____)

Section 10.70 Decertification

a)   If, as a result of random monitoring, field examinations on-site reviews, complaints and/or contact with Department personnel, the Certification Manager obtains any information evidencing that:

1)   Aa certified DBE, MBE, WBE or joint venture does not meet the eligibility standards;

2)   Aa false statement was made in a Certification Application or Recertification Application;

3)   Aa certified DBE, MBE, WBE or joint venture's size, organization, ownership or control has changed, resulting in a violation of the eligibility standards;

4)   Aa certified DBE, MBE, WBE or joint venture has gone out of business; or

5)   Tthe certified DBE, MBE, WBE or joint venture is engaging in any activity prohibited by this Part or by 49 CFR 23 including but not limited to the failure to perform a commercially useful function on any contract or subcontract;

the Certification Manager shall begin the decertification process.

b)   Any certified DBE, MBE, WBE or joint venture which the Certification Manager proposes to decertify, pursuant to this Part, shall be examined in the same manner as an applicant for certification in accordance with the standards set forth in Section 10.50 of this Part. The Certification Manager shall notify the certified concern of his/her intention to examine the certification and the reasons therefor.

c)   The concern so notified shall supply all requested information to the Certification Section. Any concern which does not supply such additional information or documentation as requested shall be decertified.

d)   Following the examination of the concern, the Certification Analyst shall draft an audit determination. The audit determination shall set forth findings and conclusions of the desk audit and any field examination and shall make a recommendation as to whether or not to decertify. The Management Committee shall render a decision based upon the audit determination and the supporting record, but the Management Committee shall not be required to follow the Certification Analyst's recommendation. The DBE, MBE or WBE shall not be decertified unless the Management Committee finds that the audit determination and the supporting record establish that the concern does not meet the eligibility standards set forth in Section 10.40 of this Part, and that cause for decertification exists.

1) If the recommendation is not to decertify, then the DBE, MBE, or WBE shall be notified that based upon the information obtained through the investigation, it will not be decertified.

2) If the decision is to decertify, then a Notice of Decertification shall be sent to the DBE, MBE or WBE by certified mail, return receipt requested. The Notice shall include:

A) ~~An~~ statement of the reasons for decertification;

B) ~~T~~the provisions of 49 CFR 23 and this Part which support decertification; and,

C) ~~An~~ statement that the Notice of Decertification is final unless a review is requested.

e) A DBE, MBE or WBE who receives a Notice of Decertification may file a written Request for Review by the Certification Review Committee within twenty business days of receipt of the Notice of Decertification. The Request for Review shall be filed with the Bureau Chief. If the DBE, MBE or WBE does not file a Request for Review within twenty business days of receipt of the Notice of Decertification, then the DBE, MBE or WBE shall be deemed to have waived its opportunity to file a Request for Review. The filing of the Request shall stay the effect of the Notice of Decertification pending determination of the review.

1) The Request for Review shall detail the assailed findings, indicate the error(s) made in the application of the standards listed under Section 10.70(a) and shall be confined to factual and legal issues essential to the ultimate and just determination of the review. The Request shall not exceed ten pages in length, excluding a separate preface and summary of the argument which shall not exceed one page. A reply to the Request shall be filed by the Certification Manager within ten business days of receipt of the Request and shall be restricted to the same requirements as to length and format.

2) The decision of the Certification Review Committee shall be made on the record of the application including all submissions, the audit determination and the Notice of Decerti-

fication. No new or additional documentation or information shall be considered by the Certification Review Committee without a showing by the party presenting such documentation or information that it was not available or, through due diligence, could not have been made available. When there is insufficient information to render a decision and/or clarify information submitted in the Request for Review, the Certification Review Committee, upon fifteen calendar days notice to the applicant and the Certification Manager, may schedule a meeting at a time and date convenient to all parties, at which time both parties may make oral presentations addressing the issues in the Request for Review.

3) If the Certification Review Committee does not agree with the audit recommendation to decertify and believes the eligibility standards contained in 49 CFR 23 have been met, the recommendation for decertification will be reversed. The file shall be returned to the Certification Manager with directions not to decertify the DBE, MBE or WBE in accordance with Section 10.70(d)(1).

4) If the Certification Review Committee affirms the decision to decertify, then the decision of the Certification Review Committee affirming the Notice of Decertification shall be mailed to the DBE, MBE or WBE. Service shall be by certified mail, return receipt requested.

5) Once the Certification Review Committee has made a final decision to decertify, that determination goes into effect immediately with respect to program participation, and the concern shall be removed from the DBE/MBE/WBE Directory. Except as provided in 49 CFR 23.55, the decertification by the Certification Review Committee shall be final.

f) Any concern believing that it has wrongly been decertified as a disadvantaged, minority, woman-owned business or joint venture by the Department may do either one of the following:

1) Correct deficiencies listed in the Notice of Decertification and reapply for certification after the passage of ~~ninety~~ one hundred-eighty calendar days from the date of the Certification Review Committee decision by filing a Certification Application; or

2) File an appeal in writing, signed and dated, with the United States Department of Transportation within one hundred-

DEPARTMENT OF TRANSPORTATION

NOTICE OF PROPOSED AMENDMENTS

eighty calendar days after the date of the final Certification Review Committee decision.

(Source: Amended at __ Ill. Reg. _____, effective _____)

Section 10.80 Challenge

a) Any third party may challenge the socially and economically disadvantaged status of any individual presumed to be socially and economically disadvantaged pursuant to 49 CFR 23.62, provided that the challenged individual is an owner of a concern certified by or seeking certification from the Department as a DBE. Only a signed, written challenge which includes all information available to the challenging party shall be accepted by the Certification Manager. An individual who has a current certification pursuant to Section 8(a) of the Small Business Act, 15 U.S.C. 687(a), may not be challenged. During the pendency of a challenge, the presumption that the challenged party is a socially and economically disadvantaged individual shall remain in effect.

b) The Certification Manager shall evaluate the information provided by the challenging party to determine whether the challenged party is in fact not socially and economically disadvantaged in accordance with 49 CFR 23.62 and 49 CFR 23, Subpart D, Appendix C.

   1) Should the Certification Manager determine the information presented in is insufficient to substantiate that the challenged party is not socially and economically disadvantaged, the Certification Manager shall so inform the challenging party in writing. This decision is final and terminates the proceeding.

   2) Should the Certification Manager determine the information presented is sufficient to substantiate that the challenged party is not socially and economically disadvantaged, the Certification Manager shall begin a proceeding as herein provided.

      A) The Certification Manager shall serve the challenged party with a written Notice of Challenge. Service shall be by certified mail, return receipt requested. The Notice shall include:

         i) As a statement that the status of a socially and economically disadvantaged individual has been challenged;

DEPARTMENT OF TRANSPORTATION

NOTICE OF PROPOSED AMENDMENTS

         ii) Identification of the challenging party;

         iii) A summary of the grounds for the challenge;

         iv) Identification of all information or documents submitted in support of the challenge; and,

         v) An statement that the challenged party shall have fifteen business days after receipt within which to respond to the challenge, providing the Certification Manager with information sufficient to permit evaluation of the socially and economically disadvantaged status of the individual. Failure to provide the requested information within the specified time shall result in decertification or a denial of certification.

B) The Certification Manager shall evaluate the available information in accordance with the socially and economically disadvantaged standards referenced in Section 10.30 of this Part and make a proposed determination of whether the challenged party meets the standard.

C) The Certification Manager shall notify both parties of this proposed determination in writing, setting forth the reasons for the proposal. The Certification Manager shall provide an opportunity to the parties for a meeting at which the parties shall have the opportunity to respond to this proposed determination in writing and in person. If the request for a meeting is not filed within twenty business days of receipt of the proposed determination, the Certification Manager shall make a final determination based on the available information.

D) Upon receipt by the Certification Manager of the written request for a meeting, the Certification Manager shall schedule a meeting within forty-five days of receipt of the request for a meeting. The meeting shall be informal and no rules of evidence shall apply. There shall be no presentation of witnesses and no cross-examination. The Certification Manager shall give the challenged and challenging parties twenty business days notice of the meeting date.

DEPARTMENT OF TRANSPORTATION

NOTICE OF PROPOSED AMENDMENTS

E) The Certification Manager shall inform the parties in writing of the final determination, setting forth the reasons for the decision.

F) A party which is challenged and found not to be socially and economically disadvantaged under this Section may file a written Request for Review by the Certification Review Committee within twenty business days of receipt of the decision of the Certification Manager. The Request for Review shall be filed with the Bureau Chief. If the party does not file a Request for Review within twenty business days of receipt of the decision of the Certification Manager, then the party shall be deemed to have waived its opportunity to file a Request for Review. The filing of the Request shall stay the effect of the notification that the challenged party is not socially and economically disadvantaged pending determination of the review.

  ~~+~~ i) The Request for Review shall detail the assailed findings, indicate the error(s) made in the application of 49 CFR 23.62 and shall be confined to factual and legal issues essential to the ultimate and just determination of the review. The Request shall not exceed ten pages in length, excluding a separate preface and summary of the argument which shall not exceed one page. A reply to the Request shall be filed by the Certification Manager within ten business days of receipt of the Request and shall be restricted to the same requirements as to length and format.

  ~~2~~ ii) The decision of the Certification Review Committee shall be made on the record of the €challenge. No new or additional documentation or information shall be considered by the Certification Review Committee without a showing by the party presenting such documentation or information that it was not available or, through due diligence, could not have been made available. When there is insufficient information to render a decision and/or clarify information submitted in the Request for Review, the Certification Review Committee, upon fifteen calendar days notice to the applicant and the

DEPARTMENT OF TRANSPORTATION

NOTICE OF PROPOSED AMENDMENTS

    Certification Manager, may schedule a meeting at a time and date convenient to all parties, at which time both parties may make oral presentations addressing the issues in the Request for Review.

  ~~5~~ iii) If the Certification Review Committee believes the information reviewed is sufficient to reverse the decision of the Certification Manager, then the file shall be returned to the Certification Manager with directions to allow the party's socially and economically disadvantaged status to stand.

  ~~4~~ iv) If the Certification Review Committee believes the information reviewed is sufficient to affirm the decision that the challenged party is not socially and economically disadvantaged, then the decision of the Certification Review Committee affirming the final determination shall be mailed to the challenged party. Service shall be by certified mail, return receipt requested.

G) Once the Certification Review Committee has made a final decision on a challenge matter, that determination goes into effect immediately with respect to the Department's contracts. Except as provided in 49 CFR 23.55, the decision by the Certification Review Committee shall be final for all contracts being let at the time of the final determination.

H) The party adversely affected by the final determination of the Certification Review Committee may file an appeal in writing, signed and dated, with the United States Department of Transportation within one hundred-eighty calendar days after the date of the final determination.

(Source: Amended at ___ Ill. Reg. _____, effective _____)

ILLINOIS LIQUOR CONTROL COMMISSION

NOTICE OF ADOPTED AMENDMENTS

1) Heading of the Part: The Illinois Liquor Control Commission

2) Code Citation: 11 Ill. Adm. Code 100

3) Section Numbers: Adopted Action:
    100.50   Amendment
    100.70   Amendment
    100.160   Amendment
    100.170   Amendment
    100.210   Amendment
    100.230   Amendment
    100.350   Amendment

4) Statutory Authority: Ill. Rev. Stat. 1987 ch.43 par. 108(2).

5) Effective date of Amendments: November 7, 1988

6) Does this rulemaking contain an automatic repeal date? No.

7) Does this amendment contain incorporations by reference? No.

8) Date filed in Agency's Principal Office: October 26, 1988.

9) Notice(s) of Proposal Published in Illinois Register:
    March 25, 1988, 12 Ill. Reg. 5591.

10) Has JCAR issued Statement of Objections to these rules? No.

11) Difference(s) between proposal and final version:

    a) Section 100.50, subsection (a), line 3, add the words "distilled
        spirits (27 C.F.R 5) and Federal Alcohol Regulation No. 7 relating
        to the advertising..." and in subsection (b), after the words
        "alcoholic beverage", the words, "in any newspaper or magazine"
        should be crossed out.

    b) Section 100.230(c) add the words "reverses or modifies the action
        of the Local Liquor Control Commission", and the words, "the
        licensee may continue the operation of the licensed business" are
        not underlined.

    c) Section 100.350 Procedure, etc... Subsection (b), eliminates the
        words "by the appellant licensee" in line 4 and moves it to the
        end of the subsection with the additional words, "pays for the
        transcript and five additional copies".

    d) Section 100.50(c)(1) the word "periodically" is changed to
        "annually"

ILLINOIS LIQUOR CONTROL COMMISSION

NOTICE OF ADOPTED AMENDMENTS

    e) Headings were added to §100.70(b)

        (5) Wine Labels

        (6) Malt Beverage Labels

        (7) Distilled Spirit Labels

12) Have all the changes agreed upon by the agency and JCAR been made as
    indicated in the agreement letter issued by JCAR? Yes.

13) Will these amendments replace an emergency rule (amendments, epealer)
    currently in effect? No.

14) Are there any amendments pending on this Part? No.

15) Summary and Purpose of Amendments:

The amendment to Section 100.50 is necessitated by P.A. 85-142,
effective January 1, 1988, which mandates periodic updates of the dollar
limitations in the Liquor Control Act (Ill. Rev. Stat. 1987 ch.43 par. 123(i)
and (ii); The amendment to Section 100.50(b) is to enable the Commission to
regulate television and radio advertising as well as print advertising.

The amendment to Section 100.70 is to conform the Illinois rules to that of
the Federal Bureau of Alcohol, Tobacco and Firearms rules as well as that of
most States.

The amendment to Sections 100.160, 100.170 and 100.210(a) is required by the
innovation of wine products being served by the tap, similar to malt beverage
products. The amendment to Section 100.210(c) is necessitated by the Federal
Revenue Act of 1987, effective January 1, 1988, which repealed the
requirement for Special Occupation Tax Stamps for special events.

The amendment to Section 100.230 is necessitated by the changes made in the
Illinois Liquor Control Act, relating to a licensees ceasing all activity
otherwise authorized by the license pending appeal and decision by the State
Commission.

16) Information and questions regarding this adopted amendment shall be
    directed to:

    Name: Peter M. Carlson
    Address: 100 West Randolph, Suite 5-300, Chicago, Illinois
    Telephone: 312-917-6188

The full text of the Adopted Rule(s) (Amendments) begins on the next page:

ILLINOIS LIQUOR CONTROL COMMISSION

NOTICE OF ADOPTED AMENDMENT(S)

TITLE 11: ALCOHOL, HORSE RACING, AND LOTTERY
SUBTITLE A: ALCOHOL
CHAPTER I: ILLINOIS LIQUOR CONTROL COMMISSION

PART 100
THE ILLINOIS LIQUOR CONTROL COMMISSION

ILLINOIS LIQUOR CONTROL COMMISSION

NOTICE OF ADOPTED AMENDMENT(S)

AUTHORITY: Implementing and authorized by Section 12(2) of Article III of the Liquor Control Act (Ill. Rev. Stat. 1987, ch. 43, par. 108(2)).

SOURCE: Rules and Regulations of the Illinois Liquor Commission, amended March 31, 1977; amended July 7, 1977; amended at 3 Ill. Reg. 12, p. 65, effective March 22, 1979; codified at 5 Ill. Reg. 10706; amended at 8 Ill. Reg. 6041, effective April 19, 1984; amended at 12 Ill. Reg. __19387__, effective November 7, 1988 .

Section 100.50 Advertising

a) General Requirements:
Federal Alcohol Administration Regulation No. 4 relating to the advertising of wine (27 CFR Part 4), Federal Alcohol Administration Regulation No. 5 relating to the advertising of distilled spirits (27 CFR Part 5) and Federal Alcohol Regulation No. 7 relating to the advertising of malt beverages (27 CFR Part 7), and all amendments thereto are hereby adopted and made a part of this Rule§ection for advertising of wine, distilled spirits and malt beverages insofar as the Federal regulations and amendments are not contrary to, or inconsistent with, the provisions of the laws of Illinois or the Rules--and--Regulations-of-the-Illinois-Liquor-Control-Commission this Part.

b) Newspaper-and-Magazine Advertising:
1) No manufacturer, distributor, importing distributor, or retailer, or the agent or representative thereof, may advertise any alcoholic beverage in any newspaper-or-magazine medium intended for circulation, viewing or listening within this State unless such advertisement is in conformity with the provisions of this Article Part.
2) Such advertisement shall conform to the approved label upon the immediate container of the alcoholic liquor so advertised.
3) Such advertisement shall not refer to the alcoholic content of malt beverages.
4) Such advertisements shall not contain illustrations of children nor shall they make use of any material which would make a special appeal to juveniles.
5) Such advertisements shall not contain any material which is false or untrue in any respect.

c) Cost adjustment factor:
1) A cost adjustment factor will be used to annually update the dollar limitations set forth in Section 6-6(i) and (ii) of the Liquor Control Act of 1934 (Ill. Rev. Stat. 1987, ch. 43, par. 123(i) and (ii)).
2) The cost adjustment factor is a percentage equal to the change in

ILLINOIS LIQUOR CONTROL COMMISSION

NOTICE OF ADOPTED AMENDMENT(S)

_the Bureau of Labor Statistics Consumer Price Index or 5%,
whichever is greater._

(Source: Amended at 12 Ill. Reg. __19387__ , effective
__November 7, 1988__)

Section 100.70 Labels

a) No manufacturer, distributor or importing distributor shall sell or
    deliver any package or container containing alcoholic liquor
    manufactured or delivered by such person unless the same is labeled in
    conformity with this Rule.
b) General requirements and Restrictions:
    1) Federal Alcohol Administration Regulations Nos. 4, 5 and 7
        relating to the labeling of wine, distilled spirits and malt
        beverages (27 CFR 4, 5, and 7, April ~~1964~~ 1988, not including any
        later amendments or editions), are hereby adopted and made a part
        of this Rule for labeling every package or container of wine,
        distilled spirits and malt beverages, with the following
        exceptions:
        A) Wine includes all products as defined in par. 95.03 of the
            Act and Section 100.10(h) of this Part.
        B) Alcoholic content must be stated on all wine labels.
    2) The aforesaid Regulations shall apply to wine, distilled spirits
        and malt beverages packaged purely for intrastate commerce within
        the State of Illinois to the same extent as though intended for
        interstate or foreign shipment.
    3) No manufacturer, distributor or importing distributor shall affix
        any label to any package or container containing alcoholic liquor
        for sale or delivery in the State of Illinois until such label
        has been submitted to and approved by the Federal government.
        Such manufacturer, distributor or importing distributor shall
        submit to the Illinois Liquor Control Commission a photostatic
        copy of the Federal label approval.
    4) No package or container containing alcoholic liquor labeled as
        "whiskey" or "gin" may be imported into, delivered or sold in the
        State of Illinois unless the entire alcoholic content thereof,
        except flavoring materials, is a distillate of fermented mash of
        grain or mixtures of grains. Packages or containers of alcoholic
        liquor of the type of whiskey or gin not conforming to the
        requirement must be labeled "imitation whiskey" or "imitation
        gin", as the case may be.
    5) Wine Labels
        A) Wine labels must contain the name and address of the
            manufacturer or the bottler of the product. ~~Alcoholic
            content must be stated on all wine labels.~~
        B) For the purpose of this ~~Rule~~ Section, the use of an assumed
            trade name which has been registered with the Clerk of the
            County in which the manufacturer or bottler is located, is

ILLINOIS LIQUOR CONTROL COMMISSION

NOTICE OF ADOPTED AMENDMENT(S)

acceptable.
6) Malt Beverage Labels
    A) Malt beverage labels must contain the name and address of
        the brewery which manufactured or canned or bottled the
        product.
    B) For the purpose of ~~the Rule~~ this Section, the use of an
        assumed trade name which has been registered with the Clerk
        of the County in which the manufacturer or bottler is
        located, is acceptable.
7) Distilled Spirits Labels
    A) Labels of all alcoholic liquors other than wine and malt
        beverages must contain either the phrase "Bottled By" or
        "Distilled By" (or other descriptive identification of the
        manufacturer of the product) followed by the name and
        address of the bottler or manufacturer, as the case may be.
    B) For the purpose of this ~~Rule~~ Section, the use of an assumed
        trade name which has been registered with the Clerk of the
        County in which the manufacturer or bottler is located, is
        acceptable.
8) No statement of age shall be made with respect to gins, cordials,
    liqueurs or specialties.
9) No person shall sell or offer for sale in this State any bottle,
    barrel, keg or other container of beer which shall have affixed
    thereto any label or statement showing the alcoholic content
    thereof.
10) The Commission shall withhold approval of any label if it has
    reasonable cause to believe that the wording or design contained
    on the label may, in any manner, tend to deceive the purchaser as
    to the true nature of such alcoholic liquor.

(Source: Amended at 12 Ill. Reg. __19387__ , effective
__November 7, 1988__)

Section 100.160 Sanitation

a) All licensees must conduct their business in premises which are at all
    times kept clean and sanitary. This applies not only to licensed
    premises, but to places of storage as well. This includes also the
    place of storage for materials and equipment used in the manufacture
    of alcoholic liquor.
b) Each retailer dispensing draught beer or wine shall have coils and
    other equipment used in drawing draught beer or wine cleaned at least
    once every week in some manner or means, either chemical or
    mechanical. The use of steam or hot water alone is not permissible. A
    record shall be kept of the dates when the cleaning was done, signed
    by the person who actually performed the cleaning.
c) Any manufacturer, importing distributor or distributor who pays for
    the cleaning of coils of any retailer is in violation of Section 4 of
    Article VI of the Act.

ILLINOIS LIQUOR CONTROL COMMISSION

NOTICE OF ADOPTED AMENDMENT(S)

d) No licensed manufacturer or importing distributor shall fill or refill any container of alcoholic liquor unless such person possesses upon the licensed premises adequate and sanitary equipment for cleaning, washing and sterilizing such container, and use such equipment before filling or refilling a container.

(Source: Amended at 12 Ill. Reg. ___19387___ , effective November 7, 1988   )

Section 100.170 Taps

a) Each retail licensee selling malt beverages or wine on draught for consumption on the premises, shall display a sign on, over or near each tap or faucet showing the name of the manufacturer of such beverages. This sign must be visible to patrons for a distance of at least ten (10) feet.

b) No licensee shall substitute any other brand of malt beverages or wine in place of the brand designated by such visible sign and the licensee shall be prepared at all times to serve any malt beverages, or wine that are advertised by such sign or signs upon the premises.

(Source: Amended at 12 Ill. Reg. ___19387___ , effective November 7, 1988   )

Section 100.210 Inducements

a) Distributors servicing, balancing, or inspecting draft beer or wine systems at regular intervals, and providing labor to replace or install rods, taps, faucets, fittings and lines in draft beer or wine dispensing equipment shall not be considered a subsidy. However, free cleaning of coils by a Distributor or by a company whose services are paid for by a Distributor shall be considered a subsidy, or something of value in violation of Sections 122 and 123 of the Act.

b) Courtesy Wagons and/or coil boxes and pumps may be supplied by a Distributor free of charge one time per year for a one day period to a retail liquor licensee for picnics held by said retailer for the retailer's customers. However, this is not to be construed to mean that free beer or wine may also be supplied to a retail licensee.

c) Courtesy Wagons and/or coil boxes and pumps may be supplied by a Distributor for a picnic, carnival or social event that is given by or under the auspices or sponsorship of a municipal, religious, charitable, fraternal or social organization, so long as the requisite Special Occupational Tax Stamp is procured from the Internal Revenue Service by the organization as required by 27 C.F.R. 194. (April 1984).

(Source: Amended at 12 Ill. Reg. ___19387___ , effective November 7, 1988 .)

ILLINOIS LIQUOR CONTROL COMMISSION

NOTICE OF ADOPTED AMENDMENT(S)

Section 100.230 Resumption of Business on Appeal

a) In any case where a licensee appeals to the Illinois Liquor Control Commission from an order of the Local Liquor Control Commission, fining, suspending or revoking a license, or denying a renewal application and in which latter circumstance said licensee shall have on deposit with the Local Liquor Control Commission an amount sufficient to cover the license fee for the renewal period and any bond that may be required, the licensee may resume the operation of the licensed business pending the decision of the Illinois Liquor Control Commission and the expiration of the time allowed for an application for rehearing.

b) Second or subsequent Suspension or Revocation
1) The foregoing shall not apply to the appeal of a suspension or revocation order entered by a Local Liquor Control Commissioner that is the second or subsequent such suspension or revocation placed upon that licensee within the preceding 12 month period.
2) In such event, the licensee shall cease all activity otherwise authorized by the liquor license.

c) If in the event of a hearing upon a second or subsequent revocation as stated above, the State Liquor Control Commission reverses or modifies the action of the Local Liquor Control Commissioner, the licensee may immediately resume operation of the licensed business pursuant to the terms of the State Commission's order.

b)d) If an application for rehearing is filed in either a first revocation, suspension or fine situation, or a second or subsequent revocation or fine that the State Commission has reversed or modified, the licensee may continue the operation of the licensed business until the denial of the application or if the rehearing is granted, until the decision on rehearing.

(Source: Amended at 12 Ill. Reg. ___19387___ , effective November 7, 1988   )

Section 100.350 Procedures For Filing Appeals From an Order of the Local Liquor Control Commissioner

Pursuant to Sections 3-12 and 3-13 of The Liquor Control Act of 1934 (Ill. Rev. Stat. 1987, ch. 43, pars. 108 and 108a) and Section 4 of the Illinois Administrative Procedure Act (Ill. Rev. Stat. 1987, ch. 127, par. 1004):
a) In all cases where an appeal from an order or action of the local liquor control commissioner is filed with this Commission, the party filing the appeal shall furnish along with the petition to appeal:
1) a copy of the citation and notice of hearing before the local liquor control commissioner, if any
2) a copy of the decision or order of the local liquor control commissioner
3) a copy of any local ordinances charged to be violated
4) the current State Retail Liquor License number of the

ILLINOIS LIQUOR CONTROL COMMISSION

NOTICE OF ADOPTED AMENDMENT(S)

establishment involved;

51 a statement indicating whether or not the licensee has, within the last 12 month period, had a suspension or revocation placed upon said licensee, and if so, all the details relating thereto.

b) In all cases where an appeal is to be heard upon the record, a certified official record of the proceedings taken and prepared by a certified court reporter, along with all exhibits, shall be filed by the local liquor control commissioner within 5 days after notice of the filing of such appeal, if the appellant licensee pays for the transcript and five additional copies.

c) The parties shall file six copies of any documents filed in connection with the said appeal.

d) Upon notice to the local liquor control commissioner that an appeal has been accepted by this Commission, Section 100.230 of the Illinois Liquor Control Commission shall become effective, when applicable.

e) All materials filed with this Commission shall be served upon the opposing party, or parties in interest.

f) Proof of service upon the opposing party or parties in interest shall accompany all materials filed with this Commission and served upon such parties.

g) All material filed with this Commission shall be filed at 100 West Randolph Street, Room 5-300, Chicago, Illinois 60601 or 201 West Monroe Street, Springfield, Illinois 62706.

(Source: Amended at 12 Ill. Reg. __19387__, effective November 7, 1988)

DEPARTMENT OF PUBLIC AID

NOTICE OF ADOPTED AMENDMENTS

1) The Heading of the Part: MEDICAL PAYMENT

2) Code Citation: 89 Ill. Adm. Code 140

3) Section Numbers:

Section Numbers:	Adopted Action:
140.533	Amendment
140.535	Amendment
140.543	Amendment
140.560	Amendment
140.570	Amendment
140.582	Amendment
140.583	New Section
140.584	New Section
140.590	Amendment

4) Statutory Authority:

89 Ill. Adm. Code 140.533, 140.582, 140.583 and 140.584

Sections 5-5.1 through 5-5.8b of the Illinois Public Aid Code (Ill. Rev. Stat. 1987, Ch. 23, Pars. 5-5.1 through 5-5.8b)

89 Ill. Adm. Code 140.535, 140.543, 140.560, 140.570 and 140.590

Sections 5-5.1 through 5-5.7 of the Illinois Public Aid Code (Ill. Rev. Stat. 1987, Ch. 23, Par. 5-5.1 through 5-5.7)

5) Effective Date of Amendments: November 6, 1988

6) Does this rulemaking contain an automatic repeal date?
_____Yes   X No

7) Do these Amendments contain incorporations by reference? No

8) Date Filed in Agency's Principal Office: November 6, 1988

9) Notices of Proposal Published in Illinois Register:

140.533, 140.582, 140.583, 140.584

May 27, 1988 (12 Ill. Reg. 8887)

DEPARTMENT OF PUBLIC AID

NOTICE OF ADOPTED AMENDMENTS

140.535, 140.543, 140.560, 140.570, 140.590

June 17, 1988 (12 Ill. Reg. 10348)

10) Has JCAR issued a Statement of Objections to these rules?
No

11) Differences between proposal and final version: On Second
Notice, the following phrase was added to Section
140.533(n)(3): ", or if the seminar is directly related to
government cost reporting and reimbursement."

Pursuant to agreements with the staff of the Joint
Committee on Administrative Rules the Department has:
Changed "(i.e., accountant, bookkeeper, etc.)" to "(e.g.,
accountant, bookkeeper, dietary, housekeeping)" in line 2
of Section 140.533(n)(3).

Changed the sentence beginning in line 11 of Section
140.582(b) to read: "All documentation and workpapers must
be presented in an orderly and organized manner to allow
for efficient review."

Added "and the entity must receive funding from the
Department of Mental Health and Developmental Disabilities"
after "ICF/MR" in line 4 of Section 140.583(a)(3).

Added "(see 89 Ill. Adm. Code Part 404)" after the last
sentence in Section 140.583(a)(3).

Deleted "The payment methodology shall take into account
the actual allowable costs to the facility of providing
services to the residents, and shall be adequate to
reimburse the allowable costs of a campus facility which is
economically and efficiently operated." from Section
140.583(b).

Added "(see Section 140.530 through Section 140.541)" to
the end of Section 140.583(b).

Changed "Section 140.560(a)" to "Section 140.560 above" in
line 14 of Section 140.560(a).

Added a comma after the word "more" in line 3, added a
comma after the word "licensure" in line 11 and correctly
spelled "determined" in line 6 by adding as "m" after the
"r" in Section 140.560(c).

DEPARTMENT OF PUBLIC AID

NOTICE OF ADOPTED AMENDMENTS

12) Have all the changes agreed upon by the agency and JCAR
been made as indicated in the agreement letter issued by
JCAR? Yes

13) Will these Amendments replace an Emergency Amendments
currently in effect? No

14) Are there any amendments pending on this Part? Yes

Section Numbers	Proposed Action	Illinois Register Citation
140.2	Amendment	July 15, 1988 (12 Ill. Reg. 11701)
140.3	Amendment	July 15, 1988 (12 Ill. Reg. 11701)
140.7	Amendment	July 15, 1988 (12 Ill. Reg. 11701)
140.9	Amendment	July 15, 1988 (12 Ill. Reg. 11701)
140.19	Amendment	August 12, 1988 (12 Ill. Reg. 12976)
140.100	Amendment	October 14, 1988 (12 Ill. Reg. 16421)
140.110	New Section	July 15, 1988 (12 Ill. Reg. 11701)
140.350	Amendment	April 1, 1988 (12 Ill. Reg. 5958)
140.362	Amendment	April 1, 1988 (12 Ill. Reg. 5958)
140.363	Amendment	April 1, 1988 (12 Ill. Reg. 5958)
140.364	Amendment	April 1, 1988 (12 Ill. Reg. 5958)
140.367	Amendment	April 1, 1988 (12 Ill. Reg. 5958)

DEPARTMENT OF PUBLIC AID

NOTICE OF ADOPTED AMENDMENTS

Section Numbers	Proposed Action	Illinois Register Citation
140.369	Amendment	April 1, 1988 (12 Ill. Reg. 5958)
140.370	Amendment	April 1, 1988 (12 Ill. Reg. 5958)
140.372	Amendment	April 1, 1988 (12 Ill. Reg. 5958)
140.373	Repealer	April 1, 1988 (12 Ill. Reg. 5958)
140.376	Repealer	April 1, 1988 (12 Ill. Reg. 5958)
140.390	Amendment	November 4, 1988 (12 Ill. Reg. 17643)
140.392	Amendment	November 4, 1988 (12 Ill. Reg. 17643)
140.394	Amendment	November 4, 1988 (12 Ill. Reg. 17643)
140.400	Amendment	October 28, 1988 (12 Ill. Reg. 17172)
140.441	Amendment	October 28, 1988 (12 Ill. Reg. 17172)
140.443	Amendment	October 28, 1988 (12 Ill. Reg. 17172)
140.445	Amendment	October 28, 1988 (12 Ill. Reg. 17172)
140.447	Amendment	October 28, 1988 (12 Ill. Reg. 17172)
140.512	Amendment	July 22, 1988 (12 Ill. Reg. 11995)
140.525	Amendment	October 28, 1988 (12 Ill. Reg. 17172)

DEPARTMENT OF PUBLIC AID

NOTICE OF ADOPTED AMENDMENTS

Section Numbers	Proposed Action	Illinois Register Citation
140.896	New Section	July 15, 1988 (12 Ill. Reg. 11701)

15) Summary and Purpose of Amendments:

89 Ill. Adm. Code 140.533, 140.582, 140.583 and 140.584

Section 140.533

These proposed amendments add detail to the Department's rule which explains those administrative costs which are allowable in determining the reimbursement of long term care facilities. Detail is added regarding treatment of bad debt, clerical costs, trust fees, professional services, and travel and seminar costs.

Section 140.582

This amendment describes the process a long term care facility can use to object to the findings of an audit of its cost report.

Section 140.583

This new rule describes the reimbursement methodology for campus facilities.

Section 140.584

This rule specifies how the Department will reimburse contributions into the Illinois Municipal Retirement Fund by long term care facilities owned and operated by county or municipal governments.

89 Ill. Adm. Code 140.535, 140.543, 140.560, 140.570 and 140.590

Section 140.535

Amendments to this Section specify that personal property replacement taxes are not allowable.

DEPARTMENT OF PUBLIC AID

NOTICE OF ADOPTED AMENDMENTS

Section 140.543

Amendments to this Section delete provisions relating to filing projections of capital costs by new owners.

Section 140.560

Amendments to this Section clarify cost report filing requirements for new owners of existing facilities, new facilities, and when new construction adds ten percent or more to the licensed bed capacity of a facility.

Section 140.570

Amendments to this Section specify allocation of costs when a portion of a building is vacant or used for functions other than a nursing home.

Section 140.590

Amendments to this Section specify record retention requirements for fixed asset transactions, and specify certain requirements for field audits.

16) Information and questions regarding these Adopted Amendments shall be directed to:

Name: Tom Toberman
            Division of Medical Programs

Address: Illinois Department of Public Aid
            Prescott E. Bloom Building
            201 South Grand Avenue East, 3rd Floor
            Springfield, Illinois 62762

Telephone: (217) 524-7335

The full text of the Adopted Amendments begins on the next page:

DEPARTMENT OF PUBLIC AID

NOTICE OF ADOPTED AMENDMENTS

TITLE 89: SOCIAL SERVICES
CHAPTER I: DEPARTMENT OF PUBLIC AID
SUBCHAPTER d: MEDICAL PROGRAMS

PART 140
MEDICAL PAYMENT

SUBPART A: GENERAL PROVISIONS

Section
140.1   Incorporation By Reference
140.2   Medical Assistance Programs
140.3   Covered Services Under The Medical Assistance Programs for AFDC, AFDC-MANG, AABD, AABD-MANG, RRP, Individuals Under Age 18 Not Eligible for AFDC and Pregnant Women Who Would Be Eligible if the Child Were Born
140.4   Covered Medical Services Under AFDC-MANG for non-pregnant persons who are 18 years of age or older (Repealed)
140.5   Covered Medical Services Under GA and AMI
140.6   Medical Services Not Covered
140.7   Medical Assistance Provided to Individuals Under the Age of Eighteen Who Do Not Qualify for AFDC
140.8   Medical Assistance For Qualified Severely Impaired Individuals
140.9   Medical Assistance for a Pregnant Woman Who Would Not Be Categorically Eligible for AFDC/AFDC-MANG if the Child Were Already Born
140.10   Medical Assistance Provided to Incarcerated Persons

SUBPART B: MEDICAL PROVIDER PARTICIPATION/DRUG MANUAL

Section
140.11   Enrollment Conditions for Medical Providers
140.12   Participation Requirements for Medical Providers
140.13   Definitions
140.14   Denial of Application to Participate in the Medical Assistance Program
140.15   Recovery of Money
140.16   Termination of a Vendor's Eligibility to Participate in the Medical Assistance Program
140.17   Suspension of a Vendor's Eligibility to Participate in the Medical Assistance Program
140.18   Effect of Termination on Individuals Associated with Vendor
140.19   Application to Participate or for Reinstatment Subsequent to Termination, Suspension or Barring
140.20   Submittal of Claims

SUBPART E: GROUP CARE

DEPARTMENT OF PUBLIC AID

NOTICE OF ADOPTED AMENDMENTS

DEPARTMENT OF PUBLIC AID

NOTICE OF ADOPTED AMENDMENTS

DEPARTMENT OF PUBLIC AID

NOTICE OF ADOPTED AMENDMENTS

Section
140.948 Negotiation Procedures (Recodified)
140.950 Factors Considered in Awarding ICARE Contracts
         (Recodified)
140.952 Closing an ICARE Area (Recodified)
140.954 Administrative Review (Recodified)
140.956 Payments to Contracting Hospitals (Recodified)
140.958 Admitting and Clinical Privileges (Recodified)
140.960 Inpatient Hospital Care or Services by Non-Contracting
         Hospitals Eligible for Payment (Recodified)
140.962 Payment to Hospitals for Inpatient Services or Care
         not Provided under the ICARE Program (Recodified)
140.964 Contract Monitoring (Recodified)
140.966 Transfer of Recipients (Recodified)
140.968 Validity of Contracts (Recodified)
140.970 Termination of ICARE Contracts (Recodified)
140.972 Hospital Services Procurement Advisory Board
         (Recodified)

TABLE A   Medichek Recommended Screening Procedures
TABLE B   Health Service Areas
TABLE C   Capital Cost Areas
TABLE D   Schedule of Dental Procedures
TABLE E   Time Limits for Processing of Prior Approval Requests
TABLE F   Podiatry Service Schedule
TABLE G   Travel Distance Standards
TABLE H   Staff Time and Allocation by Need Level (Recodified)
TABLE I   Staff Time and Allocation for Training Programs
TABLE J   HSA Grouping

AUTHORITY: Implementing Article III of the Illinois Health
Finance Reform Act (Ill. Rev. Stat. 1987, ch. 111 1/2, par.
6503-1 et seq.) and implementing and authorized by Articles
III, IV, V, VI, VII and Section 12-13 of the Illinois Public
Aid Code (Ill. Rev. Stat. 1987, ch. 23, pars. 3-1 et seq., 4-1
et seq., 5-1 et seq., 6-1 et seq., 7-1 et seq., and 12-13)

SOURCE: Adopted at 3 Ill. Reg. 24, p. 166, effective June 10,
1979; rule repealed and new rule adopted at 6 Ill. Reg. 8374,
effective July 6, 1982; emergency amendment at 6 Ill. Reg.
8508, effective July 6, 1982, for a maximum of 150 days;
amended at 7 Ill. Reg. 681, effective December 30, 1982;
amended at 7 Ill. Reg. 7956, effective July 1, 1983; amended at
7 Ill. Reg. 9308, effective July 1, 1983; amended at 7 Ill.
Reg. 8271, effective July 5, 1983; emergency amendment at 7
Ill. Reg. 8354, effective July 5, 1983, for a maximum of 150
days; amended at 7 Ill. Reg. 8540, effective July 15, 1983;

DEPARTMENT OF PUBLIC AID

NOTICE OF ADOPTED AMENDMENTS

amended at 7 Ill. Reg. 9382, effective July 22, 1983; amended
at 7 Ill. Reg. 12868, effective September 20, 1983; peremptory
amendment at 7 Ill. Reg. 15047, effective October 31, 1983;
amended at 7 Ill. Reg. 17358, effective December 21, 1983;
amended at 8 Ill. Reg. 254, effective December 21, 1983;
emergency amendment at 8 Ill. Reg. 580, effective January 1,
1984, for a maximum of 150 days; recodified at 8 Ill. Reg.
2483; amended at 8 Ill. Reg. 3012, effective February 22, 1984;
amended at 8 Ill. Reg. 5262, effective April 9, 1984; amended
at 8 Ill. Reg. 6785, effective April 27, 1984; amended at 8
Ill. Reg. 6983, effective May 9, 1984; amended at 8 Ill. Reg.
7258, effective May 16, 1984; emergency amendment at 8 Ill.
Reg. 7910, effective May 22, 1984, for a maximum of 150 days;
amended at 8 Ill. Reg. 7910, effective June 1, 1984; amended at
8 Ill. Reg.10032, effective June 18, 1984; emergency amendment
at 8 Ill. Reg. 10062, effective June 20, 1984, for a maximum of
150 days; amended at 8 Ill. Reg. 13343, effective July 17,
1984; amended at 8 Ill. Reg. 13779, effective July 24, 1984;
Sections 140.72 and 140.73 recodified to 89 Ill. Adm. Code 141
at 8 Ill. Reg. 16354; amended (by adding sections being
codified with no substantive change) at 8 Ill. Reg. 17899;
peremptory amendment at 8 Ill. Reg. 18151, effective September
18, 1984; amended at 8 Ill. Reg. 21629, effective October 19,
1984; peremptory amendment at 8 Ill. Reg. 21677, effective
October 24, 1984; amended at 8 Ill. Reg. 22097, effective
October 24, 1984; peremptory amendment at 8 Ill. Reg. 22155,
effective October 29, 1984; amended at 8 Ill. Reg. 23218,
effective November 20, 1984; emergency amendment at 8 Ill. Reg.
23721, effective November 21, 1984, for a maximum of 150 days;
amended at 8 Ill. Reg. 25067, effective December 19, 1984;
emergency amendment at 9 Ill. Reg. 407, effective January 1,
1985, for a maximum of 150 days; amended at 9 Ill. Reg. 2697,
effective February 22, 1985; amended at 9 Ill. Reg. 6235,
effective April 19, 1985; amended at 9 Ill. Reg. 8677,
effective May 28, 1985; amended at 9 Ill. Reg. 9564, effective
June 5, 1985; amended at 9 Ill. Reg. 10025, effective June 26,
1985; emergency amendment at 9 Ill. Reg. 11403, effective June
27, 1985, for a maximum of 150 days; amended at 9 Ill. Reg.
11357, effective June 28, 1985; amended at 9 Ill. Reg. 12000,
effective July 24, 1985; amended at 9 Ill. Reg. 12306,
effective August 5, 1985; amended at 9 Ill. Reg. 13998,
effective September 3, 1985; amended at 9 Ill. Reg. 14684,
effective September 13, 1985; amended at 9 Ill. Reg. 15503,
effective October 4, 1985; amended at 9 Ill. Reg. 16312,
effective October 11, 1985; amended at 9 Ill. Reg. 19138,
effective December 2, 1985; amended at 9 Ill. Reg. 19737,
effective December 9, 1985; amended at 10 Ill. Reg. 238,
effective December 27, 1985; emergency amendment at 10 Ill.

DEPARTMENT OF PUBLIC AID

NOTICE OF ADOPTED AMENDMENTS

Reg. 798, effective January 1, 1986, for a maximum of 150 days; amended at 10 Ill. Reg. 672, effective January 6, 1986; amended at 10 Ill. Reg. 1206, effective January 13, 1986; amended at 10 Ill. Reg. 3041, effective January 24, 1986; amended at 10 Ill. Reg. 6981, effective April 16, 1986; amended at 10 Ill. Reg. 7825, effective April 30, 1986; amended at 10 Ill. Reg. 8128, effective May 7, 1986;emergency amendment at 10 Ill. Reg. 8912, effective May 13, 1986, for a maximum of 150 days; amended at 10 Ill. Reg. 11440, effective June 20, 1986; amended at 10 Ill. Reg. 14714, effective August 27, 1986; amended at 10 Ill. Reg. 15211, effective September 12, 1986; emergency amendment at 10 Ill. Reg. 16729, effective September 18, 1986, for a maximum of 150 days; amended at 10 Ill. Reg. 18808, effective October 24, 1986; amended at 10 Ill. Reg. 19742, effective November 12, 1986; amended at 10 Ill. Reg. 21784, effective December 15, 1986; amended at 11 Ill. Reg. 698, effective December 19, 1986; amended at 11 Ill. Reg. 1418, effective December 31, 1986; amended at 11 Ill. Reg. 2323, effective January 16, 1987; amended at 11 Ill. Reg. 4002, effective February 25, 1987; Section 140.71 recodified to 89 Ill. Adm. Code 141 at 11 Ill. Reg. 4302; amended at 11 Ill. Reg. 4303, effective March 6, 1987; amended at 11 Ill. Reg. 7664, effective April 15, 1987; emergency amendment at 11 Ill. Reg. 9342, effective April 20, 1987, for a maximum of 150 days; amended at 11 Ill. Reg. 9169, effective April 28, 1987; amended at 11 Ill. Reg. 10903, effective June 1, 1987; amended at 11 Ill. Reg. 11528, effective June 22, 1987; amended at 11 Ill. Reg. 12011, effective June 30, 1987; amended at 11 Ill. Reg. 12290, effective July 6, 1987; amended at 11 Ill. Reg. 14048, effective August 14, 1987; amended at 11 Ill. Reg. 14771, effective August 25, 1987; amended at 11 Ill. Reg. 16758, effective September 28, 1987; amended at 11 Ill. Reg. 17295, effective September 30, 1987; amended at 11 Ill. Reg. 18696, effective October 27, 1987; amended at 11 Ill. Reg. 20909, effective December 14, 1987; amended at 12 Ill. Reg. 916, effective January 1, 1988; emergency amendment at 12 Ill. Reg. 1960, effective January 1, 1988, for a maximum of 150 days; amended at 12 Ill. Reg. 5427, effective March 15, 1988; amended at 12 Ill. Reg. 6246, effective March 16, 1988; amended at 12 Ill. Reg. 6728, effective March 22, 1988; Sections 140.900 thru 140.912 and 140.Table H and 140.Table I recodified to 89 Ill. Adm. Code 147.5 thru 147.205 and 147.Table A and 147.Table B at 12 Ill. Reg. 6956; amended at 12 Ill. Reg. 6927, effective April 5, 1988; Sections 140.940 thru 140.972 recodified to 89 Ill. Adm. Code 149.5 thru 149.325 at 12 Ill. Reg. 7401; amended at 12 Ill. Reg. 7695, effective April 21, 1988; amended at 12 Ill. Reg. 10497, effective June 3, 1988; amended at 12 Ill. Reg. 10717, effective June 14, 1988; emergency amendment at 12

DEPARTMENT OF PUBLIC AID

NOTICE OF ADOPTED AMENDMENTS

Ill. Reg. 11868, effective July 1, 1988, for a maximum of 150 days; amended at 12 Ill. Reg. 12509, effective July 15, 1988; amended at 12 Ill. Reg. 14271, effective August 29, 1988; emergency amendment at 12 Ill. Reg. 16921, effective September 28, 1988, for a maximum of 150 days; amended at 12 Ill. Reg. 16738, effective October 5, 1988; amended at 12 Ill. Reg. 17879, effective October 24, 1988; amended at 12 Ill. Reg. 18198 , effective November 4, 1988; amended at 12 Ill. Reg. 19396, effective November 6, 1988.

NOTE: CAPITALIZATION DENOTES STATUTORY LANGUAGE.

Section 140.533   General Administration Costs

General administration costs are allowable as follows:

a) Administrative -- Allowable costs are reasonable costs of salaries paid to the administrator and assistant administrator (reasonableness to be determined by hours worked, need for position, and prevailing salaries in the industry); central office expenses in accordance with Medicare guidelines; and miscellaneous administrative expenses not otherwise classified. Compensation paid to a nonworking officer or owner is not allowable.

b) Bad Debts -- Costs attributed to uncollectable accounts are not allowable. This includes professional fees incurred for the collection of such accounts.

c) Clerical -- Allowable costs are salaries and wages of clerical staff, office supplies, printing, postage, copier expenses, telephone and telephone leasing expense, and other miscellaneous expenses. Clerical costs relating to fund raising or other non-care activities are not allowable.

d) Contributions -- Contributions made to charitable or political organizations are not allowable.

e) Directors' Fees -- Reasonable fees paid to directors are allowable. Reasonableness will be determined by the duration of the meeting and the customary directors' fees paid by similar institutions. The director must attend the meeting in order for a director's fee to be allowable. Auditable records

DEPARTMENT OF PUBLIC AID

NOTICE OF ADOPTED AMENDMENTS

Section 140.533   General Administration Costs (Cont'd)

indicating attendance and duration of meetings must be kept.

f)   Dues, Fees, Subscriptions, Promotions -- Reasonable cost of membership in organizations reasonably related to the development and operation of patient care facilities and programs, or the rendering of patient care is allowable. The cost of membership in civic, social, or fraternal organizations is not allowable. The cost of subscriptions to professional, technical, or business related periodicals is allowable. Allowable advertising costs include: those in connection with recruiting personnel, or for procurement of scarce items or services related to patient care. Advertising costs are not allowable in connection with public relations, fund raising, or to encourage patient utilization. Trust fees are also a non-allowable expense.

g)   Employee Benefits and Payroll Taxes -- Allowable costs include retirement plans, life insurance, health insurance, malpractice insurance for the medical director, payroll taxes, uniform allowance, unemployment insurance, workmen's compensation and employee meals. Benefits claimed as costs must be required by law, a written contract, or written policies of the facility. Premiums on key-man life insurance where the corporation or facility is the beneficiary, or where similar insurance is not available to all employees are not allowable except as required by lending institutions.

h)   Good Will and Covenant not to Compete -- Costs are not allowable.

i)   Inservice Training and Education -- Allowable costs are travel, food, lodging, attendance fees, and cost of bringing training personnel to the facility. The cost of training employees or volunteers who will work in the facility is allowable. The cost of training non-employees is not allowable.

j)   License or Application Fees -- Fee for licensure of the facility as well as the license application fee are allowable costs.

DEPARTMENT OF PUBLIC AID

NOTICE OF ADOPTED AMENDMENTS

Section 140.533   General Administration Costs (Cont'd)

k)   Malpractice Insurance -- Cost of malpractice insurance for the facility is allowable.

l)   Professional Services -- Reasonable legal and accounting fees incurred incident to the operation of the facility are allowable. Legal and accounting costs incident to corporate matters not related to patient care are not allowable. Retainer fees are also not allowable. Legal fees for law suits against the State or Federal governments are not allowable. Management fees are allowable to the extent they are reasonable in relation to services performed.

m)   Property and Liability Insurance -- The cost of property and liability insurance premiums paid on care related assets is an allowable cost.

n)   Travel and Seminar -- The reasonable and necessary cost of attending meetings and seminars (related to patient care) is an allowable cost. Travel, lodging, food and registration expenses related to attending conferences and conventions beyond 50 miles of Illinois are not allowable. Conferences held in-state, or within 50 miles of Illinois are allowable under the following conditions:

      1)   The conference is specifically of an educational nature (i.e., improvements of skill levels). Meetings directed towards lobby activities are not considered educational.

      2)   Staff in attendance are those involved in supervising and providing direct care to clients.

      3)   Costs associated with other than direct care staff (e.g., accountant, bookkeeper, dietary, housekeeping) are allowable when attendance at a conference was at the request of, or sponsored by, the state, or if the seminar is directly related to government cost reporting and reimbursement.

o)   Utilization Review -- Reasonable expenses incurred in utilization review in skilled cases are allowable.

(Source: Amended at 12 Ill. Reg. 19396 , effective November 6, 1988)

NOTICE OF ADOPTED AMENDMENTS

Section 140.535   Costs for Interest, Taxes and Rent

a) Allowable costs for interest expenses

1) Interest -- Reasonable and necessary interest on both current and capital indebtedness is an allowable cost provided that the indebtedness is related to patient care. No interest cost shall be recognized to the extent it exceeds payment used on 125 percent of the prevailing mortgage rate at the time of the loan. Interest paid on loans from the providers' donor-restricted funds or qualified pension fund is allowable. Interest income from unrestricted funds must be used to offset allowable interest expense. Interest incurred during construction must be capitalized and amortized over the life of the asset. Interest penalties are not allowable costs. Interest on loans to purchase capital stock are not allowable costs.

2) Effective for the rate year beginning July 1, 1984, for sales occuring January 1, 1978, and after, where the increased capital cost is deemed unreasonable, and adjustment to interest expense is made, the principal on which interest is computed must be reduced by the excess of the purchase price over the calculated reasonable capital expense.

b) Rent -- Reasonable amounts expended for the rental of care related assets are allowable insofar as they represent arms length transactions between the owners of the property and the party claiming the expense. Subleases are not an allowable expense. Rents paid to related organizations are not an allowable expense. (Capital cost of related organizations must be itemized). Real estate and personal property taxes included in rental amounts should be claimed as a tax expense.

c) Taxes -- Real estate and personal property taxes on care related assets are allowable capital costs. Special assessments on land which represent capital improvements such as sewers, water, and pavements must be capitalized and depreciated over their estimated useful lives. Fines and penalties associated with

NOTICE OF ADOPTED AMENDMENTS

Section 140.535   Costs for Interest, Taxes and Rent

property taxes are not an allowable cost. The personal property replacement tax is not allowable.

(Source: Amended at 12 Ill. Reg. 19396 , effective November 8, 1988)

Section 140.543   Time Standards for Filing Cost Reports

a) Except as provided in subsections (b) and (c) below, the cost report must be filed within 90 days of the end of the facility's fiscal year. One extension up to 60 days shall be granted for circumstances which will not allow a cost report to be properly completed before the due date of the report. The written request for an extension must be submitted to the Office of Health Finance prior to the original due date. All requests shall be judged based upon the individual circumstances to determine the length of the extension.

b) Change of Ownership -- The-new-owner-of-a-new-lessee-of-a-previously-licensed-facility-may-file-a-projection-of-capital-costs-at-the-time-of-closing-if-signing-of-the-lease.--Whether-or-not-such-a-report-is-filed,-The new owner or lessee must file a cost report 9 months after acquisition (covering the first 6 months of operation). A change of ownership is dated from the closing of the sale or from the date of the oldest lease agreement between the present incumbents of a lease. The facility must also file a cost report within 90 days of the close of its first complete fiscal year.

1) A change of corporate stock ownership does not constitute a change in ownership.

2) The Department will not recognize any subsequent transaction by the lessee as a new acquisition for purposes of capital reimbursement. Capital costs are allowed only when a facility is constructed, sold or leased for the first time. The Department will recognize the one lease as a new acquisition.

DEPARTMENT OF PUBLIC AID

NOTICE OF ADOPTED AMENDMENTS

Section 140.543   Time Standards for Filing Cost Reports
(Cont'd.)

c) New Facility - A facility which is licensed for the
first time must file a projection of capital costs
before any warrants will be released to the facility.
A full cost report must be filed within 9 months after
opening the facility (covering at least the first 6
months of operation). The facility must also file a
cost report within 90 days of the close of its first
complete fiscal year.

(Source: Amended at 12 Ill. Reg. 19396 , effective November
6, 1988)

Section 140.560   Components of the Base Rate Determination

a) Except-as-specified-in-this-Section-and-Sections-
140.561-through-140.563,-rates-will-be-calculated-from-
the-facility's-cost-report-submitted-for-its-fiscal-
year-ending-more-than-one-year-but-less-than-2-years-
prior-to-the-beginning-of-the-rate-year.

Except as specified otherwise in this Section, rates will be
calculated from the facility's cost report submitted from its
full fiscal year ending during the calendar year ended 18
months prior to the beginning of the rate year. For example,
cost reports for fiscal years ending in calendar year 1986 are
used in the rate calculation for the rate year to begin on July
1, 1988.

1a) In the case of a change in ownership of a
previously certified facility, the rate issued to
the previous owner will be in effect for the
remainder of the rate year. A new rate will be
calculated for the next rate year based on the
new owner's cost report if a cost report covering
a minimum of the first six months of operation is
received by the Finance Section prior to July
1st. If a cost report covering the first six or
more months of operation for the new owner cannot
be filed with the Finance Section prior to July
1st, the rate will be calculated based upon the
prior owner's cost report filed in accordance
with Section 140.560 above. A cost report which
has not been completed in accordance with the
Department's rules and cost report instructions

DEPARTMENT OF PUBLIC AID

NOTICE OF ADOPTED AMENDMENTS

Section 140.560   Components of the Base Rate Determination
(Cont'd)

will not be considered as received until all cost
report pages are properly completed.

2b) In the case of a new facility, capital reimbursement will be assigned on the receipt of the first
cost report (which may be an abbreviated cost
report.) The support reimbursement will be set
at the median for that region until-the-rate-can-
be-replaced-by-a-support-rate-calculated-on-the-
basis-of-the-second-cost-report,-which-contains-
actual-historical-cost-information. The facility
must then file a six month cost report,
(beginning with date the first patient was
admitted) which contains actual historical cost
information. The capital and support rates will
then be recalculated based upon this cost
report. Rates so calculated will go into effect
on the first day of the first month after the six
month cost report is received by the Finance
Section.

c) When a construction addition to the building will
increase the licensed bed capacity by 10 percent
or more, the facility may file a revised cost
report reflecting the increased capital
investment. If this revised cost report is filed
within 30 days of the date of the increase in
licensure as determined by the Illinois
Department of Public Health, any increase in the
capital rate will be effective on the effective
date of licensure increase. If the revised cost
report is filed more than 30 days after the
effective date of increase in licensure, any
increase in the capital rate will be effective on
the first day of the first month after the report
is received by the Finance Section.

3d) Once a rate for an individual facility has been
calculated, a new rate will not be calculated
during the course of the rate year except as
provided in subsections (a)(1)-and-(a)(2) (b) and
(c) above.,-or-when-an-addition-to-the-facility-
increased-capacity-by-10-percent-or-more-or-
when-major-improvements-would-raise-the-weighted-
average-year.--If-a-new-rate-is-calculated,-it-

DEPARTMENT OF PUBLIC AID

NOTICE OF ADOPTED AMENDMENTS

Section 140.560   Components of the Base Rate Determination
                   (Cont'd)

~~shall-be-effective-on-the-first-day-of-the-
rate-year-subsequent-to-the-improvement.~~

e)   If a facility incurs building construction
     improvements which would raise the base year
     grouping, then the nursing home may file a
     revised cost report which reports the increased
     capital investment. The base year is defined in
     Section 140.570(b)(2) and Section 140.Table J
     shows the groupings. If the improvements have
     been completed and put into use prior to the
     forthcoming rate year and the cost report
     reflecting increased capital costs is filed prior
     to the beginning of the next rate year, then any
     increase in the capital rate will be effective on
     the first day of the rate year.

~~b)   No-change-in-individual-facility-costs-received-after-
     November-1-will-affect-the-group-averages-for-the-
     following-year.--Individual-facility-cost-reports-
     filed-after-August-1-but-prior-to-November-1-will-be-
     included-in-the-group-averages-if-at-the-time-the-
     report-is-filed,-the-Department-has-not-initiated-
     calculation-of-rates.~~

(Source: Amended at 12 Ill. Reg. 19396 , effective November
6, 1988)

Section 140.570   Capital Rate Component Determination

a)   Capital rates for all long term care facilities--
     except State Institutions, Specialized Living Centers,
     and those rented pursuant to arm's length transactions
     prior to September 1, 1981, shall be reimbursed in the
     manner described in Sections 140.570 through 140.573.
     Capital rates for facilities rented prior to September
     1, 1981 are set forth in Section 140.574. Capital
     rates for Specialized Living Centers are set forth in
     140.579.

b)   The terms used in Sections 140.570 through 140.574 are
     defined as follows.

DEPARTMENT OF PUBLIC AID

NOTICE OF ADOPTED AMENDMENTS

Section 140.570   Capital Rate Component Determination (Cont'd)

1)   "Arm's-length transaction" means a transaction
     between a buyer and a seller both free to act,
     each seeking his own best economic interest. A
     transaction between related parties as defined in
     Section 140.537 is not considered to be an
     arm's-length transaction.

2)   "Base Year" refers to the weighted average year
     of investment in the actual construction of the
     building. The Base Year is determined using the
     components of the building cost, which are
     included in the Original Building Base Cost, and
     the corresponding years of acquisition or
     construction. The year of each component of the
     total investment is multiplied by the cost of
     each year's investment. The sum of these
     products is then divided by the total Original
     Building Base Cost to yield an average year of
     construction. Any fractional portion of the Base
     Year derived from this calculation will be
     truncated. The Base Year will not change due to
     sale or lease of the building subsequent to
     January 1, 1978.

3)   "Capital Days" are used to convert all capital
     items to per diem amounts. If a facility's
     occupancy rate is above 93%, then capital days
     shall be equal to the actual patient days. If
     occupancy is below 93%, then 93% of available bed
     days (the number of licensed beds multiplied by
     the number of calendar days in a period) shall be
     the capital days.

4)   Building Basis:

     A)   "Original Building Base Cost" means either
          the cost of construction or the cost of the
          latest purchase of the building in an
          arm's-length transaction prior to January 1,
          1978. The allowable cost of subsequent
          improvements to the building will be
          included in the original building base
          cost. The original building base cost will
          not change due to sales or leases of the
          facility after January 1, 1978. In the case
          of a nursing home building constructed after

DEPARTMENT OF PUBLIC AID

NOTICE OF ADOPTED AMENDMENTS

Section 140.570   Capital Rate Component Determination (Cont'd)

January 1, 1978, the allowable construction cost plus the cost of subsequent improvements will be the original building base cost.

B)   "Current Owner's Base Cost" means the purchase price properly allocated to the long term care portion of the building resulting from the current building owner's purchase in an arm's-length transaction. For any transaction after July 18, 1984, the current owner's base cost must be adjusted according to the provisions in Section 140.573(b).

C)   If a portion of the building is vacant or is used for functions other than a nursing home, then a portion of the building's original building base cost and the current owner's base cost will not be used in the rate calculation. This cost allocation will be based upon the proportion of the total square feet in the building being used for nursing home functions.

5)   "Ceiling or group ceiling" means the per diem amount from Section 140.TABLE J based upon the Base Year and Health Service Area (HSA) (See Section 140.TABLE B) grouping for the facility.

6)   "Dodge Construction Index" means the index of changes in construction costs from year-to-year developed from the annual publication Dodge Construction Systems Costs as published by McGraw-Hill Cost Information Systems.

7)   "Equipment Basis" means the purchase price of the movable equipment being used for long term care purposes resulting from the purchase in an arm's-length transaction. Any purchase of previously used equipment from another nursing home after July 18, 1984 must have the Equipment Basis adjusted according to the provisions in Section 140.573(b).

DEPARTMENT OF PUBLIC AID

NOTICE OF ADOPTED AMENDMENTS

Section 140.570   Capital Rate Component Determination (Cont'd)

8)   "Vehicle Basis" means the purchase price of the vehicle used for nursing home operation. Only one automobile will be allowed to be included in the vehicle basis for each facility. If a portion of the use of the vehicle is for personal purposes or for purposes other than operation of the nursing home then this portion of the cost must not be included in the vehicle basis. The facility is responsible for maintaining records which document the portion of the vehicle's use for nursing home operation.

9)   "Fair Rental Percentage" means the percent rate of return on investment to be used in the rate calculation. This percentage shall be the average Treasury Bill 91 day return rate for the previous 12 months, except that the minimum Fair Rental Percentage will be 9.13 percent and the maximum shall be 12 percent.

10)   "FRV" means "Fair Rental Value". Refer to Section 140.571.

11)   "Rounded Average Year" refers to the average year of construction of the building and building improvements. This year is used to determine the proper construction inflation factor. The average year of construction shall be determined by multiplying the year of each component of the total investment to yield an average year of construction or acquisition. This average age is rounded to the nearest whole year. A separate rounded average year must be calculated for the Original Building Base Cost and for the Current Owner's Base Cost.

12)   "Updated Cost" or "Inflated Cost" refers to the appropriate cost updated for inflation.

c)   Any items of fixed equipment which are no longer in use or are not providing significant value for inpatient long term care purposes must not be reported on the cost report fixed asset schedules for land, buildings, equipment and vehicle. For example, portions of a building not being used

DEPARTMENT OF PUBLIC AID

NOTICE OF ADOPTED AMENDMENTS

Section 140.570   Capital Rate Component Determination (Cont'd)

for nursing home operations must not be reported. Any assets which were removed from the cost report depreciation schedules prior to the 1986 cost report due to the asset being fully depreciated may not now be included in the building or equipment basis. Also, if a vehicle is used partially for personal purposes or purposes other than operation of the nursing home then this portion of the cost must not be included in the vehicle cost section of the cost report.

d)   No asset may be included in the building or equipment basis unless complete documentation for the cost and year of purchase or construction is maintained. This data must be maintained to facilitate efficient audit reviews by representatives of the Department.

(Source: Amended at 12 Ill. Reg. 19396 , effective November 6, 1988)

Section 140.582   Cost Adjustments

a)   Cost adjustments will be made on a minimum occupancy standard. Facilities having utilization levels below the standard will have their per patient day cost adjusted as if occupancy were at the standard.

   1)   For capital costs, a standard of 93 percent occupancy or actual, whichever is larger, shall be used.

   2)   For operating costs (support and nursing), a standard of actual or one-third of the difference between the actual occupancy and 93 percent, if the occupancy rate is below 93 percent, shall be used.

   3)   The number of licensed beds in the cost reporting year shall be used in the calculation of the minimum occupancy standard.

b)   On-site audits and desk audits shall be made to verify the accuracy and reasonableness of reported costs. Adjustments will be made for costs which are not

DEPARTMENT OF PUBLIC AID

NOTICE OF ADOPTED AMENDMENTS

Section 140.582   Cost Adjustments (Cont'd.)

allowable under the Department's rules or are not adequately supported by the facility's records. The Department will notify the nursing home regarding any adjustments made to the cost report as a result of a desk audit. Any objections to these adjustments must be summarized in a letter with all appropriate documentation enclosed to support the requested revision. All documentation and workpapers must be presented in an orderly and organized manner to allow for efficient review. The letter explaining the objections and all supporting documentation must be received by the Department within 45 days of the date of the letter notifying the nursing home regarding cost report adjustments. In order to provide for the efficient and accurate processing of the cost data and payment rates, no further revisions will be made to the desk audit adjustments at the request of the facility or its representatives for information submitted after this 45 day period.

c)   Any non-exempt income or contributions available to or received by the recipient or the facility from any source on behalf of the recipient must be deducted in determining the amount of payment authorized by the Department.

(Source: Amended at 12 Ill. Reg. 19396 , effective November 6, 1988)

Section 140.583   Campus Facilities

a)   A "campus facility" is defined as an entity which consists of a long term care facility (or group of facilities if the facilities are on the same contiguous parcel of real estate) which meets all of the following criteria as of May 1, 1987:

   1)   The entity provides care for both children and adults.

   2)   Residents of the entity reside in three or more separate buildings with congregate and small group living arrangements on a single campus.

DEPARTMENT OF PUBLIC AID

NOTICE OF ADOPTED AMENDMENTS

Section 140.583   Campus Facilities (Cont'd)

3) The entity provides three or more separate licensed levels of care on the same campus. One of these licensed levels of care must be ICF/MR and the entity must receive funding from the Department of Mental Health and Developmental Disabilities. The facility must also be licensed as a child care institution by the Department of Children and Family Services (see 89 Ill. Adm. Code 404).

b) Allowable costs will be determined under the same guidelines as used for other types of facilities providing services for ICF/MR residents (see Sections 140.530 through 140.541).

c) The campus facility reimbursement rate will be determined using the following steps:

1) Determine the total allowable cost for all residential campus services. Costs for day training, education, and day care services shall not be included in the calculation of the campus facility rate.

2) Obtain the per diem cost by dividing the total allowable cost by the adjusted patient days. The adjusted patient days will be determined in accordance with Section 140.582.

3) The operating costs are adjusted for inflation. The inflation factors will be determined in accordance with the provisions of Section 140.550. The inflated per diem operating costs are added to the per diem capital costs to obtain the updated total per diem cost.

4) The updated total per diem cost is compared to the ceiling. The lower of the two amounts will be the prospective payment rate.

5) The ceiling will be determined at 115% of the average rate being paid to the Specialized Living Centers for ICF/MR residents.

(Source: Added at 12 Ill. Reg. 19396 , effective November 6, 1988)

DEPARTMENT OF PUBLIC AID

NOTICE OF ADOPTED AMENDMENTS

Section 140.584   Illinois Municipal Retirement Fund (IMRF)

This Section applies to long term care facilities which are owned and operated by county or municipal governments and which make payments into the Illinois Municipal Retirement Fund (IMRF).

a) For purposes of this Section, a facility shall be deemed to have paid into the IMRF any and all sums paid into said fund on account of persons employed in the facility, regardless of whether or not such payments were made out of funds specifically designated by the county or municipal government for the facility, other specific funds, county or municipal general funds, or any other funds controlled or expended by the county or municipal governing body.

b) The cost report for the county or municipal facility must separately identify IMRF costs in the section of the cost report which requests details regarding employee benefits and payroll taxes.

c) No facility receiving reimbursement for IMRF costs under this Section shall receive reimbursement for the same costs under Section 140.533(g).

d) The IMRF addition to the support rate will be calculated as follows:

1) The total IMRF costs will be divided by adjusted patient days to obtain IMRF per diem cost. The adjusted patient days will be determined in accordance with Section 140.582.

2) The IMRF per diem cost is adjusted for inflation. The inflation factors will be determined in accordance with the provisions of Section 140.550.

3) The inflated IMRF per diem cost from subsection (d)(2) will be added to the support rate determined in accordance with Section 140.561.

(Source: Added at 12 Ill. Reg. 19396 , effective November 6, 1988)

Section 140.590   Audit and Record Requirements

a)   All audits shall be conducted according to audit
     principles set forth in the Department's audit
     guidelines.

b)   Maintenance of records

     1)   All accounting, financial, medical and other
          relevant records of the provider and related
          organizations shall be kept for a minimum of 3
          years following the date of the filing of the
          cost report. This must include a copy of the
          general ledger trial balance indicating how
          ledger entries were allocated to specific
          schedules and lines. Records relating to all
          fixed asset transactions must be maintained for a
          minimum of three years following the year in
          which the assets are last recorded in the cost
          report.

     2)   The records must be kept in good order in an
          auditable form.

     3)   All provider and related organization records
          shall be made available to the State auditors or
          their designees and furnished on their request at
          a single location. If a facility is selected for
          field audit and some records are maintained at a
          location outside the State of Illinois, it is the
          responsibility of the facility to pay for the
          expense of transporting the records to one
          location in Illinois or to pay for the expense of
          transporting the audit team to the out-of-state
          location. This would include the expense of
          lodging and meals.

c)   Failure of the provider or related organization to
     furnish needed records or answer essential inquiries
     shall result in the suspension or termination of
     Public Aid payments. The suspension of payments shall
     take effect after written notice to the provider and
     continue until such time as full cooperation is
     received.

d)   Final audit results will be communicated to the
     facility within 90 days of the completion of the field
     audit.

Section 140.590   Audit and Record Requirements (Cont'd.)

e)   In the event that costs are determined to be
     overstated, the facility shall be liable for a penalty
     of 5 percent of the overstatement. The Department may
     also recover any payments, or portions of payments,
     made to the facility as a result of incorrect
     statements.

(Source: Amended at 12 Ill. Reg. 19396, effective November
6, 1988)

DEPARTMENT OF PUBLIC HEALTH

NOTICE OF ADOPTED RULES

1) Heading of the Part:

   Toxic Art Supplies Code

2) Code Citation: 77 Ill. Adm. Code 848

3) Section Numbers: Adopted Action:

   848.100   New Section
   848.110   New Section
   848.120   New Section
   848.130   New Section
   848.200   New Section
   848.210   New Section
   848.215   New Section
   848.220   New Section
   848.225   New Section
   848.230   New Section
   848.235   New Section
   848.240   New Section
   848.300   New Section
   848.310   New Section
   848.315   New Section
   848.320   New Section
   848.325   New Section
   848.330   New Section
   848.335   New Section
   848.340   New Section
   848.345   New Section
   848.350   New Section
   848.355   New Section
   848.360   New Section
   848.365   New Section
   848.370   New Section
   848.375   New Section
   Appendix A   New Section

4) Statutory Authority:

   Toxic Art Supplies in Schools Act
   Ill. Rev. Stat. 1987, ch. 122, par. 1601 et seq.

5) Effective Date of Rules:

   January 1, 1989

6) Does this Rulemaking Contain an Automatic Repeal Date? Yes ___ No X

   If "yes", please specify date:

DEPARTMENT OF PUBLIC HEALTH

NOTICE OF ADOPTED RULES

7) Does this Rulemaking Contain Any Incorporations by Reference? Yes X No___

   If "yes," please specify type: 6.02(a) X or 6.02(b)___

   If "6.02(b)," was a copy of the approval form issued by the Joint
   Committee attached to this rulemaking? Yes ___ No X

8) Date Filed in Agency's Principal Office:

   January 1, 1989

9) Date Notice(s) of Proposal was Published in Illinois Register:

   November 6, 1987 - 11 Ill. Reg. 18098

10) Has the Joint Committee on Administrative Rules issued a Statement of
    Objections to this/these Rules? Yes ___ No X

    If "yes," please complete the following:

    A)   Statement of Objection: _____, ___ Ill. Reg. _____

    B)   Agency Response: _____, ___ Ill. Reg. _____

    C)   Date Agency Response Submitted for Approval to the Joint Committee:

11) Difference Between Proposal and Final Version:

    The following changes were made in response to comments received during
    the first notice or public comment period:

    Numerous products have been added to the lists.

    The following changes were made in response to comments and suggestions of
    the Joint Committee on Administrative Rules:

    1.   Section headings have been changed and do not appear in all capital
         letters.

    2.   The headings for Section 848.375 now agree with the table of contents
         and the text.

    3.   In Section 848.110, in the definitions of "Potential Human
         Carcinogen" and "Toxic Substance", have been indented 1/2 inch.

    4.   In Section 848.130 (Now Section 848.120), the label for subsection
         (d) must has been changed from a capital letter to a lower case
         letter. Also, a heading has been developed for this subsection.

DEPARTMENT OF PUBLIC HEALTH

NOTICE OF ADOPTED RULES

5. In Section 848.140 (Now Section 848.130), the two unlabeled paragraphs at the beginning have been labeled. In addition, the "Brand Names" and "Manufacturers" have been indented.

6. In Section 848.200(a), the name and address of the Manual has been idented.

7. Deleted Section 848.120 and Section 848.130 (b)(2)(A)-(1) in their entirety.

8. The following has been added to Section 848.130 (b)(1) "as required under 29 CFR 1915 (1988)."

9. Replaced "Staff" with "Illinois Department of Public Health" in Section 848.130 (b)(4) (Now Section 848.120(b)(3)).

10. The following has been added to Section 848.120 (b)(3): "Review of recommendations of any of the Illinois Department of Public Health approved voluntary art and craft material certifying organizations."

11. The following has been added to Section 848.130 (c)(2) (Now Section 848.120(c)(2)): "GOOD CAUSE" shall mean when the Department, through its evaluation or based upon the findings and conclusions of an approved organization, finds that an art or craft material is hazardous.

12. The following has been added to the end of Section 848.130 (d)(1) (Now Section 848.120(d)G)) "if manufacturers do not voluntarily submit this information."

13. Section 848.300 has been redrafted as follows: "The art and craft materials classified and labeled as toxic by the following approved voluntary certifying organizations have been classified as toxic."

14. In the 8th line in Section 848.100 "can" was changed to cannot."

15. In Section 848.130 (Now Section 848.120) the "D" was changed to "d)".

16. The name "ASTM" has been written out in Sectin 848.110.

17. All citations to the Illinois Revised Statutes have been updated.

    In addition, various typographical, grammatical and form changes were made in response to the comments for the Administrative Code Division and the Joint Committee on Administrative Rules.

12) <u>Have all the changes agreed upon by the Agency and the Joint Committee been made as indicated in the agreement letter issued by the Joint Committee?</u>

DEPARTMENT OF PUBLIC HEALTH

NOTICE OF ADOPTED RULES

The Department has made all the changes to which it agreed with the Joint Committee.

13) <u>Will the Rules Replace an Emergency Rule Currently in Effect?</u>

Yes ___ No _X_

14) <u>Are there any other Amendments Pending on this Part?</u> Yes ___ No _X_

If Yes:

Section Numbers	Proposed Action	Ill. Reg. Citation

15) <u>Summary and Purpose of Rules:</u>

The Toxic Art Supplies in Schools Act requires the Department to review the contents of Art and Craft materials and develop a list of art and craft products for use by students in grades K through 6, and to assure that such toxic products are properly labeled to assure safe use of such products by children in grades 7 through 12. These adopted rules contain lists of those materials which can and cannot be used in schools.

16) <u>Information and Questions regarding this Adopted Rulemaking shall be directed to:</u>

Mr. Robert John Kane, Division of Governmental Affairs, Department of Public Health, 525 West Jefferson, Second Floor, Springfield, Illinois 62761, 217/782-6187.

<u>The full text of the Adopted Rules begins on the next page:</u>

DEPARTMENT OF PUBLIC HEALTH

NOTICE OF ADOPTED RULES

TITLE 77: PUBLIC HEALTH
CHAPTER I: DEPARTMENT OF PUBLIC HEALTH
SUBCHAPTER P: HAZARDOUS AND POISONOUS SUBSTANCES

PART 848
TOXIC ART SUPPLIES CODE

SUBPART A: GENERAL PROVISIONS

Section

DEPARTMENT OF PUBLIC HEALTH

NOTICE OF ADOPTED RULES

AUTHORITY: Implementing and authorized by Section 9 of the Toxic Art·Supplies in Schools Act (Ill. Rev. Stat. 1987, ch. 122, par. 1601 et seq., in particular 1609) and Section 55.39 of the Civil Administrative Code (Ill. Rev. Stat. 1987, ch. 127, par. 55.39).

SOURCE: Adopted at 12 Ill. Reg. 19429___, effective January 1, 1989.

NOTE: Capitalization denotes statutory language.

SUBPART A: GENERAL PROVISIONS

Section 848.100   Purpose and Applicability

The Toxic Art Supplies in Schools Act requires the Department to develop lists of art or craft materials which cannot be purchased or ordered for use in kindergarten through sixth grade. These lists are distributed by the State Superintendent of Education to all the school districts in Illinois as well as making the lists available to preschools, child care centers, and other businesses and organizations which involve children in the use of art or craft materials. This Part contains the standards for inclusion and removal of a product on the list of products which can not be purchased or ordered by schools as well as the list of materials which can be purchased or ordered.

Section 848.110   Definitions

"Act" means the Toxic Art Supplies in Schools Act (Ill. Rev. Stat. 1987, ch. 122, par. 1601 et seq.)

"ART OR CRAFT MATERIAL" MEANS ANY RAW OR PROCESSED MATERIAL OR MANUFACTURED PRODUCT MARKETED OR BEING REPRESENTED BY THE MANUFACTURER OR REPACKAGERS AS BEING SUITABLE FOR USE IN THE DEMONSTRATION OR THE CREATION OF ANY WORK OF VISUAL OR GRAPHIC ART IN ANY MEDIUM. SUCH MEDIA MAY INCLUDE, BUT NEED NOT BE LIMITED TO, PAINTINGS, DRAWINGS, PRINTS, SCULPTURE, CERAMICS, ENAMELS, JEWELRY, STAINED GLASS, PLASTIC SCULPTURE, PHOTOGRAPHS, AND LEATHER AND TEXTILE GOODS.
(Section, 3(a) of the Act)

"DEPARTMENT" MEANS THE ILLINOIS DEPARTMENT OF PUBLIC HEALTH.
(Section 3(e) of the Act)

"HUMAN CARCINOGEN" MEANS ANY SUBSTANCE LISTED AS A HUMAN CARCINOGEN BY THE INTERNATIONAL AGENCY FOR RESEARCH ON CANCER OR BY THE NATIONAL TOXICOLOGY PROGRAM OF THE U.S. DEPARTMENT OF HEALTH AND HUMAN SERVICES.
(Section 3(b) of the Act)

Section 848.110 (cont.)

"Nontoxic" means art or craft materials which have been determined by the Department to be safe for use in grades K through 6.

"POTENTIAL HUMAN CARCINOGEN" MEANS ONE OF THE FOLLOWING:

ANY SUBSTANCE WHICH DOES NOT MEET THE DEFINITION OF HUMAN CARCINOGEN, BUT FOR WHICH THERE EXISTS SUFFICIENT EVIDENCE OF CARCINOGENICITY IN ANIMALS, AS DETERMINED BY THE INTERNATIONAL AGENCY FOR RESEARCH ON CANCER OR THE NATIONAL TOXICOLOGY PROGRAM OF THE U.S. DEPARTMENT OF HEALTH AND HUMAN SERVICES; OR

ANY CHEMICAL SHOWN TO BE CHANGED BY THE HUMAN BODY INTO A HUMAN CARCINOGEN.
(Section 3(c) of the Act)

"Toxic" means art or craft materials which have been determined by the Department to be hazardous for use in grades K through 6 because it CONTAINS AN INGREDIENT WHICH IS A TOXIC SUBSTANCE IF THE INGREDIENT, WHETHER AN INTENTIONAL INGREDIENT OR AN IMPURITY, CONSTITUTES 1% OR MORE BY WEIGHT OF THE PRODUCT.
(Section 3(d) of the Act)

"TOXIC SUBSTANCE" MEANS ANY OF THE FOLLOWING:

HUMAN CARCINOGENS;

POTENTIAL HUMAN CARCINOGENS;

ANY SUBSTANCE HAVING A POTENTIAL FOR CAUSING A CHRONIC ADVERSE HEALTH EFFECT AS DETERMINED PURSUANT TO THE AMERICAN SOCIETY FOR TESTING AND MATERIALS (ASTM) STANDARD D 4236 OR LATEST REVISION.

FOR THE PURPOSES OF THIS ACT, AN ART OR CRAFT MATERIAL SHALL BE PRESUMED TO CONTAIN AN INGREDIENT WHICH IS A TOXIC SUBSTANCE IF THE INGREDIENT, WHETHER AN INTENTIONAL INGREDIENT OR AN IMPURITY, CONSTITUTES 1% OR MORE BY WEIGHT OF THE PRODUCT.
(Section 3(d) of the Act)

Section 848.120   Inclusion on Nontoxic or Toxic List of Materials

a)   Art or craft materials are classified as nontoxic or toxic for grades K through 6 based upon an evaluation of the potential health hazard (acute or chronic effects) by ingestion, inhalation, skin absorption or combination during any reasonably foreseeable use of the product by students in the classroom.

Section 848.120 (cont.)

b)   This evaluation of art and craft materials consists of a review of the following to determine the potential health hazards:

1)   Review of Material Safety Data Sheet (MSDS) as required under 29 CFR 1915 (1988).

2)   Review of recommendations of any of the Illinois Department of Public Health approved voluntary art and craft material certifying organizations.

3)   Consultation with Illinois Department of Public Health Toxicologist.

c)   THE DEPARTMENT SHALL CONSIDER THE FINDINGS AND CONCLUSIONS OF A VOLUNTARY ART AND CRAFT MATERIAL CERTIFYING ORGANIZATION AS TO THE APPROPRIATENESS OF PLACEMENT OF ANY PRODUCT ON THE DEPARTMENT'S ART AND CRAFT MATERIALS EXCLUSION LIST IF:

1)   SUCH VOLUNTARY CERTIFYING ORGANIZATION BASES ITS FINDINGS AND CONCLUSIONS UPON THE FINDINGS OF AN INDEPENDENT CERTIFIED TOXICOLOGIST; AND

2)   SUCH VOLUNTARY CERTIFYING ORGANIZATION DISCLOSES TO THE DEPARTMENT THE STANDARDS AND PROCEDURES USED BY ITS CERTIFYING TOXICOLOGIST FOR DETERMINING WHETHER ART AND CRAFT MATERIALS CONTAIN TOXIC SUBSTANCES CAUSING CHRONIC ILLNESS AND IF SO, WHETHER SUCH SUBSTANCES CAN REASONABLY BE EXPECTED TO POSE OR NOT TO POSE A RISK OF ADVERSE HEALTH EFFECTS.   THE DEPARTMENT MAY DETERMINE TO ADD ANY PRODUCT TO SUCH ART AND CRAFT MATERIALS EXCLUSION LIST FOR GOOD CAUSE.   (GOOD CAUSE shall mean when the department, through its evaluation or based upon the findings and conclusion of an approved organization, finds that an art or craft material is hazardous).   SUCH DETERMINATION SHALL AFFORD DUE CONSIDERATION TO UNIFORM DETERMINATIONS BY OTHER STATE HEALTH DEPARTMENTS OR AGENCIES AND VOLUNTARY CERTIFYING ORGANIZATIONS AS SPECIFIED ABOVE ON THIS SUBJECT.
(Section 9(b) of the Act)

d)   Exclusion List Development:

1)   IN DEVELOPING THE EXCLUSION LISTS, THE DEPARTMENT MAY, AS A CONDITION OF PLACEMENT ON SUCH LIST, DEMAND, UNDER APPROPRIATE PROVISIONS OF CONFIDENTIALITY TO PROTECT A MANUFACTURER'S TRADE SECRETS, SUBMISSION OF SUCH LISTS OF INGREDIENTS AND THE RESULTS OF TESTS, STUDIES, FINDINGS AND AN ANALYSIS AS MAY BE EXTANT FROM MANUFACTURERS IF MANUFACTURERS DO NOT VOLUNTARILY SUBMIT THIS INFORMATION.
(Section 9(a) of the Act)

DEPARTMENT OF PUBLIC HEALTH

NOTICE OF ADOPTED RULES

Section 848.120 (cont.)

    2) If the requested information is not provided, then the art or craft materials in question shall be listed as toxic because insufficient information exists to determine the potential health hazards.

Section 848.130   Exemptions

a) Exemption of Art and Craft Products from Act Requirements. IF THE DEPARTMENT FINDS THAT, BECAUSE THE TOXIC SUBSTANCES CONTAINED IN AN ART OR CRAFT MATERIAL CANNOT BE INGESTED, INHALED OR OTHERWISE ABSORBED INTO THE BODY DURING ANY REASONABLY FORESEEABLE USE OF THE PRODUCT IN SUCH A MANNER AS TO POSE A RISK OF ADVERSE HEALTH EFFECTS, THE DEPARTMENT SHALL EXEMPT THE PRODUCT FROM THE REQUIREMENTS OF THIS ACT.
(Section 8 of the Act)

b) Exempt Products. The following products are exempt from the requirements of this Act:

BRAND NAMES	MANUFACTURERS
Klean Klay (Modeling clay)	Art Chemical Products, Inc.
Pariscraft (Sculpture tape)	Hunt-Bienfang Co.

SUBPART B: NONTOXIC ART AND CRAFT MATERIALS

Section 848.200   Nontoxic Art and Craft Materials (Approved)

The art and craft materials classified and labeled as nontoxic by the following voluntary certifying organizations are approved as nontoxic materials:

a) The Certified Products and Certified Labeling Bureau of the Art and Craft Materials Institute, Inc. (ACMI)

    Manual of Procedure of the Certified Products and Certified Labeling Bureau (1986)
715 Boylston Street
Boston, MA 02116

b) American Art Clay Co., Inc.
4717 West Sixteenth Street
Indianapolis, IN 46222-2598

DEPARTMENT OF PUBLIC HEALTH

NOTICE OF ADOPTED RULES

Section 848.200 (cont.)

c) Pencil Makers Association, Inc. (PMA)
Manual of Procedure for the PMA
Certification Program (1986)
66 East Main Street
Moorestown, NJ 08057

Section 848.210   Nontoxic Art and Craft Materials (Specific)

The following Sections list those art and craft materials considered to be nontoxic by the Department in addition to these approved under Section 848.200. The list consists of generic headings in alphabetical order. Under the generic headings, the individual materials brand name and manufacturer are listed. See Appendix A California List.

Section 848.215 Adhesives, Cements, Glues, Pastes, Wheat Pastes

BRAND NAMES	MANUFACTURERS
Blackhawk Paste	Conros Corporation
Elmer's Carpenters Wood Glue (All Sizes)	Consumers Products Division Division of Borden, Inc.
Elmer's Glue All (All Sizes)	Consumers Products Division Division of Borden, Inc.
Elmer's School Glue (All Sizes)	Consumers Products Division Division of Borden, Inc.
Elmer's Sno-Drift (All Sizes)	Consumers Products Division Division of Borden, Inc.
Golden Harvest Wallpaper Paste - Wheat	Krause Milling Co.
LePage's All Purpose White Glue (W-6912 HBF)	LePage's, Inc.
LePage's Arts and Craft Glue (295 and 296)	LePage's, Inc.
LePage's Mucilage	LePage's, Inc.
LePage's White Paste	LePage's Inc.
LePage's White School Glue (W-6914 HBF)	LePage's Inc.

DEPARTMENT OF PUBLIC HEALTH

NOTICE OF ADOPTED RULES

Section 848.215 (cont.)

BRAND NAMES	MANUFACTURERS
Metylan (Walocel)	The Henneux Co.
Pritt Glue Stick	Conros Corporation
Reliable Wheat Paste	Reliable Paste & Chemical Co.
Ross Glitter Glue	Conros Corp.
Ross School Glue	Conros Corp.
Ross Wheat Paste	Conros Corp.
Ross White Paste	Conros Corp.
UHU Glu Stic (U26-U125)	Faber-Castell Corp.

Section 848.220 Clays, Inks, Waxes

BRAND NAMES	MANUFACTURERS
Beeswax	Felbing Co., Inc.
Higgins T-100 Ink (Black)	Faber-Castell Corp.
Higgins Waterproof Color Drawing Inks 44625-44705 (All Colors)	Faber-Castell Corp.
Roma Plastilina	Standard Clay Mines
White Bleached Beeswax Cakes	Frank B. Ross Co., Inc.

Section 848.225 Cleaner, Preservative, Starch, Water Softener

Calgon	FMC Corp.
Giv-Gard DXN	Givaudan Corp.
Higgins Pen Cleaner #4506	Faber-Castell Corp.
Sta-Flo Liquid Starch	The Dial Corp.

DEPARTMENT OF PUBLIC HEALTH

NOTICE OF ADOPTED RULES

Section 848.230 Drawing Materials: Crayons, Markers, Pastels, Pencils

BRAND NAMES	MANUFACTURERS
Copynot Pencils #151	Eberhard Faber, Inc.
El Marko Watercolor Markers (Blue, Red, Black, Green, Purple, Orange, Brown)	Gillette Medical Evaluation Laboratories
Magic Markers (Water-Based)	Magic Marker Industries, Inc.
Sanford's Oil Pastels	Sanford Corp.
Spectracolor (Graphite and Colored Core Pencils)	Faber-Castell Corp.
Staonal #2 (All Colors)	Binney & Smith, Inc.
Ultra Wax Crayons Large #80CS6	AMS Distributing, Inc.

Section 848.235 Dyes, Pigments

BRAND NAMES	MANUFACTURERS
FDFC Blue Dye #1	Virginia Dare Extract Co., Inc.
FDFC Red Dye #40	Virginia Dare Extract Co., Inc.
Keystone Oil Yellow 3G	Keystone Ingham Corp.

Section 848.240 Glitter, Gloss, Linseed Oil, Paint

BRAND NAMES	MANUFACTURERS
Fox Tempera Watercolors	Fox Supply Company
Glitter Products (Silver, Gold, Red, Purple, Royal Blue, Kelly Green)	Glitterex Corp.
Glitter (Silver)	Walco-Linck, Inc.

DEPARTMENT OF PUBLIC HEALTH

NOTICE OF ADOPTED RULES

Section 848.240 (cont.)

BRAND NAMES	MANUFACTURERS
Linseed Oil	Binney & Smith, Inc.
Mod Podge Matte & Gloss	Plaid Enterprises, Inc.

SUBPART C: TOXIC ART AND CRAFT MATERIALS

Section 848.300   Toxic Art and Craft Materials (Approved)

The art and craft materials classified and labeled as toxic by the following approved voluntary certifying organizations have been classified as toxic.

a) The Certified Products and Certified Labeling
Bureau of the Art and Craft Materials Institute, Inc.
Manual of Procedure of the Certified
Products and Certified Labeling Bureau (1986)
715 Boylston Street
Boston, MA 02116

b) American Art Clay Co., Inc.
4717 West Sixteenth Street
Indianapolis, IN 46222-2598

Section 848.310   Toxic Art and Craft Materials (Specific)

The following sections list those art and craft materials considered to be toxic by the Department in addition to those approved under Section 848.300. The list consists of generic headings in alphabetical order. Under the generic headings, the individual materials brand name and manufacturer are listed. The numeral in parenthesis following the brand name in this listing represents relative route(s) of exposure: (1) Ingestion, (2) Inhalation and (3) Dermal (eyes and/or skin contact).

Section 848.315 Adhesives, Cements, Glues, Pastes, Wheat Pastes

BRAND NAMES	MANUFACTURERS
Amaco Kiln Cement (Moist & Dry) (2)*	American Art Clay Co., Inc.
Bond Cement #484 Tacky & #4219 (1,3)	Bond Adhesives Co.
Carter's Rubber Cement (2,3)	Dennison Mfg. Co.
Duco Cement (2,3)	Devcon Corp.

DEPARTMENT OF PUBLIC HEALTH

NOTICE OF ADOPTED RULES

Section 848.315 (cont.)

BRAND NAMES	MANUFACTURERS
Elmer's Epoxy Glue (E-601, Part 1 and Part 2) (2,3)	Consumer Products Division Division of Borden, Inc.
Elmer's Rubber Cement (E-904) (2,3)	Consumer Products Division Division of Borden, Inc.
Elmer's Solvent Contact Cement (2,3)	Consumer Products Division Division of Borden, Inc.
GR-R-Rip (10-115) (3,2)	GC Electronics
Pigmented Liquid Glue (3,2)	Nazdar Co.
Ross Epoxy Glue (Hardener & Resin Components) (3,2)	Henkel Corp.
Ross Super Glue (3,2)	Henkel Corp.
Rubber Cement 4RC (2,3)	Lepage's Inc.
Sanford's Rubber Cement (2)	Sanford Corp.
Scotch Brand 6065 Spray Mount Adhesive (2,3)	3M - 3M Center
Scotch Photo Mount Spray Adhesive (2,3)	3M - 3M Center
Thermogrip 6384 (3,2)	Emhart Bostik Division
Tri-Tix (Rubber Cream Glue) (2,1)	Lakeside Plastics, Inc.

Section 848.320 Alloys, Clays, Grogs, Minerals, Molding Rubber, Plasters,
Plastic Sculptures, Powders, Talcs, Waxes

BRAND NAMES	MANUFACTURERS
Aluminum Base Alloy A380.1 (2)	U.S. Reduction Co.
Amaco Casting Compound (Plaster) (3)	American Art Clay Co., Inc.
Amaco Fireclay Brick Grog (2)	American Art Clay Co., Inc.
Amaco Setstone (Pottery Plaster) (1,2)	American Art Clay Co., Inc.

DEPARTMENT OF PUBLIC HEALTH

NOTICE OF ADOPTED RULES

Section 848.320 (cont.)

BRAND NAMES	MANUFACTURERS
Amaco Rubber Latex (Molding Rubber) (2)	American Art Clay Co., Inc.
Apex 400 Nepheline Syenite (2)	Imcore Division IMC Industry Group
Celluclay (1,2,3)	Activa Products
Ceramitalc 10 AC, HDT, No. 1, 10A (Same as Nytal) (2)	R. T. Vanderbilt Co., Inc.
Chevron Refined Wax 143 (3)	Chevron Environmental Health Center, Inc.
Cobalt Carbonate (2,3,1)	The Hall Chemical Co.
Cobalt Oxide (70-73% Co) (2,3,1)	The Hall Chemical Co.
Diazo Resin (2,3)	Ulano Corp.
Excel SLIP (2,1)	Excel, Inc.
Feldspar G-200 (2)	The Feldspar Corp.
Goldart Clay (2,3)	Cedar Heights Clay Co., Inc.
Hydrocal White Gypsum Cement, Southard (1,2,3)	United States Gypsum Co.
Industrial Plasters - Pottery, Moulding, Gauging, Art, Casting, and Dental (20 Varieties) (1,2,3)	United States Gypsum Company
Jordan Ball Clay (2)	Cyprus Industrial Minerals Co.
KT#1-4 (Ball Clay) (2)	Kentucky-Tennessee Clay Co.
Microcrystalline Wax (Victory Brown) (3,2)	Petrolite Corp.
Microtalc, Talcron, Cercron (2)	Pfizer, Inc.
Microthene (MA 778-00) (High Density Polyethylene Powder) (2,3)	U.S. Industrial Chemicals Co.

DEPARTMENT OF PUBLIC HEALTH

NOTICE OF ADOPTED RULES

Section 848.320 (cont.)

BRAND NAMES	MANUFACTURERS
Microthene (MN 711-20) (Low Density Polyethylene Powder) (2,3)	U.S. Industrial Chemicals Co.
NCR Grog - 48/F Mesh (2)	Maryland Refractories Co.
Nepheline Syenite Peak (270 Mesh) (2)	Imcore Division IMC Industry Group
Nytal 99, 100, 100 HR, 200, 300, 300 H, 400 (Same as Ceramitalc) (2)	R. T. Vanderbilt Co., Inc.
Old Mine #4 (Ball Clay) (2)	Kentucky-Tennessee Clay Co.
Plasticizer (Flexicizer) (3,2)	Loes Enterprises, Inc.
Plasticizer - Brown (PD 700A/83 PC 04) (3,2)	Loes Enterprises, Inc.
Plasticizer - Yellow (PD 400A/30 PC 01) (3,2)	Loes Enterprises, Inc.
Plasticizer - Green (PD 514/50 PC 04) (3,2)	Loes Enterprises, Inc.
Plasticizer - Red (T 6609) (3,2)	Loes Enterprises, Inc.
Plasticizer - Black (PD 808/90 PC 02) (3,2)	Loes Enterprises, Inc.
Plasticizer - Red (PD 210 IP/25 PC 03) (3,2)	Loes Enterprises, Inc.
Plasticizer - Blue (40 PC 03) (3,2)	Loes Enterprises, Inc.
Plasticizer - Orange (PD 303A/15 PC 01) (3,2)	Loes Enterprises, Inc.
Plasticizer - Yellow (81 PC 02) (3,2)	Loes Enterprises, Inc.
Plastisol (2)	Loes Enterprises, Inc.
Polyform - Modeling Material - Plastigel (2,3,1)	Polyform Products Co.
Redart Clay (2,3)	Cedar Heights Clay Co., Inc.

DEPARTMENT OF PUBLIC HEALTH

NOTICE OF ADOPTED RULES

DEPARTMENT OF PUBLIC HEALTH

NOTICE OF ADOPTED RULES

Section 848.320 (cont.)

BRAND NAMES	MANUFACTURERS
Rutland Tile Grout (2,3)	Rutland, Inc.
Soda Ash Natural Light 100#, Salsoda, Trona Soda Ash (2,3,1)	Thompson-Hayward Chemical Co.
Sodium Silicate – Liquid Grade 40 (2,3,1)	Diamond Shamrock Chemicals Co.
Superfine Aluminum Leaf No. 200 (Aluminum Flake Powder) (2)	Crescent Bronze Powder Co., Inc.
True Albany Slip Clay (2)	Hammill & Gillespie, Inc.
USG No. 1 Casting Plaster (1,2,3)	United States Gypsum Co.
USG No. 1 Moulding Plaster, Regular, Southard (1,2,3)	United States Gypsum Co.
USG No. 1 Pottery Plaster, Southard (1,2,3)	United States Gypsum Co.

Section 848.325 Bleaches

BRAND NAMES	MANUFACTURERS
Bleach #1 (3,2,1)	Star Chemical Co.
Bleach #2 (3,2,1)	Star Chemical Co.
Clorox Liquid Bleach (3,2,1)	The Clorox Co.
Lady Lee Bleach (3,2,1)	Barton Chemical Corp.

Section 848.330 Cleaners, Correction Fluids, Degreasers, Solvents, Thinners, Turpentines

BRAND NAMES	MANUFACTURERS
Acrylic Remover (3,2,1)	Starkey Chemical Process Co.

Section 848.330 (cont.)

BRAND NAMES	MANUFACTURERS
Air Brush Solvent (3,2,1)	Starkey Chemical Process Co.
Amaco Metal Cleaner (3,2)	American Art Clay Co., Inc.
Blanket Wash #61A (3,2,1)	Polychrome Corp.
Brasso (3,2,1)	Airwick Industries, Inc.
Carbon and Paint Remover – BAC #20 (3,2,1)	Build-All Corp.
Carter's Rubber Cement Thinner (2,3)	Dennison Mfg., Co. Dennison Carter's Div.
Epoxy and Lacquer Thinner (3,2,1)	DeSoto, Inc.
Filler Remover (3,2,1)	Nazdar Co.
Film Adherent (3,2,1)	Nazdar Co.
Film Adhering Liquid (2,3)	Advance Process Supply Co.
Gum Spirits of Turpentine (2,3,1)	Sunnyside Corp.
High Flash Parts Degreasing Solvent – BAC #50 (2,3,1)	Build-All Corp.
Inhibited Liquid Cleaner – Degreaser – BAC #140 (2,3,1)	Build-All Corp.
Lacquer Thinner 457 (2,3,1)	Sunnyside Corp.
Liquid Paper Correction Fluid (2,1,3)	Gillette Medical Evaluation Laboratories
Liquid Paper Just For Copies Correction Fluid (2,1,3)	Gillette Medical Evaluation Laboratories
Low Temperature Powdered Cleaner – Degreaser BAC #120 (3,2,1)	Build-All Corp.
Marker Board Cleaner (1,3)	W. M. Barr & Co.
Methylene Chloride – PPG (2,3,1)	PPG Industries, Inc.

DEPARTMENT OF PUBLIC HEALTH

NOTICE OF ADOPTED RULES

Section 848.330 (cont.)

BRAND NAMES	MANUFACTURERS
Methylene Chloride (2,3,1)	Sunnyside Corp.
Mineral Spirits 135 (2,3,1)	Jefco Laboratories, Inc.
Mineral Spirits (Syoleum) (2,3,1)	Sunnyside Corp.
Paint Thinner (Clear Mineral Spirits) (2,3,1)	Desoto, Inc.
Parts Degreasing Solvent – BAC #40 (2,3,1)	Build-All Corp.
Plate Cleaner #257 (2,3,1)	Polychrome Corp.
Powdered Cleaner – Degreaser – BAC #100 (3,1,2)	Build-All Corp.
Powdered Paint Stripper – BAC #160 (3,1,2)	Build-All Corp.
Powdered Rust Stripper – BAC #180 (3,1,2)	Build-All Corp.
Reclaimed SLD Thinner (2,3,1)	Ashland Chemical Co.
Rectified Turpentine (2,3,1)	Baldwin Oils and Commodities, Inc.
Regular Film Remover (2,3,1)	Advance Process Supply Co.
Reliable Steam Distilled Turpentine (2,3,1)	Reliable Paste & Chemical Co.
Rez-N-Bond #1 (2,3,1)	Schwartz Chemical Co.
Rust Inhibitor – BAC #80 (2,3,1)	Build-All Corp.
Savogran Kwikeeze Paint Brush Cleaner (2,3,1)	Savogran
Screen Wash (2,3,1)	Nazdar Co.
Screen Wash (EM 4733/975) (2,3,1)	E-M Company
Screen Wash 512 (2,3,1)	Sunnyside Corp.

DEPARTMENT OF PUBLIC HEALTH

NOTICE OF ADOPTED RULES

Section 848.330 (cont.)

BRAND NAMES	MANUFACTURERS
Stain Out (IS)	Stainout Co.
Sun Mineral Spirits (2,3,1)	Elroy Turpentine Co.
Ulano Screen Degreaser Liquid #3 (3,1)	Ulano Corp.
Ulano Stencil Remover #4 (3,1)	Ulano Corp.
VM & P Naphtha (2,3,1)	Sunnyside Corp.
Water Wash Brush Cleaner (2,3,1)	E. E. Zimmerman Co.
Wax Free Remover #4 (3,2,1)	Star Chemical Co.
Xylene (3,2,1)	Drake Petroleum Co.

Section 848.335 Compressed Gas, Deflocculent

BRAND NAMES	MANUFACTURERS
Amaco Deflocculent (3)	American Art Clay Co., Inc.
Isotron (R) 12 (2,3)	Pennwalt Corp.

Section 848.340 Drawing Materials: Markers Pencils

BRAND NAMES	MANUFACTURERS
Deluxe Marker (2,3,1)	Sanford Corp.
El Marko Permanent Marker – Black (2,3,1)	Gillette Medical Evaluation Laboratories
Expresso Pens (2,3,1)	Sanford Corp.
Magic Marker (Permanent) (2,3,1)	Magic Marker Industries, Inc.
Markettes (580/590-680/690) (2,3,1)	Eberhard Farber, Inc.
Marks-A-Lot Markers (IS)	Dennison Manufacturing Co.
Sharple Markers (2,3,1)	Sanford Corp.
Stabilo Pen 68 Markers (IS)	Schwan-Stabilo Schwanhauser Gmbh & Co.

DEPARTMENT OF PUBLIC HEALTH
NOTICE OF ADOPTED RULES

Section 848.345 Dyes, Mordants, Pigments

BRAND NAMES	MANUFACTURERS
Dylon Cold Water Dyes (2)	Farquhar International Ltd.
Dylon Cold Fixative (2,3)	Farquhar International Ltd.
Pigment 2820 (2,3)	Andrews Paper & Chemical Co., Inc.
Rit All Purpose Concentrated Tint & Dye (37 Colors) (1,2)	Special Products A Unit of Best Foods
Rit Liquid Dye (24 Colors) (3,1)	Special Products A Unit of Best Foods
Sal Ammoniac (2,3,1)	L. B. Allen Co., Inc.
Tandy Acrylic Cova Dye (1,3)	Tandy Dye Co.
Tandy's Super Leather Dye (2,3,1)	Tandy Dye Co.

Section 848.350 Hair Sprays

BRAND NAMES	MANUFACTURERS
Aqua Net Hair Spray (2,3)	Faberge, Inc.
Helene Curtis Hair Spray (2,3)	Helene Curtis, Inc.
VO5 Hair Spray (2,3)	Alberto - Culver Co.

Section 848.355 Inks

BRAND NAMES	MANUFACTURERS
Airset Textile Yellow SG (2,3)	Advance Process Supply Co.
Airset Textile Brite Red (2,3)	Advance Process Supply Co.
Airset Textile Jet Black (2,3)	Advance Process Supply Co.
Airset Textile Perm Green (2,3)	Advance Process Supply Co.
Aqua Set Opaque White (2,3)	Advance Process Supply Co.
Aqua Set Yellow G (2,3)	Advance Process Supply Co.
Aqua Set Green (2,3)	Advance Process Supply Co.

DEPARTMENT OF PUBLIC HEALTH
NOTICE OF ADOPTED RULES

Section 848.355 (cont.)

BRAND NAMES	MANUFACTURERS
Aqua Set Ultra Blue (2,3)	Advance Process Supply Co.
Aqua Set Bright Red Y (2,3)	Advance Process Supply Co.
Aqua Set Brown (2,3)	Advance Process Supply Co.
Aqua Set Black (2,3)	Advance Process Supply Co.
Black Drawing Ink - 9065 (3,1)	KOH-I-NOOR Rapidograph, Inc.
Black Drawing Ink - 9066 (518 Special) - 50 (3,1)	KOH-I-NOOR Rapidograph, Inc.
Black Drawing Ink - 9085 (518 T) - 17 (3,1)	KOH-I-NOOR Rapidograph, Inc.
Black Drawing Ink 6-115 (3,1)	Iovite, Inc.
Calligraphy Ink (3,1)	Dixon Ticonderoga-Almar Industries
Opaque White Flat Poster Ink (3,2,1)	Nazdar Co.
Penstix (Black Fibrewriter Ink) (2,3,1)	Brevillier-Urban
Screen Process Textile Ink - Orange (3,2,1)	Nazdar Co.
Solvent Containing Ink (3,2)	Mark-Tex Industrial Inks
Universal Fountain Concentrate PR-130 (3,2,1)	Polychrome Corp.

Section 848.360 Patching Compounds

BRAND NAMES	MANUFACTURERS
Sears Wood Filler (3,1)	Norton & Son, Inc.

DEPARTMENT OF PUBLIC HEALTH

NOTICE OF ADOPTED RULES

Section 848.365 Photographic and Lithographic Processing Chemicals

BRAND NAMES	MANUFACTURERS
Blue Toner (2,3)	Edwal Scientific Prod. Div.
Citric Acid, Anhydrous (3)	Philip Brothers Chem., Inc.
Colored Toners (Green, Brown, Yellow, Red) (2,3)	Edwal Scientific Prod. Div.
Developer #922 (3,2,1)	Polychrome Corp.
Developer Part A (#122A) (3,2)	Polychrome Corp.
Developer Part B (#122B) (3)	Polychrome Corp.
Ethol LPD Paper Developer Liquid Concentrate (2,3)	Ethol Chemicals, Inc.
Fixer Part 1 (#124) (3,2,1)	Polychrome Corp.
HI-FI Developer - Part A (3,2)	Ulano Corp.
HI-FI Developer - Part B (3,2)	Ulano Corp.
ID 11 Plus Developer (2,3,1)	Ilford, Inc.
Ilford Multigrade Developer (3,1)	Ilford, Inc.
Ilfospeed Fixer (3,1)	Ilford, Inc.
Kodafix (3)	Eastman Kodak Co.
Kodak S11 Activator (3)	Eastman Kodak Co.
Kodak S11 Deactivator (3,2)	Eastman Kodak Co.
Kodak Dektol Developer (3)	Eastman Kodak Co.
Kodak HC-110 Developer (3)	Eastman Kodak Co.
Kodak Developer D-76 (3,2)	Eastman Kodak Co.
Kodak Ektaflo Developer - Type 2 (3,2)	Eastman Kodak Co.

DEPARTMENT OF PUBLIC HEALTH

NOTICE OF ADOPTED RULES

Section 848.365 (cont.)

BRAND NAMES	MANUFACTURERS
Kodak Ektaflo Fixer (3)	Eastman Kodak Co.
Kodak Ektaflo Stop Bath (3,2,1)	Eastman Kodak Co.
Kodak Ektamatic S-30 Stabilizer (2,3)	Eastman Kodak Co.
Kodak Ektamatic S-40 Stabilizer (3)	Eastman Kodak Co.
Kodak Farmer's Reducer, Part A (3,2,1)	Eastman Kodak Co.
Kodak Farmer's Reducer, Part B (3,2)	Eastman Kodak Co.
Kodak Film Cleaner (1,2,3)	Eastman Kodak Co. Kodak Flexicolor
Developer Replenisher, Part A (3)	Eastman Kodak Co.
Kodak Flexicolor Developer Replenisher, Part B (3)	Eastman Kodak Co.
Kodak Hobby - Pac Color Negative Fixer (3,2)	Eastman Kodak Co.
Kodak Hypo Clearing Agent (3)	Eastman Kodak Co.
Kodak Indicator Stop Bath (3,2)	Eastman Kodak Co.
Kodak Lens Cleaner (3,1)	Eastman Kodak Co.
Kodak Liquid Hardener (3)	Eastman Kodak Co.
Kodak Microdol-X Developer (3,2,1)	Eastman Kodak Co.
Kodak Photo-Flo 200 Solution (3)	Eastman Kodak Co.
Kodak Potassium Ferricyanide (3,2,1)	Eastman Kodak Co.
Kodak Rapid Fixer, Part A (3,2,1)	Eastman Kodak Co.
Kodak Rapid Fixer, Part B (2,3)	Eastman Kodak Co.
Kodak Rapid Selenium Toner (1,3)	Eastman Kodak Co.

DEPARTMENT OF PUBLIC HEALTH

NOTICE OF ADOPTED RULES

Section 848.365 (cont.)

BRAND NAMES	MANUFACTURERS
Kodak Sepia Toner, Part A (2,3)	Eastman Kodak Co.
Kodak Sepia Toner, Part B (2,3)	Eastman Kodak Co.
Kodalith Developer, Part A (3,2)	Eastman Kodak Co.
Kodalith Developer, Part B (3)	Eastman Kodak Co.
Liquid Light (2,3,1)	Rockland Colloid Corp.
Maskoid Reducer (2,3,1)	Andrew Jeri Co., Inc.
Act Activator (3)	Multigraphics
AM 50 Plate Developer (2,3,1)	Multigraphics
AM 50 Plate Finisher (2,3,1)	Multigraphics
AM Multigraphics FPC Finisher/Preserver/Cleaner (2,3,1)	Multigraphics
Adhesive (83-9-101847) (2,3,1)	Multigraphics
Adhesive (Various) (3,1)	Multigraphics
All Purpose Fountain Solution (2,1)	Multigraphics
Anti-Static Spray (2,3,1)	Multigraphics
Aqua-Flo Varnish (3,1)	Multigraphics
Black Ink M-450, Multilith SF Inks (2,3)	Multigraphics
Blakout Solution (1,2)	Multigraphics
Blankdust (2,3)	Multigraphics
Burnishine Putz Pomade (3,1)	Multigraphics
CML Oil Base Inks (3)	Multigraphics
Clean Print (1)	Multigraphics

DEPARTMENT OF PUBLIC HEALTH

NOTICE OF ADOPTED RULES

Section 848.365 (cont.)

BRAND NAMES	MANUFACTURERS
Copier Toner Remover (2,3,1)	Multigraphics
Deglaze II (2,3,1)	Multigraphics
Duro-vis Lubricating Oil (2,3,1)	Multigraphics
EP3 Dry Toner (2)	Multigraphics
Electrostatic Developer (Xerox) (3,2,1)	Multigraphics
Electrostatic Image Remover Pen (3)	Multigraphics
Electrostatic Master Conversion Solution (3,1)	Multigraphics
Electrostatic Master Liquid Developer (2,3,1)	Multigraphics
Electrostatic Masters (2)	Multigraphics
Electrostatic Solution (3,1)	Multigraphics
Electrostatic Toner (Xerox) (2,1)	Multigraphics
Electrostatic Toners (Xerox) (2,3)	Multigraphics
Film Cleaner (2,3)	Multigraphics
Formula 100 (3,1)	Multigraphics
Formula 200 (3,1)	Multigraphics
Formula 300 (2,3,1)	Multigraphics
Foto Plate 8 Developer Desensitizer (3,1)	Multigraphics
Fuser Oil (3,1)	Multigraphics
Fuser Oil (agent) (3,1)	Multigraphics
Glass Cleaner (2,3)	Multigraphics

ILLINOIS REGISTER

DEPARTMENT OF PUBLIC HEALTH

NOTICE OF ADOPTED RULES

Section 848.365 (cont.)

BRAND NAMES	MANUFACTURERS
High Density Liquid Developer (2,3,1)	Multigraphics
High Yield Toner (2,3)	Multigraphics
Image Remover Pen Pretreatment Fluid (2,3,1)	Multigraphics
Ink Anti-Skin Spray (2,3,1)	Multigraphics
Isopropyl Alcohol 99% (2,3,1)	Multigraphics
Liquid Cobalt Drier (3,1)	Multigraphics
Liquid Toner (3,2,1)	Multigraphics
M & M Metricolor Inks (2,3,1)	Multigraphics
Multicolor Clear Tack Reducer (2,3,1)	Multigraphics
Multicolor Rubber Base Inks (2,3,1)	Multigraphics
Multilith Blankrola II Solvent (2,3,1)	Multigraphics
Multilith Blankrola Solvent (2,3,1)	Multigraphics
Multilith CS Ink (2,3,1)	Multigraphics
Multilith Clean N' Easy (2,3,1)	Multigraphics
Multilith Cylinder Cleaner (2,3,1)	Multigraphics
Multilith Deglazing Solvent (2,3,1)	Multigraphics
Multilith Deletion Fluid (2,3,1)	Multigraphics
Multilith Developer/Finisher (2,3,1)	Multigraphics
Multilith Electrostatic Dispersant (2,3,1)	Multigraphics
Multilith Electrostatic Solution (3,1)	Multigraphics
Multilith Electrostatic Solution II (3,1)	Multigraphics

DEPARTMENT OF PUBLIC HEALTH

NOTICE OF ADOPTED RULES

Section 848.365 (cont.)

BRAND NAMES	MANUFACTURERS
Multilith Fountain Solution Concentrate (1,3)	Multigraphics
Multilith Hand Cleaner (2,1)	Multigraphics
Multilith Keepeze (1)	Multigraphics
Multilith Master Cleaner (2,3)	Multigraphics
Multilith MBM Ink (3,1)	Multigraphics
Multilith ML/MLS Inks & Varnishes (2,3,1)	Multigraphics
Multilith MLPC Ink (2,3,1)	Multigraphics
Multilith MLPD Ink (2,3)	Multigraphics
Multilith Padding Compound (2,1,3)	Multigraphics
Multilith Platex Green Solution (2,3,1)	Multigraphics
Multilith Platex Solution (3,1)	Multigraphics
Multilith Press Cleaner (2,3,1)	Multigraphics
Multilith Pump Conditioning Solvent (2,3,1)	Multigraphics
Multilith Repelex Concentrate (3,1)	Multigraphics
Multilith Simflo Fountain Concentrate (1,3)	Multigraphics
Multilith Surface Conditioner (3,1)	Multigraphics
Multipurpose Fountain Solution Concentrate (3,1)	Multigraphics
Offset Gum Solution (1,3)	Multigraphics
Optics Cleaner 2000 (1)	Multigraphics
Paste Drier (2,3,1)	Multigraphics

DEPARTMENT OF PUBLIC HEALTH
NOTICE OF ADOPTED RULES

Section 848.365 (cont.)

BRAND NAMES	MANUFACTURERS
PhotoDirect Activator Concentrate (3,1)	Multigraphics
PhotoDirect Stop Bath Concentrate (3,1)	Multigraphics
Preservative Solution (2,1,3)	Multigraphics
ProGraphic Developer Part A (2,3,1)	Multigraphics
ProGraphic Developer Part B (3,1)	Multigraphics
ProGraphic Hardener Concentrate (2,3,1)	Multigraphics
ProGraphic Rapid Fixer Concentrate (2,3,1)	Multigraphics
Rapid Graphic Developer Concentrate (2,3,1)	Multigraphics
Rapid Graphic Fixer (Premix) (3,1)	Multigraphics
Rubber Base Plus Inks (3,1)	Multigraphics
Simflo Electrostatic Solution Concentrate (3,1)	Multigraphics
Smooth Lith (2,3,1)	Multigraphics
Spray Adhesive (2,1)	Multigraphics
Spray Powder (2,3)	Multigraphics
TSC Electrostatic Developer/Toner (2,1)	Multigraphics
Toner 7700 (3,2)	Multigraphics
Triton Finisher (2,3,1)	Multigraphics
Triton Negative Image Remover (2,3,1)	Multigraphics
Triton Negative Plate Developer (2,3,1)	Multigraphics
Photo Maskold Frisket (2,3,1)	Andrew Jeri Co., Inc.
Potassium Ferrocyanide (1)	Graymor Chemical Co., Inc.

DEPARTMENT OF PUBLIC HEALTH
NOTICE OF ADOPTED RULES

Section 848.365 (cont.)

BRAND NAMES	MANUFACTURERS
Red Potassium Prussiate (1)	Graymor Chemical Co., Inc.
Rodinal (3,1)	Agfa-Gevart, Inc.

Section 848.370 Soldering Materials

BRAND NAMES	MANUFACTURERS
Allen Solder Paste P-200 (2)	L. B. Allen Co., Inc.
Duratec Brand Type TLR and Filter Rosin-Core Solder (2)	SPC Technology
Duratec TLC-6008 Tin/Lead Cream (2)	SPC Technology
Resin Core Solder #44 (2)	Kester Solder
Ribbon Lead/Acoustilead (2,1)	Federated-Fry Metals, Inc.
Silver Alloy Solder Sheet (A6045, A6047, A6056, A6061, A6074) (2,1,3)	TSI, Inc.
Silver Alloy Solder Wire (B6061, B6003, B6032, B6040, B6045, B6047, B6074) (2,1,3)	TSI, Inc.
Solder (2)	Kester Solder
Solder (2,1)	M.C. CAnfield Sons
Solid Solder Bar, Wire and Ingot (2)	Ames Metal Products Co.
Solid Solder Bar, Wire and Ingot (2)	Ames Metal Products Co.
Sta-Brite Solder (DI-603) (2)	J.W. Harris Co., Inc.

Section 848.375 Surface Coating Materials: Antiquing Agents, Finishes, Fixatives, Glazes, Lacquers, Linseed Oil, Paints, Stains, Shellacs, Sealers

BRAND NAMES	MANUFACTURERS
Amaco Enameling Oil (3,2)	American Art Clay Co., Inc.

Section 845.375 (cont.)

BRAND NAMES	MANUFACTURERS
Americolor Conestoga White #100 (2,3,1)	Minwax Co., Inc.
Bellini Matte Medium #745 (2,3)	Spraylat Corp.
Bellini Oil Painting Medium #765 (2,3,1)	Spraylat Corp.
Black Stencil Filler (3,2)	Nazdar Co.
Boiled Linseed Oil (1)	Sunnyside Corp.
Bulls Eye Cut White or Orange Shellac Solution 3# (2,1)	William Zinsser & Co., Inc.
Bulls Eye Cut White or Orange Shellac 4# (2,1)	William Zinsser & Co., Inc.
Certified Pure White or Pure Orange Shellac (2,1)	Advance Process Supply Co.
Clear Aerosol Products (All Pigmented Lacquer Aerosols) (2,3,1)	Star Chemical Co.
Clear Finish Gloss 38 (2,1)	Pratt & Lambert, Inc.
Clear Gloss HH Lacquer (2,3)	James B. Day Co.
Deft Interior Semi-Gloss Clear Wood Finish (Brushing) (2,3)	Deft, Inc.
Effecto Enamel Flat Black (2,1)	Pratt & Lambert, Inc.
Finisher #963 (3,2,1)	Polychrome Corp.
Gloss TM-186 (2)	Aerosol Systems, Inc.
Hi Gloss Fix-It (2,1)	Plaid Enterprises, Inc.
Interior Spray Stain and Sealer (2,3)	Deft, Inc.
Kleer Vinyl Sealer Paint Additive (3,1)	The Muralo Co., Inc.

Section 848.375 (cont.)

BRAND NAMES	MANUFACTURERS
Krylon Crystal Clear Spray Coating (2,1)	Consumer Products Division Division of Borden, Inc.
Krylon 1306 Workable Fixatif Spray Coat (2,3)	Consumer Products Division Division of Borden, Inc.
Latex Gesso - White (3,1)	Daniel Boone Paint Co., Inc.
Lead Bearing Jewelry Enamels (Frit) (1,2)	Thompson Enamel
Lime Sulfur (Liver of Sulphur) (2,3)	Miller Chemical & Fertilizer Co.
Marine Spar Varnish (2,3)	Barrett Varnish Co.
Matte (TM 225) (2)	Aerosol Systems, Inc.
Neat-Lac (Lacquer) (2,3)	James B. Day & Co.
Oil Gesso - White (2,3)	Daniel Boone Paint Co., Inc.
Orr Lac Brand Paint (2,3,1)	Spray Products Corp.
Pearl (TM 166) (2)	Aerosol Systems, Inc.
Pencils, Underglaze (Black, Blue, Brown, Green, Pink, Yellow) (3,1)	Chem-Clay Corp.
Porcelain Mist (TM 2228) (2)	Aerosol Systems, Inc.
PPG Brilliant Red Gloss Enamel (2,3,1)	PPG Industries, Inc.
PPG Brilliant Yellow Quick Dry Enamel (2,3,1)	PPG Industries, Inc.
PPG Clear Gloss Spar Varnish (2,3,1)	PPG Industries, Inc.
PPG Int. Clear Varnish (2,3,1)	PPG Industries, Inc.
PPG Oil Stain Base Medium (2,3,1)	PPG Industries, Inc.

DEPARTMENT OF PUBLIC HEALTH

NOTICE OF ADOPTED RULES

Section 848.375 (cont.)

BRAND NAMES	MANUFACTURERS
PPG Pitts-Pts. Quick Dry Autumn Brown Enamel (2,3,1)	PPG Industries, Inc.
PPG Quick Enamel Arch. Gloss White (2,3,1)	PPG Industries, Inc.
PPG Quick Dry Ivy Green Enamel (2,3,1)	PPG Industries, Inc.
PPG Speedhide House and Trim, Black (2,3,1)	PPG Industries, Inc.
PPG Wrought Iron Flat Black Quick Dry Enamel (2,3,1)	PPG Industries, Inc.
Scott's Liquid Gold for Wood (Regular and Lemon Liquid) (3,1,2)	Scott's Liquid Gold, Inc.
Shellac - White/Orange (2,3,1)	E. E. Zimmerman Co.
Sparvar (Aerosol Spray Coating) (2,3)	Borden, Inc.
Spray Matte Fixative S-202 (2,3)	Aerosol Systems, Inc.
Spray Pla Enamels - Testors (84 Varieties) (2,3,1)	The Testor Corp.
Strip-O-Matic (2,3,1)	Marcon Products, Inc.
Super Gloss S-203 (TM 1397) (2,3)	Aerosol Systems, Inc.
Super Gloss (TM 1558A) (2,3)	Aerosol Systems, Inc.
Transparent Filler (3,2,1)	Nazdar Co.
Vapex F.W.F. Tint Base High Hiding White (2,1)	Pratt & Lambert
Varmor Clear Finish Gloss (2,1)	Pratt & Lambert
Varnish - Graham Clear Wood Finish Paint (2,3,1)	Graham Paint & Varnish Co.
Wood Finish Cherry #235 (2,3,1)	Minwax Co., Inc.

DEPARTMENT OF PUBLIC HEALTH

NOTICE OF ADOPTED RULES

Section 848.375 (cont.)

BRAND NAMES	MANUFACTURERS
Wood Finish Colonial Maple #223 (2,3,1)	Minwax Co., Inc.
Wood Finish Dark Walnut #2716 (2,3,1)	Minwax Co., Inc.
Wood Finish Driftwood #2126 (2,3,1)	Minwax Co., Inc.
Wood Finish Early American #230 (2,3,1)	Minwax Co., Inc.
Wood Finish Ebony #2718 (2,3,1)	Minwax Co., Inc.
Wood Finish Fruitwood #241 (2,3,1)	Minwax Co., Inc.
Wood Finish Golden Oak #210B (2,3,1)	Minwax Co., Inc.
Wood Finish Ipswich Pine #221 (2,3,1)	Minwax Co., Inc.
Wood Finish Jacobean #2750 (2,3,1)	Minwax Co., Inc.
Wood Finish Natural #209 (2,3,1)	Minwax Co., Inc.
Wood Finish Provincial #211 (2,3,1)	Minwax Co., Inc.
Wood Finish Puritan Pine #218 (2,3,1)	Minwax Co., Inc.
Wood Finish Red Mahogany #225 (2,3,1)	Minwax Co., Inc.
Wood Finish Special Walnut #224 (2,3,1)	Minwax Co., Inc.

Appendix A   California List

The following art and craft materials have been evaluated by the California Department of Health Services and are incorporated into this document under the authority granted under the "Toxic Art Supplies in Schools Act" Ill. Rev. Stat. 1985, Ch. 122, Par. 1609 (2). These products are acceptable for use by students in kindergarten and grades 1-12. The table of contents appearing on the next page is for use with the California list.

K-6 List

CATEGORY	MANUFACTURER	PRODUCT
ADHESIVES		
Polymer		
	Binney & Smith	Crayola Art & Craft Glue
	Ceramichrome, Inc.	Ed's Glue
	Rich Art Color Co.	Rich Glu White Glue
	The Slomons Group	Drape 'n Shape

DEPARTMENT OF PUBLIC HEALTH

NOTICE OF ADOPTED RULES

K-6 List

CATEGORY	MANUFACTURER	PRODUCT
	The Slomons Group	Quik
	The Slomons Group	Sobo
	The Slomons Group	Stitchless
	The Slomons Group	Thik 'n Tacky
	The Slomons Group	Velverette
	The Slomons Group	Woodwiz
School Paste		
	Binney & Smith	Crayola White
	Dixon Ticonderoga	Holdtu
	Dixon Ticonderoga	Stixit
	Lindow Manufacturing	Lindco
	Rich Art Color Co.	Rich Art School Paste
Glues		
	American Tombow	Tombow Adhesive Sticks
	American Tombow	Tombow Liquid Glue
	Artis, Inc.	Aleene's Tacky Glue
	Artis, Inc.	Aleene's Tacky Designer Glue
	Artis, Inc.	Aleene's Fabric Stiffner
	Artis, Inc.	Aleene's White Craft Glue/School
Glue		
	Delta/Shiva	Rainbow Glue
	Dixon Ticonderoga	Prang Roll On
	Lindow Manufacturing	Lindco School
	A. Ludwig Klein & Son	#53 Cementing Liquid
	A. Ludwig Klein & Son	Dusseldorf Thick Cement

BEADS, CRAFT

	Cillus Company	HAMA Beads, Pegboards

BLOCK PRINTING INKS & MEDIUMS

Water Soluble

	Dick Blick Co.	Dick Blick
	Cardinal School	Cardinal
	Delta/Shiva	Shiva Water Base
	Demco Manufacturing	Demco Blockprint

**CAUTION: In this product line, only the colors listed are acceptable
          for K-6 use.

DEPARTMENT OF PUBLIC HEALTH

NOTICE OF ADOPTED RULES

K-6 List

CATEGORY	MANUFACTURER	PRODUCT
	Dixon Ticonderoga	Prang
	Graphic Chemical & Ink	Graphic
	Hunt Manufacturing	Speedball
	Hunt Manufacturing	Speedball Drier
	Hunt Manufacturing	Speedball Reducer #1
	Hunt Manufacturing	Speedball Reducer #2
	NASCO International	NASCO Bulk-Ink
	Pyramid of Urbana	Pyra-Print Water Base
	Rock Paint Distribution	Peacock
	Triarco Arts & Crafts	Triarco Tri-Ink
CHALKS		
Charcoal		
	Berol USA	Berol Charcoal Pencil
	Dick Blick Co.	Dick Blick
Extruded Colored (Chalkboard)		
	Binney & Smith (Canada)	Crayola Sanigene
	Dixon Ticonderoga	Hyga-Color
	J. L. Hammett Co.	Hammett's
	NationArt, Inc.	3B Blackboardbest
	NationArt, Inc.	Omyacolor
	NationArt, Inc.	Robercolor
	School Mate, Inc.	School Mate
	Weber Costello	Omega
	Weber Costello	Ritebrite
Extruded Sightsaving (Chalkboard)		
	Binney & Smith	Crayola Anti-Dust
	Binney & Smith	Crayola E-Z-Syte
	Binney & Smith (Canada)	Crayola Sanigene
	Dixon Ticonderoga	Forsythe
	Dixon Ticonderoga	Velvatex
	J. L. Hammett Co.	Hammett's
	NationArt, Inc.	3B Blackboardbest

**CAUTION: In this product line, only the colors listed are acceptable
          for K-6 use.

DEPARTMENT OF PUBLIC HEALTH

NOTICE OF ADOPTED RULES

K-6 List

CATEGORY	MANUFACTURER	PRODUCT
	NationArt, Inc.	Omyacolor
	NationArt, Inc.	Robercolor
	School Mate, Inc.	School Mate
	Weber Costello	Alphasite
	Weber Costello	Ritebrite

Extended White (Chalkboard)

	Binney & Smith	Crayola An-Du-Septic
	Binney & Smith	Crayola Anti-Dust
	Binney & Smith (Canada)	Crayola Sanigene
	Dixon Ticonderoga	Dovercliff
	Dixon Ticonderoga	Hygieia
	J. L. Hammett Co.	Hammett's
	NationArt, Inc.	3B Blackboardbest
	NationArt, Inc.	Omyacolor
	NationArt, Inc.	Robercolor
	School Mate, Inc.	School Mate
	Weber Costello	Alpha
	Weber Costello	Ritebrite
	Weber Costello	Webco

Extruded Colored (Paper & Crafts)

	Binney & Smith	Crayola Colored Act
	Dixon Ticonderoga	Prang Pastello
	Dixon Ticonderoga	Prang Poster Pastello
	Weber Costello	Alphacolor

Molded Colored (Chalkboard)

	Binney & Smith	Crayola Colored

Molded White (Chalkboard)

	Binney & Smith	Crayola
	Binney & Smith	Crayola Enameled
	Binney & Smith (Canada)	Crayola Swan
	Coloron, Inc.	Avalon/Coloron Nu-Chalk
	Dixon Ticonderoga	Colorart

**CAUTION: In this product line, only the colors listed are acceptable for K-6 use.

DEPARTMENT OF PUBLIC HEALTH

NOTICE OF ADOPTED RULES

K-6 List

CATEGORY	MANUFACTURER	PRODUCT
	Montrose Products	Futura
	Dixon Ticonderoga	Prang Sidewalk
	Dixon Ticonderoga	Waltham

Molded Colored (Paper & Crafts)

	Avalon Industries	Avalon Nu-Chalk
	Binney & Smith	Crayola Colored Drawing
	Binney & Smith	Crayola Colored Poster
	Binney & Smith (Canada)	Crayola Colorex
	Binney & Smith (Canada)	Crayola Goodhue
	Dixon Ticonderoga	Ambrite
	Dixon Ticonderoga	Excello Squares
	Dixon Ticonderoga	Freart
	Dixon Ticonderoga	Lecturers
	Dixon Ticonderoga	Prang Color Chalk
	Dixon Ticonderoga	Prang Fluorescent
	Dixon Ticonderoga	Prang Lecturers

CLAYS

Modeling (Permanently Plastic, Non-Hardening)

	American Art Clay	Amaco HBX-2
	American Art Clay	Amaco Plast-I-Clay
	American Art Clay	Artone Venus A-18
	American Art Clay	Permoplast
	Binney & Smith	Clayola
	Binney & Smith	Crayola Claytime Clay
	Coloron, Inc.	Avalon/Coloron
	Coloron, Inc.	Color Craft
	Dixon Ticonderoga	Prang
	J. L. Hammett Co.	Hammett's
	Havo, B. V.	Creatherm
	NationArt, Inc.	Plasticolor
	Sargent Art	Sargent
	School Mate, Inc.	Schoolmate
	Van Aken Int'l	Leisure Clay
	Van Aken Int'l	Van Aken

**CAUTION: In this product line, only the colors listed are acceptable for K-6 use.

DEPARTMENT OF PUBLIC HEALTH

NOTICE OF ADOPTED RULES

K-6 List

CATEGORY	MANUFACTURER	PRODUCT
Modeling Dough		
	American Art Clay	Amaco
	American Art Clay	Super Dough
Paper Mache'		
	American Art Clay	Claycrete
Powdered Sculpting & Modeling Mediums		
	American Art Clay	Sculptamold
Self-Hardening		
	American Art Clay	Amaco Marble
	American Art Clay	Amaco Mexican Pottery
	Duncan Enterprises	Doll Composition Body
	Products Chimiques	Darwi
	The Friendly Plastic Co.	Friendly Plastic Compound Sticks
	The Friendly Plastic Co.	Friendly Plastic Compound Pellets

CRAYONS

Hard Molded		
	Binney & Smith	Artista II
Molded		
	Binney & Smith	Crayola
	Binney & Smith	Crayola Easy Off
	Binney & Smith	Crayola Fabric
	Binney & Smith	Crayolet
	Binney & Smith	Peacock
	Binney & Smith	Crayola So-Big
	Coloron, Inc.	Color Craft
	Dixon Ticonderoga	American Crayon
	Dixon Ticonderoga	My First Crayon
	Dixon Ticonderoga	Prang Colorart
	Dixon Ticonderoga	Prang
	Dixon Ticonderoga	Prang Wipe-Off Wash-Off
	J. L. Hammett Co.	Art Utility

**CAUTION: In this product line, only the colors listed are acceptable
for K-6 use.

DEPARTMENT OF PUBLIC HEALTH

NOTICE OF ADOPTED RULES

K-6 List

CATEGORY	MANUFACTURER	PRODUCT
	Pentel of America	GL1-16 Plastic
	Pentel of America	PTC2-25 Soft
	Sargent Art	Gothic
	Sargent Art	Sargent
	Winsor & Newton	Reeves Giant Wax
Oil Pastels		
	Dixon Ticonderoga	Sketcho**
		all except Cadmiums & Vermilio
	Winsor & Newton	Reeves**
		all except Cadmiums & Vermilio
Pressed		
	Berol USA	Prismacolor Art Stix
	Dixon Ticonderoga	Color Classics
	Dixon Ticonderoga	Crayograph
	Dixon Ticonderoga	Kantroll
	Dixon Ticonderoga	Kindograph
	J. L. Hammett Co.	Art Utility
	Sargent Art	Sargent
Water Color		
	Dixon Ticonderoga	Prang Payons
	Weber Costello	Alphacolor
	Winsor & Newton	Reeves Paintstix

DRAWING & LETTERING INKS & MEDIUMS

Non-Waterproof		
	Hunt Manufacturing	Osmiroid
	Hunt Manufacturing	Speedball Pigmented Opaque
	Royal Talens	Ecoline**
		White
		Lemon Yellow
		Light Orange
		Deep Orange
		Saffron Yellow
		Carmine

**CAUTION: In this product line, only the colors listed are acceptable
for K-6 use.

DEPARTMENT OF PUBLIC HEALTH

NOTICE OF ADOPTED RULES

K-6 List

CATEGORY	MANUFACTURER	PRODUCT
		Magenta
		Light Rose
		Pastel Red
		Pastel Rose
		Deep Ochre
		Burnot Sienna
		Sepia
		Reddish Brown
		Ultramarine Light
		Ultramarine Deep
		Ultramarine Violet
		Prussian Blue
		Turquoise Blue
		Red Violet
		Blue Violet
		Sky Blue (cyan)
		Pastel Violet
		Pastel Blue
		Deep Green
		Bluish Green
		Fir Green
		Pastel Green
		Black
		Cold Grey
		Gold
Technical		
	Hunt Manufacturing	Speedball Technical Black
	Salis International	Dr. Ph. Martin's Tech
	Steig Products	FW White Technical
	Steig Products	Pen-Opake Technical White
Waterproof		
	Duro	Duro India
	Hunt Manufacturing	Speedball Black
	Hunt Manufacturing	Speedball
	Hunt Manufacturing	Speedball Super Black India
	Rock Paint Distrib'g	Black Velvet
	Salis International	Dr. PH. Martin's Black Star Hicarb

**CAUTION: In this product line, only the colors listed are acceptable
for K-6 use.

DEPARTMENT OF PUBLIC HEALTH

NOTICE OF ADOPTED RULES

K-6 List

CATEGORY	MANUFACTURER	PRODUCT
	Salis International	Dr. PH. Martin's Black Star Matt
	Salis International	Dr. PH. Martin's Permadraft
	Steig Products	Calli Black
	Steig Products	Calli Colored
	Steig Products	FW India
	Steig Products	FW Waterproof
	Steig Products	Luma Pearlescent
	Steig Products	Re-White Correction Fluid
	Steig Products	True Flow India
	Winsor & Newton	Artists' Drawing**
		Liquid Indian Ink
		Gold Ink
		Silver Ink
ETCHING INKS AND MEDIUMS		
Grounds		
	Graphic Chemical & Ink	Graphic Hard Transparent
	Graphic Chemical & Ink	Graphic Soft Transparent
Inks		
	Graphic Chemical & Ink	Graphic
	Martin/F. Weber Co.	Weber
	Daniel Smith, Inc.	Daniel Smith, Inc.**
		Standard Black
		Stiff Black
		Vine Black
		Traditional Black
	Duro	Duro India
	Hunt Manufacturing	Speedball Black
	Hunt Manufacturing	Speedball
	Hunt Manufacturing	Speedball Super Black India
	Rock Paint Distrib'g	Black Velvet
	Salis International	Dr. PH. Martin's Black Star Hica
	Salis International	Dr. PH. Martin's Black Star Matt
	Salis International	Dr. PH. Martin's Permadraft
	Steig Products	Calli Black
	Steig Products	Calli Colored
	Steig Products	FW India

**CAUTION: In this product line, only the colors listed are acceptable
for K-6 use.

DEPARTMENT OF PUBLIC HEALTH

NOTICE OF ADOPTED RULES

K-6 List

CATEGORY	MANUFACTURER	PRODUCT
	Steig Products	FW Waterproof
	Steig Products	Luma Pearlescent
	Steig Products	Re-White Correction Fluid
	Steig Products	True Flow India
	Winsor & Newton	Artists' Drawing**
		Liquid Indian Ink
		Gold Ink
		Silver Ink

ETCHING INKS AND MEDIUMS

Grounds

	Graphic Chemical & Ink	Graphic Hard Transparent
	Graphic Chemical & Ink	Graphic Soft Transparent

Inks

	Graphic Chemical & Ink	Graphic
	Martin/F. Weber Co.	Weber
	Daniel Smith, Inc.	Daniel Smith, Inc.**
		Standard Black
		Stiff Black
		Vine Black
		Traditional Black
		Traditional Relief Black
		Intense Black
		Artists' Preferred Black
		Creamy French Black
		Graphite
		Etching Silver
		Transparent Base
		Opaque White
		Etching Yellow
		Process Yellow
		Thalo Green
		Thalo Viridian
		Chromium Green Oxide
		Ultramarine Blue
		Thalo Purple
		Thalo Turquoise

**CAUTION: In this product line, only the colors listed are acceptable
        for K-6 use.

DEPARTMENT OF PUBLIC HEALTH

NOTICE OF ADOPTED RULES

K-6 List

CATEGORY	MANUFACTURER	PRODUCT
		Thalo Blue
		Process Blue
		Indigo
		Indian Red
		Alizarin Crimson
		Naphthol Red
		Thalo Red
		Process Magenta
		Mars Violet
		Burnt Sienna
		Burnt Umber
		Raw Sienna
		Raw Umber
		Dark Brown
		Sepia

Mediums

	Graphic Chemical & Ink	Graphic Sureset
	Martin/F. Weber Co.	Martin/F. Weber Plate Oil

GESSOS & PAINTING GROUNDS

	Binney & Smith	Liquitex Gesso
	Duro Art Industries	Duro Gesso
	Golden Artists Colors	Golden Black Gesso
	Golden Artists Colors	Golden Gesso
	Hunt Manufacturing	Speedball Acrylic Artists Gesso
	Martin/F. Weber Co.	Martin/F. Weber Economy Gesso
	Martin/F. Weber Co.	Permalba Gesso
	Winsor & Newton	Acrylic Gesso Primer

GLITTER

	Conros Corp.	Ross Glitter Colors
	Glitterex Corp.	Glitter

GRAPHIC MASKING LIQUIDS

	Hunt Manufacturing	Speedball Red Ruby

**CAUTION: In this product line, only the colors listed are acceptable
        for K-6 use.

DEPARTMENT OF PUBLIC HEALTH

NOTICE OF ADOPTED RULES

K-6 List

CATEGORY	MANUFACTURER	PRODUCT
MARKERS		
Water Colors		
	Berol USA	Colorific 8500
	Binney & Smith	Crayola Coloring
	Binney & Smith	Crayola Drawing
	Binney & Smith	Crayola Washable
	Chartpak	Aqua**
		Cerulean Blue
		Brown
		Cobalt
		Blue Steel
		Dark Red
		Flesh
		Light Blue
		Sky Blue
		Orange
		Pink
		Red
		Umber
		Paynes Gray
		Prussian Blue
		Beige
		Sepia
	Chartpak	AVH Audio Visual**
		Red
		Orange
		Yellow
		Brown
		Black
		Blue
		Green
		Purple
	Chartpak	Chiz' 1 I**
		Rubine
		Light Blue
		Pink
		Redwood
		Orange

**CAUTION: In this product line, only the colors listed are acceptable
            for K-6 use.

DEPARTMENT OF PUBLIC HEALTH

NOTICE OF ADOPTED RULES

K-6 List

CATEGORY	MANUFACTURER	PRODUCT
		Umber
		Red
		Dark Red
		Blue
		Magenta
		Flesh
		Sepia
		Brown
		Non-repro Blue
	Chartpak	Chiz'l II**
		Rubine
		Light Blue
		Pink
		Redwood
		Orange
		Umber
		Red
		Dark Red
		Blue
		Magenta
		Flesh
		Sepia
		Brown
		Non-repro Blue
	Chartpak	NRBP
	Chartpak	Techmarker**
		Rubine
		Light Blue
		Pink
		Redwood
		Orange
		Umber
		Red
		Dark Red
		Blue
		Magenta
		Flesh
		Sepia

**CAUTION: In this product line, only the colors listed are acceptable
            for K-6 use.

ILLINOIS REGISTER

DEPARTMENT OF PUBLIC HEALTH

NOTICE OF ADOPTED RULES

K-6 List

CATEGORY	MANUFACTURER	PRODUCT
		Brown
		Non-repro Blue
	Dixon Ticonderoga	8040 Highlighter
	Dixon Ticonderoga	Prang
	Dixon Ticonderoga	Prang Brush Pens
	Eberhard Faber	Colorbrite
	Eberhard Faber	7500 Vurite
	Eberhard Faber	Wiff
	Gillette	Paper Mate Large; Blue, Red, Black,
		Green, Purple, Yellow, Brown, Orange
	Gillette	Paper Mate El Marko; Blue, Red, Black,
		Green, Purple, Yellow, Brown, Orange
	Gillette	Paper Mate Highlighting Marker;
		Blue, Green, Yellow, Pink
	Hunt Manufacturing	Speedball Fine & Medium Paint**
		Antique White
		Violet
		Spring Green
		Cranberry
		White
		Pink
		Olive Green
		Pumpkin
		Rose
		Lilac
		Blue
		Green
		Colonial Blue
		Brown
		Navy Blue
		Black
		Baby Blue
		Brick Red
		Goldenrod
		Orange
		Yellow
		Red
	Sanford Corp.	Mr. Sketch Scented Instant

**CAUTION: In this product line, only the colors listed are acceptable for K-6 use.

DEPARTMENT OF PUBLIC HEALTH

NOTICE OF ADOPTED RULES

K-6 List

CATEGORY	MANUFACTURER	PRODUCT
	Steig Products	Steig Lightfast
MEDIUMS & VARNISHES, ACRYLIC POLYMER		
Mediums		
	Binney & Smith	Liquitex Gel
	Binney & Smith	Liquitex Matte
	Binney & Smith	Liquitex Modeling Paste
	Binney & Smith	Liquitex Polymer
	Binney & Smith	Liquitex Retarding
	Dick Blick Co.	Blickrylic Gel
	Dick Blick Co.	Blickrylic Polymer
	Dick Blick Co.	Blickrylic Retarder
	Dick Blick Co.	Strokemaster Gel
	Dick Blick Co.	Strokemaster Gesso
	Dick Blick Co.	Strokemaster Gloss
	Dick Blick Co.	Strokemaster Matte
	Dick Blick Co.	Strokemaster Modeling Paste
	Dick Blick Co.	Strokemaster Retarder
	Cardinal School	Cardinal Acrylic Gel
	Cardinal School	Cardinal Acrylic Polymer
	Cardinal School	Cardinal Acrylic Retarder
	Ceramichrome, Inc.	Deco Art Extender
	Chroma Acrylics	Jo Sonja All Purpose Sealer
	Chroma Acrylics	Jo Sonja Flow
	Chroma Acrylics	Jo Sonja Retarder
	Chroma Acrylics	Jo Sonja Tannin Blocking Sealer
	Chroma Acrylics	Jo Sonja Textile
	Chroma Acrylics	Jo Sonja Texture Paste
	Delta/Shiva	Shiva Gel
	Delta/Shiva	Shiva Gesso
	Delta/Shiva	Shiva Gloss
	Delta/Shiva	Shiva Modeling Paste
	Delta/Shiva	Shiva Retarder
	Alois K. Diethelm AG	Lascaux Modeling Paste A & B
	Alois K. Diethelm AG	Lascaux Paint & Varnish
	Duncan Enterprises	Nonfired Snow
	Duncan Enterprises	Nonfired Thickener & Extender
	Duro Art Industries	Matte
	Duro Art Industries	Polymer Gel

**CAUTION: In this product line, only the colors listed are acceptable for K-6 use.

DEPARTMENT OF PUBLIC HEALTH

NOTICE OF ADOPTED RULES

K-6 List

CATEGORY	MANUFACTURER	PRODUCT
	Duro Art Industries	Polymer Gloss
	Golden Artists Colors	Acrylic Flow Release
	Golden Artists Colors	Film Modifier
	Golden Artists Colors	Fluid Matte
	Golden Artists Colors	Gel
	Golden Artists Colors	Matte
	Golden Artists Colors	Modeling Paste
	Golden Artists Colors	Polymer 100, 500, 700
	Golden Artists Colors	Retarder
	Hunt Manufacturing	Speedball Gel
	Hunt Manufacturing	Speedball Gloss
	Hunt Manufacturing	Speedball Matte
	Hunt Manufacturing	Speedball Modeling Paste
	Lefranc & Bourgeois	Flashe
	Lefranc & Bourgeois	Polyflashe Gel
	Lefranc & Bourgeois	Polyflashe Gesso
	Lefranc & Bourgeois	Polyflashe Modeling Paste
	Lefranc & Bourgeois	Polyflashe Opaque
	Lefranc & Bourgeois	Polyflashe Retarder
	Lefranc & Bourgeois	Polyflashe
	Martin/F. Weber Co.	Permalba Gel
	Martin/F. Weber Co.	Permalba Gloss
	Martin/F. Weber Co.	Permalba Matte
	Martin/F. Weber Co.	Permalba Modeling Paste
	Martin/F. Weber Co.	Permalba Retarder
	Mayco Colors	Hi-Gloss Sealer
	Mayco Colors	Matt Sealer
	NASCO International	Bulkrylic Gel
	NASCO International	Bulkrylic Polymer
	NASCO International	Bulkrylic Retarder
	Pyramid of Urbana	Pyra-Crylic Gel
	Pyramid of Urbana	Pyra-Crylic Polymer
	Pyramid of Urbana	Pyra-Crylic Retarder
	Rock Paint Distributing	Peacock Gel
	Rock Paint Distributing	Peacock Polymer
	Rock Paint Distributing	Peacock Retarder
	Royal Talens	Rembrandt Casein Tempera Binde
	Royal Talens	Rembrandt Glossy
	Royal Talens	Rembrandt Mat

**CAUTION: In this product line, only the colors listed are acceptable
          for K-6 use.

DEPARTMENT OF PUBLIC HEALTH

NOTICE OF ADOPTED RULES

K-6 List

CATEGORY	MANUFACTURER	PRODUCT
	Royal Talens	Rembrandt Retarder
	Salis International	Dr. PH. Martin's Spectralite Color Extender
	Sennilier	Peintex Epaississant
	Triarco Arts & Crafts	Tri-Crylic Gel
	Triarco Arts & Crafts	Tri-Crylic Polymer
	Triarco Arts & Crafts	Tri-Crylic Retarder
	Utrecht Mfg. Co.	Acrylic Gel
	Utrecht Mfg. Co.	Acrylic Matte
	Winsor & Newton	Flow Improver
	Winsor & Newton	Gel
	Winsor & Newton	Gloss
	Winsor & Newton	Matt
	Winsor & Newton	Retarder
	Zipatone, Inc.	Aqua-Tec Gesso
	Zipatone, Inc.	Aqua-Tec Matte
	Zipatone, Inc.	Aqua-Tec Modeling Paste
	Zipatone, Inc.	Aqua-Tec Polymer
Varnishes		
	Binney & Smith	Liquitex Matte
	Dick Blick Co.	Strokemaster Matte
	Chroma Acrylics	Jo Sonja Polyurethane
	Alois K. Diethelm AG	Lascaux Transparent
	Golden Artists Colors	Matte
	Martin/F. Weber Co.	Polymer
	Winsor & Newton	Aquatole
	Winsor & Newton	Gloss
	Winsor & Newton	Matt
	Zipatone, Inc.	Aqua-Tec Matte
	Zipatone, Inc.	Aqua-Tec Polymer
MEDIUMS & VARNISHES, WATER COLOR		
	Duncan Enterprises	Thin N Shade
	M. Grumbacher, Inc.	Misket
	Salis International	Dr. PH. Martin's Color-Out
	Salis International	Dr. PH. Martin's Frisket Mask Liquid
	Steig Products	Colorflex
	Steig Products	Luma Liquid Mask

**CAUTION: In this product line, only the colors listed are acceptable
          for K-6 use.

DEPARTMENT OF PUBLIC HEALTH

NOTICE OF ADOPTED RULES

K-6 List

CATEGORY	MANUFACTURER	PRODUCT
	Steig Products	Wax-Grip
	Winsor & Newton	Aquapasto
	Winsor & Newton	Art Masking Fluid
	Winsor & Newton	Art Masking Fluid Colourless
	Winsor & Newton	Prepared Size
	Winsor & Newton	Watercolour Medium
MEDIUMS, MULTI-PURPOSE		
	Dick Blick Co.	Multi-Gel
	Sails International	Dr. PH. Martin's Photo Ace
NATURAL PRODUCTS		
	Hawk, Inc.	Hawk Straw & String Products
	Winter Woods	Bulrush
	Winter Woods	Snake Grass
	Winter Woods	Ostrich Fern Fronds
	Winter Woods	Sponge Mushrooms
	Winter Woods	Red Pine Cones
	Winter Woods	Excelsior
	Winter Woods	Sheet Moss
	Winter Woods	Exotic Reindeer Moss
	Winter Woods	Cedar Cones
	Winter Woods	Ponderosa Pine Cones
	Winter Woods	Tamarack Cones
	Winter Woods	Red Cap Lichen
	Winter Woods	White Pine Cones
	Winter Woods	Sensitive Fern Fronds
	Winter Woods	Norway Spruce Cones
	Winter Woods	Lake Driftwood
	Winter Woods	Red Pine Cones
	Winter Woods	Hoof Mushrooms
	Winter Woods	Goldenrod
	Winter Woods	Angel Hair Lichen
	Winter Woods	Black Spruce Cones
	Winter Woods	Gitchee Gumee Pebbles
	Winter Woods	Antler Lichen
	Winter Woods	Wild Wood Cucumbers
	Winter Woods	Cone Flowers
	Winter Woods	White Spruce Cones

**CAUTION: In this product line, only the colors listed are acceptable
for K-6 use.

DEPARTMENT OF PUBLIC HEALTH

NOTICE OF ADOPTED RULES

K-6 List

CATEGORY	MANUFACTURER	PRODUCT
	Winter Woods	Coral Moss
NEEDLECRAFT		
	Needlecraft Corp. of America	WonderArt Needlepoint
	Needlecraft Corp. of America	WonderArt Counted Cross Stitch
	Needlecraft Corp. of America	Sunset Stamped Cross Stitch
	Needlecraft Corp. of America	Sunset Stitchery
	Needlecraft Corp. of America	Sunset Counted Cross Stitch
	Needlecraft Corp. of America	Sunset Needlepoint
PAINTS		
Acrylics, Artists		
	Binney & Smith	Liquitex** all except Cadmiums & Vermill
	Dick Blick Co.	Blickrylic** all except Cadmiums & Vermill
	Dick Blick Co.	Strokemaster** all except Cadmiums & Vermill
	Cardinal School	Cardinal Acrylic** all except Cadmiums & Vermill
	Ceramichrome, Inc.	Decoart Americana** all except Cadmiums & Vermill
	Ceramichrome, Inc.	Deco Art** all except Cadmiums & Vermill
	Chroma Acrylics	Atelier** Alizarin
		Black
		Brilliant Green
		Brown Oxide
		Burnt Sienna
		Burnt Umber
		Cerulean Blue Hue
		Cobalt Blue Hue

**CAUTION: In this product line, only the colors listed are acceptable
for K-6 use.

DEPARTMENT OF PUBLIC HEALTH

NOTICE OF ADOPTED RULES

K-6 List

CATEGORY	MANUFACTURER	PRODUCT
		Diox. Purple
		Gold Oxide
		Green Oxide
		Hooker's Green Hue
		Indian Red Oxide
		Lemon (Arylide) Yellow
		Mars Black
		Naples Yellow Deep
		Napthol Crimson
		Napthol Red Light
		Napthol Scarlet
		Paynes Grey
		Prussian Blue
		Pthalo Blue
		Pthalo Green
		Quin. Red Violet
		Raw Sienna
		Raw Umber
		Red Oxide
		Sap Green
		Terre Verte Hue
		Titanate Turquoise
		Trans Golden Yellow
		Trans Magenta
		Trans Red Oxide
		Ultramarine Blue
		White (Titanium)
		Yellow Lt. (Arylide)
		Yellow Mid. (Arylide)
		Yellow Oxide
	Color Craft	Createx Poster/Fabric**
		all except Cadmiums & Vermilions
	Delta/Shiva	Shiva Signatex**
		all except Cadmiums & Vermilions
	Demco Manufacturing	Demcryl**
		all except Cadmiums & Vermilions
	Duro Art Industries	Duro**
		all except Cadmiums & Vermilions
	Golden Artists Colors	Fluid
		all except Cadmiums & Vermilions

**CAUTION: In this product line, only the colors listed are acceptable
for K-6 use.

DEPARTMENT OF PUBLIC HEALTH

NOTICE OF ADOPTED RULES

K-6 List

CATEGORY	MANUFACTURER	PRODUCT
	Golden Artists Colors	Golden**
		all except Cadmiums & Vermilions
	M. Grumbacher	Hyplar Colors**
		all except Cadmiums & Vermilions
	Hunt Manufacturing	Speedball**
		all except Cadmiums & Vermilions
	Lefranc & Bourgeois	Polyflashe**
		all except Cadmiums & Vermilions
	Fratelli Maimeri	Brera**
		all except Cadmiums & Vermilions
	Martin/F. Weber Co.	Permalba**
		all except Cadmiums & Vermilions
	Martin/F. Weber Co.	Priscilla's Basecoat**
		all except Cadmiums & Vermilions
	Martin/F. Weber Co.	Weber Acrylic Base**
		all except Cadmiums & Vermilions
	NASCO International	Bulkrylic**
		all except Cadmiums & Vermilions
	Pyramid of Urbana	Pyra-Crylic**
		all except Cadmiums & Vermilions
	Rock Paint Distributing	Peacock**
		all except Cadmiums & Vermilions
	Royal Talens	Decorfin**
		all except Cadmiums & Vermilions
	Royal Talens	Rembrandt**
		all except Cadmiums & Vermilions
	Royal Talens	Talens Relief**
		all except Cadmiums & Vermilions
	Sennelier	Peintex**
		all except Cadmiums & Vermilions
	Triarco Arts & Crafts	Tri-Crylic**
		all except Cadmiums & Vermilions
	Utrecht Mfg. Co.	Utrecht**
		Viridian
		Green Earth Hue
		Sap Green
		Raw Sienna
		Raw Umber
		Burnt Sienna

**CAUTION: In this product line, only the colors listed are acceptable
for K-6 use.

DEPARTMENT OF PUBLIC HEALTH

NOTICE OF ADOPTED RULES

K-6 List

CATEGORY	MANUFACTURER	PRODUCT
		English Red, Light
		Paynes Gray
		Ivory Black
		Mars Black
		Titanium White
		Utrecht White
		Zinc Oxide
		Priming White
		Hansa Yellow, Light
		Mars Yellow
		Yellow Ochre
		Alizarin Crimson
		Ultramarine Blues & Cobalt Blue Hue
		Phthalocyanine Blue
		Cerulean Blue Hue
	Winsor & Newton	Artists' Colours**
		Azo Yellow Light
		Azo Yellow Medium
		Azo Yellow Medium
		Bronze
		Burnt Sienna
		Burnt Umber
		Chromium Oxide Green
		Dioxazine Purple
		Gold
		Hooker's Green
		Indo Orange Red
		Ivory Black
		Mars Black
		Naphthol Crimson
		Olive Green
		Paynes Grey
		Permanent Green Light
		Phthalo Blue
		Phthalo Green
		Quinacridone Red
		Quinacridone Violet
		Raw Sienna

**CAUTION: In this product line, only the colors listed are acceptable for K-6 use.

DEPARTMENT OF PUBLIC HEALTH

NOTICE OF ADOPTED RULES

K-6 List

CATEGORY	MANUFACTURER	PRODUCT
		Raw Umber
		Red Iron Oxide
		Sap Green
		Silver
		Titanium White
		Ultramarine Blue
		Yellow Ochre
	Zipatone, Inc.	Bocour Aqua-Tec**
		all except Cadmiums & Vermilio
Acrylics, Washable		
	Chroma Acrylics	Chromacryl**
		all except Cadmiums & Vermilio
	Duncan Enterprises	Doll Composition Primer**
		all except Cadmiums & Vermilio
	Duncan Enterprises	Mask N Peel**
		all except Cadmiums & Vermilio
	Duncan Enterprises	Natural Touch Drybrushing**
		all except Cadmiums & Vermilio
	Duncan Enterprises	Prep Coat**
		all except Cadmiums & Vermilio
	Duncan Enterprises	Ultra Metallics**
		all except Cadmiums & Vermilio
	Koh-I-Noor	Top Color**
		all except Cadmiums & Vermilio
		Blue Violet
		Light Purple
		Cobalt Violet Light (imit.)
		Cobalt Violet Deep (imit.)
		Violet Extra Deep
		Stable Violet
		Madder Lake Purple
		Violet Lake
		Persian Violet
		Bister
	Royal Talens	Extra Fine**
		White
		Yellow
		Deep Yellow

**CAUTION: In this product line, only the colors listed are acceptable for K-6 use.

K-6 List

CATEGORY	MANUFACTURER	PRODUCT
		Lemon Yellow
		Greenish Yellow
		Naples Yellow
		Carmine
		Carmine Hue
		Scarlet
		Indian Red
		Rose
		Talens Rose
		Deep Rose (magenta)
		Flesh Tint
		Bordeaux
		Light Brown
		Deep Brown
		Burnt Umber
		Burnt Sienna
		Sepia
		Havana Brown
		Light Blue (cyan)
		Ultramarine Light
		Ultramarine Deep
		Prussian Blue
		Cobalt Blue (ultram.)
		Turquoise Blue
		Orient Blue
		Azure Blue
		Mauve
		Cerulean Blue (phthalo.)
		Violet
		Red Violet
		Blue Violet
		Lilac
		Light Green
		Deep Green
		Emerald Green
		Viridian
	Koh-I-Noor	Top Color Metallic**
		all except Cadmiums & Vermilions
	Rich Art Color Co.	Rich Cryl**
		all except Cadmiums & Vermilions

**CAUTION: In this product line, only the colors listed are acceptable
for K-6 use.

K-6 List

CATEGORY	MANUFACTURER	PRODUCT
Caseins		
	Delta/Shiva	Shiva Colors**
		all except Cadmiums & Vermilions
Designer Colors (Gouache)		
	Koh-I-Noor	Designers' Colors**
		all except Cadmiums & Vermilions
	Lefranc & Bourgeois	Linel 35 GT**
		Permanent White
		Prussian Blue
		Turquoise Blue
		Cobalt Blue (imit.)
		Cerulean Blue
		Ultramarine Deep
		Cyan
		Vandyke Brown
		Raw Sepia
		Primary Yellow
		Persian Yellow Lemon
		Persian Yellow Light
		Persian Yellow Middle
		Persian Yellow Deep
		Persian Orange Light
		Ivory Black
		Velvet Black
		Yellow Ochre
		Red Ochre
		Carmine Imitation
		Crimson Lake
		Chinese Red
		Persian Red Light
		Magenta Red
		Burnt Umber
		Raw Umber
		Burnt Sienna
		Raw Sienna
		Olive Green
		Veronese Green (imit.)
		Emerald Oxide of Chromium (imit.)

**CAUTION: In this product line, only the colors listed are acceptable
for K-6 use.

DEPARTMENT OF PUBLIC HEALTH

NOTICE OF ADOPTED RULES

K-6 List

CATEGORY	MANUFACTURER	PRODUCT
		Japan Green Light
		Japan Green Deep
		Light Green Deep
		Persian Violet Light
		Persian Violet Deep
	Lefranc & Bourgeois	Linel 650**
		Permanent White
		Titanium White
		Super Hiding White
		Insulating White
		Cobalt Blue
		Azure Blue (#650 035)
		Hoggar Blue
		Sky Blue
		Indian Blue
		Light Blue
		Prussian Blue
		Turquoise Blue
		Ash Blue
		Cerulean Blue
		Orient Blue
		Marine Blue Light
		Marine Blue Medium
		France Blue
		Persian Blue
		Delft Blue
		Mineral Blue
		Indigo (imit.)
		Light Ultramarine
		Deep Ultramarine
		Red Brown
		Toledo Brown
		Vandyke Brown
		Warm Sepia
		Sepia
		Brown Pink
		Asia Yellow
		Carthusian Yellow
		Japanese Yellow Lemon
		Indian Yellow (imit.)
		Japanese Yellow Light
		Japanese Yellow Deep

**CAUTION: In this product line, only the colors listed are acceptable
             for K-6 use.

DEPARTMENT OF PUBLIC HEALTH

NOTICE OF ADOPTED RULES

K-6 List

CATEGORY	MANUFACTURER	PRODUCT
		Monaco Yellow
		Naples Yellow (imit.)
		Orange Lead (imit.)
		Persian Yellow Lemon
		Persian Yellow Light
		Persian Yellow Medium
		Persian Yellow Deep
		Persian Orange Light
		Persian Orange Deep
		Blue Grey
		Yellow Grey
		Paynes Grey
		Mouse Grey
		Deep Black
		Ivory Black
		Velvet Black
		Yellow Ochre
		Red Ochre
		Lemon Ochre
		Carmine (imit.)
		Carmine Extra-Fine
		Brilliant Red
		Turkish Red
		Crimson Lake
		Madder Lake Deep
		Carthame Rose
		Tyrian Rose
		Bordeaux Red
		China Red
		Mars Red
		Phoenician Red
		Ruby Red Light
		Ruby Red Deep
		Venetian Red
		Persian Red Light
		Persian Red Deep
		Madder Lake Light
		Madder Lake Garnet
		Geranium Lake
		Havana Lake
		Bengal Pink
		Cassel Earth

**CAUTION: In this product line, only the colors listed are acceptable
             for K-6 use.

DEPARTMENT OF PUBLIC HEALTH

NOTICE OF ADOPTED RULES

K-6 List

CATEGORY	MANUFACTURER	PRODUCT
		Burnt Umber
		Raw Umber
		Burnt Sienna
		Raw Sienna
		Armor Green
		Celadon Green
		Corot Green
		Cypress Gren
		Olive Green
		Water Green
		Pinaster Green
		Rich Green Deep
		Brilliant Green
		Viridian (imit.)
		Persian Green Light
		Japanese Green Light
		Japanese Green Deep
		Persian Green Deep
		Transparent Green-Blue
		Ultramarine Pink (imit.)
		Bayeux Violet
		Olive Green
		Brilliant Green Deep
		Bluish Green
		Moss Green
		Fir Green
		Turquoise Green
		Chrom. Oxide Green
		Middle Green
		Black
		Neutral Grey 1
		Neutral Grey 2
		Neutral Grey 3
		Neutral Grey 4
		Neutral Grey 5
		Silver
		Light Gold
		Deep Gold
	Turner Colour Works	Turner Design**
		all except Cadmiums & Vermilions

**CAUTION: In this product line, only the colors listed are acceptable
for K-6 use.

DEPARTMENT OF PUBLIC HEALTH

NOTICE OF ADOPTED RULES

K-6 List

CATEGORY	MANUFACTURER	PRODUCT
	Winsor & Newton	Designers'**
		Carthamus Pink
		Magenta
		Mistletoe Green
		Myosotis Blue
		Olive Green
		Oxide of Chromium
		Peacock Blue
		Sky Blue
		Vandyke Brown
		Viridian
		Yellow Ochre
		Gold
		Silver
Enamels		
	American Art Clay	Amaco Art
	American Art Clay	Amaco Art
	American Art Clay	Amaco Counterenamel
	Decart, Inc.	DEKA-Gloss
	Thompson Enamel	Hot Glass Colors**
		Tr. Yellow
		Tr. Orange Yellow
		Tr. Copper Ruby
		Clear
	Thompson Enamel	Led Free Opaques
	Thompson Enamel	Lead Free Transparents
Fabric		
	Decart, Inc.	Deka-Permanent
	Sennelier	Super Tinfix Dyes
Finger Paint, Dry		
	Binney & Smith	Crayola

**CAUTION: In this product line, only the colors listed are acceptable
for K-6 use.

DEPARTMENT OF PUBLIC HEALTH

NOTICE OF ADOPTED RULES

K-6 List

CATEGORY	MANUFACTURER	PRODUCT
Finger Paint, Liquid		
	Binney & Smith	Crayola
	Dick Blick Co.	Strokemaster
	Coloron, Inc.	Color Craft
	Dixon Ticonderoga	Prang
	J. L. Hammett Co.	Art Utility
	Palmer Paint	Palmer
	Rich Art Color Co.	Rich Art
	Sargent Art	Sargent
	Weber Costello	Alphacolor
Foam Paints		
	X-tra Art, Inc.	Rainbow Foam Paints
Tempera, Cake		
	Binney & Smith (Canada)	Crayola
	Dixon Ticonderoga	Prang
	Weber Costello	Alphacolor
	Winsor & Newton	Reeves Temperablock
Tempera, Liquid		
	Binney & Smith	Artista II
	Binney & Smith	Crayola
	Binney & Smith	Crayola Fluorescent
	Binney & Smith	Tem-Pra-Tone
	Dick Blick Co.	Blick City
	Dick Blick Co.	Strokemaster
	Coloron, Inc.	Color Craft
	Coloron, Inc.	Spectrum
	C2F, Inc.	Pro Art
	Cardinal School	Cardinal School
	Chroma Acrylics	Chromacryl Tempra I
	Chroma Acrylics	Chromacryl Tempra II

**CAUTION: In this product line, only the colors listed are acceptable
       for K-6 use.

DEPARTMENT OF PUBLIC HEALTH

NOTICE OF ADOPTED RULES

K-6 List

CATEGORY	MANUFACTURER	PRODUCT
	H. S. Crocker Co.	Sierra
	Delta/Shiva	Shiva Professional Artists
	Dixon Ticonderoga	American Crayon
	Dixon Ticonderoga	Colorart
	Dixon Ticonderoga	Prang
	J. L. Hammett Co.	Art Utility
	J. L. Hammett Co.	Hammett School Tempera
	NASCO International	NASCO Country School
	Palmer Paint	Liquid Tempra
	Palmer Paint	Ultra Tempra
	Pentel of America	YNGP-12 Poster Colors
	Pyramid of Urbana	Pyramid PPC
	Rich Art Color Co.	Liq Fesco/Rich Gel
	Rich Art Color Co.	Rich Art School
	Rock Paint Distributing	Peacock
	Sargent Art	Gothic
	Sargent Art	Sargent
	Sax Arts & Crafts	True Color
	Sax Arts & Crafts	Versatemp
	Triarco Arts & Crafts	Triarco
	Utrecht Mfg. Co.	Utrecht
	Van Aken Int'l	Jazz
	Van Aken Int'l	Leisure Tone
	Weber Costello	Alphabrite
	Weber Costello	Alphacolor
	Weber Costello	Webco
Tempera, Powder		
	Binney & Smith	Artista II
	Binney & Smith	Crayola
	Dick Blick Co.	Blick City
	Coloron, Inc.	Color Craft
	Coloron, Inc.	Spectrum
	Dixon Ticonderoga	American Crayon
	Dixon Ticonderoga	Colorart
	Dixon Ticonderoga	Prang
	Dixon Ticonderoga	Prang Media Mixer
	J. L. Hammett Co.	Art Utility
	Palmer Paint	Palmer Dry Tempra

**CAUTION: In this product line, only the colors listed are acceptable
       for K-6 use.

DEPARTMENT OF PUBLIC HEALTH

NOTICE OF ADOPTED RULES

K-6 List

CATEGORY	MANUFACTURER	PRODUCT
	Rich Art Color Co.	Fresco
	Sargent Art	Gothic
	Sargent Art	Sargent
	Weber Costello	Alphabrite
	Weber Costello	Webco
Vinyls		
	Lefranc & Bourgeois	Flashe**
		White
		Cobalt Blue
		Electric Blue
		Hoggar Blue
		Ultramarine Blue
		Prussian Blue
		Touareg Blue
		Sepia Brown
		Lemon Yellow
		Gold Yellow
		Naples Yellow Shade
		Senegal Yellow
		Orange
		Brilliant Orange Permanent
		Black
		Yellow Ochre
		Red Ochre
		Tyrian Rose
		Breughel Red
		Carmine Red
		Oriental Red
		Ruby Red
		Raw Umber
		Burnt Sienna
		Raw Sienna
		Verdaccio
		Chrome Green
		Armor Green
		Emerald Oxide of Chromium
		Light Green
		Green Oxide of Chromium
		Spring Green

**CAUTION: In this product line, only the colors listed are acceptable
for K-6 use.

DEPARTMENT OF PUBLIC HEALTH

NOTICE OF ADOPTED RULES

K-6 List

CATEGORY	MANUFACTURER	PRODUCT
		Veronese Green Shade
		Violet
		Bayeux Violet
		Violet Permanent
		White (Fluorescent)
		Light Blue (Fluorescent)
		Light Yellow (Fluorescent)
		Light Orange (Fluorescent)
		Fire Red (Fluorescent)
		Grenadine (Fluorescent)
		Bengal Red (Fluorescent)
		Light Green (Fluorescent)
		Yellow Green (Fluorescent)
Water Colors, Dry Pan		
	Daler-Rowney	Rowney Artists**
		Brown Madder (Alizarin)
		Brown Pink
		Burnt Sienna
		Burnt Umber
		Carmine
		Chinese White
		Chrome Orange
		Cobalt Blue
		Cobalt Green
		Coeruleum
		Crimson Alizarin
		Crimson Lake
		French Ultramarine
		Gamboge (Hue)
		Hooker's Green 1
		Hooker's Green 2
		Indian Red
		Indian Yellow
		Indigo
		Ivory Black
		Lemon Yellow
		Light Red
		Monestial Blue
		Monestial Green

**CAUTION: In this product line, only the colors listed are acceptable
for K-6 use.

DEPARTMENT OF PUBLIC HEALTH

NOTICE OF ADOPTED RULES

K-6 List

CATEGORY	MANUFACTURER	PRODUCT
		Naples Yellow
		Olive Green
		Paynes Grey
		Permanent Blue
		Permanent Magenta
		Permanent Mauve
		Permanent Red
		Permanent Rose
		Permanent Yellow
		Prussian Blue
		Purple Lake
		Purple Madder (Alizarin)
		Raw Sienna
		Raw Umber
		Rose Dore
		Sap Green
		Scarlet Alizarin
		Scarlet Lake
		Sepia (Permanent Sepia)
		Terre Verte (Hue)
		Vandyke Brown
		Venetian Red
		Violet Alizarin
		Viridian
		Yellow Ochre
	M. Grumbacher, Inc.	See for yourself**
		all except Cadmiums & Vermilions
	Koh-I-Noor	Fine Watercolors – 725**
		all except Cadmiums & Vermilions
	Winsor & Newton	Reeves Water Colour Tablets**
		all except Cadmiums & Vermilions
	Winsor & Newton	Sketchers**
		all except Cadmiums & Vermilions
Water Colors, Semi-Moist		
	Binney & Smith	Artista/II/Peacock**
		all except Cadmiums & Vermilions
	Binney & Smith	Crayola**
		all except Cadmiums & Vermilions

**CAUTION: In this product line, only the colors listed are acceptable
for K-6 use.

DEPARTMENT OF PUBLIC HEALTH

NOTICE OF ADOPTED RULES

K-6 List

CATEGORY	MANUFACTURER	PRODUCT
	Binney & Smith (Canada)	Crayola**
		all except Cadmiums & Vermilic
	Coloron, Inc.	Color Craft**
		all except Cadmiums & Vermilic
	Dixon Ticonderoga	American Crayon
	Dixon Ticonderoga	Colorart
	Dixon Ticonderoga	Kopy Kat
	Dixon Ticonderoga	Prang
	J.L. Hammett Co.	Art Utility**
		all except Cadmiums & Vermilic
	Royal Talens	Rembrandt**
		Chinese White
		Naples Yellow Light
		Naples Yellow Reddish
		Yellow Ochre
		Gold Ochre
		Raw Sienna
		Gamboge
		Indian Yellow
		Talens Yellow Lemon
		Talens Yellow Light
		Talens Yellow
		Talens Yellow Deep
		Talens Orange
		Transparent Oxide Yellow
		Carmine
		Madder Lake Light
		Rose Madder
		Madder Lake Deep
		Brown Madder Alizarine
		Purple Madder Alizarine
		Light Oxide Red
		Indian Red
		Talens Red Deep
		Rembrandt Rose
		Transparent Oxide Red
		Vandyke Brown
		Raw Umber
		Burnt Umber
		Burnt Sienna

**CAUTION: In this product line, only the colors listed are acceptable
for K-6 use.

K-6 List

CATEGORY	MANUFACTURER	PRODUCT
	Binney & Smith (Canada)	Crayola**
		all except Cadmiums & Vermilions
	Coloron, Inc.	Color Craft**
		all except Cadmiums & Vermilions
	Dixon Ticonderoga	American Crayon
	Dixon Ticonderoga	Colorart
	Dixon Ticonderoga	Kopy Kat
	Dixon Ticonderoga	Prang
	J.L. Hammett Co.	Art Utility**
		all except Cadmiums & Vermilions
	Royal Talens	Rembrandt**
		Chinese White
		Naples Yellow Light
		Naples Yellow Reddish
		Yellow Ochre
		Gold Ochre
		Raw Sienna
		Gamboge
		Indian Yellow
		Talens Yellow Lemon
		Talens Yellow Light
		Talens Yellow
		Talens Yellow Deep
		Talens Orange
		Transparent Oxide Yellow
		Carmine
		Madder Lake Light
		Rose Madder
		Madder Lake Deep
		Brown Madder Alizarine
		Purple Madder Alizarine
		Light Oxide Red
		Indian Red
		Talens Red Deep
		Rembrandt Rose
		Transparent Oxide Red
		Vandyke Brown
		Raw Umber
		Burnt Umber
		Burnt Sienna

**CAUTION: In this product line, only the colors listed are acceptable
for K-6 use.

K-6 List

CATEGORY	MANUFACTURER	PRODUCT
		Sepia (modern)
		Transparent Oxide Brown
		Ultramarine Light
		Ultramarine Deep
		Prussian Blue
		Cobalt Blue (ultram.)
		Rembrandt Blue
		Turquoise Blue
		Mauve
		Indigo (modern)
		Cerulean Blue (phthalo.)
		Violet
		Emerald Green
		Viridian
		Yellowish Green
		Permanent Green Light
		Olive Green
		Sap Green
		Terre Verte
		Rembrandt Green
		Hooker's Green Light
		Hooker's Green Deep
		Rembrandt Bluish Green
		Chromium Oxide Green
		Ivory Black
		Paynes Grey
		Neutral Tint
		Charcoal Grey
	Salis International	Dr. PH. Martin's Bleed Proof White
	Salis International	Dr. PH. Martin's Flo-2 White
	Salis International	Dr. PH. Martin's Graph-X White
	Salis International	Dr. PH. Martin's Radiant Concentrated
	Sargent Art	Sargent (22 series)**
		all except Cadmiums & Vermilions
	Sargent Art	Sargent (66 series)**
		all except Cadmiums & Vermilions
	Steig Products	Inkable White
	Steig Products	Luma Brilliant Concentrated**
		all except Cadmiums & Vermilions
	Steig Products	Luma Solar Chromatic**
		all except Cadmiums & Vermilions

**CAUTION: In this product line, only the colors listed are acceptable
for K-6 use.

ILLINOIS REGISTER

DEPARTMENT OF PUBLIC HEALTH

NOTICE OF ADOPTED RULES

K-6 List

CATEGORY	MANUFACTURER	PRODUCT
	Steig Products	Luma White High Opacity
	Steig Products	Pro Black
	Steig Products	Pro White Retouch White
	Steig Products	Q White Retouch White
	Steig Products	Steig White
	Winsor & Newton	Artists' Professional**
		Bright Red
		Burnt Umber
		Carmine
		Davy's Gray
		French Ultramarine
		Light Red
		Mauve
		Naples Yellow
		Olive Green
		Oxide of Chromium
		Permanent Blue
		Prussian Green
		Purple Lake
		Purple Madder Aliz.
		Raw Sienna
		Raw Umber
		Rose Madder Gen.
		Sap Green
		Sepia
		Terre Verte
		Vandyke Brown
		Venetian Red
		Viridian
		Warm Sepia
		Winsor Blue
		Winsor Emerald
		Winsor Green
		Winsor Red
		Winsor Violet
		Yellow Ochre
Water Colors, Tube		
	Binney and Smith	Liquitex**

**CAUTION: In this product line, only the colors listed are acceptable
for K-6 use.

DEPARTMENT OF PUBLIC HEALTH

NOTICE OF ADOPTED RULES

K-6 List

CATEGORY	MANUFACTURER	PRODUCT
		all except Cadmiums & Vermilions
	Daler-Rowney	Rowney Artists**
		Alizarin Green
		Brown Madder (Alizarin)
		Brown Pink
		Burnt Sienna
		Burnt Umber
		Carmine
		Chinese White
		Chrome Orange
		Cobalt Blue
		Cobalt Green
		Coeruleum
		Crimson Alizarin
		Crimson Lake
		French Ultramarine
		Gamboge (Hue)
		Hooker's Green 1
		Hooker's Green 2
		Indian Red
		Indian Yellow
		Indigo
		Ivory Black
		Lemon Yellow
		Light Red
		Monestial Blue
		Monestial Green
		Naples Yellow
		Olive Green
		Paynes Grey
		Permanent Blue
		Permanent Magenta
		Permanent Mauve
		Permanent Red
		Permanent Rose
		Permanent Yellow
		Prussian Blue
		Purple Lake
		Purple Madder (Alizarin)

**CAUTION: In this product line, only the colors listed are acceptable
for K-6 use.

DEPARTMENT OF PUBLIC HEALTH

NOTICE OF ADOPTED RULES

K-6 List

CATEGORY	MANUFACTURER	PRODUCT
		Raw Sienna
		Raw Umber
		Rose Dore
		Sap Green
		Scarlet Alizarin
		Scarlet Lake
		Sepia (Permanent Sepia)
		Terre Verte (Hue)
	Delta/Shiva	Shiva Transparent**
		Alizarin Crimson
		Burnt Sienna
		Burnt Umber
		Chinese White
		Chrome Oxide Green (Lt.)
		Citron
		Cobalt Blue Genuine
		Emerald Green
		Hooker's Green
		Ivory Black
		Light Green
		Light Red
		Mars Violet
		Paynes Gray
		Vandyke Brown
		Venetian Red
		Violet Alizarin
		Viridian
		Yellow Ochre
		Permanent Violet
		Permasol Blue
		Permasol Yellow (Gamboge)
		Prussian Blue
		Raw Sienna
		Raw Umber
		Rose Crimson
		Rose Madder
		Scarlet Red
		Sepia
		Shiva Blue Deep (Phthalo)
		Shiva blue Light (Phthalo)

** CAUTION: In this product line, only the colors listed are acceptable
for K-6 use.

DEPARTMENT OF PUBLIC HEALTH

NOTICE OF ADOPTED RULES

K-6 List

CATEGORY	MANUFACTURER	PRODUCT
		Shiva Green (Phthalo)
		Shiva Orange
		Shiva Yellow Light
		Shiva Yellow Medium
		Shiva Yellow Pale
		Terra Verte
		Ultramarine Blue
		Ultramarine Cobalt Blue
		Viridian
		Yellow Ochre
	M. Grumbacher, Inc.	Academy**
		all except Cadmiums & Vermilions
	Holbein Works, Ltd.	Holbein**
		Brown Madder
		Naples Yellow
		Aureolin
		Indian Yellow
		Perm. Yellow Orange
		Perm. Yellow Deep
		Perm. Yellow Light
		Perm. Yellow Lemon
		Lemon Yellow
		Jaune Brilliant #1
		Jaune Brilliant #2
		Yellow Ochre
		Greenish Yellow
		Yellow Grey
		Green Grey
		Sap Green
		Hooker's Green
		Viridian
		Viridian (tint)
		Compose Green #1
		Compose Green #2
		Compose Green #3
		Olive Green
		Terre Verte
		Perm. Green #1
		Perm. Green #2
		Perm. Green #3

**CAUTION: In this product line, only the colors listed are acceptable
for K-6 use.

DEPARTMENT OF PUBLIC HEALTH

NOTICE OF ADOPTED RULES

K-6 List

CATEGORY	MANUFACTURER	PRODUCT
		Emerald Green Nova
		Cobalt Green
		Blue Grey
		Cobalt blue (tint)
		Indigo
		Prussian Blue
		Ultramarine Deep
		Ultramarine Light
		Peacock Blue
		Turquoise Blue
		Compose Blue
		Paynes Grey
		Neutral Tint
		Sepia
		Mars Violet
		Mineral Violet
		Permanent Violet
		Permanent Magenta
		Violet Grey
		Indian Red
		Light Red
		Burnt Sienna
		Burnt Umber
		Vandyke Brown
		Row Umber
		Raw Sienna
		Grey of Grey
		Davy's Grey
		Ivory Black
		Peach Black
		Chinese White
	Hunt Manufacturing	Speedball Professional**
		all except Cadmiums & Vermilions
	Kooh-I-Noor	Chinese White**
		all except Cadmiums & Vermilions
	Lefranc & Bourgeois	Aquarelle 600**
		Silver white (Subst.)
		Chinese White
		Cerulean Blue
		Cobalt Blue

**CAUTION: In this product line, only the colors listed are acceptable
        for K-6 use.

DEPARTMENT OF PUBLIC HEALTH

NOTICE OF ADOPTED RULES

K-6 List

CATEGORY	MANUFACTURER	PRODUCT
		Hoggar Blue
		Hortensia Blue
		Indian Blue
		Prussian Blue
		Touareg Blue
		Blue Verditer (Subst.)
		Permanent Indigo
		Ultramarine Deep
		Ultramarine Light
		Antwerp Blue
		Mars Brown
		Transparent Brown
		Vandyke Brown
		Warm Sepia
		Raw Sepia
		Gamboge
		Flanders Yellow
		Helios Yellow
		Indian Yellow (Subst.)
		Naples Yellow (Subst.)
		Sahara Yellow
		Gallstone
		Chrome Yellow Lemon
		Paynes Grey
		Ivory Black
		Peach Black
		Yellow Ochre
		Red Ochre
		Brilliant Orange
		Mars Orange
		Madder Carmine
		Carmine Permanent
		Coral
		Crimson Lake
		Alizarin Crimson
		Deep Madder
		Rose Madder
		Carthamus Rose
		Malmaison Rose
		Tyrian Rose
		Angelico Red

**CAUTION: In this product line, only the colors listed are acceptable
        for K-6 use.

K-6 List

CATEGORY	MANUFACTURER	PRODUCT
		Breughel Red
		Ruby Red
		Uccello Red
		Venetian Red
		Bright Red
		Burnt Umber
		Raw Umber
		Burnt Sienna
		Raw Sienna
		Terre Verte
		Antioche Green Light
		Armor Green
		Ambusson Green
		Chrome Green 1 (Subst.)
		Cyprus Green 2 Permanent
		Viridian
		Hooker's Green
		Warm Green
		Olive Green
		Chromim Oxide Green
		Green Lake Permanent
		Sap Green
		Bayeux Violet
		Egypt Violet
		Violet Extra-Light
		Neutral Tint
		Permanent Violet
	Martin/F. Weber Co.	Weber**
		all except Cadmiums & Vermilions
	Pentel of America	PAW-18
	Pentel of America	SW-15 Water Color Dyes
	Pentel of America	WF-25
	Royal Telans	Rembrandt**
		Chinese White
		Naples Yellow Light
		Naples Yellow Reddish
		Yellow Ochre
		Gold Ochre
		Raw Sienna
		Gamboge
		Indian Yellow
		Talens Yellow Lemon

**CAUTION: In this product line, only the colors listed are acceptable
for K-6 use.

K-6 List

CATEGORY	MANUFACTURER	PRODUCT
		Talens Yellow Light
		Talens Yellow
		Talens Yellow Deep
		Talens Orange
		Transparent Oxide Yellow
		Carmine
		Madder Lake Light
		Rose Madder
		Madder Lake Deep
		Brown Madder Alizarine
		Purple Madder Alizarine
		Light Oxide Red
		Indian Red
		Talens Red Deep
		Rembrandt Rose
		Transparent Oxide Red
		Vandyke Brown
		Raw Umber
		Burnt Umber
		Burnt Sienna
		Transparent Oxide Brown
		Ultramarine Light
		Ultramarine Deep
		Prussian Blue
		Cobalt Blue (ultram.)
		Rembrandt Blue
		Turquoise Blue
		Mauve
		Indigo (modern)
		Cerulean Blue (phthalo.)
		Violet
		Emerald Green
		Viridian
Yellowish Green		
		Permanent Green Light
		Olive Green
		Sap Green
		Terre Verte

**CAUTION: In this product line, only the colors listed are acceptable
for K-6 use.

DEPARTMENT OF PUBLIC HEALTH

NOTICE OF ADOPTED RULES

K-6 List

CATEGORY	MANUFACTURER	PRODUCT
		Rembrandt Green
		Hooker's Green Light
		Hooker's Green Deep
		Rembrandt Bluish Green
		Chromium Oxide Green
		Ivory Black
		Paynes Grey
		Neutral Tint
		Charcoal Grey
	Royal Talens	Talens**
		Chinese White
		Yellow Ochre
		Raw Sienna
		Gamboge
		Carmine
		Madder Lake Deep
		Light Oxide Red
		Van Dyck Brown
		Raw Umber
		Burnt Umber
		Burnt Sienna
		Sepia (modern)
		Ultramarine Deep
		Prussian Blue
		Cobalt Blue (ultram.)
		Turquoise Blue
		Indigo (modern)
		Cerulean Blue (phthalo.)
		Violet
		Red Violet
		Phthalo Blue
		Emerald Green
		Viridian
		Yellowish Green
		Permanent Green Light
		Olive Green
		Sap Green
		Hooker's Green Deep
		Ivory Black

**CAUTION: In this product line, only the colors listed are acceptable
for K-6 use.

DEPARTMENT OF PUBLIC HEALTH

NOTICE OF ADOPTED RULES

K-6 List

CATEGORY	MANUFACTURER	PRODUCT
		Paynes Grey
	Sakura of America	Special Water Colors
	Utrecht Mfg. Co.	Utrecht**
		Alizarin Crimson
		Ultramarine Blue
		Phthalocyanine Blue
		Permanent Green
		Viridian
		Phthalocyanine Green
		Permanent Violet
		Yellow Ochre
		Burnt Sienna
		Raw Sienna
		Raw Umber
		Ivory Black
		Paynes Gray
	Winsor & Newton	Artists' Professional**
		Alizarin Crimson
		Antwerp Blue
		Aurora Yellow
		Blue Black
		Bright Red
		Brown Madder Aliz.
		Burnt Sienna
		Burnt Umber
		Carmine
		Cerulean Blue
		Charcoal Grey
		Crimson Lake
		Davy's Gray
		Franch Ultramarine
		Gold Ochre
		Indian Red
		Indigo
		Ivory Black
		Light Red
		Magenta
		Mars Black
		Mars Brown
		Mars Orange
		Mars Red

**CAUTION: In this product line, only the colors listed are acceptable
for K-6 use.

DEPARTMENT OF PUBLIC HEALTH

NOTICE OF ADOPTED RULES

K-6 List

CATEGORY	MANUFACTURER	PRODUCT
		Mars Violet
		Mars Yellow
		Mauve Blue Shade
		Mauve Red Shade
		New Blue
		Olive Green
		Oxide of Chromium
		Paynes Gray
		Permanent Blue
		Permanent Magenta
		Permanent Rose
		Prussian Blue
		Prussian Green
		Purple Lake
		Purple Madder Aliz.
		Raw Sienna
		Raw Umber
		Rose Dore
		Rose Madder Deep
		Rose Madder Genuine
		Sap Green
		Scarlet Lake
		Terra Rosa
		Terre Verte
		Titanium White
		Trans. Gold Ochre
		Ultramarine Deep
		Underpainting White
		Vandyke Brown
		Venetian Red
		Viridian
		Winsor Blue
		Winsor Emerald
		Winsor Green
		Winsor Lemon
		Winsor Orange
		Winsor Red
		Winsor Violet
		Winsor White
		Winsor Yellow

**CAUTION: In this product line, only the colors listed are acceptable
        for K-6 use.

DEPARTMENT OF PUBLIC HEALTH

NOTICE OF ADOPTED RULES

K-6 List

CATEGORY	MANUFACTURER	PRODUCT
		Yellow Ochre
		Yellow Ochre Pale
		Zinc White
	Winsor & Newton	London**
		Burnt Sienna
		Cerulean Blue
		Chinese White
		Cobalt Blue
		Cobalt Violet
		French Ultramarine
		Hooker's Green Dark
		Hooker's Green Light
		Indian Red
		Light Red
		Paynes Gray
		Phthalo Blue
		Prussian Blue
		Raw Sienna
		Rose Madder
		Sap Green
		Vandyke Brown
		Viridian
		Yellow Ochre
PASTELS		
Oil Pastels		
	Pentel of America	PHN-36 Oil Pastels
	Pentel of America	PTA-50 Oil Pastels
	Pentel of America	PTS-15 Pentel Dye Sticks
	Sakura Color Products	Cray-Pas
	Sakura Color Products	Chubbies
	Sakura Color Products	Deluxe Sticks
	Sakura Color Products	For Artists' Use
	Sakura Color Products	Jumbo
	Sakura Color Products	Junior
	Sakura Color Products	Large Size
	Sakura Color Products	Square Sticks

**CAUTION: In this product line, only the colors listed are acceptable
        for K-6 use.

ILLINOIS REGISTER

DEPARTMENT OF PUBLIC HEALTH

NOTICE OF ADOPTED RULES

K-6 List

CATEGORY	MANUFACTURER	PRODUCT
	Sakura Color Products	Square Type
	Sakura Color Products	Super
	Sanford	Regular Oil Pastels
	Sanford	Square Sticks
	Sanford	Jumbo Oil Pastels
Soft Pastels		
	Royal Talens	Rembrandt
PENS, PENCILS		
Ball Point		
	Gillette	Paper Mate Medium Point Stick; Blue, Red, Black, Green
	Gillette	Paper Mate Fine Point Stick; Blue, Red, Black
	Gillette	Paper Mate Ball Pen
	Gillette	Paper Mate Malibu Pen
	Gillette	Paper Mate Contour Pen
	Gillette	Paper Mate Profile Pen – Slim
	Gillette	paper Mate Profile Pen – Regular
	Gillette	Paper Mate Profile Slim Set
	Gillette	Paper Mate Executive Slim Gold Pen
	Gillette	Paper Mate Executive Slim Chrome Pen
	Gillette	Paper Mate gold Antique Pen (Burgandy)
	Gillette	Paper Mate Gold Antique Pen (Black)
	Gillette	Paper Mate Chrome Antique Pen
	Gillette	Paper Mate Gold Lacquer Pen
	Gillette	Paper Mate Profile Slim Pen
	Gillette	Paper Mate Executive Slim Gold Pen & Pencil Set
	Gillette	Paper Mate Executive Slim chrome Pen & Pencil Set
	Gillette	Paper Mate gold Antique Pen & Pencil Set (Burgandy)
	Gillette	Paper Mate Gold Antique Pen & Pencil Set (Black)

**CAUTION: In this product line, only the colors listed are acceptable for K-6 use.

DEPARTMENT OF PUBLIC HEALTH

NOTICE OF ADOPTED RULES

K-6 List

CATEGORY	MANUFACTURER	PRODUCT
	Gillette	Paper Mate Chrome Antique Pen & Penc Set
	Gillette	Paper Mate Gold Lacquer Pen & Pencil Set
	Gillette	Paper Mate Eraser Mate
	Gillette	Paper Mate Eraser Mate 2, Medium & Fine Point; blue, Red, Black
	Gillette	Paper Mate Accu-Point Fine Point; Blue, Red, Black, Green
	Gillette	Paper Mate Accu-Point Extra Fine Point; Blue, Red, Black, Green
	Gillette	Paper Mate Roller Stick; Blue, Red, Black, Green
	Gillette	Paper Mate Metal Roller; Blue, Red, Black, Green
	Gillette	Paper Mate Write Bros. Retractable, Medium & Fine Point; blue, Black
	Gillette	Paper Mate Write Bros. Prof. Fine Point Stick; Blue, Red, Black
	Gillette	Paper Mate Write Bros. Medium Point Stick; Blue, Red, Black, Green
	Gillette	Write Bros. Fine Point Stick; Blue, Red, Black
	Gillette	Paper Mate Eraser Mate Ball Point Refills
	Gillette	Paper Mate Standard Refills, Medium Fine Point Blue, Black
	Gillette	Paper Mate Powerpoint Refill, Medium Point; Blue, Red, Black
	Gillette	Paper Mate Powerpoint Refill, Fine Point; Blue, Black
	Gillette	Paper Mate Jumbo Refill, Medium & Fine Point; Blue, Black
	Gillette	Paper Mate Jumbo Powerpoint Refill, Medium & Fine Point; Blue, Black
Fountain Pens, Inks		
	Gillette	Paper Mate Gold Fountain Pen – Mediu Point, Fine Point

**CAUTION: In this product line, only the colors listed are acceptable for K-6 use.

DEPARTMENT OF PUBLIC HEALTH

NOTICE OF ADOPTED RULES

K-6 List

CATEGORY	MANUFACTURER	PRODUCT
	Gillette	Paper Mate Chrome Fountain Pen – Medium Point, Fine Point
	Gillette	Paper Mate Burgandy Antique Fountain Pen – Medium Point, Fine Point
	Gillette	Paper Mate black Antique Fountain Pen Medium Point, Fine Point
	Gillette	Paper Mate Fountain Pen Cartridges; Blue, Black
Pencils, Leads		
	Binney & Smith	Crayola Colored Pencils
	Gillette	Paper Mate Sharpwriter
	Gillette	Paper Mate Advancer – .5MM, .7MM
	Gillette	Paper Mate Advancer 100 – .5MM, .7MM
	Gillette	Paper Mate Advancer Cassette 1000, .5MM, .7MM
	Gillette	Paper Mate Advancer Leads & Eraser Refill, .5MM, .7MM
	Gillette	Paper Mate Advancer Cassette Refill .5MM, .7MM
	Gillette	Paper Mate Advancer Eraser Refill
	Gillette	Paper Mate .7MM Leads
	Gillette	Paper Mate Erasers
Plastic Point Pens		
	Gillette	Paper Mate Extra Fine Plastic Point; Blue, Red, Black, Green
Porous Tip Pens		
	Gillette	Paper Mate Nylon Fiber Porous Point; Blue, Red, black, Green, Purple, Yellow, Brown, Orange
	Gillette	Paper Mate Flair Point Guard; Blue, Red, black, Green, Purple, Brown, Orange
	Gillette	Paper Mate Ultra Fine Flair; Blue, Red

DEPARTMENT OF PUBLIC HEALTH

NOTICE OF ADOPTED RULES

K-6 List

CATEGORY	MANUFACTURER	PRODUCT
	Gillette	Black, Green Paper Mate Hardhead Flair; Blue, Red Black, Green
SCREEN PRINTING INKS & MEDIUMS		
Acrylic		
	Hunt Manufacturing	Speedball Permanent

**CAUTION: In this product line, only the colors listed are acceptable for K-6 use.

SECRETARY OF STATE

NOTICE OF ADOPTED AMENDMENT

1) The Heading of the Part: Freedom of Information

2) Code Citation: 2 Ill. Adm. Code 551

3) Section numbers: Adopted Action:
   551.140   Amendment

4) Statutory Authority: Implementing and authorized by the Freedom of
   Information Act (Ill. Rev. Stat. 1987, ch. 116, par. 201 et seq.).

5) Effective Date of Amendment: November 7, 1988

6) Does this rulemaking contain an automatic repeal date? No

7) Does this amendment contain incorporations by reference? No

8) Date Filed in Agency's Principal Office: November 7, 1988

9) Notice of Proposal Published in Illinois Register: N/A

10) Has JCAR issued a Statement of Objections to these amendments? N/A

11) Differences between proposal and final version: N/A

12) Have all the changes agreed upon by the agency and JCAR been made as
    indicated in the agreement letter issued by JCAR? N/A

13) Will these amendments replace an emergency rule amendment currently in
    effect? No

14) Are there any amendments pending on this Part? No

15) Summary and Purpose of Amendment:

    The purpose is to show that the appeal authority in Freedom of
    Information matters is the Deputy Secretary of State, whose title was
    formerly the Assistant Secretary of State. There is no substantive
    change in procedure in this amendment.

16) Information and questions regarding these adopted amendments shall be
    directed to:

    Philip S. Howe
    Counsel to the Secretary
    298 Centennial Building
    Springfield, Illinois 62706
    (217)785-3094

SECRETARY OF STATE

NOTICE OF ADOPTED AMENDMENT

The full text of the Adopted Amendment begins on the next page:

SECRETARY OF STATE

NOTICE OF ADOPTED AMENDMENT

TITLE 2: GOVERNMENTAL ORGANIZATION
SUBTITLE C: CONSTITUTIONAL OFFICERS
CHAPTER III: SECRETARY OF STATE

PART 551
FREEDOM OF INFORMATION

SUBPART A: SUMMARY AND PURPOSE

Section
551.10   Summary and Purpose
551.20   Definitions
551.30   Principal Office
551.40   Availability of Records

SUBPART B: REQUEST PROCEDURES

Section
551.110   Inspection of Records at Department Offices
551.120   Notice of Denial
551.130   Requests
551.140   Appeal Procedure to Secretary of State
551.150   Fees

Appendix A   FREEDOM OF INFORMATION REQUEST FORM

AUTHORITY: Implementing and authorized by the Freedom of Information Act (Ill. Rev. Stat. 1987, ch. 116, par. 201 et seq.).

SOURCE: Adopted at 8 Ill. Reg. 10045, effective July 1, 1984; amended at 12, Ill. Reg. ___19515___, effective November 7, 1988.

Section 551.140 Appeal Procedure to Secretary of State

a)   Any person requesting a record who has been denied access by a Department Director or Freedom of Information Officer may appeal such denial to the Secretary of State, pursuant to Section 10 of the FOIA.

b)   The appeal request must be in writing and addressed to the Assistant Deputy Secretary of State, Room 208 213, Capitol Building, Springfield, Illinois. It shall contain a copy of the original request, a copy of the denial received by the requestor, and a statement of the reasons why the appeal should be granted.

(Source: Amended at 12 Ill. Reg. ___19515___, effective November 7, 1988)

DEPARTMENT OF PUBLIC HEALTH

NOTICE OF EMERGENCY AMENDMENTS

1)   Heading of the Part:

Clinical Laboratories and Blood Banks

2)   Code Citation:

77 Ill. Adm. Code 450

3)   Section Numbers: Emergency Action:

450.440   New Section
450.450   New Section
450.1300   New Section
450.1310   New Section
450.1320   New Section
450.1330   New Section

4)   Statutory Authority:

Illinois Clinical Laboratory Act
Ill. Rev. Stat. 1987, ch. 111 1/2, par. 621-101 et seq., as amended by Public Act 85-1251, effective August 30, 1988.

5)   Effective Date of Rule(s):

October 28, 1988

6)   If the Emergency Amendments are to Expire Before the End of the 150-day Period, Please Specify the Date on Which it is to Expire:

Not Applicable

7)   Date Filed in Agency's Principal Office:

October 28, 1988

8)   Reason for Emergency:

Public Act 85-1251, effective August 30, 1988 specifies that the Department of Public Health promulgate emergency rules implementing the provisions of the Act within 60 days of the effective date of the Public Act.

9)   A Complete Description of the Subjects and Issues Involved:

This rulemaking specifies what laboratory tests are considered health screening tests, what entities can perform health screening activities,

DEPARTMENT OF PUBLIC HEALTH

NOTICE OF EMERGENCY AMENDMENTS

9) A Complete Description of the Subjects and Issues Involved: (continued)

and how health screening activities are to be conducted.

The Department has solicited and received numerous recommendations concerning what laboratory tests should be listed as health screening tests. After a review of all recommendations and the recent legislation, the Department has decided upon the following approach.

In response to HB 3911 and HB 3303, the Department proposes to adopt only two specific exclusive lists of tests: (1) a list of tests for health screening, which is included in this rulemaking and (2) a list of tests for the registration class which the Department anticipates proposing in February of 1989 under HB 3303. All remaining tests would be either "simple" or "complex" under the provisions of HB 3303. The lists of tests would be as follows:

A "HEALTH SCREENING" test "MEANS THE PERFORMANCE OF ANY OF THE DEPARTMENT LISTED TESTS FOR THE PURPOSE OF ASSESSING A PHASE OF THE GENERAL STATE OF HEALTH OF HUMAN SUBJECTS" in the context of an off-site health screening event such as a health fair. Tests designed as health screening tests may be conducted at the principal location of the laboratory without the protocol required by these rules.

A. Health Screening Test list pursuant HB 3911 - Public Act 85-1251, effective August 30, 1988.

    1. Blood total cholesterol testing by finger stick method, and
    2. Blood glucose testing by finger stick method.

B. DRAFT registration class tests pursuant to HB 3303 - Public Act 85-1025, effective June 30, 1988.

    1.   Any tests performed by a Physician, Dentist or Podiatrist;
    2.   Hematocrit;
    3.   Hemoglobin;
    4.   Blood lead level testing;
    5.   Chemical Urinalysis testing;
    6.   Sickle cell anemia testing;
    7.   Sperm count testing;
    8.   Pin worm testing;
    9.   Blood cholesterol testing;
    10. Blood glucose testing;
    11. Occult blood testing;
    12. Urine pregnancy testing (semi-quantitative chorionic gonadotropin), and
    13. Triglycerides.

DEPARTMENT OF PUBLIC HEALTH

NOTICE OF EMERGENCY AMENDMENTS

9) A Complete Description of the Subjects and Issues Involved: (continued)

Under the existing clinical laboratory rules (77 Ill. Adm. Code 450.30(b)(7)) and until new rules pursuant to HB 3303 are adopted circa July 1, 1989, local health department laboratories are exempt from licensure in the following situation:

PUBLIC HEALTH LABORATORIES WHICH MEET THE PROVISIONS OF SECTION 1-103(e) OF THE ILLINOIS CLINICAL LABORATORY ACT AND WHICH RESTRICT THEIR CLINICAL LABORATORY TESTING TO THE FOLLOWING: SMEARS AND CULTURES FOR NEISSERIA GONORRHEAE, WET MOUNTS FOR YEAST OR TRICHOMONAS, SYPHILIS SEROLOGY, SEMI/QUANTITATIVE CHORIONIC GONADOTROPIN, GLUCOSE, URINALYSIS (LIMITED TO DIP-STICK AND MICROSCOPIC FOR RED AND WHITE CELLS), HEMATOCRIT, HEMOGLOBIN, AND RBC SICKLE CELL SCREENING.

Pursuant to HB 3911 and emergency rules to be adopted circa October 28, 1988, local health departments will also be able to conduct health screenings without a license or permit if done on a not for profit or free of charge basis. The health screening tests can be in addition to those tests presently permissible without a license.

Both the present rules and the health screening rules will be combined and explained further in future amendments pursuant to HB 3303 which will be drafted later this year.

NOTICE OF PUBLIC HEARING ON EMERGENCY AMENDMENTS AND PROPOSED AMENDMENTS

The Department will conduct public hearings on these EMERGENCY RULES and the identical PROPOSED AMENDMENTS at the following times and places:

Date, Time and Location of Public Hearings:

1:00 PM
December 8, 1988
Illinois Department of Public Health
First Floor Training Room
525 West Jefferson
Springfield, Illinois 62761

10:00 AM
December 9, 1988
Ninth Floor, Room 40
State of Illinois Center
100 West Randolph Street
Chicago, Illinois 60601

DEPARTMENT OF PUBLIC HEALTH

NOTICE OF EMERGENCY AMENDMENTS

9) A Complete Description of the Subjects and Issues Involved: (continued)

Other Pertinent Information:

The hearings will be for the sole purpose of gathering public comment. Persons interested in presenting testimony at this hearing are advised that the Department will adhere to the following procedures in the conduct of the hearing:

1. Each person presenting oral testimony shall provide to the hearing officer a written (preferably typed) copy of such testimony at the time the oral testimony is presented. No oral testimony shall be accepted without such written copy of the testimony being provided.

2. Each person presenting oral testimony will be limited to fifteen (15) minutes for the presentation of such testimony.

3. No person will be recognized to speak for a second time until all persons wishing to testify have done so. All testimony shall conclude at the specific times except that an individual in the midst of presenting testimony shall be allowed to complete his/her testimony.

4. In order to provide for a balanced presentation of views and to facilitate the orderly conduct of the hearing, the Hearing Officer may impose such other rules of procedure, including the order of call of witnesses, as he/she deems necessary.

10) Are there any proposed amendments to this Part Pending? No.

Section Numbers   Proposed Action   Ill. Reg. Citation

11) Statement of Statewide Policy Objectives:

This rulemaking is required by Public Act 85-1251. The Department believes any expansion or contraction of a state mandate is necessary in order to protect the public from inaccurate testing procedures.

12) Information and Questions Regarding this Rule shall be directed to:

Robert John Kane, Administrative Rules Coordinator, Illinois Department of Public Health, 525 West Jefferson-Second Floor, Springfield, Illinois 62761, (217) 782-6187.

The full text of the Emergency Amendments begins on the next page:

DEPARTMENT OF PUBLIC HEALTH

NOTICE OF EMERGENCY AMENDMENTS

TITLE 77: PUBLIC HEALTH
CHAPTER I: DEPARTMENT OF PUBLIC HEALTH
SUBCHAPTER d: LABORATORIES AND BLOOD BANKS

PART 450
CLINICAL LABORATORIES AND BLOOD BANKS

SUBPART A: GENERAL

Section
450.10   Definitions
450.20   Laboratories and Blood Banks
450.30   Laboratories required to be licensed

SUBPART B: DIRECTORS OF CLINICAL LABORATORIES

Section
450.210 Qualification of the Director of a Clinical Laboratory
450.220 Operational Participation of the Director
450.230 Number of Laboratories Permitted to Operate

SUBPART C: LOCATION, CONSTRUCTION AND SANITATION

Section
450.310 Location
450.320 Conformance to local ordinances
450.330 Safety and Sanitation Requirements

SUBPART D: QUALIFICATIONS OF PERSONNEL HAVING REPONSIBILITY FOR
            THE CONDUCT AND OPERATION OF THE LABORATORY

Section
450.410 Supervisor
450.420 Medical Technologist
450.430 Cytotechnologist
450.440 Technician
EMERGENCY
450.450 Laboratory Assistant
EMERGENCY

SUBPART E: EQUIPMENT

Section
450.510 Facilities and Equipment
450.520 Preventive Maintenance of Equipment and Instruments
450.530 Glassware
450.540 Lancets, Needles and Syringes
450.550 Electrical Equipment

ILLINOIS REGISTER

DEPARTMENT OF PUBLIC HEALTH

NOTICE OF EMERGENCY AMENDMENTS

DEPARTMENT OF PUBLIC HEALTH

NOTICE OF EMERGENCY AMENDMENTS

Authority: Implementing and authorized by the Illinois Blood Bank Act (Ill.
Rev. Stat. 1987, ch. 111 1/2, par. 601-101 et seq.), The Blood Labeling Act
(Ill. Rev. Stat. 1987, ch. 111 1/2, par. 620-3.1) and the Illinois Clinical
Laboratory Act (Ill. Rev. Stat. 1987, ch. 111 1/2, par. 621 et seq.).

SOURCE: Amended November 16, 1970; amended at 2 Ill. Reg., p. 87, effective
November 5, 1978; amended at 4 Ill. Reg. 33, p. 224, 225 and 228, effective
August 6, 1980; amended at 6 Ill. Reg. 4151, effective April 5, 1982; amended
at 7 Ill. Reg. 7643, effective June 14, 1983; codified at 8 Ill. Reg. 19488;
amended at 9 Ill. Reg. 20709, effective January 3, 1986; emergency amendment
at 10 Ill. Reg. 377, effective January 3, 1986; for a maximum of 150 days,
amended at 10 Ill. Reg. 10712, effective June 3, 1986; amended at 12 Ill. Reg.
10018, effective May 27, 1988; emergency amendment at 12 Ill. Reg. 19518 ,
effective October 28, 1988, for a maximum of 150 days.

SUBPART D: QUALIFICATIONS OF PERSONNEL HAVING RESPONSIBILITY
FOR THE CONDUCT AND OPERATION OF THE LABORATORY

Section 450.440 Technician
EMERGENCY

An individual who meets one of the following qualifications shall qualify as a
technician:

    a) Successful completion of 60 semester hours of academic credit
        including chemistry and biology as well as a structured curriculum in
        medical laboratory techniques at an accredited institution or has an

DEPARTMENT OF PUBLIC HEALTH

NOTICE OF EMERGENCY AMENDMENTS

associate degree based on a course of study including those subjects from an accredited institution; or

b)   High school graduate or equivalent and has completed at least 1 year in a technician training program in a school accredited by an accrediting agency approved by the U.S. Office of Education; or

c)   High school graduate or equivalent and has successfully completed an official military medical laboratory procedures course of at least 50 weeks duration and has held the military enlisted occupational specialty of Medical Laboratory Specialist (Laboratory Technician).

(Source: Emergency rule added at 12 Ill. Reg. _19518_ , effective October 28, 1988, for a maximum of 150 days)

Section 450.450 Laboratory Assistant
EMERGENCY

A laboratory assistant is an individual who is employed in a laboratory and meets the education and experience requirements set forth by that laboratory director and who functions only under the direct supervision of a director, supervisor or technologist.

(Source: Emergency rule added at 12 Ill. Reg. _19518_ , effective October 28, 1988, for a maximum of 150 days).

SUBPART M: HEALTH SCREENING

Section 450.1300 Health Screening and Approved Health Screening Tests
EMERGENCY

a)   "HEALTH SCREENING" MEANS THE PERFORMANCE OF ANY OF THE FOLLOWING TESTS FOR THE PURPOSE OF ASSESSING A PHASE OF THE GENERAL STATE OF HEALTH OF HUMAN SUBJECTS (Section 2-102.1 of the Act):

1)   Blood total cholesterol testing by finger stick method, and

2)   Blood glucose testing by finger stick method.

b)   Health screening activities may only be conducted by the following entities:

1)   LABORATORIES WHICH ONLY PERFORM HEALTH SCREENINGS ON A NOT-FOR-PROFIT OR FREE-OF-CHARGE BASIS. NOT-FOR-PROFIT OR FREE-OF-CHARGE BASIS means screenings performed for a fee calculated to recover the actual cost of the test material and equipment and direct labor costs, excluding any cost associated with test interpretation or other administrative costs or with no direct cost to the recipient;

DEPARTMENT OF PUBLIC HEALTH

NOTICE OF EMERGENCY AMENDMENTS

2)   LICENSED OR PERMITTED LABORATORIES; and

3)   Licensed Hospital laboratories which are exempt from regulation under the Act and not precluded from such activities under the Hospital Licensing Act (Ill. Rev. Stat. 1987, ch. 111 1/2, par. 142 et seq.).(Section 2-102.1(a)(3) and (b) of the Act)

c)   ANY ENTITIES WHICH CONDUCT MORE THAN ONE HEALTH SCREENING EVENT PER calendar YEAR SHALL FILE ESTABLISHED PROTOCOLS WITH THE DEPARTMENT IN ACCORDANCE WITH the provisions of this Subpart. A health screening event, as used in this Section, shall mean any day or continuous series of days not exceeding five on which health screening activities are conducted in the same location other than the principal location of the laboratory such as a health fair. Tests listed as health screening tests may be conducted at the principal location of the laboratory without the protocol required by this Subpart. (Section 2-102.1(a)(2) of the Act).

d)   AGENCY NOTE: Health screening tests should not be used as diagnostic tests.

(Source: Emergency rule added at 12 Ill. Reg. _19518_ , effective October 28, 1988, for a maximum of 150 days).

Section 450.1310 Protocol for Conducting Health Screening
EMERGENCY

a)   Any entity which performs health screening shall establish a protocol for health screening activities which is APPROVED BY A PHYSICIAN LICENSED TO PRACTICE MEDICINE IN ALL ITS BRANCHES. (Section 2-102.1(a)(1) of the Act)

b)   The protocol for conducting the health screening shall:

1)   indicate the test(s) to be conducted;

2)   indicate the way in which results shall be reported to the test subject including any available oral counseling and health professional referral program;

3)   indicate how confidentiality will be maintained with provisions which allow the testing personnel, test subject and test subject's representative access to the test results;

4)   include a written quality control program to assure accurate and precise test values as set by the physician signing the protocol

DEPARTMENT OF PUBLIC HEALTH

NOTICE OF EMERGENCY AMENDMENTS

and a description of the steps to be taken if the control values fall outside acceptable limits as set by the physician in the written quality control program;

5) include the step by step instructions for the following:

   i) specimen collection, handling, transport, storage and disposal;

   ii) patient preparation;

   iii) type and volume of specimen needed and the established rejection criteria;

   iv) proper specimen identification;

   v) proper reagent use, such as labeling, proper lot number usage, expiration dates, and storage requirements, and

   vi) instrument operation and calibration in accordance with the manufacturer's instructions.

6) include a detailed procedure for all quantitative methodologies, to be performed at least once each twelve hours, to determine method linearity over the reportable range of values for each analyte and instrument;

7) include directions for the use of one reference material and one calibrator or two reference materials with different concentrations once each 24 hour period in which the analyzer is used;

8) include a description of the training required of all staff conducting specific health screening tests;

9) include a copy of educational materials for each individual screening test given to each test subject;

10) be available to all health screening personnel at the test site;

11) be sent to the Department at least 30 days prior to the initial testing date if more than one health screening event is conducted by that entity in a calendar year. Such protocols will be effective for one year. An existing protocol may be renewed by submitting a letter from the physician who signed the protocol specifying that no changes have been made in the protocol and that the protocol will be used for health screenings over the next year. This letter must be submitted

DEPARTMENT OF PUBLIC HEALTH

NOTICE OF EMERGENCY AMENDMENTS

within 30 days prior to the expiration of the existing protocol;

12) be signed, dated, and approved by a physician licensed to practice medicine in all its branches no earlier than three months prior to submission date;

13) include, for not-for-profit or free-of-charge operations, a statement from the physician who signs the protocol that the education and experience of the staff members are adequate to assure proper specimen collection, specimen handling, instrument operation, quality assurance, record-keeping, reporting of results, and proper sanitary conditions to protect the test subjects and the environment;

14) include a copy of the document to be given to each test subject which discloses the purpose and limitations of each individual screening test to be conducted;

15) state whether the testing to be conducted will be done on a NOT-FOR-PROFIT OR FREE-OF-CHARGE basis or for-profit basis. If the testing is conducted on a NOT-FOR-PROFIT basis, then the calculations used to determine the actual cost of the test material and equipment must be included.

16) include copies of any forms used in the course of conducting health screening activities;

17) indicate how documentation and quality control items are traceable to each individual analyte and instruments used in the health screening process and how records shall be maintained;

18) indicate how records of test subject results and documentation of quality control items shall be maintained for two years, and

19) document the basis for any fee charged to the recipient indicating whether testing is being done on a for-profit or not-for-profit basis.

(Source: Emergency rule added at 12 Ill. Reg. 19526, effective October 28, 1988, for a maximum of 150 days)

Section 450.1320 Application for a Permit to Conduct Health Screening EMERGENCY

THE OWNER OF A CLINICAL LABORATORY WHICH IS OPERATED AND MAINTAINED EXCLUSIVELY FOR THE PURPOSE OF CONDUCTING HEALTH SCREENING TESTS BY A PERSON, CORPORATION, ORGANIZATION, ASSOCIATION OR GROUP WHICH PROVIDES HEALTH

DEPARTMENT OF PUBLIC HEALTH

NOTICE OF EMERGENCY AMENDMENTS

SCREENING SERVICES IN ACCORDANCE WITH SECTION 2-102.1 of the Act EITHER
DIRECTLY OF INDIRECTLY ON A FOR-PROFIT BASIS MUST OBTAIN A PERMIT FROM THE
DEPARTMENT. APPLICATION SHALL BE MADE ON A FORM PRESCRIBED BY THE
DEPARTMENT. THE APPLICATION SHALL BE ACCOMPANIED BY AN APPLICATION FEE OF $
200 FOR EACH SUCH PERMIT. THE APPLICATION SHALL BE UNDER OATH (i.e. signed by
the owner or authorized officer and notarized). THE PERMIT SHALL EXPIRE JULY
1, 1989, AND THE APPLICATION SHALL CONTAIN THE FOLLOWING INFORMATION:

a) THE NAME AND LOCATION OF THE OWNER'S PRINCIPAL PLACE OF BUSINESS;

b) THE NAME OF THE OWNER OF SUCH FACILITY AND OF THE DIRECTOR THEREOF;

c) When the owner is a corporation the names and addresses of all
persons owning five percent or more of shares of the corporation;

d) a completed personnel form for the director(s), the anticipated
schedule of hours for the director(s) to be at the laboratory during
hours of testing, and other laboratories directed by the director(s);

e) A DESCRIPTION OF THE PROGRAM AND SERVICES PROVIDED BY SUCH CLINICAL
LABORATORY;

f) the name of the laboratory assistant(s) or technician(s) employed and
a completed personnel form for each laboratory assistant or
technician;

g) the name of the person(s) who is in charge of the total laboratory
operation at the test site and a personnel form(s) for that person;

h) a statement signed by the director indicating that the person in
charge of the total laboratory operation at the test site has the
education and training necessary to assure proper specimen
collection, specimen handling, instrument operation, recordkeeping,
reporting of results to assure confidentiality of test subjects and
results, and proper sanitary conditions to protect the test subjects
and environment;

i) an explanation of the location where all equipment and supplies are
kept when not at the test site and the location where all records are
kept relating to the laboratory operations at the test sites; and

j) a copy of the physician approved protocol.

(Source: Emergency rule added at 12 Ill. Reg. 19518 , effective October
28, 1988, for a maximum of 150 days)

DEPARTMENT OF PUBLIC HEALTH

NOTICE OF EMERGENCY AMENDMENTS

Section 450.1330 Reporting and Notification
EMERGENCY

a) All health screening entities shall file a protocol with the
Department in accordance with Section 450.1310 of this Part.

b) All health screening entities shall notify the Department of all
health screening sites including street address, city, zip code and
any other identifying data that are available at least seven days
prior to any health screening event.

c) All health screening entities shall notify the Department of all
personnel anticipated to conduct any health screening event including
name, professions, training background, street address, city, zip
code at least seven days prior to any health screening event.

(Source: Emergency rule added at 12 Ill. Reg. 19518, effective October 28,
1988, for a maximum of 150 days)

DEPARTMENT OF REVENUE

NOTICE OF MODIFICATION TO EMERGENCY AMENDMENTS IN RESPONSE TO
AN OBJECTION OF THE JOINT COMMITTEE ON ADMINISTRATIVE RULES

1) Heading of the Part: Retailers' Occupation Tax

2) Code Citation: 86 Ill. Adm. Code 130

3) Section numbers: 130.2000

4) Notice of Emergency Amendments published in the Illinois Register:

September 9, 1988 , 12 Ill. Reg. 14401
(Issue date)

5) JCAR Statement of Objection to Emergency Amendments published in the
Illinois Register:

October 28, 1988 , 12 Ill. Reg. 17450
(Issue date)

6) Effective date of original emergency rulemaking: September 1, 1988

7) Date agency submitted this modification to JCAR for approval: November 3, 1988

8) Summary of Action Taken by the Agency?

Rule was redrafted in accordance with the objections of the Joint Committee.

The full text of the Section(s) of the emergency amendments being modified
begins on the next page:

DEPARTMENT OF REVENUE

NOTICE OF MODIFICATION TO EMERGENCY AMENDMENTS IN RESPONSE TO AN
OBJECTION OF THE JOINT COMMITTEE ON ADMINISTRATIVE RULES

TITLE 86: REVENUE
CHAPTER I: DEPARTMENT OF REVENUE

PART 130
RETAILERS' OCCUPATION TAX

SUBPART A: NATURE OF TAX

Section
130.101 Character and Rate of Tax
130.115 Responsibility of Trustees, Receivers, Executors or Administrators
130.110 Occasional Sales
130.111 Sale of Used Motor Vehicles by Leasing or Rental Business
130.115 Habitual Sales
130.120 Nontaxable Transactions

SUBPART B: SALE AT RETAIL

Section
130.201 The Test of a Sale at Retail
130.205 Sales for Transfer Incident to Service
130.210 Sales of Tangible Personal Property to Purchasers for Resale
130.215 Further Illustrations
130.220 Sales to Lessors of Tangible Personal Property

SUBPART C: CERTAIN STATUTORY EXEMPTIONS

Section
130.305 Farm Machinery and Equipment
130.310 Food, Drugs, Medicines and Medical Appliances
130.315 Fuel Sold for Use in Vessels on Rivers Bordering Illinois
130.320 Gasohol
130.325 Graphic Arts Machinery and Equipment Exemption
130.330 Manufacturing Machinery and Equipment
EMERGENCY
130.335 Pollution Control Facilities
130.340 Rolling Stock
130.345 Oil Field Exploration, Drilling and Production Equipment
130.350 Coal Exploration, Mining, Off Highway Hauling, Processing,
         Maintenance and Reclamation Equipment

SUBPART D: GROSS RECEIPTS

Section
130.401 Meaning of Gross Receipts
130.405 How to Avoid Paying Tax on State or Local Tax Passed on to the
         Purchaser
130.410 Cost of Doing Business Not Deductible
130.415 Transportation and Delivery Charges
130.420 Finance or Interest Charges--Penalties--Discounts
130.425 Traded-In Property
130.430 Deposit or Prepayment on Purchase Price

19533
88   ILLINOIS REGISTER
                 DEPARTMENT OF REVENUE

         NOTICE OF MODIFICATION TO EMERGENCY AMENDMENTS IN RESPONSE TO AN
             OBJECTION OF THE JOINT COMMITTEE ON ADMINISTRATIVE RULES

                 ILLINOIS REGISTER   19534
                                                         88
                 DEPARTMENT OF REVENUE

         NOTICE OF MODIFICATION TO EMERGENCY AMENDMENTS IN RESPONSE TO AN
             OBJECTION OF THE JOINT COMMITTEE ON ADMINISTRATIVE RULES

DEPARTMENT OF REVENUE

NOTICE OF MODIFICATION TO EMERGENCY AMENDMENTS IN RESPONSE TO AN
OBJECTION OF THE JOINT COMMITTEE ON ADMINISTRATIVE RULES

Section
130.1501 Claims for Credit—Limitations—Procedure
130.1505 Disposition of Credit Memoranda by Holders Thereof
130.1510 Refunds
130.1515 Interest

SUBPART P: PROCEDURE TO BE FOLLOWED UPON
SELLING OUT OR DISCONTINUING BUSINESS
Section
130.1601 When Returns are Required After a Business is Discontinued
130.1605 When Returns Are Not Required After Discontinuation of a Business
130.1610 Cross Reference to Bulk Sales Regulation

SUBPART Q: NOTICE OF SALES OF GOODS IN BULK
Section
130.1701 General Information

SUBPART R: POWER OF ATTORNEY
Section
130.1801 When Powers of Attorney May be Given
130.1805 Filing of Power of Attorney With Department
130.1810 Filing of Papers by Agent Under Power of Attorney

SUBPART S: SPECIFIC APPLICATIONS
Section
130.1901 Addition Agents to Plating Baths
130.1905 Agricultural Producers
130.1910 Antiques, Curios, Art Work, Collectors' Coins, Collectors' Postage
Stamps and Like Articles
130.1915 Auctioneers and Agents
130.1920 Barbers and Beauty Shop Operators
130.1925 Blacksmiths
130.1930 Chiropodists, Osteopaths and Chiropractors
130.1935 Computer Software
130.1940 Construction Contractors and Real Estate Developers
130.1945 Co-operative Associations
130.1950 Dentists
130.1951 Enterprise Zones
130.1955 Farm Chemicals
130.1960 Finance Companies and Other Lending Agencies:- Installment Contracts
- Repossessions
130.1965 Florists and Nurserymen
130.1970 Hatcheries
130.1975 Operators of Games of Chance and Their Suppliers
130.1980 Optometrists, Oculists and Opticians
130.1985 Pawnbrokers
130.1990 Peddlers, Hawkers and Itinerant Vendors

DEPARTMENT OF REVENUE

NOTICE OF MODIFICATION TO EMERGENCY AMENDMENTS IN RESPONSE TO AN
OBJECTION OF THE JOINT COMMITTEE ON ADMINISTRATIVE RULES

130.1995 Personalizing Tangible Personal Property
130.2000 Persons Engaged in the Printing, Graphic Arts or Related Occupations, and Their Suppliers
EMERGENCY
130.2005 Persons Engaged in Nonprofit Service Enterprises and in Similar
Enterprises Operated As Businesses, and Suppliers of Such Persons
130.2006 Sales by Teacher-Sponsored Student Organizations
130.2007 Exemption Identification Numbers
130.2010 Persons Who Rent or Lease the Use of Tangible Personal Property to
Others
130.2015 Persons Who Repair or Otherwise Service Tangible Personal Property
130.2020 Physicians and Surgeons
130.2025 Picture-Framers
130.2030 Public Amusement Places
130.2035 Registered Pharmacists and Druggists
130.2040 Retailers of Clothing
130.2045 Retailers on Premises of the Illinois State Fair, County Fairs, Art
Shows, Flea Markets and the Like
130.2050 Sales and Gifts By Employers to Employees
130.2055 Sales by Governmental Bodies
130.2060 Sales of Alcoholic Beverages, Motor Fuel and Tobacco Products
130.2065 Sales of Automobiles for Use In Demonstration
130.2070 Sales of Containers, Wrapping and Packing Materials and Related
Products
130.2075 Sales To Construction Contractors, Real Estate Developers and
Speculative Builders
130.2080 Sales to Governmental Bodies
130.2085 Sales to or by Banks and Savings and Loan Associations
130.2090 Sales to Railroad Companies
130.2095 Sellers of Gasohol, Coal, Coke, Fuel Oil and Other Combustibles
130.2100 Sellers of Feeds and Breeding Livestock
130.2105 Sellers of Newspapers, Magazines, Books, Sheet Music and Phonograph
Records and their Suppliers
130.2110 Sellers of Seeds and Fertilizer
130.2115 Sellers of Machinery, Tools and the Like
130.2120 Suppliers of Persons Engaged in Service Occupations and Professions
130.2125 Trading Stamps and Discount Coupons
130.2130 Undertakers and Funeral Directors
130.2135 Vending Machines
130.2140 Vendors of Curtains, Slip Covers, Floor Covering and Other Similar
Items made to Order
130.2145 Vendors of Meals
130.2150 Vendors of Memorial Stones and Monuments
130.2155 Vendors of Signs
130.2156 Vendors of Steam
130.2160 Vendors of Tangible Personal Property Employed for Premiums,
Advertising, Prizes, Etc.

NOTICE OF MODIFICATION TO EMERGENCY AMENDMENTS IN RESPONSE TO AN
OBJECTION OF THE JOINT COMMITTEE ON ADMINISTRATIVE RULES

130.2165 Veterinarians
130.2170 Warehousemen

AUTHORITY: Implementing the Illinois Retailers' Occupation Tax Act (Ill.
Rev. Stat. 1987, ch. 120, pars. 440 et seq.) and authorized by Section 39b3
of the Civil Administrative Code of Illinois (Ill. Rev. Stat. 1987, ch. 127,
par. 39b3).

SOURCE: Adopted July 1, 1933; amended at 2 Ill. Reg. 50, p. 71, effective
December 10, 1978; amended at 3 Ill. Reg. 12, p. 4, effective March 19, 1979;
amended at 3 Ill. Reg. 13, pp. 93 and 95, effective March 25, 1979; amended
at 3 Ill. Reg. 21, p. 164, effective June 3, 1979; amended at 3 Ill. Reg. 25,
p. 229, effective June 17, 1979; amended at 3 Ill. Reg. 44, p. 193, effective
October 19, 1979; amended at 3 Ill. Reg. 46, p. 52, effective November 2,
1979; amended at 4 Ill. Reg. 24, pp. 520, 539, 564 and 571, effective June 1,
1980; amended at 5 Ill. Reg. 818, effective January 2, 1981; amended at 5
Ill. Reg. 3014, effective March 11, 1981; amended at 5 Ill. Reg. 12782,
effective November 2, 1981; amended at 6 Ill. Reg. 2860, effective March 3,
1982; amended at 6 Ill. Reg. 6780, effective May 24, 1982; codified at 6 Ill.
Reg. 8229; recodified at 6 Ill. Reg. 8999; amended at 6 Ill. Reg. 15225,
effective December 3, 1982; amended at 7 Ill. Reg. 7990, effective June 15,
1983; amended at 8 Ill. Reg. 5319, effective April 11, 1984; amended at 8
Ill. Reg. 19062, effective September 26, 1984; amended at 10 Ill. Reg. 1937,
effective January 10, 1986; amended at 10 Ill. Reg. 12067, effective July 1,
1986; amended at 10 Ill. Reg. 19538, effective November 5, 1986; amended at
10 Ill. Reg. 19772, effective November 5, 1986; amended at 11 Ill. Reg. 4325,
effective March 2, 1987; amended at 11 Ill. Reg. 6252, effective March 20,
1987; amended at 11 Ill. Reg. 18284, effective October 27, 1987; amended at
11 Ill. Reg. 18767, effective October 28, 1987; amended at 11 Ill. Reg.
19138, effective October 29, 1987; amended at 11 Ill. Reg. 19696, effective
November 23, 1987; amended at 12 Ill. Reg. 5652, effective March 15, 1988;
emergency amendments at 12 Ill. Reg. 14401, effective September 1, 1988, for
a maximum of 150 days, modified in response to an objection of the Joint Committee on Administrative Rules at 12 Ill. Reg.19531, effective Nov. 4, 1988,
not to exceed the 150 day time limit of the original rulemaking.

NOTE: Capitalization denotes statutory language.

Section 130.2000 Persons Engaged in the Printing, Graphic Arts or Related
Occupations, and Their Suppliers
EMERGENCY

a) Classification of Businesses

Falling into the classification of persons engaged in the graphic
arts or related occupations are printers, book binders,

NOTICE OF MODIFICATION TO EMERGENCY AMENDMENTS IN RESPONSE TO AN
OBJECTION OF THE JOINT COMMITTEE ON ADMINISTRATIVE RULES

typographers, portrait or commercial photographers, commercial
artists, portrait painters, sign painters, photostaters, and
blueprinters and photofinishers. This list is illustrative, but not
exhaustive. Persons falling under this Part may or may not qualify
for the graphic arts machinery and equipment exemption set forth in
Section 130.3.5. Effective September 1, 1988, retailers of photoprocessing products are subject to Retailers' Occupation Tax. This
includes photofinishers, portrait and studio photographers,
free-lance and other photographers engaged in the business of selling the products of photoprocessing. Photoprocessing products
include, but are not limited to, negatives, prints, motion picture
and slides. Magnetic video tape is not included, nor are other
graphic arts processes such as printing, lithography, photographers,
film makers, and other servicemen, are required to collect
Retailers' Occupation Tax on the photoprocessing component of their
total service charge when they sell products of photoprocessing.
The tax on the photoprocessing component will apply regardless of
whether the photographer performs the photoprocessing in-house, or
engages a third-party photoprocessor. Photoprocessing includes, but
is not limited to: developing films, positives and negatives,
transparencies, tinting, coloring, making and enlarging prints.
Photoprocessing does not include color separation and typesetting by
photographic means in the graphic arts industry. The charge for
in-house photoprocessing may not be less than the photoprocessor's
cost price of materials. If a charge for the photoprocessing
component is not separately stated, tax is imposed on 50% of the
entire selling price.

1) EXAMPLE: The commercial photographer receives an assignment to
   shoot a specified layout from an advertising agency. The
   photographer selects the location, hires the models, arranges
   for the make-up, rents the equipment and shoots the scene. The
   photographer sends the undeveloped film to an outside
   photoprocessing laboratory for development. The photographer's
   bill for the sale of the photograph includes a charge for his
   artistic and other services and a separately-stated charge for
   the photoprocessing component which is either the charge made
   to him by the photoprocessing laboratory or such an amount plus
   his customary mark-up. The tax should only be applied to the
   photoprocessing component.

2) EXAMPLE: The same facts as above except the photographer does
   not separately state a charge for the photoprocessing component
   and bills his client a lump sum. A tax is collected on 50% of
   the lump sum price.

3) EXAMPLE: A portrait photographer photographs a family in his

DEPARTMENT OF REVENUE

NOTICE OF MODIFICATION TO EMERGENCY AMENDMENTS IN RESPONSE TO AN
OBJECTION OF THE JOINT COMMITTEE ON ADMINISTRATIVE RULES

studio and develops the film in-house. The photographer's bill
includes a sitting fee and a separately-stated charge for the
product of photoprocessing. A tax is collected on the photoprocessing charge only.

b) Persons Engaged in the Graphic Arts--When Liable For Tax

1) Persons engaged in the graphic arts or related occupations may,
under certain circumstances, be considered to be engaged in the
business of selling tangible personal property to purchasers'
for use or consumption, in which event they incur Retailers'
Occupation Tax liability. This is the case, for example, when
they sell to purchasers for use or consumption tangible personal property which is standard enough to be stocked for sale
or offered for sale from catalogues or other sales literature,
or which otherwise is sold at retail apart from the seller's
engaging in a service occupation. Illustrations would include
legal forms, pictures or other items which are stocked for sale
or offered for sale to the public generally, or products of
photoprocessing.

2) Effective August 1, 1961, a person who is engaged in the
graphic arts also incurs Retailers' Occupation Tax liability on
his receipts from sales, to users, of items which he produces
on special order if such item serves substantially the same
function as stock or standard items of tangible personal property that are sold at retail. Items which "serve substantially
the same function" are those which, when produced on special
order, could be sold substantially as produced to someone other
than the original purchaser at substantially the same price.

c) Persons Engaged in the Graphic Arts--When Not Liable For Tax

1) A photostater who is employed to reproduce material for his
customer by the photostating process, or a printer who is
employed to print material for his customer in accordance with
copy supplied to the printer by the customer or otherwise in
accordance with the customer's specifications and special
order, or a person who otherwise engages primarily in the
transaction in furnishing graphic arts' services is not engaged
in such transaction in the business of selling tangible
personal property within the meaning of the Act, if the item so
produced does not serve substantially the same function as
stock or standard items of tangible personal property that are
sold at retail, but is engaged in such transaction primarily in
a service occupation.

DEPARTMENT OF REVENUE

NOTICE OF MODIFICATION TO EMERGENCY AMENDMENTS IN RESPONSE TO AN
OBJECTION OF THE JOINT COMMITTEE ON ADMINISTRATIVE RULES

2) To the extent to which any such person engages in a service
occupation, he is not liable for Retailers' Occupation Tax on
his receipts therefrom, including receipts from both labor and
tangible personal property. For further illustrations, see
Section 130.1995(b) of this Part.

3) If the tax exemption described in this Section would otherwise
apply, the person supplying the printed item or other item that
is produced through the graphic arts' processes to the user
will not lose that exemption because of the fact that he farms
the work of producing the item out to someone else.

d) Suppliers of Persons Engaged in the Graphic Arts--When Liable For Tax

1) When persons who are engaged in the business of selling tangible personal property sell any such tangible personal property, for use or consumption, to persons engaged in the graphic
arts or related occupations, such vendors incur Retailers'
Occupation Tax liability unless such purchases qualify for the
graphic arts exemption (see Section 130.325). This class of
sales includes, but is not limited to, sales of machinery,
tools, equipment, office supplies and other tangible personal
property which the purchasers retain and use or consume. This
class of sales also includes sales of plates, film,
pre-sensitized plates, alcohol, chemicals, etc., which are
consumed by those engaged in the graphic arts or related
occupations in the course of the performance of their work.

2) It is not material whether the plates, film, pre-sensitized
plates, alcohol, chemicals, etc., are consumed in the course of
producing, by the graphic arts' processes, items which have a
commercial value, or whether the plates, film, pre-sensitized
plates, alcohol, chemicals, etc., are consumed in producing, on
special order, items of noncommercial value.

3) Likewise, this class of sales includes sales of film to
photographers who use such film in producing negatives which
remain the property of such photographers.

4) Furthermore, this class of sales includes sales of paper stock,
ink, duplicating materials (stencil sheet masters, offset masters and spirit masters) and other tangible personal property
to printers and other graphic arts' servicemen who incorporate
such tangible personal property as ingredients into items which
remain the property of such servicemen instead of being resold
by them in some manner.

DEPARTMENT OF REVENUE

NOTICE OF MODIFICATION TO EMERGENCY AMENDMENTS IN RESPONSE TO AN
OBJECTION OF THE JOINT COMMITTEE ON ADMINISTRATIVE RULES

e) Suppliers of Persons Engaged in the Graphic Arts--When Not Liable
    For Tax

    1) Persons who sell tangible personal property to persons who are
        engaged in the graphic arts or related occupations and who
        resell such property to others are not required to remit Retail-
        ers' Occupation Tax measured by their gross receipts from such
        sales. This class of sales includes sales of ink, paper stock,
        developing paper, sensitized paper, bookbindings, metal, wood,
        glue, brads, staples, binding tape and other tangible personal
        property where such property is purchased by persons engaged in
        the graphic arts or related occupations and incorporated by
        them into printed matter, pictures or other tangible personal
        property which they sell.

    2) It is not material whether the ink, paper, developing paper and
        other similar items are resold as ingredients of articles which
        have a commercial value or whether the ink, paper stock, devel-
        oping paper and other similar items are resold as ingredients
        of articles which are produced on special order and which have
        no commercial value.

f) Liability Under the Service Occupation Tax

    For information concerning the application of the Service Occupation
    Tax to purchases, by graphic arts' servicemen, of tangible personal
    property which they retransfer as an incident to rendering service,
    see the Service Occupation Tax, 86 Ill. Adm. Code 140.

(Source: Modified in response to an objection of the Joint Committee on
Administrative Rules at 12 Ill. Reg. 19531 , effective November 4, 1988 ,
not to exceed the 150 day time limit of the original rulemaking.)

DEPARTMENT OF PUBLIC HEALTH

NOTICE OF PUBLIC HEARING ON PROPOSED AMENDMENTS

1) Heading of the Part:

    Drinking Water Systems

2) Code Citation:

    77 Ill. Adm. Code 900

3) Register Citation to Notice of Proposed Amendments:

    12 Ill. Reg. 1706 - October 28, 1988

4) Date, Time and Location of Public Hearing:

    RESCHEDULED FROM: 10:00 AM - November 30, 1988

    RESCHEDULED TO: 10:00 AM - December 16, 1988

    Illinois Department of Public Health
    First Floor Hearing Room
    525 West Jefferson
    Springfield, Illinois 62761

5) Other Pertinent Information:

    The hearings will be for the sole purpose of gathering public comment on
    the Proposed Amendments. Persons interested in presenting testimony at
    this hearing is advised that the Department will adhere to the following
    procedures in the conduct of the hearing:

    1. Each person presenting oral testimony shall provide to the hearing
        officer a written (preferably typed) copy of such testimony at the
        time the oral testimony is presented. No oral testimony shall be
        accepted without such written copy of the testimony being provided.

    2. Each person presenting oral testimony will be limited to fifteen (15)
        minutes for the presentation of such testimony.

    3. No person will be recognized to speak for a second time until all
        persons wishing to testify have done so. All testimony shall
        conclude at the specific times except that an individual in the midst
        of presenting testimony shall be allowed to complete his/her
        testimony.

    4. In order to provide for a balanced presentation of views and to
        facilitate the orderly conduct of the hearing, the Hearing Officer
        may impose such other rules of procedure, including the order of call

: HEALTH

ED PROPOSED AMENDMENTS

ary.

public hearings shall be directed to Mr. Robert
tment of Public Health, Division of Governmental
n, Second Floor, Springfield, Illinois 62761.

DEPARTMENT OF PUBLIC HEALTH

NOTICE OF PUBLIC HEARING ON PROPOSED AMENDMENTS

1) Heading of the Part:

Illinois Water Well Construction Code

2) Code Citation:

77 Ill. Adm. Code 920

3) Register Citation to Notice of Proposed Amendments:

12 Ill. Reg. 17233 - October 28, 1988

4) Date, Time and Location of Public Hearing:

RESCHEDULED FROM: 10:00 AM - November 30, 1988

RESCHEDULED TO: 10:00 AM - December 16, 1988

Illinois Department of Public Health
First Floor Hearing Room
525 West Jefferson
Springfield, Illinois 62761

5) Other Pertinent Information:

The hearings will be for the sole purpose of gathering public comment on
the Proposed Amendments. Persons interested in presenting testimony at
this hearing is advised that the Department will adhere to the following
procedures in the conduct of the hearing:

1. Each person presenting oral testimony shall provide to the hearing
officer a written (preferably typed) copy of such testimony at the
time the oral testimony is presented. No oral testimony shall be
accepted without such written copy of the testimony being provided.

2. Each person presenting oral testimony will be limited to fifteen (15)
minutes for the presentation of such testimony.

3. No person will be recognized to speak for a second time until all
persons wishing to testify have done so. All testimony shall
conclude at the specific times except that an individual in the midst
of presenting testimony shall be allowed to complete his/her
testimony.

4. In order to provide for a balanced presentation of views and to
facilitate the orderly conduct of the hearing, the Hearing Officer

C HEALTH

ROPOSED AMENDMENTS

    dure, including the order of call
ary.

lic hearings shall be directed to Mr. Robert
t of Public Health, Division of Governmental
second Floor, Springfield, Illinois 62761.

DEPARTMENT OF PUBLIC HEALTH

NOTICE OF PUBLIC HEARING ON PROPOSED AMENDMENTS

1) **Heading of the Part:**

    Illinois Water Well Pump Installation Code

2) **Code Citation:**

    77 Ill. Adm. Code 925

3) **Register Citation to Notice of Proposed Amendments:**

    12 Ill. Reg. 17252 - October 28, 1988

4) **Date, Time and Location of Public Hearing:**

    RESCHEDULED FROM: 10:00 AM - November 30, 1988

    RESCHEDULED TO: 10:00 AM - December 16, 1988

    Illinois Department of Public Health
    First Floor Hearing Room
    525 West Jefferson
    Springfield, Illinois 62761

5) **Other Pertinent Information:**

    The hearings will be for the sole purpose of gathering public comment on
    the Proposed Amendments. Persons interested in presenting testimony at
    this hearing is advised that the Department will adhere to the following
    procedures in the conduct of the hearing:

    1.   Each person presenting oral testimony shall provide to the hearing
        officer a written (preferably typed) copy of such testimony at the
        time the oral testimony is presented. No oral testimony shall be
        accepted without such written copy of the testimony being provided.

    2.   Each person presenting oral testimony will be limited to fifteen (15)
        minutes for the presentation of such testimony.

    3.   No person will be recognized to speak for a second time until all
        persons wishing to testify have done so. All testimony shall
        conclude at the specific times except that an individual in the midst
        of presenting testimony shall be allowed to complete his/her
        testimony.

    4.   In order to provide for a balanced presentation of views and to
        facilitate the orderly conduct of the hearing, the Hearing Officer

MENT OF PUBLIC HEALTH

HEARING ON PROPOSED AMENDMENTS

rules of procedure, including the order of call
deems necessary.

contact Person:

blic hearings shall be directed to Mr. Robert
nt of Public Health, Division of Governmental
Second Floor, Springfield, Illinois 62761.

DEPARTMENT OF PUBLIC HEALTH

NOTICE OF PUBLIC HEARING ON PROPOSED RULES

1) Heading of the Part:

Private Sewage Mound Code

2) Code Citation:

77 Ill. Adm. Code 906

3) Register Citation to Notice of Proposed Amendments:

12 Ill. Reg. 19332 - November 18, 1988

4) Date, Time and Location of Public Hearing:

RESCHEDULED FROM: 10:00 AM - November 30, 1988

RESCHEDULED TO: 10:00 AM - December 16, 1988

Illinois Department of Public Health
First Floor Hearing Room
525 West Jefferson
Springfield, Illinois 62761

5) Other Pertinent Information:

The hearings will be for the sole purpose of gathering public comment on
the Proposed Amendments. Persons interested in presenting testimony at
this hearing is advised that the Department will adhere to the following
procedures in the conduct of the hearing:

1. Each person presenting oral testimony shall provide to the hearing
officer a written (preferably typed) copy of such testimony at the
time the oral testimony is presented. No oral testimony shall be
accepted without such written copy of the testimony being provided.

2. Each person presenting oral testimony will be limited to fifteen (15)
minutes for the presentation of such testimony.

3. No person will be recognized to speak for a second time until all
persons wishing to testify have done so. All testimony shall
conclude at the specific times except that an individual in the midst
of presenting testimony shall be allowed to complete his/her
testimony.

4. In order to provide for a balanced presentation of views and to
facilitate the orderly conduct of the hearing, the Hearing Officer

DEPARTMENT OF PUBLIC HEALTH

NOTICE OF PUBLIC HEARING ON PROPOSED RULES

may impose such other rules of procedure, including the order of call
of witnesses, as he/she deems necessary.

6) **Name and Address of Agency Contact Person:**

Questions regarding these public hearings shall be directed to Mr. Robert
John Kane, Illinois Department of Public Health, Division of Governmental
Affairs, 525 West Jefferson, Second Floor, Springfield, Illinois 62761.

JOINT COMMITTEE ON ADMINISTRATIVE RULES
ILLINOIS GENERAL ASSEMBLY

SECOND NOTICES RECEIVED

The following second notices were received by the Joint Committee on
Administrative Rules during the period of October 31, 1988 through
November 4, 1988 and have been scheduled for review by the Committee at its
December 15, 1988 meeting. Other items not contained in this published list
may also be considered by the Joint Committee at its scheduled December
meeting. Members of the public wishing to express their views with respect to
a proposed rule should submit written comments to the Joint Committee at the
following address: Joint Committee on Administrative Rules, 509 South Sixth
Street, Room 500, Springfield, IL 62701.

Second Notice Expires	Agency and Rule	Start of First Notice	Scheduled for Consideration by JCAR
12/19/88	Department of Financial Institutions, Illinois Credit Union Act (38 Ill. Adm. Code 190).	9/9/88 12 Ill. Reg. 14097	December 15, 1988
12/19/88	Department of Commerce and Community Affairs, Illinois Small Business Development Program (14 Ill. Adm. Code 570)	12/28/87 11 Ill. Reg. 20714	December 15, 1988
12/19/88	Department of Professional Regulation, Medical Practice Act, Repeal of (68 Ill. Adm. Code 1280)	5/20/88 12 Ill. Reg. 8536	December 15, 1988
12/19/88	Department of Professional Regulation, Medical Practice Act of 1987 (68 Ill. Adm. Code 1285)	5/20/88 12 Ill. Reg. 8571	December 15, 1988
12/19/88	Department of Children and Family Services, Reports of Child Abuse and Neglect (89 Ill. Adm. Code 300)	7/22/88 12 Ill. Reg. 11953	December 15, 1988
12/19/88	Department of Children and Family Services, Confidentiality of Personal Information of Persons Served by the Department (89 Ill. Adm. Code 431)	7/22/88 12 Ill. Reg. 11922	December 15, 1988

le	Start of First Notice	Scheduled for Consideration by JCAR
en and rvices apartment 302)	9/2/88 12 III. Reg. 13814	December 15, 1988

PROCLAMATION
88-508
Kristallnacht 50th Anniversary

WHEREAS, Kristallnacht, the Night of Broken Glass, in Nazi Germany and Austria led to the culmination of the first period of persecution of the Jewish people, a period marked by legal disenfranchisement, social segregation, pressured emigration, and systematic exclusion from economic life; and

WHEREAS, Kristallnacht was a Pogrom in the tradition of a long European history of violent anti-Semitism; and

WHEREAS, this Pogrom was not spontaneous nor even mob directed, but instigated by the State of Germany with the full cooperation of those who were sworn to protect the powerless and the weak; and

WHEREAS, Kristallnacht led to the death of 36 Jews; the arrest and deportation of 30,000 Jews to concentration camps; the setting afire of 26 synagogues; the looting of 7,000 Jewish shops and businesses; and a fine of 1 billion marks levied upon the victims - the Jewish community; and

WHEREAS, Kristallnacht signaled the beginning of the second period of Jewish persecution - officially directed violence and murder that culminated in the "Final Solution" - the destruction of the European Jewish Community and the liquidation of 6,000,000 Jews - 1 1/2 Million of whom were children;

THEREFORE, I, James R. Thompson, Governor of the State of Illinois, designate November 9-10, 1988, as an official day of commemoration and memory for the 50TH ANNIVERSARY OF KRISTALLNACHT. The State of Illinois also commends the teaching of mutual tolerance and understanding so as to prevent any reoccurence of that tragic and fateful event.

Issued October 27, 1988. Filed November 7, 1988.

PROCLAMATION
88-509
Erna I. Gans Day

PROCLAMATION
88-510
Fecha Conmemorativa Del Descubrimiento De Puerto Rico

WHEREAS, Erna I. Gans is an outstanding member of the Jewish community in both the United States and countries abroad; and

WHEREAS, as a survivor of the infamous Holocaust, Mrs. Gans is president of the Holocaust Memorial Foundation of Illinois and was appointed by President Reagan to the United States Memorial Council; and

WHEREAS, she is vice-president of the Institute of Sociological Research and Development, serves as the International Commissioner of B'nai B'rith, and is a member of many other community groups; and

WHEREAS, Mrs. Gans is also successful in the private sector, serving as president of International Label and Printing; and

WHEREAS, she will receive the Third Annual Humanitarian Award from the Holocaust Memorial Foundation for her dedication to the Jewish cause;

THEREFORE, I, James R. Thompson, Governor of the State of Illinois, proclaim November 13, 1988, as ERNA I. GANS DAY in Illinois in honor of her unyielding service as a citizen of our state, not only to the Jewish community, but to all of the many people who have benefitted from her selflessness.

POR CUANTO, Puerto Rico conmemora el 19 de Noviembre, la efemeride del Descubrimiento de la Isla por Cristobal Colon, en 1493; y

POR CUANTO, la comunidad puertorriquena es una fuerza cultural vigorosa en el Estado de Illinois, una comunidad que continuaca enriqueciendo la vida de los ciudadanos de Illinois a traves de sus contribuciones a la cultura y economia; y

POR CUANTO, es necesario que los demas grupos etnicos de Chicago, tomen en cuenta esta contribucion de los puertorriquenos en esta ciudad; y

POR CUANTO, la oficina del Departamento del Trabajo y Recursos Humanos del Estado Libre Asociado de Puerto Rico en la ciudad de Chicago, observara esta efemeride con un acto civico cultural el 18 de Noviembre de 1988; y

POR CUANTO, yo, James R. Thompson, Gobernador del Estado de Illinois, resuelvo proclamar el 19 de Noviembre de 1988, como FECHA CONMEMORATIVA DEL DESCUBRIMIENTO DE PUERTO RICO, reconociendo la comunidad puertorriquena y su contribucion al desarrollo del Estado de Illinois.

Issued October 31, 1988. Filed November 7, 1988.

Issued October 31, 1988. Filed November 7, 1988.

PROCLAMATION
88-511
Gettysburg Address 125th Anniversary

WHEREAS, Abraham Lincoln was probably the greatest President who ever served our country, and he is synonymous with the state of Illinois where he lived and is buried; and

WHEREAS, his famous Gettysburg Address of 1863, which he took only a few minutes to deliver, was not recognized a classic speech until many years later; and

WHEREAS, this piece consummately reflects the sorrow of the Civil War era and those people's hope and belief that this strong, free nation would survive;

THEREFORE, I, James R. Thompson, Governor of the State of Illinois, observe the 125TH ANNIVERSARY OF THE GETTYSBURG ADDRESS in Illinois, urging all citizens to honor this event and recognize the liberty and unity that the United States of America continues to preserve.

Issued October 31, 1988. Filed November 7, 1988.

PROCLAMATION
88-512
Harry Caray Day

WHEREAS, since 1982, Harry Caray has been the broadcasting voice of Illinois' Chicago Cubs baseball team, and previously he had been an announcer for the Chicago White Sox; and

WHEREAS, he will be "roasted" at a benefit dinner November 19 in Las Vegas, with proceeds going to the Maryville City Youth Academy in Des Plaines, Illinois; and

WHEREAS, Maryville, the largest residential child care agency in Illinois, has recently been appointed to be the administrator of Cuneo Memorial Hospital in Chicago, which will offer counseling and educational programs for youths awaiting placement in foster and group homes; and

WHEREAS, Maryville has been a favorite charity of Harry Caray, and the roast is expected to raise more than $150,000 for this worthy cause;

THEREFORE, I, James R. Thompson, Governor of the State of Illinois, proclaim November 19, 1988, as HARRY CARAY DAY in Illinois, honoring this celebrated figure and his many contributions to the community.

Issued October 31, 1988. Filed November 7, 1988.

PROCLAMATION
88-513
Honors Dr. And Mrs. Alfred C. Golden

WHEREAS, Dr. Alfred C. Golden and Mrs. Mary L. Golden have served their church, their community and Chicago proper as dedicated and committed religious, civic leaders; and

WHEREAS, Dr. Golden has pastored the New Morgan Park Church of God In Christ for 37 years. He has given his service to numerous positions in the Church of God In Christ denomination and currently serves as the First Administrative Assistant of the Northern Illinois Jurisdiction under the leadership of Bishop Isaiah Roberts; and

WHEREAS, Mrs. Golden has shared her expertise, skills and been the inspirational catalyst and model for women of the civic community and Church of God In Christ denomination throughout the world. She has administered her talents in various church offices and currently serves as the International President of the Pastors and Ministers Wives Department, the State President of the Pastors and Ministers Wives Department of Northern Illinois Jurisdiction, and the President of the New Morgan Park Church of God In Christ Music Department; and

WHEREAS, Dr. Golden has been instrumental in the moral and ethical teaching of hundreds of youths; and

WHEREAS, Dr. and Mrs. Golden have been distinctive civic leaders in the New Morgan Park community and adjacent neighborhoods;

THEREFORE, I, James R. Thompson, Governor of the State of Illinois, proclaim November 1-6, 1988, as the week to honor DR. AND MRS. ALFRED C. GOLDEN, and I encourage all religious and civic organizations to recognize the valuable contributions of these two great people to their community and the City of Chicago.

Issued October 31, 1988. Filed November 7, 1988.

PROCLAMATION
88-514
Operating Room Nurses Day

WHEREAS, operating room nurses in Illinois provide necessary and valuable support for doctors throughout the state; and

WHEREAS, surgery today is a highly technical, sophisticated and exacting procedure aided by the expertise of operating room nurses. Registered nurses not only help patients physically, but work to allay patients' fears, preparing them for surgery and for recuperation; and

WHEREAS, registered nurses act as the patient's advocate during surgery, a much needed service during a crucial point in the patient's life;

THEREFORE, I, James R. Thompson, Governor of the State of Illinois, proclaim November 14, 1988, as OPERATING ROOM NURSES DAY in Illinois. On behalf of the citizens of this state, I thank these nurses who dedicate their careers to the care of others.

Issued October 31, 1988. Filed November 7, 1988.

PROCLAMATION
88-515
Veterans Day

PROCLAMATION
88-516
Women In Charge Day

WHEREAS, the men and women who have served in the Armed Forces of the United States of America have made major contributions toward the preservation of the freedom of this nation and her people; and

WHEREAS, the services performed by these millions of gallant Americans have demonstrated the willingness of our nation to meet the challenge of those forces wishing to subjugate individual determination through armed conflict; and

WHEREAS, the Congress of the United States of America has designated the 11th day of November of each year as Veterans Day; and

WHEREAS, Veterans Day has become a significant part of our national heritage as we recognize the important contributions of the millions of our citizens whose military service has had a profound effect on history; and

WHEREAS, the unselfishness of all those who served in the United States Armed Forces is a quality for which we all are grateful:

THEREFORE, I, James R. Thompson, Governor of the State of Illinois, proclaim November 11, 1988, as VETERANS DAY in Illinois, in conjunction with the national observance. I ask that the day be observed with appropriate ceremonies in honor of those who have served the national purpose to preserve the principles of justice, freedom and democracy.

WHEREAS, the Women In Charge conference was established to promote women leaders in the non-profit sector; and

WHEREAS, the Women In Charge conference has created an environment in which women may learn job skills, share life-enhancing experiences, and plan effective strategies for success; and

WHEREAS, Women In Charge has for six consecutive years inspired women to positions of leadership and power for positive change in the workplace and to benefit all society;

THEREFORE, I, James R. Thompson, Governor of the State of Illinois, proclaim November 17, 1988, as WOMEN IN CHARGE DAY in Illinois, in recognition of the achievements and contributions of women leaders in the non-profit sector.

Issued October 31, 1988. Filed November 7, 1988.

Issued October 31, 1988. Filed November 7, 1988.

PROCLAMATION
88-517
Hispanic State Employment Day

WHEREAS, Hispanics presently number 19.4 million (8.1%) of the U.S. population, and by the year 2010, will be the largest minority group in the United States; and

WHEREAS, according to the Bureau of the Census, Illinois with approximately 801,000 Hispanics, ranks fifth among the top 10 states with Hispanic populations; and

WHEREAS, cities like Joliet, Aurora, Chicago Heights, West Chicago, Elgin, Rockford, Sterling, Moline, Waukegan and Chicago have experienced significant increases of language minority groups, of which Hispanics are the largest; and

WHEREAS, state government is committed to meet the challenge of providing services to this population in the areas of education, housing, health, business, employment and training opportunities; and

WHEREAS, the 85th General Assembly passed House Bill 1645, which I signed into law in October 1987, calling for the Department of Central Management Services to "develop and implement a plan to increase the number of Hispanic employees at all levels," as a vehicle to expand the state's capacity to provide services to Hispanics in the State of Illinois; and

WHEREAS, the Department of Central Management Services, the state agency responsible for personnel, has developed the Hispanic Employment Plan under the direction of Director Michael E. Tristano and Assistant Director Rose Mary Bombela;

THEREFORE, I, James R. Thompson, Governor of the State of Illinois, proclaim November 4, 1988, as HISPANIC STATE EMPLOYMENT DAY in Illinois in recognition of the contributions of Hispanic employees to the vitality and growth of our great state.

Issued November 2, 1988. Filed November 7, 1988.

ACTION CODES   JCAR - Joint Committee on Administrative Rules

A – Adopted Rule	P – Proposed Rule
AR – Adopted Repealer	PF – Prohibited Filing Ordered by JCAR
C – Notice of Corrections	PP – Peremptory or Court ordered Rules
CC – Codification Changes	PR – Proposed Repealer
E – Emergency Rule	R – Refusal to meet JCAR objection
ER – Emergency Repealer	RC – Statement of Recommendation
M – Modification to meet JCAR objections	S – Suspension ordered by JCAR
O – JCAR Statement of Objections	W – Withdrawal to meet JCAR objections

EXAMPLE:

AGRICULTURE, DEPARTMENT OF
8 Ill. Adm. Code 285   Ill. Grain Insurance Act (P-18048/85; A-6818)

TITLE — PART — ACTION CODE — PAGE NUMBER
PAGE NUMBER — ACTION CODE
PREVIOUS VOLUME

ALL RULES ARE LISTED BY PART NUMBER AND HEADING ONLY. (FOR ACTION ON SPECIFIC SECTIONS, PLEASE REFER TO THE SECTIONS AFFECTED INDEX.) IF THERE ARE ANY QUESTIONS, PLEASE CONTACT THE ADMINISTRATIVE CODE DIVISION AT (217) 782-9786.

AGING, DEPARTMENT ON
89 Ill. Adm. Code 240   Community Care Program (A-7980) (P-10821)
89 Ill. Adm. Code 230   Older Americans Act Programs (P-12137) (E-12540) (P-14777)

AGRICULTURE, DEPARTMENT OF
8 Ill. Adm. Code 1   Administrative Rules (Formal Administrative Proceedings; Contested Cases; Petitions; Declaratory Rulings; Public Disclosure) (P-4743; A-11439)
8 Ill. Adm. Code 30   Animal Control Act (P-15999/87; A-2216)
8 Ill. Adm. Code 110   Animal Diagnostic Laboratory Act (P-15669/87; A-3379) (P-19153)
8 Ill. Adm. Code 25   Animal Welfare Act (P-15676/87; A-8265) (P-19164)
8 Ill. Adm. Code 75   Bovine Brucellosis (P-15686/87; A-3386) (P-19172)
8 Ill. Adm. Code 20   Definitions (P-15695/87; A-8275) (P-19178)
8 Ill. Adm. Code 85   Diseased Animals (P-15704/87; A-8283) (P-19185)
8 Ill. Adm. Code 700   Farmland Preservation Act (P-18833/87; A-5235) (P-14786) (P-17139)
8 Ill. Adm. Code 675   Groundwater Use Guidelines (P-3539; A-10416) (E-3790)
8 Ill. Adm. Code 80   Ill. Bovine Tuberculosis Eradication Act (P-15716/87; A-8295) (P-19196)
8 Ill. Adm. Code 90   Ill. Dead Animals Disposal Act (P-19201)
8 Ill. Adm. Code 250   Ill. Pesticide Act (P-7035; A-12784)
8 Ill. Adm. Code 250   Ill. Pesticide Act of 1979 (P-7035)
8 Ill. Adm. Code 115   Ill. Pseudorabies Control Act (P-15720/87; A-3394) (P-19218)
8 Ill. Adm. Code 230   Ill. Seed Law (P-1679; A-10437)
8 Ill. Adm. Code 240   Insect Pest & Plant Disease Act (P-20295/87; A-8299)
8 Ill. Adm. Code 40   Livestock Auction Markets (P-15737/87; A-3411)
8 Ill. Adm. Code 610   Livestock Dealer Licensing (P-19205)

AGRICULTURE, DEPARTMENT OF (CONT'D)
8 Ill. Adm. Code 125   Meat & Poultry Inspection Act (PP-2154) (P-17331/87; A-3417) (PP-4879) (PP-6313) (PP-6819) (PP-13621) (PP-19116) (P-19211)
2 Ill. Adm. Code 700   Organizational Chart, Description, Rulemaking Procedure, & Programs (A-6648)
8 Ill. Adm. Code 290   Standardbred & Thoroughbred Horse Breeding & Racing Programs (P-8171; A-14515)
8 Ill. Adm. Code 100   Swine Brucellosis (P-15743/87; A-3432)
8 Ill. Adm. Code 105   Swine Disease Control & Eradication Act (P-15751/87; A-3440)
8 Ill. Adm. Code 600   Weights & Measures Act (P-18841/87; A-8306) (P-10271; A-15528)

ALCOHOLISM AND SUBSTANCE ABUSE, DEPARTMENT OF
77 Ill. Adm. Code 2055   Drug Abuse Programs (PR-5683)
77 Ill. Adm. Code 2056   Driving Under the Influence Programs (P-20303/87; O-9174; RC-9176; R-11317; A-11138) (PR-20336/87; AR-11136)
77 Ill. Adm. Code 2058   Licensure of Alcoholism & Substance Abuse Treatment, Intervention & Research Programs (P-5760; O-11322; R-14735; A-14524)
77 Ill. Adm. Code 2000   Rules of Practice & Procedure in Administrative Hearings (PR-5845)
77 Ill. Adm. Code 2070   Schedule of Controlled Substances (P-3147)
77 Ill. Adm. Code 2090   Subacute Alcoholism & Substance Abuse Treatment Services (P-10994) (E-11273; O-14457)

ATTORNEY GENERAL
14 Ill. Adm. Code 200   Franchise Disclosure Act (P-1; A-9424; C-10804) (E-1124)
14 Ill. Adm. Code 470   Retail Advertising (P-15239)

BANKING BOARD OF ILLINOIS, STATE
38 Ill. Adm. Code 900   Hearings for Removal of Directors, Officers, Employees or Agents of a State Bank (P-10277; A-17074)

BANKS AND TRUST COMPANIES, COMMISSIONER OF
38 Ill. Adm. Code 305   Bank Branches (P-4295; A-11178)
38 Ill. Adm. Code 310   Electronic Fund Transfers (P-5489; RC-15792; A-17774)
38 Ill. Adm. Code 330   Lending Limits (P-20372/87; A-7991) (P-10282; A-17280)
38 Ill. Adm. Code 357   Reduction in the Number of Required Directors (P-3865; A-10663)
38 Ill. Adm. Code 356   Reimbursement to Banks for Financial Records (P-3158; A-11182)
38 Ill. Adm. Code 355   Statutory Bad Debts (P-3869; A-10667)

CAPITOL DEVELOPMENT BOARD
71 Ill. Adm. Code 50   Bonding Guidelines (P-10957/87; A-9845)
71 Ill. Adm. Code 400   Ill. Accessibility Code (PR-6649/87; AR-5243) (P-6597/87; O-19830/87; M-5473; A-5245)
44 Ill. Adm. Code 1050   Insurance & Surety Companies (P-10968/87; A-9856) (P-13377)
44 Ill. Adm. Code 950   Prequalification & Suspension of Contractors (P-10972/87; A-9860)
44 Ill. Adm. Code 980   Prequalification of Architects & Engineers (P-13691)
44 Ill. Adm. Code 910   Procurement Practices (P-10974/87; A-9864)
44 Ill. Adm. Code 1000   Selection of Architects/Engineers (A/E) (P-12140; A-17815)

CARNIVAL-AMUSEMENT SAFETY BOARD
56 Ill. Adm. Code 6000   Carnival & Amusement Ride Inspection Law (P-20699/87; A-11186)

CENTRAL MANAGEMENT SERVICES, DEPARTMENT OF
80 Ill. Adm. Code 3100   Auto Liability (P-2041; A-9487)
89 Ill. Adm. Code 1300   Day Care (P-19223)
44 Ill. Adm. Code 5010   Marking, Inventory, Transfer & Disposal of State-Owned Personal Property (P-14907/87; A-10671)
80 Ill. Adm. Code 302   Merit & Fitness (P-4969/87; A-5634) (P-10569) (P-15813) (E-16214)
80 Ill. Adm. Code 310   Pay Plan (PP-3811) (PP-5459) (P-16009/87; A-6073) (P-17955/87; A-6073) (P-7453; A-14630) (E-7754) (PP-7783) (P-7889) (PP-8135) (PP-9745) (E-11778; O-15764) (P-12599) (E-12895; C-13359; C-13716; O-15766) (PP-13306; O-15769)
80 Ill. Adm. Code 2150   Service-Connected Days Benefit Administration (P-10285)

CI - 7

CI - 8

PROCLAMATIONS (CONT'D)

88-475	With Walker Day	17564
88-476	Higher Education Week	17565
88-477	Scottish Culture Week	17566
88-478	Slovenian Day	17567
88-479	National Grandeloquent Gala Days	18006
88-480	Family Health Month	18007
88-481	Salute the 25th Anniversary of Ill. Gifted Education	18008
88-482	Statewide Affordable Housing Week	18009
88-483	Forest Products Week	18010
88-484	Ill. Cottage Industry Awareness Day	18011
88-485	Mutual Ground, Inc. Day	18012
88-486	United Nations Day	18013
88-487	Ill. Olympian Salute Week	18014
88-488	Max Davidson Day/Max Davidson Month/Max Davidson Year	18015
88-489	Home Care Week	18016
88-490	HARP of Little City Day	18017
88-491	Infection Control Week	18018
88-492	The Old Style Marathon/Chicago Day	18019
88-493	Coast Guard Recognition Day	19137
88-494	Honor Isreal Day	19138
88-495	10th Anniversary of Zanies Comedy Nite Club	19139
88-496	James O'Grady Day	19140
88-497	Alzheimer's Disease Public Awareness Month	19141
88-498	Broadcast Journalist Day	19142
88-499	Community Education Day	19143
88-500	Hospice Week	19144
88-501	Ill. Paralegal Association Day	19145
88-502	Lupus Awareness Month	19146
88-503	Victory Week	19147
88-504	Worldwide Peace Day	19148
88-505	The Month of the Awakening Child	19149
88-506	Chicago Abused Women Coalition Day	19150
88-507	Environmental Health Practitioners' Week	19151
88-508	Kristallnacht 50th Anniversary	19552
88-509	Erna I. Gans Day	19553
88-510	Fecha Conmemorativa Del Descubrimiepto De Puerto Rico	19554
88-511	Gettysburg Address 125th Anniversary	19555
88-512	Harry Caray Day	19556
88-513	Honors Dr. & Mrs. Alfred C. Golden	19557
88-514	Operating Rooms Nurses Day	19558
88-515	Veterans Day	19559
88-516	Women In Charge Day	19560
88-517	Hispanic State Employment Day	19561

The Sections Affected Index lists, by Title, each Section of a codified Part on which rulemaking activity has occurred in this volume of the Register and is divided into two parts: the first lists the Sections on which rulemaking occurred in the previous issues of this volume year; the second lists the Sections on which rulemaking activity occurred in this issue of the Register. (The headings at the top of each page indicate the two parts: the first part shows the previous issue numbers inclusively and the date of the last published issue; the second lists the current issue number and date.) The columns in both parts indicate the type of rulemaking activity and the action taken along with the page number on which the first page of the notice of rulemaking activity appeared. If a Section on which action is being taken in the current volume (calendar year) of the Register was proposed in a previous volume, the last two digits of the previous volume's year appear immediately after the page number sequenced by a slash. (e.g. 1 Ill. Adm. Code 100.280 was proposed last year and adopted this year. The action entry reads: (P-8577/86; A-724)) The codes for both columns are listed below. For a complete listing of the Titles of the Illinois Administrative Code, please refer to 1 Ill. Adm. Code 100.140 or contact the Administrative Code Division.

TYPE OF RULEMAKING		ACTION CODES	
am = amendment to existing Section	A = Adopted rule	O = JCAR Objection
co = codification changes	C = Correction	P = Proposed rule
n = new Section	CC = Codification Changes	PP = Prohibited Filing
r = repeal of existing Section	E = Emergency rule	PE = Peremptory rule
ro = recodified	F = Failure to Remedy	R = Refusal to Modify or Withdraw
# = renumbered	Objections	RC = JCAR Recommendation
	M = Modification	S = Suspended rule
		W = Withdrawal of Proposed rule

TITLE 1				TITLE 2 (CONT'D)		
300.100	n	(P-8511)		1176.20	am	(A-14689)
300.200	n	(P-8511)		1176.100	am	(A-14689)
300.300	n	(P-8511)		1176.110	am	(A-14689)
300.400	n	(P-8511)		1176.200	am	(A-14689)
300.Ap. A	n	(P-8511)		1176.210	am	(A-14689)
				1176.300	am	(A-14689)
TITLE 2				1176.310	am	(A-14689)
550.10	am	(A-17969)		1176.400	am	(A-14689)
550.210	am	(A-7726) (A-17969)		1176.420	am	(A-14689)
550.Th. A	am	(A-7726)		1176.Ex. A	r	(A-14689)
552.10	n	(A-3022)		1176.Ex. B	r	(A-14689)
552.20	n	(A-3022)		1325.10	ro	(A-2976)
700.10	am	(A-6648)		1325.20	ro	(A-2976)
700.30	am	(A-6648)		1325.30	ro	(A-2976)
700.100	am	(A-6648)		1325.40	ro	(A-2976)
1150.10	ro	(A-2976)		1325.50	ro	(A-2976)
1150.20	ro	(A-2976)		1326.110	ro	(A-2913)
1150.30	ro	(A-2976)		1326.120	ro	(A-2913)
1150.40	ro	(A-2976)		1326.210	ro	(A-2913)
1150.50	ro	(A-2976)		1326.220	ro	(A-2913)
1151.110	ro	(A-2913)		1326.310	ro	(A-2913)
1151.120	ro	(A-2913)		1326.320	ro	(A-2913)
1151.210	ro	(A-2913)		1326.410	ro	(A-2913)
1151.220	ro	(A-2913)		1326.420	ro	(A-2913)
1151.310	ro	(A-2913)		1326.510	ro	(A-2913)
1151.320	ro	(A-2913)		1326.520	ro	(A-2913)
1151.410	ro	(A-2913)		1326.530	ro	(A-2913)
1151.420	ro	(A-2913)		1375.100	n	(A-17377)
1151.510	ro	(A-2913)		1375.110	n	(A-17377)
1151.520	ro	(A-2913)		1375.200	n	(A-17377)
1151.530	ro	(A-2913)		1375.210	n	(A-17377)
1176.10	am	(A-14689)		1375.220	n	(A-17377)

TITLE 2 (CONT'D)

1375.230	n	(A-17377)
1375.240	n	(A-17377)
1375.250	n	(A-17377)
1375.260	n	(A-17377)
1375.270	n	(A-17377)
1375.280	n	(A-17377)
1375.290	n	(A-17377)
1375.300	n	(A-17377)
1375.310	n	(A-17377)
1375.320	n	(A-17377)
1375.330	n	(A-17377)
1375.340	n	(A-17377)
1375.350	n	(A-17377)
1375.360	n	(A-17377)
1375.370	n	(A-17377)
1375.380	n	(A-17377)
1375.390	n	(A-17377)
1375.400	n	(A-17377)
1375.410	n	(A-17377)
1375.420	n	(A-17377)
1375.430	n	(A-17377)
1375.440	n	(A-17377)
1375.Ap. A	n	(A-17377)
1376.100	n	(A-17368)
1376.110	n	(A-17368)
1376.120	n	(A-17368)
1376.130	n	(A-17368)
1376.140	n	(A-17368)
1376.150	n	(A-17368)
1376.160	n	(A-17368)
1376.170	n	(A-17368)
1376.180	n	(A-17368)
1376.190	n	(A-17368)
1376.Ap. A	n	(A-17368)
1376.Ap. B	n	(A-17368)
1875.10	am	(A-16712)
1875.20	am	(A-16712)
1875.220	am	(A-16712)
1875.230	am	(A-16712)

TITLE 5

1.10	am	(P-4743; A-11439)
20.1	n	(P-15695/87; A-8275)
25.15	n	(P-15676/87; A-8265)
25.20	am	(P-15676/87; A-8265)
25.50	am	(P-15676/87; A-8265)
25.50	am	(P-15676/87; A-8265)
25.80	am	(P-15676/87; A-8265)
25.110	am	(P-15676/87; A-8265)
25.120	am	(P-15676/87; A-8265)
30.10	am	(P-15999/87; A-2216)
30.20	am	(P-15999/87; A-2216)
30.90	am	(P-15999/87; A-2216)
30.140	am	(P-15999/87; A-2216)
30.170	n	(P-15999/87; A-2216)
40.5	am	(P-15737/87; A-3411)

TITLE 8 (CONT'D)

40.60	am	(P-15737/87; A-3411)
40.160	am	(P-15737/87; A-3411)
40.170	am	(P-15737/87; A-3411)
40.230	am	(P-15737/87; A-3411)
75.5	am	(P-15686/87; A-3386)
75.50	am	(P-15686/87; A-3386)
75.130	am	(P-15686/87; A-3386)
75.190	am	(P-15686/87; A-3386)
80.10	am	(P-15716/87; A-8295)
80.110	am	(P-15716/87; A-8295)
85.5	am	(P-15704/87; A-8283)
85.10	am	(P-15704/87; A-8283)
85.15	am	(P-15704/87; A-8283)
85.50	am	(P-15704/87; A-8283)
85.75	am	(P-15704/87; A-8283)
85.95	am	(P-15704/87; A-8283)
100.10	am	(P-15743/87; A-3432)
100.30	n	(P-15743/87; A-3432)
105.5	am	(P-15751/87; A-3440)
105.10	r	(P-15751/87; A-3440)
105.40	r	(P-15751/87; A-3440)
105.41	r	(P-15751/87; A-3440)
105.42	r	(P-15751/87; A-3440)
105.44	r	(P-15751/87; A-3440)
105.46	r	(P-15751/87; A-3440)
105.60	r	(P-15751/87; A-3440)
105.70	r	(P-15751/87; A-3440)
105.80	r	(P-15751/87; A-3440)
110.10	am	(P-15669/87; A-3379)
110.90	am	(P-15669/87; A-3379)
110.190	n	(P-15669/87; A-3379)
115.10	n	(P-15720/87; A-3994)
115.15	n	(P-15720/87; A-3994)
115.20	am	(P-15720/87; A-3994)
115.30	n	(P-15720/87; A-3994)
115.40	n	(P-15720/87; A-3994)
115.50	n	(P-15720/87; A-3994)
115.60	n	(P-15720/87; A-3994)
115.70	n	(P-15720/87; A-3994)
115.80	n	(P-15720/87; A-3994)
115.90	n	(P-15720/87; A-3994)
115.100	n	(P-15720/87; A-3994)
125.10	am	(P-17331/87; A-3417)
125.90	am	(P-17331/87; A-3417)
125.100	am	(P-17331/87; A-3417) (PP-19116)
125.110	am	(P-2154)
125.190	am	(P-17331/87; A-3417) (PP-19116)
125.200	am	(P-17331/87; A-3417) (PP-19116)
125.250	am	(PP-13621)
125.260	n	(P-17331/87; A-3417) (PP-6313) (PP-13621)
125.270	am	(PP-6313)
125.280	am	(PP-4879) (PP-6819)
125.300	am	(PP-13621)
125.305	n	(P-17331/87; A-3417)
125.310	am	(PP-2154)

TITLE 8 (CONT'D)

125.360	am	(PP-13621)
125.390	am	(P-17331/87; A-3417) (PP-6313)
230.50	am	(P-1679; A-10437)
230.70	am	(P-1679; A-10437)
230.80	am	(P-1679; A-10437)
230.90	am	(P-1679; A-10437)
230.140	am	(P-1679; A-10437)
230.150	am	(P-1679; A-10437)
230.160	r	(P-1679; A-10437)
230.220	am	(P-1679; A-10437)
230.230	r	(P-1679; A-10437)
240.40	am	(P-20295/87; A-8299)
240.60	am	(P-20295/87; A-8299)
240.90	am	(P-20295/87; A-8299)
240.120	am	(P-20295/87; A-8299)
240.140	am	(P-20295/87; A-8299)
240.160	am	(P-20295/87; A-8299)
250.10	am	(P-7035; A-12784)
250.20	am	(P-7035; A-12784)
250.70	am	(P-7035; A-12784)
250.80	am	(P-7035; A-12784)
250.90	am	(P-7035; A-12784)
250.100	am	(P-7035; A-12784)
250.110	am	(P-7035; A-12784)
250.120	am	(P-7035; A-12784)
250.130	am	(P-7035; A-12784)
250.160	am	(P-7035; A-12784)
250.170	am	(P-7035; A-12784)
250.180	n	(P-7035; A-12784)
250.190	n	(P-7035; A-12784)
250.200	n	(P-7035; A-12784)
290.215	am	(P-8171; A-14515)
600.1	n	(P-18841/87; A-8306)
600.1	r	(P-10271; A-15524)
600.10	r	(P-18841/87; A-8306)
600.20	r	(P-18841/87; A-8306)
600.30	r	(P-18841/87; A-8306)
600.40	r	(P-18841/87; A-8306)
600.50	r	(P-18841/87; A-8306)
600.60	r	(P-18841/87; A-8306)
600.70	r	(P-18841/87; A-8306)
600.80	r	(P-18841/87; A-8306)
600.90	r	(P-18841/87; A-8306)
600.100	r	(P-18841/87; A-8306)
600.110	r	(P-18841/87; A-8306)
600.120	r	(P-18841/87; A-8306)
600.130	r	(P-18841/87; A-8306)
600.150	r	(P-18841/87; A-8306)
600.250	r	(P-18841/87; A-8306)
600.300	am	(P-18841/87; A-8306)
600.310	am	(P-18841/87; A-8306)
600.350	r	(P-18841/87; A-8306)
600.360	r	(P-18841/87; A-8306)
600.370	r	(P-18841/87; A-8306)
600.380	r	(P-18841/87; A-8306)
600.450	r	(P-18841/87; A-8306)

TITLE 8 (CONT'D)

600.460	r	(P-18841/87; A-8306)
600.470	r	(P-18841/87; A-8306)
600.480	r	(P-18841/87; A-8306)
600.490	r	(P-18841/87; A-8306)
600.500	r	(P-18841/87; A-8306)
600.510	r	(P-18841/87; A-8306)
600.520	r	(P-18841/87; A-8306)
600.530	r	(P-18841/87; A-8306)
600.540	r	(P-18841/87; A-8306)
600.550	r	(P-18841/87; A-8306)
600.560	r	(P-18841/87; A-8306)
600.680	r	(P-18841/87; A-8306)
600.730	r	(P-18841/87; A-8306)
600.840	am	(P-18841/87; A-8306)
600.Tb. A	r	(P-18841/87; A-8306)
675.10	n	(P-3539; A-10416) (E-3790)
675.20	n	(P-3539; A-10416) (E-3790)
675.30	n	(P-3539; A-10416) (E-3790)
675.40	n	(P-3539; A-10416) (E-3790)
675.50	n	(P-3539; A-10416) (E-3790)
675.60	n	(P-3539; A-10416) (E-3790)
675.70	n	(P-3539; A-10416) (E-3790)
675.80	n	(P-3539; A-10416) (E-3790)
675.90	n	(P-3539; A-10416) (E-3790)
675.100	n	(P-3539; A-10416) (E-3790)
675.110	n	(P-3539; A-10416) (E-3792)
675.120	n	(P-3539; A-10416) (E-3790)
675.130	n	(P-3539; A-10416) (E-3790)
675.140	n	(P-3539; A-10416) (E-3790)
700.Ap. B	am	(P-18833/87; A-5235)
700.Ap. I	r	(P-14786)
700.Ap. G	am	(P-17139)
1400.10	am	(P-12119/87; A-11219) (P-13832)
1400.140	am	(P-12119/87; A-11219) (P-13832)
1400.147	am	(P-5545)
1400.149	am	(P-5545)
1400.160	am	(P-12119/87; A-11219)

TITLE 11

100.50	am	(P-5591; C-10241)
100.70	am	(P-5591)
100.160	am	(P-5591)
100.170	am	(P-5591)
100.210	am	(P-5591)
100.230	am	(P-5591; C-10241)
100.350	am	(P-5591; C-10241)
208.10	n	(P-13926)
208.20	n	(P-13926)
208.30	n	(P-13926)
208.40	n	(P-13926)
208.100	n	(P-13926)
208.110	n	(P-13926)
208.120	n	(P-13926)
404.60	am	(P-13936)
404.200	am	(P-13936)
405.130	am	(P-10999/87; A-206)

TITLE 11 (CONT'D)

Section		Reference
414.10	r	(P-14653/87; A-14687)
414.20	r	(P-14653/87; A-14687)
422.20	am	(P-13922)
435.10	n	(E-6805) (P-11008/87; A-11235)
435.20	n	(E-6805) (P-11008/87; A-11235)
435.30	n	(E-6805) (P-11008/87; A-11235)
435.40	n	(E-6805) (P-11008/87; A-11235)
435.50	n	(E-6805) (P-11008/87; A-11215)
435.60	n	(E-6805) (P-11008/87; A-11235)
435.70	n	(E-6805) (P-11008/87; A-11235)
435.80	n	(E-6805) (P-11008/87; A-11235)
435.90	n	(E-6805) (P-11008/87; A-11235)
435.100	n	(E-6805) (P-11008/87; A-11235)
435.110	n	(E-6805) (P-11008/87; A-11235)
435.120	n	(E-6805) (P-11008/87; A-11235)
435.130	n	(E-6805) (P-11008/87; A-11235)
435.140	n	(E-6805) (P-11008/87; A-11235)
435.150	n	(E-6805) (P-11008/87; A-11235)
435.160	n	(E-6805) (P-11008/87; A-11235)
435.170	n	(P-17058)
436.10	n	(P-11003/87; A-6304)
436.20	n	(P-11003/87; A-6304)
436.28	n	(P-11003/87; O-4925; RC-4927; R-6329)
436.30	n	(P-11003/87; A-6304)
436.40	n	(P-11003/87; A-6304)
436.50	n	(P-11003/87; A-6304)
436.60	n	(P-11003/87; A-6304)
436.70	n	(P-11003/87; A-6304)
436.80	n	(P-11003/87; A-6304)
436.90	n	(P-11003/87; A-6304)
436.100	n	(P-11003/87; A-6304)
436.110	n	(P-11003/87; A-6304)
436.120	n	(P-11003/87; A-6304)
436.130	n	(P-11003/87; O-4925; R-6329; A-6304)
436.140	n	(P-11003/87; A-6304)
502.40	am	(P-18105)
502.120	am	(P-17755)
502.600	am	(P-17755)
508.30	am	(P-11463/87; A-1910) (P-4779)
508.35	am	(P-4779)
508.50	am	(P-4779)
508.60	am	(P-11463/87; O-19918/87; M-2030; A-1910) (P-4779)
508.70	am	(P-4779)
508.80	am	(P-4779)
509.90	am	(P-4677)
1308.20	am	(P-17766)
1308.30	n	(P-17766)
1308.40	n	(P-17766)
1409.120	am	(P-17761)
1409.130	n	(P-17761)
1409.132	r	(P-17761)
1410.10	am	(P-4345)
1410.15	r	(P-4345)

TITLE 11 (CONT'D)

Section		Reference
1770.10	r	(P-10331)
1770.10	n	(P-10298)
1770.20	r	(P-10331)
1770.20	n	(P-10298)
1770.30	r	(P-10331)
1770.30	n	(P-10298)
1770.40	r	(P-10331)
1770.40	n	(P-10298)
1770.50	r	(P-10331)
1770.50	n	(P-10298)
1770.60	r	(P-10331)
1770.60	n	(P-10298)
1770.70	r	(P-10331)
1770.70	n	(P-10298)
1770.80	r	(P-10331)
1770.80	n	(P-10298)
1770.90	r	(P-10331)
1770.90	n	(P-10298)
1770.100	r	(P-10331)
1770.100	n	(P-10298)
1770.110	r	(P-10331)
1770.110	n	(P-10298)
1770.120	r	(P-10331)
1770.120	n	(P-10298)
1770.130	r	(P-10331)
1770.130	n	(P-10298)
1770.140	r	(P-10331)
1770.140	n	(P-10298)
1770.150	r	(P-10331)
1770.150	n	(P-10298)
1770.160	r	(P-10331)
1770.160	n	(P-10298)
1770.170	r	(P-10331)
1770.170	n	(P-10298)
1770.180	r	(P-10331)
1770.180	n	(P-10298)
1770.190	r	(P-10331)
1770.190	n	(P-10298)
1770.200	r	(P-10331)
1770.200	n	(P-10298)
1770.210	r	(P-10331)
1770.220	n	(P-10298)

TITLE 14

Section		Reference
176.11	am	(P-17770)
180.10	n	(P-11130; O-15757; R-17036; A-17431)
180.11	n	(P-11130; O-15757; R-17036; A-17431)
180.12	n	(P-11130; O-15757; R-17036; A-17431)
180.13	n	(P-11130; O-15757; R-17036; A-17431)
180.14	n	(P-11130; O-15757; R-17036; A-17431)
200.100	am	(P-1; A-9424)

TITLE 14 (CONT'D)

Section		Reference
200.101	am	(P-1; A-9424)
200.105	am	(P-1; A-9424)
200.107	am	(P-1; A-9424)
200.109	am	(P-1; A-9424)
200.110	am	(P-1; A-9424)
200.111	r	(P-1; A-9424)
200.300	am	(P-1; A-9424)
200.201	n	(P-1; A-9424)
200.202	n	(P-1; A-9424)
200.304	am	(P-1; A-9424)
200.305	am	(P-1; A-9424)
200.400	n	(P-1; A-9424)
200.404	n	(P-1; A-9424)
200.500	am	(P-1; A-9424; C-10804)
200.501	n	(P-1; A-9424)
200.502	am	(P-1; A-9424)
200.503	am	(P-1; A-9424)
200.505	n	(P-1; A-9424)
200.506	n	(P-1; A-9424)
200.507	n	(P-1; A-9424; C-10804)
200.508	n	(P-1; A-9424)
200.600	am	(P-1; A-9424)
200.601	r	(P-1; A-9424; (E-1124)
200.603	r	(P-1; A-9424; C-10804)
200.603	n	(P-1; A-9424; C-10804)
200.603	am	(E-1124)
200.604	am	(P-1; A-9424) (E-1124)
200.605	am	(P-1; A-9424)
200.700	r	(P-1; A-9424)
200.701	am	(P-1; A-9424)
200.702	am	(P-1; A-9424)
200.703	r	(P-1; A-9424)
200.800	am	(P-1; A-9424)
200.1000	r	(P-1; A-9424) (E-1124)
200.1001	r	(P-1; A-9424) (E-1124)
200.Ap. A	am	(P-1; A-9424)
IL A	am	(P-1; A-9424)
IL I	r	(P-1; A-9424)
IL J	r	(P-1; A-9424)
IL L	am	(P-1; A-9424)
IL M	n	(P-1; A-9424)
IL N	n	(P-1; A-9424)
200.Ap. C	am	(P-1; A-9424)
IL B	am	(P-1; A-9424)
IL C	n	(P-1; A-9424)
200.Ap.F	am	(P-1; A-9424)
IL A	n	(P-1; A-9424)
IL B	n	(P-1; A-9424)
470.110	n	(P-15239)
470.120	n	(P-15239)
470.210	n	(P-15239)
470.220	n	(P-15239)
470.230	n	(P-15239)
470.240	n	(P-15239)
470.250	n	(P-15239)
470.260	n	(P-15239)

TITLE 14 (CONT'D)

Section		Reference
470.270	n	(P-15239)
470.280	n	(P-15239)
470.290	n	(P-15239)
470.310	n	(P-15239)
500.60	am	(P-9275)
500.90	am	(P-9275)
520.100	n	(P-17346/87; O-7826; R-11318; A-11201)
520.210	am	(P-5856; A-17823)
520.300	n	(P-17346/87; O-7826; R-11318; A-11201)
520.320	am	(P-17346/87; O-7826; R-11318; A-11201)
520.700	n	(P-17346/87; O-7826; R-11318; A-11201)
520.710	n	(P-17346/87; O-7826; R-11318; A-11201)
520.720	am	(P-17346/87; O-7826; R-11318; A-11201)
520.730	n	(P-17346/87; O-7826; R-11318; A-11201)
520.900	am	(P-5856; A-17823)
520.910	am	(P-5856; A-17823)
520.920	am	(P-5856; A-17823)
520.930	am	(P-5856; A-17823)
520.1000	am	(P-15419/87; A-4115)
520.1010	am	(P-15419/87; A-4115)
520.1020	am	(P-15419/87; A-4115)
520.1030	am	(P-15419/87; A-4115)
550.20	am	(P-14350/87; A-2226)
550.40	am	(P-14350/87; A-2226)
550.50	am	(P-14350/87; A-2226)
550.60	am	(P-14350/87; A-2226)
590.10	am	(P-15249)
590.80	n	(P-15249)
590.81	n	(P-15249)
590.90	n	(P-15249)
590.91	n	(P-15249)
590.92	n	(P-15249)
590.93	n	(P-15249)
620.10	am	(P-14797) (E-15207)
620.30	am	(P-14797) (E-15207)
620.40	am	(P-14797) (E-15207)
620.50	am	(P-14797) (E-15207)
620.60	am	(P-14797) (E-15207)
620.70	am	(P-14797) (E-15207)
620.80	am	(P-14797) (E-15207)
620.90	am	(P-14797) (E-15207)
630.20	am	(P-4987)
630.40	am	(P-4987)
640.10	n	(P-7926)
640.20	n	(P-7926)
640.30	n	(P-7926)
640.40	n	(P-7926)
640.50	n	(P-7926)
640.60	n	(P-7926)

TITLE 14 (CONT'D)

Section		
640.70	n	(P-7926)
640.80	n	(P-7926)
640.90	n	(P-7926)
640.100	n	(P-7926)
640.110	n	(P-7926)
640.120	n	(P-7926)
640.130	n	(P-7926)
640.140	n	(P-7926)
640.150	n	(P-7926)
640.160	n	(P-7926)
640.170	n	(P-7926)
910.10	n	(P-12539/87; A-3480)
910.20	n	(P-12539/87; A-3480)
910.30	n	(P-12539/87; A-3480)
910.40	n	(P-12539/87; A-3480)
910.50	n	(P-12539/87; A-3480)
910.60	n	(P-12539/87; A-3480)
910.70	n	(P-12539/87; A-3480)
910.80	n	(P-12539/87; A-3480)

TITLE 17

Section		
510.10	am	(P-5081; A-11724)
510.20	am	(P-5081; A-11724)
520.20	am	(P-14567/87; A-1815)
520.30	am	(P-14567/87; A-1815)
530.20	am	(P-4999; A-12016)
530.70	am	(P-4999; A-12016)
530.80	am	(P-4999; A-12016)
530.90	am	(P-4999; A-12016)
530.100	am	(P-4999; A-12016)
530.105	am	(P-4999; A-12016)
530.110	am	(P-4999; A-12016)
530.120	am	(P-4999; A-12016)
550.10	am	(P-5094; A-11730)
550.20	am	(P-5094; A-11730)
550.30	am	(P-5094; A-11730)
570.10	am	(P-5087; A-12034)
570.40	am	(P-5087; A-12034) (E-16261)
590.10	am	(P-5027; A-12200) (E-16233)
590.20	am	(P-5027; A-12200)
590.30	am	(P-5027; A-12200)
590.40	am	(P-5027; A-12200) (E-16233)
590.50	am	(P-5027; A-12200)
590.60	am	(P-5027; A-12200) (E-16233)
590.Ex. A	am	(P-5027; A-12200)
650.10	am	(P-74; A-8003)
650.20	am	(P-74; A-8003)
650.21	n	(P-74; A-8003)
650.22	n	(P-74; A-8003)
650.23	n	(P-74; A-8003)
650.30	am	(P-5525; A-12055)
650.40	am	(P-74; A-8003)
650.50	am	(P-74; A-8003)
650.60	am	(P-5525; A-12055) (P-74; A-8003)
650.70	am	(P-5525) (P-74; A-8003)
670.20	am	(P-5117; A-12042)

TITLE 17 (CONT'D)

Section		
670.30	am	(P-5117; A-12042)
670.40	am	(P-5117; A-12042)
670.55	am	(P-5117; A-12042)
670.60	am	(P-5117; A-12042)
690.20	am	(P-5104; A-12246)
690.30	am	(P-5104; A-12246)
710.10	am	(P-19471/87; A-5342)
710.20	am	(P-19471/87; A-5342)
710.30	am	(P-19471/87; A-5342)
710.50	am	(P-19471/87; A-5342)
710.60	am	(P-19471/87; A-5342)
720.10	am	(P-5111; A-12254)
720.20	am	(P-5111; A-12254)
720.40	am	(P-5111; A-12254)
730.20	am	(P-5016; A-12186)
730.30	am	(P-5016; A-12186)
740.10	am	(P-5130; A-12261)
740.20	am	(P-5130; A-12261)
810.30	am	(P-19435/87; A-5306) (E-6981) (P-10580; A-15982)
810.40	am	(P-19435/87; A-5306) (E-6981) (L-18255) (P-10580; A-15982)
810.70	am	(P-19435/87; A-5306)
810.90	am	(P-19435/87; A-5306)
830.20	am	(P-4761; A-11714)
830.60	am	(P-4761; A-11714)
850.50	am	(P-2183; A-7996)
850.60	am	(P-2183; A-7996)
850.80	am	(P-2183; A-7996)
930.20	am	(P-5522; A-11720)
930.45	n	(P-5522; A-11720)
950.10	r	(P-13121/87; A-1813)
950.10	n	(P-13116/87; A-1808)
950.20	r	(P-13121/87; A-1813)
950.20	n	(P-13116/87; A-1808)
950.30	r	(P-13121/87; A-1813)
950.30	n	(P-13116/87; A-1808)
950.40	n	(P-13116/87; A-1808)
950.50	n	(P-13116/87; A-1808)
950.60	n	(P-13116/87; A-1808)
1535.10	am	(P-8197; A-16018)
1535.60	am	(P-8197; A-16018)
1540.10	am	(P-14463/87; A-5296)
1540.20	am	(P-14463/87; A-5296)
1540.30	am	(P-14463/87; A-5296)
1540.40	am	(P-14463/87; A-5296)
1545.10	n	(P-12103/87; A-2274; RC-7829)
1545.20	n	(P-12103/87; A-2274; RC-7829)
1545.30	n	(P-12103/87; A-2274; RC-7829)
1545.40	n	(P-12103/87; A-2274; RC-7829)
1545.50	n	(P-12103/87; A-2274; RC-7829)
1545.60	n	(P-12103/87; A-2274; RC-7829)
1545.70	n	(P-12103/87; A-2274; RC-7829)
1545.80	n	(P-12103/87; A-2274; RC-7829)
1545.90	n	(P-12103/87; A-2274; RC-7829)
1590.20	am	(P-5072; A-12807)

TITLE 17 (CONT'D)

Section		
1590.50	am	(P-5072; A-12807)
1590.80	am	(P-5072; A-12807)
1590.90	am	(P-5072; A-12807)
1590.100	am	(P-5072; A-12807)
1590.120	am	(P-5072; A-12807)
2030.30	am	(E-8745) (P-10575; A-16707) (E-12111) (P-13820)

TITLE 28

Section		
205.10	am	(P-10980/87; A-8351)
205.15	n	(P-10980/87; A-8351)
205.17	n	(P-10980/87; A-8351)
205.20	am	(P-10980/87; A-8351)
205.40	am	(P-10980/87; A-8351)
205.50	am	(P-10980/87; A-8351)
504.10	am	(P-12727/87; A-8351)
504.12	n	(P-12727/87; A-8351)
504.15	n	(P-12727/87; A-8351)
504.20	am	(P-12727/87; A-8351)
504.30	am	(P-12727/87; A-8351)
504.40	am	(P-12727/87; A-8351)
504.50	am	(P-12727/87; A-8351)
504.60	am	(P-12727/87; A-8351)
504.70	am	(P-12727/87; A-8351)
504.80	am	(P-12727/87; A-8351)
504.90	am	(P-12727/87; A-8351)
504.100	am	(P-12727/87; A-8351)
504.120	am	(P-12727/87; A-8351)
504.130	am	(P-12727/87; A-8351)
504.150	am	(P-12727/87; A-8351)
504.170	am	(P-12727/87; A-8351)
504.202	n	(P-12727/87; A-8351)
504.205	n	(P-12727/87; A-8351)
504.210	am	(P-12727/87; A-8351)
504.230	am	(P-12727/87; A-8351)
504.240	am	(P-12727/87; A-8351)
504.250	am	(P-12727/87; A-8351)
504.260	am	(P-12727/87; A-8351)
504.270	am	(P-12727/87; A-8351)
504.275	n	(P-12727/87; A-8351)
504.300	am	(P-12727/87; A-8351)
504.400	am	(P-12727/87; A-8351)
504.401	n	(P-12727/87; A-8351)
504.405	n	(P-12727/87; A-8351)
504.410	am	(P-12727/87; A-8351)
504.420	am	(P-12727/87; A-8351)
504.430	am	(P-12727/87; A-8351)
504.440	am	(P-12727/87; A-8351)
504.450	am	(P-12727/87; A-8351)
504.460	am	(P-12727/87; A-8351)
504.470	am	(P-12727/87; A-8351)
504.480	am	(P-12727/87; A-8351)
504.500	am	(P-12727/87; A-8351)
504.510	am	(P-12727/87; A-8351)
504.600	am	(P-12727/87; A-8351)

TITLE 28 (CONT'D)

Section		
504.602	am	(P-12727/87; A-8351)
504.605	n	(P-12727/87; A-8351)
504.610	am	(P-12727/87; A-8351)
504.620	am	(P-12727/87; A-8351)
504.630	am	(P-12727/87; A-8351)
504.640	r	(P-12727/87; A-8351)
504.650	am	(P-12727/87; A-8351)
504.660	n	(P-12727/87; A-8351)
504.700	am	(P-12727/87; A-8351)
504.710	am	(P-12727/87; A-8351)
504.715	n	(P-12727/87; A-8351)
504.720	am	(P-12727/87; A-8351)
504.730	am	(P-12727/87; A-8351)
504.800	am	(P-12727/87; A-8351)
504.802	n	(P-12727/87; A-8351)
504.805	n	(P-12727/87; A-8351)
504.810	am	(P-12727/87; A-8351)
504.820	am	(P-12727/87; A-8351)
504.830	am	(P-12727/87; A-8351)
504.840	am	(P-12727/87; A-8351)
504.850	am	(P-12727/87; A-8351)
504.900	n	(P-12727/87; A-8351)
504.905	n	(P-12727/87; A-8351)
504.910	n	(P-12727/87; A-8351)
504.920	n	(P-12727/87; A-8351)
504.930	n	(P-12727/87; A-8351)
504.940	n	(P-12727/87; A-8351)
504.Th. A	am	(P-12727/87; A-8351)
504.Th. B	am	(P-12727/87; A-8351)
504.Th. C	am	(P-12727/87; A-8351)
525.510	am	(P-3542; A-9664)
701.5	n	(P-313; A-12274)
701.10	am	(P-313; A-12274)
701.20	am	(P-313; A-12274)
701.30	am	(P-313; A-12274)
701.40	am	(P-313; A-12274)
701.60	am	(P-313; A-12274)
701.70	am	(P-313; A-12274)
701.80	am	(P-313; A-12274)
701.90	am	(P-313; A-12274)
701.100	am	(P-313; A-12274)
701.110	am	(P-313; A-12274)
701.120	am	(P-313; A-12274)
701.130	am	(P-313; A-12274)
701.140	am	(P-313; A-12274)
701.150	am	(P-313; A-12274)
701.160	am	(P-313; A-12274)
701.170	am	(P-313; A-12274)
701.180	am	(P-313; A-12274)
701.200	am	(P-313; A-12274)
701.210	am	(P-313; A-12274)
701.220	am	(P-353; A-12274)
701.250	am	(P-313; A-12274)
701.260	am	(P-313; A-12274)
701.270	am	(P-313; A-12274)
702.5	n	(P-378; A-12340)

TITLE 20 (CONT'D)

Section	Type	Reference
702.10	am	(P-379; A-12340)
702.20	am	(P-378; A-12340)
702.30	am	(P-378; A-12340)
702.40	am	(P-378; A-12340)
702.50	am	(P-378; A-12340)
702.60	am	(P-378; A-12340)
702.70	am	(P-378; A-12340)
702.80	am	(P-378; A-12340)
702.90	am	(P-378; A-12340)
702.110	am	(P-378; A-12340)
702.120	am	(P-378; A-12340)
702.130	am	(P-378; A-12340)
702.140	am	(P-378; A-12340)
702.150	am	(P-378; A-12340)
702.160	am	(P-378; A-12340)
702.170	am	(P-378; A-12340)
702.180	am	(P-378; A-12340)
702.190	am	(P-378; A-12340)
702.200	am	(P-378; A-12340)
702.210	am	(P-378; A-12340)
702.220	am	(P-378; A-12340)
702.230	am	(P-378; A-12340)
702.240	am	(P-378; A-12340)
702.250	am	(P-378; A-12340)
702.260	am	(P-378; A-12340)
703.1	n	(P-443; A-12405)
703.5	n	(P-443; A-12405)
703.10	am	(P-443; A-12405)
703.20	am	(P-443; A-12405)
703.40	am	(P-443; A-12405)
703.50	am	(P-443; A-12405)
703.60	am	(P-443; A-12405)
703.70	am	(P-443; A-12405)
703.80	am	(P-443; A-12405)
703.90	am	(P-443; A-12405)
703.110	am	(P-443; A-12405)
703.120	am	(P-443; A-12405)
703.130	am	(P-443; A-12405)
703.140	am	(P-443; A-12405)
703.150	am	(P-443; A-12405)
703.160	am	(P-443; A-12405)
703.170	am	(P-443; A-12405)
703.190	am	(P-443; A-12405)
703.200	am	(P-443; A-12405)
703.210	am	(P-443; A-12405)
703.240	am	(P-443; A-12405)
720.5	n	(P-489; A-12452)
720.10	am	(P-489; A-12452)
720.30	am	(P-489; A-12452)
720.50	am	(P-489; A-12452)
720.60	am	(P-489; A-12452)
720.70	am	(P-489; A-12452)
720.100	am	(P-489; A-12452)
720.130	am	(P-489; A-12452)
720.150	am	(P-489; A-12452)
720.160	am	(P-489; A-12452)
1280.10	n	(P-10497/87; A-8458)
1280.20	n	(P-10497/87; A-8458)
1280.30	n	(P-10497/87; A-8458)
1280.40	n	(P-10497/87; A-8458)
1290.10	n	(P-9415)
1290.20	n	(P-9415)
1290.30	n	(P-9415)
1290.40	n	(P-9415)
1290.50	n	(P-9415)
1290.60	n	(P-9415)
1290.70	n	(P-9415)
1291.10	n	(P-9420; O-15760)
1291.20	n	(P-9420; O-15760)
1291.30	n	(P-9420; O-15760)
1291.40	n	(P-9420; O-15760)
1295.10	n	(P-17064)
1295.20	n	(P-17064)
1295.30	n	(P-17064)
1295.40	n	(P-17064)
1295.50	n	(P-17064)
1295.60	n	(P-17064)
1295.70	n	(P-17064)
1295.80	n	(P-17064)
1520.10	am	(P-12110/87; O-7832; R-8750; A-8649)
1520.45	n	(P-12110/87; O-7832; R-8750; A-8649)
1520.50	am	(P-12110/87; O-7832; R-8750; A-8649)
1550.10	n	(P-7800/87; A-7585)
1550.20	n	(P-7800/87; A-7585)
1550.30	n	(P-7800/87; A-7585)
1550.40	n	(P-7800/87; A-7585)
1550.50	n	(P-7800/87; A-7585)
1550.60	n	(P-7800/87; A-7585)
1550.70	n	(P-7800/87; A-7585)
1610.70	am	(P-4774; P-14106)
1720.30	am	(P-11454/87; A-3728)
1720.Ap. A	n	(P-11454/87; A-3728)

TITLE 23

Section	Type	Reference
1.260	am	(P-9385/87; A-4800)
1.290	n	(P-9385/87; O-19868/87; M-4884; A-4800)
1.330	n	(P-9385/87; A-4800)
1.420	n	(P-9385/87; O-19868/87; M-4884; A-4800)
25.10	am	(P-1694; A-16022)
25.20	am	(P-1694; A-16022)
25.30	am	(P-1694; A-16022)
25.40	am	(P-1694; A-16022)
25.80	am	(P-1694; A-16022)
25.705	n	(P-11894/87; A-3709)
25.710	n	(P-11894/87; A-3709)
25.715	n	(P-11894/87; A-3709)

TITLE 23 (CONT'D)

Section	Type	Reference
25.720	n	(P-11894/87; A-3709)
25.725	n	(P-11894/87; A-3709)
25.730	n	(P-11894/87; A-3709)
25.735	n	(P-11894/87; A-3709)
25.740	n	(P-11894/87; A-3709)
25.745	n	(P-11894/87; A-3709)
25.750	n	(P-11894/87; A-3709)
25.755	n	(P-11894/87; A-3709)
25.760	n	(P-11894/87; O-19860/87; M-3828; A-3709; F-4942)
25.765	n	(P-11894/87; A-3709)
25.770	n	(P-11894/87; A-3709)
25.775	n	(P-11894/87; A-3709)
25.780	n	(P-11894/87; A-3709)
50.40	am	(P-20377/87; A-9882)
50.50	am	(P-20377/87; A-9882)
110.10	am	(P-12625)
110.20	am	(P-12625)
110.25	am	(P-12625)
110.30	am	(P-12625)
110.40	am	(P-12625)
110.50	am	(P-12625)
110.60	am	(P-12625)
110.70	am	(P-12625)
110.80	am	(P-12625)
110.90	am	(P-12625)
110.110	am	(P-12625)
110.7a. A	am	(P-12625)
110.7a. B	am	(P-12625)
110.7a. C	am	(P-12625)
110.7a. D	am	(P-12625)
120.10	am	(P-9402/87; A-4147)
120.30	am	(P-9402/87; A-4147)
120.40	am	(P-9402/87; A-4147)
120.50	am	(P-9402/87; A-4147)
120.60	am	(P-9402/87; A-4147)
120.70	am	(P-9402/87; A-4147)
120.80	am	(P-9402/87; A-4147)
120.90	am	(P-9402/87; A-4147)
120.100	am	(P-9402/87; A-4147)
120.110	am	(P-9402/87; A-4147)
120.120	am	(P-9402/87; A-4147)
120.200	am	(P-9402/87; A-4147)
120.210	am	(P-9402/87; A-4147)
120.240	am	(P-9402/87; A-4147)
120.245	n	(P-9402/87; A-4147)
210.10	am	(P-6873; A-16052)
210.110	am	(P-6873; A-16052)
210.120	am	(P-6873; A-16052)
210.140	am	(P-6873; A-16052)
226.525	am	(P-17151)
226.525	am	(P-17151)
226.544	n	(P-17151)
226.570	am	(P-17151)
226.572	r	(P-17151)
226.605	am	(P-17151)
230.10	am	(P-12747)
230.30	am	(P-12747)
230.60	am	(P-12747)
254.110	r	(P-4451/87; A-2282)
254.120	am	(P-4451/87; A-2282)
254.130	am	(P-4451/87; A-2282)
254.140	am	(P-4451/87; A-2282)
254.150	am	(P-4451/87; A-2282)
254.210	am	(P-4451/87; A-2282)
254.220	am	(P-4451/87; A-2282)
254.230	am	(P-4451/87; A-2282)
254.240	am	(P-4451/87; A-2282)
254.250	am	(P-4451/87; A-2282)
254.310	am	(P-4451/87; O-15357; HC-238; R-3116; A-2282) (P-8777)
254.320	am	(P-4451/87; A-2282)
254.330	r	(P-4451/87; A-2282)
254.340	r	(P-4451/87; A-2282)
254.340	n	(P-4451/87; A-2282)
254.340	am	(P-8777)
254.350	am	(P-4451/87; RC-238; A-2282)
254.360	am	(P-4451/87; A-2282)
254.370	am	(P-4451/87; A-2282) (P-8777)
254.380	am	(P-4451/87; A-2282)
254.390	am	(P-4451/87; A-2282) (P-8777)
254.395	am	(P-4451/87; O-15357/87; R-3116; A-2282)
254.398	am	(P-4451/87; A-2282)
254.410	am	(P-4451/87; A-2282)
254.420	am	(P-4451/87; A-2282)
254.440	am	(P-4451/87; A-2282)
254.450	am	(P-4451/87; A-2282)
254.460	am	(P-4451/87; A-2282)
254.470	am	(P-4451/87; A-2282)
254.480	am	(P-4451/87; A-2282)
254.490	r	(P-4451/87; A-2282)
254.510	am	(P-4451/87; A-2282)
254.610	am	(P-4451/87; O-15357/87; R-3116; A-2282) (P-8777)
254.620	am	(P-4451/87; O-15357/87; R-3116; A-2282)
254.620	r	(P-8777)
254.630	am	(P-4451/87; O-15357/87; R-3116; A-2282)
254.640	am	(P-4451/87; O-15357/87; R-3116; A-2282)
254.710	am	(P-4451/87; A-2282)
254.720	am	(P-4451/87; A-2282)
254.730	am	(P-4451/87; A-2282)
254.740	am	(P-4451/87; A-2282)
254.750	am	(P-4451/87; A-2282)
254.760	r	(P-4451/87; A-2282)
254.810	am	(P-4451/87; A-2282)
254.820	am	(P-4451/87; A-2282)
254.910	am	(P-4451/87; A-2282)
254.920	am	(P-4451/87; A-2282)

TITLE 26 (CONT'D)

106.507	n	(P-1722; O-11335; R-12549; A-12684)
106.601	n	(P-6904; A-12817)
106.602	n	(P-6904; A-12817)
106.602	am	(P-14865)
106.603	n	(P-6904; A-12817)
106.604	n	(P-6904; A-12817)
106.604	am	(P-14865)
106.605	n	(P-6904; A-12817)
106.701	n	(P-14865)
106.702	n	(P-14865)
106.703	n	(P-14865)
106.704	n	(P-14865)
106.705	n	(P-14865)
106.706	n	(P-14865)
106.707	n	(P-14865)
106.708	n	(P-14865)
106.709	n	(P-14865)
106.710	n	(P-14865)
106.711	n	(P-14865)
106.712	n	(P-14865)
106.713	n	(P-14865)
106.714	n	(P-14865)
106.801	n	(P-14865)
106.802	n	(P-14865)
106.803	n	(P-14865)
106.804	n	(P-14865)
106.805	n	(P-14865)
106.806	n	(P-14865)
106.807	n	(P-14865)
106.808	n	(P-14865)
106.901	n	(P-14865)
106.902	n	(P-14865)
106.903	n	(P-14865)
106.904	n	(P-14865)
106.905	n	(P-14865)
106.906	n	(P-14865)
106.907	n	(P-14865)
107.100	r	(P-14933)
107.101	r	(P-14933)
107.Ap. A	r	(P-14933)
161.202	r	(P-16343)
201.281	am	(P-5154)
201.401	n	(P-5154)
201.402	n	(P-5154)
201.403	n	(P-5154)
201.404	r	(P-5154)
201.405	n	(P-5154)
201.406	n	(P-5154)
201.407	n	(P-5154)
201.408	n	(P-5154)
203.103	am	(P-10407/87; A-6118)
203.104	am	(P-10407/87; A-6118)
203.107	am	(P-10407/87; A-6118)
203.110	am	(P-10407/87; A-6118)
203.112	n	(P-10407/87; A-6118)

203.113	am	(P-10407/87; A-6118)
203.116	am	(P-10407/87; A-6118)
203.117	n	(P-10407/87; A-6118)
203.123	n	(P-10407/87; A-6118)
203.124	n	(P-10407/87; A-6118)
203.125	n	(P-10407/87; A-6118)
203.126	#	(P-10407/87; A-6118)
203.127	n	(P-10407/87; A-6118)
203.128	am	(P-10407/87; A-6118)
203.131	am	(P-10407/87; A-6118)
203.134	am	(P-10407/87; A-6118)
203.136	n	(P-10407/87; A-6118)
203.145	n	(P-10407/87; A-6118)
203.150	am	(P-10407/87; A-6118)
203.155	r	(P-10407/87; A-6118)
203.201	am	(P-10407/87; A-6118)
203.202	am	(P-10407/87; A-6118)
203.203	am	(P-10407/87; A-6118)
203.204	r	(P-10407/87; A-6118)
203.205	am	(P-10407/87; A-6118)
203.206	am	(P-10407/87; A-6118)
203.207	am	(P-10407/87; A-6118)
203.208	am	(P-10407/87; A-6118)
203.209	am	(P-10407/87; A-6118)
203.210	am	(P-10407/87; A-6118)
203.211	n	(P-10407/87; A-6118)
203.301	am	(P-10407/87; A-6118)
203.302	am	(P-10407/87; A-6118)
203.303	am	(P-10407/87; A-6118)
203.304	r	(P-10407/87; A-6118)
203.305	am	(P-10407/87; A-6118)
203.306	am	(P-10407/87; A-6118)
203.601	am	(P-10407/87; A-6118)
203.602	am	(P-10407/87; A-6118)
203.603	r	(P-10407/87; A-6118)
203.701	n	(P-10407/87; A-6118)
211.122	am	(P-14197/87; A-7284; O-19898/87; R-1642; A-787) (P-14992/87; A-7621) (P-15294)
212.113	am	(P-1729; A-12492)
212.121	am	(P-1729; A-12492)
212.123	am	(P-1729; A-12492)
212.124	am	(P-1729; A-12492)
212.126	n	(P-1729; A-12492)
214.101	am	(P-8219)
214.102	am	(P-8219)
214.104	am	(P-8219)
214.382	am	(P-8219)
214.562	n	(P-9337; A-17387)
215.102	am	(P-12835/87; P-13788/87; A-815) (P-14617/87; A-7650)
215.103	am	(P-12835/87; P-13788/07; A-815)
215.104	am	(P-12835/87; P-13788/07; A-815) (P-15412)
215.105	am	(P-14617/87; A-7650) (P-15412)

TITLE 26 (CONT'D)

215.121	am	(P-12835/87; P-13788/87; A-815)
215.122	am	(P-12835/87; P-13788/87; A-815)
215.141	am	(P-12835/87; P-13788/87; A-815)
215.142	am	(P-12835/87; P-13788/87; A-815)
215.204	am	(P-12835/87; P-13788/87; O-19904/87; R-1644; A-815) (P-14617/87; A-7650)
215.205	am	(P-12835/87; P-13788/87; O-19904/87; R-1644; A-7650)
215.206	am	(P-9787)
215.207	am	(P-12835/87; P-13788/87; O-19904/87; R-1644; A-815)
215.245	am	(P-7483)
215.260	n	(P-14224/87; A-7311)
215.261	n	(P-14224/87; A-7311)
215.263	n	(P-14224/87; A-7311; O-7846)
215.264	n	(P-14224/87; A-7311)
215.267	n	(P-14224/87; A-7311)
215.420	am	(P-15412)
215.430	am	(P-15412)
215.432	am	(P-15412)
215.435	am	(P-15412)
215.437	am	(P-15412)
215.438	n	(P-15412)
215.439	#	(P-15412)
215.439	am	(P-15412)
215.442	am	(P-12835/87; P-13788/87; A-815)
215.443	am	(P-12835/87; P-13788/87; A-815)
215.444	am	(P-12835/87; P-13788/87; A-815)
215.480	n	(P-14617/87; A-7650)
215.481	n	(P-14617/87; A-7650)
215.482	n	(P-14617/87; A-7650)
215.483	n	(P-14617/87; A-7650)
215.484	n	(P-14617/87; A-7650)
215.485	n	(P-14617/87; A-7650)
215.486	n	(P-14617/87; A-7650)
215.487	n	(P-14617/87; A-7650)
215.488	n	(P-14617/87; A-7650)
215.489	n	(P-14617/87; A-7650)
215.620	n	(P-14224/87; A-7311)
215.621	n	(P-14224/87; A-7311)
215.623	n	(P-14224/87; A-7311)
215.624	n	(P-14224/87; A-7311)
215.625	n	(P-14224/87; A-7311)
215.628	n	(P-14224/87; A-7311)
215.630	n	(P-14224/87; A-7311)
215.636	n	(P-14224/87; A-7311)
215.920	n	(P-14224/87; A-7311)
215.923	n	(P-14224/87; A-7311)
215.926	n	(P-14224/87; A-7311)
215.940	n	(P-14224/87; A-7311)
215.943	n	(P-14224/87; A-7311)
215.946	n	(P-14224/87; A-7311)
215.960	n	(P-14224/87; A-7311)
215.963	n	(P-14224/87; A-7311)
215.966	n	(P-14224/87; A-7311)

215.Ap. D	am	(P-15412)
216.122	n	(P-16615)
260.101	n	(P-16336)
260.102	r	(P-16336)
260.201	r	(P-16336)
260.202	r	(P-16336)
260.203	r	(P-16336)
260.204	r	(P-16336)
260.205	r	(P-16336)
260.206	-	(P-16336)
263.101	r	(P-16352)
263.102	r	(P-16352)
263.103	r	(P-16352)
263.201	r	(P-16352)
263.202	r	(P-16352)
263.301	r	(P-16352)
263.302	r	(P-16352)
263.304	r	(P-16352)
263.305	r	(P-16352)
263.306	r	(P-16352)
263.307	r	(P-16352)
263.308	r	(P-16352)
263.309	r	(P-16352)
263.401	r	(P-16352)
263.402	r	(P-16352)
263.501	r	(P-16352)
276.102	am	(P-17051)
277.101	r	(P-16346)
277.102	r	(P-16346)
277.103	r	(P-16346)
277.201	r	(P-16346)
277.202	r	(P-16346)
277.301	r	(P-16346)
277.302	r	(P-16346)
277.401	r	(P-16346)
277.402	r	(P-16346)
283.101	r	(P-16319)
283.102	r	(P-16319)
283.103	r	(P-16319)
283.201	r	(P-16319)
283.202	r	(P-16319)
283.203	r	(P-16319)
283.204	r	(P-16319)
283.301	r	(P-16319)
283.302	r	(P-16319)
283.303	r	(P-16319)
283.401	r	(P-16319)
283.402	r	(P-16319)
283.403	r	(P-16319)
283.404	r	(P-16319)
283.405	r	(P-16319)
283.501	r	(P-16319)
283.502	r	(P-16319)
283.503	r	(P-16319)
283.504	r	(P-16319)
283.505	r	(P-16319)

TITLE 38 (CONT'D)

Section		Citation
307.7802	n	(P-5507/87; A-2592)
307.7901	n	(P-5507/87; A-2592)
307.7902	n	(P-5507/87; A-2592)
307.7903	n	(P-5507/87; A-2592)
307.7904	n	(P-5507/87; A-2592)
307.8100	n	(P-5507/87; A-2592)
307.8110	am	(P-16396)
307.8101	n	(P-5507/87; A-2592)
307.8102	n	(P-5507/87; A-2592)
307.8103	n	(P-5507/87; A-2592)
307.8104	n	(P-5507/87; A-2592)
307.8105	n	(P-5507/87; A-2592)
307.8106	n	(P-5507/87; A-2592)
307.8107	n	(P-5507/87; A-2592)
307.8108	n	(P-5507/87; A-2592)
307.8109	n	(P-5507/87; A-2592)
307.8110	n	(P-5507/87; A-2592)
307.Ap. A	r	(P-5507/87; A-2592)
309.201	am	(A-2495)
309.203	am	(A-2495)
309.204	am	(A-2495)
309.281	am	(P-15839)
310.101	n	(P-5453/87; A-2502)
310.102	n	(P-5453/87; A-2502)
310.103	n	(P-5453/87; A-2502)
310.104	n	(P-5453/87; A-2502)
310.105	n	(P-5453/87; A-2502)
310.107	n	(P-5453/87; A-2502)
310.107	am	(P-16384)
310.110	am	(P-16384)
310.110	n	(P-5453/87; A-2502)
310.201	n	(P-5453/87; A-2502)
310.202	n	(P-5453/87; A-2502)
310.210	n	(P-5453/87; A-2502)
310.211	n	(P-5453/87; A-2502)
310.220	n	(P-5453/87; A-2502)
310.221	n	(P-5453/87; A-2502)
310.222	n	(P-5453/87; A-2502)
310.230	n	(P-5453/87; A-2502)
310.232	n	(P-5453/87; A-2502)
310.233	n	(P-5453/87; A-2502)
310.301	n	(P-5453/87; A-2502)
310.302	n	(P-5453/87; A-2502)
310.303	n	(P-5453/87; A-2502)
310.310	n	(P-5453/87; A-2502)
310.311	n	(P-5453/87; A-2502)
310.312	n	(P-5453/87; A-2502)
310.320	n	(P-5453/87; A-2502)
310.330	n	(P-5453/87; A-2502)
310.340	n	(P-5453/87; A-2502)
310.341	n	(P-5453/87; A-2502)
310.343	n	(P-5453/87; A-2502)
310.350	n	(P-5453/87; A-2502)
310.351	n	(P-5453/87; A-2502)
310.400	n	(P-5453/87; A-2502)
310.401	n	(P-5453/87; A-2502)
310.402	n	(P-5453/87; A-2502)
310.403	n	(P-5453/87; A-2502)
310.410	n	(P-5453/87; A-2502)
310.411	n	(P-5453/87; A-2502)
310.412	n	(P-5453/87; A-2502)
310.413	n	(P-5453/87; A-2502)
310.414	n	(P-5453/87; A-2502)
310.415	n	(P-5453/87; A-2502)
310.420	n	(P-5453/87; A-2502)
310.421	n	(P-5453/87; A-2502)
310.430	n	(P-5453/87; A-2502)
310.431	n	(P-5453/87; A-2502)
310.432	n	(P-5453/87; A-2502)
310.441	n	(P-5453/87; A-2502)
310.442	n	(P-5453/87; A-2502)
310.443	n	(P-5453/87; A-2502)
310.444	n	(P-5453/87; A-2502)
310.501	n	(P-5453/87; A-2502)
310.502	n	(P-5453/87; A-2502)
310.503	n	(P-5453/87; A-2502)
310.504	n	(P-5453/87; A-2502)
310.505	n	(P-5453/87; A-2502)
310.510	n	(P-5453/87; A-2502)
310.521	n	(P-5453/87; A-2502)
310.522	n	(P-5453/87; A-2502)
310.524	n	(P-5453/87; A-2502)
310.531	n	(P-5453/87; A-2502)
310.532	n	(P-5453/87; A-2502)
310.533	n	(P-5453/87; A-2502)
310.541	n	(P-5453/87; A-2502)
310.542	n	(P-5453/87; A-2502)
310.543	n	(P-5453/87; A-2502)
310.544	n	(P-5453/87; A-2502)
310.545	n	(P-5453/87; A-2502)
310.546	n	(P-5453/87; A-2502)
310.547	n	(P-5453/87; A-2502)
310.601	n	(P-5453/87; A-2502)
310.602	n	(P-5453/87; A-2502)
310.603	n	(P-5453/87; A-2502)
310.604	n	(P-5453/87; A-2502)
310.605	n	(P-5453/87; A-2502)
310.606	n	(P-5453/87; A-2502)
310.610	n	(P-5453/87; A-2502)
310.621	n	(P-5453/87; A-2502)
310.631	n	(P-5453/87; A-2502)
310.632	n	(P-5453/87; A-2502)
310.633	n	(P-5453/87; A-2502)
310.634	n	(P-5453/87; A-2502)
310.701	n	(P-5453/87; A-2502)
310.702	n	(P-5453/87; A-2502)
310.703	n	(P-5453/87; A-2502)
310.704	n	(P-5453/87; A-2502)
310.705	n	(P-5453/87; A-2502)
310.706	n	(P-5453/87; A-2502)
310.711	n	(P-5453/87; A-2502)
310.712	n	(P-5453/87; A-2502)

Section		Citation
310.713	n	(P-5453/87; A-2502)
310.714	n	(P-5453/87; A-2502)
310.721	n	(P-5453/87; A-2502)
310.722	n	(P-5453/87; A-2502)
310.801	n	(P-5453/87; A-2502)
310.901	n	(P-5453/87; A-2502)
310.902	n	(P-5453/87; A-2502)
310.903	n	(P-5453/87; A-2502)
310.904	n	(P-5453/87; A-2502)
310.905	n	(P-5453/87; A-2502)
310.906	n	(P-5453/87; A-2502)
365.101	n	(P-18030)
365.102	n	(P-18030)
365.103	n	(P-18030)
365.104	n	(P-18030)
365.201	n	(P-18030)
365.202	n	(P-18030)
365.203	n	(P-18030)
365.204	n	(P-18030)
365.301	n	(P-18030)
365.302	n	(P-18030)
365.302	n	(P-18030)
365.304	n	(P-18030)
365.401	n	(P-18030)
365.402	n [3]	(P-18030)
365.403	n	(P-18030)
365.404	n	(P-18030)
365.405	n	(P-18030)
365.406	n	(P-18030)
365.501	n	(P-18030)
365.502	n	(P-18030)
365.503	n	(P-18030)
365.504	n	(P-18030)
365.505	n	(P-18030)
365.506	n	(P-18030)
365.601	n	(P-18030)
365.602	n	(P-18030)
365.603	n	(P-18030)
365.604	n	(P-18030)
365.605	n	(P-18030)
365.606	n	(P-18030)
365.607	n	(P-18030)
365.701	n	(P-18030)
365.702	n	(P-18030)
365.703	n	(P-18030)
365.704	n	(P-18030)
365.705	n	(P-18030)
365.706	n	(P-18030)
365.707	n	(P-18030)
365.801	n	(P-18030)
365.802	n	(P-18030)
365.901	n	(P-18030)
365.902	n	(P-18030)
365.903	n	(P-18030)
365.904	n	(P-18030)
365.905	n	(P-18030)
365.1001	n	(P-18030)
365.1002	n	(P-18030)
365.1003	n	(P-18030)
365.1101	n	(P-18030)
365.1102	n	(P-18030)
373.102	am	(P-13125/87; O-19883/87; R-1641; A-3472)
373.103	am	(P-13125/87; O-19883/87; R-1641; A-3472)
373.202	am	(P-13125/87; O-19883/87; R-1641; A-3472)
373.203	am	(P-13125/87; O-19883/87; R-1641; A-3472)
373.204	am	(P-13125/87; O-19883/87; R-1641; A-3472)
373.205	n	(P-13125/87; O-19883/87; R-1641; A-3472)
378.101	n	(P-12753)
378.102	n	(P-12753)
378.103	n	(P-12753)
378.201	n	(P-12753)
378.202	n	(P-12753)
378.203	n	(P-12753)
378.204	n	(P-12753)
378.301	n	(P-12753)
378.302	n	(P-12753)
378.Ap. A	n	(P-12753)
378.Ap. B	n	(P-12753)
378.Ap. C	n	(P-12753)
378.Ap. D	n	(P-12753)
378.Ap. E	n	(P-12753)
660.101	n	(P-19563/87; A-9018)
660.102	n	(P-19563/87; A-9018)
660.103	n	(P-19563/87; A-9018)
660.201	n	(P-19563/87; A-9018)
660.202	n	(P-19563/87; A-9018)
660.203	n	(P-19563/87; A-9018)
661.101	n	(P-19480/87; A-8926)
661.102	n	(P-19480/87; A-8926)
661.103	n	(P-19480/87; A-8926)
661.201	n	(P-19480/87; A-8926)
661.202	n	(P-19480/87; O-7835; R-9169; A-8926)
661.203	n	(P-19480/87; O-7835; R-9169; A-8926)
661.204	n	(P-19480/87; O-7835; R-9169; A-8926)
661.205	n	(P-19480/87; A-8926)
661.301	n	(P-19480/87; O-7835; R-9169; A-8926)
661.302	n	(P-19480/87; A-8926)
661.303	n	(P-19480/87; A-8926)
661.304	n	(P-19480/87; A-8926)
661.305	n	(P-19480/87; A-8926)
661.306	n	(P-19480/87; A-8926)
661.307	n	(P-19480/87; A-8926)

TITLE 38 (CONT'D)

661.401	n	(P-19480/87; A-8926)
661.402	n	(P-19480/87; A-8926)
661.403	n	(P-19480/87; A-8926)
661.404	n	(P-19480/87; A-8926)
661.405	n	(P-19480/87; A-8926)
661.406	n	(P-19480/87; A-8926)
661.407	n	(P-19480/87; A-8926)
661.408	n	(P-19480/87; A-8926)
661.501	n	(P-19480/87; A-8926)
661.502	n	(P-19480/87; A-8926)
661.601	n	(P-19480/87; A-8926)
661.602	n	(P-19480/87; A-8926)
661.701	n	(P-19480/87; A-8926)
661.702	n	(P-19480/87; A-8926)
661.703	n	(P-19480/87; A-8926)
661.704	n	(P-19480/87; A-8926)
661.705	n	(P-19480/87; O-7835; R-9169; A-8926)
661.Ap. A	n	(P-19480/87; A-8926)
661.Ap. B	n	(P-19480/87; A-8926)
661.Ap. C	n	(P-19480/87; A-8926)
671.101	n	(P-3877; A-14134)
671.102	n	(P-3877; A-14134)
671.105	n	(P-3877; A-14134)
671.104	n	(P-3877; A-14134)
671.201	n	(P-3877; A-14134)
671.202	n	(P-3877; A-14134)
671.301	n	(P-3877; A-14134)
671.302	n	(P-3877; A-14134)
671.303	n	(P-3877; A-14134)
671.304	n	(P-3877; A-14134)
671.305	n	(P-3877; A-14134)
671.306	n	(P-3877; A-14134)
671.Ap. A	n	(P-3877; A-14134)
671.Ap. B	n	(P-3877; A-14134)
671.Ap. C	n	(P-3877; A-14134)
671.Ap. D	n	(P-3877; A-14134)
671.Ap. E	n	(P-3877; A-14134)
671.Ap. F	n	(P-3877; A-14134)
Tb. A	n	(P-3877; A-14134)
Tb. B	n	(P-3877; A-14134)
680.107	am	(P-17981/87; A-8442)
680.202	am	(P-17981/87; A-8442)
680.203	am	(P-17981/87; A-8442)
680.302	am	(P-17981/87; A-8442)
680.305	am	(P-17981/87; A-8442)
680.501	am	(P-17981/87; A-8442)
702.104	am	(P-16368/87; A-2579) (P-17368/87; A-6673)
702.110	am	(P-17266/87; A-6673)
702.181	am	(P-6490; A-13083)
702.184	am	(P-6490; A-13083)
702.187	am	(P-6490; A-13083)
703.121	am	(P-6476; A-13069)
703.123	am	(P-15444)
703.141	am	(P-6476; A-13069)

TITLE 38 (CONT'D)

703.155	am	(P-6476; A-13069)
703.159	n	(P-6476; A-13069)
703.160	n	(P-6476; A-13069)
703.185	am	(O-16374/87; A-2584) (P-6476; A-13069)
703.187	n	(P-6476; A-13069)
703.188	n	(P-6476; A-13069)
704.101	am	(P-17383/87; A-6687)
704.106	am	(P-17383/87; A-6687)
704.122	am	(P-17383/87; A-6687)
704.143	am	(P-17167)
704.151	n	(P-8229; A-13700)
704.161	am	(P-8229; A-13700)
720.110	am	(P-15327)
720.111	am	(P-16320/87; A-2450) (P-6392; A-12999) (P-15327)
721.103	am	(P-16327/87; A-2456)
721.104	am	(P-15347)
721.105	am	(P-15347)
721.106	am	(P-16327/87; A-2456)
721.133	am	(P-16327/87; A-2456) (P-6397; A-13006) (P-15347)
721.Ap. H	am	(P-6397) (P-15347)
721.Ap. I	am	(P-3211; A-12070)
Tb. A	am	(P-3211; A-12070)
Tb. B	am	(P-3211; A-12070)
722.110	am	(P-15449)
722.142	am	(P-6501; A-13129)
722.144	-	(P-6501; A-13129)
722.151	am	(P-15449)
722.170	am	(P-6501; A-131129)
724.101	am	(P-15455)
724.113	am	(P-6507; A-13135)
724.198	am	(P-6507; A-13135)
724.199	am	(P-6507; A-13135)
724.200	am	(P-6507; A-13135)
724.201	am	(P-6507; A-13135)
724.247	am	(P-6507; A-13135)
724.251	am	(P-6507; A-13135)
724.Ap.I	n	(P-6507; A-13135) (P-15455)
725.101	am	(P-6434; A-13027) (P-15402)
725.113	am	(P-6434; A-13027)
725.247	am	(P-6434; A-13027)
725.328	am	(P-16357/87; A-2485)
726.120	am	(P-16383/87; A-2900)
726.131	am	(P-16383/87; A-2900)
726.134	am	(P-16383/87; A-2900)
726.135	am	(P-16383/87; A-2900)
726.143	am	(P-16383/87; A-2900)
726.144	am	(P-16383/87; A-2900)
728.101	am	(P-6453; A-13046)
728.102	am	(P-6453; A-13046)
728.103	am	(P-6453; A-13046)
728.104	am	(P-6453; A-13046)
728.105	am	(P-6453; A-13046)
728.106	am	(P-6453; A-13046)

TITLE 38 (CONT'D)

728.107	am	(P-6453; A-13046)
728.130	am	(P-6453; A-13046)
728.132	n	(P-6453; A-13046)
728.139	n	(P-6453; A-13046)
728.140	am	(P-6453; A-13046)
728.142	am	(P-6453; A-13046)
728.150	am	(P-6453; A-13046)
728.Ap. C	n	(P-6453; A-13046)
807.105	n	(P-7166)
807.700	n	(P-5168; A-15566)
808.100	n	(P-9326)
808.101	n	(P-9326)
808.102	n	(P-9326)
808.110	n	(P-9326)
808.111	n	(P-9326)
808.121	n	(P-9326)
808.Ap. A	n	(P-9326)
810.101	n	(P-7157)
810.102	n	(P-7157)
810.103	n	(P-7157)
810.104	n	(P-7157)
811.101	n	(P-7172)
811.102	n	(P-7172)
811.103	n	(P-7172)
811.104	n	(P-7172)
811.105	n	(P-7172)
811.106	n	(P-7172)
811.107	n	(P-7172)
811.108	n	(P-7172)
811.109	n	(P-7172)
811.110	n	(P-7172)
811.111	n	(P-7172)
811.201	n	(P-7172)
811.202	n	(P-7172)
811.203	n	(P-7172)
811.204	n	(P-7172)
811.205	n	(P-7172)
811.301	n	(P-7172)
811.302	n	(P-7172)
811.303	n	(P-7172)
811.304	n	(P-7172)
811.305	n	(P-7172)
811.306	n	(P-7172)
811.307	n	(P-7172)
811.308	n	(P-7172)
811.309	n	(P-7172)
811.310	n	(P-7172)
811.311	n	(P-7172)
811.312	n	(P-7172)
811.313	n	(P-7172)
811.314	n	(P-7172)
811.315	n	(P-7172)
811.316	n	(P-7172)
811.317	n	(P-7172)
811.318	n	(P-7172)
811.319	n	(P-7172)

TITLE 38 (CONT'D)

811.320	n	(P-7172)
811.321	n	(P-7172)
811.322	n	(P-7172)
811.401	n	(P-7172)
811.402	n	(P-7172)
811.403	n	(P-7172)
811.404	n	(P-7172)
811.405	n	(P-7172)
811.406	n	(P-7172)
811.501	n	(P-7172)
811.502	n	(P-7172)
811.503	n	(P-7172)
811.504	n	(P-7172)
811.505	n	(P-7172)
811.506	n	(P-7172)
811.507	n	(P-7172)
811.508	n	(P-7172)
811.509	n	(P-7172)
811.600	n	(P-7172)
811.700	n	(P-7172)
811.701	n	(P-7172)
811.702	n	(P-7172)
811.703	n	(P-7172)
811.704	n	(P-7172)
811.705	n	(P-7172)
811.706	n	(P-7172)
811.707	n	(P-7172)
811.708	n	(P-7172)
811.709	n	(P-7172)
811.710	n	(P-7172)
811.711	n	(P-7172)
811.712	n	(P-7172)
811.713	n	(P-7173)
811.714	n	(P-7172)
811.715	n	(P-7172)
812.101	n	(P-7074)
812.102	n	(P-7074)
812.103	n	(P-7074)
812.104	n	(P-7074)
812.105	n	(P-7074)
812.106	n	(P-7074)
812.107	n	(P-7074)
812.108	n	(P-7074)
812.109	n	(P-7074)
812.110	n	(P-7074)
812.111	n	(P-7074)
812.112	n	(P-7074)
812.113	n	(P-7074)
812.114	n	(P-7474)
812.115	n	(P-7074)
812.116	n	(P-7074)
812.201	n	(P-7074)
812.202	n	(P-7074)
812.203	n	(P-7074)
812.204	n	(P-7074)
812.301	n	(P-7074)

TITLE 35 (CONT'D)

Section		Reference
812.302	n	(P-7074)
812.303	n	(P-7074)
812.304	n	(P-7074)
812.305	n	(P-7074)
812.306	n	(P-7074)
812.307	n	(P-7074)
812.308	n	(P-7074)
812.309	n	(P-7074)
812.310	n	(P-7074)
812.311	n	(P-7074)
812.312	n	(P-7074)
812.313	n	(P-7074)
812.314	n	(P-7074)
812.315	n	(P-7074)
812.316	n	(P-7074)
812.317	n	(P-7074)
812.318	n	(P-7074)
813.101	n	(P-7123)
813.102	n	(P-7123)
813.103	n	(P-7123)
813.104	n	(P-7123)
813.105	n	(P-7123)
813.106	n	(P-7123)
813.107	n	(P-7123)
813.108	n	(P-7123)
813.109	n	(P-7123)
813.110	n	(P-7123)
813.111	n	(P-7123)
813.201	n	(P-7123)
813.202	n	(P-7123)
813.203	n	(P-7123)
813.204	n	(P-7123)
813.301	n	(P-7123)
813.302	n	(P-7123)
813.303	n	(P-7123)
813.304	n	(P-7123)
813.305	n	(P-7123)
813.401	n	(P-7123)
813.402	n	(P-7123)
813.403	n	(P-7123)
813.501	n	(P-7123)
813.502	n	(P-7123)
813.503	n	(P-7123)
814.101	n	(P-7097)
814.102	n	(P-7097)
814.103	n	(P-7097)
814.104	n	(P-7097)
814.105	n	(P-7097)
814.106	n	(P-7097)
814.201	n	(P-7097)
814.202	n	(P-7097)
814.301	n	(P-7097)
814.401	n	(P-7097)
814.402	n	(P-7097)
814.501	n	(P-7097)

TITLE 35 (CONT'D)

Section		Reference
814.502	n	(P-7097)
815.101	n	(P-7115)
815.102	n	(P-7115)
815.201	n	(P-7115)
815.202	n	(P-7115)
815.203	n	(P-7115)
815.204	n	(P-7115)
815.301	n	(P-7115)
815.302	n	(P-7115)
815.303	n	(P-7115)
815.401	n	(P-7115)
815.402	n	(P-7115)
815.501	n	(P-7115)
815.502	n	(P-7115)
815.503	n	(P-7115)
849.101	n	(E-8485) (P-15828)
849.102	n	(E-8485) (P-15828)
849.103	n	(E-8485)
849.104	n	(E-8485) (P-15828)
849.105	n	(E-8485) (P-15828)
849.106	n	(P-15828)
855.201	am	(P-17358/87; A-6094)
855.202	am	(P-17358/87; A-6094)
855.203	am	(P-17358/87; A-6094)
855.204	am	(P-17358/87; A-6094)
855.205	am	(P-17358/87; A-6094)
855.206	am	(P-17358/87; A-6094)
855.207	am	(P-17358/87; A-6094)
855.210	am	(P-17358/87; A-6094)
855.211	r	(P-17358/87; A-6094)
855.212	am	(P-17358/87; A-6094)
855.213	n	(P-17358/87; A-6094)
857.201	am	(P-16294/87; O-3125; R-4725; A-4703)
858.101	am	(P-17599)
858.103	am	(P-17599)
858.107	am	(P-17599)
858.201	am	(P-17599)
858.202	am	(P-17599)
858.203	am	(P-17599)
858.204	#	(P-17599)
858.204	am	(P-17599)
858.205	#	(P-17599)
858.205	am	(P-17599)
858.206	n	(P-17599)
858.207	n	(P-17599)
858.208	n	(P-17599)
858.302	am	(P-17599)
858.303	am	(P-17599)
858.304	#	(P-17599)
858.304	am	(P-17599)
858.305	#	(P-17599)
858.305	am	(P-17599)
858.306	#	(P-17599)
858.307	n	(P-17599)
858.308	n	(P-17599)

TITLE 35 (CONT'D)

Section		Reference
858.309	n	(P-17599)
858.310	n	(P-17599)
858.401	am	(P-17599)
860.210	am	(P-94; A-16074)
870.207	am	(P-5534)
870.209	r	(P-5534)
870.210		(P-5534)
870.211	r	(P-5534)
870.213	n	(P-5534)
870.214	n	(P-5534)
870.309	r	(P-5534)
870.310		(P-5534)

TITLE 38

Section		Reference
100.10	r	(P-13745/87; A-10462)
100.20	r	(P-13745/87; A-10462)
100.30	r	(P-13745/87; A-10462)
100.40	r	(P-13745/87; A-10462)
100.50	r	(P-13745/87; A-10462)
100.60	r	(P-13745/87; A-10462)
100.70	r	(P-13745/87; A-10462)
100.80	r	(P-13745/87; A-10462)
100.90	r	(P-13745/87; A-10462)
100.100	r	(P-13745/87; A-10462)
100.110	r	(P-13745/87; A-10462)
100.120	r	(P-13745/87; A-10462)
100.130	r	(P-13745/87; A-10462)
100.140	r	(P-13745/87; A-10462)
100.150	r	(P-13745/87; A-10462)
100.160	r	(P-13745/87; A-10462)
100.170	r	(P-13745/87; A-10462)
100.180	r	(P-13745/87; A-10462)
100.190	r	(P-13745/87; A-10462)
100.200	r	(P-13745/87; A-10462)
100.210	r	(P-13745/87; A-10462)
100.220	r	(P-13745/87; A-10462)
100.230	r	(P-13745/87; A-10462)
100.240	r	(P-13745/87; A-10462)
100.250	r	(P-13745/87; A-10462)
100.Tb.A	r	(P-13745/87; A-10462)
100.Tb.B	r	(P-13745/87; A-10462)
110.70	am	(P-13782/87; A-10456)
125.40	am	(P-6894; A-17834)
160.170	am	(P-6899; A-17844)
190.5	am	(P-6888; A-17838)
190.10	am	(P-18473/87; A-10464) (P-14097)
190.50	am	(P-14097)
190.140	am	(P-18473/87; A-10464) (P-14097)
190.160	am	(P-18473/87; A-10464) (P-14097)
190.180	am	(P-18473/87; A-10464) (P-14097)
305.10	n	(P-4295; A-11178)
305.20	n	(P-4295; A-11178)
305.30	n	(P-4295; A-11178)
305.40	n	(P-4295; A-11178)
310.110	r	(P-5489; A-17774)
310.210	am	(P-5489; A-17774)

TITLE 38 (CONT'D)

Section		Reference
310.310	am	(P-5489; A-17774)
310.320	am	(P-5489; A-17774)
310.330	n	(P-5489; A-17774)
310.340	n	(P-5489; A-17774)
310.350	n	(P-5489; A-17774)
310.360	n	(P-5489; A-17774)
310.370	n	(P-5489; A-17774)
310.410	am	(P-5489; A-17774)
310.420	r	(P-5489; A-17774)
310.430	n	(P-5489; A-17774)
310.440	r	(P-5489; A-17774)
310.610	am	(P-5489; A-17774)
310.620	am	(P-5489; A-17774)
310.630	am	(P-5489; A-17774)
310.640	r	(P-5489; A-17774)
310.650	n	(P-5489; A-17774)
310.660	n	(P-5489; A-17774)
310.670	n	(P-5489; A-17774)
310.680	n	(P-5489; A-17774)
310.690	n	(P-5489; A-17774)
310.700	n	(P-5489; A-17774)
310.710	am	(P-5489; A-17774)
310.810	am	(P-5489; A-17774)
310.820	n	(P-5489; RC-15732; A-17774)
310.830	n	(P-5489; A-17774)
310.840	n	(P-5489; A-17774)
310.850	n	(P-5489; A-17774)
310.860	n	(P-5489; A-17774)
310.870	n	(P-5489; A-17774)
310.880	n	(P-5489; A-17774)
310.890	n	(P-5489; A-17774)
310.910	n	(P-5489; A-17774)
330.10	n	(P-20372/87; A-7991)
330.20	n	(P-20372/87; A-7991)
330.100	n	(P-20372/87; A-7991)
330.110	n	(P-20372/87; A-7991)
330.120	am	(P-10282; A-17280)
355.10	n	(P-3869; A-10667)
355.20	n	(P-3869; A-10667)
355.30	n	(P-3869; A-10667)
355.40	n	(P-3869; A-10667)
356.10	n	(P-3158; A-11182)
356.20	n	(P-3158; A-11182)
356.30	n	(P-3158; A-11182)
356.40	n	(P-3158; A-11182)
357.10	n	(P-3865; A-10663)
357.20	n	(P-3865; A-10663)
400.1520	am	(P-7977; A-15165) (E-8106; O-11364)
400.1800	n	(P-7977; A-15165) (E-8106; O-11364)
400.1810	n	(P-7977; A-15165) (E-8106; O-11364)
400.1905	n	(P-7977; A-15165) (E-8106; O-11364)

TITLE 38 (CONT'D)

Section		Actions
400.1910	n	(P-7977; A-15165) (E-8106; O-11364)
400.1915	n	(P-7977; A-15165) (E-8106; O-11364)
400.1920	n	(P-7977; A-15165) (E-8106; O-11364)
400.1925	n	(P-7977; A-15165) (E-8106; O-11364)
400.1930	n	(P-7977; A-15165) (E-8106; O-11364)
400.1935	n	(P-7977; A-15165) (E-8106; O-11364)
400.1940	n	(P-7977; A-15165) (E-8106; O-11364)
400.1945	n	(P-7977; A-15165) (E-8106; O-11364)
400.1950	n	(P-7977; A-15165) (E-8106; O-11364)
400.1955	n	(P-7977; A-15165) (E-8106; O-11364)
400.1970	n	(P-7977; A-15165) (E-8106; O-11364)
400.1972	n	(P-7977; A-15165) (E-8106; O-11364)
400.1975	n	(P-7977; A-15165) (E-8106; O-11364)
400.1980	n	(P-7977; A-15165) (E-8106; O-11364)
400.1982	n	(P-7977; A-15165) (E-8106; O-11364)
400.1985	n	(P-7977; A-15165) (E-8106; O-11364)
400.1990	n	(P-7977; A-15165) (E-8106; O-11364)
400.1993	n	(P-7977; A-15165) (E-8106; O-11364)
400.1997	n	(P-7977; A-15165) (E-8106; O-11364)
400.2005	n	(P-7977; A-15165) (E-8106; O-11364)
400.2010	n	(P-7977; A-15165) (E-8106; O-11364)
400.2020	n	(P-7977; A-15165) (E-8106; O-11364)
400.2030	n	(P-7977; A-15165) (E-8106; O-11364)
400.2040	n	(P-7977; A-15165) (E-8106; O-11364)
400.2050	n	(P-7977; A-15165) (E-8106; O-11364)
400.2060	n	(P-7977; A-15165) (E-8106; O-11364)
400.2070	n	(P-7977; A-15165) (E-8106; O-11364)
400.2105	n	(P-7977; A-15165) (E-8106; O-11364)

TITLE 38 (CONT'D)

Section		Actions
400.2110	n	(P-7977; A-15165) (E-8106; O-11364)
400.2120	n	(P-7977; A-15165) (E-8106; O-11364)
400.2200	n	(P-7977; A-15165) (E-8106; O-11364)
400.2300	n	(P-7977; A-15165) (E-8106; O-11364)
400.2310	n	(P-7977; A-15165) (E-8106; O-11364)
400.2320	n	(P-7977; A-15165) (E-8106; O-11364)
400.2330	n	(P-7977; A-15165) (E-8106; O-11364)
400.2340	n	(P-7977) (E-8106; O-11364)
400.2400	n	(P-7977; O-14453; M-15230; A-15165) (E-8106; O-11364)
400.2410	n	(P-7977; A-15165) (E-8106; O-11364)
400.2420	n	(P-7977; A-15165) (E-8106; O-11364)
400.2500	n	(P-7977; A-15165) (E-8106; O-11364)
400.2510	n	(P-7977; A-15165) (E-8106; O-11364)
400.2520	n	(P-7977; A-15165) (E-8106; O-11364)
400.2530	n	(P-7977; A-15165) (E-8106; O-11364)
400.2540	n	(P-7977; A-15165) (E-8106; O-11364)
400.2550	n	(P-7977) (E-8106; O-11364)
450.10	r	(P-2201; A-8683) (E-3041)
450.20	r	(P-2201; A-8683) (E-3041)
450.30	r	(P-2201; A-8683) (E-3041)
450.40	r	(P-2201; A-8683) (E-3041)
450.50	r	(P-2201; A-8683) (E-3041)
450.60	r	(P-2201; A-8683) (E-3041)
450.70	r	(P-2201; A-8683) (E-3041)
450.80	r	(P-2201; A-8683) (E-3041)
450.90	r	(P-2201; A-8683) (E-3041)
450.100	r	(P-2201; A-8683) (E-3041)
450.110	r	(P-2201; A-8683) (E-3041)
450.110	n	(P-2203; RC-7851; A-8685) (E-3079; O-7866)
450.115	n	(P-2201; A-8683) (E-3041)
450.120	r	(P-2201; A-8683) (E-3041)
450.120	n	(P-2203; RC-7851; A-8685) (E-3079; O-7866)
450.125	n	(P-2203; RC-7851; A-8685) (E-3079; O-7866)
450.130	r	(P-2201; A-8683) (E-3041)
450.130	n	(P-2203; RC-7851; A-8685) (E-3079; O-7866)
450.140	n	(P-2201; A-8683) (E-3041)

TITLE 38 (CONT'D)

Section		Actions
450.140	n	(P-2203; RC-7851; A-8685) (E-3079; O-7866)
450.150	r	(P-2201; A-8683) (E-3041)
450.150	n	(P-2203; RC-7851; A-8685) (E-3079; O-7866)
450.160	n	(P-2203; A-8683) (E-3041)
450.170	n	(P-2203; RC-7851; A-8685) (E-3079; O-7866)
450.175	n	(P-2203; RC-7851; A-8685) (E-3079; O-7866)
450.185	n	(P-2203; RC-7851; A-8685) (E-3079; O-7866)
450.190	n	(E-3079; O-7866)
450.210	n	(P-2203; RC-7851; A-8685) (E-3079; O-7866)
450.220	n	(P-2203; RC-7851; A-8685) (E-3079; O-7866)
450.230	n	(P-2203; RC-7851; A-8685) (E-3079; O-7866)
450.240	n	(P-2203; RC-7851; A-8685) (E-3079; O-7866)
450.250	n	(P-2203; RC-7851; A-8685) (E-3079; O-7866)
450.260	n	(P-2203; RC-7851; A-8685) (E-3079; O-7866)
450.270	n	(P-2203; RC-7851; A-8685) (E-3079; O-7866)
450.280	n	(P-2203; RC-7851; A-8685) (E-3079; O-7866)
450.290	n	(P-2203; RC-7851; A-8685) (E-3079; O-7866)
450.310	n	(P-2203; RC-7851; A-8685; O-9191) (E-3079; O-7866)
450.320	n	(P-2203; RC-7851; A-8685; O-9191) (E-3079; O-7866)
450.330	n	(P-2203; RC-7851; A-8685) (E-3079; O-7866)
450.340	n	(P-2203; RC-7851; A-8685) (E-3079; O-7866)
450.350	n	(P-2203; RC-7851; A-8685) (E-3079; O-7866)
450.410	n	(P-2203; RC-7851; A-8685) (E-3079; O-7866)
450.420	n	(P-2203; RC-7851; A-8685) (E-3079; O-7866)
450.430	n	(P-2203; RC-7851; A-8685) (E-3079; O-7866)
450.440	n	(P-2203; RC-7851; A-8685) (E-3079; O-7866)
450.450	n	(P-2203; RC-7851; A-8685) (E-3079; O-7866)
450.460	n	(P-2203; RC-7851; A-8685) (E-3079; O-7866)
450.470	n	(P-2203; RC-7851; A-8685) (E-3079; O-7866)
450.480	n	(P-2203; RC-7851; A-8685) (E-3079; O-7866)

TITLE 38 (CONT'D)

Section		Actions
450.490	n	(P-2203; RC-7851; A-8685; O-9191) (E-3079; O-7866)
450.610	n	(P-2203; RC-7851; A-8685) (E-3079; O-7866)
450.620	n	(P-2203; RC-7851; A-8685) (E-3079; O-7866)
450.630	n	(P-2203; RC-7851; A-8685) (E-3079; O-7866)
450.640	n	(P-2203; RC-7851; A-8685) (E-3079; O-7866)
450.650	n	(P-2203; RC-7851; A-8685) (E-3079; O-7866)
450.660	n	(P-2203; RC-7851; A-8685) (E-3079; O-7866)
450.710	n	(P-2203; RC-7851; A-8685) (E-3079; O-7866)
450.720	n	(P-2203; RC-7851; A-8685) (E-3079; O-7866)
450.730	n	(P-2203; RC-7851; A-8685) (E-3079; O-7866)
450.740	n	(P-2203; RC-7851; A-8685) (E-3079; O-7866)
450.750	n	(P-2203; RC-7851; A-8685) (E-3079; O-7866)
450.810	n	(P-2203; RC-7851; A-8685) (E-3079; O-7866)
450.820	n	(P-2203; RC-7851; A-8685) (E-3079; O-7866)
450.830	n	(P-2203; RC-7851; A-8685) (E-3079; O-7866)
450.840	n	(P-2203; RC-7851; A-8685) (E-3079; O-7866)
450.850	n	(P-2203; RC-7851; A-8685) (E-3079; O-7866)
450.860	n	(P-2203; RC-7851; A-8685) (E-3079; O-7866)
450.910	n	(P-2203; RC-7851; A-8685) (E-3079; O-7866)
450.920	n	(P-2203; RC-7851; A-8685) (E-3079; O-7866)
450.930	n	(P-2203; RC-7851; A-8685) (E-3079; O-7866)
450.940	n	(P-2203; RC-7851; A-8685) (E-3079; O-7866)
450.950	n	(P-2203; RC-7851; A-8685) (E-3079; O-7866)
450.1010	n	(P-2203; RC-7851; A-8685) (E-3079; O-7866)
450.1020	n	(P-2203; RC-7851; A-8685) (E-3079; O-7866)
450.1030	n	(P-2203; RC-7851; A-8685) (E-3079; O-7866)
450.1040	n	(E-3079; O-7866)
450.1110	n	(P-2203; RC-7851; A-8685) (E-3079; O-7866)
450.1120	n	(P-2203; RC-7851; A-8685) (E-3079; O-7866)

TITLE 38 (CONT'D)

Section		Reference
450.1130	n	(P-2203; RC-7851; A-8685) (E-3079; O-7866)
450.1140	n	(P-2203; RC-7851; A-8685)
450.1150	n	(P-2203; RC-7851; A-8685) (E-3079; O-7866)
450.1160	n	(P-2203; RC-7851; A-8685) (E-3079; O-7866)
450.1170	n	(P-2203; RC-7851; A-8685) (E-3079; O-7866)
450.1210	n	(P-2203; RC-7851; A-8685) (E-3079; O-7866)
450.1220	n	(P-2203; RC-7851; A-8685) (E-3079; O-7866)
450.1230	n	(P-2203; RC-7851; A-8685) (E-3079; O-7866)
450.1240	n	(P-2203; RC-7851; A-8685) (E-3079; O-7866)
450.1250	n	(P-2203; RC-7851; A-8685) (E-3079; O-7866)
450.1305	n	(P-2203; RC-7851; A-8685) (E-3079; O-7866)
450.1310	n	(P-2203; RC-7851; A-8685) (E-3079; O-7866)
450.1315	n	(P-2203; RC-7851; A-8685) (E-3079; O-7866)
450.1320	n	(P-2203; RC-7851; A-8685) (E-3079; O-7866)
450.1325	n	(P-2203; RC-7851; A-8685) (E-3079; O-7866)
450.1330	n	(P-2203; RC-7851; A-8685) (E-3079; O-7866)
450.1335	n	(P-2203; RC-7851; A-8685) (E-3079; O-7866)
450.1340	n	(P-2203; RC-7851; A-8685) (E-3079; O-7866)
450.1345	n	(P-2203; RC-7851; A-8685) (E-3079; O-7866)
450.1350	n	(P-2203; RC-7851; A-8685) (E-3079; O-7866)
450.1355	n	(P-2203; RC-7851; A-8685) (E-3079; O-7866)
450.1360	n	(P-2203; RC-7851; A-8685) (E-3079; O-7866)
450.1410	n	(P-2203; RC-7851; A-8685) (E-3079; O-7866)
450.1420	n	(P-2203; RC-7851; A-8685) (E-3079; O-7866)
450.1510	n	(P-9406; A-17093) (E-9721; O-12582)
450.1520	n	(P-9406; A-17093) (E-9721; O-12582)
450.1530	n	(P-9406; A-17093) (E-9721; O-12582)
450.1540	n	(P-9406; A-17093) (E-9721; O-12582)
450.1550	n	(P-9406; A-17093) (E-9721; O-12582)
450.1560	n	(P-9406; A-17093) (E-9721; O-12582)
450.1570	n	(P-9406; A-17093) (E-9721; O-12582)
450.1580	n	(P-9406; A-17093) (E-9721; O-12582)
450.1590	n	(P-9406; A-17093) (E-9721; O-12582)
450.1595	n	(P-9406; A-17093) (E-9721; O-12582)
450.1600	n	(P-9406; A-17093) (E-9721; O-12582)
450.1610	n	(P-9406; A-17093) (E-9721; O-12582)
450.1620	n	(P-9406; A-17093) (E-9721; O-12582)
450.1630	n	(P-9406; A-17093) (E-9721; O-12582)
450.1640	n	(P-9406; A-17093) (E-9721; O-12582)
450.1650	n	(P-9406; A-17093) (E-9721; O-12582)
450.1660	n	(P-9406; A-17093) (E-9721; O-12582)
450.1670	n	(P-9406; A-17093) (E-9721; O-12582)
450.1680	n	(P-9406; A-17093) (E-9721; O-12582)
450.1690	n	(P-9406; A-17093) (E-9721; O-12582)
450.1700	n	(P-9406; A-17093) (E-9721; O-12582)
450.1710	n	(P-9406; A-17093) (E-9721; O-12582)
450.1720	n	(P-9406; A-17093) (E-9721; O-12582)
450.1730	n	(P-9406; A-17093) (E-9721; O-12582)
450.1740	n	(P-9406; A-17093) (E-9721; O-12582)
450.1750	n	(P-9406; A-17093) (E-9721; O-12582)
450.1760	n	(P-9406; A-17093) (E-9721; O-12582)
450.1770	n	(P-9406; A-17093) (E-9721; O-12582)
450.1780	n	(P-9406; A-17093) (E-9721; O-12582)
450.1790	n	(P-9406; A-17093) (E-9721; O-12582)
450.Ap. A	r	(P-2201; A-8683) (E-3041)
450.Ap. B	r	(P-2201; A-8683) (E-3041)
900.110	am	(P-10277; A-17074)
900.120	am	(P-10277; A-17074)

TITLE 41

Section		Reference
100.1	n	(P-7816/87; A-8017)
100.3	n	(P-7816/87; A-8017)
100.4	n	(P-7816/87; A-8017)
100.5	n	(P-7816/87; A-8017)
100.5	r	(P-7822/87; A-8015)
100.7	n	(P-7816/87; A-8017)
100.10	r	(P-7822/87; A-8015)
100.11	r	(P-7822/87; A-8015)
100.20	r	(P-7822/87; A-8015)
100.30	r	(P-7822/87; A-8015)
100.40	r	(P-7822/87; A-8015)
100.50	r	(P-7822/87; A-8015)
100.60	r	(P-7822/87; A-8015)
100.70	r	(P-7822/87; A-8015)
100.80	r	(P-7822/87; A-8015)
100.81	r	(P-7822/87; A-8015)
100.82	r	(P-7822/87; A-8015)
100.85	r	(P-7822/87; A-8015)
100.90	r	(P-7822/87; A-8015)
100.100	r	(P-7822/87; A-8015)
100.110	r	(P-7822/87; A-8015)
100.120	r	(P-7822/87; A-8015)
100.130	r	(P-7822/87; A-8015)
100.140	r	(P-7822/87; A-8015)
100.150	r	(P-7822/87; A-8015)
100.160	r	(P-7822/87; A-8015)
100.170	r	(P-7822/87; A-8015)
100.180	r	(P-7822/87; A-8015)
100.190	r	(P-7822/87; A-8015)
100.200	r	(P-7822/87; A-8015)
100.210	r	(P-7822/87; A-8015)
100.220	r	(P-7822/87; A-8015)
100.225	r	(P-7822/87; A-8015)
100.240	r	(P-7822/87; A-8015)
100.300	r	(P-7822/87; A-8015)
100.Ap. A	n	(P-7816/87; A-8017)
120.900	am	(P-5142)
120.1200	am	(P-5142)
120.1210	am	(P-5142)
120.1260	am	(P-5142)
170.75	r	(P-1889/087; A-8023)

TITLE 44

Section		Reference
1.2215	am	(P-6351; O-12551; W-17978)
536.10	n	(P-13729)
536.20	n	(P-13729)
536.30	n	(P-13729)
536.40	n	(P-13729)
536.50	n	(P-13729)
536.60	n	(P-13729)
536.70	n	(P-13729)
536.80	n	(P-13729)
536.90	n	(P-13729)
536.100	n	(P-13729)
536.110	n	(P-13729)
536.120	n	(P-13729)

TITLE 44 (CONT'D)

Section		Reference
536.130	n	(P-13729)
536.140	n	(P-13729)
536.150	n	(P-13729)
910.140	am	(P-10976/87; A-9864)
950.110	am	(P-10972/87; A-9860)
980.110	am	(P-13691)
1000.110	am	(P-12140; A-17815)
1000.120	am	(P-12140; A-17815)
1000.130	am	(P-12140; A-17815)
1050.110	am	(P-13377)
1050.120	am	(P-10968/87; A-9856) (P-13377)
1050.140	n	(P-13377)
1300.10	n	(P-15048) (E-15227)
1300.20	n	(P-15048) (E-15227)
1300.30	n	(P-15048) (E-15227)
5010.110	am	(P-14907/87; A-10671)
5010.210	am	(P-14907/87; A-10671)
5010.220	am	(P-14907/87; A-10671)
5010.240	am	(P-14907/87; A-10671)
5010.250	n	(P-14907/87; A-10671)
5010.260	n	(P-14907/87; A-10671)
5010.300	r	(P-14907/87; A-10671)
5010.310	am	(P-14907/87; A-10671)
5010.320	am	(P-14907/87; A-10671)
5010.400	am	(P-14907/87; A-10671)
5010.410	am	(P-14907/87; A-10671)
5010.420	r	(P-14907/87; A-10671)
5010.430	r	(P-14907/87; A-10671)
5010.435	s	(P-14907/87; A-10671)
5010.450	r	(P-14907/87; A-10671)
5010.460	am	(P-14907/87; A-10671)
5010.470	am	(P-14907/87; A-10671)
5010.480	am	(P-14907/87; A-10671)
5010.485	n	(P-14907/87; A-10671)
5010.490	am	(P-14907/87; A-10671)
5010.500	am	(P-14907/87; A-10671)
5010.510	am	(P-14907/87; A-10671)
5010.520	s	(P-14907/87; A-10671)
5010.610	am	(P-14907/87; A-10671)
5010.650	am	(P-14907/87; A-10671)
5010.660	am	(P-14907/87; A-10671)
5010.670	am	(P-14907/87; A-10671)
5010.710	am	(P-14907/87; A-10671)
5010.730	am	(P-14907/87; A-10671)
5010.740	am	(P-14907/87; A-10671)
5010.780	am	(P-14907/87; A-10671)
5010.800	am	(P-14907/87; A-10671)
5010.1010	am	(P-14907/87; A-10671)
5010.1130	am	(P-14907/87; A-10671)
5010.1140	am	(P-14907/87; A-10671)
5010.1160	am	(P-14907/87; A-10671)
5010.1170	am	(P-14907/87; A-10671)
5010.1240	am	(P-14907/87; A-10671)
5010.1260	am	(P-14907/87; A-10671)
5010.1300	am	(P-14907/87; A-10671)
5010.1400	n	(P-14907/87; A-10671)

TITLE 44 (CONT'D)

5010.1500	n	(P-14907/87; A-10671)
5010.1510	n	(P-14907/87; A-10671)
5010.1600	n	(P-14907/87; A-10671)

TITLE 47

1.35	n	(P-4403)
1.60	n	(P-4403)
1.70	am	(P-4403)
1.85	n	(P-4403)
1.100	am	(P-4403)
1.105	n	(P-4403)
1.110	am	(P-4403)
1.130	am	(P-4403)
1.160	n	(P-4403)
1.170	n	(P-4403)
1.175	n	(P-4403)
1.180	n	(P-4403)
1.185	n	(P-4403)
1.190	n	(P-4403)
1.195	n	(P-4403)
10.10	n	(P-13737/87; A-9868)
10.20	n	(P-13737/87; A-9868)
10.30	n	(P-13737/87; A-9868)
10.40	n	(P-13737/87; A-9868)
10.50	n	(P-13737/87; A-9868)
10.60	n	(P-13737/87; A-9868)
10.70	n	(P-13737/87; A-9868)
10.80	n	(P-13737/87; A-9868)
10.90	n	(P-13737/87; A-9868)
10.100	n	(P-13737/87; A-9868)
10.110	n	(P-13737/87; A-9868)
10.120	n	(P-13737/87; A-9868)
10.130	n	(P-13737/87; A-9868)
100.30	am	(P-4976/87; A-757)
100.80	am	(P-4976/87; A-757) (P-9287)
100.85	n	(P-4299; A-15530)
100.110	am	(P-4976/87; O-18390/87; M-1638; A-757)
100.115	n	(P-2173; A-14639)
100.120	am	(P-4976/87; A-757)
100.130	am	(P-4976/87; A-757)
100.140	am	(P-4976/87; A-757)
100.210	n	(P-4976/87; A-757)
100.220	n	(P-4976/87; A-757)
100.230	n	(P-4976/87; A-757)
100.240	n	(P-4976/87; A-757)
100.240	am	(P-9287)
100.250	n	(P-4976/87; O-18390/87; M-1638; A-757)
100.250	n	(P-9287)
100.260	n	(P-4976/87; A-757)
100.270	n	(P-4976/87; O-18390/87; R-1638; A-757)
100.270	n	(P-9287)
100.280	n	(P-4976/87; O-18390/87; M-1638; A-757)

TITLE 47 (CONT'D)

100.280	am	(P-9287)
100.290	n	(P-4976/87; A-757)
100.290	am	(P-9287)
100.Ap. A	n	(P-2173; A-14639) (P-9287)
100.Ap. B	n	(P-2173; A-14639) (P-9287)
100.Ap. C	n	(P-2173; A-14639) (P-9287)
100.Ap. D	n	(P-9287) (A-14639)
100.Ap. E	n	(P-9287)
100.Ap. F	n	(P-9287)
110.80	n	(P-12073/87; A-2254)
110.90	am	(P-12073/87; A-2254)
110.100	am	(P-12073/87; A-2254)
120.50	am	(P-14185/87; A-751) (P-4751; A-17311)
120.70	am	(P-4751; A-17311)
120.80	n	(P-4751; A-17311)
120.90	am	(P-4751; A-17311)
120.110	n	(P-8521)
120.115	n	(P-8521)
160.10	n	(P-14936/87; O-3119; RC-3122; R-3827; A-3676)
160.20	n	(P-14938/87; O-3119; RC-3122; R-3827; A-3676)
160.30	n	(P-14938/87; O-3119; RC-3122; R-3827; A-3676)
160.40	n	(P-14938/87; O-3119; RC-3122; R-3827; A-3676)
160.50	n	(P-14938/87; O-3119; RC-3122; R-3827; A-3676)
160.60	n	(P-14938/87; O-3119; RC-3122; R-3827; A-3676)
160.70	n	(P-14938/87; O-3119; RC-3122; R-3827; A-3676)
160.80	n	(P-14938/87; O-3119; RC-3122; R-3827; A-3676)
160.80	am	(P-9271)
160.90	n	(P-14938/87; O-3119; RC-3122; R-3827; A-3676)

TITLE 50

350.202	am	(P-2057)
601.10	n	(P-11985)
601.20	n	(P-11985)
601.30	n	(P-11985)
601.40	n	(P-11985)
601.50	n	(P-11985)
601.60	n	(P-11985)
601.70	n	(P-11985)
601.80	n	(P-11985)
601.90	n	(P-11985)
601.100	n	(P-11985)
601.110	n	(P-11985)
601.120	n	(P-11985)
601.130	n	(P-11985)
601.140	n	(P-11985)
754.Ex. B	am	(P-2057)

TITLE 50 (CONT'D)

919.10	am	(P-13535)
919.20	am	(P-13535)
919.30	am	(P-13535)
919.40	am	(P-13535)
919.50	am	(P-13535)
919.60	am	(P-13535)
919.70	am	(P-13535)
919.80	am	(P-13535)
919.90	am	(P-13535)
919.Ex. A	am	(P-13535; C-17456)
925.50	am	(P-12945)
941.10	n	(P-12948)
941.20	n	(P-12948)
941.30	n	(P-12948)
941.40	n	(P-12948)
941.50	n	(P-12948)
951.10	am	(P-17987/87; A-2426)
951.20	r	(P-17987/87; A-2426)
951.30	n	(P-17987/87; A-2426)
951.40	n	(P-17987/87; A-2426)
951.50	n	(P-17987/87; A-2426)
951.60	n	(P-17987/87; A-2426)
951.70	n	(P-17987/87; A-2426)
951.80	n	(P-17987/87; A-2426)
1102.10	n	(P-18480/87; A-18151)
1102.20	n	(P-18480/87; A-18151)
1102.30	n	(P-18480/87; A-18151)
1102.40	n	(P-18480/87; A-18151)
1102.50	n	(P-18480/87; A-18151)
1102.60	n	(P-18480/87; A-18151)
1405.10	am	(P-99)
1405.20	am	(P-99)
1405.30	am	(P-99)
1405.40	am	(P-99)
1405.50	am	(P-99)
1405.60	am	(P-99)
1405.70	am	(P-99)
1405.80	am	(P-99)
1405.90	n	(P-99)
2007.60	am	(P-18896/87; A-6921)
2009.10	n	(P-5568; A-17346)
2009.20	n	(P-5568; A-17346)
2009.30	n	(P-5568; A-17346)
2009.40	n	(P-5568; A-17346)
2009.50	n	(P-5568; A-17346)
2009.60	n	(P-5568; A-17346)
2009.70	n	(P-5568)
2009.Ex. A	n	(P-5568; A-17346)
2009.Ex. B	n	(P-5568)
2011.10	n	(P-13558)
2011.20	n	(P-13558)
2011.30	n	(P-13558)
2011.40	n	(P-13558)
2011.50	n	(P-13558)
2011.60	n	(P-13558)
2011.70	n	(P-13558)

TITLE 50 (CONT'D)

2011.Ap. A	n	(P-13558)
2501.20	am	(P-15785/87; O-240; R-11899; A-11751)
2502.10		(A-205; W-6331)
2502.20	r	(A-205; W-6331)
2801.10	am	(P-20718/87; A-11754)
2801.20	am	(P-20718/87; A-11754)
2801.30	am	(P-20718/87; A-11754)
2801.40	r	(P-20718/87; A-11754)
2801.40	m	(P-20718/87; A-11754)
2801.50	am	(P-20718/87; A-11754)
2801.60	r	(P-20718/87; A-11754)
2801.60	n	(P-20718/87; A-11754)
2801.70	r	(P-20718/87; A-11754)
2801.70	n	(P-20718/87; A-11754)
2801.80	r	(P-20718/87; A-11754)
2801.80	n	(P-20718/87; A-11754)
2801.90	am	(P-20718/87; A-11754)
2801.100	am	(P-20718/87; A-11754)
2801.110	am	(P-20718/89; A-11754)
2801.130	am	(P-20718/89; A-11754)
2801.130	n	(P-20718/89; A-11754)
2801.140	n	(P-20718/87; A-11754)
2901.A	n	(P-20718/87; A-11754)
2903.10	n	(P-14589/87; A-6669)
2903.20	n	(P-14589/87; A-6669)
2903.30	n	(P-14589/87; A-6669)
2903.40	n	(P-14589/87; A-6669)
2903.50	n	(P-14589/87; A-6669)
6301.Ex. A	am	(P-14301)
6302.40	am	(P-15269)
6701.10	n	(P-17617)
6701.20	n	(P-17617)
6701.30	n	(P-17617)
6701.Ex. A	n	(P-17617)

TITLE 56

350.30	am	(P-15272)
350.280	am	(P-9783; O-15739; RC-15742; R-17128; A-17086)
350.300	am	(P-15272)
350.310	am	(P-15272)
350.320	am	(P-15272)
350.330	am	(P-15272)
350.340	am	(P-15272)
350.350	am	(P-15272)
350.360	am	(P-15272)
350.370	am	(P-15272)
350.380	am	(P-15272)
350.400	am	(P-15272)
350.410	am	(P-15272)
350.420	am	(P-15272)
350.430	am	(P-15272)
350.440	am	(P-15272)
2610.130	am	(P-13097/87; A-4128)
2610.Ap. A	r	(P-13097/87; A-4128)

TITLE 56 (CONT'D)

2610.Ap. B	r	(P-13097/87; A-4128)
2630.83	am	(P-62; A-15961)
2630.84	am	(P-62; A-15961)
2630.110	n	(P-82; A-15961)
2712.100	am	(A-11679/86; O-11355; RC-11359)
2712.105	am	(A-11679/86; O-11355; RC-11359)
2720.115	am	(P-8201; A-14660)
2720.130	am	(P-8201; A-14660)
2712.201	n	(P-15257)
2712.202	n	(P-15257)
2712.203	n	(P-15257)
2712.205	n	(P-15257)
2712.207	n	(P-15257)
2712.210	n	(P-15257)
2720.270	am	(P-8201; A-14660)
2725.110	am	(P-11387; A-16060)
2725.120	am	(P-17973/87; A-14653)
2730.105	am	(P-8211; A-15072)
2730.130	n	(P-8211; A-15072)
2760.105	am	(P-88; O-11331; R-13632; A-13604) (E-222; O-4949)
2760.150	am	(P-11393; A-16070)
2765.50	am	(P-90; A-11740) (E-225; O-4955)
2765.55	am	(P-90; A-11740) (E-225; O-4955)
2765.68	am	(P-90; A-11740) (E-225; O-4955)
2765.90	am	(P-13531)
2765.200	n	(P-11021; O-15735; R-17439; A-17542)
2770.100	am	(P-11978; A-18143)
2770.105	am	(P-11978; A-18143)
2770.110	am	(P-20481/87; O-9178; R-11319; A-11213) (P-13825)
2770.400	am	(P-86; A-12473) (E-210; O-4947)
2770.405	am	(P-86; A-12473) (E-210; O-4947)
2770.410	am	(P-86; A-12473) (E-210; O-4947)
2770.501	am	(P-86; A-12473) (E-210; O-4947)
2835.10	am	(P-92; A-11746) (E-231; O-4957)
2835.Tb. A	am	(P-92; A-11746) (E-231; O-4957)
2920.50	am	(P-7956; A-16066)
2920.65	n	(P-17592)
2920.80	n	(P-17592)
2960.105	n	(P-6880; A-13596)
2960.110	n	(P-6880; A-13596)
6000.10	n	(P-20699; A-11186)
6000.40	am	(P-20699; A-11186)
6000.50	am	(P-20699; A-11186)
6000.65	n	(P-20699; A-11186)
6000.80	am	(P-20699; A-11186)
6000.180	am	(P-20699; A-11186)
6000.220	am	(P-20699; A-11186)
6000.280	am	(P-20699; A-11186)
6000.300	n	(P-20699; A-11186)

TITLE 59

106.15	am	(P-18087)
106.35	am	(P-3903; A-10472)

TITLE 59 (CONT'D)

106.45	am	(P-3903; A-10472)
106.65	am	(P-12154; A-18158)
106.85	am	(P-12154; A-18158)
130.10	n	(P-5406/87; A-5356)
130.15	n	(P-5406/87; A-5356)
130.20	n	(P-5406/87; A-5356)
130.30	n	(P-5406/87; A-5356)
130.40	n	(P-5406/87; A-5356)
130.50	n	(P-5406/87; A-5356)
130.51	n	(P-5406/87; A-5356)
130.60	n	(P-5406/87; A-5356)
130.70	n	(P-5406/87; A-5356)
130.80	n	(P-5406/87; A-5356)
130.90	n	(P-5406/87; A-5356)
130.100	n	(P-5406/87; A-5356)
130.110	n	(P-5406/87; O-248; RC-252; M-5474; A-5356)
130.120	n	(P-5406/87; A-5356)
130.130	n	(P-5406/87; A-5356)
130.140	n	(P-5406/87; O-248; RC-252; M-5474; A-5356)
130.150	n	(P-5406/87; O-248; RC-252; M-5474; A-5356)
130.160	n	(P-5406/87; A-5356)
130.170	n	(P-5406/87; A-5356)
130.180	n	(P-5406/87; A-5356)
130.190	n	(P-5406/87; A-5356)
130.200	n	(P-5406/87; A-5356)
130.210	n	(P-5406/87; A-5356)
130.220	n	(P-5406/87; A-5356)
130.230	n	(P-5406/87; A-5356)
130.240	n	(P-5406/87; A-5356)
130.250	n	(P-5406/87; A-5356)
130.Tb. A	n	(P-5406/87; A-5356)
130.Tb. B	n	(P-5406/87; A-5356)

TITLE 68

110.5	rn	(A-2964)
110.10	rn	(A-2964)
110.20	rn	(A-2964)
110.30	rn	(A-2964)
110.40	rn	(A-2964)
110.50	rn	(A-2964)
110.60	rn	(A-2964)
110.70	rn	(A-2964)
110.80	rn	(A-2964)
110.90	rn	(A-2964)
110.100	rn	(A-2964)
110.110	rn	(A-2964)
110.120	rn	(A-2964)
110.130	rn	(A-2964)
110.140	rn	(A-2964)
110.150	rn	(A-2964)
110.170	rn	(A-2964)
110.180	rn	(A-2964)

TITLE 68 (CONT'D)

110.190	rn	(A-2964)
110.200	rn	(A-2964)
110.210	rn	(A-2964)
110.220	rn	(A-2964)
110.230	rn	(A-2964)
110.240	rn	(A-2964)
110.250	rn	(A-2964)
110.270	rn	(A-2964)
110.Ap. A	rn	(A-2964)
110.Ap. B	rn	(A-2964)
110.Ap. C	rn	(A-2964)
120.10	rn	(A-2980)
120.20	rn	(A-2980)
120.30	rn	(A-2980)
120.40	rn	(A-2980)
120.50	rn	(A-2980)
120.60	rn	(A-2980)
150.10	rn	(A-2933)
150.20	rn	(A-2933)
150.30	rn	(A-2933)
150.40	rn	(A-2933)
150.50	rn	(A-2933)
150.60	rn	(A-2933)
150.70	rn	(A-2933)
150.80	rn	(A-2933)
150.81	rn	(A-2933)
150.82	rn	(A-2933)
150.83	rn	(A-2933)
150.85	rn	(A-2933)
150.90	rn	(A-2933)
150.100	rn	(A-2933)
160.10	rn	(A-2935)
160.20	rn	(A-2935)
160.30	rn	(A-2935)
160.40	rn	(A-2935)
160.50	rn	(A-2935)
160.60	rn	(A-2935)
160.70	rn	(A-2935)
160.80	rn	(A-2935)
170.10	rn	(A-2936)
170.20	rn	(A-2936)
170.30	rn	(A-2936)
170.40	rn	(A-2936)
170.50	rn	(A-2936)
170.60	rn	(A-2936)
170.70	rn	(A-2936)
170.80	rn	(A-2936)
170.90	rn	(A-2936)
170.100	rn	(A-2936)
170.110	rn	(A-2936)
170.120	rn	(A-2936)
170.130	rn	(A-2936)
180.10	rn	(A-2915)
180.20	rn	(A-2915)
180.30	rn	(A-2915)
180.40	rn	(A-2915)

TITLE 68 (CONT'D)

180.50	rn	(A-2915)
180.60	rn	(A-2915)
180.65	rn	(A-2915)
180.70	rn	(A-2915)
180.80	rn	(A-2915)
180.90	rn	(A-2915)
180.95	rn	(A-2915)
180.100	rn	(A-2915)
180.110	rn	(A-2915)
180.120	rn	(A-2915)
180.130	rn	(A-2915)
180.Ap. A	rn	(A-2915)
180.Ap. B	rn	(A-2915)
180.Ap. C	rn	(A-2915)
200.10	rn	(A-2917)
200.20	rn	(A-2917)
200.30	rn	(A-2917)
200.35	rn	(A-2917)
200.40	rn	(A-2917)
200.45	rn	(A-2917)
200.50	rn	(A-2917)
200.60	rn	(A-2917)
200.70	rn	(A-2917)
200.80	rn	(A-2917)
210.10	rn	(A-2919)
210.20	rn	(A-2919)
210.30	rn	(A-2919)
210.40	rn	(A-2919)
210.50	rn	(A-2919)
210.60	rn	(A-2919)
210.70	rn	(A-2919)
210.80	rn	(A-2919)
210.90	rn	(A-2919)
210.100	rn	(A-2919)
210.110	rn	(A-2919)
210.120	rn	(A-2919)
210.130	rn	(A-2919)
210.140	rn	(A-2919)
210.150	rn	(A-2919)
210.160	rn	(A-2919)
210.170	rn	(A-2919)
210.180	rn	(A-2919)
210.190	rn	(A-2919)
210.200	rn	(A-2919)
210.210	rn	(A-2919)
210.220	rn	(A-2919)
210.230	rn	(A-2919)
210.235	rn	(A-2919)
210.240	rn	(A-2919)
210.250	rn	(A-2919)
220.110	rn	(A-2926)
220.120	rn	(A-2926)
220.130	rn	(A-2926)
220.140	rn	(A-2926)
220.150	rn	(A-2926)
220.210	rn	(A-2926)

TITLE 68 (CONT'D)

Section		Reference
350.30	ro	(A-2960)
350.40	ro	(A-2960)
350.50	ro	(A-2960)
350.60	ro	(A-2960)
350.70	ro	(A-2960)
350.80	ro	(A-2960)
350.90	ro	(A-2960)
350.100	ro	(A-2960)
350.110	ro	(A-2960)
350.115	ro	(A-2960)
350.120	ro	(A-2960)
360.10	ro	(A-2963)
360.20	ro	(A-2963)
360.30	ro	(A-2962)
360.40	rn	(A-2962)
360.50	ro	(A-2963)
360.55	rn	(A-2962)
360.60	rn	(A-2962)
360.70	rn	(A-2962)
360.80	rn	(A-2962)
360.85	rn	(A-2962)
360.90	rn	(A-2962)
360.Ap. A	rn	(A-2962)
360.Ap. B	rn	(A-2962)
370.10	rn	(A-2969)
370.20	rn	(A-2969)
370.30	rn	(A-2969)
370.40	rn	(A-2969)
370.50	rn	(A-2969)
370.60	rn	(A-2969)
370.70	rn	(A-2969)
370.80	rn	(A-2969)
370.90	rn	(A-2969)
370.100	rn	(A-2969)
370.110	rn	(A-2969)
370.120	rn	(A-2969)
370.200	rn	(A-2969)
370.210	rn	(A-2969)
370.220	rn	(A-2969)
370.230	rn	(A-2969)
370.240	rn	(A-2969)
370.250	rn	(A-2969)
370.260	rn	(A-2969)
370.270	rn	(A-2969)
370.280	rn	(A-2969)
370.290	rn	(A-2969)
370.300	rn	(A-2969)
370.310	rn	(A-2969)
370.320	rn	(A-2969)
370.325	rn	(A-2969)
370.325	rn	(E-21008/87; O-4966)
370.330	rn	(A-2969)
370.340	rn	(A-2969)
370.350	rn	(A-2969)
370.360	rn	(A-2969)
370.370	rn	(A-2969)

TITLE 68 (CONT'D)

Section		Reference
380.210	rn	(A-2942)
380.220	rn	(A-2942)
380.230	rn	(A-2942)
380.240	rn	(A-2942)
380.250	rn	(A-2942)
380.260	rn	(A-2942)
380.270	rn	(A-2942)
380.280	rn	(A-2942)
380.290	rn	(A-2942)
380.300	rn	(A-2942)
380.310	rn	(A-2942)
380.320	rn	(A-2942)
380.Ap. A	rn	(A-2942)
400.10	rn	(A-2972)
400.20	rn	(A-2972)
400.30	rn	(A-2972)
400.40	rn	(A-2973)
400.50	rn	(A-2972)
400.60	rn	(A-2972)
400.65	rn	(A-2972)
400.70	rn	(A-2972)
400.80	rn	(A-2972)
400.90	rn	(A-2972)
420.5	rn	(A-2944)
420.7	rn	(A-2944)
420.10	rn	(A-2944)
420.15	rn	(A-2944)
420.20	rn	(A-2944)
420.25	rn	(A-2944)
420.30	rn	(A-2944)
420.35	rn	(A-2944)
420.40	rn	(A-2944)
420.45	rn	(A-2944)
420.50	rn	(A-2944)
420.55	rn	(A-2944)
420.56	rn	(A-2944)
420.60	rn	(A-2944)
420.65	rn	(A-2944)
420.70	rn	(A-2944)
420.80	rn	(A-2944)
420.85	rn	(A-2944)
420.90	rn	(A-2944)
420.95	rn	(A-2944)
420.100	rn	(A-2944)
420.105	rn	(A-2944)
420.115	rn	(A-2944)
430.300	rn	(A-2973)
430.500	rn	(A-2973)
430.800	rn	(A-2973)
430.1010	rn	(A-2973)
430.1020	rn	(A-2973)
430.2010	rn	(A-2973)
430.2020	rn	(A-2973)
430.2030	rn	(A-2973)
430.2040	rn	(A-2973)
430.3010	rn	(A-2973)

TITLE 68 (CONT'D)

Section		Reference
430.3020	rn	(A-2973)
430.4010	rn	(A-2973)
430.5010	rn	(A-2973)
430.5030	rn	(A-2973)
430.5040	rn	(A-2973)
430.5050	rn	(A-2973)
430.6010	rn	(A-2973)
430.6020	rn	(A-2973)
430.6030	rn	(A-2973)
430.Ap. A	rn	(A-2973)
430.Ap. B	rn	(A-2973)
450.10	rn	(A-2977)
450.15	rn	(A-2977)
450.17	rn	(A-2977)
450.20	rn	(A-2977)
450.30	rn	(A-2977)
450.40	rn	(A-2977)
450.50	rn	(A-2977)
450.60	rn	(A-2977)
450.70	rn	(A-2977)
450.80	rn	(A-2977)
450.90	rn	(A-2977)
450.100	rn	(A-2977)
450.110	rn	(A-2977)
450.120	rn	(A-2977)
450.130	rn	(A-2977)
450.140	rn	(A-2977)
450.150	rn	(A-2977)
450.170	rn	(A-2977)
450.180	rn	(A-2977)
450.185	rn	(A-2977)
450.190	rn	(A-2977)
450.195	rn	(A-2977)
450.200	rn	(A-2977)
450.210	rn	(A-2977)
450.215	rn	(A-2977)
450.220	rn	(A-2977)
450.230	rn	(A-2977)
450.240	rn	(A-2977)
450.250	rn	(A-2977)
450.260	rn	(A-2977)
450.270	rn	(A-2977)
450.280	rn	(A-2977)
450.290	rn	(A-2977)
450.Ap. A	rn	(A-2977)
460.10	rn	(A-2946)
460.20	rn	(A-2946)
460.30	rn	(A-2946)
460.40	rn	(A-2946)
460.50	rn	(A-2946)
460.60	rn	(A-2946)
460.70	rn	(A-2946)
470.10	rn	(A-2981)
470.20	rn	(A-2981)
470.30	rn	(A-2981)
470.40	rn	(A-2981)

TITLE 68 (CONT'D)

Section		Reference
470.50	rn	(A-2981)
470.60	rn	(A-2981)
470.70	rn	(A-2981)
470.80	rn	(A-2981)
470.90	rn	(A-2981)
470.100	rn	(A-2981)
480.10	rn	(A-2947)
480.20	rn	(A-2947)
480.30	rn	(A-2947)
480.40	rn	(A-2947)
480.45	rn	(A-2947)
480.50	rn	(A-2947)
480.60	rn	(A-2947)
500.5	rn	(A-2982)
500.10	rn	(A-2982)
500.11	rn	(A-2982)
500.15	rn	(A-2982)
500.20	rn	(A-2982)
500.25	rn	(A-2982)
500.30	rn	(A-2982)
500.35	rn	(A-2982)
500.45	rn	(A-2982)
500.50	rn	(A-2982)
500.55	rn	(A-2982)
500.60	rn	(A-2982)
500.65	rn	(A-2982)
500.70	rn	(A-2982)
505.10	rn	(A-2918)
505.20	rn	(A-2918)
505.30	rn	(A-2918)
505.40	rn	(A-2918)
505.50	rn	(A-2918)
505.60	rn	(A-2918)
505.70	rn	(A-2918)
1110.5	rn	(A-2964)
1110.10	rn	(A-2964)
1110.20	rn	(A-2964)
1110.30	rn	(A-2964)
1110.40	rn	(A-2964)
1110.50	rn	(A-2964)
1110.60	rn	(A-2964)
1110.70	rn	(A-2964)
1110.80	rn	(A-2964)
1110.90	rn	(A-2964)
1110.100	rn	(A-2964)
1110.110	rn	(A-2964)
1110.120	rn	(A-2964)
1110.130	rn	(A-2964)
1110.140	rn	(A-2964)
1110.150	rn	(A-2964)
1110.160	rn	(A-2964)
1110.170	rn	(A-2964)
1110.180	rn	(A-2964)
1110.190	rn	(A-2964)
1110.200	rn	(A-2964)
1110.210	rn	(A-2964)

TITLE 68 (CONT'D)

1110.220	re	(A-2964)
1110.230	re	(A-2964)
1110.240	re	(A-2964)
1110.250	re	(A-2964)
1110.270	re	(A-2964)
1110.Ap. A	re	(A-2964)
1110.Ap. B	re	(A-2964)
1110.Ap. C	re	(A-2964)
1120.10	re	(A-2980)
1120.20	re	(A-2980)
1120.30	re	(A-2980)
1120.40	re	(A-2980)
1120.50	re	(A-2980)
1120.60	re	(A-2980)
1150.20	re	(A-2933)
1150.30	re	(A-2933)
1150.40	re	(A-2933)
1150.50	re	(A-2933)
1150.60	re	(A-2933)
1150.70	re	(A-2933)
1150.80	re	(A-2933)
1150.90	re	(A-2933)
1150.100	re	(A-2933)
1150.110	re	(A-2933)
1160.20	re	(A-2935)
1160.30	re	(A-2935)
1160.40	re	(A-2935)
1160.50	re	(A-2935)
1160.60	re	(A-2935)
1160.70	re	(A-2935)
1160.80	re	(A-2935)
1170.10	re	(A-2936)
1170.20	re	(A-2936)
1170.30	re	(A-2936)
1170.40	re	(A-2936)
1170.50	re	(A-2936)
1170.60	re	(A-2936)
1170.70	re	(A-2936)
1170.80	re	(A-2936)
1170.90	re	(A-2936)
1170.100	re	(A-2936)
1170.110	re	(A-2936)
1170.120	re	(A-2936)
1170.130	re	(A-2936)
1175.110	n	(P-19179/87; O-17443; RC-17447)
1175.110	n	(P-19179/87; O-17443;RC-17447)
1175.200	n	(P-19179/87; O-17443; RC-17447)
1175.205	n	(P-19179/87; O-17443; RC-17447)
1175.210	n	(P-19179/87; O-17443; RC-17447)
1175.215	n	(P-19179/87; O-17443; RC-17447)
1175.220	n	(P-19179/87; O-17443; RC-17447)
1175.225	n	(P-19179/87; O-17443; RC-17447)
1175.230	n	(P-19179/87; O-17443; RC-17447)
1175.235	n	(P-19179/87; O-17443; RC-17447)
1175.240	n	(P-19179/87; O-17443; RC-17447)
1175.245	n	(P-19179/87; O-17443; RC-17447)

TITLE 68 (CONT'D)

1175.255	n	(P-19179/87; O-17443; RC-17447)
1175.300	n	(P-19179/87; O-17443; RC-17447)
1175.305	n	(P-19179/87; O-17443; RC-17447)
1175.310	n	(P-19179/87; O-17443; RC-17447)
1175.315	n	(P-19179/87; O-17443; RC-17447)
1175.320	n	(P-19179/87; O-17443; RC-17447)
1175.325	n	(P-19179/87; O-17443; RC-17447)
1175.330	n	(P-19179/87; O-17443; RC-17447)
1175.335	n	(P-19179/87; O-17443; RC-17447)
1175.340	n	(P-19179/87; O-17443; RC-17447)
1175.345	n	(P-19179/87; O-17443; RC-17447)
1175.350	n	(P-19179/87; O-17443; RC-17447)
1175.355	n	(P-19179/87; O-17443; RC-17447)
1175.360	n	(P-19179/87; O-17443; RC-17447)
1175.365	n	(P-19179/87; O-17443; RC-17447)
1175.370	n	(P-19179/87; O-17443; RC-17447)
1175.400	n	(P-19179/87; O-17443; RC-17447)
1175.405	n	(P-19179/87; O-17443; RC-17447)
1175.410	n	(P-19179/87; O-17443; RC-17447)
1175.415	n	(P-19179/87; O-17443; RC-17447)
1180.10	re	(A-2915)
1180.20	re	(A-2915)
1180.30	re	(A-2915)
1180.40	re	(A-2915)
1180.50	re	(A-2915)
1180.60	re	(A-2915)
1180.65	re	(A-2915)
1180.70	re	(A-2915)
1180.80	re	(A-2915)
1180.90	re	(A-2915)
1180.95	re	(A-2915)
1180.100	re	(A-2915)
1180.110	re	(A-2915)
1180.120	re	(A-2915)
1180.130	re	(A-2915)
1180.Ap. A	re	(A-2915)
1180.Ap. C	re	(A-2915)
1200.20	am	(P-7966; A-16718)
1200.30	re	(A-2917)
1200.30	am	(P-7966; A-16718)
1200.35	re	(A-2917)
1200.40	re	(A-2917)
1200.45	re	(A-2917)
1200.45	am	(P-7966; A-16718)
1200.50	re	(A-2917)
1200.50	am	(P-7966; A-16718)
1200.60	re	(A-2917)
1200.70	re	(A-2917)
1200.80	re	(A-2917)
1210.10	re	(A-2919)
1210.20	re	(A-2919)
1210.30	re	(A-2919)
1210.40	re	(A-2919)
1210.50	re	(A-2919)
1210.60	re	(A-2919)
1210.70	re	(A-2919)

TITLE 68 (CONT'D)

1210.80	re	(A-2919)
1210.90	re	(A-2919)
1210.100	re	(A-2919)
1210.110	re	(A-2919)
1210.120	re	(A-2919)
1210.130	re	(A-2919)
1210.140	re	(A-2919)
1210.150	re	(A-2919)
1210.160	re	(A-2919)
1210.170	re	(A-2919)
1210.180	re	(A-2919)
1210.190	re	(A-2919)
1210.200	re	(A-2919)
1210.210	re	(A-2919)
1210.220	re	(A-2919)
1210.230	re	(A-2919)
1210.235	re	(A-2919)
1210.240	re	(A-2919)
1210.250	re	(A-2919)
1220.110	re	(A-2926)
1220.110	am	(P-5867)
1220.120	re	(A-2926)
1220.120	am	(P-5867)
1220.130	re	(A-2926)
1220.130	am	(P-5867)
1220.140	re	(A-2926)
1220.150	re	(A-2926)
1220.150	r	(P-5867)
1220.160	n	(P-5867)
1220.210	re	(A-2926)
1220.220	re	(A-2926)
1220.220	am	(P-5867)
1220.230	re	(A-2926)
1220.231	re	(A-2926)
1220.231	am	(P-5867)
1220.240	re	(A-2926)
1220.240	am	(P-5867)
1220.250	re	(A-2926)
1220.260	n	(P-5867)
1220.310	re	(A-2926)
1220.320	re	(A-2926)
1220.330	re	(A-2926)
1220.335	re	(A-2926)
1220.340	re	(A-2926)
1220.340	r	(P-5867)
1220.350	n	(P-5867)
1220.400	n	(P-5867)
1220.410	re	(A-2926)
1220.410	am	(P-5867)
1220.421	re	(A-2926)
1220.421	am	(P-5867)
1220.425	n	(P-5867)
1220.431	re	(A-2926)
1220.431	r	(P-5867)
1220.435	r	(A-2926)
1220.435	am	(P-5867)

TITLE 68 (CONT'D)

1220.441	re	(A-2926)
1220.500	n	(P-5867)
1220.510	n	(P-5867)
1220.520	n	(P-5867)
1220.530	n	(P-5867)
1220.540	n	(P-5867)
1220.550	n	(P-5867)
1220.560	n	(P-5867)
1220.Ap. A	re	(A-2926)
1220.Ap. A	r	(P-5867)
1220.Ap. B	re	(A-2926)
1220.Ap. B	am	(P-5867)
1220.Ap. C	re	(A-2926)
1220.Ap. C	am	(P-5867)
1230.10	re	(A-2929)
1230.20	re	(A-2929)
1230.30	re	(A-2929)
1230.40	re	(A-2929)
1230.50	re	(A-2929)
1230.60	re	(A-2929)
1230.70	re	(A-2929)
1230.80	re	(A-2929)
1230.90	re	(A-2929)
1230.100	re	(A-2929)
1230.110	re	(A-2929)
1230.120	re	(A-2929)
1230.130	re	(A-2929)
1230.140	re	(A-2929)
1230.150	re	(A-2929)
1230.160	re	(A-2929)
1240.5	re	(A-2967)
1240.10	re	(A-2967)
1240.15	re	(A-2967)
1240.20	re	(A-2967)
1240.25	re	(A-2967)
1240.30	re	(A-2967)
1240.35	re	(A-2967)
1240.40	re	(A-2967)
1240.45	re	(A-2967)
1240.50	re	(A-2967)
1240.55	re	(A-2967)
1240.60	re	(A-2967)
1240.65	re	(A-2967)
1240.70	re	(A-2967)
1250.110	re	(A-2931)
1250.120	re	(A-2931)
1250.130	re	(A-2931)
1250.140	re	(A-2931)
1250.150	re	(A-2931)
1250.160	re	(A-2931)
1250.170	re	(A-2931)
1250.190	re	(A-2931)
1250.200	re	(A-2931)
1250.205	re	(A-2931)
1250.210	re	(A-2931)
1260.11	re	(A-2948)

TITLE 68 (CONT'D)

Section		Ref
1260.12	ro	(A-2948)
1260.13	ro	(A-2948)
1260.14	ro	(A-2948)
1260.15	ro	(A-2948)
1260.16	ro	(A-2948)
1260.17	re	(A-2948)
1260.18	ro	(A-2948)
1260.19	ro	(A-2948)
1260.21	ro	(A-2948)
1260.22	ro	(A-2948)
1260.31	ro	(A-2948)
1260.32	re	(A-2948)
1260.33	ro	(A-2948)
1260.41	ro	(A-2948)
1260.42	ro	(A-2948)
1270.10	ro	(A-2950)
1270.15	ro	(A-2950)
1270.20	ro	(A-2950)
1270.30	ro	(A-2950)
1270.40	ro	(A-2950)
1270.50	re	(A-2950)
1270.60	ro	(A-2950)
1280.10	ro	(A-2953)
1280.10	r	(P-8536)
1280.13	n	(E-12116)
1280.20	ro	(A-2953)
1280.20	r	(P-8536)
1280.30	ro	(A-2953)
1280.30	r	(P-8536)
1280.40	ro	(A-2953)
1280.40	r	(P-8536)
1280.50	re	(A-2953)
1280.50	r	(P-8536)
1280.55	ro	(A-2953)
1280.55	r	(P-8536)
1280.60	ro	(A-2953)
1280.60	r	(P-8536)
1280.70	ro	(A-2953)
1280.70	r	(P-8536)
1280.80	ro	(A-2953)
1280.80	am	(P-4440)
1280.80	r	(P-8536) (P-4440; W-8752)
1280.85	re	(A-2953)
1280.85	r	(P-8536)
1280.95	ro	(A-2953)
1280.105	ro	(A-2953)
1280.105	r	(P-8536)
1280.107	ro	(A-2953)
1280.107	r	(P-8536)
1280.110	ro	(A-2953)
1280.110	r	(P-8536)
1285.10	n	(P-8571)
1285.20	n	(P-8571)
1285.30	n	(P-8571)
1285.40	n	(P-8571)
1285.50	n	(P-8571)

Section		Ref
1285.60	n	(P-8571)
1285.70	n	(P-8571)
1285.80	n	(P-8571)
1285.90	n	(P-8571)
1285.100	n	(P-8571)
1285.110	n	(P-8571)
1285.120	n	(P-8571)
1285.130	n	(P-8571)
1285.140	n	(P-8571)
1285.200	n	(P-15880)
1285.205	n	(P-15880)
1285.210	n	(P-15880)
1285.215	n	(P-15880)
1285.220	n	(P-15880)
1285.225	n	(P-15880)
1285.230	n	(P-15880)
1285.235	n	(P-15880)
1285.240	n	(P-15880; C-19125)
1285.245	n	(P-15880)
1285.250	n	(P-15880)
1285.255	n	(P-15880)
1285.260	n	(P-15880)
1285.265	n	(P-15880)
1285.270	n	(P-15880)
1285.275	n	(P-15880)
1285.310	n	(P-15880)
1285.320	n	(P-15880)
1290.10	ro	(A-2951)
1290.10	r	(P-15854)
1290.20	re	(A-2951)
1290.20	r	(P-15854)
1290.30	ro	(A-2951)
1290.30	r	(P-15854)
1290.35	re	(A-2951)
1290.35	r	(P-15854)
1290.40	re	(A-2951)
1290.40	r	(P-15854)
1290.50	re	(A-2951)
1290.50	r	(P-15854)
1290.55	ro	(A-2951)
1290.55	r	(P-15854)
1290.60	re	(A-2951)
1290.60	r	(P-15854)
1290.70	re	(A-2951)
1290.70	r	(P-15854)
1290.80	re	(A-2951)
1290.80	r	(P-15854)
1290.90	re	(A-2951)
1290.90	r	(P-15854)
1290.100	re	(A-2951)
1290.100	r	(P-15854)
1290.110	re	(A-2951)
1290.110	r	(P-15854)
1290.120	ro	(A-2951)
1290.120	r	(P-15854)
1290.130	ro	(A-2951)

TITLE 68 (CONT'D)

Section		Ref
1290.130	r	(P-15854)
1290.135	re	(A-2951)
1290.135	r	(P-15854)
1290.140	re	(A-2951)
1290.140	r	(P-15854)
1290.150	re	(A-2951)
1290.150	r	(P-15854)
1290.160	re	(A-2951)
1290.160	r	(P-15854)
1290.170	re	(A-2951)
1290.170	r	(P-15854)
1290.180	re	(A-2951)
1290.180	r	(P-15854)
1290.190	re	(A-2951)
1290.190	r	(P-15854)
1300.20	re	(A-2938)
1300.25	ro	(A-2938)
1300.25	am	(P-4431; O-11338; RC-11342; R-12130; A-12088)
1300.27	ro	(A-2938)
1300.30	ro	(A-2938)
1300.40	ro	(A-2938)
1300.41	ro	(A-2938)
1300.42	ro	(A-2938)
1300.43	ro	(A-2938)
1300.44	ro	(A-2938)
1300.44	am	(P-4431; A-12088)
1300.45	re	(A-2938)
1300.48	ro	(A-2938)
1300.50	ro	(A-2938)
1310.10	ro	(A-2955)
1310.10	r	(P-14938)
1310.20	ro	(A-2955)
1310.20	am	(P-14938)
1310.30	ro	(A-2955)
1310.30	am	(P-14938)
1310.40	re	(A-2955)
1310.40	am	(P-14938)
1310.50	ro	(A-2955)
1310.50	am	(P-14938)
1310.60	ro	(A-2955)
1310.60	am	(P-14938)
1310.70	ro	(A-2955)
1310.70	am	(P-14938)
1310.75	ro	(A-2955)
1310.75	am	(P-14938)
1310.80	ro	(A-2955)
1310.80	am	(P-14938)
1310.85	ro	(A-2955)
1310.90	ro	(A-2955)
1315.90	ro	(A-2940)
1315.100	ro	(A-2940)
1315.110	ro	(A-2940)
1315.120	ro	(A-2940)
1315.130	re	(A-2940)

Section		Ref
1315.140	re	(A-2940)
1315.150	ro	(A-2940)
1315.160	ro	(A-2940)
1315.165	ro	(A-2940)
1315.170	re	(A-2940)
1315.180	ro	(A-2940)
1315.200	ro	(A-2940)
1320.20	ro	(A-1821)
1320.20	am	(P-8606)
1320.30	ro	(A-1821)
1320.30	am	(P-8606)
1320.40	ro	(A-1821)
1320.40	am	(P-8606)
1320.45	n	(E-1925) (P-4448)
1320.50	ro	(A-1821)
1320.50	am	(P-8606)
1320.55	ro	(A-1821)
1320.55	am	(P-8606)
1320.60	ro	(A-1821)
1320.60	am	(P-8606)
1320.70	ro	(A-1821)
1320.70	am	(P-8606)
1320.80	ro	(A-1821)
1320.80	am	(P-8606)
1320.90	ro	(A-1821)
1320.90	am	(P-8606)
1320.95	n	(P-8606)
1320.100	ro	(A-1821)
1320.100	am	(P-8606)
1320.110	ro	(A-1821)
1320.110	am	(P-8606)
1320.120	ro	(A-1821)
1320.200	ro	(A-1821)
1320.210	re	(A-1821)
1320.220	re	(A-1821)
1320.230	ro	(A-1821)
1320.240	re	(A-1821)
1320.250	re	(P-8606)
1320.260	re	(A-1821)
1320.270	ro	(A-1821)
1320.300	n	(P-4448; A-11447)
1320.310	n	(P-8606)
1330.10	ro	(A-2957)
1330.20	ro	(A-2957)
1330.30	re	(A-2957)
1330.30	am	(P-8606)
1330.50	ro	(A-2957)
1330.50	ro	(A-2957)
1330.55	ro	(A-2957)
1330.60	ro	(A-2957)
1330.70	am	(P-5906; A-17394)
1330.70	ro	(A-2957)
1330.80	ro	(A-2957)
1330.90	ro	(A-2957)
1330.90	am	(P-5906; A-17394)
1330.91	ro	(A-2957)

TITLE 68 (CONT'D)

Section		Reference
1330.91	am	(P-5906; A-17394)
1330.92	re	(A-2957)
1330.92	am	(P-5906; A-17394)
1330.93	re	(A-2957)
1330.93	am	(P-5906; A-17394)
1330.94	re	(A-2957)
1330.94	am	(P-5906; A-17394)
1330.95	n	(P-5906; A-17394)
1330.100	re	(A-2957)
1330.110	ro	(A-2957)
1330.120	re	(A-2957)
1330.130	ro	(A-2957)
1330.130	am	(P-5906; A-17394)
1330.140	n.	(P-5906; A-17394)
1340.20	re	(A-2959)
1340.30	ro	(A-2959)
1340.30	am	(P-20500/87; A-8030)
1340.40	re	(P-20500/87; A-8030)
1340.50	ro	(A-2959)
1340.55	re	(A-2959)
1340.60	re	(A-2959)
1340.65	re	(A-2959)
1340.70	re	(A-2959)
1350.10	n	(A-2960)
1350.20	re	(A-2960)
1350.30	ro	(A-2960)
1350.40	ro	(A-2960)
1350.50	ro	(A-2960)
1350.60	ro	(A-2960)
1350.70	ro	(A-2960)
1350.80	re	(A-2960)
1350.90	re	(A-2960)
1350.100	re	(A-2960)
1350.110	ra	(A-2960)
1350.115	re	(A-2960)
1350.120	ro	(A-2960)
1360.10	re	(A-2962)
1360.10	r	(P-14963)
1360.20	re	(A-2962)
1360.20	am	(P-14963)
1360.30	ro	(A-2962)
1360.30	am	(P-14963)
1360.40	ro	(A-2962)
1360.40	am	(P-14963)
1360.45	n	(P-14963)
1360.50	ro	(A-2962)
1360.50	am	(P-14963)
1360.55	am	(P-14963)
1360.60	ro	(A-2962)
1360.60	am	(P-14963)
1360.65	am	(P-14963)
1360.70	ro	(A-2962)
1360.70	am	(P-14963)
1360.75	n	(P-14963)
1360.80	re	(A-2962)
1360.80	r	(P-14963)
1360.85	am	(A-2962)
1360.85	am	(P-14963)
1360.90	re	(A-2962)
1360.90	am	(P-14963)
1360.Ap. A	re	(A-2962)
1360.Ap. A	r	(P-14963)
1360.Ap. B	re	(A-2962)
1360.Ap. B	r	(P-14963)
1370.10	re	(A-2969)
1370.20	re	(A-2969)
1370.30	re	(A-2969)
1370.40	ro	(A-2969)
1370.50	re	(A-2969)
1370.60	re	(A-2969)
1370.70	re	(A-2969)
1370.80	re	(A-2969)
1370.90	re	(A-2969)
1370.100	re	(A-2969)
1370.110	re	(A-2969)
1370.120	re	(A-2969)
1370.200	re	(A-2969)
1370.210	re	(A-2969)
1370.220	re	(A-2969)
1370.230	re	(A-2969)
1370.240	re	(A-2969)
1370.250	re	(A-2969)
1370.260	re	(A-2969)
1370.270	re	(A-2969)
1370.280	re	(A-2969)
1370.290	re	(A-2969)
1370.300	ro	(A-2969)
1370.310	re	(A-2969)
1370.320	re	(A-2969)
1370.325	ra	(A-2969)
1370.325	n	(P-20506/87; A-11452)
1370.330	ra	(A-2969)
1370.340	re	(A-2969)
1370.350	re	(A-2969)
1370.360	re	(A-2969)
1370.370	re	(A-2969)
1380.210	re	(A-2942)
1380.220	re	(A-2942)
1380.230	re	(A-2942)
1380.240	re	(A-2942)
1380.250	re	(A-2942)
1380.260	re	(A-2942)
1380.270	re	(A-2942)
1380.280	re	(A-2942)
1380.290	ro	(A-2942)
1380.300	ro	(A-2942)
1380.310	re	(A-2942)
1380.320	re	(A-2942)
1380.Ap. A	re	(A-2942)
1400.10	re	(A-2972)

TITLE 68 (CONT'D)

Section		Reference
1400.20	re	(A-2972)
1400.30	re	(A-2972)
1400.40	ro	(A-2972)
1400.50	ro	(A-2972)
1400.60	ro	(A-2972)
1400.65	re	(A-2972)
1400.70	ro	(A-2972)
1400.80	re	(A-2972)
1400.90	re	(A-2972)
1420.10	re	(A-2944)
1420.20	re	(A-2944)
1420.30	re	(A-2944)
1420.40	re	(A-2944)
1420.50	re	(A-2944)
1420.60	re	(A-2944)
1420.70	re	(A-2944)
1420.80	ro	(A-2944)
1420.90	ro	(A-2944)
1420.100	ro	(A-2944)
1420.110	ro	(A-2944)
1430.300	ro	(A-2973)
1430.500	ro	(A-2973)
1430.800	ro	(A-2973)
1430.1010	re	(A-2973)
1430.1020	re	(A-2973)
1430.2010	re	(A-2973)
1430.2020	ro	(A-2973)
1430.2030	re	(A-2973)
1430.2040	ra	(A-2973)
1430.3010	ro	(A-2973)
1430.3020	ro	(A-2973)
1430.4010	ro	(A-2973)
1430.5010	re	(A-2973)
1430.5030	ro	(A-2973)
1430.5040	ro	(A-2973)
1430.5050	ro	(A-2973)
1430.6010	ro	(A-2973)
1430.6020	ro	(A-2973)
1430.6030	re	(A-2973)
1430.Ap. A	ro	(A-2973)
1430.Ap. B	re	(A-2973)
1450.10	re	(A-2977)
1450.15	ro	(A-2977)
1450.15	am	(P-17422/87; A-8036)
1450.17	re	(A-2977)
1450.17	am	(P-17422/87; A-8036)
1450.18	n	(P-17422/87; A-8036)
1450.20	re	(A-2977)
1450.20	am	(P-17422/87; A-8036)
1450.30	re	(A-2977)
1450.30	am	(P-17422/87; A-8036)
1450.40	ro	(A-2977)
1450.40	am	(P-17422/87; A-8036)
1450.50	ro	(A-2977)
1450.50	am	(P-17422/87; A-8036)
1450.60	ro	(A-2977)
1450.60	am	(P-17422/87; A-8036)
1450.70	re	(A-2977)
1450.70	am	(P-17422/87; A-8036)
1450.80	ro	(A-2977)
1450.90	re	(A-2977)
1450.90	am	(P-17422/87; A-8036)
1450.100	re	(A-2977)
1450.110	re	(A-2977)
1450.110	am	(P-17422/87; A-8036)
1450.120	re	(A-2977)
1450.140	re	(A-2977)
1450.150	re	(A-2977)
1450.150	am	(P-17422/87; A-8036)
1450.170	re	(A-2977)
1450.170	am	(P-17422/87; A-8036)
1450.180	re	(A-2977)
1450.180	am	(P-17422/87; A-8036)
1450.185	re	(A-2977)
1450.190	re	(A-2977)
1450.195	re	(A-2977)
1450.200	re	(A-2977)
1450.210	re	(A-2977)
1450.215	re	(A-2977)
1450.220	re	(A-2977)
1450.230	re	(A-2977)
1450.240	re	(A-2977)
1450.250	re	(A-2977)
1450.260	re	(A-2977)
1450.270	re	(A-2977)
1450.280	re	(A-2977)
1460.10	ro	(A-2946)
1460.20	re	(A-2946)
1460.40	re	(A-2946)
1460.50	ro	(A-2946)
1460.60	re	(A-2946)
1460.70	re	(A-2946)
1470.10	ro	(A-2981)
1470.20	re	(A-2981)
1470.30	re	(A-2981)
1470.40	re	(A-2981)
1470.50	ro	(A-2981)
1470.60	re	(A-2981)
1470.70	re	(A-2981)
1470.80	re	(A-2981)
1470.90	re	(A-2981)
1470.100	re	(A-2981)
1480.10	re	(A-2947)
1480.20	re	(A-2947)
1480.30	re	(A-2947)
1480.40	re	(A-2947)
1480.45	re	(A-2947)
1480.50	re	(A-2947)
1480.60	re	(A-2947)
1500.5	re	(A-2982)
1500.10	re	(A-2982)

TITLE 68 (CONT'D)

1500.10	am	(P-18100)
1500.11	ro	(A-2982)
1500.11	am	(P-18100)
1500.15	ro	(A-2982)
1500.20	ro	(A-2982)
1500.25	ro	(A-2982)
1500.30	ro	(A-2982)
1500.35	ro	(A-2982)
1500.45	ro	(A-2982)
1500.50	ro	(A-2982)
1500.55	ro	(A-2982)
1500.60	ro	(A-2982)
1500.65	ro	(A-2982)
1500.70	ro	(A-2982)
1505.10	ro	(A-2918)
1505.20	ro	(A-2918)
1505.30	ro	(A-2918)
1505.40	ro	(A-2918)
1505.50	ro	(A-2918)
1505.60	ro	(A-2918)
1505.70	ro	(A-2918)

TITLE 71

50.110	am	(P-10957/87; A-9845)
50.120	am	(P-10957/87; A-9845)
200.20	am	(P-13326)
250.109	am	(P-13529)
290.1203	am	(P-13518)
290.1204	am	(P-13518)
400.110	r	(P-6649/87; A-5243)
400.110	n	(P-6597/87; A-5245)
400.120	r	(P-6649/87; A-5243)
400.120	n	(P-6597/87; A-5245)
400.130	r	(P-6649/87; A-5243)
400.130	n	(P-6597/87; A-5245)
400.140	r	(P-6649/87; A-5243)
400.140	n	(P-6597/87; A-5245)
400.150	r	(P-6649/87; A-5243)
400.150	n	(P-6597/87; A-5245)
400.160	r	(P-6649/87; A-5243)
400.160	n	(P-6597/87; A-5245)
400.170	r	(P-6649/87; A-5243)
400.170	n	(P-6597/87; A-5245)
400.180	r	(P-6649/87; A-5243)
400.180	n	(P-6597/87; A-5245)
400.190	n	(P-6597/87; A-5245)
400.210	r	(P-6649/87; A-5243)
400.210	n	(P-6597/87; A-5245)
400.220	r	(P-6649/87; A-5243)
400.230	r	(P-6649/87; A-5243)
400.231	r	(P-6649/87; A-5243)
400.233	r	(P-6649/87; A-5243)
400.234	r	(P-6649/87; A-5243)
400.240	r	(P-6649/87; A-5243)
400.250	r	(P-6649/87; A-5243)
400.260	r	(P-6649/87; A-5243)

TITLE 71 (CONT'D)

400.270	r	(P-6649/87; A-5243)
400.280	r	(P-6649/87; A-5243)
400.281	r	(P-6649/87; A-5243)
400.282	r	(P-6649/87; A-5243)
400.283	r	(P-6649/87; A-5243)
400.290	r	(P-6649/87; A-5243)
400.300	r	(P-6649/87; A-5243)
400.310	r	(P-6649/87; A-5243)
400.310	n	(P-6597/87; A-5245)
400.320	n	(P-6597/87; A-5245)
400.330	n	(P-6597/87; A-5245)
400.350	n	(P-6597/87; O-19830/87; M-5473; A-5245)
400.410	r	(P-6649/87; A-5243)
400.410	n	(P-6597/87; A-5245)
400.420	r	(P-6649/87; A-5243)
400.420	n	(P-6597/87; A-5245)
400.430	r	(P-6649/87; A-5243)
400.440	r	(P-6649/87; A-5243)
400.450	r	(P-6649/87; A-5243)
400.460	r	(P-6649/87; A-5243)
400.470	r	(P-6649/87; A-5243)
400.480	r	(P-6649/87; A-5243)
400.490	r	(P-6649/87; A-5243)
400.500	r	(P-6649/87; A-5243)
400.510	r	(P-6649/87; A-5243)
400.510	n	(P-6597/87; O-19830/87; M-5473; A-5243)
400.520	r	(P-6649/87; A-5243)
400.520	n	(P-6597/87; A-5245)
400.530	r	(P-6649/87; A-5243)
400.610	r	(P-6649/87; A-5243)
400.610	n	(P-6597/87; A-5245)
400.620	r	(P-6649/87; A-5243)
400.620	n	(P-6597/87; A-5245)
400.630	r	(P-6649/87; A-5243)
400.630	n	(P-6597/87; A-5245)
400.710	r	(P-6649/87; A-5243)
400.710	n	(P-6597/87; A-5245)
400.810	r	(P-6649/87; A-5243)
400.820	r	(P-6649/87; A-5243)
400.830	r	(P-6649/87; A-5243)
400.910	r	(P-6649/87; A-5243)
400.920	r	(P-6649/87; A-5243)
400.1010	r	(P-6649/87; A-5243)
400.1110	r	(P-6649/87; A-5243)
400.1210	r	(P-6649/87; A-5243)
400.1310	r	(P-6649/87; A-5243)
400.1400	r	(P-6649/87; A-5243)
400.1410	r	(P-6649/87; A-5243)
400.1420	r	(P-6649/87; A-5243)
400.1430	r	(P-6649/87; A-5243)
400.1510	r	(P-6649/87; A-5243)
400.1610	r	(P-6649/87; A-5243)
400.1620	r	(P-6649/87; A-5243)
400.1630	r	(P-6649/87; A-5243)

TITLE 71 (CONT'D)

400.1640	r	(P-6649/87; A-5243)
400.1710	r	(P-6649/87; A-5243)
400.1800	r	(P-6649/87; A-5243)
400.1810	r	(P-6649/87; A-5243)
400.1820	r	(P-6649/87; A-5243)
400.1830	r	(P-6649/87; A-5243)
400.1840	r	(P-6649/87; A-5243)
400.1850	r	(P-6649/87; A-5243)
400.1860	r	(P-6649/87; A-5243)
400.1870	r	(P-6649/87; A-5243)
400.1880	r	(P-6649/87; A-5243)
400.1890	r	(P-6649/87; A-5243)
400.1900	r	(P-6649/87; A-5243)
400.2010	r	(P-6649/87; A-5243)
400.2020	r	(P-6649/87; A-5243)
400.2030	r	(P-6649/87; A-5243)
400.2040	r	(P-6649/87; A-5243)
400.2050	r	(P-6649/87; A-5243)
400.2060	r	(P-6649/87; A-5243)
400.2110	r	(P-6649/87; A-5243)
400.Th. A	r	(P-6649/87; A-5243)
400.Ap. A	r	(P-6649/87; A-5243)
400.Ap. B	r	(P-6649/87; A-5243)
400.Ap. C	r	(P-6649/87; A-5243)
400.Ap. D	r	(P-6649/87; A-5243)
400.Ap. E	r	(P-6649/87; A-5243)
1510.100	n	(P-14813)
1510.110	n	(P-14813)
1510.120	n	(P-14813)
1510.130	n	(P-14813)
1510.140	n	(P-14813)
1510.150	n	(P-14813)
1510.160	n	(P-14813)
1510.170	n	(P-14813)
1510.180	n	(P-14813)
1510.200	n	(P-14813)
1510.210	n	(P-14813)
1510.220	n	(P-14813)
1510.230	n	(P-14813)
1510.240	n	(P-14813)
1510.300	n	(P-14813)
1510.310	n	(P-14813)
1510.320	n	(P-14813)
1510.330	n	(P-14813)

TITLE 77

100.13	am	(P-13377/87; W-10555)
200.100	r	(P-17673)
200.101		(P-17673)
200.150		(P-17673)
200.201		(P-17573)
200.202		(P-17673)
200.203		(P-17673)
200.204		(P-17673)
200.205		(P-17673)
200.206		(P-17673)

TITLE 77 (CONT'D)

200.207	r	(P-17673)
200.208	r	(P-17673)
200.209	r	(P-17673)
200.210	r	(P-17673)
200.301	r	(P-17673)
200.302	r	(P-17673)
200.303	r	(P-17673)
200.401	r	(P-17673)
200.402	r	(P-17673)
200.403	r	(P-17673)
200.404	r	(P-17673)
200.405	r	(P-17673)
200.406	r	(P-17673)
200.501	r	(P-17673)
200.502	r	(P-17573)
200.503	r	(P-17673)
200.504	r	(P-17673)
200.601	r	(P-17673)
200.602	r	(P-17673)
200.603	r	(P-17673)
200.604	r	(P-17673)
200.605	r	(P-17673)
200.701	r	(P-17673)
200.702	r	(P-17673)
200.703	r	(P-17673)
200.704	r	(P-17673)
200.705		(P-17673)
200.706	r	(P-17673)
200.707		(P-17673)
200.708		(P-17673)
200.801		(P-17673)
200.802		(P-17673)
200.803		(P-17673)
200.804		(P-17673)
200.805		(P-17673)
200.806		(P-17673)
200.807		(P-17673)
200.808		(P-17673)
200.809		(P-17673)
200.810		(P-17673)
200.811		(P-17673)
200.812		(P-17673)
200.813		(P-17673)
200.814		(P-17673)
200.815		(P-17673)
200.816	r	(P-17673)
200.817	r	(P-17673)
200.818		(P-17673)
200.819		(P-17673)
200.820		(P-17673)
200.821		(P-17673)
200.822		(P-17673)
200.823		(P-17673)
200.824		(P-17673)
200.825		(P-17673)
200.826		(P-17673)

TITLE 77 (CONT'D)

Section		Reference
200.901	r	(P-17673)
200.902	r	(P-17673)
200.903		(P-17673)
200.904		(P-17673)
200.905	r	(P-17673)
200.906	r	(P-17673)
200.907		(P-17673)
200.908		(P-17673)
200.909		(P-17673)
200.910		(P-17673)
200.911	-	(P-17673)
200.912		(P-17673)
200.913		(P-17673)
200.914	r	(P-17673)
200.915		(P-17673)
200.916	.	(P-17673)
200.917		(P-17673)
200.918	r	(P-17673)
200.919		(P-17673)
200.920	r	(P-17673)
200.921	r	(P-17673)
200.922	-	(P-17673)
200.923		(P-17673)
200.924		(P-17673)
200.925		(P-17673)
200.926		(P-17673)
200.927	r	(P-17673)
200.928	r	(P-17673)
200.929	r	(P-17673)
200.930		(P-17673)
200.931		(P-17673)
200.932		(P-17673)
200.933	r	(P-17673)
200.1001	r	(P-17673)
200.1002	r	(P-17673)
200.1003	r	(P-17673)
200.1004	r	(P-17673)
200.1005	r	(P-17673)
200.1006	r	(P-17673)
200.1007		(P-17673)
200.1008	r	(P-17673)
205.115	n	(P-12585/87; A-3743)
205.330	am	(P-12585/87; A-3743)
205.620	am	(P-5604; A-15573)
205.620	n	(P-12585/87; A-3743)
205.810	am	(P-12585/87; A-3743)
205.1400	am	(P-12585/87; A-3743)
205.1410	am	(P-12585/87; A-3743)
240.10	r	(P-18940/87; A-15581)
240.10	n	(P-18958/87; A-15581)
240.20	r	(P-18940/87; A-15581)
240.20	n	(P-18958/87; O-14443; R-15725; A-15583)
240.30	r	(P-18940/87; A-15581)
240.30	n	(P-18958/87; O-14443; RC-14450; R-15725; A-15583)
240.40	r	(P-18940/87; A-15581)
240.40	n	(P-18958/87; O-14443; RC-14450; R-15725; A-15583)
240.50	r	(P-18940/87; A-15581)
240.50	n	(P-18958/87; O-14443; RC-14450; R-15725; A-15583)
240.60	r	(P-18940/87; A-15581)
240.60	n	(P-18958/87; O-14443; RC-14450; R-15725; A-15583)
240.70	r	(P-18940/87; A-15581)
240.80	n	(P-18958/87; O-14443; R-15725; A-15583)
240.90	n	(P-18958/87; A-15583)
240.100	n	(P-18958/87; A-15583)
240.110	n	(P-18958/87; A-15583)
240.120	n	(P-18958/87; O-14443; R-15725; A-15583)
250.525	n	(P-5611; A-16760)
250.540	n	(P-4523; A-15080)
250.550	n	(P-5611; A-16760)
250.725	n	(P-5611; A-16760)
250.730	am	(P-4523; A-15080)
250.1720	am	(P-5611; A-16760)
250.Tb.C	r	(P-4523; A-15080)
250.Tb.D	r	(P-4523; A-15080)
250.Tb.G	am	(P-4523; A-15080)
300.110	am	(E-18477)
300.120	am	(E-18477)
300.130	am	(E-18477)
300.150	am	(E-18477)
300.160	am	(E-18477)
300.200	am	(E-18477)
300.210	am	(E-18477)
300.220	am	(E-18477)
300.230	am	(E-18477)
300.250	am	(E-18477)
300.272	am	(E-18477)
300.274	am	(E-18477)
300.276	am	(E-18477)
300.277	n	(E-18477)
300.278	am	(E-18477)
300.282	am	(P-3989; A-16811)
300.284	am	(E-18477)
300.290	am	(E-18477)
300.300	am	(E-18477)
300.330	am	(E-18477)
300.340	n	(P-21578/86; A-1052)
300.510	am	(E-18477)
300.610	am	(E-18477)
300.620	n	(P-13581) (E-18477)
300.630	am	(E-18477)
300.640	am	(E-18477)
300.650	am	(E-18477)
300.660	am	(E-18477)
300.670	am	(E-18477)

TITLE 77 (CONT'D)

Section		Reference
300.680	am	(E-18477)
300.690	am	(E-18477)
300.690	n	(P-3989; O-15748; R-17034; A-16811)
300.810	am	(E-18477)
300.820	am	(E-18477)
300.830	am	(E-18477)
300.1010	am	(E-18477)
300.1020	am	(P-13581) (E-18477)
300.1030	am	(P-13581)
300.1040	am	(E-18477)
300.1050	am	(E-18477)
300.1210	am	(P-21578/86; A-1052) (E-18477)
300.1220	am	(P-21578/86; A-1052) (E-18477)
300.1230	am	(P-21578/86; A-1052)
300.1410	am	(P-21578/86; A-1052) (E-18477)
300.1420	am	(E-18477)
300.1430	am	(E-18477)
300.1610	am	(E-18477)
300.1620	am	(E-18477)
300.1630	am	(P-21578/86; A-1052) (E-18477)
300.1640	am	(E-18477)
300.1650	am	(E-18477)
300.1810	am	(P-21578/86; A-1052) (E-18477)
300.1810	r	(P-3989; O-15748; R-17034; A-16811)
300.1810	n	(P-3969; O-15748; R-17034; A-16811)
300.1820	r	(P-3989; O-15748; R-17034; A-16811)
300.1820	n	(P-3989; O-15748; R-17034; A-16811)
300.1820	am	(E-18477)
300.1830	am	(E-18477)
300.1830	r	(P-3989; O-15748; R-17034; A-16811)
300.1830	n	(P-3989; O-15748; R-17034; A-16811)
300.1840	am	(P-21578/86; A-1052) (E-18477)
300.1840	r	(P-3989; O-15748; R-17034; A-16811)
300.1840	n	(P-3989; O-15748; R-17034; A-16811)
300.1850	n	(P-3989; O-15748; R-17034; A-16811)
300.1860	n	(P-3989; O-15748; R-17034; A-16811)
300.1860	am	(E-18477)
300.1870	am	(E-18477)
300.1870	n	(P-3989; O-15748; R-17034; A-16811)
300.1880	n	(P-3989; O-15748; R-17034; A-16811)
300.1880	am	(E-18477)
300.2010	am	(E-18477)
300.2020	am	(E-18477)
300.2030	am	(E-18477)
300.2040	am	(E-18477)
300.2060	am	(E-18477)
300.2070	am	(E-18477)
300.2080	am	(E-18477)
300.2090	am	(E-18477)
300.2110	am	(E-18477)
300.2210	am	(E-18477)
300.2220	am	(E-18477)
300.2410	am	(E-18477)
300.2420	am	(E-18477)
300.2430	am	(E-18477)
300.2610	am	(E-18477)
300.2620	am	(E-18477)
300.2830	am	(E-18477)
300.2640	am	(E-18477)
300.2810	am	(E-18477)
300.2820	am	(E-18477)
300.2830	am	(E-18477)
300.2840	am	(E-18477)
300.2850	am	(E-18477)
300.2860	am	(E-18477)
300.2870	am	(E-18477)
300.2880	am	(E-18477)
300.2890	am	(E-18477)
300.2900	am	(P-21578/86; A-1052) (E-18477)
300.2910	am	(E-18477)
300.2920	am	(E-18477)
300.2930	am	(E-18477)
300.2940	am	(E-18477)
300.3010	am	(E-18477)
300.3020	am	(P-21578/86; A-1052) (E-18477)
300.3030	am	(E-18477)
300.3040	am	(E-18477)
300.3050	am	(E-18477)
300.3060	am	(P-21578/86; A-1052) (E-18477)
300.3070	am	(E-18477)
300.3080	am	(E-18477)
300.3090	am	(E-18477)
300.3100	am	(E-18477)
300.3110	am	(E-18477)
300.3120	am	(E-18477)
300.3130	am	(E-18477)
300.3140	am	(P-21578/86; A-1052) (E-18477)
300.3210	am	(E-18477)
300.3220	am	(E-18477)
300.3230	am	(E-18477)
300.3240	am	(E-18477)
300.3250	am	(E-18477)
300.3260	am	(P-21578/86; A-1052) (E-18477)
300.3270	am	(E-18477)
300.3280	am	(E-18477)
300.3290	am	(E-18477)
300.3300	am	(P-21578/86; A-1052) (E-18477)
300.3310	am	(E-18477)

TITLE 77 (CONT'D)

Section		Reference
350.1620	am	(E-18705)
350.1620	r	(P-4016; O-15751; R-17033; A-16838)
350.1620	n	(P-4016; O-15751; R-17033; A-16838)
350.1630	r	(P-4016; O-15751; R-17033; A-16838)
350.1630	n	(P-4016; O-15751; R-17033; A-16838)
350.1640	r	(P-4016; O-15751; R-17033; A-16838)
350.1640	am	(E-18705)
350.1640	n	(P-4016; O-15751; R-17033; A-16838)
350.1650	r	(P-4016; O-15751; R-17033; A-16838)
350.1650	n	(P-4016; O-15751; R-17033; A-16838)
350.1650	am	(E-18705)
350.1660	am	(P-21506/86; A-979)
350.1660	r	(P-4016; R-17033; A-16838)
350.1660	n	(P-4016; O-15751; R-17033; A-16838)
350.1670	n	(P-4016; O-15751; R-17033; A-16838)
350.1680	n	(P-4016; O-15751; R-17033; A-16838)
350.1680	am	(E-18705)
350.1690	am	(E-18705)
350.1690	n	(P-4016; O-15751; R-17033; A-16838)
350.1810	am	(E-18705)
350.1820	am	(E-18705)
350.1830	am	(E-18705)
350.1840	am	(E-18705)
350.1860	am	(E-18705)
350.1870	am	(E-18705)
350.1880	am	(E-18705)
350.1890	am	(E-18705)
350.1910	am	(E-18705)
350.2010	am	(E-18705)
350.2020	am	(E-18705)
350.2030	am	(E-18705)
350.2210	am	(E-18705)
350.2220	am	(E-18705)
350.2410	n	(E-18705)
350.2420	am	(E-18705)
350.2430	am	(E-18705)
350.2610	am	(E-18705)
350.2620	am	(E-18705)
350.2630	am	(E-18705)
350.2640	am	(E-18705)
350.2650	am	(E-18705)
350.2660	am	(E-18705)
350.2670	am	(E-18705)

Section		Reference
350.2680	am	(E-18705)
350.2690	am	(E-18705)
350.2700	am	(P-21506/86; A-979) (E-18705)
350.2710	am	(E-18705)
350.2720	am	(E-18705)
350.2730	am	(E-18705)
350.2740	am	(E-18705)
350.2930	am	(P-21506/86; A-979) (E-18705)
350.2930	am	(E-18705)
350.2940	am	(E-18705)
350.2950	am	(E-18705)
350.2960	am	(P-21506/86; A-979) (E-18705)
350.2970	am	(E-18705)
350.2980	am	(E-18705)
350.2990	am	(E-18705)
350.3000	am	(E-18705)
350.3010	am	(E-18705)
350.3020	am	(E-18705)
350.3030	am	(E-18705)
350.3040	am	(E-18705)
350.3210	am	(E-18705)
350.3220	am	(E-18705)
350.3230	am	(E-18705)
350.3240	am	(E-18705)
350.3250	am	(E-18705)
350.3260	am	(P-21506/86; A-979) (E-18705)
350.3300	am	(P-21506/86; A-979)
350.3920	am	(P-21506/86; A-979)
350.3270	am	(E-18705)
350.3280	am	(E-18705)
350.3290	am	(E-18705)
350.3300	am	(E-18705)
350.3310	am	(E-18705)
350.3320	am	(E-18705)
350.3330	am	(E-18705)
350.3710	am	(E-18705)
350.3720	am	(E-18705)
350.3730	am	(E-18705)
350.3740	am	(E-18705)
350.3750	am	(E-18705)
350.3760	am	(E-18705)
350.3770	am	(E-18705)
350.3790	am	(E-18705)
350.3800	am	(E-18705)
350.3820	am	(E-18705)
350.3840	am	(E-18705)
350.3860	am	(E-18705)
350.3870	am	(E-18705)
350.3880	am	(E-18705)
350.3890	am	(E-18705)
350.3910	am	(E-18705)
350.3920	am	(E-18705)
350.3930	am	(E-18705)
350.3950	am	(E-18705)
350.3960	am	(E-18705)
350.3970	am	(E-18705)

TITLE 77 (CONT'D)

Section		Reference
350.3980	am	(E-18705)
350.3990	am	(E-18705)
350.4000	am	(E-18705)
350.4010	am	(E-18705)
350.4030	am	(E-18705)
390.110	am	(E-18243)
390.120	am	(E-18243)
390.130	am	(E-18243)
390.150	am	(E-18243)
390.160	am	(E-18243)
390.200	am	(E-18243)
390.210	am	(E-18243)
390.220	am	(E-18243)
390.230	am	(E-18243)
390.250	am	(E-18243)
390.272	am	(E-18243)
390.276	am	(E-18243)
390.277	n	(E-18243)
390.278	am	(E-18243)
390.282	am	(P-3958; A-16780) (E-18243)
390.284	am	(E-18243)
390.290	am	(E-18243)
390.300	am	(E-18243)
390.330	am	(E-18243)
390.340	n	(P-21457/86; A-931)
390.500	am	(E-18243)
390.610	am	(E-18243)
390.620	am	(E-18243)
390.630	am	(E-18243)
390.640	am	(E-18243)
390.650	am	(E-18243)
390.660	am	(E-18243)
390.670	am	(E-18243)
390.680	am	(E-18243)
390.690	am	(E-18243)
390.700	am	(E-18243)
390.700	n	(P-3958; O-15745; R-17032; A-16780)
390.820	am	(E-18243)
390.830	am	(E-18243)
390.1010	am	(E-18243)
390.1020	am	(E-18243)
390.1030	am	(E-18243)
390.1040	am	(E-18243)
390.1050	am	(E-18243)
390.1070	am	(E-18243)
390.1080	am	(E-18243)
390.1090	am	(E-18243)
390.1100	am	(E-18243)
390.1120	am	(E-18243)
390.1310	am	(E-18243)
390.1320	am	(E-18243)
390.1330	am	(E-18243)
390.1410	am	(E-18243)
390.1420	am	(E-18243)

Section		Reference
390.1430	am	(E-18243)
390.1440	am	(E-18243)
390.1450	am	(E-18243)
390.1610	am	(E-18243)
390.1610	r	(P-3958; A-16780)
390.1610	n	(P-3958; O-15745; R-17032; A-16780)
390.1620	am	(E-18243)
390.1620	r	(P-3958; O-15745; R-17032; A-16780)
390.1620	n	(P-3958; O-15745; R-17032; A-16780)
390.1630	r	(P-3958; O-15745; R-17032; A-16780)
390.1630	n	(P-3958; O-15745; R-17032; A-16780)
390.1640	r	(P-3958; O-15745; R-17032; A-16780)
390.1640	n	(P-3958; O-15745; R-17032; A-16780)
390.1640	am	(P-21457/86; A-931) (E-18243)
390.1650	am	(E-18243)
390.1650	n	(P-3958; O-15745; R-17032; A-16780)
390.1660	n	(P-3958; O-15745; R-17032; A-16780)
390.1670	n	(P-3958; O-15745; R-17032; A-16780)
390.1680	n	(P-3958; O-15745; R-17032; A-16780)
390.1680	am	(E-18243)
390.1690	am	(E-18243)
390.1690	n	(P-3958; O-15745; R-17032; A-16780)
390.1810	am	(E-18243)
390.1820	am	(E-18243)
390.1830	am	(E-18243)
390.1840	am	(E-18243)
390.1860	am	(E-18243)
390.1870	am	(E-18243)
390.1880	am	(E-18243)
390.1890	am	(E-18243)
390.1900	am	(E-18243)
390.1920	am	(E-18243)
390.2010	am	(E-18243)
390.2020	am	(E-18243)
390.2030	am	(E-18243)
390.2210	am	(E-18243)
390.2220	am	(E-18243)
390.2230	am	(E-18243)
390.2410	am	(E-18243)
390.2420	am	(E-18243)
390.2430	am	(E-18243)
390.2440	am	(E-18243)
390.2610	am	(E-18243)
390.2620	am	(E-18243)

TITLE 77 (CONT'D)

390.2630	am	(E-18243)
390.2640	am	(E-18243)
390.2650	am	(E-18243)
390.2660	am	(P-21457/86; A-931) (E-18243)
390.2670	am	(E-18243)
390.2680	am	(E-18243)
390.2690	am	(E-18243)
390.2700	am	(P-21457/86; A-931) (E-18243)
390.2710	am	(E-18243)
390.2720	am	(E-18243)
390.2730	am	(E-18243)
390.2740	am	(E-18243)
390.2910	am	(E-18243)
390.2920	am	(P-21457/86; A-931) (E-18243)
390.2930	am	(E-18243)
390.2940	am	(E-18243)
390.2950	am	(E-18243)
390.2960	am	(E-18243)
390.2970	am	(E-18243)
390.2980	am	(E-18243)
390.2990	am	(E-18243)
390.3000	am	(E-18243)
390.3010	am	(E-18243)
390.3020	am	(E-18243)
390.3030	am	(E-18243)
390.3040	am	(P-21457/86; A-931) (E-18243)
390.3210	am	(P-21457/86; A-931) (E-18243)
390.3220	am	(E-18243)
390.3230	am	(E-18243)
390.3240	am	(E-18243)
390.3250	am	(E-18243)
390.3260	am	(P-21457/86; A-931) (E-18243)
390.3270	am	(E-18243)
390.3280	am	(E-18243)
390.3290	am	(E-18243)
390.3300	am	(P-21457/86; A-931) (E-18243)
390.3310	am	(E-18243)
390.3320	am	(E-18243)
390.3330	am	(E-18243)
450.10	am	(P-12136/87; W-3831)
450.20	am	(P-12136/87; W-3831)
450.30	am	(P-12136/87; W-3831)
450.210	am	(P-12136/87; W-3831)
450.220	am	(P-12136/87; W-3831)
450.330	am	(P-604; A-10018)
450.410	am	(P-12136/87; W-3831)
450.560	r	(P-12136/87; W-3831)
450.730	n	(P-604; A-10018)
450.830	am	(P-604; A-10018) (P-12136/87; W-3831)
450.835	n	(P-604; A-10018)
450.840	am	(P-604; A-10018) (P-12136/87; W-3831)
450.860	am	(P-12136/87; W-3831)
450.940	am	(P-12136/87; W-3831)
450.950	am	(P-12136/87; W-3831)

450.1010	am	(P-604; A-10018) (P-12136/87; W-3831)
450.1150	am	(P-12136/87; W-3831)
450.1200	n	(P-604; A-10018)
460.130	am	(P-584; A-9998)
460.140	am	(P-584; A-9998)
460.150	n	(P-584; A-9998)
460.500	n	(P-584; A-9998)
470.10	am	(P-708; A-10179)
470.20	m	(P-708; A-10179)
470.30	am	(P-708; A-10179)
470.40	n	(P-708; A-10179)
470.50	n	(P-708; A-10179)
470.60	am	(P-708; A-10179)
470.70	n	(P-708; A-10179)
470.80	n	(P-708; A-10179)
510.40	am	(P-9384)
510.130	n	(P-9384)
520.10	am	(P-11340/87; A-7405)
520.40	amt	(P-11340/87; A-7405)
535.10	am	(P-4478)
535.20	am	(P-4478)
535.60	am	(P-4478)
535.200	am	(P-4478)
535.210	am	(P-4478)
535.220	am	(P-4478)
535.230	am	(P-4478)
535.240	am	(P-4478)
535.260	n	(P-4478)
535.265	n	(P-4478)
535.270	n	(P-4478)
535.700	am	(P-4478)
542.10	n	(P-4544)
542.20	n	(P-4544)
542.30	n	(P-4544)
542.40	n	(P-4544)
542.50	n	(P-4544)
542.60	n	(P-4544)
542.70	n	(P-4544)
542.80	n	(P-4544)
542.90	n	(P-4544)
542.100	n	(P-4544)
545.10	am	(P-4560)
545.20	am	(P-4560)
545.25	am	(P-4560)
545.30	am	(P-4560)
545.40	am	(P-4560)
545.50	am	(P-4560)
545.60	am	(P-4560)
545.65	n	(P-4560)
545.70	r	(P-4560)
545.80	am	(P-4560)
545.90	am	(P-4560)
545.100	am	(P-4560)
545.Ap. A	am	(P-4560)
545.Ap. B	am	(P-4560)

TITLE 77 (CONT'D)

595.10	am	(P-2657; A-3757)
595.100	am	(P-2657; A-3757)
595.110	am	(P-2657; A-3757) (P-4230; A-3757)
595.200	am	(P-2657; A-3757)
595.210	am	(P-2657; A-3757) (P-4230; A-3757)
595.300	am	(P-2657; A-3757)
595.310	am	(P-2657; A-3757)
595.320	am	(P-2657; A-3757)
595.Ap. A	n	(A-3757)
595.Ap. B	n	(A-3757)
600.1210	am	(P-3809/87; W-3832)
600.1220	am	(P-3809/87; W-3832)
682.700	n	(P-7552/87; A-4720)
690.100	am	(P-629; A-10045)
690.200	am	(P-629; A-10045)
690.290	r	(P-629; A-10045)
690.340	r	(P-629; A-10045)
690.430	r	(P-629; A-10045)
690.440	r	(P-629; A-10045)
690.450	am	(P-629; A-10045)
690.475	n	(P-629; A-10045)
690.500	r	(P-629; A-10045)
690.505	n	(P-629; A-10045)
690.520	am	(P-629; A-10045)
690.550	am	(P-629; A-10045)
690.580	am	(P-629; A-10045)
690.620	am	(P-629; A-10045)
690.640	r	(P-629; A-10045)
690.690	am	(P-629; A-10045)
690.695	n	(P-629; A-10045)
690.720	am	(P-629; A-10045)
690.750	n	(P-629; A-10045)
690.1000	am	(P-629; A-10045)
690.1010	n	(P-629; A-10045)
690.1100	r	(P-629; A-10045)
690.1200	am	(P-629; A-10045)
693.10	n	(P-677; A-10097)
693.15	n	(P-677; A-10097)
693.20	n	(P-677; A-10097)
693.30	n	(P-677; A-10097)
693.35	n	(P-677; A-10097)
693.40	n	(P-677; A-10097)
693.50	n	(P-677; A-10097)
693.60	n	(P-677; A-10097)
693.70	n	(P-677; A-10097)
693.80	n	(P-677; A-10097)
693.90	r	(P-677; A-10097)
693.100	n	(P-677; A-10097)
693.110	n	(P-677; A-10097)
693.120	n	(P-677; A-10097)
693.130	n	(P-677; A-10097)
693.140	n	(P-677; A-10097)
697.10	n	(P-546; A-9952) (E-1601)
697.20	n	(P-546; A-9952) (E-1601; RC-4969)

697.30	n	(P-546; A-9952)
697.40	n	(P-546; A-9952) (E-1601)
697.100	n	(P-546; A-9952) (E-1601; RC-4969)
697.110	n	(P-546; A-9952) (E-1601)
697.120	n	(P-546; O-9181; RC-9186; R-10236; A-9952) (E-1601)
697.130	n	(P-546; O-9181; RC-9186; R-10236; A-9952) (E-1601)
697.140	n	(P-546; A-9952) (E-1601)
697.150	n	(P-546; A-9952) (E-1601)
697.160	n	(P-546; A-9952) (E-1601)
697.170	n	(P-546; A-9952) (E-1601)
697.180	n	(P-546; A-9952) (E-1601)
697.200	n	(P-546; A-9952) (E-1601)
697.210	n	(P-546; A-9952) (E-1601)
697.220	n	(P-546; A-9952) (E-1601)
697.300	n	(P-546; A-9952)
697.400	n	(P-546; A-9952)
697.410	n	(P-546; A-9952)
697.420	n	(P-546; A-9952)
697.Ap. A	n	(P-546; A-9952) (E-1601)
697.II. A	n	(P-546; A-9952) (E-1601)
697.II. B	n	(P-546; A-9952) (E-1601)
697.Ap.B	n	(P-546; A-9952)
700.10	am	(P-12777)
700.20	n	(P-12777)
700.30	am	(P-12777)
725.5	r	(P-7265)
725.10	n	(P-7272)
725.10	r	(P-7265)
725.15	n	(P-7272)
725.20	n	(P-7272)
725.30	r	(P-7272)
725.30	r	(P-7265)
725.40	n	(P-7272)
725.40	r	(P-7265)
725.41	n	(P-7272)
725.42	n	(P-7272)
725.43	n	(P-7272)
725.44	n	(P-7272)
725.45	r	(P-7265)
725.50	n	(P-7272)
725.50	r	(P-7265)
725.51	n	(P-7272)
725.60	n	(P-7272)
725.60	r	(P-7265)
725.65	r	(P-7265)
725.70	n	(P-7272)
725.70	r	(P-7265)
725.71	n	(P-7272)
725.80	n	(P-7272)
725.80	r	(P-7265)
750.10	am	(P-14113) (E-14380)
750.140	am	(P-14113) (E-14380)
750.1100	am	(P-3200; A-17918)

TITLE 77 (CONT'D)

790.3820 am (P-10065/87; P-13837/87; A-1823)
790.3860 am (P-10065/87; P-13837/87; A-1823)
790.3900 am (P-16425) (E-16937)
790.3907 n (P-10065/87; P-13837/87; A-1823)
790.3907 am (P-7575; A-12846) (E-7743)
  (P-10650; A-15101) (E-10745)
  (P-12991) (E-13255)
790.3910 am (P-12991) (E-13255) (P-16425)
  (E-16937)
790.3920 n (P-7575; A-12846) (E-7743)
790.3945 am (P-1771; A-10133) (E-1984)
  (P-16425) (E-16937)
790.3960 am (P-10065/87; P-13837/87; A-1823)
790.3980 am (P-10065/87; P-13837/87; A-1823)
  (P-10650; A-15101) (E-10745)
790.3996 am (P-1771; A-10133) (E-1984)
790.4012 am (P-1771; A-10133) (E-1984)
  (P-10065/87; P-13837/87; A-1823)
  (P-7575; A-12846) (E-7743)
  (P-10650; A-15101) (E-10745)
  (P-16425) (E-16937)
790.4040 am (P-1771; A-10133) (E-1984)
  (P-10065/87; P-13837/87; A-1823)
  (P-7575; A-12846) (E-7743)
  (P-10650; A-15101) (E-10745)
  (P-16425) (E-16937)
790.4060 am (P-10065/87; P-13837/87; A-1823)
790.4100 am (P-1771; A-10133) (E-1984)
  (P-10065/87; P-13837/87; A-1823)
  (P-7575; A-12846) (E-7743)
  (P-12991) (E-13255) (P-16425)
  (E-16937)
790.4140 am (P-10065/87; P-13837/87; A-1823)
790.4150 am (P-7575; A-12846) (E-7743)
790.4173 n (P-10065/87; P-13837/87; A-1823)
790.4180 am (P-1771; A-10133) (E-1984)
790.4220 am (P-10065/87; P-13837/87; A-1823)
  (P-16425) (E-16937)
790.4260 am (P-10065/87; P-13837/87; A-1823)
790.4300 am (P-1771; A-10133) (E-1984)
790.4396 am (P-1771; A-10133) (E-1984)
  (P-10065/87; P-13837/87; A-1823)
  (P-7575; A-12846) (E-7743)
  (P-10650; A-15101) (E-10745)
  (P-12991) (E-13255) (P-16425)
  (E-16937)
790.4398 am (P-1771; A-10133) (E-1984)
  (P-10065/87; P-13837/87; A-1823)
  (P-7575; A-12846) (E-7743)
  (P-10650; A-15101) (E-10745)
  (P-12991) (E-13255) (P-16425)
  (E-16937)
790.4420 am (P-10065/87; P-13837/87; A-1823)
790.4430 am (P-16425) (E-16937)
790.4460 am (P-16425) (E-16937)

TITLE 77 (CONT'D)

790.4580 am (P-7575; A-12846) (E-7743)
  (P-16425) (E-16937)
790.4630 am (P-10065/87; P-13837/87; A-1823)
  (P-16425) (E-16937)
790.4660 am (P-16425) (E-16937)
790.4665 n (P-1771; A-10133) (E-1984)
790.4670 am (P-10065/87; P-13837/87; A-1823)
  (P-10650; A-15101) (E-10745)
  (P-12991) (E-13255)
790.4680 am (P-10065/87; P-13837/87; A-1823)
  (P-7575; A-12846) (E-7743)
  (P-10650; A-15101) (E-10745)
  (P-12991) (E-13255)
790.4700 am (P-1771; A-10133) (E-1984)
790.4720 n (P-7575; A-12846) (E-7743)
790.4720 am (P-10650; A-15101) (E-10745)
  (P-12991) (E-13255) (P-16425)
  (E-16937)
790.4740 am (P-10065/87; P-13837/87; A-1823)
  (P-10650; A-15101) (E-10745)
  (P-12991) (E-13255) (P-16425)
  (E-16937)
790.4780 am (P-10065/87; P-13837/87; A-1823)
  (P-7575; A-12846) (E-7743)
790.4820 am (P-16425) (E-16937)
790.4840 n (P-1771; A-10133) (E-1984)
790.4960 n (P-16425) (E-16937)
790.4980 am (P-10065/87; P-13837/87; A-1823)
790.5060 am (P-10065/87; P-13837/87; A-1823)
  (P-16425) (E-16937)
790.5100 am (P-10065/87; P-13837/87; A-1823)
790.5140 am (P-10065/87; P-13837/87; A-1823)
  (P-12991) (E-13255) (P-16425)
  (E-16937)
790.5180 am (P-10065/87; P-13837/87; A-1823)
  (P-16425) (E-16937)
790.5220 am (P-1771; A-10133) (E-1984)
  (P-10065/87; P-13837/87; A-1823)
  (P-7575; A-12846) (E-7743)
  (P-10650; A-15101) (E-10745)
  (P-12991) (E-13255)
790.5300 am (P-16425) (E-16937)
790.5312 n (P-1771; A-10133) (E-1984)
  (P-12991) (E-13255)
790.5340 am (P-16425) (E-16937)
790.5420 am (P-16425) (E-16937)
790.5460 am (P-10065/87; P-13837/87; A-1823)
790.5483 n (P-16425) (E-16937)
  (E-7743)
790.5483 am (P-10650; A-15101) (E-10745)
  (P-7575; A-12846) (P-12991)
  (E-13255) (P-16425) (E-16937)
790.5500 am (P-1771; A-10133) (E-1984)
790.5520 n (P-16425) (E-16937)

TITLE 77 (CONT'D)

790.5530 am (P-16425) (E-16937)
790.5540 am (P-16425) (E-16937)
790.5544 am (P-10065/87; P-13837/87; A-1823)
  (P-7575; A-12846) (E-7743)
  (P-10650; A-15101) (E-10745)
  (P-12991) (E-13255) (P-16425)
  (E-16937)
790.5560 am (P-16425) (E-16937)
790.5580 am (P-16425) (E-16937)
790.5630 am (P-12991) (E-13255)
790.5640 (P-12991) (E-13255)
790.5720 fi (P-10650; A-15101) (E-10745)
790.5740 am (P-10065/87; P-13837/87; A-1823)
790.5792 am (P-1771; A-10133) (E-1984)
  (P-10065/87; P-13837/87; A-1823)
  (P-7575; A-12846) (E-7743)
  (P-10650; A-15101) (E-10745)
  (P-12991) (E-13255) (P-16425)
  (E-16937)
790.5795 am (P-16425) (E-16937)
790.5802 fim (P-1771; A-10133) (E-1984)
  (P-10065/87; P-13837/87; A-1823)
790.5807 n (P-10650; A-15101) (E-10745)
790.5807 am (P-16425) (E-16937)
790.5820 am (P-12991) (E-13255) (P-16425)
  (E-16937)
790.5830 am (P-1771; A-10133) (E-1984)
  (P-10065/87; P-13837/87; A-1823)
  (P-7575; A-12846) (E-7743)
  (P-12991) (E-13255) (P-16425)
  (E-16937)
790.5835 n (P-10650; A-15101)
790.5837 n (P-12991) (E-13255)
790.5840 n (P-7575; A-12846) (E-7743)
  (E-10745)
790.5840 am (P-16425) (E-16937)
790.5872 am (P-16425) (E-16937)
790.5893 n (P-10065/87; P-13837/87; A-1823)
790.5893 am (P-7575; A-12846) (E-7743)
  (P-16425) (E-16937)
790.5900 am (P-10650; A-15101) (E-10745)
  (P-12991) (E-13255)
790.5924 n (P-10065/87; P-13837/87; A-1823)
790.5924 am (P-12991) (E-13255) (P-16425)
  (E-16937)
790.5940 am (P-7575; A-12846) (E-7743)
  (P-12991) (E-13255) (P-16425)
  (E-16937)
790.5980 am (P-10065/87; P-13837/87; A-1823)
  (P-16425) (E-16937)
790.6140 am (P-10065/87; P-13837/87; A-1823)
  (P-16425) (E-16937)
790.6180 am (P-1771; A-10133) (E-1984)
  (P-10065/87; P-13837/87; A-1823)
790.6260 am (P-10650; A-15101) (E-10745)
  (P-16425) (E-16937)
790.6275 am (P-10065/87; P-13837/87; A-1823)
  (P-12991) (E-13255) (P-16425)
  (E-16937)

TITLE 77 (CONT'D)

790.6277 am (P-1771; A-10133) (E-1984)
  (P-10065/87; P-13837/87; A-1823)
  (P-7575; A-12846) (E-7743)
  (P-10650; A-15101) (E-10745)
790.6280 am (P-16425) (E-16937)
790.6284 n (P-10650; A-15101) (E-10745)
790.6284 am (P-16425) (E-16937)
790.6300 am (P-10065/87; P-13837/87; A-1823)
790.6370 am (P-1771; A-10133) (E-1984)
  (P-10065/87; P-13837/87; A-1823)
  (P-10650; A-15101) (E-10745)
  (P-12991) (E-13255)
790.6375 am (P-16425) (E-16937)
790.6420 am (P-1771; A-10133) (E-1984)
  (P-10065/87; P-13837/87; A-1823)
790.6435 am (P-10650; A-15101) (E-10745)
790.6435 fim (P-10650; A-15101) (E-10745)
790.6445 am (P-10065/87; P-13837/87; A-1823)
  (P-16425) (E-16937)
790.6450 am (P-10065/87; P-13837/87; A-1823)
  (P-16425) (E-16937)
790.6452 am (P-16425) (E-16937)
790.6454 n (P-16425) (E-16937)
790.6456 am (P-10065/87; P-13837/87; A-1823)
  (P-10650; A-15101) (E-10745)
  (P-12991) (E-13255) (P-16425)
  (E-16937)
790.6460 am (P-10065/87; P-13837/87; A-1823)
790.6480 am (P-10065/87; P-13837/87; A-1823)
790.6500 am (P-10065/87; P-13837/87; A-1823)
790.6540 am (P-16425) (E-16937)
790.6544 am (P-10065/87; P-13837/87; A-1823)
790.6580 am (P-16425) (E-16937)
790.6621 n (P-16425) (E-16937)
790.6670 am (P-1771; A-10133) (E-1984)
  (P-7575; A-12846) (E-7743)
  (P-16425) (E-16937)
790.6740 am (P-1771; A-10133) (E-1984)
790.6780 am (P-10650; A; A-15101) (E-10745)
  (P-12991) (E-13255) (P-16425)
  (E-16937)
790.6800 am (P-10065/87; P-13837/87; A-1823)
  (P-10650; A-15101) (E-10745)
790.6820 am (P-10065/87; P-13837/87; A-1823)
790.6875 n (P-10065/87; P-13837/87; A-1823)
790.6875 am (P-16425) (E-16937)
790.6946 am (P-10065/87; P-13837/87; A-1823)
790.6960 am (P-12991) (E-13255) (P-16425)
  (E-16937)
790.6980 am (P-16425) (E-16937)
790.7020 am (P-10065/87; P-13837/87; A-1823)
  (P-16425) (E-16937)
790.7060 r (P-7575; A-12846) (E-7743)
790.7130 n (P-7575; A-12846) (E-7743)
  (E-10745)

TITLE 77 (CONT'D)

3100.510	re	(A-2922)
3100.520	re	(A-2922)
3100.530	re	(A-2922)

TITLE 80

150.10	am	(P-16438)
150.210	am	(P-12855/87; A-1118) (P-2207; A-10736)
150.510	am	(P-16438)
150.520	am	(P-16438)
150.530	am	(P-16438)
150.565	am	(P-16438)
150.665	am	(P-16438)
150.680	am	(P-16438)
150.Ap. A	n	(P-2207; A-10736)
150.Ap. B	n	(P-2207; A-10736)
250.50	am	(P-16281/87; A-3457) (P-6389; C-12559; M-17127; A-17029) (P-17569)
250.60	am	(P-16281/87; A-3457)
302.90	am	(P-4969/87; A-5634)
302.91	n	(P-4969/87; A-5634)
302.105	n	(P-10569)
302.800	r	(P-15813) (E-16214)
302.800	n	(P-15813) (E-16214)
302.810	r	(P-15813) (E-16214)
302.810	n	(P-15813) (E-16214)
302.820	r	(P-15813) (E-16214)
302.820	n	(P-15813) (E-16214)
302.822	r	(P-15813) (E-16214)
302.822	n	(P-15813) (E-16214)
302.824	r	(P-15813) (E-16214)
302.824	n	(P-15813) (E-16214)
302.825	r	(P-15813) (E-16214)
302.825	n	(P-15813) (E-16214)
302.830	r	(P-15813) (E-16214)
302.830	n	(P-15813) (E-16214)
302.840	r	(P-15813) (E-16214)
302.840	n	(P-15813) (E-16214)
302.841	r	(P-15813) (E-16214)
302.842	r	(P-15813) (E-16214)
302.846	r	(P-15813) (E-16214)
302.846	n	(P-15813) (E-16214)
302.850	r	(P-15813) (E-16214)
302.850	n	(P-15813) (E-16214)
302.860	r	(P-15813) (E-16214)
302.860	n	(P-15813) (E-16214)
302.863	r	(P-15813) (E-16214)
302.863	n	(P-15813) (E-16214)
310.40	am	(P-7889) (P-12599)
310.110	am	(P-7889) (E-11778; O-15764) (P-12599)
310.130	am	(P-7889) (E-11778; O-15764) (P-12599)

TITLE 80 (CONT'D)

310.230	am	(P-16009/87; A-6073) (P-17955/87; A-6073) (P-7453; A-14630) (E-7734)
310.280	am	(P-16009/87; A-6073)
310.290	am	(P-16009/87; A-6073) (P-7889) (E-11778; O-15764) (P-12599) (E-12895)
310.300	am	(P-7889) (P-12599)
310.440	am	(P-7889) (P-12599)
310.450	am	(E-11778) (P-12599) (E-12895; O-15766)
310.455	am	(P-7889) (P-12599) (E-12895)
310.456	am	(P-7889) (P-12599) (E-12895)
310.500	am	(P-7889)
310.530	am	(P-7889) (E-11778) (P-12599) (E-12895; O-15766)
310.540	am	(P-7889) (E-11778) (P-12599) (E-12895; O-15766) (E-12895; C-13359)
310.Ap. A	am	(PP-3811) (PP-5459) (PP-7783) (PP-7783) (PP-8135) (PP-9745) (PP-13306; O-15769)
		(PP-13306)
Tb. D	am	(PP-13306)
Tb. H	am	(PP-7783) (PP-13306; O-15769)
Tb. I	am	(PP-7783) (PP-13306)
Tb. J	am	(PP-7783) (PP-13306; O-15769)
Tb. L	n	(PP-8135)
Tb. O	am	(PP-7783) (PP-13306; O-15769)
Tb. P	am	(PP-3811) (PP-13306; O-15769)
Tb. Q	am	(PP-5459)
Tb. R	am	(PP-13306; O-15769)
Tb. U	am	(PP-9745)
Tb. V	am	(PP-7783)
Tb. Y	am	(PP-7783)
Tb. Z	am	(PP-13306)
310.Ap. B	am	(P-16009/87; A-6073) (P-7889) (E-11778; O-15764) (P-12599)
310.Ap. C	am	(P-7889) (P-12599) (E-12895; C-13716; O-15766)
310.Ap. D	am	(P-7889) (P-12599) (E-12895; O-15766)
420.210	am	(P-17464/87; A-6766)
420.330	am	(P-17464/87; A-6766)
420.340	am	(P-17464/87; A-6766)
420.350	am	(P-17464/87; A-6766)
420.380	am	(P-17464/87; A-6766)
420.400	am	(P-17464/87; A-6766)
420.420	am	(P-17464/87; A-6766)
420.430	am	(P-17464/87; A-6766)
420.435	n	(P-17464/87; A-6766)
420.610	am	(P-17464/87; A-6766)
420.645	n	(P-17464/87; A-6766)
420.720	am	(P-17464/87; A-6766)
420.760	am	(P-17464/87; A-6766)
420.800	am	(P-17464/87; A-6766)

TITLE 80 (CONT'D)

420.820	am	(P-17464/87; A-6766)
420.850	am	(P-17464/87; A-6766)
1125.10	am	(E-13707) (P-16375)
1125.20	am	(E-13707) (P-16375)
1125.30	r	(E-13707)
1125.30	am	(P-16375)
1125.50	n	(E-13707)
1125.50	r	(P-16375)
1125.70	am	(E-13707) (P-16375)
1125.80	am	(E-13707) (P-16375)
1125.90	r	(E-13707) (P-16375)
1125.100	n	(E-13707) (P-16375)
1135.10	n	(P-14504)
1135.20	n	(P-14504)
1135.30	n	(P-14504)
1200.60	am	(P-11025)
1200.90	am	(P-11025)
1200.140	n	(P-11025)
1210.100	am	(P-11039)
1210.160	am	(P-11039)
1220.40	am	(P-11052)
1230.50	am	(P-11031)
1230.60	am	(P-11031)
1230.70	am	(P-11031)
1230.150	am	(P-11051)
1570.40	am	(P-14122)
1570.60	r	(P-14122)
1570.70	am	(P-14122)
1570.80	am	(P-14122)
1570.90	am	(P-14122)
1570.100	am	(P-14122)
1570.110	r	(P-14122)
1570.120	am	(P-14122)
1570.150	r	(P-14122)
1570.160	am	(P-14122)
1650.180	am	(P-9390; A-16896)
1650.210	am	(P-9390; A-16896)
1650.230	am	(P-9390; A-16896)
1650.271	n	(P-9390; A-16896)
1650.350	am	(P-9390; A-16896)
1650.410	am	(P-9390; A-16896)
2000.70	am	(P-17266)
2110.30	am	(P-7912; A-17283) (E-11795)
2110.210	am	(P-7912; A-17283) (E-11795)
2110.220	am	(P-7912; A-17283) (E-11795)
2110.240	r	(P-7912; A-17283) (E-11795)
2110.330	am	(P-7912; A-17283) (E-11795)
2110.420	am	(P-7912; A-17283) (E-11795)
2110.440	am	(P-7912; A-17283) (E-11795)
2110.510	am	(P-7912; A-17283) (E-11795)
2110.530	am	(P-7912; A-17283) (E-11795)
2110.540	am	(P-7912; A-17283) (E-11795)
2110.610	am	(P-7912; A-17283) (E-11795)
2110.710	am	(P-7912; A-17283) (E-11795)
2120.10	n	(P-8180; A-17296) (E-11810)
2120.20	n	(P-8180; A-17296) (E-11810)

TITLE 80 (CONT'D)

2120.30	n	(P-8180; A-17296) (E-11810)
2120.110	n	(P-8180; A-17296) (E-11810)
2120.120	n	(P-8180; A-17296) (E-11810)
2120.210	n	(P-8180; A-17296) (E-11810)
2120.220	n	(P-8180; A-17296) (E-11810)
2120.230	n	(P-8180; A-17296) (E-11810)
2120.310	n	(P-8180; A-17296) (E-11810)
2120.320	n	(P-8180; A-17296) (E-11810)
2120.330	n	(P-8180; A-17296) (E-11810)
2120.340	n	(P-8180; A-17296) (E-11810)
2120.410	n	(P-8180; A-17296) (E-11810)
2120.420	n	(P-8180; A-17296) (E-11810)
2120.430	n	(P-8180; A-17296) (E-11810)
2120.440	n	(P-8180; A-17296) (E-11810)
2120.510	n	(P-8180; A-17296) (E-11810)
2120.520	n	(P-8180; A-17296) (E-11810)
2120.530	n	(P-8180; A-17296) (E-11810)
2120.540	n	(P-8180; A-17296) (E-11810)
2120.610	n	(P-8180; A-17296) (E-11810)
2120.620	n	(P-8180; A-17296) (E-11810)
2120.710	n	(P-8180; A-17296) (E-11810)
2120.720	n	(P-8180; A-17296) (E-11810)
2120.730	n	(P-8180; A-17296) (E-11810)
2120.740	n	(P-8180; A-17296) (E-11810)
2120.750	n	(P-8180; A-17296) (E-11810)
2120.760	n	(P-8180; A-17296) (E-11810)
2120.770	n	(P-8180; A-17296) (E-11810)
2120.780	n	(P-8180; A-17296) (E-11810)
2120.790	n	(P-8180; A-17296) (E-11810)
2120.800	n	(P-8180; A-17296) (E-11810)
2120.810	n	(P-8180)
2150.1	n	(P-10285)
2150.2	n	(P-10285)
2150.5	n	(P-10285)
2150.10	n	(P-10285)
2650.1	r	(E-6871) (E-6975; O-11352)
2650.1	r	(E-10191)
2650.5	r	(E-6871) (E-6975; O-11352)
2650.5	r	(E-10191)
2650.10	r	(E-6871) (E-6975; O-11352)
2650.10	r	(E-10191)
2650.15	r	(E-6871) (E-6975; O-11352)
2650.15	r	(E-10191)
2650.20	n	(E-6871) (E-6975; O-11352)
2650.20	r	(E-10191)
2650.25	n	(E-6871) (E-6975; O-11352)
2650.25	r	(E-10191)
2650.30	n	(E-6871) (E-6975; O-11352)
2650.30	r	(E-10191)
2650.50	n	(E-6871) (E-6975; O-11352)
2650.50	r	(E-10191)
2800.5	r	(P-10373/87; A-749)
2800.10	r	(P-10373/87; A-749)
2800.20	r	(P-10373/87; A-749)
2800.30	r	(P-10373/87; A-749)
2800.100	n	(P-10363/87; O-19842/87; R-1636; A-738)

TITLE 80 (CONT'D)

2800.110	n	(P-10363/87; O-19842/87; R-1636; A-738)
2800.200	r	(P-10373/87; A-749)
2800.200	n	(P-10363/87; O-19842/87; R-1636; A-738)
2800.210	r	(P-10373/87; A-749)
2800.210	n	(P-10363/87; O-19842/87; R-1636; A-738)
2800.220	r	(P-10373/87; A-749)
2800.220	n	(P-10363/87; O-19842/87; R-1636; A-738)
2800.230	r	(P-10373/87; A-749)
2800.230	n	(P-10363/87; O-19842/87; R-1636; A-738)
2800.240	r	(P-10373/87; A-749)
2800.240	n	(P-10363/87; O-19842/87; R-1636; A-738)
2800.250	r	(P-10373/87; A-749)
2800.250	n	(P-10363/87; O-19842/87; R-1636; A-738)
2800.260	r	(P-10373/87; A-749)
2800.260	n	(P-10363/87; O-19842/87; R-1636; A-738)
2800.270	r	(P-10373/87; A-749)
2800.270	n	(P-10363/87; O-19842/87; R-1636; A-738)
2800.280	r	(P-10373/87; A-749)
2800.290	r	(P-10373/87; A-749)
2800.295	r	(P-10373/87; A-749)
2800.298	r	(P-10373/87; A-749)
2800.300	r	(P-10373/87; A-749)
2800.300	n	(P-10363/87; O-19842/87; R-1636; A-738)
2800.310	r	(P-10373/87; A-749)
2800.320	r	(P-10373/87; A-749)
2800.330	r	(P-10373/87; A-749)
2800.340	r	(P-10373/87; A-749)
2800.350	r	(P-10373/87; A-749)
2800.360	r	(P-10373/87; A-749)
2800.400	r	(P-10373/87; A-749)
2800.400	n	(P-10363/87; O-19842/87; R-1636; A-738)
2800.410	r	(P-10373/87; A-749)
2800.410	n	(P-10363/87; O-19842/87; R-1636; A-738)
2800.420	r	(P-10373/87; A-749)
2800.430	r	(P-10373/87; A-749)
2800.440	r	(P-10373/87; A-749)
2800.500	r	(P-10373/87; A-749)
2800.500	n	(P-10363/87; O-19842/87; R-1636; A-738)
2800.510	r	(P-10373/87; A-749)
2800.520	r	(P-10373/87; A-749)
2800.530	r	(P-10373/87; A-749)
2800.540	r	(P-10373/87; A-749)
2800.550	r	(P-10373/87; A-749)

TITLE 88 (CONT'D)

2800.600	r	(P-10373/87; A-749)
2800.600	n	(P-10363/87; O-19842/87; R-1636; A-738)
2800.610	r	(P-10373/87; A-749)
2800.620	.	(P-10373/87; A-749)
2800.700	s	(P-10373/87; A-749)
2800.700	n	(R-1636; A-738)
2800.710	r	(P-10373/87; A-749)
2800.710	n	(P-10363/87; O-19842/87; R-1636; A-738)
2800.720	.	(P-10373/87; A-749)
2800.730	r	(P-10373/87; A-749)
2800.740	r	(P-10373/87; A-749)
2800.800	r	(P-10373/87; A-749)
2800.Th. A	r	(P-10373/87; A-749)
3000.300	am	(P-5629; A-11626)
3000.Ap. A	am	(P-5629; A-11626)
3100.100	n	(P-2041; A-9487)
3100.200	n	(P-2041; A-9487)
3100.300	n	(P-2041; A-9487)
3100.400	n	(P-2041; A-9487)
3100.500	n	(P-2041; A-9487)
3100.600	n	(P-2041; A-9487)
3100.700	n	(P-2041; A-9487)
3100.800	n	(P-2041; A-9487)
3100.900	n	(P-2041; A-9487)
3100.1000	n	(P-2041; A-9487)
3100.1100	n	(P-2041; A-9487)
3100.1200	n	(P-2041; A-9487)

TITLE 83

215.10	am	(P-18026)
215.30	am	(P-18026)
270.5	n	(P-19983/87; W-1640) (P-293; A-7580)
270.10	r	(P-19983/87; W-1640) (P-293; A-7580)
270.20	r	(P-19983/87; W-1640) (P-293; A-7580)
270.30	am	(P-19983/87; W-1640) (P-293; A-7580)
325.5	.	(P-18021)
325.10	r	(P-18021)
325.20	r	(P-18021)
415.20	am	(P-3873; A-11710)
440.10	n	(P-3162)
440.100	n	(P-3162)
440.200	n	(P-3162)
440.210	n	(P-3162)
440.220	n	(P-3162)
440.240	n	(P-3162)
440.300	n	(P-3162)
440.310	n	(P-3162)
440.400	n	(P-3162)
440.410	n	(P-3162)
440.420	n	(P-3162)

TITLE 83 (CONT'D)

440.430	n	(P-3162)
440.500	n	(P-3162)
440.510	n	(P-3162)
440.520	n	(P-3162)
440.600	n	(P-3162)
440.610	n	(P-3162)
440.620	n	(P-3162)
440.630	n	(P-3162)
440.640	n	(P-3162)
440.650	n	(P-3162)
440.660	n	(P-3162)
440.700	n	(P-3162)
440.800	n	(P-3162)
440.810	n	(P-3162)
440.900	n	(P-3162)
440.910	n	(P-3162)
535.10	n	(P-9314)
535.100	n	(P-9314)
535.110	n	(P-9314)
535.200	n	(P-9314)
535.205	n	(P-9314)
535.210	n	(P-9314)
535.220	n	(P-9314)
535.300	n	(P-9314)
535.305	n	(P-9314)
535.310	n	(P-9314)
535.320	n	(P-9314)
535.330	n	(P-9314)
535.340	n	(P-9314)
535.350	n	(P-9314)
535.400	n	(P-9314)
535.410	n	(P-9314)
535.500	n	(P-9314)
535.510	n	(P-9314)
590.10	re	(A-12997)
595.10	re	(A-12998)
595.110	re	(A-12998)
595.120	re	(A-12998)
595.120	am	(P-16309)
595.130	re	(A-12998)
710.1	n	(P-305; A-9645) (E-1295)
710.3	n	(P-305; A-9645) (E-1295)
710.4	n	(P-305; A-9645) (E-1295)
710.5	r	(P-308; A-9659) (E-1309)
710.10	r	(P-308; A-9659) (E-1309)
710.11	n	(P-305; A-9645) (E-1295)
710.13	n	(P-305; A-9645) (E-1295)
710.14	n	(P-305; A-9645) (E-1295)
710.15	r	(P-308; A-9659) (E-1309)
710.16	n	(P-305; A-9645) (E-1295)
710.17	n	(P-305; A-9645) (E-1295)
710.18	n	(P-305; A-9645) (E-1295)
710.19	n	(P-305; A-9645) (E-1295)
710.20	r	(P-308; A-9659) (E-1309)
710.22	n	(P-305; A-9645) (E-1295)
710.23	n	(P-305; A-9645) (E-1295)

TITLE 83 (CONT'D)

710.25	r	(P-308; A-9659) (E-1309)
710.25	n	(P-305; A-9645) (E-1295)
710.27	n	(P-305; A-9645) (E-1295)
710.30	r	(P-308; A-9659) (E-1309)
710.35	r	(P-308; A-9659) (E-1309)
710.40	r	(P-308; A-9659) (E-1309)
710.45	r	(P-308; A-9659) (E-1309)
710.50	r	(P-308; A-9659) (E-1309)
710.70	r	(P-308; A-9659) (E-1309)
710.75	r	(P-308; A-9659) (E-1309)
710.80	r	(P-308; A-9659) (E-1309)
710.85	r	(P-308; A-9659) (E-1309)
710.90	r	(P-308; A-9659) (E-1309)
710.100	r	(P-308; A-9659) (E-1309)
710.110	r	(P-308; A-9659) (E-1309)
710.120	r	(P-308; A-9659) (E-1309)
710.130	r	(P-308; A-9659) (E-1309)
710.140	r	(P-308; A-9659) (E-1309)
710.150	r	(P-308; A-9659) (E-1309)
710.160	r	(P-308; A-9659) (E-1309)
710.165	r	(P-308; A-9659) (E-1309)
710.170	r	(P-308; A-9659) (E-1309)
710.200	r	(P-308; A-9659) (E-1309)
710.210	r	(P-308; A-9659) (E-1309)
710.220	r	(P-308; A-9659) (E-1309)
710.225	r	(P-308; A-9659) (E-1309)
710.230	r	(P-308; A-9659) (E-1309)
710.240	r	(P-308; A-9659) (E-1309)
710.250	r	(P-308; A-9659) (E-1309)
710.260	r	(P-308; A-9659) (E-1309)
710.300	r	(P-308; A-9659) (E-1309)
710.310	r	(P-308; A-9659) (E-1309)
710.320	r	(P-308; A-9659) (E-1309)
710.400	r	(P-308; A-9659) (E-1309)
710.500	r	(P-308; A-9659) (E-1309)
710.510	r	(P-308; A-9659) (E-1309)
710.520	r	(P-308; A-9659) (E-1309)
710.530	r	(P-308; A-9659) (E-1309)
710.600	r	(P-308; A-9659) (E-1309)
710.610	r	(P-308; A-9659) (E-1309)
710.620	r	(P-308; A-9659) (E-1309)
710.630	r	(P-308; A-9659) (E-1309)
710.640	r	(P-308; A-9659) (E-1309)
710.650	r	(P-308; A-9659) (E-1309)
710.700	r	(P-308; A-9659) (E-1309)
710.800	r	(P-308; A-9659) (E-1309)
710.810	r	(P-308; A-9659) (E-1309)
710.820	r	(P-308; A-9659) (E-1309)
710.830	r	(P-308; A-9659) (E-1309)
710.840	r	(P-308; A-9659) (E-1309)
710.850	r	(P-308; A-9659) (E-1309)
710.855	r	(P-308; A-9659) (E-1309)
710.860	r	(P-308; A-9659) (E-1309)
710.870	r	(P-308; A-9659) (E-1309)
710.880	r	(P-308; A-9659) (E-1309)
710.890	r	(P-308; A-9659) (E-1309)

TITLE 83 (CONT'D)

Section		Reference
710.900	r	(P-308; A-9659) (E-1309)
710.905	r	(P-308; A-9659) (E-1309)
710.910	r	(P-308; A-9659) (E-1309)
710.1001	r	(P-308; A-9659) (E-1309)
710.1002	r	(P-308; A-9659) (E-1309)
710.1003	r	(P-308; A-9659) (E-1309)
710.1004	r	(P-308; A-9659) (E-1309)
710.1007	r	(P-308; A-9659) (E-1309)
710.1011	r	(P-308; A-9659) (E-1309)
710.1012	r	(P-308; A-9659) (E-1309)
710.1020	r	(P-308; A-9659) (E-1309)
710.1030	r	(P-308; A-9659) (E-1309)
710.1040	r	(P-308; A-9659) (E-1309)
710.1050	r	(P-308; A-9659) (E-1309)
710.1060	r	(P-308; A-9659) (E-1309)
710.1130	r	(P-308; A-9659) (E-1309)
710.1140	r	(P-308; A-9659) (E-1309)
710.1150	r	(P-308; A-9659) (E-1309)
710.1160	r	(P-308; A-9659) (E-1309)
710.1180	n	(P-305; A-9645) (E-1295)
710.1171	r	(P-308; A-9659) (E-1309)
710.1172	r	(P-308; A-9659) (E-1309)
710.1180	r	(P-308; A-9659) (E-1309)
710.1181	n	(P-305; A-9645) (E-1295)
710.1190	n	(P-305; A-9645) (E-1295)
710.1191	n	(P-305; A-9645) (E-1295)
710.1200	n	(P-305; A-9645) (E-1295)
710.1201	r	(P-308; A-9659) (E-1309)
710.1201	n	(P-305; A-9645) (E-1295)
710.1202	r	(P-308; A-9659) (E-1309)
710.1310	r	(P-308; A-9659) (E-1309)
710.1220	r	(P-308; A-9659) (E-1309)
710.1230	r	(P-308; A-9659) (E-1309)
710.1260	r	(P-308; A-9659) (E-1309)
710.1270	r	(P-308; A-9659) (E-1309)
710.1290	r	(P-308; A-9659) (E-1309)
710.1300	r	(P-308; A-9659) (E-1309)
710.1310	r	(P-308; A-9659) (E-1309)
710.1320	r	(P-308; A-9659) (E-1309)
710.1330	r	(P-308; A-9659) (E-1309)
710.1341	r	(P-308; A-9659) (E-1309)
710.1342	r	(P-308; A-9659) (E-1309)
710.1350	r	(P-308; A-9659) (E-1309)
710.1360	r	(P-308; A-9659) (E-1309)
710.1370	r	(P-308; A-9659) (E-1309)
710.1380	r	(P-308; A-9659) (E-1309)
710.1390	r	(P-308; A-9659) (E-1309)
710.1401	n	(P-305; A-9645) (E-1295)
710.1438	n	(P-305; A-9645) (E-1295)
710.1500	r	(P-308; A-9659) (E-1309)
710.1510	r	(P-305; A-9659) (E-1309)
710.1520	r	(P-308; A-9659) (E-1309)
710.1531	r	(P-308; A-9659) (E-1309)
710.1532	r	(P-308; A-9659) (E-1309)
710.1541	r	(P-308; A-9659) (E-1309)

TITLE 83 (CONT'D)

Section		Reference
710.1542	r	(P-308; A-9659) (E-1309)
710.1550	r	(P-308; A-9659) (E-1309)
710.1560	r	(P-308; A-9659) (E-1309)
710.1570	r	(P-308; A-9659) (E-1309)
710.1581	r	(P-308; A-9659) (E-1309)
710.1582	r	(P-308; A-9659) (E-1309)
710.1591	r	(P-308; A-9659) (E-1309)
710.1592	r	(P-308; A-9659) (E-1309)
710.1600	r	(P-308; A-9659) (E-1309)
710.1620	r	(P-308; A-9659) (E-1309)
710.1630	r	(P-308; A-9659) (E-1309)
710.1640	r	(P-308; A-9659) (E-1309)
710.1650	r	(P-308; A-9659) (E-1309)
710.1660	r	(P-308; A-9659) (E-1309)
710.1670	r	(P-308; A-9659) (E-1309)
710.1680	r	(P-308; A-9659) (E-1309)
710.1690	r	(P-308; A-9659) (E-1309)
710.1700	r	(P-308; A-9659) (E-1309)
710.1710	r	(P-308; A-9659) (E-1309)
710.1720	r	(P-308; A-9659) (E-1309)
710.1730	r	(P-308; A-9659) (E-1309)
710.1740	r	(P-308; A-9659) (E-1309)
710.1760	r	(P-308; A-9659) (E-1309)
710.1790	r	(P-308; A-9659) (E-1309)
710.1800	r	(P-308; A-9659) (E-1309)
710.1810	r	(P-308; A-9659) (E-1309)
710.2000	n	(P-305; A-9645) (E-1295)
710.2002	n	(P-305; A-9645) (E-1295)
710.2010	r	(P-308; A-9659) (E-1309)
710.2020	r	(P-308; A-9659) (E-1309)
710.2030	r	(P-308; A-9659) (E-1309)
710.2110	r	(P-308; A-9659) (E-1309)
710.2120	r	(P-308; A-9659) (E-1309)
710.2210	r	(P-308; A-9659) (E-1309)
710.2231	n	(P-305; A-9645) (E-1295)
710.2232	n	(P-305; A-9645) (E-1295)
710.2310	r	(P-308; A-9659) (E-1309)
710.2320	r	(P-308; A-9659) (E-1309)
710.2340	r	(P-308; A-9659) (E-1309)
710.2350	r	(P-308; A-9659) (E-1309)
710.2410	r	(P-308; A-9659) (E-1309)
710.2421	r	(P-308; A-9659) (E-1309)
710.2422	r	(P-308; A-9659) (E-1309)
710.2423	r	(P-308; A-9659) (E-1309)
710.2424	r	(P-308; A-9659) (E-1309)
710.2430	r	(P-308; A-9659) (E-1309)
710.2440	r	(P-308; A-9659) (E-1309)
710.2610	r	(P-308; A-9659) (E-1309)
710.2620	r	(P-308; A-9659) (E-1309)
710.2640	r	(P-308; A-9659) (E-1309)
710.2690	n	(P-305; A-9645) (E-1295)
710.2750	r	(P-308; A-9659) (E-1309)
710.2770	r	(P-308; A-9659) (E-1309)
710.3000	r	(P-308; A-9659) (E-1309)
710.3010	r	(P-308; A-9659) (E-1309)
710.3020	r	(P-308; A-9659) (E-1309)

TITLE 83 (CONT'D)

Section		Reference
710.3030	r	(P-308; A-9659) (E-1309)
710.3040	r	(P-308; A-9659) (E-1309)
710.3060	r	(P-308; A-9659) (E-1309)
710.3070	r	(P-308; A-9659) (E-1309)
710.3080	r	(P-308; A-9659) (E-1309)
710.3090	r	(P-308; A-9659) (E-1309)
710.3120	r	(P-308; A-9659) (E-1309)
710.3130	r	(P-308; A-9659) (E-1309)
710.3140	r	(P-308; A-9659) (E-1309)
710.3150	r	(P-308; A-9659) (E-1309)
710.3160	r	(P-308; A-9659) (E-1309)
710.3170	r	(P-308; A-9659) (E-1309)
710.3230	r	(P-308; A-9659) (E-1309)
710.3260	r	(P-308; A-9659) (E-1309)
710.3270	r	(P-308; A-9659) (E-1309)
710.3350	r	(P-308; A-9659) (E-1309)
710.3360	r	(P-308; A-9659) (E-1309)
710.3380	r	(P-308; A-9659) (E-1309)
710.3390	r	(P-308; A-9659) (E-1309)
710.3400	r	(P-308; A-9659) (E-1309)
710.3600	r	(P-308; A-9659) (E-1309)
710.3650	r	(P-308; A-9659) (E-1309)
710.3700	r	(P-308; A-9659) (E-1309)
710.3750	r	(P-308; A-9659) (E-1309)
710.3800	r	(P-308; A-9659) (E-1309)
710.4000	r	(P-308; A-9659) (E-1309)
710.4010	n	(P-305; A-9645) (E-1295)
710.4020	r	(P-308; A-9659) (E-1309)
710.4020	n	(P-305; A-9645) (E-1295)
710.4100	n	(P-305; A-9645) (E-1295)
710.4110	n	(P-305; A-9645) (E-1295)
710.4130	r	(P-308; A-9659) (E-1309)
710.4150	r	(P-308; A-9659) (E-1309)
710.4160	r	(P-308; A-9659) (E-1309)
710.4340	n	(P-305; A-9645) (E-1295)
710.4350	n	(P-305; A-9645) (E-1295)
710.4999	n	(P-305; A-9645) (E-1295)
710.5000	r	(P-308; A-9659) (E-1309)
710.5010	r	(P-308; A-9659) (E-1309)
710.5030	r	(P-308; A-9659) (E-1309)
710.5040	r	(P-308; A-9659) (E-1309)
710.5060	r	(P-308; A-9659) (E-1309)
710.5080	r	(P-308; A-9659) (E-1309)
710.5081	r	(P-308; A-9659) (E-1309)
710.5082	r	(P-308; A-9659) (E-1309)
710.5082	n	(P-305; A-9645) (E-1295)
710.5083	r	(P-308; A-9659) (E-1309)
710.5083	n	(P-305; A-9645) (E-1295)
710.5090	r	(P-308; A-9659) (E-1309)
710.5091	r	(P-308; A-9659) (E-1309)
710.5092	r	(P-308; A-9659) (E-1309)
710.5093	r	(P-308; A-9659) (E-1309)
710.5100	r	(P-308; A-9659) (E-1309)
710.5110	r	(P-308; A-9659) (E-1309)
710.5120	r	(P-308; A-9659) (E-1309)
710.5160	r	(P-308; A-9659) (E-1309)

TITLE 83 (CONT'D)

Section		Reference
710.5210	r	(P-308; A-9659) (E-1309)
710.5230	r	(P-308; A-9659) (E-1309)
710.5240	r	(P-308; A-9659) (E-1309)
710.5250	r	(P-308; A-9659) (E-1309)
710.5260	r	(P-308; A-9659) (E-1309)
710.5270	r	(P-308; A-9659) (E-1309)
710.5280	r	(P-308; A-9659) (E-1309)
710.5300	r	(P-308; A-9659) (E-1309)
710.5999	r	(P-305; A-9645) (E-1295)
710.6021		(P-308; A-9659) (E-1309)
710.6022	r	(P-308; A-9659) (E-1309)
710.6023	r	(P-308; A-9659) (E-1309)
710.6024	r	(P-308; A-9659) (E-1309)
710.6025	r	(P-308; A-9659) (E-1309)
710.6026	r	(P-308; A-9659) (E-1309)
710.6027	r	(P-308; A-9659) (E-1309)
710.6028	r	(P-308; A-9659) (E-1309)
710.6030	r	(P-308; A-9659) (E-1309)
710.6040	r	(P-308; A-9659) (E-1309)
710.6050	r	(P-308; A-9659) (E-1309)
710.6060	r	(P-308; A-9659) (E-1309)
710.6070	r	(P-308; A-9659) (E-1309)
710.6080	r	(P-308; A-9659) (E-1309)
710.6090	r	(P-308; A-9659) (E-1309)
710.6100	r	(P-308; A-9659) (E-1309)
710.6110	r	(P-308; A-9659) (E-1309)
710.6120	r	(P-308; A-9659) (E-1309)
710.6130	r	(P-308; A-9659) (E-1309)
710.6150	r	(P-308; A-9659) (E-1309)
710.6140	r	(P-308; A-9659) (E-1309)
710.6210	r	(P-308; A-9659) (E-1309)
710.6220	r	(P-308; A-9659) (E-1309)
710.6240	r	(P-308; A-9659) (E-1309)
710.6260	r	(P-308; A-9659) (E-1309)
710.6270	r	(P-308; A-9659) (E-1309)
710.6290	r	(P-308; A-9659) (E-1309)
710.6300	r	(P-308; A-9659) (E-1309)
710.6310	r	(P-308; A-9659) (E-1309)
710.6320	r	(P-308; A-9659) (E-1309)
710.6330	r	(P-308; A-9659) (E-1309)
710.6340	r	(P-308; A-9659) (E-1309)
710.6350	r	(P-308; A-9659) (E-1309)
710.6400	r	(P-308; A-9659) (E-1309)
710.6420	r	(P-308; A-9659) (E-1309)
710.6430	r	(P-308; A-9659) (E-1309)
710.6440	r	(P-308; A-9659) (E-1309)
710.6450	r	(P-308; A-9659) (E-1309)
710.6460	r	(P-308; A-9659) (E-1309)
710.6470	r	(P-308; A-9659) (E-1309)
710.6480	r	(P-308; A-9659) (E-1309)
710.6490	r	(P-308; A-9659) (E-1309)
710.6500	r	(P-308; A-9659) (E-1309)
710.6570	r	(P-308; A-9659) (E-1309)
710.6580	r	(P-308; A-9659) (E-1309)
710.6610	r	(P-308; A-9659) (E-1309)
710.6620	r	(P-308; A-9659) (E-1309)
710.6630	r	(P-308; A-9659) (E-1309)

TITLE 83 (CONT'D)

Section		Citation
710.6640	r	(P-303; A-9659) (E-1309)
710.6650	r	(P-303; A-9659) (E-1309)
710.6680	r	(P-303; A-9659) (E-1309)
710.6690	r	(P-303; A-9659) (E-1309)
710.6710	r	(P-303; A-9659) (E-1309)
710.6720	r	(P-303; A-9659) (E-1309)
710.6730	r	(P-303; A-9659) (E-1309)
710.6740	r	(P-303; A-9659) (E-1309)
710.6750	r	(P-303; A-9659) (E-1309)
710.6760	r	(P-303; A-9659) (E-1309)
710.6770	r	(P-303; A-9659) (E-1309)
710.7020	r	(P-303; A-9659) (E-1309)
710.7040	r	(P-303; A-9659) (E-1309)
710.7050	r	(P-303; A-9659) (E-1309)
710.7060	r	(P-303; A-9659) (E-1309)
710.7070	r	(P-303; A-9659) (E-1309)
710.7250	r	(P-305; A-9645) (E-1295)
710.7450	r	(P-305; A-9645) (E-1295)
710.9000	n	(P-305; A-9645) (E-1295)
711.5	n	(P-298; A-9495) (E-1136)
711.10	n	(P-298; A-9495) (E-1136)
711.15	n	(P-298; A-9495) (E-1136)
711.20	n	(P-298; A-9495) (E-1136)
711.25	n	(P-298; A-9495) (E-1116)
711.100	n	(P-298; A-9495) (E-1136)
711.105	n	(P-298; A-9495) (E-1136)
711.110	n	(P-298; A-9495) (E-1136)
711.115	n	(P-298; A-9495) (E-1136)
711.200	n	(P-298; A-9495) (E-1136)
711.205	n	(P-298; A-9495) (E-1136)
711.210	n	(P-298; A-9495) (E-1136)
711.215	n	(P-298; A-9495) (E-1136)
711.220	n	(P-298; A-9495) (E-1136)
711.225	n	(P-298; A-9495) (E-1136)
711.230	n	(P-298; A-9495) (E-1136)
711.235	n	(P-298; A-9495) (E-1136)
711.245	n	(P-298; A-9495) (E-1136)
711.250	n	(P-298; A-9495) (E-1136)
711.255	n	(P-298; A-9495) (E-1136)
711.260	n	(P-298; A-9495) (E-1136)
711.265	n	(P-298; A-9495) (E-1136)
711.270	n	(P-298; A-9495) (E-1136)
711.275	n	(P-298; A-9495) (E-1136)
711.280	n	(P-298; A-9495) (E-1136)
711.285	n	(P-298; A-9495) (E-1136)
711.290	n	(P-298; A-9495) (E-1136)
711.305	n	(P-298; A-9495) (E-1136)
711.309	n	(P-298; A-9495) (E-1136)
711.310	n	(P-298; A-9495) (E-1136)
711.315	n	(P-298; A-9495) (E-1136)
711.320	n	(P-298; A-9495) (E-1136)
711.325	n	(P-298; A-9495) (E-1136)
711.330	n	(P-298; A-9495) (E-1136)
711.335	n	(P-298; A-9495) (E-1136)
711.340	n	(P-298; A-9495) (E-1136)
711.345	n	(P-298; A-9495) (E-1136)
711.350	n	(P-298; A-9495) (E-1136)
711.355	n	(P-298; A-9495) (E-1136)
711.360	n	(P-298; A-9495) (E-1136)
711.365	n	(P-298; A-9495) (E-1136)
711.370	n	(P-298; A-9495) (E-1136)
711.375	n	(P-298; A-9495) (E-1136)
711.1220	n	(P-298; A-9495) (E-1136)
711.1439	n	(P-298; A-9495) (E-1136)
711.2002	n	(P-298; A-9495) (E-1136)
711.2003	n	(P-298; A-9495) (E-1136)
711.2004	n	(P-298; A-9495) (E-1136)
711.2005	n	(P-298; A-9495) (E-1136)
711.2111	n	(P-298; A-9495) (E-1136)
711.2112	n	(P-298; A-9495) (E-1136)
711.2113	n	(P-298; A-9495) (E-1136)
711.2114	n	(P-298; A-9495) (E-1136)
711.2115	n	(P-298; A-9495) (E-1136)
711.2116	n	(P-298; A-9495) (E-1136)
711.2121	n	(P-298; A-9495) (E-1136)
711.2122	n	(P-298; A-9495) (E-1136)
711.2123	n	(P-298; A-9495) (E-1136)
711.2134	n	(P-298; A-9495) (E-1136)
711.2211	n	(P-298; A-9495) (E-1136)
711.2212	n	(P-298; A-9495) (E-1136)
711.2215	n	(P-298; A-9495) (E-1136)
711.2220	n	(P-298; A-9495) (E-1136)
711.2231	n	(P-298; A-9495) (E-1136)
711.2232	n	(P-298; A-9495) (E-1136)
711.2311	n	(P-298; A-9495) (E-1136)
711.2321	n	(P-298; A-9495) (E-1136)
711.2341	n	(P-298; A-9495) (E-1136)
711.2351	n	(P-298; A-9495) (E-1136)
711.2362	n	(P-298; A-9495) (E-1136)
711.2411	n	(P-298; A-9495) (E-1136)
711.2421	n	(P-298; A-9495) (E-1136)
711.2422	n	(P-298; A-9495) (E-1136)
711.2423	n	(P-298; A-9495) (E-1136)
711.2424	n	(P-298; A-9495) (E-1136)
711.2425	n	(P-298; A-9495) (E-1136)
711.2426	n	(P-298; A-9495) (E-1136)
711.2431	n	(P-298; A-9495) (E-1136)
711.2441	n	(P-298; A-9495) (E-1136)
711.2681	n	(P-298; A-9495) (E-1136)
711.2682	n	(P-298; A-9495) (E-1136)
711.2690	n	(P-298; A-9495) (E-1136)
711.3100	n	(P-298; A-9495) (E-1136)
711.3200	n	(P-298; A-9495) (E-1136)
711.3410	n	(P-298; A-9495) (E-1136)
711.3420	n	(P-298; A-9495) (E-1136)
711.3500	n	(P-298; A-9495) (E-1136)
711.3600	n	(P-298; A-9495) (E-1136)
711.4100	n	(P-298; A-9495) (E-1136)
711.4340	n	(P-298; A-9495) (E-1136)
711.6112	n	(P-298; A-9495) (E-1136)
711.6113	n	(P-298; A-9495) (E-1136)
711.6114	n	(P-298; A-9495) (E-1136)

TITLE 83 (CONT'D)

Section		Citation
711.6115	n	(P-298; A-9495) (E-1136)
711.6116	n	(P-298; A-9495) (E-1136)
711.6121	n	(P-298; A-9495) (E-1136)
711.6122	n	(P-298; A-9495) (E-1136)
711.6123	n	(P-298; A-9495) (E-1136)
711.6124	n	(P-298; A-9495) (E-1136)
711.6211	n	(P-298; A-9495) (E-1136)
711.6212	n	(P-298; A-9495) (E-1136)
711.6215	n	(P-298; A-9495) (E-1136)
711.6230	n	(P-298; A-9495) (E-1136)
711.6231	n	(P-298; A-9495) (E-1136)
711.6232	n	(P-298; A-9495) (E-1136)
711.6311	n	(P-298; A-9495) (E-1136)
711.6341	n	(P-298; A-9495) (E-1136)
711.6351	n	(P-298; A-9495) (E-1136)
711.6362	n	(P-298; A-9495) (E-1136)
711.6411	n	(P-298; A-9495) (E-1136)
711.6421	n	(P-298; A-9495) (E-1136)
711.6422	n	(P-298; A-9495) (E-1136)
711.6423	n	(P-298; A-9495) (E-1136)
711.6424	n	(P-298; A-9495) (E-1136)
711.6425	n	(P-298; A-9495) (E-1136)
711.6426	n	(P-298; A-9495) (E-1136)
711.6431	n	(P-298; A-9495) (E-1136)
711.6441	n	(P-298; A-9495) (E-1136)
711.6511	n	(P-298; A-9495) (E-1136)
711.6512	n	(P-298; A-9495) (E-1136)
711.6531	n	(P-298; A-9495) (E-1136)
711.6532	n	(P-298; A-9495) (E-1136)
711.6533	n	(P-298; A-9495) (E-1136)
711.6534	n	(P-298; A-9495) (E-1136)
711.6535	n	(P-298; A-9495) (E-1136)
711.6540	n	(P-298; A-9495) (E-1136)
711.6561	n	(P-298; A-9495) (E-1136)
711.6562	n	(P-298; A-9495) (E-1136)
711.6563	n	(P-298; A-9495) (E-1136)
711.6564	n	(P-298; A-9495) (E-1136)
711.6565	n	(P-298; A-9495) (E-1136)
711.6611	n	(P-298; A-9495) (E-1136)
711.6612	n	(P-298; A-9495) (E-1136)
711.6613	n	(P-298; A-9495) (E-1136)
711.6621	n	(P-298; A-9495) (E-1136)
711.6622	n	(P-298; A-9495) (E-1136)
711.6623	n	(P-298; A-9495) (E-1136)
711.6711	n	(P-298; A-9495) (E-1136)
711.6712	n	(P-298; A-9495) (E-1136)
711.6721	n	(P-298; A-9495) (E-1136)
711.6722	n	(P-298; A-9495) (E-1136)
711.6723	n	(P-298; A-9495) (E-1136)
711.6724	n	(P-298; A-9495) (E-1136)
711.6725	n	(P-298; A-9495) (E-1136)
711.6726	n	(P-298; A-9495) (E-1136)
711.6727	n	(P-298; A-9495) (E-1136)
711.6728	n	(P-298; A-9495) (E-1136)
711.6790	n	(P-298; A-9495) (E-1136)
711.7110	n	(P-298; A-9495) (E-1136)
711.7130	n	(P-298; A-9495) (E-1136)
711.7140	n	(P-298; A-9495) (E-1136)
711.7150	n	(P-298; A-9495) (E-1136)
711.7160	n	(P-298; A-9495) (E-1136)
711.7210	n	(P-298; A-9495) (E-1136)
711.7220	n	(P-298; A-9495) (E-1136)
711.7230	n	(P-298; A-9495) (E-1136)
711.7240	n	(P-298; A-9495) (E-1136)
711.7250	n	(P-298; A-9495) (E-1136)
711.7350	n	(P-298; A-9495) (E-1136)
711.9370	n	(P-298; A-9495) (E-1136)
711.7400	n	(P-298; A-9495) (E-1136)
711.7510	n	(P-298; A-9495) (E-1136)
711.7520	n	(P-298; A-9495) (E-1136)
711.7530	n	(P-298; A-9495) (E-1136)
711.7540	n	(P-298; A-9495) (E-1136)
711.7610	n	(P-298; A-9495) (E-1136)
711.7620	n	(P-298; A-9495) (E-1136)
711.7630	n	(P-298; A-9495) (E-1136)
711.7640	n	(P-298; A-9495) (E-1136)
712.5	n	(P-302; A-9588) (E-1236)
712.10	n	(P-302; A-9588) (E-1236)
712.15	n	(P-302; A-9588) (E-1236)
712.20	n	(P-302; A-9588) (E-1236)
712.25	n	(P-302; A-9588) (E-1236)
712.100	n	(P-302; A-9588) (E-1236)
712.105	n	(P-302; A-9588) (E-1236)
712.110	n	(P-302; A-9588) (E-1236)
712.115	n	(P-302; A-9588) (E-1236)
712.200	n	(P-302; A-9588) (E-1236)
712.205	n	(P-302; A-9588) (E-1236)
712.210	n	(P-302; A-9588) (E-1236)
712.215	n	(P-302; A-9588) (E-1236)
712.235	n	(P-302; A-9588) (E-1236)
712.245	n	(P-302; A-9588) (E-1236)
712.250	n	(P-302; A-9588) (E-1236)
712.255	n	(P-302; A-9588) (E-1236)
712.260	n	(P-302; A-9588) (E-1236)
712.265	n	(P-302; A-9588) (E-1236)
712.270	n	(P-302; A-9588) (E-1236)
712.280	n	(P-302; A-9588) (E-1236)
712.285	n	(P-302; A-9588) (E-1236)
712.290	n	(P-302; A-9588) (E-1236)
712.305	n	(P-302; A-9588) (E-1236)
712.315	n	(P-302; A-9588) (E-1236)
712.320	n	(P-302; A-9588) (E-1236)
712.335	n	(P-302; A-9588) (E-1236)
712.345	n	(P-302; A-9588) (E-1236)
712.350	n	(P-302; A-9588) (E-1236)
712.355	n	(P-302; A-9588) (E-1236)
712.360	n	(P-302; A-9588) (E-1236)
712.365	n	(P-302; A-9588) (E-1236)
712.370	n	(P-302; A-9588) (E-1236)
712.375	n	(P-302; A-9588) (E-1236)
712.1220	n	(P-302; A-9588) (E-1236)
712.1439	n	(P-302; A-9588) (E-1236)

TITLE 83 (CONT'D)

712.2002	n	(P-302; A-9588) (E-1236)
712.2003	n	(P-302; A-9588) (E-1236)
712.2004	n	(P-302; A-9588) (E-1236)
712.2005	n	(P-302; A-9588) (E-1236)
712.2006	n	(P-302; A-9588) (E-1236)
712.2007	n	(P-302; A-9588) (E-1236)
712.2110	n	(P-302; A-9588) (E-1236)
712.2111	n	(P-302; A-9588) (E-1236)
712.2113	n	(P-302; A-9588) (E-1236)
712.2114	n	(P-302; A-9588) (E-1236)
712.2115	n	(P-302; A-9588) (E-1236)
712.2116	n	(P-302; A-9588) (E-1236)
712.2121	n	(P-302; A-9588) (E-1236)
712.2122	n	(P-302; A-9588) (E-1236)
712.2123	n	(P-302; A-9588) (E-1236)
712.2124	n	(P-302; A-9588) (E-1236)
712.2210	n	(P-302; A-9588) (E-1236)
712.2220	n	(P-302; A-9588) (E-1236)
712.2230	n	(P-302; A-9588) (E-1236)
712.2310	n	(P-302; A-9588) (E-1236)
712.2311	n	(P-302; A-9588) (E-1236)
712.2321	n	(P-302; A-9588) (E-1236)
712.2341	n	(P-302; A-9588) (E-1236)
712.2410	n	(P-302; A-9588) (E-1236)
712.2680	n	(P-302; A-9588) (E-1236)
712.2690	n	(P-302; A-9588) (E-1236)
712.3100	n	(P-302; A-9588) (E-1236)
712.3200	n	(P-302; A-9588) (E-1236)
712.3400	n	(P-302; A-9588) (E-1236)
712.3500	n	(P-302; A-9588) (E-1236)
712.3600	n	(P-302; A-9588) (E-1236)
712.4100	n	(P-302; A-9588) (E-1236)
712.4340	n	(P-302; A-9385) (E-1236)
712.5300	n	(P-302; A-9394) (E-1236)
712.6110	n	(P-302; A-9383) (E-1236)
712.6120	n	(P-302; A-9528) (E-1236)
712.6210	u	(P-302; A-9528) (E-1236)
712.6220	n	(P-302; A-9589) (E-1236)
712.6230	n	(P-302; A-9588) (E-1236)
712.6310	n	(P-302; A-9588) (E-1236)
712.6410	n	(P-302; A-9588) (E-1236)
712.6510	n	(P-302; A-9588) (E-1236)
712.6530	n	(P-302; A-9586) (E-1236)
712.6540	n	(P-302; A-9588) (E-1236)
712.6560	n	(P-302; A-9588) (E-1236)
712.6610	n	(P-302; A-9519) (E-1236)
712.6620	n	(P-302; A-9588) (E-1236)
712.6710	n	(P-302; A-9394) (E-1236)
712.6720	n	(P-302; A-9588) (E-1236)
712.6790	n	(P-302; A-9588) (E-1236)
712.7100	n	(P-302; A-9588) (E-1236)
712.7210	n	(P-302; A-9588) (E-1236)
712.7220	n	(P-302; A-9588) (E-1236)
712.7230	n	(P-302; A-9588) (E-1236)
712.7340	n	(P-302; A-9588) (E-1236)

TITLE 83 (CONT'D)

712.7250	n	(P-302; A-9588) (E-1236)
712.7350	n	(P-302; A-9588) (E-1236)
712.7370	n	(P-302; A-9583) (E-1236)
712.7400	n	(P-302; A-9588) (E-1236)
712.7500	n	(P-302; A-9588) (E-1236)
712.7600	n	(P-302; A-9588) (E-1236)
755.10	n	(P-11587/87; A-3687)
755.15	n	(P-11587/87; A-3687)
755.20	n	(P-11587/87; A-3687)
755.25	n	(P-11587/87; A-3687)
755.100	n	(P-11587/87; A-3687)
755.105	n	(P-11587/87; A-3687)
755.110	n	(P-11587/87; A-3687)
755.115	r	(P-11587/87; A-3687)
755.120	n	(P-11587/87; A-3687)
755.125	n	(P-11587/87; A-3687)
755.130	n	(P-11587/87; A-3687)
755.135	n	(P-11587/87; A-3687)
755.145	n	(P-11587/87; A-3687)
755.200	n	(P-11587/87; A-3687)
755.210	n	(P-11587/87; A-3687)
755.220	n	(P-11587/87; A-3687)
755.225	n	(P-11587/87; A-3687)
755.230	n	(P-11587/87; A-3687)
755.300	n	(P-11587/87; A-3687)
755.305	n	(P-11587/87; A-3687)
755.310	n	(P-11587/87; A-3687)
755.400	n	(P-11587/87; A-3687)
755.405	n	(P-11587/87; A-3687)
755.410	n	(P-11587/87; A-3687)
755.415	n	(P-11587/87; A-3687)
756.10	n	(P-7455; O-14428; R-17437; A-17321)
756.15	n	(P-7455; A-17321)
756.20	n	(P-7455; A-17321)
756.100	n	(P-7455; A-17321)
756.105	n	(P-7455; O-14428)
756.110	n	(P-7455x; A-17321)
756.115	n	(P-7455; O-14428)
756.120	n	(P-7455; A-17321)
756.125	n	(P-7455; A-17321)
756.200	n	(P-7455; A-17321)
756.205	n	(P-7455; A-17321)
756.210	n	(P-7455; A-17321)
756.215	n	(P-7455; A-17321)
756.220	n	(P-7455; A-17321)
756.225	n	(P-7455; O-14428; R-17437; A-17321)
756.300	n	(P-7455; A-17321)
756.305	n	(P-7455; A-17321)
756.310	n	(P-7455; A-17321)
757.10	n	(P-14799)
757.15	n	(P-14799)
757.100	n	(P-14799)
757.105	n	(P-14799)
757.110	n	(P-14799)

TITLE 83 (CONT'D)

757.115	n	(P-14799)
757.120	n	(P-14799)
757.200	n	(P-14799)
757.205	n	(P-14799)
757.Ex. A	n	(P-14799)

TITLE 86

100.5200	am	(P-5175/87; A-6748)
100.5250	r	(P-5175/87; A-6748)
100.5300	r	(P-5175/87; A-6748)
100.5350	r	(P-5175/87; A-6748)
100.5400	r	(P-5175/87; A-6748)
100.5500	am	(P-5175/87; A-6748)
100.5550	r	(P-5175/87; A-6748)
100.5700	n	(P-17083/87; A-4865)
100.5702	n	(P-17083/87; A-4865)
100.5704	n	(P-17083/87; A-4865)
100.5706	n	(P-17083/87; A-4865)
100.5708	n	(P-17083/87; A-4865)
100.5716	n	(P-17083/87; A-4865)
100.5712	n	(P-17083/87; A-4865)
100.5714	n	(P-17083/87; A-4865)
100.7030	am	(P-12215/87; A-11766)
100.9010	am	(P-14263/87; A-14307)
100.9020	am	(P-14263/87; A-14307)
100.9060	am	(P-14263/87; A-14307)
100.9070	am	(P-14263/87; A-14307)
100.9080	am	(P-14263/87; A-14307)
100.9100	r	(P-14263/87; A-14307)
100.9110	am	(P-14263/87; A-14307)
100.9120	r	(P-14263/87; A-14307)
100.9130	am	(P-14263/87; A-14307)
100.9200	am	(P-14263/87; A-14307)
110.145	am	(P-14317/87; A-14546)
130.330	am	(E-14401)
130.801	am	(P-18301/87; A-5652)
130.805	am	(P-18301/87; A-5652)
130.810	am	(P-18301/87; A-5652)
130.825	am	(P-18301/87; A-5652)
130.901	am	(P-11084)
130.1501	am	(P-11084)
130.1505	am	(P-11084)
130.1515	am	(P-11084)
130.2000	am	(E-14461; O-17450)
140.140	am	(P-14419; O-17451)
140.145	am	(P-14419; O-17453)
140.1401	n	(P-11108)
140.1405	am	(P-11108)
140.1415	am	(P-11119)
160.150	am	(P-11119)
160.155	am	(P-11119)
160.165	am	(P-11119)
180.101	am	(P-11056)
210.135	n	(P-11060)
428.100	n	(P-9400; A-15159)
428.110	n	(P-9400; A-15159)

TITLE 86 (CONT'D)

428.120	n	(P-9400; A-15159)
428.130	n	(P-9400; A-15159)
432.100	n	(E-11297) (P-15027)
432.110	n	(E-11297) (P-15027)
432.120	n	(E-11297) (P-15027)
432.130	n	(E-11297) (P-15027)
432.140	n	(E-11297) (P-15027)
432.150	n	(E-11297) (P-15027)
432.160	n	(E-11297) (P-15027)
437.170	n	(E-11297) (P-15027)
432.190	n	(E-11297) (P-15027)
432.190	n	(E-11297) (P-15027)
432.200	n	(E-11297) (P-15027)
440.10	am	(P-11063)
440.30	am	(P-11063)
440.90	am	(P-11063)
450.10	am	(P-11077)
480.110	am	(P-11077)
525.101	n	(E-16828)
530.165	am	(P-11104)

TITLE 89

102.120	am	(P-17663)
102.270	am	(P-14977/87; A-3735)
102.280	am	(P-18007/87; A-3735)
103.20	am	(P-3952; C-9757; A-14681) (P-7667)
103.100	am	(P-162; A-9142)
104.101	n	(P-162; A-9142)
104.102	am	(P-162; A-9142)
104.104	am	(P-162; A-9142)
104.202	am	(P-18084/87; W-9755)
104.207	am	(P-18084/87; W-9755)
104.209	am	(P-18084/87; W-9755)
104.210	am	(P-18084/87; W-9755)
104.212	am	(P-18084/87; W-9755)
104.221	am	(P-18084/87; W-9755)
104.230	am	(P-18084/87; W-9755)
104.231	n	(P-18084/87; W-9755)
104.241	n	(P-18084/87; W-9755)
104.250	am	(P-18084/87; W-9755)
104.260	am	(P-18084/87; W-9755)
104.280	am	(P-18084/87; W-9755)
110.20	am	(P-5176; A-11457)
110.30	am	(P-5176; A-11457)
110.40	am	(P-5176; A-11457)
111.90	am	(P-15844/87; A-8711)
111.101	am	(P-15844/87; A-8711) (P-15920)
112.10	am	(P-16040/87; A-3487)
112.20	am	(P-19259/87; O-4890; R-6824; A-6694)
112.70	am	(P-8437; A-14172)
112.74	am	(P-18007/87; A-7336)
112.76	am	(P-18007/87; A-7336)
112.78	am	(P-8437; A-14172) (P-17047/87; W-10554)

TITLE 89 (CONT'D)

112.79	am	(P-8837; A-14172)
112.82	am	(P-10007/87; A-7336) (P-8837; A-14172)
112.83	n	(E-18781/87; RC-260) (P-18491/87; O-4895; RC-4897; M-6325; A-6159)
112.86	am	(P-3223; A-9032)
112.87	n	(P-3223; A-9032)
112.88	n	(P-3223; A-9032)
112.89	n	(P-3223; A-9032)
112.90	n	(P-3223; A-9032)
112.91	n	(P-3223; A-9032)
112.93	n	(P-3223; A-9032)
112.95	n	(P-3223; A-9032)
112.98	n	(P-1743; RC-7849; A-7673) (E-1929)
112.110	am	(P-14940/87; P-15829/87; A-844) (P-20732/87; A-10481)
112.127	am	(P-20732/87; A-10481)
112.251	am	(P-14940/87; P-15829/87; A-844)
112.252	am	(P-14940/87; P-15829/87; A-844) (P-15905)
112.253	am	(P-14940/87; P-15829/87; A-844) (P-15905)
112.254	am	(P-14940/87; P-15829/87; A-844) (P-15905)
112.302	am	(P-7520; A-14669)
112.308	am	(P-3911; A-9032) (P-8837; A-14172)
112.315	am	(P-10435/87; A-6694)
112.320	am	(P-15575/87; A-2126) (P-4453) (P-20732/87; A-10481)
113.10	am	(P-16032/87; A-3497) (P-3923; A-9023)
113.20	am	(P-19585/87; O-4900; R-6324; A-6151)
113.70	am	(P-17999/87; A-8662)
113.107	am	(P-20747/87; A-9699)
113.130	am	(P-15475)
113.141	no	(P-20487/87; A-5642) (P-12953) (P-12953; A-17849)
113.142	am	(P-15442/87; A-864) (P-15898)
113.143	no	(20487/87; A-9699) (P-12953) (P-12953; A-17849)
113.247	am	(P-11674/87; E-11828; R-14736) (P-11674; A-17849)
113.253	am	(P-20014/87; A-7687)
113.260	am	(P-20012/87; A-7687)
113.302	am	(P-13828/87; O-19910/87; R-2160; A-2137) (P-7529; A-14669)
113.303	am	(P-8827; A-14162)
113.247	am	(E-11828; O-14460; R-14736)
114.10	am	(P-16397/87; A-3505) (P-3932; A-9699)
114.52	re	(A-2984)
114.80	am	(P-3556; A-9699)

114.100	r	(P-18027/87; A-6170)
114.108	am	(P-3250; A-9108)
114.109	n	(P-3250; A-9108)
114.110	n	(P-3250; A-9108)
114.110	re	(A-2984)
114.111	n	(P-3250; A-9108)
114.113	n	(P-3250; A-11483)
114.115	n	(P-3250; A-9108)
114.117	n	(P-3250; A-9108)
114.120	n	(E-18311/87; RC-263) (P-18027/87; A-6170)
114.120	am	(P-11839) (S-14463)
114.121	n	(E-18311/87; RC-263) (P-18027/87; A-6170)
114.122	n	(P-18027/87; A-6170)
114.122	am	(P-14111) (E-14364) (P-11839) (E-14463)
114.123	am	(P-18027/87; RC-4912) (P-18027/87; A-6170)
114.124	n	(P-18027/87; RC-4912) (P-18491/87; A-6170)
114.125	n	(P-18027/87; A-6170)
114.126	n	(P-18027/87; A-6170)
114.127	n	(P-18027/87; A-6170)
114.127	am	(P-14996)
114.128	n	(P-18027/87; A-6170) (P-17621)
114.129	n	(P-18027/87; A-6170)
114.130	n	(P-18027/87; A-6170)
114.130	am	(P-8872; A-14255)
114.140	n	(E-18791/87; RC-276) (P-18491/87; O-4904; RC-4909; M-6326; A-6170)
114.210	am	(P-20755/87; A-9940)
114.220	am	(P-18932/87; O-4906; R-6826; A-6719) (P-10619; A-16729)
114.223	am	(P-20755/87; A-9940)
114.350	am	(P-15850/87; A-889)
114.351	am	(P-15850/87; A-889) (P-15924)
114.352	am	(P-15850/87; A-889) (P-15924)
114.353	am	(P-15850/87; A-889) (P-15924)
114.400	am	(P-6345; A-11474)
114.402	am	(P-8872; A-14255)
114.420	am	(P-16050/87; A-3505)
116.520	am	(P-8236; A-14207; C-15772)
117.10	am	(P-15471/87; A-2985)
117.20	am	(P-7571; A-13608)
117.40	am	(P-10373)
117.70	r	(P-8635; A-14296)
118.100	am	(P-20497/87; A-6301)
118.200	n	(P-2190; A-8068) (E-3037)
118.200	r	(P-11412)
120.10	am	(P-4463) (P-7540; W-11321)
120.11	n	(P-11676) (E-11839; O-14463; R-15721)
120.20	am	(P-6554; A-12835) (E-11839; O-14463)

TITLE 89 (CONT'D)

120.31	n	(P-7540; W-11321) (P-11676) (E-11839; O-14463; R-15721)
120.40	am	(P-6554; A-12835) (E-11839; O-14463) (P-17633)
120.60	am	(P-4463) (P-11676) (E-11839; O-14463; R-15721)
120.61	am	(P-5391; A-11483)
120.64	n	(P-11676) (E-11839; O-14463; R-15721)
120.80	am	(P-11408) (E-11632)
120.310	am	(P-16058/87; A-3516) (P-3942; A-9132)
120.311	am	(P-19620/87; O-4915; R-6327; A-6234)
120.318	am	(P-18050/87; A-8672)
120.335	am	(P-14952/87; P-15449/87; A-904) (P-19620/87; O-4915; R-6327; A-6234) (P-12964; A-17867) (E-13243)
120.380	am	(P-11676) (E-11839; O-14463; R-15721)
120.381	am	(P-11676) (E-11839; O-14463; R-15721)
120.382	am	(P-14952/87; P-15449/87; A-904) (P-11676) (E-11839; O-14463; R-15721) (P-15938)
120.390	am	(P-7540; W-11321) (P-11676) (E-11839; O-14463; R-15721)
120.391	am	(P-11676) (E-11839; O-14463; R-15721)
120.392	am	(P-11676) (E-11839; O-14463; R-15721)
120.335	am	(P-12964; A-17867)
121.1	am	(P-13362/87; O-19914/87; R-4235; A-4304) (P-1745; A-9678)
121.7	am	(P-1745; A-9678) (E-1941)
121.19	n	(P-19603/87; A-9922)
121.20	am	(PP-11855/87; O-15401/87; R-236) (P-19603/87; A-9922)
121.23	n	(P-19603/87; A-9922)
121.24	n	(P-19603/87; A-9922)
121.25	n	(P-19603/87; A-9922)
121.26	n	(P-19603/87; A-9922)
121.27	n	(P-19603/87; A-9922)
121.31	am	(P-1745; A-9678) (E-1941) (P-13915) (E-14045) (PP-16271)
121.50	am	(P-14950/87; A-877)
121.51	am	(P-14950/87; A-877)
121.58	am	(P-14950/87; A-877)
121.60	am	(PP-15704)
121.61	am	(PP-15704)
121.63	am	(P-8246; A-12824) (PP-15704)
121.64	am	(PP-15704)
121.70	am	(P-1745; A-9678) (E-1941)
121.72	am	(P-1745; A-9678) (E-1941) (P-19603/87; A-9922)
121.120	am	(PP-16271)

121.140	n	(P-5180; A-11463)
121.151	n	(P-1745; A-9678) (E-1941)
140.2	am	(P-19632/87; O-4920; R-6828; A-6728) (P-7553; W-11654) (P-11701) (E-11868; O-14466; R-15723)
140.3	am	(P-1765; O-14440; R-17031; A-16738) (E-1960) (P-11701) (E-11868; O-14466; R-15723)
140.5	am	(P-1765; O-14440; R-17031; A-16738) (E-1960)
140.7	am	(P-11701) (E-11868; O-14466; R-15723)
140.8	n	(P-15457/87; O-256; R-1646; A-916)
140.9	am	(P-7553; W-11654) (P-11701) (E-11868; R-15723)
140.10	am	(P-14963/87; A-7695)
140.11	am	(P-18039/87; W-9756)
140.12	am	(P-18039/87; W-9756)
140.13	am	(P-18039/87; W-9756)
140.14	am	(P-18039/87; W-9756)
140.15	am	(P-18039/87; W-9756)
140.16	am	(P-18039/87; W-9756)
140.17	am	(P-18039/87; W-9756)
140.18	am	(P-18039/87; W-9756)
140.19	am	(P-18039/87; W-9756) (P-12976)
140.21	am	(P-18039/87; W-9756)
140.22	am	(P-18039/87; W-9756)
140.27	am	(P-18039/87; W-9756)
140.28	am	(P-18039/87; W-9756)
140.35	am	(P-18039/87; W-9756)
140.51	am	(P-1765; O-14440)
140.97	am	(P-3273; A-10497)
140.100	am	(P-16421) (E-16921)
140.101	n	(P-17392; A-17879)
140.102	n	(P-17392; A-17879)
140.103	n	(P-17392; A-17879)
140.104	n	(P-17392; A-17879)
140.110	n	(P-11701) (E-11868)
140.350	am	(P-5958)
140.362	am	(P-5958)
140.363	am	(P-5958)
140.364	am	(P-5958)
140.367	am	(P-5958)
140.369	am	(P-5958)
140.370	am	(P-5958)
140.372	am	(P-5958)
140.373	am	(P-5958)
140.376	am	(P-5958)
140.390	am	(P-17643)
140.392	am	(P-17643)
140.394	am	(P-17643)
140.400	am	(P-17172)
140.420	am	(P-4317; A-12509)

TITLE 89 (CONT'D)

Section		Citation
140.421	am	(P-4317; A-12509)
140.441	am	(P-17172)
140.443	am	(P-17172)
140.445	am	(P-17172)
140.447	am	(P-17172)
140.452	n	(P-9433/87; A-6927)
140.453	n	(P-9433/87; A-6927)
140.454	n	(P-9433/87; A-6927)
140.455	n	(P-9433/87; A-6927)
140.456	am	(P-9433/87; A-6927)
140.460	am	(P-9433/87; A-6927)
140.469	n	(P-1765; O-14440; R-17031; A-16738) (E-1960)
140.473	am	(P-1765; O-14440; R-17031; A-16738) (E-1960)
140.485	am	(P-510; W-2161)
140.486	am	(P-510; W-2161)
140.487	am	(P-510; W-2161)
140.488	n	(P-510; W-2161)
140.506	am	(P-2076; A-12509)
140.512	am	(P-11995)
140.523	am	(P-1358497; A-5427)
140.525	am	(P-3273; O-12563; R-14427; A-14271) (P-9344; A-18198)
140.526	am	(P-9344; A-18198)
140.529	am	(P-16067/87; A-6927) (P-9344; A-18198)
140.533	am	(P-8887)
140.535	am	(P-10348)
140.543	am	(P-10348)
140.560	am	(P-10348)
140.562	n	(P-1765; A-10717) (E-1960)
140.570	am	(P-10348)
140.582	am	(P-8887)
140.583	n	(P-8887)
140.584	n	(P-8887)
140.590	am	(P-10348)
140.895	n	(P-1765; A-10717) (E-1960)
140.896	n	(P-11701) (E-11868)
140.900	rn	(P-1045487; O-3128; R-6328; A-6246)
140.901	am	(P-1045487; O-3128; R-6328; A-6246)
140.901	rn	(A-6956)
140.902	am	(P-1045487; O-3128; R-6328; A-6246)
140.902	rn	(A-6956)
140.903	rn	(A-6956)
140.903	am	(P-1045487; O-3128; R-6328; A-6246)
140.906	re	(A-6956)
140.907	rn	(A-6956)
140.908	re	(A-6956)
140.909	re	(A-6956)
140.910	rn	(A-6956)
140.911	re	(A-6956)

TITLE 89 (CONT'D)

Section		Citation
140.912	rn	(A-6956)
140.940	rn	(A-7401)
140.942	rn	(A-7401)
140.944	rn	(A-7401)
140.946	rn	(A-7401)
140.948	rn	(A-7401)
140.950	rn	(A-7401)
140.952	rn	(A-7401)
140.952		(A-3273)
140.954	rn	(A-7401)
140.956	rn	(A-7401)
140.958	rn	(A-7401)
140.960	rn	(A-7401)
140.962	rn	(A-7401)
140.964	rn	(A-7401)
140.966	rn	(A-7401)
140.968	rn	(A-7401)
140.970	rn	(A-7401)
140.972	rn	(A-7401)
140.Th. A	r	(P-510; W-2161)
140.Th. D	am	(P-4317; A-12509)
140.Th. H	am	(P-1045487; O-3128; R-6328; A-6246)
140.Th. H	re	(A-6956)
140.Th. I	am	(P-1045487; O-3128; R-6328; A-6246)
140.Th. I	re	(A-6956)
141.200	am	(P-20022/87; A-7358) (P-9804; A-14219) (E-10197)
141.400	am	(P-20022/87; A-7358) (P-15483) (E-15667)
141.480	am	(P-15483) (E-15667)
141.560	am	(P-20022/87; A-7358) (P-9804; A-14219) (E-10197) (P-15483) (E-15667)
141.640	am	(P-20022/87; A-7358)
141.720	am	(P-9804; A-14219) (E-10197)
141.800	am	(P-20022/87; A-7358) (P-9804; A-14219) (E-10197) (P-15483)
141.880	am	(P-20022/87; A-7358) (P-9804; A-14219) (E-10197)
141.1000	am	(P-20022/87; A-7358)
141.1160	am	(P-20022/87; A-7358) (P-15483)
141.1200	am	(P-20022/87; A-7358) (P-9804; A-14219) (E-10197)
141.1240	am	(P-15483) (E-15667)
141.1280	am	(P-9804; A-14219) (E-10197) (P-15483) (E-15667)
141.1320	am	(P-20022/87; A-7358)
141.1480	am	(P-15483) (E-15667)
141.1520	am	(P-9804; A-14219) (E-10197) (P-15483) (E-15667)
141.1680	am	(P-9804; A-14219) (E-10197) (P-15483) (E-15667)

TITLE 89 (CONT'D)

Section		Citation
141.1760	am	(P-15483) (E-15667)
141.1840	am	(P-20022/87; A-7358)
141.2160	am	(P-20022/87; A-7358)
141.2280	am	(P-20022/87; A-7358) (P-15483) (E-15667)
141.2360	am	(P-20022/87; A-7358) (P-15483) (E-15667)
141.2400	am	(P-20022/87; A-7358) (P-15483) (E-15667)
141.2680	am	(P-9804; A-14219) (E-10197)
141.2720	am	(P-20022/87; A-7358) (P-9804; A-14219) (E-10197)
141.2760	am	(P-15483) (E-15667)
141.2840	am	(P-9804; A-14219) (E-10197)
141.2920	am	(P-20022/87; A-7358)
141.2960	am	(P-20022/87; A-7358) (P-9804; A-14219) (E-10197) (P-15483) (E-15667)
141.3040	am	(P-9804; A-14219) (E-10197)
141.3080	am	(P-20022/87; A-7358)
141.3280	am	(P-20022/87; A-7358)
141.3440	am	(P-15483) (E-15667)
141.3480	am	(P-15483) (E-15667)
141.3560	am	(P-20022/87; A-7358) (P-9804; A-14219) (E-10197)
141.3760	am	(P-9804; A-14219) (E-10197)
141.3800	am	(P-9804; A-14219) (E-10197) (P-15483) (E-15667)
141.3840	am	(P-15483) (E-15667)
141.3920	am	(P-20022/87; A-7358)
141.4000	am	(P-15483) (E-15667)
141.4040	am	(P-20022/87; A-7358) (P-9804; A-14219) (E-10197) (P-15483) (E-15667)
141.4160	am	(P-15483) (E-15667)
141.4200	am	(P-20022/87; A-7358) (P-9804; A-14219) (E-10197)
141.4440	am	(P-20022/87; A-7358) (P-15483) (E-15667)
141.4520	am	(P-15483) (E-15667)
141.4560	am	(P-9804; A-14219) (E-10197)
141.4640	am	(P-20022/87; A-7358)
141.4720	am	(P-15483) (E-15667)
141.4760	am	(P-9804; A-14219) (E-10197) (P-15483) (E-15667)
147.5	re	(A-6956)
147.25	re	(A-6956)
147.50	re	(A-6956)
147.75	re	(A-6956)
147.75	am	(P-10627)
147.100	re	(A-6956)
147.100	am	(P-10627)
147.105	re	(A-6956)
147.125	re	(A-6956)

TITLE 89 (CONT'D)

Section		Citation
147.150	re	(A-6956)
147.175	re	(A-6956)
147.200	re	(A-6956)
147.205	re	(A-6956)
147.205	am	(P-17201)
147.Th. A	re	(A-6956)
147.Th. A	urn	(P-10627)
147.Th. B	re	(A-6956)
147.Th. B	am	(P-10627)
149.5	re	(A-7401)
149.25	re	(A-7401)
149.50	re	(A-7401)
149.75	re	(A-7401)
149.100	re	(A-7401)
149.105	re	(A-7401) (P-13917)
149.125	re	(A-7401)
149.125	am	(P-3273; A-13095)
149.150	re	(A-7401)
149.175	re	(A-7401)
149.200	re	(A-7401)
149.205	re	(A-7401)
149.225	re	(A-7401)
149.250	re	(A-7401)
149.275	re	(A-7401)
149.300	re	(A-7401)
149.305	re	(A-7401)
149.325	re	(A-7401)
160.60	am	(P-120; A-9065) (E-1563)
160.70	am	(P-120; A-9065) (E-1563)
160.75	am	(P-120; A-9065) (E-1563) (P-13899)
160.80	n	(P-120; A-9065) (E-1563)
160.80	am	(P-9797; W-12919) (P-12770; A-18185)
165.40	am	(P-11402; A-18192)
165.42	am	(P-11402; A-18192)
165.70	am	(P-10543)
165.100	am	(P-10543)
230.360	am	(P-14777)
230.362	am	(P-14777)
230.365	am	(P-14777)
230.510	n	(P-12137) (E-12540)
230.520	n	(P-12137) (E-12540)
230.530	n	(P-12137) (E-12540)
230.540	n	(P-12137) (E-12540)
230.550	n	(P-12137) (E-12540)
230.560	n	(P-12137) (E-12540)
230.570	n	(P-12137) (E-12540)
230.580	n	(P-12137) (E-12540)
240.100	re	(A-7980)
240.110	am	(P-10821)
240.110	re	(A-7980)
240.120	am	(P-10821)
240.120	re	(A-7980)
240.130	re	(A-7980)
240.131	re	(A-7980)

TITLE 92 (CONT'D)

Section		Citation
452.Tb. E	r	(P-16447)
452.Ex. A	r	(P-16447)
522.16	n	(P-6011; A-16163)
522.10	r	(P-6045; A-16201)
522.20	n	(P-6011; C-6829)
522.20	r	(P-6045; A-16201)
522.30	n	(P-6011; A-16163)
522.30	r	(P-6045; A-16201)
522.40	n	(P-6011; A-16163)
522.50	n	(P-6011; A-16163)
522.60	n	(P-6011; A-16163)
522.70	n	(P-6011; O-12566; RC-12574; M-14738; A-16163)
522.80	n	(P-6011; A-16163)
522.90	n	(P-6011; O-12566; RC-12574; R-14738; A-16163)
522.100	n	(P-6011; A-16163)
522.110	n	(P-6011; A-16163)
522.120	n	(P-6011; A-16163)
522.130	n	(P-6011; O-12566; RC-12574; R-14738; A-16163)
522.150	n	(P-6011; A-16163)
522.160	n	(P-6011; A-16163)
522.170	n	(P-6011; A-16163)
522.180	n	(P-6011; A-16163)
522.190	n	(P-6011; A-16163)
522.200	n	(P-6011; A-16163)
522.210	n	(P-6011; A-16163)
522.220	n	(P-6011; A-16163)
522.230	n	(P-6011; A-16163)
522.240	n	(P-6011; A-16163)
522.301	r	(P-6045; A-16201)
522.302	r	(P-6045; A-16201)
522.303	r	(P-6045; A-16201)
522.304	r	(P-6045; A-16201)
522.305	r	(P-6015; A-16201)
522.306	r	(P-6045; A-16201)
522.307	r	(P-6045; A-16201)
522.308	r	(P-6045; A-16201)
522.309	r	(P-6045; A-16201)
522.310	r	(P-6045; A-16201)
522.311	r	(P-6045; A-16201)
522.312	r	(P-6045; A-16201)
522.313	r	(P-6015; A-16201)
522.314	r	(P-6045; A-16201)
522.315	r	(P-6045; A-16201)
522.316	r	(P-6045; A-16201)
522.317	r	(P-6045; A-16201)
522.318	r	(P-6045; A-16201)
522.319	r	(P-6045; A-16201)
522.320	r	(P-6045; A-16201)
522.400	r	(P-6045; A-16201)
522.401	r	(P-6045; A-16201)
522.402	r	(P-6045; A-16201)
522.403	r	(P-6045; A-16201)
522.404	r	(P-6045; A-16201)
522.405	r	(P-6045; A-16201)
522.407	r	(P-6045; A-16201)
522.500	r	(P-6045; A-16201)
522.600	r	(P-6045; A-16201)
522.601	r	(P-6045; A-16201)
522.602	r	(P-6045; A-16201)
522.603	r	(P-6045; A-16201)
522.604	r	(P-6045; A-16201)
522.700	r	(P-6045; A-16201)
522.800	r	(P-6045; A-16201)
522.801	r	(P-6045; A-16201)
522.802	r	(P-6045; A-16201)
522.803	r	(P-6045; A-16201)
522.900	r	(P-6045; A-16201)
522.1000	r	(P-6045; A-16201)
522.Ex.A	r	(P-6045; A-16201)
522.Ex.B	r	(P-6045; A-16201)
522.Ex.C	r	(P-6045; A-16201)
522.Il. A	n	(P-6011; A-16163)
522.Il. B	n	(P-6011; A-16163)
522.Il. C	n	(P-6011; A-16163)
522.Il. D	n	(P-6011; A-16163)
522.Il. E	n	(P-6011; A-16163)
522.Il. F	n	(P-6011; A-16163)
522.Il. G	n	(P-6011; A-16163)
522.Il. H	n	(P-6011; A-16163)
522.Il. I	n	(P-6011; A-16163)
534.10	n	(P-18143/87; O-4929; RC-4935; R-9172; A-12884)
534.20	n	(P-18143/87; O-4929; RC-4935; R-9172; A-12884)
534.30	n	(P-18143/87; O-4929; RC-4935; R-9172; A-12884)
534.110	n	(P-18143/87; O-4929; RC-4935; R-9172; A-12884)
534.210	n	(P-18143/87; O-4929; RC-4935; R-9172; A-12884) (P-15952)
534.220	n	(P-18143/87; O-4929; RC-4935; R-9172)
546.200	am	(P-16085/87; A-4214)
546.350	am	(P-16085/87; A-4214)
554.101	am	(P-1797; A-13232)
554.111	am	(P-1797; A-13232)
554.408	am	(P-1797; A-13232)
554.504	am	(P-1797; A-13232)
554.903	am	(P-1797; A-13232)
708.10	n	(P-5200)
708.20	n	(P-5200)
708.40	n	(P-5200)
708.50	n	(P-5200)
708.60	n	(P-5200)
708.70	n	(P-5200)
708.80	n	(P-5200)

ILLINOIS REGISTER
VOL. 12, THRU ISSUE #46   SECTIONS AFFECTED INDEX   THRU NOVEMBER 14, 1988

TITLE 92 (CONT'D)

Section		Citation
708.90	n	(P-5200)
708.100	n	(P-5200)
708.110	n	(P-5200)
708.120	n	(P-5200)
708.130	n	(P-5200)
708.140	n	(P-5200)
708.150	n	(P-5200)
708.160	n	(P-5200)
708.170	n	(P-5200)
708.180	n	(P-5200)
810.10	n	(P-5225; A-16203)
810.20	n	(P-5225; A-16203)
810.30	n	(P-5225; A-16203)
810.40	n	(P-5225; A-16203)
810.50	n	(P-5225; A-16203)
810.60	n	(P-5225; A-16203)
810.70	n	(P-5225; A-16203)
810.80	n	(P-5225; A-16203)
810.90	n	(P-5225; A-16203)
1000.41	n	(P-17269)
1003.10	n	(P-8639; A-14719)
1003.20	n	(P-8639; A-14719)
1003.30	n	(P-8639; A-14719)
1003.40	n	(P-8639; A-14719)
1003.50	n	(P-8639; A-14719)
1003.60	n	(P-8639; A-14719)
1003.70	n	(P-8639; A-14719)
1010.240	am	(P-8257; A-14711)
1010.440	n	(P-16432)
1010.451	n	(P-8920; A-15193)
1020.10	am	(P-4792; O-11346; RC-11349; R-12920; A-13612)
1020.20	am	(P-3607; A-17962)
1020.25	n	(P-3607)
1030.15	n	(P-13010)
1030.50	am	(P-10117/87; A-3027)
1030.65	n	(P-10117/87; A-3027)
1030.86	n	(P-17275)
1030.92	n	(P-4694; A-13221)
1030.94	n	(P-9840; A-16915)
1030.115	n	(P-10117/87; A-3027)
1040.20	am	(P-4077; A-15625)
1040.30	n	(P-17259)
1040.32	n	(P-11475/87; A-2148)
1040.32	am	(P-8913; A-16153)
1040.40	n	(P-17259)
1040.42	n	(P-10655; A-16906)
1040.43	n	(P-10655; A-16906)
1040.65	am	(P-6916; A-14351)
1040.66	n	(P-15947)
1040.70	n	(P-9409; A-17090)
1060.5	n	(P-11417)
1060.10	am	(P-11417)
1060.20	am	(P-11417)
1060.30	am	(P-11417)
1060.80	am	(P-11417)
1060.90	am	(P-11417)
1060.100	am	(P-11417)
1060.110	am	(P-11417)
1060.140	am	(P-11417)
1060.150	am	(P-11417)
1060.160	am	(P-11417)
1060.230	am	(P-11417)
1060.250	n	(P-20512/87; A-13203)
1100.5	n	(P-20770/87; A-8448)
1100.7	n	(P-20770/87; A-8448)
1100.10	am	(P-20770/87; A-8448)
1100.20	n	(P-20770/87; A-8448)
1100.30	n	(P-20770/87; A-8448)
1205.10	am	(P-7947; O-14432; RC-14436; A-15540)
1205.100	am	(P-7947; O-14432; BC-14436; R-15719; A-15540)
1205.110	am	(P-7947; O-14432; RC-14436; R-15719; A-15540)
1205.115	n	(P-7947; O-14432; RC-14436; R-15719; A-15540)
1205.210	am	(P-7947; O-14432; RC-14436; R-15719; A-15540)
1206.20	am	(P-18885/87; A-6089)
1207.40	n	(P-2047; A-10453)
1235.10	n	(P-17045)
1235.15	n	(P-17045)
1235.20	n	(P-17045)
1235.25	n	(P-17045)
1235.30	n	(P-17045)
1235.35	n	(P-17045)
1235.40	n	(P-17045)
1235.45	n	(P-17045)
1235.50	n	(P-17045)
1235.55	n	(P-17045)
1304.10	n	(P-13381)
1460.5	n	(P-13385)
1460.10	.	(P-13385)
1460.15	r	(P-13385)
1460.20	r	(P-13385)
1460.25	r	(P-13385)
1460.30	r	(P-13385)
1460.35	r	(P-13385)
1460.40	n	(P-13385)
1460.45	r	(P-13385)
1460.50	n	(P-13385)
1460.100	r	(P-13385)
1460.105	r	(P-13385)
1460.110	r	(P-13385)
1460.115	r	(P-13385)
1460.120	r	(P-13385)
1460.125	n	(P-13385)
1460.130		(P-13385)
1460.135		(P-13385)
1460.140		(P-13385)
1460.145		(P-13385)

TITLE 92 (CONT'D)

Section		Reference
1460.150	r	(P-13385)
1460.155	rs	(P-13385)
1460.160	*	(P-13385)
1460.165		(P-13385)
1460.170		(P-13385)
1460.175	.	(P-13385)
1460.180		(P-13385)
1460.185	*	(P-13385)
1460.190		(P-13385)
1460.195		(P-13385)
1460.200		(P-13385)
1460.205	*	(P-13385)
1460.210		(P-13385)
1460.215	r	(P-13385)
1460.220		(P-13385)
1460.225		(P-13385)
1460.235		(P-13385)
1460.240		(P-13385)
1460.245		(P-13385)
1460.250		(P-13385)
1460.255		(P-13385)
1460.260		(P-13385)
1460.265		(P-13385)
1460.270	r	(P-13385)
1460.275	r	(P-13385)
1460.280		(P-13385)
1460.285		(P-13385)
1460.290		(P-13385)
1460.295		(P-13385)
1460.300		(P-13385)
1460.305		(P-13385)
1460.310		(P-13385)
1460.315		(P-13385)
1460.320		(P-13385)
1460.325		(P-13385)
1460.330		(P-13385)
1460.335	r	(P-13385)
1470.20	am	(PP-12122)
1470.700	n	(PP-12122)
1470.Ex. A	n	(PP-12122)
1710.160	n	(PP-1630; RC-4944)
1800.10	am	(P-4417; A-11707)
1800.10	rn	(A-12997)
1810.10	rn	(A-12998)
1810.20	rn	(A-12998)
1810.30	rn	(A-12998)
1810.110	rn	(A-12998)
1810.120	rn	(A-12996)
1810.130	rn	(A-12998)
2000.10	am	(P-2050)
2000.25	n	(P-2050)
2000.30	am	(P-2050)

TITLE 95

Section		Reference
102.5	am	(P-15865/87; A-14731)
102.10	am	(P-15865/87; A-14731)

TITLE 95 (CONT'D)

Section		Reference
102.20	am	(P-15865/87; A-14731)
102.30	am	(P-15865/87; A-14731)
106.10	am	(P-14679/87; A-14361)
107.10	am	(P-14673/87; A-14356)
107.20	am	(7-14673/87; A-14356)
107.30	am	(7-14673/87; A-14356)
107.40	am	(7-14673/87; A-14356)
107.50	am	(7-14673/87; A-14356)
108.10	am	(P-14687/87; A-4225; C-14469)
108.20	am	(P-14687/87; A-4225; C-14469)
108.30	am	(P-14687/87; A-4225; C-14469)
108.40	am	(P-14687/87; A-4225; C-14469)
108.50	am	(P-14687/87; A-4225; C-14469)
108.60	am	(P-14687/87; A-4225; C-14469)
108.70	am	(P-14687/87; A-4225; C-14469)
108.90	am	(P-14687/87; A-4225; C-14469)
108.110	am	(P-14687/87; A-4225; C-14469)
108.120	am	(P-14687/87; A-4225; C-14469)
108.130	am	(P-14687/87; A-4225; C-14469)
108.140	am	(P-14687/87; A-4225; C-14469)
108.150	am	(P-14687/87; A-4225; C-14469)
108.160	am	(P-14687/87; A-4225; C-14469)
108.170	am	(P-14687/87; A-4225; C-14469)
109.10	am	(P-14681/87; A-3785)
109.20	am	(P-14681/87; A-3785)
109.30	am	(P-14681/87; A-3785)
109.40	am	(P-14681/87; A-3785)
109.50	am	(P-14681/87; A-3785)
109.70	am	(P-14681/87; A-3785)
109.90	am	(P-14681/87; A-3785)
109.100	am	(P-14681/87; A-3785)
109.110	am	(P-14681/87; A-3785)
120.5	n	(P-16419/87; A-15200)
120.10	n	(P-16419/87; A-15200)
120.20	n	(I-16419/87; A-15200)
120.30	n	(P-16419/87; RC-3136; A-15200)

This part of the Sections Affected Index lists only those Sections on which rulemaking is occurring in this issue of the *Illinois Register*. For previous action on these Sections in this volume of the *Register*, please refer to the first part of this index which begins on page SAI-1.

TITLE 2

Section		Reference
551.140	am	(A-19515)

TITLE 8

Section		Reference
20.1	am	(P-19178)
25.20	am	(P-19164)
25.30	am	(P-19164)
25.50	am	(P-19164)
25.130	am	(P-19164)
75.5	am	(P-19172)
75.190	am	(P-19172)
80.10	am	(P-19196)
80.20	am	(P-19196)
80.110	am	(P-19196)
85.5	am	(P-19185)
85.10	am	(P-19185)
85.15	am	(P-19185)
85.50	am	(P-19185)
85.75	am	(P-19185)
90.10	am	(P-19201)
90.110	am	(P-19201)
110.50	am	(P-19153)
110.80	am	(P-19153)
110.90	am	(P-19153)
110.110	am	(P-19153)
110.120	am	(P-19153)
115.10	am	(P-19218)
115.20	am	(P-19218)
125.60	am	(P-19211)
125.80	am	(P-19211)

TITLE 11

Section		Reference
100.50	am	(A-19387)
100.70	am	(A-19387)
100.160	am	(A-19387)
100.170	am	(A-19387)
100.210	am	(A-19387)
100.230	am	(A-19387)
100.350	am	(A-19387)

TITLE 23

Section		Reference
120.10	am	(P-19266)
120.60	am	(P-19266)
120.110	am	(P-19266)
120.130	n	(P-19266)
120.200	am	(P-19266)
120.210	am	(P-19266)
120.235	n	(P-19266)
200.10	am	(P-19279)
200.30	am	(P-19279)
200.40	am	(P-19279)
200.80	am	(P-19279)
200.100	am	(P-19279)

TITLE 35

Section		Reference
211.101	am	(P-19296)
211.122	am	(P-19296)
243.108	am	(P-19290)
243.120	n	(P-19290)

TITLE 44

Section		Reference
1.2215	am	(P-19225)

TITLE 68

Section		Reference
610.10	am	(P-19205)
610.20	am	(P-19205)
610.30	am	(P-19205)
610.40	am	(P-19205)
610.60	am	(P-19205)

TITLE 74

Section		Reference
280.10	am	(P-19259)
280.30	am	(P-19259)
280.Ap. A	n	(P-19259)
280.Ap. B	n	(P-19259)

TITLE 77

Section		Reference
450.440	n	(P-19327) (E-19518)
450.450	n	(P-19327) (E-19518)
450.1300	n	(P-19327) (E-19518)
450.1310	n	(P-19327) (E-19518)
450.1320	n	(P-19327) (E-19518)
450.1330	n	(P-19327) (E-19518)
848.100	n	(A-19429)
848.110	n	(A-19429)
848.130	n	(A-19429)
848.130	n	(A-19429)
848.200	n	(A-19429)
848.210	n	(A-19429)
848.215	n	(A-19429)
848.220	n	(A-19429)
848.225	n	(A-19429)
848.230	n	(A-19429)
848.235	n	(A-19429)
848.240	n	(A-19429)
848.300	n	(A-19429)
848.310	n	(A-19429)
848.315	n	(A-19429)
848.320	n	(A-19429)
848.325	n	(A-19429)
848.330	n	(A-19429)
848.335	n	(A-19429)
848.340	n	(A-19429)
848.345	n	(A-19429)
848.350	n	(A-19429)
848.355	n	(A-19429)
848.360	n	(A-19429)

CPSIA information can be obtained
at www.ICGtesting.com
Printed in the USA
BVHW040917050219
539516BV00009B/379/P

9 780260 851802